Lecture Notes in Computer Science 4671

Commenced Publication in 1973
Founding and Former Series Editors:
Gerhard Goos, Juris Hartmanis, and Jan van Leeuwen

Victor Malyshkin (Ed.)

Parallel Computing Technologies

9th International Conference, PaCT 2007
Pereslavl-Zalessky, Russia, September 3-7, 2007
Proceedings

 Springer

Volume Editor

Victor Malyshkin
Russian Academy of Sciences
Institute of Computational Mathematics and Mathematical Geophysics
Supercomputer Software Department
pr.Lavrentieva 6, ICM MG RAS, 630090 Novosibirsk, Russia
E-mail: malysh@ssd.sscc.ru

Library of Congress Control Number: 2007931744

CR Subject Classification (1998): D, F.1-2, C, I.6

LNCS Sublibrary: SL 1 – Theoretical Computer Science and General Issues

ISSN 0302-9743

ISBN 978-3-540-73939-5 Springer Berlin Heidelberg New York

Springer is a part of Springer Science+Business Media

springer.com

© Springer-Verlag Berlin Heidelberg 2007

Typesetting: Camera-ready by author, data conversion by Scientific Publishing Services, Chennai, India
Printed on acid-free paper   SPIN: 12099672   06/3180   5 4 3 2 1 0

Preface

PaCT-2007 (Parallel Computing Technologies) was a four-day conference held in Pereslavl-Zalessky, September 3–7, 2007. This was the ninth international conference in the PaCT series. The conferences are held in Russia every odd year. The first conference, PaCT-91, was held in Novosibirsk (Academgorodok), September 7–11, 1991. The next PaCT conferences were held in Obninsk (near Moscow), August 30 - September 4, 1993, in St.Petersburg, September 12-15, 1995, in Yaroslavl, September 9–12 1997, in Pushkin (near St.Petersburg), September 6–10, 1999, in Academgorodok (Novosibirsk), September 3-7, 2001, in Nizhni Novgorod, September 15–19, 2003, in Krasnoyarsk, September 5–9, 2005. Since 1995 all the PaCT proceedings have been published by Springer in the LNCS series.

PaCT-2007 was jointly organized by the Institute of Computational Mathematics and Mathematical Geophysics of the Russian Academy of Sciences (RAS) and the Program Systems Institute of the RAS (Pereslavl-Zalessky).

The purpose of the conference was to bring together scientists working on theory, architecture, software, hardware and the solution of large-scale problems in order to provide integrated discussions on parallel computing technologies.

The conference attracted about 100 participants from around the world. Authors from 25 countries submitted 98 papers. Of those, 37 papers were selected for the conference as regular papers; there were also 2 invited papers. In addition there were a number of posters presented. All the papers were internationally reviewed by at least three referees.

A demo session was organized for the participants, and different tools were submitted for a demonstration and tutorial. One of them was the Open TS: Dynamic Parallelization System for Multicore CPUs, SMPs, Clusters and GRIDs.

In conjunction with PaCT-2007, the Russian – Taiwan symposium on Methods and Tools of Parallel Programming of Multicomputers was held in Pereslavl-Zalessky, September 2–3, 2007. The symposium was organized by the Institute of Computational Mathematics and Mathematical Geophysics of RAS (Novosibirsk, Russia), the Institute of Program Systems RAS (Pereslavl-Zalessky) and the Chung Hua University (Taiwan). The symposium attracted 22 papers and 4 tools demonstrations and tutorials. Of those, 16 were selected for the symposium as regular papers; there was also 1 invited paper.

Many thanks to our sponsors: the Russian Academy of Sciences, the Russian Fund for Basic Research, National Scientific Council (Taiwan), IBM, Microsoft, Intel, and T-Platforms for their financial support.

June 2007   Victor Malyshkin

Organization

PaCT-2007 was organized by the Supercomputer Software Department, Institute of Computational Mathematics and Mathematical Geophysics SB RAS (Novosibirsk) in cooperation with the Program Systems Institute of RAS (Pereslavl-Zalessky).

Conference Chair	Victor Malyshkin	(Russian Academy of Sciences)
Conference Co-chair	Sergei Abramov	(Russian Academy of Sciences)
Organizing Committee	V. Malyshkin	Co-chairman (Novosibirsk)
	S. Abramov	Co-chairman (Pereslavl-Zalessky)
	O. Bandman	Publication Chair (Novosibirsk)
	Yu. Fomina	Secretary (Pereslavl-Zalessky)
	S. Nechaev	Secretary (Novosibirsk)
	V. Yumaguzhina	Vice-Chair (Pereslavl-Zalessky)

Program Committee

V. Malyshkin	Russian Academy of Sciences, Russia
S. Abramov	Russian Academy of Sciences, Russia
S. Bandini	University of Milano - Bicocca, Italy
O. Bandman	Russian Academy of Sciences, Russia
T. Casavant	University of Iowa, USA
A. Chambarel	University of Avignon, France
P. Degano	State University of Pisa, Italy
B. Goossens	University Paris 7 Denis Diderot, France
S. Gorlatch	Technical University of Berlin, Germany
Yu. Karpov	State Technical University, St.Petersburg, Russia
V. Kasyanov	Russian Academy of Sciences, Russia
K.-C. Li	Providence University, Taiwan
T. Ludwig	University of Heidelberg, Germany
G. Mauri	Università degli Studi di Milano - Bicocca, Italy
D. Petcu	Western University of Timisoara, Romania
M. Raynal	IRISA, Rennes, France
B. Roux	CNRS-Universites d'Aix-Marseille, France
P. Sloot	University of Amsterdam. The Netherlands
V. Sokolov	Yaroslavl State University
C. Trinitis	LRR, Munich, Germany
M. Valero	Barcelona Supercomputer Center, Spain
I. Virbitskaite	Russian Academy of Sciences, Russia
V. Vshivkov	Russian Academy of Sciences, Russia
S. El Yacoubi	University of Perpignan, France

MTPP Organizers

Steering Co-chairs

Victor E. Malyshkin, Russian Academy of Sciences, Russia
Ching-Hsien Hsu, Chung Hua University, Taiwan

International Advisory Board

Chung-Ta King, National Tsing Hua University, Taiwan
Hai Jin, Huazhong University of Science and Technology, China
Laurence T. Yang, St.Francis Xavier Univ. Canada
Ce-Kuen Shieh, National Cheng Kung University, Taiwan
B.Glinskii, Russian Academy of Sciences, Russia
V.Kas'yanov, Russian Academy of Sciences, Russia
V.Gergel, University of Nizhni Novgorod, Russia

General Co-chairs

Yeh-Ching Chung, National Tsing Hua University, Taiwan
Sergey Abramov, Institite of Program Systems RAS, Russia

Program Co-chairs

Kuan-Ching Li, Providence University, Taiwan
Arutyun Avetisyan,Russian Academy of Sciences, Russia

Local Arrangements Chair

Valeria Yumaguzhina, University of Pereslavl-Zalessky, Russia

Publication Chair

Olga Bandman, Russian Academy of Sciences, Russia

Program Committee

Pangfeng Liu, National Taiwan University, Taiwan
Jan-Jan Wu, Academia Sinica, Taiwan
Tsung-Chuan Huang, National Sun Yat-Sen University, Taiwan
Jong Hyuk Park, Hanwha S&C Co., Ltd., Korea
Jingling Xue, University of New South Wales, Australia
Cho-Li Wang, Hong Kong University, Hong Kong
Jenq-Kuen Lee, National Tsing Hua University, Taiwan

Chien-Min Wang, Academia Sinica, Taiwen
Weijia Jia, City University of HongKong, China
John Morris, University of Auckland, New Zealand
Jiannong Cao, Hong Kong Polytechnic University, Hong Kong
Satoshi Matsuoka, Tokyo Institute of Technology, Japan
Yuri Karpov, State Technical University of Saint Petersburg, Russia
O. Bandman, Russian Academy of Sciences, Russia
M. Valero, Barcelona Supercomputer Center, Spain
T. Ludwig, Ruprecht-Karls-Universität Heidelberg, Germany
B. Glinskii, Russian Academy of Sciences, Russia
V. Kas'yanov, Russian Academy of Sciences, Russia
Yong-Kee Jun, Gyeongsang National University, South Korea

Referees

M. Aldinucci	G. Italiano	M. Raynal
R. Andonov	Y.-K. Jun	B. Roux
R. Arapbaev	Yu. Karpov	F.-X. Roux
S. Arykov	V. Kas'yanov	M. Schellmann
A. Avetisyan	K. Kedzierski	D. Shkurko
E. Badouel	S. Kireev	P. Sloot
T. Bair	E. Kouzmin	P. Sobe
S. Bandini	N. Kuchin	V. Sokolov
O. Bandman	V. Kuzin	S. Sorokin
T. Casavant	K-C Li	A Stasenko
D. Chaly	Ch.-Ch. Lin	V. Subotic
H-Ya. Chang	P. Liu	D. Tack
Ye-Ch. Chung	J. Llosa	E. Timofeev
P. Degano	T. Ludwig	P. Trifonov
M. D. Marino	V. Malyshkin	C. Trinitis
P. Dortman	N. Malyshkin	M. Valero
F. Gadducci	S. Manzoni	I. Virbitskaite
A. Glebovsky	V. Marjanovic	V. Vshivkov
M. Gluhankov	V. Markova	J. Walters
B. Goossens	G. Mauri	Ch.-M. Wang
S. Gorlatch	Yu. Medvedev	H.-H. Wang
M. Gorodnichev	J. Mueller	T.-H. Weng
N. Gribovskaya	S. Nechaev	J.-J. Wu
A. Grishin	M. Ostapkevich	R. Yahyapour
R. Grossi	D. Parello	Ch.-T. Yang
R. Guanciale	D. Petcu	G. Zabinyako
Zh. Hu.	S. Piskunov	
K-Ch. Huang	K. Pyjov	

Table of Contents

Models and Languages

Applications

Techniques for Parallel Programming Supporting

Cellular Automata

Methods and Tools of Parallel Programming of Multicomputers

Looking for a Definition of
Dynamic Distributed Systems*

R. Baldoni[1], M. Bertier[2], M. Raynal[2], and S. Tucci-Piergiovanni[1]

[1] IRISA, Campus de Beaulieu, 35042 Rennes, France
[2] Computer Science Department, University *La Sapienza*, Roma, Italy
{marin.bertier,raynal}@irisa.fr,
{baldoni,sara.tucci}@dis.uniroma1.it

Abstract. This paper is a position paper on the nature of dynamic systems. While there is an agreement on the definition of what a static distributed system is, there is no agreed definition on what a dynamic distributed system is. This paper is a first step in that direction. To that end, it emphasizes two orthogonal dimensions that are present in any dynamic distributed system, namely the varying and possibly very large number of entities that currently define the system, and the fact that each of these entities knows only a few other entities (its neighbors) and possibly will never be able to know the whole system it is a member of. To illustrate the kind of issues one has to cope with in dynamic systems, the paper considers, as a "canonical" problem, a simple data aggregation problem. It shows the type of dynamic systems in which that problem can be solved and the ones in which it cannot be solved. The aim of the paper is to give the reader an idea of the subtleties and difficulties encountered when one wants to understand the nature of dynamic distributed systems.

1 Introduction

The nature of distributed computing. Distributed computing arises when the problem to solve involves several entities such that each entity has only a partial knowledge of the many parameters involved in the problem. According to the context, these entities are usually called processes, nodes, sites, sensors, actors, peers, agents, etc. The entities communicate and exchange data through a communication medium (usually an underlying network).

While *parallelism* and *real-time* can be respectively characterized by the words "efficiency" and "on time computing", distributed computing can be characterized by the word "uncertainty". This uncertainty is created by asynchrony, failures, unstable behaviors, non-monotonicity, system dynamism, mobility, low computing capability, scalability requirements, etc. Mastering one form or another of uncertainty is pervasive in all distributed computing problems. So, a fundamental issue of distributed computing consists in finding concepts and mechanisms that are general and powerful enough to allow reducing (or even eliminating) the underlying uncertainty.

---

* This work has been done in the context of the European Network of Excellence ReSIST (Resilience for Survivability in IST).

V. Malyshkin (Ed.): PaCT 2007, LNCS 4671, pp. 1–14, 2007.
© Springer-Verlag Berlin Heidelberg 2007

Static reliable asynchronous distributed systems. A distributed system (the software and hardware layer on top of which the distributed applications are executed) can be characterized by behavioral properties and structural properties. These properties define a computation model.

The static reliable asynchronous model is the most popular one. *Static* means that the number of entities is fixed. *Reliable* means that neither the entities nor the communication medium suffer failures. *Asynchronous* means that there is no particular assumption on the speed of the processes, or on message transfer delays. Moreover, the underlying network is usually considered as fully connected: any entity can send messages to, or receive messages from, any other entity (this means that the message routing is hidden at the abstraction level offered by this distributed computing model).

An important result associated with this distributed computing model is the determination of a consistent global state (sometimes called a snapshot). It has been shown [5] that the "best" that can be done is the computation of a global state (of the upper layer distributed application) with the following consistency guarantees: the computed global state is such that (1) the application could have passed through it, but (2) has not necessarily passed through it. There is no way to know whether or not the actual execution passed through that global state. This is one of the fundamental facets of the uncertainty encountered in static distributed systems.

Static unreliable asynchronous distributed systems. The simplest static unreliable asynchronous model is characterized by the fact that processes may crash. The most famous result for this model is the impossibility to solve the consensus problem as soon as a process may crash [6] (the consensus problem is a coordination - -or agreement- - problem. It consists in designing a deterministic protocol in which all the processes that do not crash reach a common decision based on their initial opinions). The impossibility to solve this problem comes from the net effect of asynchrony and failures. One way to solve consensus despite asynchrony and failures consists in enriching the asynchronous model with appropriate devices called failure detectors [3,10] (so, the resulting computing model is no longer fully asynchronous).

Fortunately, problems simpler than consensus can be solved in this model. Let us consider the reliable broadcast problem [8] as an example. This problem consists in providing the processes with a broadcast primitive such that all the processes that do not crash deliver all the messages that are broadcast (while the faulty processes are allowed to deliver only a subset of these messages). Let a correct process be a process that never crash. This problem can easily be solved as soon as any two correct processes remain forever connected through a path made up of reliable channels and correct processes.

So, when we proceed from the static reliable asynchronous distributed computing model to its unreliable counterpart, there are problems that can still be solved, while other problems become impossible to solve if asynchrony is not restricted (e.g., by using failure detectors, or considering their "ultimate" endpoint, namely, a synchronous system).

Dynamic distributed systems. Since a recent past, there are a lot of papers (mainly in the peer-to-peer literature) that propose protocols for what they call *dynamic systems*. These protocols share the following: the entities can join and leave the system at will. This dynamicity dimension constitutes a new attribute of the uncertainty that characterizes distributed computing. Unfortunately, (to our knowledge) there is no clear definition of what a dynamic system is. This paper is a first step in that direction. To that end, it proposes to investigate two dimensions of dynamicity. The first is on the number of entities that compose the system: is there an upper bound that is known? How many entities can coexist at any given time? etc. The second dimension is "geographical". More precisely, it is related to the fact that it is not possible to provide the entities with an abstraction offering a logical point-to-point bidirectional link to each pair of entities. So, this dimension is on the notion of entity neighborhood (locality) and the fact that the processes can or cannot know an upper bound on the network diameter.

Content of the paper. The paper is made up of 4 sections. Section 2 proposes parameters that should be taken into account when one wants to precisely define a dynamic system model. Considering a very simple dynamic system, Section 3 investigates what can be computed in this model. To that end a simple aggregation problem is used as a "canonical" problem. Section 4 provides a few concluding remarks.

The spirit of the paper is more the spirit of a position paper with a pedagogical flavor than the spirit of a traditional research paper. We do think that a precise definition of what a dynamic distributed system is (or maybe what families of dynamic distributed systems are) is hardly needed. This paper is a very first endeavor towards this goal.

2 Elements for Defining a Dynamic Distributed System

Informally, *a dynamic system is a continually running system in which an arbitrarily large number of processes are part of the system during each interval of time* and, *at any time, any process can directly interact with only an arbitrary small part of the system.* This section proposes and investigates two attributes that should be part of the definition of any dynamic distributed system.

2.1 Modeling the Dynamic Size of the System in Terms of Number of Entities

In a dynamic system, entities may join and leave the system at will. Consequently, at any point on time, the system is composed of all processes (entities) that have joined and have not yet left the system. We call *system run* (or simply a run) a total order on the join and leave events (issued by the processes) that respect their real time occurrence order.

In order to model entities continuously arriving to and departing from the system, we assume the infinite arrival model (as defined in [9]), where, in each run, infinitely many processes $P = \{\ldots, p_i, p_j, p_k \ldots\}$ may join the system. However, several models can be defined, that differ in the assumptions on the number of processes that can *concurrently* be part of the system [7,9]. Using the notation introduced in [1], the following infinite arrival models can be defined:

- M^b: The number of processes concurrently inside the system is bounded by a constant b in all runs.
- M^n: The number of processes concurrently inside the system is bounded in each run, but may be unbounded when we consider the union of all the runs.

- M: The number of processes that join the system in a single run may grow to infinity as the time passes.

In the first model, the maximum number of processes in each run is bounded by a constant b that is the same for all the runs. When it is known, that constant can be used by the protocols defined for that system.

In the second model, the maximum number of processes in each run is bounded, but that bound may vary from one run to another. It follows that no protocol can rely on such a bound as a protocol does not know in advance the particular run that will be produced.

In the third model, the number of processes concurrently inside the system is finite when we consider any finite time interval, but may be infinite in an infinite interval of time. This means that the only way for a system to have an infinite number of processes is the passage of time.

2.2   Modeling the Dynamic Size of the System in Terms of Geography

The previous models [7,9] implicitly assume that, at any time, the communication network is fully connected: any process knows any other process that is concurrently in the system, and can send it - -or receive from it- - messages directly through a point-to-point channel.

Our aim is here to relax this (sometimes unrealistic) assumption, and take into account the fact that, at any time, each process has only a partial view of the system, i.e., it can directly interact with only a subset of the processes that are present in the system (this part is called its *neighborhood*). So, we consider the following *geographical* attributes for the definition of a dynamic distributed system.

- At any time, the system can be represented by a graph $G = (P, E)$, where P is the set of processes currently in the system and E is a set of pairs (p_i, p_j) that describe a symmetric neighborhood relation connecting some pairs of processes. $(p_i, p_j) \in E$ means that there is a bidirectional reliable channel connecting p_i and p_j.
- The dynamicity of the system, i.e., the arrivals and departures of processes, is modeled through additions and removals of vertices and edges in the graph.
  - The addition of a process p_i to a graph G brings to another graph G' obtained from G by including p_i and a certain number of new edges (p_i, p_j) where the p_j are the processes to which p_i is directly connected.
  - The removal of a process p_i to a graph G brings to another graph G' obtained from G by suppressing the vertex p_i and all the edges involving p_i.
  - Some new edges can be added to the graph, and existing edges can be suppressed from the graph. Each such addition/deletion brings the graph G into another graph G'.
- Let $\{G_n\}_{run}$ denote the sequence of graphs through which the system passes during a given run. Each $G_n \in \{G_n\}_{run}$ is a *connected graph the diameter of which can be greater than one* for all runs.

As we have seen, an infinite arrival model allows capturing a dynamicity dimension of dynamic distributed systems. Making different assumptions on the diameters of the graphs in the sequences $\{G_n\}_{run}$ allows capturing another dynamicity dimension related to the "geography" of the system. More specifically, we consider the following possible attributes. In the following $\{D_n\}_{run}$ denotes the set of the diameters of the graphs $\{G_n\}_{run}$.

- *Bounded and known diameter.* In this case the diameter is always bounded by b, i.e., for each $D_n \in \{D_n\}_{run}$ we have $D_n \leq b$ for all the runs, and that bound is known by the protocols designed for that model.
- *Bounded and unknown diameter.* In this case all the diameters $\{D_n\}_{run}$ are finite in each run, but the union of $\{D_n\}_{run}$ for all runs can be unbounded. In that case, as an algorithm cannot know in which run it is working, it follows that the maximal diameter remains unknown to the protocol. So, in that model, a protocol has no information on the diameter.
- *Unbounded diameter.* In this case, the diameter is possibly growing indefinitely in a run, i.e., the limit of $\{D_n\}_{run}$ can go to infinity.

2.3 Dynamic Models Definition

A model is denoted as $M^{N,D}$ where N is on the number of processes and D is on the graph diameter, both parameters can assume the value b, n, ∞ to indicate respectively a number of entities/diameter never exceeding a known bound, a number of entities/diameter never exceeding an unknown bound and a number of entities/diameter possibly growing indefinitely (in the following, if a parameter may indifferently assume any value, we denote that as $*$). Possible models are $M^{b,b}$, $M^{n,b}$, $M^{\infty,b}$ ([1]), $M^{n,n}$, $M^{\infty,n}$ and $M^{\infty,\infty}$.

Note that the previous models characterize only the *dynamicity* of the system without considering other more classical aspects such as the level of synchrony or the type of failures. Clearly, any of these models can be refined further by specifying these additional model attributes as usually done in static systems.

To be able to establish the impact of geographical assumptions on a problem solving in dynamic distributed systems, we only consider, in this paper, synchronous systems or asynchronous system completed with perfect failure detectors. In other words, we assume that a node can have reliable information about nodes in its neighborhood.

3   An illustrating Example: One-Time Query

3.1   The One-Time Query Problem

To illustrate and investigate the previous attributes of a dynamic distributed system, we consider the *One-Time Query* problem as defined in [2]. This problem can informally be defined as follows. A process (node) issues a query in order to aggregate data that are distributed among a set of processes (nodes). The issuing process does not know (i) if there exist nodes holding a value matched by the query, (ii) where these nodes are, (iii) how many they are. However, the query has to complete in a meaningful way in spite of the uncertainty in which the querying node works.

---

[1] An instance of the model $M^{\infty,b}$ is M^{∞} of [1] where the diameter is implicitly set to 1.

The One-Time Query problem, as stated in [2] requires that the query, issued by a node p_i aggregates *at least* all the values held by the nodes that are in the system and are connected to p_i during the whole duration of the query (query time interval).

Unfortunately, this specification has been intended for a model slightly different from the more general model proposed in the previous section. In fact, the system is intended to be *monotonous* in the sense that it can be represented by a graph G defined at the beginning of the computation (query) and from which edges can be removed as time passes, but to which no new edges can be added as time passes. Differently, in the previous models, the system is *dynamic* in the sense that nodes/edges additions and nodes/edges deletions are allowed. As we are about to see, while the One-Time Query problem -as defined above- cannot be solved in a dynamic system, a weaker version of it can be. It is also important to notice (as we will show later) that this weaker version cannot be solved in $M^{\infty,\infty}$.

One-Time Query specification. The specification that follows is due to [2]. Let $query(Q)$ denote the operation a process invoke to aggregate the set of values $V = \{v_1, v_2, \ldots\}$ present in the system and that match the query. The aim for the process that issues the query is to compute $v = Q(V)$. Given that setting, the problem is defined by the following properties (this means that any protocol solving the problem has to satisfy these properties):

- **Termination:** $query(Q)$ completes in a finite time.
- **Validity:** The set V of data obtained for computing $query(Q)$ includes at least the values held by processes that are member of the system during the whole query time interval.

3.2   The WILDFIRE Algorithm

In [2] the following algorithm (called WILDFIRE) to solve the problem is proposed. This algorithm relies on the following assumptions:

- synchronous channels with a known upper bound δ,
- a known upper bound on the network diameter D.

Algorithm description. The principle of this algorithm is simple. Each process which receives a so-called query-update message updates its current value to a new one, computed by aggregating the current value and the received value, then it spreads the new value to its neighbors.

The initiator of the query just sends its initial value to its neighbors in a query-update message and waits for at least $2 * D * \delta$ time before returning its value. $D * \delta$ is the time required to inform all nodes in the network about the query, and the same duration is required to transmit values to the initiator.

As the initiator, all nodes which receive a query-update message for the first time, initiate a timeout and when this timeout expires, they stop to process all new query-update messages.

In [2], the authors propose to reduce the number of messages exchanged by sending a query-update message only when there is new information: (i) if the remote value doesn't change the local value, then the node doesn't send any message (except for the first reception of the query-update message), (ii) if the aggregate value is equal to the remote one, then the node transmits the new value to its neighbors except the sender of the remote value.

INITIALIZATION
1   $active \leftarrow false$;
2   $v \leftarrow initial\_value$;

LAUNCH(Q)
3   $active \leftarrow true$;
4   $d \leftarrow D$; % D is the upper bound on the network diameter. %
5   **send** [QUERY-UPDATE $(Q, d-1, v)$] **to** $neighbors$;
6   **set** $timeout\ T \leftarrow 2d * \delta$;
7   **when** $(T\ elapses)$ **do**
8     $active \leftarrow false$;
9   **return** (v);

RECEPTION
10   **when** (**receive** [QUERY-UPDATE(Q, d, rv)] **from** p_j) **do**
11   **if** $(\neg active)$
12   **then set** $timeout\ T \leftarrow 2d * \delta$; % We consider negligible process step's executions w.r.t. message delays. %
13   **if** $(T\ not\ yet\ elapsed)$
14   **then** $temp \leftarrow aggregate(v, rv)$;
15   **if** $(temp! = v\ \textbf{or}\ \neg active)$
16   **then** $active \leftarrow true; v \leftarrow temp$;
17   **send** [QUERY-UPDATE,$(Q, d-1, v)$] **to** $neighbors - p_j$;
18   **if** $(v! = rv)$
19   **then send** [QUERY-UPDATE,$(Q, d-1, v)$] **to** p_j

Fig. 1. The WILDFIRE Algorithm

3.3   The One-Time Query Problem for Dynamic Models

One-Time Query problem solvability. The WILDFIRE algorithm solves the one-time query problem in a monotonous network but does not solve it in a dynamic network (in none of the models presented in the previous section, neither in $M^{*,b}$). More generally, the one-time query specification introduced so far is too strong, and cannot be satisfied by any algorithm if the network graph can change by *adding* edges *during the query completion* [2]. However, if an edge is added during a query, the following bad scenario can happen.

Description on a bad scenario. Let us consider the querying process p_A and a process p_E (i) inside the system when the query starts and (ii) connected to p_A through a given path. Let us suppose that an edge joining p_A and p_E is *added after* the query started and remains up until the query ends. Let us also suppose that the path previously connecting p_A and p_E is removed (due to a crash of some process in the path) before the query ends. Formally, p_A is always connected to p_B throughout the entire duration of the query (as herein assumed by all dynamic models), but its value could not be retrieved as described in Figure 2 where t_q is the time the query starts.

---

[2] The addition of edges during the query completion is reasonable as the query takes an arbitrary long time spanning the entire graph and in order to maintain connectivity edges addition may be needed in spite of edges removals occurring at arbitrary times.

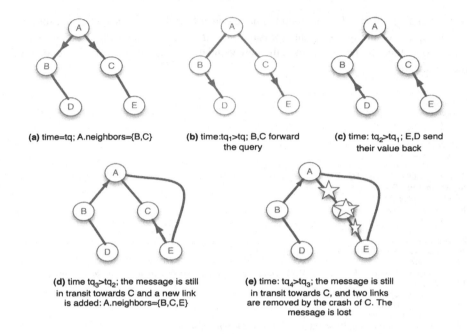

(a) time=tq; A.neighbors={B,C}

(b) time:tq_1>tq; B,C forward the query

(c) time: tq_2>tq_1; E,D send their value back

(d) time tq_3>tq_2; the message is still in transit towards C and a new link is added: A.neighbors={B,C,E}

(e) time: tq_4>tq_3; the message is still in transit towards C, and two links are removed by the crash of C. The message is lost

Fig. 2. Bug Example

The problem lies in the fact that the process p_E replies to the query but the message containing the reply is exchanged through a path that is removed before the query completes, and is consequently lost before it reaches the querying process.

Then, to retrieve this value, p_E should be forced to send again the reply back (this can be done by assuming a detection of the path removal that triggers a new sending on the new path). However, by the nature of the infinite arrival model, the substitution of a path with a new one during the query could happen infinitely often in all dynamic models in which the diameter is not bounded by one (see Fig. 3). In all these models the query may never complete violating termination.

One-Time Query specification for dynamic models. The specification of the one-time query problem in case of a dynamic model is here refined bringing to the definition of the Dynamic One-Time Query Specification. This new specification states that the values to include in the query computation are at least those coming from nodes that belong to the graph G defined at time the query starts, and remain connected, during the whole query interval, to the querying process through a subgraph of G. More formally, the Dynamic One-Time Query specification satisfies the following two properties:

– **Termination:** $query(Q)$ completes in a finite time.
– **Dynamic Validity:** For each run, $query(Q)$ will compute the result including in V at least the values held by each process that, during the whole query interval, remains connected to the querying process through a subgraph of the graph G that represents the network at the time the query is started.

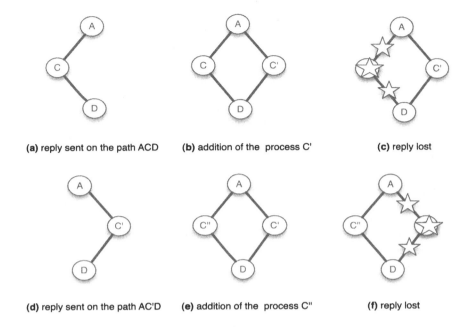

(a) reply sent on the path ACD   **(b)** addition of the process C'   **(c)** reply lost

(d) reply sent on the path AC'D   **(e)** addition of the process C''   **(f)** reply lost

Fig. 3. Bad Pattern of Graphs Changing

It is important to note (and easy to see) that the dynamic one-time query specification is satisfied by the WILDFIRE algorithm in the model $M^{*,b}$ with $b > 1$. In the following we will explore if there exist solutions without assuming a known upper bound on the diameter.

3.4   The DEPTHSEARCH Algorithm

The algorithm that follows (called DEPTHSEARCH) solves the one-time query problem as defined just previously. That protocol relies on the following assumptions.

- asynchronous model enriched with a perfect failure detector (the faulty processes are deleted from the set *neighborhood*),
- unique process identifiers,
- a finite diameter of the network (not known in advance).

Algorithm description. This algorithm works in a different way than WILDFIRE. In WILDFIRE, many query-update messages are exchanged all over the network at the same time. In the DEPTHSEARCH algorithm only one message (query or reply) is transmitted at one time. The only case, in which two different queries co-exist, is the consequence of a disconnection between two nodes, but in any case only one query is taken into account.

This algorithm manages several sets:

- The set values that contains all values currently collected,
- The set replied that contains the identifiers of the nodes that have provided their value,

– querying contains the identifiers of the nodes that have sent a querying message and are waiting for replies from their neighborhood. These nodes (except the query initiator) are also nodes that have to provide their value to some other querying process.

This algorithm works similarly to a depth-first tree traversal algorithm (it traverses the nodes that compose the system). When a node p_i receives a query message, it checks if some of its neighbors have not yet received the query message yet by checking the querying and replied set. If some of them have not yet received a query message, then p_i sends to the first of them (say p_j) a query message and waits until it receives a reply from p_j.

When the node p_i receives a reply message from p_j, or if p_j is no more in the p_i's neighborhood (p_i is failed or is disconnected), the node p_i sends a query message to the next neighbor that has not yet received a query message. When all p_i's neighgbors have received a query message or are no longer in the p_i's neighborhood, then p_i sends back a reply message with the values and replied set updated or, if p_i is the query initiator, it returns the set of values.

INITIALIZATION
1   $querying \leftarrow \emptyset$;   % set of processes forwarding the query %;
2   $replied \leftarrow \emptyset$;   % set of processes replied to the query %;
3   $targets \leftarrow \emptyset$;   % set of processes to query by the local process %;
4   $values \leftarrow \{local\_value\}$;   % set of processes to query by the local process %;
5   $neighborhood$ % set of correct neighbors provided and updated by the perfect failure detector %

REQUEST (Q)
6   $targets \leftarrow neighborhood$; % This line freezes the neighbor set %;
7   $querying \leftarrow querying \cup \{local\_id\}$;
8   **for each** $i := 1$ *to* $|targets|$
9   **if** $(targets[i] \notin \{querying\} \cup \{replied\})$
10   **then send** [QUERY,$(Q, querying, replied)$] **to** $n[i]$;
11   **wait until** (**receive** [REPLY,$r\_values, r\_replied$] **from** $n[i] \lor n[i] \notin neighborhood$);
12   **if** $(n[i] \in neighborhood)$
13   **then** $values \leftarrow values \cup r\_values$;
14              $replied \leftarrow replied \cup r\_replied$

LAUNCH (Q)
15   REQUEST (Q);
16   **return** $(values)$

RECEPTION
17   **when** (**receive** [QUERY,$(Q, r\_querying, r\_replied)$] **from** p_j) **do**
18     $querying \leftarrow r\_querying$;
19     $replied \leftarrow r\_replied$;
20   REQUEST (Q);
21     $replied \leftarrow replied \cup \{local\_id\}$;
22   **send** [REPLY,$(values, replied)$] **to** p_j;

Fig. 4. The DEPTHSEARCH Algorithm

Algorithm illustration. To illustrate the protocol behaviour, let us consider the computation related to a query initiated by a node p_A in the network shown in Figure 5. In this scenario p_A starts to query the first process in the $p_A.targets = (B, C, D)$ set, p_B does the same with its $p_B.targets = (A, C, E)$ set where $p_B.querying =$

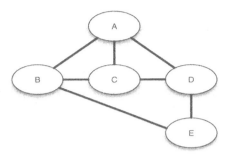

Fig. 5. Graph Representing the Network during the A's Query

$p_A.querying = \{A\}$. Then p_B queries p_C, piggybacking the list of querying processes, that now is $\{A,B\}$. Then, p_C does not query anyone and gives back a reply to p_B, with a list of *replied* processes equal to $\{C\}$. At this point, p_B queries p_E. Let us consider the case in which the edge (p_B, p_E) breaks, then p_B ends and becomes part of *replied* giving back to p_A the value come from p_B, v_b, and the value from p_C, v_c. Then, p_A avoids to query p_C as part of *replied* and queries directly p_D, piggybacking the list of $p_A.querying$ still containing only A and the list of *replied* equal to $\{B,C\}$. Then p_D avoids to query p_C and it queries only p_E. p_E receives the query with the following information: querying processes $\{A,D\}$, replied processes $\{B,C\}$. Then, the process p_E terminates the querying phase and sends back a reply to p_D containing v_E. p_D terminates the querying phase also as its pending list is empty (targets-querying-replied) and sends back the reply containing v_E, v_D. p_A terminates the querying phase, computes the result on the values of all nodes, and returns.

DEPTHSEARCH *correctness proof.* In the following we formally prove that the DEPTH-SEARCH algorithm solves the dynamic one time query problem in any model with a bounded but unknown diameter (Theorem 1). In particular, Lemma 1 proves that the DEPTHSEARCH algorithm satisfies **Dynamic Validity** while Lemma 2 proves that the algorithm satisfies **Termination**.

Lemma 1 (Dynamic Validity). DEPTHSEARCH *satisfies the* **Dynamic Validity** *property in the* $M^{\infty,n}$ *model.*

Proof. (Sketch) Let G be the graph representing the network when the query starts and let us consider the maximal connected subgraph G' of G at the time the query ends which includes the query initiator p_A. Let us assume by contradiction that when the query ends, p_A does not comprise in its *values* set the value of one node p_X in the graph G'.

Since p_X belongs to G', then there exists a non-empty set of paths (generally non-independent) which connect p_A and p_X belonging to G' (and G). Without loss of generality let us suppose that there exists only one of such paths $P = \{p_A, ..., p_X\}$.

Let us first observe that when a process p_i receives a query q, the query has actually traversed a sequence of processes which are in the querying state and always comprising the initiator p_A. Let us call this sequence as the query path for the received query. By construction (line 9) no process in the sequence is in the *replied* set of any process of the sequence. Then, if p_i replies back to the query, its value starts to flow back on the query path, and each processes which receives it, stores p_i in the *replied* set and the p_i's local value in the *values* set. On the other hand, if the query path breaks, then the flowing of the value towards p_A could block. All nodes which did not receive the value back are a prefix of the broken query path and are still in their querying phase (a node is in the querying phase at least the time its succesor in the path is in the querying phase). None of these processes have p_i in the *replied* set then, a new query path reaching p_i with this prefix is still possible. Moreover, even disconnected nodes which have p_i in the replied set, will renew this set excluding p_i when they receive a new query (line 19) from one of the querying nodes of this prefix.

Let us now consider the case of p_X. p_X will have the path P connecting it to p_A which is up for the whole time interval. However, it could receive a query from another query path which breaks before p_A gets the value of p_X. This could happen more than once, depending on the graph G topology and changes while the algorithm work. Without loss of generality let us suppose that only two paths connect p_A to p_i, i.e. P and a path F which shares with P a non-empty prefix pfx, and the F is the first explored by the algorithm. Let us also suppose that the path F breaks leaving nodes of pfx without the value of p_X. In this case the last node of pfx, let's say p_l, once revealed the disconnection explores another path with the same prefix pfx. Without loss of generality we can now suppose it will explore P. In fact we can assume that all other explored paths before P could complete correclty bringing then the p_l to query its successor in P (by the accuracy property of the failure detector no nodes in the path P can be excluded), this successor does the same as each process between p_l and p_X, leading then to query p_X. By contradiction we assumed that p_X was not in the p_A values when p_A stops to be querying, however when p_A stops to be querying the value of p_X has been surely flowed on the path P leading to a contradiction. $\square_{Lemma\ 1}$

Lemma 2. *The DEPTHSEARCH algorithm satisfies* **Termination** *in the model* $M^{\infty,n}$.

Proof. The only statement blocks the protocol is the wait statement at line 11. Let us call as querying process a process which sent the query message to some node and is waiting for a reply, i.e. a process blocked at statement 11. By the completeness property of the failure detector no querying process can block due to a failure of a node in its neighborhood. Then, let us suppose that no failures happen during the query interval, this also implies that the graph representing the network when the query starts can only grow during this time. By the pseudo-code, a querying node waits a reply from each neighbor which was in the neighborhood when the query is received (line 6). Then, even if in the model $M^{\infty,n}$, a node could have an always growing neighborhood, the neighborhood to wait from never grows, i.e. each querying node p_i has to wait a reply from a bounded number of neighbors n_i. Starting from p_A (the initiator) the query message starts to flow in the graph involving the first neighbor of p_A, which in turn involves its first neighbor and so on. Let us denote as $\{p_1^1, p_1^2, p_1^3...\}$ the sequence of processes in which p_1^i is the first neighbor of the process p_1^{i-1}. A first observation on the diameter of the graph which is bounded as the model implies, leads to conclude that this sequence is bounded when all these processes are one different to the other.

On the other hand, since the *querying* set, sent along with the query, includes all the sequence $\{p_1^1, \dots p_1^{i-1}\}$ when arrives at p_1^i, the query stops to flow when (i) either the last process is reached (in the case it contains all different processes) (ii) the first time a process is repeated in the sequence (which means that the sequence contained a loop). Let us denote as p_1^i this last node, it will reply back by letting the process p_1^{i-1} to query its second neighbor. A second observation about the arbitrary order of neighbors in the neighborhoods which make indistinguishable a sequence of processes through where a query flows from another leads to assume $n_i = 1$ for each p_i without lossing generality. This means that each querying process starting from p_1^{i-1} will unblock p_1^{i-2} by replying back its value. All querying processes in the system will eventually unblock preserving Termination.
$$\square_{Lemma\ 2}$$

Theorem 1. *The* DEPTHSEARCH *algorithm solves the dynamic one time query problem in the model* $M^{\infty,n}$.

Proof. It immediately follows from Lemma 1 and Lemma 2. $\square_{Theorem\ 1}$

3.5   Impossibility of Solving the Dynamic One-Time Query Problem in $M^{\infty,\infty}$

This proof is simple. It is based on the race among the message that arrives at a process p_i just a moment before a new process p_{i+1} joins linking to p_i. The race is infinite as a diameter always growing makes possible stretching the path by one infinitely often.

Theorem 2. *The dynamic one-time query problem cannot be solved in the model* $M^{\infty,\infty}$.

Proof. Let us suppose by contradiction that given any operation $query()$, (i) $query()$ will take a finite time Δ, (ii) the operation gathers values from all processes inside the graph for the whole time duration and which are connected to the querying process through the graph defined at the time the query starts or its subgraphs.

Let consider a process p_i invoking a $query()$ operation at some point of time t_q. Let us suppose that a time t_0 (initial time) the network graph consists of a finite path of processes denoted as $\{p_i, \dots p_k\}$. Then, let us suppose that this path infinitely grows along the time, without loss of generality, let us suppose that the path length is increased by 1, by adding a process p_h^i, each δ time interval. Then after $t_0 + n\delta$ the graph consists of the path $\{p_i \dots p_k, p_h^1, p_h^2 \dots p_h^n\}$.

Let us now consider a run R in which $t_q = k\delta + t_0$. In this case all processes $\{p_i \dots p_k, p_h^1, p_h^2 \dots p_h^k\}$ must necessarily receive the query message in order to be involved in the $query()$ operation as the specification requires. This also implies that the process p_h^{k-1} must send the query message to p_h^k. By construction p_h^k belongs to p_h^{k-1}'s neighborhood before the time t_r in which p_h^{k-1} receives the query message.

Now we consider a run R' with the same scenario as R but with $t_q = (k-1)\delta + t_0$ and the time at which p_h^{k-1} receives the query message is again t_r where $t_r > k\delta + t_0$; As p_h^{k-1} cannot determine t_q, then R and R' are indistinguishable for p_h^{k-1}. This means that in R', p_h^{k-1} will relay the message to p_h^k.

This implies that, each process receiving a query message must relay it to the neighborhood defined at the time the query message has been received. Each $query()$ operation can terminate only when a reply has been gathered by all these processes.

Then, consider a run in which each process p_h^i receives the query message at time $t_r^i > (i+1)\delta$. The number of processes will receive the query message will be infinite and Δ is infinite as well, getting a contradiction. $\qquad\qquad \square_{Theorem\ 2}$

4   Conclusion

The aim of this position paper was the investigation of two attributes that characterize dynamic distributed systems, namely the varying size of the system (according to process joins and departures), and its "geography" captured by the notion of process neighborhood. In order to illustrate these notions, the paper has considered the One-Time query problem as a benchmark problem. It has been shown that (1) the traditional definition of this problem has to be weakened in order the problem can be solved in some dynamic models, and (2) it cannot be solved in all dynamic models. The quest for a general definition of what a "dynamic distributed system" is (a definition on which the distributed system and network communities could agree) still remains a holy grail quest.

References

1. Aguilera, M.K.: A Pleasant Stroll Through the Land of Infinitely Many Creatures. ACM SIGACT News, Distributed Computing Column 35(2), 36–59 (2004)
2. Bawa, M., Gionis, A., Garcia-Molina, H., Motwani, R.: The Price of Validity in Dynamic Networks. In: Proc. ACM Int'l Conference on Management of Data (SIGMOD), pp. 515–526. ACM Press, New York (2004)
3. Chandra, T., Toueg, S.: Unreliable Failure Detectors for Reliable Distributed Systems. Journal of the ACM 43(2), 225–267 (1996)
4. Chandra, T., Hadzilacos, V., Toueg, S.: The Weakest Failure Detector for Solving Consensus. Journal of the ACM 43(4), 685–722 (1996)
5. Chandy, K.M., Lamport, L.: Distributed Snapshots: Determining Global States of Distributed Systems. ACM Trans. on Computer Systems 3(1), 63–75 (1985)
6. Fischer, M.J., Lynch, N.A., Paterson, M.S.: Impossibility of Distributed Consensus with One Faulty Process. Journal of the ACM 32(2), 374–382 (1985)
7. Gafni, E., Merritt, M., Taubenfeld, G.: The concurrency hierarchy, and algorithms for unbounded concurrency. In: Proc. 20th ACM Symposium on Principles of Distributed Computing (PODC '01), pp. 161–16 (2001)
8. Hadzilacos, V., Toueg, S.: Reliable Broadcast and Related Problems. In: Distributed Systems, pp. 97–145. ACM Press, New York (1993)
9. Merritt, M., Taubenfeld, G.: Computing with Infinitely Many Processes. In: Herlihy, M.P. (ed.) DISC 2000. LNCS, vol. 1914, pp. 164–178. Springer, Heidelberg (2000)
10. Raynal, M.: A Short Introduction to Failure Detectors for Asynchronous Distributed Systems. ACM SIGACT News, Distr. Computing Column 36(1), 53–70 (2005)

Adaptive Workflow Nets for Grid Computing*

Carmen Bratosin, Kees van Hee, and Natalia Sidorova

Department of Mathematics and Computer Science
Eindhoven University of Technology
P.O. Box 513, 5600 MB Eindhoven, The Netherlands
c.c.bratosin@tue.nl, k.m.v.hee@tue.nl, n.sidorova@tue.nl

Abstract. Existing grid applications commonly use workflows for the orchestration of grid services. Existing workflow models however suffer from the lack of adaptivity. In this paper we define Adaptive Grid Workflow nets (AGWF nets) appropriate for modeling grid workflows and allowing changes in the process structure as a response to triggering events/exceptions. Moreover, a recursion is allowed, which makes the model especially appropriate for a number of grid applications. We show that soundness can be verified for AGWF nets.

Keywords: workflows, Petri nets, grid computing, coordination, modeling, verification.

1 Introduction

The notion of workflow appeared first in the world of enterprize information systems, where the execution of business processes is divided over several components, each with its own task. One of these components is a workflow engine that takes care of the control flow only. This separation of concerns is very fruitful and allows designers to prove (partial) correctness of the designed system.

Almost all the existing grid applications currently also use the idea of workflow to model processes. From the grid point of view, a workflow is a mean for the automation of processes, which involves the orchestration of a set of grid services, agents and actors that must be combined together to solve a problem or to define a new service [5]. The most common model used for grid workflows is the Directed Acyclic Graph (DAG). Although DAGs are intuitive for process descriptions, their modeling power has limitations (e.g. they does not support loop patterns and does not allow dynamic process changes driven by events happened in the system).

In [6], we introduced Adaptive Workflow Nets (AWF nets), an extension of workflow Petri nets [2,3] with the nesting concept [10]. AWF nets allow to include dynamic process changes and a fault handling mechanism into a model without forcing the user to get into implementation details. In this paper we

---

* This research is supported by the GLANCE NWO project "Workflow Management for Large Parallel and Distributed Applications".

V. Malyshkin (Ed.): PaCT 2007, LNCS 4671, pp. 15–21, 2007.

define Adaptive Grid Workflow nets (AGWF nets), a subclass of AWF nets appropriate for modeling grid workflows. AGWF nets allow changes in the process structure as a response to triggering events/exceptions (adaptivity). They make use of a pattern library, which easies reusability. Exception transitions are used as a solution to the robustness problem. Moreover, a (restricted form of) recursion is allowed, which makes it especially appropriate for a number of grid applications.

An important correctness property of workflow nets is soundness [2,3], which means that each computation *can* always terminate without leaving garbage[1]. In this paper we show that soundness can be checked for AGWF nets.

Related work. The advantages of the use of colored Petri nets for modeling grid workflows are considered in [9]. Tokens represent there real data and the net is used to model the interactions between different software resources. Similar graph representations can be found in [4,11]. Neither one however considers flexibility and adaptivity aspects.

The rest of the paper is organized as follows. In Section 2 we give basic definitions. In Section 3 we introduce the notion of adaptive grid workflow nets and formulate the soundness criterium for them. In Section 4 we discuss the obtained results and indicate directions for future work.

2   Preliminaries

$\mathbb{N}$ denotes the set of natural numbers. A *bag (multiset)* M over a set P is a mapping $M: P \to \mathbb{N}$. The set of all bags over P is also denoted by $\mathbb{N}^P$. We use $+$ and $-$ for the sum and the difference of two bags and $=, <, >, \leq, \geq$ for comparisons of bags, which are defined in the standard way. We overload the set notation, writing $\emptyset$ for the empty bag and $\in$ for the element inclusion. We write e.g. $M = 2[p] + [q]$ for a bag M with $M(p) = 2$, $M(q) = 1$ and $M(r) = 0$ for all $r \in P \setminus \{p, q\}$.

A *Petri net* is a tuple $N = \langle P, T, F, l \rangle$, where: (1) P and T are two disjoint non-empty finite sets of *places* and *transitions* respectively, elements of the set $P \cup T$ are called *nodes* of N; (2) $F \subseteq (P \times T) \cup (T \times P)$ is a *flow relation* between places and transitions and conversely; (3) l is a labeling function for transitions mapping each $t \in T$ to some label $l(t) \in \Sigma$, where Σ is a finite set of labels.

Let $N = \langle P, T, F, l \rangle$ be a Petri net and $T' \subseteq T$. The *projection* $N_{|T'}$ of N on T' is the net $\langle P, T', F', l' \rangle$, where $F' = \{(x,y)|(x,y) \in F \wedge x, y \notin T \setminus T'\}$ and $l': T' \to \Sigma$ with $l'(t) = l(t)$ for all $t \in T'$.

Markings are states (configurations) of a net interpreted as bags over P. A *marked net* is a tuple (N, M), where N is a net and M is its marking.

Given a node $n \in (P \cup T)$, the *preset* $^\bullet n$ and the *postset* $n^\bullet$ of t are the sets $\{n'|(n',n) \in F\}$ and $\{n''|(n,n'') \in F\}$ respectively. We will say that a node n

---

[1] Note that soundness differs from the halting problem, which is the property that a computation *will* always terminate.

is a *source* node iff $^\bullet n = \emptyset$ and n is a *sink* node iff $n^\bullet = \emptyset$. A *path* of a net is a sequence $\langle x_0, \ldots, x_n \rangle$ of nodes such that $\forall i : 1 \leq i \leq n : x_{i-1} \in {}^\bullet x_i$.

We define the firing relation $\longrightarrow$ as $M + {}^\bullet t \xrightarrow{t} M + t^\bullet$ for any marking M and transition t. $M \xrightarrow{t}$ is an abbreviation of $\exists M' :: M \xrightarrow{t} M'$. For $\sigma = t_1 \ldots t_n$, we write $M \xrightarrow{\sigma} M'$ iff $M \xrightarrow{t_1} \cdots \xrightarrow{t_n} M'$. Next, $M \xrightarrow{*} M'$ iff $\exists \sigma :: M \xrightarrow{\sigma} M'$ and $\mathcal{R}(N, M)$ denotes $\{M' \mid M \xrightarrow{*} M'\}$, the markings of N reachable from M.

A *workflow net* is a Petri net with one initial (source) place i and one final (sink) place f and every place and transition of the net being on a directed path from the initial to the final place. The initial marking of a workflow net is $[i]$ and the (desired) final marking is $[f]$.

3   Adaptive Grid Workflow Nets

In this section we define *Adaptive Grid Workflow nets* (AGWF-nets) and formulate the soundness criterium for them. We start with introducing a notion of Extended Workflow nets (EWF-nets), which form the basis for AGWF-nets.

Extended Workflow nets [6,7] are an extension of Workflow nets [2,3] that simplifies the modeling of exceptions by making a clear distinction between normal termination and termination caused by an exception. When an exception occurs, it is observed by some upper layer, which handles it. The execution of the EWF net is then terminated.

We consider a partition of the set of transitions $T = T_e \cup T_n$, where T_e is the set of *exception transitions* and T_n is the set of non-exception transitions. The set Σ of labels is partitioned into $\Sigma_e \cup \Sigma_n$ accordingly.

Definition 1 (Extended workflow net). *A net $N = \langle P, T_e \cup T_n, F, l \rangle$ is an extended workflow net (EWF net) iff (1) the net $N_{|T_n}$ is a workflow net; (2) for all $t \in T_e$, $t^\bullet = \emptyset$, ${}^\bullet t \neq \emptyset$, and ${}^\bullet t \subseteq P \setminus \{f\}$; (3) for all $t \in T_e$, $l(t) \in \Sigma_e$, and for all $t \in T_n$, $l(t) \in \Sigma_n$.*

As usual, the state of the net is given by its marking. The initial marking consists of a single token on the initial place. The only change in the semantics w.r.t. the standard semantics of Petri nets is that exception transitions terminate the execution of the net.

We allow standard algebraic operations on EWF nets: Two (unmarked) nets can be combined to produce a new net by means of sequential ($\cdot$) and parallel ($\|$) composition and choice ($+$). Parallel composition can also be applied to marked nets, and sequential composition to a marked net and an unmarked net.

Adaptive workflow nets. In [6], we introduced a class of nets, called *adaptive workflow nets* (AWF nets), allowing more flexibility and adaptivity than existing workflow systems. By adaptivity we understand an ability to modify processes in a structured way as response to some triggering events, for instance by extending a process with a subprocess. In [7] we considered a non-recursive subclass of AWF nets from [6] that is well-suited for modeling business workflows and showed how to verify their soundness using abstractions. Recursion is however essential for a number of grid applications. Here we describe a recursive subclass of adaptive workflow systems appropriate for grid applications for which soundness is still decidable.

Let $Var = \{v, \ldots\}$ be a finite set of *variable* names and *Con* a finite set of *constant* names. We assume a given library of process descriptions to be used as basic building blocks for constructing more complex processes by using net expressions. A net expression e and a token expression te are inductively defined as: $e := c \mid e + e \mid e\|e \mid e.e$, $te := \mathfrak{b} \mid ce$ and $ce := v \mid ce\|ce \mid ce.e \mid init(e)$, where $v \in Var$, $c \in Con$. The sets of all net expressions and token expressions are denoted by *Expr* and *CExpr*, respectively. The expressions in *Expr* will be interpreted as adaptive workflow nets while the expressions in *CExpr* denote either black tokens ($\mathfrak{b}$) or marked adaptive workflow nets. Given an expression $e \in CExpr$, the set of variables appearing in it is denoted $Var(e)$ and the set of constants in it is denoted by $Con(e)$.

Firings of the adaptive net can depend on firings in the net tokens, which is modelled by the guards of transitions expressed in the guard language $\mathcal{G}$. A guard g is defined as $g := \top \mid final(v) \mid e(v)$, where $v \in Var$ and $e \in \Sigma_e$. A guard $final(v)$ is called *termination guard* and $e(v) \in \mathcal{G}$ is called an *exception guard*. The set of all guards is denoted by $\mathcal{G}$. Intuitively, the guard $\top$ of a transition t means that the firing of t does not depend on the internal states of the net tokens, $e(v)$ means that the firing of t is conditioned by the firing of an exception transition with label e in the token net v, whereas $final(v)$ means that it is conditioned by the token net v having reached the final marking $[(f, \mathfrak{b})]$.

We define now nested workflow nets as extended EWF nets.

Definition 2 (Adaptive workflow net). *A Adaptive Workflow net $\mathcal{N}$ is a tuple $\langle P, T, F, \mathcal{E}, g, l \rangle$, where $\langle P, T, F, l \rangle$ is an EWF net called* system net *and the extensions $\mathcal{E}, g$ are defined by:*

- *$\mathcal{E} \colon F \to CExpr$ are arc expressions such that*
  1. *All input arcs for transitions are mapped either to the black token or to variables, i.e. for every $(p, t) \in F$, $\mathcal{E}(p, t) \in Var \cup \{\mathfrak{b}\}$;*
  2. *Every two variables on two different input arcs of a transition are distinct, i.e. for all (p, t), $(p', t) \in F$ with $p \neq p'$, $Var(\mathcal{E}(p, t)) \cap Var(\mathcal{E}(p', t)) = \emptyset$;*
  3. *Every variable on the outgoing arc of a transition also occurs in the expression of some incoming arc of this transition, i.e. for all $(t, p) \in F$, $v \in Var(\mathcal{E}(t, p))$ implies $v \in Var(\mathcal{E}(p', t))$ for some $(p', t) \in F$;*
  4. *All outgoing arcs of the initial place and incoming arcs of the final place are mapped to the black token, i.e. for all $t \in i^\bullet$, $\mathcal{E}(i, t) = \mathfrak{b}$ and for all $t \in {}^\bullet f$, $\mathcal{E}(t, f) = \mathfrak{b}$.*
- *g is a function that maps transitions from T to expressions from $\mathcal{G}$ such that the variable of a guard $g(t)$ $(t \in T)$ appears in the expression of some incoming arc of t and does not appear in any outgoing arc of t, i.e. $Var(g(t)) \subseteq \bigcup_{p \in {}^\bullet t} Var(\mathcal{E}(p, t))$ and $Var(g(t)) \cap \bigcup_{p \in t^\bullet} Var(\mathcal{E}(t, p)) = \emptyset$.*

For the sake of brevity, we define the semantics of AWF nets at an informal level. An *adaptive workflow net* can be seeing as a special colored EWF net (the system net), whose tokens can be either (marked) adaptive workflow nets themselves, called *token nets*, or black tokens. Transitions with *true* as a guard may fire if there are enough tokens on their input places, like in classical Petri nets. A transition t guarded by $final(x)$ may fire if there are enough tokens on its input places and the place connected to t by the arc with variable x contains a token net that has reached its final state $[(f, \flat)]$. This token will then be consumed from p during the firing. A transition t guarded by $e(x)$ may fire if there are enough tokens on its input places and some transition with label e is enabled in a token net contained in the place connected to t by the arc with variable x. Again, it is this token that will be used in the transition firing. Note that since we require that the output arc expressions do not contain variables from the transition guard, the net token x gets destroyed. The output token nets are computed according to the corresponding arc expressions where variables are substituted by the token nets from the input places, participating in the firing.

Soundness. Soundness is an important property of adaptive workflow nets stating that at any moment of system run there is a chance to terminate properly by reaching the final marking, also when no exception occurs in token nets. We define soundness for adaptive nets as proper termination of every reachable marking by firing only non-exceptional transitions without synchronizing on exceptions:

Definition 3 (Soundness for AWF nets). *An AWF net $\mathcal{N}$ is called* sound *iff $\mathcal{N}$ is quasi-live, and for all M such that $[(i, \flat)] \xrightarrow{\sigma} M$, for some transition sequence $\sigma \in T_n^*$, there exists σ' such that $M \xrightarrow{\sigma'} [(f, \flat)]$, and for all t from σ', $t \in T_n$ and $g(t) \in \{final(v), \top\}$.*

In [7] we defined a non-recursive subclass of AWF-nets for which soundness can be algorithmically checked:

1. $\mathfrak{N}_1$ and $\mathfrak{M}_1$ are the sets of all EWF nets and marked EWF nets, respectively;
2. $\langle P, T, F, \mathcal{E}, g, l \rangle \in \mathfrak{N}_{k+1}$, for $k \geq 1$, iff for all $a \in F$ and $c \in Con(\mathcal{E}(a))$, $\ell(c) \in \mathfrak{N}_k$. A marking M of $N \in \mathfrak{N}_{k+1}$ is a multiset over $P \times (\mathfrak{M}_k \cup \{\flat\})$. $\mathfrak{M}_{k+1} \stackrel{\text{def}}{=} \{(N, M) | N = \langle P, T, F, \mathcal{E}, g, l \rangle \in \mathfrak{N}_{k+1} \wedge M \in \mathbb{N}^{P \times (\mathfrak{M}_k \cup \{\flat\})}\}$ is called the set of marked nets of level at most k.

Note that $\mathfrak{N}_j \subseteq \mathfrak{N}_{j+1}$ and $\mathfrak{M}_j \subseteq \mathfrak{M}_{j+1}$, for all $j \geq 1$.

Since we want to have at least a restricted form of recursion for grid applications and still have an analyzable class of models, we introduce a form of well-foundedness for the recursion in Adaptive Grid Workflow nets.

Let $\mathcal{N}$ be a given AGWF net. We define the net collection $Coll(\mathcal{N})$ of $\mathcal{N}$ as the union of the set of constants (nets) used on the arc expressions of $\mathcal{N}$ and the net collections of these constant nets. The net collection of an AGWF net can be computed by using standard fixed point algorithms. By inspecting the net collection, one can easily check whether a net belongs to $\cup_{j\in\mathbb{N}}\mathfrak{M}_j$.

Definition 4 (Adaptive Grid Workflow net). *An* Adaptive Grid Workflow net *(AGFW net) is an AWF net such that every net from Coll($\mathcal{N}$) allows a firing sequence $[(i, \mathfrak{b})] \xrightarrow{\sigma} [(f, \mathfrak{b})]$ such that for any transition t from σ, we have $g(t) \in \{final(v), \top\}$ and for any $(t, p) \in F$, $Con(Expr(t, p)) \subseteq \cup_{j\in\mathbb{N}}\mathfrak{M}_j$.*

Note that the property required is checked at the level of EWF-nets, i.e. classical Petri nets, and not at the nested level. Intuitively, we require that there is at least one execution with *bounded nesting* allowed in every net involved in the process.

Now we show that soundness can be checked for AGWF nets. To reduce the verification of soundness to a finite problem, we introduce the abstraction α that replaces every token net in the AGWF net by a colored token with the set of exceptions of the net token as its color. An adaptive workflow net is thus abstracted by a colored EWF net whose color set is finite since the number of exceptions is finite. The guards of the type *final(v)* are replaced by $\top$ in the abstract net, and the guards $e(v)$ are replaced by the guards $e \in \alpha(v)$. Parallel and sequential composition, as well as choice, are abstracted to the union of the sets of exceptions, and constants in the arc expressions are substituted by their sets of exceptions. Now we can formulate our main result:

Theorem 5 (Soundness check). *An AGWF net $\mathcal{N}$ is sound iff for every net $\mathcal{N}' \in Coll(\mathcal{N})$ the following properties hold: (1) $\alpha(\mathcal{N}')$ is quasi-live, and (2) for all abstract markings M_α reachable by firings of non-exception transitions in $\alpha(\mathcal{N}')$, i.e. $[(i, \mathfrak{b})] \xrightarrow{\sigma} M_\alpha$ with $\sigma \in T_n^*$, we have $M_\alpha \xrightarrow{\sigma'} [(f, \mathfrak{b})]$, where $g^\alpha(t) = \top$ for all $t \in \sigma'$.*

4   Conclusion

In this paper, we introduced adaptive grid workflow nets. Exceptions transition are used to model faults (e.g. failure of a job). The idea of nested nets is used to make models adaptable. A library of workflow nets is used to increase the reusability and achieve separation of concerns in process modeling. We showed that an important correctness property called soundness can be verified on this class of nets by using abstraction techniques. We conjecture that another important property of adaptive workflow systems called circumspectness[2] is also decidable for AGWF nets.

Our next step is to extend the workflow engine YASPER [8] for handling AGWF nets, and extend the existing translation of classical workflow nets to WS BPEL [1] for our model by incorporating the nesting mechanism and patterns for standard exception handling mechanisms.

---

[2] Circumspectness ensures that whenever an exception happens, the upper layer net is able to handle it.

References

1. Web Services Business Process Execution Language Version 2.0. WS-BPEL TC OASIS (2005) http://www.oasis-open.org/committees/download.php/11601/
2. van der Aalst, W.M.P.: The Application of Petri Nets to Workflow Management. The Journal of Circuits, Systems and Computers 8(1), 21–66 (1998)
3. van der Aalst, W.M.P., van Hee, K.M.: Workflow Management: Models, Methods, and Systems. MIT Press, Cambridge (2002)
4. Deelman, E., Blythe, J., Gil, Y., Kesselman, C., Mehta, G., Patil, S., Su, M.-H., Vahi, K., Livny, M.: Pegasus: Mapping scientific workflows onto the Grid. In: Dikaiakos, M.D. (ed.) AxGrids 2004. LNCS, vol. 3165, pp. 11–20. Springer, Heidelberg (2004)
5. Fox, G.C., Gannon, D.: Workflow in Grid Systems. Concurrency and Computation: Practice and Experience 18(10), 1009–1019 (2006)
6. van Hee, K., Lomazova, I.A., Oanea, O., Serebrenik, A., Sidorova, N., Voorhoeve, M.: Nested nets for adaptive systems. In: Donatelli, S., Thiagarajan, P.S. (eds.) ICATPN 2006. LNCS, vol. 4024, pp. 241–260. Springer, Heidelberg (2006)
7. van Hee, K., Lomazova, I.A., Oanea, O., Serebrenik, A., Sidorova, N., Voorhoeve, M.: Checking properties of adaptive workflow nets. In: CS&P 2006 - Concurrency 2006, Specification and Programming, 27-29 September 2006, Germany, pp. 92–103 (2006) (An extended version is to appear in Fundamenta Informaticae)
8. van Hee, K., Oanea, O., Post, R., Somers, L., van der Werf, J.M.E.M.: Yasper: a tool for workflow modeling and analysis. In: ACSD, pp. 279–282. IEEE Computer Society, Los Alamitos (2006)
9. Hoheisel, A.: User tools and languages for graph-based Grid workflows. Concurrency and Computation: Practice and Experience 18(10), 1101–1113 (2006)
10. Lomazova, I.A.: Modeling dynamic objects in distributed systems with Nested Petri nets. Fundamenta Informaticae 51(1-2), 121–133 (2002)
11. Oinn, T.M., Addis, M., Ferris, J., Marvin, D., Senger, M., Greenwood, R.M., Carver, T., Glover, K., Pocock, M.R., Wipat, A., Li, P.: Taverna: a tool for the composition and enactment of bioinformatics workflows. Bioinformatics 20(17), 3045–3054 (2004)

A Stochastic Semantics for BioAmbients

Linda Brodo[1], Pierpaolo Degano[2], and Corrado Priami[3]

[1] Dipartimento di Scienze dei Linguaggi - via Tempio 9, I-07100 Sassari, Italia
brodo@uniss.it
[2] Dipartimento di Informatica - Largo Pontecorvo 3, I-56127 Pisa, Italia
degano@di.unipi.it
[3] The Microsoft Research - University of Trento Centre for Computational and
Systems Biology - Piazza Manci 17, I-38100 Povo (Tn), Italia
priami@cosbi.eu

Abstract. We consider BioAmbients, a calculus for specifying biological
entities and for simulating and analysing their behaviour. We extend
BioAmbients to take quantitative information into account by defining
a stochastic semantics, based on a simulation stochastic algorithm, to
determine the actual rate of transitions.

Keywords: Process Calculi, Stochastic Operational Semantics, Systems
Biology.

1 Introduction

The classical research in Biology has followed a *reductionistic* approach by focusing on the understanding of the activities of single molecules. A model of
a complete biological system is then obtained by simply putting together its
components. This methodology lacks in expressive power because the whole is
more complex that the simple sum of individuals. Then, there has been a shift
from the description of components towards the specification of their overall
behaviour and interactions. This was made evident during the Human Genome
Project [1]: an enormous quantity of biological data have been collected and still
there are no satisfactory simulators of the dynamics of even a few genes. A new
branch of Biology is now emerging called *Systems Biology* [13]. Its main challenges are to develop theoretical and technological tools for modeling, analysing
and predicting biological system behaviour.

The main mathematical models for describing living matter rely on the classical ordinary or stochastic differential equations. However, these systems of
equations rapidly grow very complex, are hardly computable and extensible, often become difficult to solve hence sometimes do not offer satisfactory analysis
tools. Recently, Regev, Silverman and Shapiro [22] brought out the similarities between distributed, concurrent, mobile computer systems and biological
systems, *e.g.* metabolic or gene regulatory networks and signalling pathways.

---

[1] Started 1990 and ended in 2003 (http://www.ornl.gov/sci/techresources/
Human_Genome/home.shtml).

V. Malyshkin (Ed.): PaCT 2007, LNCS 4671, pp. 22–34, 2007.
© Springer-Verlag Berlin Heidelberg 2007

Biological systems are made up of millions of biological components that are active simultaneously and that can interact to cooperate towards a common goal. Furthermore, the interactions between components are mainly binary and can occur only if the partners are correctly located (*e.g.* they are near enough, no membrane is dividing them, the affinity or propensity to interactions is sufficiently high). Finally, the actual interactions may change the future behaviour of the whole system even though they occur locally. All these features describe distributed, mobile concurrent computer systems as well, except maybe for those artificial systems having a smaller number of components. There are various process calculi, *e.g.* [15,12,16,5] that specify the form and the dynamic behaviour of concurrent systems, and that allow for mechanically analysing them. In this paper we focus on the BioAmbient calculus [1], a variant of the Mobile Ambients [5]. It has been specifically introduced for describing biological interactions within, or across, molecular compartments: processes represent cells, compartments model membranes, and localized communications and movements specify biological reactions.

Our main contribution (Sect. 3) is the definition of a stochastic semantics for this calculus to represent the effects of chemical and physical parameters, *e.g.* concentration of molecules, on the dynamics of living matters. Our stochastic semantics enables us to closely simulate the experiments that biologists carry on *in vivo* on *in vitro*. Several computations are run representing each one a single virtual experiment that simulate the behaviour of the biological system in hand. The computations are inspected to collect the relevant information about, *e.g.* the occurrences of selected communication or synchronizations, *i.e.* of reactions. The classical statistical analysis then applies. This methodology is known as transient analysis, and reflects the way biologists carry on their experiments. Another approach, typical of computer scientists, consists of deriving Markov chains and study the probability distribution in the steady states. We follow this one and exemplify our proposal through the analysis of a simple enzyme-substrate complex. Our example shows how the behaviour *in silico* is regulated by stochastic rates that are dynamically computed after each synchronization (Sect. 4).

There are many approaches for studying the behaviour of biological systems based on process calculi, in some cases new calculi with biologically inspired primitives have been introduced [17,9,4,19]. The first stochastic calculi applied for modelling biological systems was the stochastic π-calculus [18]. It has been used to model and perform transient analyses on some interesting biological systems [14,7,22], using simulation tools developed for the biological domain [6,20]. The relevance of the quantitative analyses in the study of biological models is arising and many works apply stochastic semantics both for simulations [10,3,11] and steady states analyses [2]. To the best of our knowledge, ours is the first stochastic semantics for Ambient-like calculi that apply the Gillespie's algorithm in a context with explicit biological compartments and steady state analysis.

2 Background

BioAmbients [1] (hereafter BioA, for short) are a variant of Mobile Ambients [5] which we assume the reader is familiar with. Each BioA process models a cell and the ambient constructor represents a cellular membrane, possibly nested.

A BioA process evolves when a pair of its sub-processes interact synchronously, representing a reaction between the involved cells. There are two kinds of interactions. The first is typical of calculi of communicating processes: it uses input and output prefixes for sending and receiving messages. The second kind of interactions involves membranes and capabilities that act on them. Such interactions consist of synchronizations between capabilities and the corresponding co-capabilities. For example, two sub-processes, enclosed each one in a membrane and lying side to side, may fuse in a single one by merging their membrane if the first one offers the capability $merge^+$ and the second one the capability $merge^-$, both on the same channel a. Formally, the process $[merge^+a.P]\|[merge^-a.Q]$ can evolve to the process $[P|Q]$. (Note that membranes have no names and that the *merge* capability makes the *open* capability useless).

BioA processes describe the behaviour of the molecules, and a specific molecule is characterized by the communication prefixes and the capabilities offered by its sub-processes. The syntax of BioA follows.

Definition 1. *Given a countable infinite set of names ranged over by $n, m, p, \ldots$ the set of BioA processes is described by the following BNF-like specification:*

Processes		Capabilities	
$P, Q ::= \mathbf{0}$	Inaction(empty)	$M, N ::= enter\, n$	Synch entry
$\mid (\nu n)P$	Restriction	$\mid accept\, n$	Accept
$\mid P|Q$	Composition	$\mid exit\, n$	Exit
$\mid A(\tilde{x})$	Agent Identifier	$\mid expel\, n$	Expel
$\mid [P]$	Ambient(membrane)	$\mid merge^+\, n$	Merge with
$\mid \pi.P$	Communication prefix	$\mid merge^-\, n$	Merge into
$\mid M.P$	Capability prefix		
$\mid \sum_{i \in I} \pi_i.P_i$	Comm Choice		
$\mid \sum_{i \in I} M_i.P_i$	Capability Choice		

Actions		Directions	
$\pi ::= \$n!\{m\}$	Output	$\$ ::= local$	Intra–ambient
$\$n?\{m\}$	Input	$\mid s2s$	Inter–siblings
		$\mid p2c$	Parent to child
		$\mid c2p$	Child to parent

As said above, the activities of BioA processes can only be synchronizations on input/output prefixes or on capabilities. The semantics of BioA is given by the reduction rules in Table 2 up to the standard congruence rules in Table 2.

We assume the classical definitions of the functions $fn(P)$ and $bn(P)$, for computing the free names and the bound names of P: bound names are defined by the restriction operator and by input prefixes; free names are the ones which are not bound. The first three rules in Table 2 define the activities on ambients.

The next four axioms prescribe how communications may occur according to the four different kinds of synchronizations. The last four rules are the usual axioms of the reduction semantics.

More in detail, the process **0** can perform no activities. The restriction operator $(\nu n)P$ creates a new bound name n whose scope is P. The parallel composition of two processes $P|Q$ interleaves the execution of the activities of P with those of Q. The two processes can also synchronize. When the synchronization is acting on membranes, the involved capability and the corresponding co-capability must share a channel and must be in a certain structural relationship (see also the example above for merging). The capability *enter n* allows a membrane to enter another one, if this is aside and offers the co-capability *accept n* on the same channel n. An *exit n* allows a nested membrane to leave its containing membrane, if this offers the corresponding co-capability *expel n*. The synchronizations on input/output prefixes allow a message to be sent from the sender to the receiver, along a channel n. Moreover, prefixes are equipped with a *direction* that specifies the relative position for the two corresponding prefixes to interact. Some constraints must hold on the position of the membranes enclosing the relevant prefixes. Indeed, if the two (processes firing the) prefixes exhibit direction *local*, then they must be within the same membrane (rule *Local* in Table 2). If the two prefixes have direction *sibling*, then they must lie in two different sibling membranes (rule *Sibling* in Table 2). When the output prefix has direction *p2c* and lies in one-level higher nested membrane enclosing the input prefix, input must have direction *c2p* (rule *ComOut* in Table 2), and symmetrically when exchanging input with output (rule *ComIn* in Table 2).

We find here convenient to adopt agent identifier $A(\tilde{x})$, instead of replication. Each identifier has a unique equation of the form $A(\tilde{x}) = P$; $\tilde{x}$ stands for the tuple $x_1, \ldots, x_n$ where all the names are different and are the only names that occur free in P. The ambient constructor $[P]$ creates a computational environment modeling a membrane in which P runs. Even though membranes have no names, sometimes in the examples we shall give them one for clarity.

Table 1. Congruence rules for BioAmbients

Par Commut	$P|Q \equiv Q|P$
Par Assoc	$P|(Q|R) \equiv (P|Q)|R$
Choice π	$\sum_{i \in I} \pi_i.P_i \equiv \sum_{i \in I} \pi_{\rho(i)}.P_{\rho(i)}$, with any permutation ρ
Choice M	$\sum_{i \in I} M_i.P_i \equiv \sum_{i \in I} M_{\rho(i)}.P_{\rho(i)}$, with any permutation ρ
Par Zero	$P|\mathbf{0} \equiv P$
Res Zero	$(\nu x)0 \equiv 0$
Res Res	$(\nu n)(\nu m)P \equiv (\nu m)(\nu n)P$
Res Par	$(\nu n)(P|Q) \equiv P|(\nu n)Q \ n \notin fn(P)$
Res Amb	$(\nu n)[P] \equiv [(\nu n)P]$
Ide	$A(\tilde{y}) \equiv P\{\tilde{y}/\tilde{x}\}$, if $A(\tilde{x}) = P$
α−conv	$P \equiv Q$ if P is obtained by α-converting Q

Table 2. Transition system for BioAmbients

In $[(T + enter\, n.P)|Q]|[(T' + accept\, n.R)|S] \;\rightarrow\; [[P|Q]|(R|S)]$

Out $[[(T + exit\, n.P)|Q]|(T' + expel\, n.R)|S)] \;\rightarrow\; [P|Q]|[R|S]$

Merge $[(T + merge^{+}\, n.P)|Q]|[(T' + merge^{-}\, n.R)|S] \;\rightarrow\; [(P|Q)|(R|S)]$

Local $(T + local\, n!\{m\}.P)|(local\, n?\{p\}.Q + T') \;\rightarrow\; P|Q\{p \leftarrow m\}$

Com Out $(T + p2c\, n!\{m\}.P)|[(c2p\, n?\{p\}.Q + T')|R] \;\rightarrow\; P|[Q\{p \leftarrow m\}|R]$

Com In $[(T + c2p\, n!\{m\}.P)|R]|(p2c\, n?\{p\}.Q + T') \;\rightarrow\; [P|R]|Q\{p \leftarrow m\}$

Sibling $[(T + s2s\, n!\{m\}.P)|R]|[(s2s\, n?\{p\}.Q + T')|S] \;\rightarrow\; [P|R]|[Q\{p \leftarrow m\}|S]$

$$\text{Res} \;\frac{P \rightarrow Q}{(\nu\, n)P \rightarrow (\nu\, n)Q} \qquad \text{Amb} \;\frac{P \rightarrow Q}{[P] \rightarrow [Q]} \qquad \text{Par} \;\frac{P \rightarrow Q}{P|R \rightarrow Q|R}$$

$$\text{Cong} \;\frac{P \equiv P',\; P \rightarrow Q,\; Q \equiv Q'}{P' \rightarrow Q'}$$

The processes $\sum_{i \in I} \pi_i.P_i$ and $\sum_{i \in I} M_i.P_i$ non-deterministically behave as the (guarded) summand $\pi_i.P_i$, and $M_i.P_i$ respectively, for some $i \in I$.

2.1   The Gillespie's Algorithm

We shall use the Gillespie's formulas to compute the rate at which a reaction occurs in a biological complex. We briefly recall them. Suppose to have a biological complex containing some molecules. Let c be the *basal rate* constant that governs the rate at which two molecules interact. This only depends on the physical properties of the two interacting molecules of the biological system, assuming temperature, pressure and volume be constant. There are two forms of molecular interactions. Symmetric molecular interactions are interactions between pairs of molecules of the same type. In this case, let N be the number of the molecules of the selected type (as volume is constant, this number equals concentration). The rate of a symmetric interaction is computed by the following formula: $c \times \frac{1}{2}(N_1 \times (N_1 - 1))$. Asymmetric interactions occur between different types of molecules. In this case, the computation of the rate takes into account the number of the molecules of the first type, N_1, and the one of the second type, N_2, and is: $c \times N_1 \times N_2$. In the next section we will also make use of a third number N_3, introduced in [6], to record combinations of corresponding prefixes in summation processes, as they can not generate any synchronizations.

2.2   Stochastic Process Calculi

Our semantics associates stochastic rates to transitions which are the parameters of exponential probability functions enjoying the forgetful property. Thus, the execution probability of each transition does not depend on the previous transitions. Instead, the dynamical computation of the stochastic rates keeps track of the variation of concentration of molecules. Then, we can simulate the stochastic behaviour of a process to perform transient analysis, by repeatedly running a specification and collecting statistical data, e.g. on the usage of enzymes. Also, we can build the stochastic transition system of the derivatives of the process for deriving the Continuous Time Markov Chain (CTMC) associated to the process, for studying the behaviour of biological systems in their steady state. We follow this line here, under the standard hypothesis that processes are finitary and cyclic, in order to generate a non singular and homogeneous matrix. By applying standard mathematical techniques we derive then the stationary probability of the system which specifies the probability of the system to be in one of the states of the transition system, at a given instant. Further analyses of the behaviour of the system can be done by the reward techniques [8], which, for example, allow us to compute the throughput of a specific activity. This measure gives the time the system takes to complete a selected interaction with respect to the overall execution time.

3   Stochastic BioAmbients

As usual, we associate a rate with each communication prefix π and with each capability M that became (π, r) and (M, r), respectively. For all prefixes we assume as given the parameter r, which represents the basal rate c discussed in Sect. 2.1. The rate at which a transition takes place is then computed through the Gillespie's formulas. Recall that the volume is constant, so concentration can be measured by counting the number of molecules as distinct prefixes present in the whole system.

Following [1], we make three assumptions on our processes for modeling symmetric and asymmetric molecular interactions. We distinguish a set of channel names $\mathcal{H}$ for characterizing symmetric interactions, as these channels can only be used in prefixes with direction *local*. Because of symmetry, summation $\sum_i (\pi_i, r_i).P_i$, offering a local prefix on $\mathcal{H}$ channel, also offers the corresponding co-action. We also prevent a process $\sum_i (\pi_i, r_i).P_i$ from offering the same prefix twice. The above holds for processes offering capabilities $\sum_i (M_i, r_i).P_i$, as well.

Table 3 depicts the BioA stochastic semantics up to the congruences in Table 2. The actual transition relation is $P \xrightarrow{(n, r')}_s Q$, in the lower part of the table, and its definition uses the auxiliary relation $P \xrightarrow{(x,y),(r,N_1,N_2,N_3)}_l Q$. In the left part of these labels, the x and the y stand for both direction and action of the prefixes involved in the communications. For brevity, we sometimes write only n, the channel name involved in the interaction, and this is always the case when capabilities are fired. The other part of the label is the tuple (r, N_1, N_2, N_3) that accumulates the number of prefixes that could have generated a synchronization equal to the fired one. This information is eventually used to compute the rate in the second part of the label of the actual transitions $P \xrightarrow{(n, r')}_s Q$, the first part records the channel name involved in the interaction, *i.e.* the kind

Table 3. Stochastic transition system for BioAmbients

S_In

$[(T + (enter\,n, r).P)|Q]|[(T' + (accept\,n, r).R)|S] \xrightarrow{(n,n),(r,N_1,N_2,0)}_l [[P|Q]|(R|S)]$
with $N_1 = In_{enter\,n}(((enter\,n, r)|Q), r)$ and $N_2 = Out_{accept\,n}(((accept\,n, r)|S), r)$

S_Out

$[[(T + (exit\,n, r).P)|Q]|(T' + (expel\,n, r).R)|S)] \xrightarrow{(n,n),(r,N_1,N_2,0)}_l [P|Q]|[R|S]$
with $N_1 = In_{exit\,n}(((exit\,n, r)|Q), r)$ and $N_2 = Out_{expel\,n}(((expel\,n, r)|S), r)$

S_Merge

$[(T + (merge^+\,n, r).P)|Q]|[(T' + (merge^-\,n, r).R)|S] \xrightarrow{(n,n),(r,N_1,N_2,0)}_l [(P|Q)|(R|S)]$
with $N_1 = In_{merge^+\,n}(((merge^+\,n, r)|Q), r)$ and $N_2 = Out_{merge^-\,n}(((merge^-\,n, r)|S), r)$

S_Local

$(T + (local\,n!\{m\}, r).P)|((local\,n?\{p\}, r).Q + T') \xrightarrow{(local\,n!\{m\}, local\,n?\{p\}),(r,N_1,N_2,N_3)}_l P|Q\{p \leftarrow m\}$
with $(r, N_1, N_2) = \begin{cases} (r, 1, 1) & n \notin \mathcal{H} \\ (\frac{r}{2}, 2, (2-1)) & n \in \mathcal{H} \end{cases}$
$N_3 = Mix_{local\,n!\{m\}}(((T + (local\,n!\{m\}, r).0) \mid ((local\,n?\{p\}, r).0 + T')), r)$

S_Com Out

$(T + (p2c\,n!\{m\}, r).P)|[((c2p\,n?\{p\}, r).Q + T')|R] \xrightarrow{(p2c\,n!\{m\}, n),(r,1,N_2,0)}_l P||Q\{p \leftarrow m\}|R]$
with $N_2 = In_{c2p\,n?\{p\}}(((c2p\,n?\{p\}, r)|R), r)$

S_Com In

$[(T + (c2p\,n!\{m\}, r).P)|R]|((p2c\,n?\{p\}, r).Q + T') \xrightarrow{(n,p2c\,n?\{p\}),(r,N_1,1,0)}_l [P|R]|Q\{p \leftarrow m\}$
with $N_1 = Out_{c2p\,n!\{m\}}(((c2p\,n!\{m\}, r)|R, r))$

S_Sibling

$[(T + (s2s\,n!\{m\}, r).P)|R]|[((s2s\,n?\{p\}, r).Q + T')|S] \xrightarrow{(n,n),(r,N_1,N_2,0)}_l [P|R]|[Q\{p \leftarrow m\}|S]$
with $N_1 = Out_{s2s\,n!\{m\}}(((s2s\,n!\{m\}, r)|R), r))$ and $N_2 = In_{s2s\,n?\{p\}}(((s2s\,n?\{p\}, r)|S), r)$

$$\text{S\_Res} \frac{P \xrightarrow{(x,y),(r,N_1,N_2,N_3)}_l Q}{(\nu n)P \xrightarrow{(x,y),(r,N_1,N_2,N_3)}_l (\nu n)Q} \qquad \text{S\_Amb} \frac{P \xrightarrow{(x,y),(r,N_1,N_2,N_3)}_l Q}{[P] \xrightarrow{(n,n),(r,N_1,N_2,N_3)}_l [Q]}, \begin{cases} x = x'n \\ \text{or} \\ x = \$nx'' \end{cases}$$

$$\text{S\_Par} \frac{P \xrightarrow{(x,y),(r,N_1,N_2,N_3)}_l Q}{P|R \xrightarrow{(x,y),(r,N_1',N_2',N_3')}_l Q|R}, \begin{cases} N_1' = N_1 + Out_x(R, r) \\ N_2' = N_2 + In_y(R, r) \\ N_3' = \begin{cases} N_3 + Mix_x(R, r) , & \text{if } x = local\,n!\pi \\ 0 & , \text{otherwise} \end{cases} \end{cases}$$

$$\text{S\_Cong} \frac{P \equiv P' \quad P' \xrightarrow{(x,y),(r,N_1,N_2,N_3)}_l Q' \quad Q' \equiv Q}{P \xrightarrow{(n,r\times(N_1\times N_2 - N_3))}_s Q}, \begin{cases} x = x'n \\ y = y'n \end{cases}$$

of biological reaction modelled. Some comments on the rules are in order. The main point here is determining the quantities N_1, N_2 and N_3. To do that we follow [6] and we use three auxiliary functions In, Out and Mix that search within a membrane the processes modelling the same molecules, *i.e.* a process offering prefixes with the *same* channel and basal rate. Actually we have a family of such functions In_α, $Out_{\overline{\alpha}}$ and $Mix_{\overline{\alpha}}$ for capabilities and directions $\alpha \in \{enter\, n,$ $exit\, n,\ merge^+ n,\ local\, n?\{p\},\ p2c\, n?\{p\},\ c2p\, n?\{p\},\ s2s\, n?\{p\}\}$ and for the corresponding co-actions $\overline{\alpha} \in \{\ accept\, n,\ expel\, n,\ merge^- n,\ local\, n!\{m\}, p2c\, n!\{m\},$ $c2p\, n!\{m\}, s2s\, n!\{m\}\}$. We give the definitions of In_α and $Mix_{\overline{\alpha}}$, as $Out_{\overline{\alpha}}$ is similarly defined by replacing any occurrence of In_α with $Out_{\overline{\alpha}}$ and α with $\overline{\alpha}$. We induce on the structure of BioA processes and take a basal rate r as an additional parameter.

$$In_\alpha(\mathbf{0}, r) = In_\alpha([P], r) \ = 0$$

$$In_\alpha((\nu\, n)P, r) \qquad = \begin{cases} In_\alpha(P, r) \text{, if } n \neq fn(\alpha) \\ \\ 0 \qquad\qquad \text{, otherwise} \end{cases}$$

$$In_\alpha(A(\tilde{y}), r) \qquad\quad = In_\alpha(P\{\tilde{y}/\tilde{x}\}, r),\ \text{if } A(\tilde{x}) = P$$

$$In_\alpha(\textstyle\sum_{i \in I}(\pi_i, r_i).P_i, r) = \#\{(\pi_i, r_i)\,|\, i \in I,\ \pi_i = \alpha,\ \text{and} \quad r_i = r\}$$

$$In_\alpha(\textstyle\sum_{i \in I}(M_i, r_i).P_i, r) = \#\{(M_i, r_i)\,|\, i \in I,\ M = \alpha\ \text{and} \quad r_i = r\}$$

$$In_\alpha(P_1 | P_2, r) \qquad\quad = In_\alpha(P_1, r) + In_\alpha(P_2, r)$$

As in [6], function $Mix_{\overline{\alpha}}$ computes the number of combinations of corresponding prefixes in summation processes, as they can not generate any synchronizations. This number is then subtracted from the global computation of synchronizations, see rule S_Cong in Table 3. $Mix_{\overline{\alpha}}$ is defined by mean of In_α and $Out_{\overline{\alpha}}$:

$$Mix_{\overline{\alpha}}(P, r) = \textstyle\sum_{i=0}^{n}(In_\alpha(S_i, r) * Out_{\overline{\alpha}}(S_i, r)), \quad \text{where } P = \prod_{i=0}^{n} S_i.$$

Actually, function $Mix_{\overline{\alpha}}$ is only applied in rule S_Local, because in the other cases compartmentalization limits the scope of prefixes that can generate similar synchronizations. The rule S_In needs not to record the involved channel and direction, because another $(enter\, n, r)$, or $(accept\, n, r)$, can only appear within Q, or S respectively — indeed summations never offer the same prefix twice. The same reason justifies the quantities N_1, N_2, and N_3. The rule uses the Gillespie's formula for asymmetric interactions in the computation of the transition rate. Similarly for rules S_Out and S_Merge. Rule S_Local records that the communication channel was n and the direction was $local$. Also, it verifies if the interaction is symmetric or asymmetric, by checking if $n \in \mathcal{H}$. Then, the Gillespie's formula is applied, with $N_1 = 2$ and $N_2 = 1$ and r divided by two, in the first case, and the with $N_1 = N_2 = 1$, in the second case. As we said before, this is the only rule where N_3 is computed, as it is not necessarily equal to zero. Rule S_Com_Out uses the asymmetric Gillespie's formula. Note that we can only have a single process offering an output on a same channel, so N_1 is 1. Symmetrically for rule S_Com_In. Computing the label in rule $S\_Sibling$ is just as in the case of rule S_Merge. Rules S_Res and S_Amb are trivial, except for the last one substitutes the pair (n, n) for (x, y) because the transition modelling the interaction is wrapped into a membrane. Rule S_Par updates the numbers N_1, N_2, and N_3 in the Gillespie's formulas. Note that the information (x, y) is crucial here because In_y and Out_x will always return $\mathbf{0}$ when x or y stand for the prefix channel name n. Also, note that output always occurs on the right hand side because the processes involved in $\rightarrow_l$ can only be rearranged, through

S_Cong, as last step of the deduction of transitions. In fact, the last rule applies the congruence rules and computes the actual transition, by determining its rate through the Gillespie's formula with basal rate r and quantities N_1, N_2, and N_3 computed so far.

The property below says that the stochastic BioA transition system conservatively extends the standard one (Table 2). Its proof is by trivial induction on the depth of the derivation of $P_s \xrightarrow{(n,r')}_s P'_s$, noting that the rules in Table 3 require the rates of the prefixes involved in an interaction to be the same.

Property 1. Given a BioA process P, let P_s be P where each prefix π or M becames (π, r) or (M, r) for suitable rate r. Then $P_s \xrightarrow{(n,r')}_s P'_s$ implies $P \to P'$.

The last property claims that the transition rate computed in Table 3 is based on a correct computation of synchronizations:

Property 2. If $P \xrightarrow{(n,r*(N_1*N_2-N_3))}_\ell P'$, then P can exactly perform $N_1 * N_2 - N_3$ different synchronizations of the same type and with the same rate, *i. e.* $P \xrightarrow{(n,r*(N_1*N_2-N_3))}_\ell P'_i$, with $i \in [1, N_1 * N_2 - N_3]$.

The proof is structured by cases on the transition rules and by induction on the lenght of the derivation.

4   An Example

Our example is taken from [21]. We consider the interactions of a simple complex, composed by an enzyme and two molecules, forming its substrate. These are graphically represented as separated ambients within which we write the names

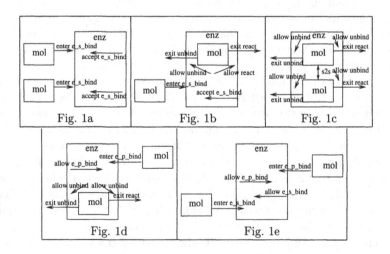

Fig. 1. BioAmbient model of the reversible bi-substrate reactions

mol and *enz* for readability. The interactions of the two molecules can only happen if both are inside an enzyme that acts as catalyser. We model the bindings between the molecules and the enzyme as two successive *enter e_s_bind* made by the two copies of *mol* that interact through the corresponding co-capabilities of *enz* (Fig. 1a). When the complex is formed, the two molecules can communicate along the channel c (Fig. 1c). Then, they can exit either via *exit react* or via *exit unbound* (Fig. 1d), coupled with the corresponding co-capabilities offered by *enz*. The whole BioA enzyme-substrate model is given below. For brevity, we detail the parameters of constant only in their definitions and we omit them otherwise (*e.g.* we write $X(\dots)$ when calling constant X). Also, here we use the *enz* and *mol*, as ambient names, which are however ignored by the semantics.

$System = mol[S(c, a, e\_s\_bind, e\_p\_bind, unbind, react)]$ |
$\qquad mol[S(c, a, e\_s\_bind, e\_p\_bind, unbind, react)]$ |
$\qquad enz[E(e\_p\_bind, e\_s\_bind, unbind, react) | E(e\_p\_bind, e\_s\_bind, unbind, react)])$
where
$S(c, a, e\_s\_bind, e\_p\_bind, unbind, react) = (enter\ e\_s\_bind, r_s).P(\dots)$
$P(c, a, e\_s\_bind, e\_p\_bind, unbind, react) =$
$\quad (s2s\ c!\{a\}, r_c).X(\dots) + (s2s\ c?\{p\}, r_c).X(\dots) + X(\dots)$
$X(c, a, e\_s\_bind, e\_p\_bind, unbind, react) =$
$\quad (exit\ unbind, r_u).S(\dots) + (exit\ react, r_r).(enter\ e\_p\_bind, r_p).P(\dots)$
$E(e\_s\_bind, e\_p\_bind, unbind, react) =$
$\quad (accept\ e\_p\_bind, r_p).ES(\dots) + (accept\ e\_s\_bind, r_s).ES(\dots)$
$ES(e\_s\_bind, e\_p\_bind, unbind, react) = (expel\ unbind, r_u).E(\dots) + (expel\ react, r_r).E(\dots)$

The complete transition system of our example is in Fig. 2. To clarify how stochastic rates are computed we show the derivation of the first transition where a *mol* ambient enters the *enz* ambient by executing the rule *S_In*. In this case, the functions In_α and $Out_{\overline{\alpha}}$ return 1, because in the ambient *mol* there is a single *enter e_s_bind* prefix, and 2, because *enz* offers two *accept e_s_bind* prefixes. The application of rule *S_Par* only changes the label by rewriting its first part (n, n), where $n = e\_s\_bind$. Finally, rule *S_Cong* computes the actual rate.

$$\frac{mol[S()|\mathbf{0}]|enz[E()|E()] \xrightarrow{((n,n)),(r_s,1,2,0)}_{\ell} enz[mol[P()|\mathbf{0}]|(ES()|E())]}{\cfrac{mol[S()|\mathbf{0}]|(mol[S()|\mathbf{0}]|enz[E()|E()]) \xrightarrow{(n,n),(r_s,1,2,0)}_{\ell} mol[S()|\mathbf{0}]|enz[mol[P()|\mathbf{0}]|(ES()|E())]}{mol[S()|\mathbf{0}]|(mol[S()|\mathbf{0}]|enz[E()|E()]) \xrightarrow{(n,2\times r_s-0)}_{s} mol[S()|\mathbf{0}]|enz[mol[P()|\mathbf{0}]|(ES()|E())]}}$$

where we assume that the basal rates be $r_s = 0.5$, $r_u = 0.6$, $r_p = 0.3, r_c = 0.4$, $r_r = 0.7$, thus the label of the above activity is $(n, 1)$. Similarly, we compute the labels of the other transitions.

The resulting vector of the stationary probability associated with each of the 10 states of Fig. 2 is:

$(0.0805\ 0.2638\ 0.1464\ 0.1603\ 0.269\ 0.0728\ 0.1164\ 0.0442\ 0.0085\ 0.0072)$.

E.g. consider S_4, ready for executing the *s2s* interaction or the two different capabilities *exit unbind* and *exit react*, the probability of the system to be in this

$S_1 \xrightarrow{(e\_s\_bind,2r_s)}_s S_2$	$S_4 \xrightarrow{(unbind,2r_r)}_s S_5$	$S_7 \xrightarrow{(e\_p\_bind,2r_p)}_s S_5$	$S_9 \xrightarrow{(unbind,2r_u)}_s S_{10}$
$S_2 \xrightarrow{(unbind,r_u)}_s S_1$	$S_4 \xrightarrow{(c,r_c)}_s S_6$	$S_8 \xrightarrow{(unbind,r_u)}_s S_3$	$S_{10} \xrightarrow{(unbind,r_u)}_s S_1$
$S_2 \xrightarrow{(react,r_r)}_s S_3$	$S_5 \xrightarrow{(unbind,r_u)}_s S_3$	$S_8 \xrightarrow{(react,r_r)}_s S_7$	$S_{10} \xrightarrow{(unbind,r_u)} S_3$
$S_2 \xrightarrow{(e\_s\_unbind,r_s)}_s S_4$	$S_5 \xrightarrow{(e\_p\_bind,r_p)}_s S_4$	$S_8 \xrightarrow{(e\_p\_bind,r_p)}_s S_9$	$S_{10} \xrightarrow{(e\_s\_bind,r_s)}_s S_9$
$S_3 \xrightarrow{(e\_p\_bind,2r_p)}_s S_2$	$S_5 \xrightarrow{(react,r_r)}_s S_7$	$S_9 \xrightarrow{(unbind,2r_u)}_s S_2$	
$S_3 \xrightarrow{(e\_s\_bind,2r_s)}_s S_5$	$S_6 \xrightarrow{(react,2r_r)}_s S_8$	$S_9 \xrightarrow{(react,2r_r)}_s S_5$	
$S_4 \xrightarrow{(unbind,2r_u)}_s S_2$	$S_6 \xrightarrow{(unbind,2r_u)}_s S_{10}$	$S_9 \xrightarrow{(react,2r_r)}_s S_8$	

where $S_1 = System$
$S_2 = enz[(E()|ES())|mol[P()]]|mol[S()]$
$S_3 = enz[E()|E()]|mol[S()]|mol[(enter\,e\_p\_bind,r_p).P()]$
$S_4 = enz[(ES()|ES())|(mol[P()]|mol[P()])]$
$S_5 = enz[(ES()|E())|mol[P()]|mol[(enter\,e\_p\_bind,r_p).P()]$
$S_6 = enz[(ES()|ES())|(mol[X()]|mol[X()])]$
$S_7 = enz[E()|E()]|mol[(enter\,e\_p\_bind,r_p).P()]|mol[(enter\,e\_p\_bind,r_p).P()]$
$S_8 = enz[(ES()|E())|mol[X()]]|mol[(enter\,e\_p\_bind,r_p).P()]$
$S_9 = enz[(ES()|ES())|mol[X()]|mol[X()]]$
$S_{10} = enz[(ES()|ES())|mol[X()]]|mol[S()]$

Fig. 2. The transition system of the BioA process *System*

state is 0.1603. The actions that have the highest execution probability, 0.2638, are those activated in S_2 that offers *exit react*, *enter e_s_bind* and *exit unbind*.

Suppose now to have the following reward array, where non zero values are assigned to the states where the capabilities can be fired:
(0 1/3 0 1/3 1/3 1/2 0 1/3 1/3 0). Then, the weighted troughtput of the *exit react* capability is 0.285, *i.e.* the system is busy firing this capability for a little more than $\frac{1}{4}$ of the whole execution time.

5   Conclusions

We have defined a stochastic operational semantics for the calculus of BioAmbients, exploiting the Gillespie's algorithm. To the best of our knowledge, this is the first such semantics, which makes the calculus usable by biologists in performing their experiments *in silico*. Through a very simple example, with no significance in biology, we show that techniques for performance evaluation typical of process calculi can help analysing the behaviour of biological systems.

Acknowledgments. We thank Alessandro Romanel for his collaboration. The second author has been partially supported by EU-FETPI GC Project IST-2005-16004 Sensoria, and by the Microsoft Research - University of Trento Centre for Computational and Systems Biology.

References

1. Regev, A., Panina, E.M., Silverman, W., Cardelli, L., Shapiro, E.: BioAmbients: An abstraction for biological compartments. Th. Comp. Sci. 325(1), 141–167 (2004)
2. Calder, M., Gilmore, S., Hillston, J.: Modelling the influence of RKIP an the ERK signalling pathway using the stochastic process algebra PEPA. In: Priami, C., Ingólfsdóttir, A., Mishra, B., Nielson, H.R. (eds.) Transactions on Computational Systems Biology VII. LNCS (LNBI), vol. 4230, pp. 1–23. Springer, Heidelberg (2006)
3. Calzone, L., Chabrier-River, N., Fages, F., Soliman, S.: Machine learning biochemical networks from temporal logic properties. In: Priami, C., Plotkin, G. (eds.) Transactions on Computational Systems Biology VI. LNCS (LNBI), vol. 4220, p. 68. Springer, Heidelberg (2006)
4. Cardelli, L.: Brane calculi - interactions of biological membranes. In: Danos, V., Schachter, V. (eds.) CMSB 2004. LNCS (LNBI), vol. 3082, pp. 257–280. Springer, Heidelberg (2005)
5. Cardelli, L., Gordon, A.: Mobile ambients. Th. Comp. Sci. 240(1), 177–213 (2000)
6. Cardelli, L., Philips, A.: A correct abstract machine for the stochastic π-calculus. In: Proc. Concurrent Models in Molecular Biology (2004)
7. Chiarugi, D., Curti, M., Degano, P., Lo Brutto, G., Marangoni, R.: Feedbacks and oscillations in the virtual cell VICE. In: Priami, C. (ed.) CMSB 2006. LNCS (LNBI), vol. 4210, p. 93. Springer, Heidelberg (2006)
8. Clark, G., Hillston, J.: Towards automatic derivation of performance measures from pepa models. In: Proc. UK Performance Engineering Workshop, pp. 65–81 (1996)
9. Danos, V., Laneve, C.: Formal molecular biology. Th. Comp. Sci. 325(1), 69–110 (2004)
10. Goss, P., Peccoud, J.: Quantitative modeling of stochastic systems in molecular biology by using stochastic petri nets. Proc. National Academy of Science USA 95, 6750–6754 (1998)
11. Heat, J., Kwiatkowska, M., Norman, G., Parker, D., Tymchyshyn, O.: Probabilistic model checking of complex biological pathways. In: Priami, C. (ed.) CMSB 2006. LNCS (LNBI), vol. 4210, p. 32. Springer, Heidelberg (2006)
12. Hoare, C.: Communicating Sequential Processes. Prentice-Hall, Englewood Cliffs (1985)
13. Kitano, H.: Foundations of Systems Biology. MIT Press, Cambridge (2002)
14. Lecca, P., Priami, C., Quaglia, P., Rossi, B., Laudanna, C., Costantin, G.: A stochastic process algebra approach to simulation of autoreactive lymphocyte recruiment. SIMULATION, 80(4) (2004)
15. Milner, R.: Communication and Concurrency. Prentice-Hall, Englewood Cliffs (1989)
16. Milner, R., Parrow, J., Walker, D.: A calculus of mobile processes (i and ii). Information and Computation 100(1), 1–72 (1992)
17. Nagasaki, M., Onami, S., Miyano, S., Kitano, H.: Bio-calculus: Its concept and an application for molecular interaction. Frontiers Science Series, 30 (2000)
18. Priami, C.: Stochastic π-calculus. The Computer Journal 38(7), 578–589 (1995)
19. Priami, C., Quaglia, P.: Beta-binders for biological interactions. In: Danos, V., Schachter, V. (eds.) CMSB 2004. LNCS (LNBI), vol. 3082, pp. 21–34. Springer, Heidelberg (2005)

20. Priami, C., Regev, A., Shapiro, E., Silverman, W.: Application of a stochastic name-passing calculus to representation and simulation of molecular processes. Information Processing Letters 80(1), 25–31 (2001)
21. Regev, A.: Computational Systems Biology: A Calculus for Biomolecular knowledge. PhD thesis, Tel Aviv University (2002)
22. Regev, A., Shapiro, E.T., Silverman, W.: Representation and simulation of biochemical processes using the π-calculus process algebra. In: Proc. Pacific Symposium on Biocomputing, vol. 6, pp. 459–470 (2001)

A Categorical Observation of Timed Testing Equivalence

Natalya Gribovskaya and Irina Virbitskaite

A.P. Ershov Institute of Informatics Systems
Siberian Division of the Russian Academy of Sciences
6, Acad. Lavrentiev avenue, 630090, Novosibirsk, Russia
Phone: +7 3833 30 40 47; Fax: +7 3833 32 34 94
`natamosk@ngs.ru, virb@iis.nsk.su`

Abstract. Timed transition systems are a widely studied model for real-time systems. The intention of the paper is to show the applicability of the general categorical framework of open maps to the setting of testing equivalence on timed transition systems, in order to transfer general concepts of equivalences to the model. In particular, we define a category of timed transition systems, whose morphisms are to be thought of as simulations, and an accompanying (sub)category of observations, to which the corresponding notion of open maps is developed. We then use the open maps framework to obtain an abstract bisimilarity which is established to coincide with timed testing equivalence.

1 Introduction

In the core of every theory of systems lies a notion of a behavioural equivalence between systems: it indicates which particular aspects of a system behaviour are considered to be observable. In concurrency theory, a variety of behavioural equivalences have been promoted, and the relationship between them has been quite well-understood (see, for example, [13,14]).

Testing [20] is one of the major equivalences of concurrency theory. Testing equivalences and preorders are defined in terms of tests which processes may and must satisfy. Two processes are considered as testing equivalent, if there is no test that can distinguish them. A test is usually itself a process applied to a process by computing both together in parallel. A particular computation is assumed to be successful if the test reaches a designated successful state, and the process guarantees the test if every computation is successful.

Recently, in an attempt to explain and unify apparent differences between the extensive amount of research within the field of behavioural equivalences, several category-theoretic approaches to the matter have appeared (see [18,19] among others). One of them was initiated by Joyal, Nielsen, and Winskel in [19] where they proposed an abstract way of capturing the notion of bisimulation through the so-called spans of open maps: first, a category of models of computations is identified, then a subcategory of observation is chosen relative to which open maps are defined; two models are bisimilar if there exists a span of open maps

V. Malyshkin (Ed.): PaCT 2007, LNCS 4671, pp. 35–46, 2007.

between the models. The abstract definition of bisimilarity makes possible a uniform definition of an equivalence over different models ranging from interleaving models like transition systems to true concurrent models like event structures and higher dimensional automata. On transition systems, abstract bisimilarity readily corresponds to interleaving bisimulation. On event structures and higher dimensional models, abstract bisimilarity leads to a slight strengthening of history preserving bisimulation, as shown in [19,25] and [8,12], respectively. Furthermore, the categorical setting turned out appropriate for defining, among others, trace and testing equivalences, barbed and weak bisimulations (see [21]). Moreover, as argued in [11], combining the open maps and presheaf approaches allows one to avoids some obstructions to a treatment of weak bisimulation on true concurrent models.

However, none of the models and approaches above has taken into account real-time. It is generally recognized that time plays an important role in many concurrent systems. This has motivated the development and extension of several models and analysis methods to support the correctness of real-time systems. As a result, timed extensions of interleaving models have been investigated thoroughly. Various recipes on how to incorporate time in transition systems — the most prominent interleaving model — are, for example, described in [2,16], whereas the incorporation of real time into equivalence notions is less advanced. There are a few papers (see, for example, [9,22,24]), where decidability questions of time-sensitive equivalences are investigated in the setting of timed interleaving models.

The contribution of the paper is to show the applicability of the general categorical framework of open maps to the setting of testing equivalence on timed transition systems, in order to transfer general concepts of equivalences to the model. In particular, we define a category of timed transition systems, whose morphisms are to be thought of as simulations, and an accompanying (sub)category of observations, to which the corresponding notion of open maps is developed. We then use the open maps framework to obtain an abstract bisimilarity which is established to coincide with timed testing equivalence.

There have been several motivations for this work. One has been given by the number of papers on timed testing. For instance, [10] and [22] have treated interleaving testing for discrete time and dense time transition models, respectively. In order to analyze the behaviour of real-time and concurrent systems, the testing approach has been extended by timing constraints in the setting of true concurrent models like timed Petri nets [5] and timed event structures [4]. A next origin of our study has been the paper [6] where the categorical setiing has been developed for different kinds of transition systems to establish correspondences with net based systems. Furthermore, in [21] abstract bisimilarity has been shown to coincide with testing equivalence on transition systems. Finally, another motivation has been the paper [17] that illustrates the use of open maps for providing an abstract characterization of bisimulation on timed transition systems. Besides, the category-theoretic approach has been applied to partial order based equivalences in the framework of timed event structures [23].

The rest of the paper is organized as follows. The basic notions and notations concerning timed transition systems and their behaviour are introduced in section 2. In the subsequent section, we define a category of timed transition systems whose morphisms are to be thought of as simulations. An accompanying (sub)category of observations and the corresponding notion of open maps are developed in section 4. Also, an alternative characterization of the open maps is provided. Further, the abstract equivalence based on spans of the open maps is shown to coincide with timed testing equivalence. Section 5 contains conclusion and some remarks on future work. In Appendix, we give a short introduction to open maps as presented in [19].

2   Timed Transition Systems

In this section, we first introduce some basic notions and notations concerning timed transition systems [2,17] and then define the notion of testing equivalence in the setting of the model.

Before doing so, it will be convenient to introduce some auxiliary notions and notations. Let $\mathbf{R}^+$ be the set of non-negative reals, and Σ a finite alphabet of actions. A *timed word over* Σ is a finite sequence of pairs $\alpha = (\sigma_1, \tau_1)$ (σ_2, τ_2) (σ_3, τ_3) ... (σ_n, τ_n) such that $\sigma_i \in \Sigma$, $\tau_i \in \mathbf{R}^+$ for all $1 \leq i \leq n$, and $\tau_i \leq \tau_{i+1}$ for all $1 \leq i < n$. A pair(σ_i, τ_i) represents an occurrence of an action σ_i at time τ_i relative to the starting time (0) of the execution. We consider a finite set V of clock variables. A *clock valuation over* V is a mapping $\nu : V \to \mathbf{R}^+$ which assigns time values to the clock variables of a system. Define $(\nu + c)(x) := \nu(x) + c$ for all clock variables $x \in V$. For a subset λ of clock variables, we shall write $\nu[\lambda \to 0](x) := 0$, if $x \in \lambda$, and $\nu[\lambda \to 0](x) := \nu(x)$, otherwise. Given a set V, we define the set $\Delta(V)$ of *clock constraints* by the following grammar: $\delta ::= c \# x$ $| x + c \# y | \delta \wedge \delta$, where $\# \in \{\leq, <, \geq, >, =\}$, c is a real valued constant and x, y are clock variables from V. We shall say that a clock constraint δ is *satisfied by a clock valuation* ν if the expression $\delta[\nu(x)/x]^1$ evaluates to true. A clock constraint δ defines a subset of $\mathbf{R}^m$ (m is the number of clock variables in V). We call the subset as the meaning of δ and denote it as $\|\delta\|_V$. A clock valuation ν defines a point in $\mathbf{R}^m$ (denoted $\|\nu\|_V$). So, the clock constraint δ is satisfied by the clock valuation ν iff $\|\nu\|_V \in \|\delta\|_V$.

We are now prepared to consider the definition of timed transition systems.

Definition 1. *A timed transition system $\mathcal{T}$ is a quintuple (S, s_0, Σ, V, T) where*

- *S is a set of states and s_0 is the initial state,*
- *Σ is a finite alphabet of actions,*
- *V is a set of clock variables,*
- *$T \subseteq S \times \Sigma \times \Delta(V) \times 2^V \times S$ is a set of transitions. We shall write $s \xrightarrow[\delta, \lambda]{\sigma} s'$ to denote a transition $(s, \sigma, \delta, \lambda, s')$.*

---

[1] $\delta[y/x]$ is the substitution of y for x in δ.

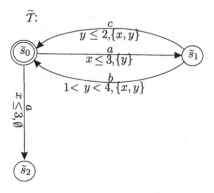

Fig. 1.

Example 1. The timed transition system $\widetilde{T}$ shown in Fig. 1 has three states $\widetilde{s}_0$ (the initial state), $\widetilde{s}_1$ and $\widetilde{s}_2$, three actions a, b and c, and two clock variables x and y. Four transitions are depicted between the states. $\diamondsuit$

Define the behaviour of timed transition systems.

Definition 2. *Let $T = (S, s_0, \Sigma, V, T)$ be a timed transition system.*

A configuration of T is a pair $\langle s, \nu \rangle$, where s is a state and ν is a clock valuation. The set of configurations of T is denoted as $Conf(T)$.

A run of T is a sequence $\langle s_0, \nu_0 \rangle \xrightarrow[\tau_1]{\sigma_1} \langle s_1, \nu_1 \rangle \xrightarrow[\tau_2]{\sigma_2} \ldots \xrightarrow[\tau_n]{\sigma_n} \langle s_n, \nu_n \rangle$ such that for all $0 < i \leq n$ there is a transition $s_{i-1} \xrightarrow[\delta_i, \lambda_i]{\sigma_i} s_i$ such that $\|\nu_{i-1} + (\tau_i - \tau_{i-1})\|_V \in \|\delta_i\|_V$ and $\nu_i = (\nu_{i-1} + (\tau_i - \tau_{i-1}))[\lambda_i \to 0]$. Here, s_0 is the initial state, ν_0 is the constant 0 function, and τ_0 is defined to be 0. A run as above is said to generate the timed word $\alpha = (\sigma_1, \tau_1)(\sigma_2, \tau_2)(\sigma_3, \tau_3) \ldots (\sigma_n, \tau_n)$. We will use $Runs(T)$ to denote the set of runs of T.

The language of T is the set $L(T) = \{\alpha = (\sigma_1, \tau_1)(\sigma_2, \tau_2) \ldots (\sigma_n, \tau_n) \mid \langle s_0, \nu_0 \rangle \xrightarrow[\tau_1]{\sigma_1} \langle s_1, \nu_1 \rangle \xrightarrow[\tau_2]{\sigma_2} \ldots \xrightarrow[\tau_n]{\sigma_n} \langle s_n, \nu_n \rangle \in Runs(T)\}$.

Example 2. To illustrate the concepts, consider the language of the timed transition system $\widetilde{T}$, shown in Fig. 1: $L(\widetilde{T}) = \{\alpha \mid \alpha\omega = (a, \tau_1)(x_1, \tau_2)(a, \tau_3) \ldots (x_n, \tau_{2n})(a, \tau_{2n+1}) \mid \tau_{2i+1} - \tau_{2i} \leq 3 \ (i = 0..n), \ x_j \in \{b, c\}, \ 1 < \tau_{2j} - \tau_{2j-1} < 4$ for $x_j = b$, $\tau_{2j} - \tau_{2j-1} \leq 2$ for $x_j = c \ (j = 1..n)\}$. $\diamondsuit$

Testing equivalences [20] are defined in terms of tests which processes may and must satisfy. Two processes are considered testing equivalent if there is no test that can distinguish them. A test is usually itself a process applied to a process by computing both together in parallel. A particular computation is assumed to be successful if the test reaches a designated successful state, and the process guarantees the test if every computation is successful. However, following the papers [1,15], we use an alternative characterization of the testing concept. Then, in timed interleaving semantics, a test consists of a timed word and a set of actions occurred at some times. A process passes this test if after every execution of the timed word, occurrences of the actions at the times are inevitable next.

Definition 3. *Let T_1 and T_2 be timed transition systems. Then,*

- *for a timed word $\alpha = (\sigma_1, \tau_1) \ldots (\sigma_n, \tau_n)$ and for a subset $L \subseteq (\Sigma \times \mathbf{R}^+)$, T_i after α **MUST** L iff for all $\langle s, \nu \rangle \in Conf(T_i)$ such that $C_0(T_i) \xrightarrow[\tau_1]{\sigma_1} \ldots$ $\xrightarrow[\tau_n]{\sigma_n} \langle s, \nu \rangle$ there exists $(\sigma, \tau) \in L$ and $\langle s', \nu' \rangle \in Conf(T_i)$ such that $\langle s, \nu \rangle \xrightarrow{\sigma} \langle s', \nu' \rangle$ $(i = 1, 2)$,*
- *T_1 and T_2 are testing equivalent iff for all timed words $\alpha = (\sigma_1, \tau_1) \ldots (\sigma_n, \tau_n)$ and for all subsets $L \subseteq (\Sigma \times \mathbf{R}^+)$ it holds:*

$$T_1 \text{ after } \alpha \text{ MUST } L \iff T_2 \text{ after } \alpha \text{ MUST } L.$$

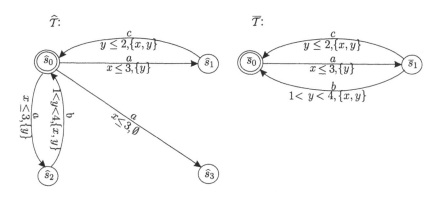

Fig. 2.

Example 3. Consider the timed transition systems shown in Fig. 1 and 2. The timed transition systems $\tilde{T}$ and $\hat{T}$ are testing equivalent, while the timed transition systems $\hat{T}$ and $\overline{T}$ are not, because $\overline{T}$ **after** $(a, 1)$ **MUST** $\{(c, 2)\}$ but it is not the case for $\hat{T}$.   ◇

3   A Category of Timed Transition Systems

In this section, we define a category of timed transition systems, $\mathcal{CTTS}_\Sigma$, and consider its useful property.

We start with introducing some auxiliary notions and notations. For a timed transition system T, we define the following:

- for $\gamma = \langle s_0, \nu_0 \rangle \xrightarrow[\tau_1]{\sigma_1} \ldots \xrightarrow[\tau_n]{\sigma_n} \langle s_n, \nu_n \rangle \in Runs(T)$,

$$tw(\gamma) = \sigma_1 \tau_1 \ldots \sigma_n \tau_n,$$

$$\mathcal{A}_T(\gamma) = \{(\sigma_{n+1}, \tau_{n+1}) \mid \exists \langle s_{n+1}, \nu_{n+1} \rangle \text{ s.t. } \langle s_n, \nu_n \rangle \xrightarrow[\tau_{n+1}]{\sigma_{n+1}} \langle s_{n+1}, \nu_{n+1} \rangle \},$$

- $SR(T)$ is the least subset of $(2^{Runs(T)} \setminus \{\emptyset\})$ such that
  - $\forall \gamma \in Runs(T) \, \exists X \in SR(T) \circ \gamma \in X$,
  - $\forall X \in SR(T) \, \forall \gamma, \gamma' \in X \circ tw(\gamma) = tw(\gamma')$,
- for $X, Y \in SR(T)$,

$$A_T(X) = \{A_T(\gamma) \mid \gamma \in X\},$$

$$tw(X) = tw(\gamma) \text{ for some } \gamma \in X,$$

$$X \xrightarrow{\sigma}_{\tau} Y \iff tw(Y) = tw(X)(\sigma, \tau).$$

Example 4. To illustrate the notions and notations defined prior to that, consider some run $\widetilde{\gamma} \in Runs(\widetilde{T})$ and some set of runs $\widetilde{X} \in SR(\widetilde{T})$ of the timed transition system $\widetilde{T}$ shown in Fig. 1. For instance, take $\widetilde{\gamma} = \langle \widetilde{s}_0, \nu_0 \rangle \xrightarrow{a}_{1} \langle \widetilde{s}_1, \nu_1 \rangle$, where $\nu_1(x) = 1, \nu_1(y) = 0$, and $\widetilde{X} = \{\langle \widetilde{s}_0, \nu_0 \rangle \xrightarrow{a}_{1} \langle \widetilde{s}_1, \nu_1 \rangle, \langle \widetilde{s}_0, \nu_0 \rangle \xrightarrow{a}_{1} \langle \widetilde{s}_2, \nu_1' \rangle\}$, where $\nu_1(x) = 1, \nu_1(y) = 0$ and $\nu_1'(x) = \nu_1'(y) = 1$. Clearly, $tw(\widetilde{\gamma}) = tw(\widetilde{X}) = (a, 1)$. Moreover, we have $A_{\widetilde{T}}(\widetilde{\gamma}) = \{(b, \tau), (c, \tau') \mid 1 < \tau - 1 < 4, \, \tau' - 1 \leq 2\}$ and $A_{\widetilde{T}}(\widetilde{X}) = \{\{(b, \tau), (c, \tau') \mid 1 < \tau - 1 < 4, \, \tau' - 1 \leq 2\}, \emptyset\}$. Next, consider $\widetilde{Y} \in SR(\widetilde{T})$ such that $tw(\widetilde{Y}) = (a, 1)(c, 2)$, i.e. $\widetilde{Y} = \{\langle \widetilde{s}_0, \nu_0 \rangle \xrightarrow{a}_{1} \langle \widetilde{s}_1, \nu_1 \rangle \xrightarrow{c}_{2} \langle \widetilde{s}_0, \nu_2 \rangle\}$, where $\nu_1(x) = 1, \nu_1(y) = 0$ and $\nu_2(x) = \nu_2(y) = 0$. We then get $\widetilde{X} \xrightarrow{c}_{2} \widetilde{Y}$. $\diamond$

Now we are ready to define the notion of a morphism.

Definition 4. *Let T and T' be timed transition systems. A map $\mu : T \to T'$ is called a* morphism, *if $\mu : SR(T) \to SR(T')$ is a function such that for all $X \in SR(T)$ it holds:*

- $tw(X) = tw(\mu(X))$,
- $\forall A' \in A_{T'}(\mu(X)) \, \exists A \in A_T(X) \circ A \subseteq A'$.

Notice, the morphisms defined prior to that are to be thought of as simulations — the morphisms reflect correspondences of timed words and matches of sets of actions occurred after the timed words at some times.

Example 5. It is easy to check that there is the (only) morphism from the timed transition system $\widetilde{T}$ in Fig. 1 to the timed transition system $\widehat{T}$ in Fig. 2. $\diamond$

Timed transition systems (with alphabet Σ) and morphisms between them form a category of timed transition systems, $CTTS_\Sigma$, in which the composition of two morphisms $\mu_1 : T_0 \longrightarrow T_1$ and $\mu_2 : T_1 \longrightarrow T_2$ is $(\mu_2 \circ \mu_1) : T_0 \longrightarrow T_2$, and the identity morphism is the identity function.

Theorem 1. $CTTS_\Sigma$ *has pullbacks.*

Proof. Assume $T_1 \xrightarrow{\mu_1} T_0 \xleftarrow{\mu_2} T_2$ to be a diagram, where $T_i = (S_i, \Sigma, s_0^i, V_i, T_i)$ $(i = 0, 1, 2)$ is an object and μ_j $(j = 1, 2)$ is a morphism of the category $CTTS_\Sigma$. Construct the system $T = (S, \Sigma, s_0, V, T)$ as follows:

- $S = \{(X, Y, D) \in \mathcal{SR}(T_1) \times \mathcal{SR}(T_2) \times 2^{(\Sigma \times \mathbf{R}^+)} \mid \mu_1(X) = \mu_2(Y) \text{ and } D \in M(X, Y)\}$, where $M(X, Y) = \{A \cap (\underset{B \in \mathcal{A}_{T_2}(Y)}{\bigcup} B) \mid A \in \mathcal{A}_{T_1}(X)\} \cup \{B \cap (\underset{A \in \mathcal{A}_{T_1}(X)}{\bigcup} A) \mid B \in \mathcal{A}_{T_2}(Y)\}$,

- $s_0 = (\{C_0(T_1)\}, \{C_0(T_2)\}, \mathcal{A}_{T_1}(C_0(T_1)) \cap \mathcal{A}_{T_2}(C_0(T_2)))$. Notice, $s_0 \in S$,

- $V = \{u\}$,

- $((X, Y, D), \sigma, (u = \tau), \emptyset, (X', Y', D')) \in T \Leftrightarrow (\sigma, \tau) \in D, X \xrightarrow[\tau]{\sigma} X', Y \xrightarrow[\tau]{\sigma} Y'$.

Due to the above construction, it is easy to see that T is a timed transition system. Consider the following properties of T:

- for $\gamma \in Runs(T)$ with $last(\gamma) = \langle (X, Y, D), \nu \rangle^2$, $\mathcal{A}_T(\gamma) = D$ and $tw(\gamma) = tw(X) = tw(Y)$. It follows from the construction of T and the definition of $\mathcal{A}_T(\gamma)$.
- for $Z \in \mathcal{SR}(T)$, $Z = \{\gamma \in Runs(T) \mid last(\gamma) = \langle (X, Y, D), \nu \rangle$ with $D \in M(X, Y)\}$. It follows from the construction of T and the definition of $\mathcal{SR}(T_1)$ and $\mathcal{SR}(T_2)$ (i.e. the uniqueness of X and Y).

Define the mappings $\pi_1 : \mathcal{SR}(T) \to \mathcal{SR}(T_1)$ and $\pi_2 : \mathcal{SR}(T) \to \mathcal{SR}(T_2)$ as follows: $\pi_1(Z) = X$ and $\pi_2(Z) = Y$, for all $Z \in \mathcal{SR}(T)$. Using the properties of T and the definition of π_i $(i = 1, 2)$, it is routine to show that π_i is a morphism. By the construction of T and the definition of π_1 and π_2, we get $\mu_1 \circ \pi_1 = \mu_2 \circ \pi_2$.

Suppose $T_1 \xleftarrow{\phi_1} T' \xrightarrow{\phi_2} T_2$ to be a diagram in the category $\mathcal{CTTS}_\Sigma$ such that $\mu_1 \circ \phi_1 = \mu_2 \circ \phi_2$. Define the mapping $\xi : \mathcal{SR}(T') \to \mathcal{SR}(T)$ as follows: $\xi(Z') = \{\gamma \in Runs(T) \mid last(\gamma) = \langle (\phi_1(Z'), \phi_2(Z'), D), \nu \rangle$ with $D \in M(\phi_1(Z'), \phi_2(Z'))\}$, for all $Z' \in \mathcal{SR}(T')$. Using the properties of T and ϕ_i $(i = 1, 2)$ being a morphism, it is straightforward to show that ξ is a morphism. The equations $\phi_1 = \pi_1 \circ \xi$ and $\phi_2 = \pi_2 \circ \xi$ follow from the definition of the morphisms ξ, π_1 and π_2. $\Diamond$

4 $\mathcal{P}_\Sigma$-Open Morphisms

In this section we first define a subcategory of observations allowing us to develop the corresponding notion of open maps (see Appendix) and then provide an alternative characterization of the open maps. Further, the abstract equivalence based on spans of the open maps is shown to coincide with testing equivalence.

Following the standards of timed transition systems and the paper [21], we choose the subcategory $\mathcal{P}_\Sigma$ of observations which are trees consisting of a 'trunk' and 'branches' of length one, except for the 'top' of the tree, where a more general branching structure is assumed.

Definition 5. *The subcategory $\mathcal{P}_\Sigma$ of the category $\mathcal{CTTS}_\Sigma$ contains objects of the form*

---

[2] For $\gamma = C_0(T) \xrightarrow[\tau_1]{\sigma_1} \ldots \xrightarrow[\tau_n]{\sigma_n} \langle (X, Y, D), \nu \rangle \in Runs(T)$, we write $last(\gamma)$ to denote $\langle (X, Y, D), \nu \rangle$.

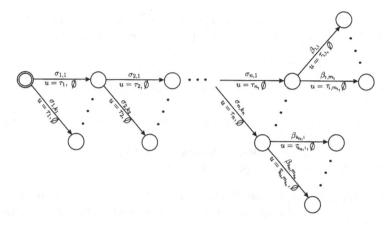

and morphisms between the objects, where $k_1, \ldots, k_n, m_1, \ldots, m_{k_n} \geq 0$.

Our next aim is to characterize $\mathcal{P}_\Sigma$-openness (see Appendix) of morphisms relative to the subcategory of observations defined prior to that.

Theorem 2. *Let T and T' be timed transition systems. Then, a morphism $\mu : T \to T'$ in $CTTS_\Sigma$ is $\mathcal{P}_\Sigma$-open iff for all $Y \in \mathcal{SR}(T')$ there exists $X \in \mathcal{SR}(T)$ such that $\mu(X) = Y$ and for all $A \in \mathcal{A}_T(X)$ there exists $A' \in \mathcal{A}_{T'}(Y)$ such that $A' \subseteq A$.*

Proof. ($\Rightarrow$) Assume $\mu : T \to T'$ to be a $\mathcal{P}_\Sigma$-open morphism. Take an arbitrary $Y \in \mathcal{SR}(T')$ such that $tw(Y) = (\sigma_1, \tau_1) \ldots (\sigma_n, \tau_n)$. Construct the system $\mathcal{O} = (O, \Sigma, o_0, X_\mathcal{O}, T_\mathcal{O})$ as follows:

- $O = \{o_0, o_i, \varsigma_i, o_n^\gamma, \vartheta_{(a,d)}^\gamma \mid i = 1..(n-1), \gamma \in Y, (a,d) \in \mathcal{A}_{T'}(\gamma)\}$,
- $X_\mathcal{O} = \{u\}$,
- $T_\mathcal{O} = \{(o_{i-1}, \sigma_i, \{u = \tau_i\}, \emptyset, o_i) \mid i = 1..(n-1)\} \cup$
  $\{(o_{i-1}, \sigma_i, \{u = \tau_i\}, \emptyset, \varsigma_i) \mid i = 1..(n-1)\} \cup$
  $\{(o_{n-1}, \sigma_n, \{u = \tau_n\}, \emptyset, o_n^\gamma) \mid \gamma \in Y\} \cup$
  $\{(o_n^\gamma, a, \{u = d\}, \emptyset, \vartheta_{(a,d)}^\gamma) \mid \gamma \in Y, (a,d) \in \mathcal{A}_{T'}(\gamma)\}$.

Due to the construction, it is easy to see that $\mathcal{O}$ is a timed transition system. For the sake of clarity, consider the set $\mathcal{SR}(\mathcal{O}) = \{Z_0, Z_1, \ldots, Z_n, Z_{(a,d)} \mid (a,d) \in \bigcup_{A' \in \mathcal{A}_{T'}(Y)} A'\}$, where $Z_0 = \{C_0(\mathcal{O})\}$; $Z_i = \{C_0(\mathcal{O}) \overset{\sigma_1}{\underset{\tau_1}{\to}} \ldots \overset{\sigma_{i-1}}{\underset{\tau_{i-1}}{\to}} \langle o_{i-1}, \nu_{i-1}\rangle \overset{\sigma_i}{\underset{\tau_i}{\to}}$ $\langle o_i, \nu_i\rangle, C_0(\mathcal{O}) \overset{\sigma_1}{\underset{\tau_1}{\to}} \ldots \overset{\sigma_{i-1}}{\underset{\tau_{i-1}}{\to}} \langle o_{i-1}, \nu_{i-1}\rangle \overset{\sigma_i}{\underset{\tau_i}{\to}} \langle\varsigma_i, \nu_i\rangle\}$ $(i = 1..n-1)$; $Z_n = \{C_0(\mathcal{O}) \overset{\sigma_1}{\underset{\tau_1}{\to}}$ $\ldots \overset{\sigma_{n-1}}{\underset{\tau_{n-1}}{\to}} \langle o_{n-1}, \nu_{n-1}\rangle \overset{\sigma_n}{\underset{\tau_n}{\to}} \langle o_n^\gamma, \nu_n\rangle \mid \gamma \in Y\}$; $Z_{(a,d)} = \{C_0(\mathcal{O}) \overset{\sigma_1}{\underset{\tau_1}{\to}} \ldots \overset{\sigma_n}{\underset{\tau_n}{\to}} \langle o_n^\gamma, \nu_n\rangle$ $\overset{a}{\underset{d}{\to}} \langle \vartheta_{(a,d)}^\gamma, \nu_{n+1}\rangle \mid \gamma \in Y, (a,d) \in \mathcal{A}_{T'}(\gamma)\}$ $((a,d) \in \bigcup_{A' \in \mathcal{A}_{T'}(Y)} A')$. Moreover, we have that $\mathcal{A}_\mathcal{O}(Z_0) = \{\{(\sigma_1, \tau_1)\}\}$; $\mathcal{A}_\mathcal{O}(Z_i) = \{\{(\sigma_{i+1}, \tau_{i+1})\}, \emptyset\}$ $(i = 1..n-1)$; $\mathcal{A}_\mathcal{O}(Z_n) = \{\mathcal{A}_{T'}(\gamma) \mid \gamma \in Y\}$; $\mathcal{A}_\mathcal{O}(Z_{(a,d)}) = \{\emptyset\}$ $((a,d) \in \bigcup_{A' \in \mathcal{A}_{T'}(Y)} A')$.

Define the mappings $\mu_1 : \mathcal{E} \to \mathcal{O}$ and $\mu_2 : \mathcal{E} \to \mathcal{T}$ as follows: $\mu_1(\{C_0(\mathcal{E})\}) = \{C_0(\mathcal{O})\}$ and $\mu_2(\{C_0(\mathcal{E})\}) = \{C_0(\mathcal{T})\}$, where $\mathcal{E} = (\{e_0\}, \Sigma, e_0, \emptyset, \emptyset)$. Clearly, μ_1 and μ_2 are morphisms. Also, define the mapping $\mu_3 : \mathcal{O} \to \mathcal{T}'$ as follows: $\mu_3(Z_i) = \{\gamma' \in Runs(\mathcal{T}') \mid tw(\gamma') = tw(Z_i)\}$ $(i = 1..n)$ and $\mu_3(Z_{(a,d)}) = \{\gamma' \in Runs(\mathcal{T}') \mid tw(\gamma') = tw(Z_{(a,d)})\}$ $((a, d) \in \bigcup_{A' \in \mathcal{A}_{\mathcal{T}'}(Y)} A')$. Due to the construction of $\mathcal{O}$ and the definition of μ_3, it should be easy to see that μ_3 is a morphism. By the definition of $\mathcal{SR}(\mathcal{T}')$, we conclude that $\mu_3(Z_n) = Y$. Clearly, we have $\mu \circ \mu_2 = \mu_3 \circ \mu_1$. Since μ is a $\mathcal{P}_\Sigma$-open morphism, there exists a morphism $\overline{\mu} : \mathcal{O} \to \mathcal{T}$ such that $\mu_2 = \overline{\mu} \circ \mu_1$ and $\mu_3 = \mu \circ \overline{\mu}$. Assume $X = \overline{\mu}(Z_n)$. Due to the commutativity property of the triangles, we have $Y = \mu(X)$. Take $A \in \mathcal{A}_\mathcal{T}(X) = \mathcal{A}_\mathcal{T}(\overline{\mu}(Z_n))$. Since $\overline{\mu}$ is a morphism, there exists $A' \in \mathcal{A}_\mathcal{O}(Z_n)$ such that $A' \subseteq A$. Moreover, we have $\mathcal{A}_\mathcal{O}(Z_n) = \mathcal{A}_{\mathcal{T}'}(Y) = \mathcal{A}_{\mathcal{T}'}(\mu(X))$. So, there exists $A' \in \mathcal{A}_{\mathcal{T}'}(\mu(X))$ such that $A' \subseteq A$.

($\Leftarrow$) Assume $\mu : \mathcal{T} \to \mathcal{T}'$ to be a morphism in $\mathcal{CTTS}_\Sigma$. Take arbitrary morphisms $\mu_1 : \mathcal{O}_1 \to \mathcal{O}_2$ in $\mathcal{P}_\Sigma$, and $\mu_2 : \mathcal{O}_1 \to \mathcal{T}$, $\mu_3 : \mathcal{O}_2 \to \mathcal{T}'$ in $\mathcal{CTTS}_\Sigma$ such that $\mu \circ \mu_2 = \mu_3 \circ \mu_1$. Define the mapping $\mu' : \mathcal{SR}(\mathcal{O}_2) \to \mathcal{SR}(\mathcal{T})$ as follows: $\mu'(Z) = \{\gamma \in Runs(\mathcal{T}) \mid tw(\gamma) = tw(Z)\}$, for all $Z \in \mathcal{SR}(\mathcal{O}_2)$. It is routine to show that μ' is a morphism. The equations $\mu_3 = \mu \circ \mu'$ and $\mu_2 = \mu' \circ \mu_1$ follow trivially. Thus, μ is a $\mathcal{P}_\Sigma$-open morphism. $\diamond$

Example 6. Consider the transition systems $\widehat{\mathcal{T}}$ and $\overline{\mathcal{T}}$ shown in Fig. 2. The (only) morphism, μ, from $\widehat{\mathcal{T}}$ to $\overline{\mathcal{T}}$ is not $\mathcal{P}_\Sigma$-open because, for instance, for $A = \emptyset \in \mathcal{A}_{\widehat{\mathcal{T}}}(\widehat{X})$ there is no $A' \in \mathcal{A}_{\overline{\mathcal{T}}}(\overline{X} = \mu(\widehat{X}))$ such that $A' \subseteq A = \emptyset$, where $\widehat{X} = \{\langle \widehat{s}_0, \nu_0 \rangle \xrightarrow[1]{a} \langle \widehat{s}_1, \nu_1 \rangle, \langle \widehat{s}_0, \nu_0 \rangle \xrightarrow[1]{a} \langle \widehat{s}_2, \nu_1' \rangle, \langle \widehat{s}_0, \nu_0 \rangle \xrightarrow[1]{a} \langle \widehat{s}_3, \nu_1'' \rangle\}$, where $\nu_1(x) = \nu_1'(x) = 1$, $\nu_1(y) = \nu_1'(y) = 0$, $\nu_1''(x) = \nu_1''(y) = 1$, and $\overline{X} = \{\langle \overline{s}_0, \nu_0 \rangle \xrightarrow[1]{a} \langle \overline{s}_1, \nu_1 \rangle\}$, where $\nu_1(x) = 1$ and $\nu_1(y) = 0$. $\diamond$

Finally, the coincidence of $\mathcal{P}_\Sigma$-bisimilarity and testing equivalence is established.

Theorem 3. *Timed transition systems are $\mathcal{P}_\Sigma$-bisimilar iff they are testing equivalent.*

Proof. ($\Rightarrow$) For a timed transition system $\mathcal{T}$, $X \in \mathcal{SR}(\mathcal{T})$ and $\alpha \in L(\mathcal{T})$, we shall write $\mathcal{A}_\mathcal{T}(\alpha) = \mathcal{A}_\mathcal{T}(X)$ if $tw(X) = \alpha$. Suppose $\mathcal{T}_1 \xleftarrow{\mu_1} \mathcal{T} \xrightarrow{\mu_2} \mathcal{T}_2$ to be a span of $\mathcal{P}_\Sigma$-open morphisms. It is easy to show that $L(\mathcal{T}_1) = L(\mathcal{T}_2)$. We shall prove that for all timed words α and for all sets $L \subseteq (\Sigma \times \mathbf{R}^+)$, if $\mathcal{T}_1$ **after** α **MUST** L, then $\mathcal{T}_2$ **after** α **MUST** L (the proof of the converse direction is similar). Take arbitrary α and L such that $\mathcal{T}_1$ **after** α **MUST** L. Two cases are admissible.

- $\alpha \in L(\mathcal{T}_1)$. This implies $\alpha \in L(\mathcal{T}_2)$. Then there exists $X_1 \in \mathcal{SR}(\mathcal{T}_1)$ and $X_2 \in \mathcal{SR}(\mathcal{T}_2)$ such that $tw(X_1) = \alpha = tw(X_2)$. Hence, we have $\mathcal{A}_{\mathcal{T}_1}(X_1) = \mathcal{A}_{\mathcal{T}_1}(\alpha)$ and $\mathcal{A}_{\mathcal{T}_2}(X_2) = \mathcal{A}_{\mathcal{T}_2}(\alpha)$. Since μ_1 is a $\mathcal{P}_\Sigma$-open morphism, for X_1 we can find $X \in \mathcal{SR}(\mathcal{T})$ such that $\mu_1(X) = X_1$ and for all $A \in \mathcal{A}_\mathcal{T}(X)$ there exists $A_1 \in \mathcal{A}_{\mathcal{T}_1}(X_1)$ such that $A_1 \subseteq A$, by Theorem 2. Next, since

μ_2 is a morphism, it follows that $X_2 = \mu_2(X) \in \mathcal{SR}(T_2)$, and for all $A_2 \in \mathcal{A}_{T_2}(X_2)$ there exists $A \in \mathcal{A}_T(X)$ such that $A \subseteq A_2$. So, we have that for all $A_2 \in \mathcal{A}_{T_2}(\alpha)$ there exists $A_1 \in \mathcal{A}_{T_1}(\alpha)$ such that $A_1 \subseteq A_2$. Since T_1 **after** α **MUST** L, it follows $A_1 \cap L \neq \emptyset$, for all $A_1 \in \mathcal{A}_{T_1}(\alpha)$. This means $A_2 \cap L \neq \emptyset$, for all $A_2 \in \mathcal{A}_{T_2}(\alpha)$. Thus, we can conclude that T_2 **after** α **MUST** L.

- $\alpha \notin L(T_1)$. Then, $\alpha \notin L(T_2)$. This implies T_2 **after** α **MUST** L.

($\Leftarrow$) Suppose T_1 and T_2 to be testing equivalent. It is easy to show that $L(T_1) = L(T_2)$. Clearly, we can define a map $\mu : T_1 \to T_2$ as a function $\mu : \mathcal{SR}(T_1) \longrightarrow \mathcal{SR}(T_2)$ such that: for all $X \in \mathcal{SR}(T_1)$, $tw(X) = tw(\mu(X))$, and for all $Y \in \mathcal{SR}(T_2)$ there exists $X \in \mathcal{SR}(T_1)$ such that $\mu(X) = Y$. Next, we shall prove that for all $A_2 \in \mathcal{A}_{T_2}(\mu(X))$ there exists $A_1 \in \mathcal{A}_{T_1}(X)$ such that $A_1 \subseteq A_2$ (the proof of the converse fact is similar). Suppose a contrary, i.e. there exists $A_2 \in \mathcal{A}_{T_2}(\mu(X))$ such that $A_1 \nsubseteq A_2$, for all $A_1 \in \mathcal{A}_{T_1}(X)$. This means that for all A_1 there exists at least one $(\sigma, \tau)_{A_1}$ such that $(\sigma, \tau)_{A_1} \in A_1 \setminus A_2$. Define $L_0 = \cup_{A_1 \in \mathcal{A}_{T_1}(X)}(\sigma, \tau)_{A_1}$. W.l.o.g. assume $tw(X) = \alpha$. We then conclude that T_1 **after** α **MUST** L_0, but $\neg(T_2$ **after** α **MUST** $L_0)$, contradicting our assumption. Thus, μ is a morphism and, moreover, a $\mathcal{P}_\Sigma$-open morphism, due to Theorem 2. $\Diamond$

5   Conclusion

In this paper, we have presented an application of Joyal, Nielsen, and Winskel's theory [19] illustrating that testing equivalence on timed transition systems can be captured by the span of open maps idea. This allows us to transfer general concepts of equivalences to the model under consideration and to apply general results from the categorical setting (e.g. the existence of canonical models and characteristic games and logics) to a concrete time-sensitive equivalence. It is worth noting that the developed here category can also be exploited to provide an open maps characterization of trace equivalence on timed transition systems.

As for future work, we plan to extend the obtained results to other observational equivalences (e.g., equivalences taking into account internal actions, etc.) and to other classes of timed models (e.g. timed Petri nets, timed local event structures, etc.). Also, we intend to exploit the approach from [11] as part of our future work. Further, it would be interesting to study the relationship of the characteristic path logic [19] to existing real-time logics [3].

References

1. Aceto, L., De Nicola, R., Fantechi, A.: Testing equivalences for event structures. In: Venturini Zilli, M. (ed.) Mathematical Models for the Semantics of Parallelism. LNCS, vol. 280, pp. 1–20. Springer, Heidelberg (1987)
2. Alur, R., Dill, D.: The theory of timed automata. Theoretical Computer Science 126, 183–235 (1994)
3. Alur, R., Henziger, T.A.: Logics and models of real time: a survey. In: Huizing, C., de Bakker, J.W., Rozenberg, G., de Roever, W.-P. (eds.) Real-Time: Theory in Practice. LNCS, vol. 600, pp. 74–106. Springer, Heidelberg (1992)

4. Andreeva, M.V., Bozhenkova, E.N., Virbitskaite, I.B.: Analysis of timed concurrent models based on testing equivalence. Fundamenta Informaticae 43(1–4), 1–20 (2000)
5. Bihler, E., Vogler, W.: Timed Petri Nets: Efficiency of asynchronous systems. In: Bernardo, M., Corradini, F. (eds.) Formal Methods for the Design of Real-Time Systems. LNCS, vol. 3185, pp. 25–58. Springer, Heidelberg (2004)
6. Badouel, E., Bednarczyk, M., Darondeau, P.: Generalized automata and their net representations. In: Ehrig, H., Juhás, G., Padberg, J., Rozenberg, G. (eds.) Unifying Petri Nets. LNCS, vol. 2128, pp. 304–345. Springer, Heidelberg (2001)
7. Borceux, F.: Handbook of Categorical Algebra, vol. 2(3). Encyclopedia of Mathematics and its Applications, vol. 51(52). Cambridge University Press (1994)
8. Cattani, G.L., Sassone, V.: Higher dimentional transition systems. In: Proc. LICS'96, pp. 55–62 (1996)
9. Čerāns, K.: Decidability of bisimulation equivalences for parallel timer processes. In: Probst, D.K., von Bochmann, G. (eds.) CAV 1992. LNCS, vol. 663, pp. 302–315. Springer, Heidelberg (1993)
10. Cleaveland, R., Zwarico, A.E.: A theory of testing for real-time. In: Proc. LICS'91, pp. 110–119 (1991)
11. Fiore, M., Cattani, G.L., Winskel, G.: Weak bisimulation and open maps. In: Proc. LICS'99, pp. 214–225 (1999)
12. Fahrenberg, U.: A Category of Higher-Dimensional Automata. In: Sassone, V. (ed.) FOSSACS 2005. LNCS, vol. 3441, pp. 187–201. Springer, Heidelberg (2005)
13. van Glabbeek, R.J.: The linear time – branching time spectrum II: the semantics of sequential systems with silent moves. Extended abstract. In: Best, E. (ed.) CONCUR 1993. LNCS, vol. 715, pp. 66–81. Springer, Heidelberg (1993)
14. Glabbeek, R., Goltz, U.: Equivalence notions for concurrent systems and refinement of action. In: Kreczmar, A., Mirkowska, G. (eds.) Mathematical Foundations of Computer Science 1989. LNCS, vol. 379, pp. 237–248. Springer, Heidelberg (1989)
15. Goltz, U., Wehrheim, H.: Causal testing. In: Penczek, W., Szałas, A. (eds.) Mathematical Foundations of Computer Science 1996. LNCS, vol. 1113, pp. 394–406. Springer, Heidelberg (1996)
16. Henzinger, T.A., Manna, Z., Pnueli, A.: Timed transition systems. In: Huizing, C., de Bakker, J.W., Rozenberg, G., de Roever, W.-P. (eds.) Real-Time: Theory in Practice. LNCS, vol. 600, pp. 226–251. Springer, Heidelberg (1992)
17. Hune, T., Nielsen, M.: Bisimulation and open maps fot timed transition systems. Fundamenta Informaticae 38, 61–77 (1999)
18. Jacobs, B., Rutten, J.: A tutorial on (Co)algebras and (Co)induction. EATCS Bulletin 62, 222–259 (1997)
19. Joyal, A., Nielsen, M., Winskel, G.: Bisimulation from open maps. Information and Computation 127(2), 164–185 (1996)
20. De Nicola, R., Hennessy, M.: Testing equiavalence for processes. Theoretical Computer Science 34, 83–133 (1984)
21. Nielsen, M., Cheng, A.: Observing behaviour categorically. In: Thiagarajan, P.S. (ed.) Foundations of Software Technology and Theoretical Computer Science. LNCS, vol. 1026, pp. 263–278. Springer, Heidelberg (1995)
22. Steffen, B., Weise, C.: Deciding testing equivalence for real-time processes with dense time. In: Borzyszkowski, A.M., Sokolowski, S. (eds.) MFCS 1993. LNCS, vol. 711, pp. 703–713. Springer, Heidelberg (1993)
23. Virbitskaite, I.B., Gribovskaya, N.S.: Open maps and observational equivalences for timed partial order models. Fundamenta Informaticae 60(1-4), 383–399 (2004)

24. Weise, C., Lenzkes, D.: Efficient scaling-invariant checking of timed bisimulation. In: Reischuk, R., Morvan, M. (eds.) STACS 97. LNCS, vol. 1200, pp. 176–188. Springer, Heidelberg (1997)
25. Winskel, G., Nielsen, M.: Models for concurrency. In: Handbook of Logic in Computer Science 4 (1995)

Appendix: Introduction to Open Maps

We briefly recall the basic definitions from [19].

First, a category which represents a model of computation has to be identified. Let us denote this category $\mathcal{M}$. A morphism $m : X \longrightarrow Y$ in $\mathcal{M}$ should intuitively be thought of as a simulation of X in Y. Then, within the category $\mathcal{M}$, we choose a subcategory of 'observation objects' and 'observation extension' morphisms between these objects. We denote this *category of observations* by $\mathcal{P}$. Given an observation (object) O in $\mathcal{P}$ and a model X in $\mathcal{M}$, then O is said to be an *observable behaviour* of X if there exists a morphism $p : O \longrightarrow Y$ in $\mathcal{M}$. We think of p as representing a particular way of realizing O in X.

Next, we identify morphisms $m : X \longrightarrow Y$ which have the property that whenever an observable behaviour of X can be extended via f in Y then that extension can be matched by an extension of the observable behaviour in X. A morphism $m : X \to Y$ in $\mathcal{M}$ is called $\mathcal{P}$-open if whenever $f : O_1 \to O_2$ in $\mathcal{P}$, $p : O_1 \to X$, $q : O_2 \to Y$ in $\mathcal{M}$ such that $m \circ p = q \circ f$, there exists a morphism $h : O_2 \to X$ in $\mathcal{M}$ such that $p = h \circ f$ and $q = m \circ h$. When no confusion is possible, we refer to $\mathcal{P}$-open morphisms as open maps.

Finally, we introduce an abstract notion of bisimilarity. As reported in [19], the open map approach provides general concepts of bisimilarity for any categorical model of computation. The definition is given in terms of spans of open maps. Two models X and Y in $\mathcal{M}$ are said to be $\mathcal{P}$-bisimilar if there exists a span $X \xleftarrow{m} Z \xrightarrow{m'} Y$ with vertex Z of $\mathcal{P}$-open morphisms.

Notice that if $\mathcal{M}$ has pullbacks, it can be shown that $\mathcal{P}$-bisimilarity is always an equivalence relation. The important observation is that pullbacks of open maps are themselves open maps [19].

From Unreliable Objects to Reliable Objects: The Case of Atomic Registers and Consensus

Rachid Guerraoui[1] and Michel Raynal[2]

[1] Distributed Programming Lab, EPFL, Lausanne, Switzerland
`rachid.guerraoui@epfl.ch`
[2] IRISA, University of Rennes 1, 35042 Rennes, France
`michel.raynal@irisa.fr`

Abstract. A *concurrent* object is an object that can be concurrently accessed by several processes. It has been shown by Maurice Herlihy that any concurrent object O defined by a sequential specification can be wait-free implemented from reliable atomic registers (shared variables) and consensus objects. *Wait-free* means that any invocation of an operation of the object O issued by a non-faulty process does terminate, whatever the behavior of the other processes (e.g., despite the fact they are very slow or even have crashed).

So, an important issue consists in providing reliable atomic registers and reliable consensus objects despite the failures experienced by the base objects from which these atomic registers and consensus objects are built. This paper considers self-implementations, i.e., the case where a reliable atomic register (resp., consensus object) is built from unreliable atomic registers (resp., unreliable consensus objects). The paper addresses the object failure model where the base objects can suffer *responsive* or *nonresponsive* crash failures. When there are solutions the paper presents corresponding algorithms, and when there is no solution, it presents the corresponding impossibility result. The paper has a tutorial flavor whose aim is to make the reader familiar with important results when one has to build resilient concurrent objects. To that aim, the paper use both algorithms from the literature and new algorithms.

1   Introduction

Concurrent object with a sequential specification. A *concurrent* object is an object that can be concurrently accessed by several processes. As any object, such an object is defined by (1) an interface providing operations that allow manipulating the object and (2) a specification describing the correct behaviors of the object. Such a specification can be sequential or not. As an example, a concurrent queue has a sequential specification. Differently, a failure detector [2,10] has no sequential specification. *Sequential specification* means that, at some abstraction level, the behavior of the object can be described as if each operation was executed instantaneously and without concurrency. Among the most popular concurrent objects defined by a sequential specification there are the shared queue (whose implementation is usually described in textbooks under the name

V. Malyshkin (Ed.): PaCT 2007, LNCS 4671, pp. 47–61, 2007.
© Springer-Verlag Berlin Heidelberg 2007

producer/consumer problem), and the shared file, also called disk or register (the implementation of which underlies the *readers/writers* problem).

Net effect of asynchrony and failures. When operations accessing a concurrent object overlap, a simple way to ensure that the sequential specification of the object is never violated consists in blocking all of them but one during some time in order that one can access the object without being bothered by the others and consequently be able to proceed in a safe way. This is traditionally solved by associating *locks* with each concurrent object [6]. (Such a lock is called a *condition* in the monitor terminology [6], and a simple way to implement a lock consists in using a semaphore.) Due to their (relative) simplicity and their effectiveness, lock-based implementations are popular.

Unfortunately, in asynchronous systems (i.e., the class of systems where no assumption on the speed of the processes is possible), the lock-based approach presents intrinsic major drawbacks. If a slow process holds a lock during a long period of time, it can delay faster processes from accessing (some parts of) the object. More severely, the lock-based approach does not prevent by itself deadlock scenarios from occurring. Preventing them requires additional mechanisms or strategies that can give rise to long waiting periods that degrade the whole system efficiency. The situation becomes even more critical in presence of failures. When a process holding a lock crashes, as the system is asynchronous, there is no way to know whether this process has crashed or is only very slow. It follows that such a crash can block the system during an arbitrarily long period (i.e., until an appropriate recovery action is started, either manually, or after the operating system becomes aware of the crash of the process).

Wait-free object implementation and consensus universality. These crucial drawbacks make a case for implementations of concurrent objects that, instead of being lock-based, allow each process that executes an object operation to progress without waiting, i.e., whatever the current state and behavior of the other processes. Such implementations of concurrent objects are known as *wait-free* [4]. Initially proposed by Lamport [8], they basically ensure that no process can be arbitrarily delayed by the other processes. It is important to notice that "wait-free" is a property of a protocol implementing an object, not a property of the object itself.

Very interestingly, it has been shown [4] that any concurrent object that has a sequential specification (as it is the case for shared queues and shared files) can have a wait-free implementation for any number of processes as soon as we are provided with *atomic registers* (shared variables) and *consensus* objects [4]. This result is called the *universality of consensus*. A *universal construction* is a wait-free algorithm that, given the specification of any sequential type T, builds a concurrent object of the type T from atomic registers and consensus objects. The most known universal construction is described in [4]; that construction is bounded. A simpler (not bounded) universal construction is described in [3].

Content of the paper. The previous discussion shows that atomic registers and consensus objects are fundamental objects as soon as one wants to build high level wait-free reliable objects. A universal construction considers that these base objects are reliable, i.e., they always provide their failure-free semantics. So, to complete the picture, it is necessary to be able to build reliable atomic registers and reliable consensus objects from unreliable base objects. Such an investigation had been done in [7]. In that paper, adopting a very theoretical point of view, the authors consider several failure models (crash, omission, Byzantine) and delineate a precise borderline separating what that can be done from what that cannot be done (impossibility results).

Although some of the algorithms it presents are new, this paper has a more pedagogical and survey flavor. Assuming that any number of processes can crash (wait-free case), the paper considers two variants of the object crash failure model, namely the *responsive* crash model, and the *nonresponsive* crash model. This difference is fundamental. In the responsive crash model, a process that invokes an operation always receives a response (a default value when the object has crashed), while it can never receive a response in the nonresponsive model after the base object has crashed (the invoking operation can then remain pending forever).

The paper is divided into 4 sections. First, the system model is presented and important definitions are stated (Section 2). Then, the responsive failure model is addressed in Section 3, while the nonresponsive failure model is considered in Section 4. In each case, (existing or new) algorithms are presented and proved correct. When no algorithm can be designed, an impossibility result is proved. As already mentioned, in addition to new algorithms, the paper has a pedagogical and survey flavor. Interestingly, the paper visits also proofs techniques that one can use to prove that objects are atomic.

2 Computation Model

2.1 Processes, Registers and Consensus Objects

Process model We consider a system made up of an arbitrary number (not necessarily finite) of sequential processes, denoted $p_1, p_2, \ldots$, such that any number of them can crash (wait-free case). Given any execution of the system, a *correct* process is a process that does not crash during that execution. A process that crashes is said to be *faulty*. A process executes correctly (i.e., according to its specification) until it possibly crashes. After it has crashed, a process executes no operation. There is no bound on the relative speed of a process with respect to another, which means that the system is *asynchronous* [1].

Shared Registers. A register [9] is an abstraction of shared variable. A *reliable atomic register* is an object that provides the processes with two operations usually called read and a write operations. Whatever the number of processes that can concurrently access such a register, the read and write operations issued by the processes appear as if they have been executed one after the other, each one being executed instantaneously at some point of the time line between its invocation event and its response event.

In the following we consider that each register has a single writer and a single reader (1W1R register). This is not at the price of generality as multi-writers multi-readers atomic registers can be built from 1W1R atomic registers (e.g., see [11]). The notion of atomic register is the ultimate of the following suite of definitions [9].

- A 1W1R *safe* register is a register such that a read operation that is not concurrent with a write operation returns the current value of the register, while a read concurrent with a write returns any value that the register can contain (let us observe that, in that case, it is possible that the returned value has never been written into the register!).
- A 1W1R *regular* register is a safe register such that any read concurrent with one or more write operations returns the value of the register before these write operations, or the value written by one of these write operations.

  It is important to see that when two read operations $r1$ and $r2$ are concurrent with two write operations $w1$ and $w2$ (see Figure 5), it is possible that the second read $r2$ obtains the value written by the first write $w1$, while the first read $r1$ obtains the value written by the second write $w2$. When it occurs, this is called a *new/old inversion*.
- A 1W1R *atomic* register is a regular register with no new/old inversion [9].

Consensus Object. A consensus object offers a single operation to its users, namely *propose*(). A process p_i invokes it at most once, and supplies a parameter value v_i. So its invocation has the form "*propose*(v_i)", and we say "p_i proposes v_i". Each process invocation returns a result. The semantic of a consensus object states that (1) all the processes that invoke *propose*() obtain a result value (termination); (2) there is single result value (agreement); and (3) the result value is a proposed value (validity). Restraining, without loss of generality, the decided value to be the value proposed in the first invocation of the *propose*() operation provides a sequential specification of the consensus object [7].

2.2 Responsive and Nonresponsive Crash Failures

Intuitively, an object crash failure occurs when the corresponding object stops working. More precisely, two different crash failure models can be distinguished: the *responsive* crash model and the *nonresponsive* crash model.

Responsive crashes. In the responsive crash failure model, an object fails if it behaves correctly until some time, after which every operation returns the default value $\perp$. This means that the object behaves according to its sequential specification until it crashes (if it ever crashes), and then satisfies the property "once $\perp$, forever $\perp$". The responsive crash model is sometimes called *fail-stop* model.

Nonresponsive crashes. In the nonresponsive crash model, an object does not return $\perp$ after it has crashed. There is no response and the invoked operation remains pending forever. The nonresponsive crash model is sometimes called *fail-silent* model.

Facing nonresponsive failures is more difficult than facing responsive failures. Indeed, in the asynchronous computation model, a process that invokes an operation on an object that has crashed and is not responsive, has no mean to know whether the object has indeed crashed or is only very slow. As we will see, some objects that can be implemented in the responsive failure model, can no longer be implemented in the nonresponsive failure model.

2.3 Notion of *t*-Resilience

As indicated above, we are interested in the wait-free construction of reliable objects from base object prone to crash (let us recall that "wait-free" means that the constructions have to work whatever the number of faulty processes). More precisely we are interested in, *self-implementation*, which means that we want to build a reliable object of type T (atomic register or consensus), from base objects of the same type T a subset of them being possibly unreliable.

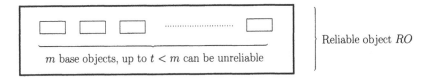

Fig. 1. Reliable object from unreliable base objects

Let us assume that the reliable object RO is built from m base objects of the same type (Figure 1). RO is said to be *t-resilient* if behaves correctly despite the crash of up to t shared base objects from which it is built. This means that, for the processes that use RO, there is no difference if none, 1, 2, etc., up to $t < m$ base objects crash. (If there are differences, those concern efficiency and could be perceived only by an external observer. Due to the asynchrony of the system model, they are "hidden" to the processes.) Differently, if more than t base object crash, there is no guarantee on the behavior of RO (that can then behave arbitrarily).

3 Registers and Consensus Objects with Responsive Failures

This section presents wait-free self-constructions of t-resilient objects from $m \geq t + 1$ base objects prone to responsive crash failures. "Self-construction" means that the reliable object that is built and the base objects from which it is built have the same type. It is easy to see that $t+1$ is a tight lower bound on the number of base objects required to mask up to t faulty base objects. If an operation on the constructed object accesses only t base objects, and all of them fail, there is no way for the constructed object to mask the base object failures. As previously indicated, these constructions concern 1W1R atomic registers and consensus.

3.1 Reliable Register When Failures Are Responsive: An Unbounded Construction

The first construction (that is present on some textbooks without proof) is based on sequence numbers. It consequently requires base atomic registers that are potentially unbounded. The $t + 1$ registers are denoted $REG[1 : (t + 1)]$. Each register $REG[i]$ is made up of two fields denoted $REG[i].sn$ (sequence number part) and $REG[i].val$ (value part). Each base register $REG[i]$ is initialized to the pair $(v_{init}, 0)$ where v_{init} is the initial value of the constructed register.

---

operation $RO.write(v)$: % invoked by the writer %
    $sn \leftarrow sn + 1$;
    for $j \in \{1, \ldots, t+1\}$ **do** $REG[j] \leftarrow (v, sn)$ **end_do**;
    return ()

operation $RO.read()$: % invoked by the reader %
    % The initial value of $last$ is $(v\_init, 0)$ %
    for $j \in \{1, \ldots, t+1\}$ **do**
        $aux \leftarrow REG[j]$;
        if $(aux \neq \perp) \land (aux.sn > last.sn)$ **then** $last \leftarrow aux$ **end_if**
    end_do;
    return $(last.val)$

Fig. 2. 1W1R t-resilient atomic register RO: construction 1

The read and write operation to access the t-resilient 1W1R register (denoted RO) are described in Figure 2. The write operation consists in writing the pair, made up of the new value plus its sequence number, in all the base registers (without specific order) sn is a variable local to the writer that is used to generate sequence numbers (it is initialized to 0).

The reader keeps in a local variable denoted $last$, and initialized to $(v_{init}, 0)$, a copy of the pair (v, sn) with the highest sequence number it has ever read. This variable allows preventing new/old inversions when base registers or the writer crash. The read operation consists in reading the base registers (in any order). Let us observe that, as at most t registers can crash, at least one register always returns a non-$\perp$ value. For all the base registers whose read returns a non-$\perp$ value, if the reader reads a more recent value, it updates $last$ accordingly. Finally, it returns the value $last.val$, i.e., the value associated with the highest sequence number it has ever seen $(last.sn)$.

It is important to notice that the read and write operations access the base registers in any order. This means that no operation on a base register depends on a previous operation on another base register. Said in another way, they could be issued in parallel, thereby favoring efficiency. (Differently, when base registers can suffer nonresponsive failures, the parallel invocation approach has to be used to cope with base operations that never answer. This is illustrated in Figure 8.) Let us also notice that the version of the construction with parallel invocations provides an optimal construction as far as time complexity is concerned.

Theorem 1. *The algorithm described in Figure 2 wait-free implements a t-resilient 1W1R atomic register from $(t + 1)$ 1W1R base atomic registers that can suffer responsive crash failures.*

Proof. As already noticed, the construction is trivially wait-free. Moreover, as each read operation returns a non-$\perp$ value, the register that is built is reliable (in the sense that it always returns a non-$\perp$ value). So, it remains to show that the register that is built is atomic. This is done by first defining a total order on the read and write operations on the constructed object, and then showing that the resulting sequence satisfies the sequential specification of a register. This second step uses the fact that there exists a total order on the accesses to the base registers (as those registers are atomic).

Let us associate with each write operation on the constructed object RO (high level write) the sequence number associated with the value it writes. Similarly, let us associate with each high level read operation the sequence number of the value it reads. Let $\widehat{S}$ be the total order on the high level read and write operations defined as follows. The high level write operations are ordered according to their sequence numbers. The high level read operations with a given sequence number are ordered just after the high level write operation with the same sequence number. If two or more read operations have the same sequence number, they are ordered in $\widehat{S}$ according to their invocation order. We have the following.

- It follows from its definition that $\widehat{S}$ includes all the operations issued by the reader and the writer (except possibly their last operation if they crash).
- Due to the way the local variable sn is used by the writer, the high level write operations appear in $\widehat{S}$ according to their invocation order.
- Similarly, the high level read operations appear in $\widehat{S}$ according to their invocation order. This is due the local variable $last$ used by the reader (the reader returns the value with the highest sequence number it has ever obtained from a base register).
- As the base registers are atomic, the base operations on these registers are totally ordered. Consequently, when we consider that total order, a base read operation that obtains the sequence number sn from a base atomic register, is after the base write operation that wrote sn into that register.
  As $\widehat{S}$ is such that a high level read operation that obtains a value whose sequence number is sn is after the snth high level write operation, it follows that $\widehat{S}$ is consistent with the occurrence order defined by the operations on the base objects.

It follows from the previous items that $\widehat{S}$ is a *linearization* of the high level read and write operations (this means that these high level operations can be totally ordered in such a way that each operation appears as if it has been executed instantaneously at some point of the time line between its invocation event and its end event [4]). Consequently, the constructed object RO is an atomic register.

$$\square_{Theorem\ 1}$$

3.2 Reliable Register When Failures Are Responsive: A Bounded Construction

Eliminating sequence numbers. When we consider the previous construction, an interesting question is the following: is it possible to design a t-resilient 1W1R atomic register from $t+1$ bounded base registers, i.e., are the sequence numbers necessary? The construction that follows shows that they are not: there is a bounded 1W1R atomic register construction. Moreover, that construction (that, to our knowledge, is new) is optimal in the sense that each base register has only to contain the value that is written. No additional control information is required.

The corresponding construction is described in Figure 4. The writer simply writes the new value in each base register, in increasing order, starting from $REG[1]$ until $REG[t+1]$. The reader scans sequentially the registers in the opposite order, starting from $REG[t+1]$. It stops just after the first read of a base register that returns a non-$\perp$ value. As at least one base register does not crash (model assumption), the reader always obtains a non-$\perp$ value. (Let us remind that, as we want to build a t-resilient object, the construction is not required to provide guarantees when more than t base objects crash.) It is important to remark that, differently from the construction described in Figure 2, each read and write operation has now to follow a predefined order when it accesses the base registers. Moreover, the order for reading and the order for writing are opposite. These orders are depicted in Figure 3 with a space-time diagram in which the "time line" of each base register is represented. A black circle indicates a base read or write operation on a base register $REG[k]$. The read stops reading base registers when it reads a non-$\perp$ value for the first time.

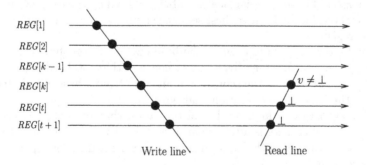

Fig. 3. Order in which the operations access the base registers

Why read and write operations have to access base registers in opposite order.
To understand why the high level read and write operations have to access the
base registers in opposite order, let us consider the following scenario where
both the read and write operations access the base registers in the same order,
from $REG[1]$ to $REG[t + 1]$. The write updates $REG[1]$ to x and crashes just
after. Then, a read obtains the value x. Sometimes later, $REG[1]$ crashes. After
that crash occurred, the reader reads $REG[1]$, obtains $\perp$, then reads $REG[2]$
and obtains y, the value that was written before x. The two high level read
operations issued by the reader suffer a new/old inversion, and consequently, the
constructed object is not atomic. Forcing the reader to access the base registers
in the reverse order (with respect to the writer) ensures that if the reader returns
v from $REG[j]$, then all the based registers $REG[k]$ such that $j < k \leq t+1$ have
crashed. More generally, as we have seen previously, if the reader and the writer
do not access the base registers in opposite order, additional control information
has to be used, such as sequence numbers.

---

operation $RO.write(v)$: % invoked by the writer %
    for j **from** 1 **to** $t + 1$ **do** $REG[j] \leftarrow v$ **end_do**;
    return ()

operation $RO.read()$: % invoked by the reader %
    for j **from** $t + 1$ **to** 1 **do**
        $aux \leftarrow REG[j]$;
        if $(aux \neq \perp)$ **then** *return* (aux) **end_if**
    end_do

Fig. 4. 1W1R t-resilient atomic register RO: construction 2

Tradeoff. It is interesting to emphasize the tradeoff between this construction
and the previous one. The construction of a 1W1R t-resilient atomic register described in Figure 2 is time-optimal (when the invocations are done in parallel),
but requires additional control information, namely, sequence numbers. Differently, the construction described in Figure 4 is space optimal (no additional
control information is required), but requires sequential invocations on the base
registers.

Theorem 2. *The algorithm described in Figure 4 wait-free implements a t-
resilient 1W1R atomic register from $(t + 1)$ 1W1R base atomic registers that
can suffer responsive crash failures. Moreover it is space optimal.*

Proof. The wait-free property follows directly from the fact there is no explicit
or implicit wait statement in the construction. Due to the assumption that at
most t base registers crash, the value returned by a high level read operation is
a value that has been previously written. Consequently, the constructed object
never returns $\perp$, and is (in that sense) a reliable register.

The proof that the constructed register is atomic is done incrementally. It is shown that the register is first safe, then regular and finally atomic. The proof for going from regularity to atomicity consists in showing that there is no new/old inversion, from which atomicity follows [9].

Safeness. Let us consider a read operation of the constructed register when there is no concurrent write operation. Safeness requires that, in this scenario, the read returns the last written value.

As (by assumption) no write operation is concurrent with the read operation, we conclude that the writer has not crashed during the last write operation issued before the read operation (otherwise, this write operation would not be terminated and consequently would be concurrent with the read operation).

The last write has updated all the non-crashed registers to the same value v. It follows that, whatever the base register from which the read operation obtains a non-$\perp$ value, it obtains and returns the value v.

Regularity. If a read operation r is concurrent with one or several write operations, we have to show that it obtains the value of the constructed register before these write operations, or a value written by one of them.

Let us first observe that a read operation cannot obtain from a base register a value that has not yet been written into it. We conclude from that observation that a high level read operation cannot return a value that has not yet been written by a write operation.

Let v be the value of the register before the concurrent high level write operation. This means that all the non-crashed base registers are equal to v before the first concurrent high level write operation. If the high level read operation obtains the value v, regularity is ensured. So, let us assume that r obtains another value v' from some register $REG[x]$. This means that $REG[x]$ has not crashed and has been updated to v' after having been updated to v. This can only be done by a concurrent high level write operation that writes v' and has been issued by the writer after the write of v. The constructed register is consequently regular.

Atomicity. We prove that there is no new/old inversion. Let us assume that two read operations $r1$ and $r2$ are such that $r1$ is invoked before $r2$, $r1$ returns $v2$ that has been written by $w2$, $r2$ returns $v1$ that has been written by $w1$, and $w1$ is before $w2$ (Figure 5). The read operation $r1$ returns $v2$ from some base register $REG[x]$. It follows from the read algorithm that all the base registers $REG[y]$ such that $x < y \le t + 1$ have crashed. It also follows from the write

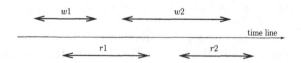

Fig. 5. Proof of no new/old inversion

algorithm that the non-crashed registers from $REG[1]$ to $REG[x-1]$ contain $v2$ or a more recent value when $r1$ returns $v2$.

As the base registers from $REG[t+1]$ until $REG[x+1]$ have crashed when $r2$ is invoked, that read operation obtains $\perp$ from all these registers. When it reads the atomic register $REG[x]$, it obtains $v2$, or a more recent value, or $\perp$.

- If it obtains $v2$ or a more recent value, there is no new/old inversion.
- If it obtains $\perp$, it continues reading from $REG[x-1]$ until it finds a base register $REG[y]$ $(y < x)$ from which it obtains a non-$\perp$ value. On another side, as the write algorithm writes the base registers in increasing order starting from $REG[1]$, it follows that no register from $REG[1]$ until $REG[x-1]$ (not crashed when read by $r2$) can contain a value older than $v2$, namely it can only contain $v2$ or a more recent value. It follows that there is no possibility of new/old inversion also in that case. $\square_{Theorem\ 2}$

---

operation $RO.read()$: % invoked by the reader %
    for j **from** *shortcut* **to** 1 **do**
        $aux \leftarrow REG[j]$;
        if $(aux \neq \perp)$ **then** $shortcut \leftarrow j$; $return\ (aux)$ **end_if**
    end_do

Fig. 6. Improving construction 2

An improvement. An easy way to improve the time efficiency of the previous read operation consists in providing the reader with a local variable (denoted *shortcut* and initialized to $t+1$), that keeps an index such that, to the reader knowledge, each $REG[k]$ has crashed, for $shortcut < k \leq t+1$. The resulting read algorithm is described in Figure 6. It is easy to see that, if after some time no more base register crashes, *shortcut* always points to the first (in descending order) non-crashed base register. This means that there is a time after which the duration of a read operation is constant.

3.3 Consensus When Failures Are Responsive: A Bounded Construction

This section presents a t-resilient consensus object RES_CONS built from $m = t+1$ base consensus objects. As for the previous register, it is easy to see that $t+1$ is a tight lower bound on the number of crash-prone base consensus objects.

The "parallel invocations" approach does not work. Before presenting a construction that builds a t-resilient consensus object, let us give an intuitive explanation of the fact that there is no solution when the invocations on the base consensus objects are done in parallel.

So, let us assume that we have $m = 2t + 1$ base consensus objects, and an invocation on the constructed object is implemented as follows: a process p_i (1) invokes in parallel $propose(v)$ on each base object, and then (2) takes the value decided by a majority of the base consensus objects. As there is a majority of base objects that are reliable, this algorithm does not block, and p_i receives decided values from a majority of base consensus objects. But, according to the values proposed by the other processes, it is possible that none of the values it receives be a majority value. It is even possible that it receives a different value from each of the $2t + 1$ base consensus objects if there are $n \geq m = 2t + 1$ processes and they all have a proposed different values to the constructed consensus object.

While this approach works for objects such as atomic registers (see below), it does not for consensus objects. This comes from the fact that registers are *data* objects, while consensus are *synchronization* objects and synchronization is inherently non-deterministic.

A t-resilient construction. The $t+1$ base consensus objects are denoted $CONS[1 : (t+1)]$. The construction (from [7]) is described in Figure 7. The variable *est* is local to the invoking process. When a process p_i invokes $RES\_CONS.propose(v)$, it first sets *est* to the value v it proposes. Then, p_i sequentially visits the base consensus objects in a predetermined order (e.g., starting from $CONS[1]$ until $CONS[t + 1]$. The important point here is that all the processes use the same visit order). At the step k, p_i invokes $CONS[k].propose(est)$. Then, if the value it obtains is different from $\bot$, p_i adopts it as its new estimate value *est*. Finally, p_i decides the value of *est* after it has visited all the base consensus objects. Let us observe that, as at least one consensus object is not faulty, all the processes that invoke $propose()$ on that object obtain the same non-$\bot$ value from it.

```
operation RES_CONS.propose(v):
(1)    est ← v;
(2)    for k from 1 to t + 1 do
(3)        aux ← CONS[k].propose(est);
(4)            if (aux ≠ ⊥) then est ← aux end_if
(5)    end_do;
(6)    return (est)
```

Fig. 7. Construction of a t-resilient consensus object RES_CONS [7]

Theorem 3. *The algorithm described in Figure 7 wait-free implements a t-resilient consensus object from $(t + 1)$ base consensus objects that can suffer responsive crash failures.*

Proof. The proof has to show that, it no more than t base consensus object crash, the object that is built satisfies the validity, agreement and wait-free termination properties of consensus.

As any $CONS[k]$ base consensus object is responsive, it follows that any $CONS[k].propose(est)$ invocation terminates (line 03). Consequently, when executed by a correct process, the **for** loop always terminates. The wait-free termination follows directly from these observations.

When a process invokes $RES\_CONS.propose(v)$, it first initializes its local variable est to the value v it proposes. Then, if est is modified, it is modified at line 04 and takes the value proposed by a process to the corresponding base consensus object. By backward induction, that value has been proposed by a process. The consensus validity property follows.

Let $CONS[x]$ be the first (in the increasing order on x) non-faulty base consensus object (by assumption, there is at least one such object). Let v be value decided by that consensus object. It follows from the agreement property of that base object, that all the processes that invoke $CONS[x].propose(est)$ decide v. From then on, only v can be proposed to the base consensus objects $CONS[x+1]$ until $CONS[t+1]$. It follows that, from $CONS[x]$, the only value proposed to a next consensus object is v. Consequently, v is the value decided by the processes that execute line 06. The agreement property follows. (As we can see, the fact that all the processes "visit" the base consensus objects in the same order -from $CONS[1]$ to $CONS[t+1]$- is central in the proof of this agreement property.)

$\square_{Theorem\ 3}$

4 Registers and Consensus Objects with Nonresponsive Failures

4.1 Reliable Register When Failures Are Not Responsive: An Unbounded Construction

Construction of a 1W1R *reliable register.* When failures are not responsive, the construction of a 1W1R atomic register is still possible but requires a higher cost in terms of base registers, namely $m \geq 2t + 1$ base registers are then required. This construction is well-known. Its principles are simple. They are:

– The use of sequence numbers, as in the construction for responsive failures (Figure 2).
– The use of the majority notion, as the model assumes at most t unreliable base registers, with $t < m/2 < m - t$. This implies that any two majorities of base objects do intersect. Moreover, any set of $t+1$ base registers contains at least one correct register.
– The parallel activation of read operations on base registers, as now it is possible that such a read operation never returns a result if the corresponding base object has crashed. Due to the majority of correct base registers, we know that a majority of these base read operations do terminate, but it is not know in advance which ones.

The construction is described in Figure 8. It is a straightforward extension of the algorithm described in Figure 2, that takes into account the fact that a base operation can never answer. So, it considers $m = 2t + 1$, and issues base read and write operations in parallel in order to prevent a possible definitive blocking that could occur if the base operations were issued sequentially. As in the algorithm described in Figure 2, the reader maintains a local variable *last* that keeps the (val, sn) pair with the highest sequence number it has ever read from a base register. This construction shows that, when one is interested

---

operation $RO.write(v)$: % invoked by the writer %
$\quad sn \leftarrow sn + 1$;
concurrently for each base register $j \in \{1, \ldots, m\}$
$\qquad\qquad\qquad$ **do** issue write (v, sn) into $REG[j]$ **end_do**;
wait until (a majority of the previous base write operations have terminated);
return ()

operation $RO.read()$: % invoked by the reader %
concurrently for each base register $j \in \{1, \ldots, m\}$
$\qquad\qquad\qquad$ **do** issue read () on $REG[j]$ **end_do**;
wait until (a majority of the previous base read operations have terminated);
let *pairs*= the set of pairs (val, sn) received from the previous read operations;
last $\leftarrow$ the pair in the set *pairs* $\cup \{last\}$ with the highest sequence number;
return (*last.val*)

Fig. 8. 1W1R t-resilient atomic register RO despite nonresponsive crashes

in building a reliable 1W1R atomic register, the price to go from base object responsive failures to nonresponsive failures, increases from $t + 1$ base registers to $2t + 1$ base registers.

Theorem 4. *The algorithm described in Figure 8 wait-free implements a t-resilient 1W1R atomic register from $m = 2t + 1$ base 1W1R atomic registers that can suffer nonresponsive crash failures.*

Proof. The proof is a simple adaptation of the proof of Theorem 1 to the context of nonresponsive crash failures. It is left to the reader as an exercise. (The fact that at least one non-faulty base register is written (read) used in Theorem 1 is replaced here by the majority of correct base registers assumption.) $\square_{Theorem\ 2}$

4.2   Consensus When Failures Are Not Responsive: An Impossibility

This section presents an impossibility result. Differently from atomic registers, no t-resilient consensus object can be built from crash-prone nonresponsive consensus objects.

Theorem 5. *There is no algorithm that wait-free implements a consensus object from crash-prone nonresponsive consensus objects and reliable atomic registers.*

Proof. The proof is by contradiction. Let us assume that there is an algorithm A that builds a consensus object from reliable atomic registers and any number x of consensus objects such that at least one of them is crash-prone and nonresponsive. Each consensus object can be simulated by an asynchronous process. (From a computability point of view, a process is as powerful as any object with a sequential specification.) It follows that A solves the consensus problem in a system made up of atomic registers and x asynchronous processes, where one of them can crash. This has shown to be impossible [4], from which we conclude that no algorithm A can be designed. $\square_{Theorem\ 5}$

References

1. Attiya, H., Welch, J.: Distributed Computing: Fundamentals, Simulations and Advanced Topics, p. 451. McGraw-Hill, New York (1998)
2. Chandra, T., Toueg, S.: Unreliable Failure Detectors for Resilient Distributed Systems. Journal of the ACM 43(2), 225–267 (1996)
3. Guerraoui, R., Raynal, M.: A Universal Construction for Wait-free Objects. In: Proc. ARES 2007 Workshop on Foundations of Fault-tolerant Distributed Computing (FOFDC 2007), IEEE Society Computer Press, Vienna (Austria) (2007)
4. Herlihy, M.P.: Wait-Free Synchronization. ACM TOPLAS 13(1), 124–149 (1991)
5. Herlihy, M.P., Wing, J.M: Linearizability: a Correctness Condition for Concurrent Objects. ACM TOPLAS 12(3), 463–492 (1990)
6. Hoare, C.A.R.: Monitors: an Operating System Structuring Concept. Comm. ACM 17(10), 549–557 (1974)
7. Jayanti, P., Chandra, T., Toueg, S.: Fault-Tolerant Wait-Free Shared Objects. Journal of the ACM 45(3), 451–500 (1998)
8. Lamport, L.: Concurrent Reading and Writing. Comm. ACM 20(11), 806–811 (1977)
9. Lamport, L.: On Interprocess Communication, Part 1: Models, Part 2: Algorirhms. Distributed Computing 1(2), 77–101 (1986)
10. Raynal, M.: A Short Introduction to Failure Detectors for Asynchronous Distributed Systems. ACM Sigact News, Distributed Computing Column 36(1), 53–70 (2005)
11. Vitányi, P., Awerbuch, B.: Atomic Shared Register Access by Asynchronous Hardware. In: Proc. 27th IEEE Symposium on Foundations of Computer Science (FOCS'86), pp. 233–243. IEEE Computer Society Press, Los Alamitos (1986)

A Functional Programming System SFP: Sisal 3.1 Language Structures Decomposition*

V.N. Kasyanov and A.P. Stasenko

A.P. Ershov Institute of Informatics Systems
Novosibirsk, 630090, Russia
kvn@iis.nsk.su, astasenko@gmail.com

Abstract. The paper describes equivalent transformations of structures of the Sisal 3.1 programming language (based on Sisal 90). These transformations are aimed to decompose the complex language structures into more simple ones that can be directly expressed by the internal representation IR1 (based on the IF1 language). Currently some description of similar transformations can be found in few works about Sisal 90 in the form of examples. A front-end compiler from Sisal 3.1 into IR1 performs these transformations, so they can help to understand better its translation strategy. The paper also briefly describes Sisal 3.1 and IR1.

Keywords: Sisal 3.1, functional programming, parallel programming, program transformation, internal representation, front-end compiler.

1   The Introduction

Using the traditional methods, it is very difficult to develop high quality portable software for parallel computers. In particular, parallel software cannot be developed on low cost sequential computers and then moved to high performance parallel computers without extensive rewriting and debugging.

As compared with imperative languages, functional languages [1] simplify the programmer's work, because an algorithm can be specified in terms of recursive function applications without special care to computing resources and it is a compiler responsibility to produce effective code. In contrast to many other functional languages, the functional language Sisal (Steams and Iterations in a Single Assignment Language) supports data types and operators typical for scientific calculations. Sisal is considered as an alternative to Fortran for supercomputers [2] and its version 1.2 was implemented for many of them.

Sisal 90 [3] is more oriented towards scientific programming. It has built-in support for complex values, array and vector operations, higher order functions, rectangular arrays, and an explicit interface to other languages like Fortran and C. Sisal 3.1 [4] that has been designed as an input language of the SFP system being under development at the Institute of Informatics Systems in Novosibirsk [5]

---

* The work was partially supported by the Russian Foundation for Basic Research (grant N 07-07-12050).

V. Malyshkin (Ed.): PaCT 2007, LNCS 4671, pp. 62–73, 2007.

is based on Sisal 90. Sisal 3.1 simplifies, improves, extends and more exactly specifies Sisal 90. Sisal 3.1 incorporates the ideas of enhanced module support, annotated programming and preprocessing of Sisal 3.0 [6]. Sisal 3.1 also supports function overloading and user-defined types which allow user-defined operations.

The SFP system is intended to support the development of portable high performance parallel computing applications. It runs under Microsoft Windows and provides target platform independent means to write, debug and translate the Sisal-programs into target platform optimized code. The SFP uses the intermediate representation IR1 [7], which is based on the intermediate form language IF1 [8] and consists of acyclic, directed, hierarchical graphs [9]. The IR1 allows the Sisal constructions to be represented in their natural form, close to their syntax. This is convenient for simplification of further optimizing transformations.

Usually, not every form of a language syntax construction can be directly represented in IR1, so compound nodes correspond to the basic forms, which are powerful enough to express all their variations. Because of that, during translation in the SFP system, some complex Sisal 3.1 structures need to be reduced to more unified objects of IR1. The peculiarities of such transformations are shown in terms of Sisal 3.1 by rewriting of complex language structures into more simple ones that can be directly represented by IR1. Such rewriting rules are described in terms of the Sisal language, because IR1 does not allow natural representation of the most complex language structures.

The rest of the paper is structured as follows. Section 2 briefly describes the most important Sisal 3.1 constructions used below. Section 3 considers the *Select* and *Forall* compound nodes of IR1 to which the most language structures can be reduced. Sections 4, 5, 6 and 7 present transformations of complex Sisal 3.1 structures into more simple ones that can be directly represented by IR1.

2   The Sisal 3.1 Language

Sisal defines calculations via a function application in a form of different expressions. Every Sisal type has the dedicated error value, which can be explicitly produced and tested. In most undefined situations Sisal expressions produce error values. Since the explanations are very brief, familiarity with the Sisal 90 user's guide [3] is recommended. As an example, consider function *QuickSort* in Listing 1.1 that recursively sorts an input array of integers.

The **let** expression in its *name definitions* defines a new scope and its names that can be used in a calculation of the *result expression list*:

let *name definitions* **in** *result expression list* **end let**

The **if** expression looks as follows, where the chosen *result expression list* will define the results of the **if** expression, so all of them should have the same number of expressions and the same sequence of expression types:

if *Boolean expression* **then** *result expression list*
{ **elseif** *Boolean expression* **then** *result expression list* }*
[**else** *result expression list*] **end if**

Listing 1.1. Sisal 3.1 function that sorts array of integers

```
type Info = array[integer];
function QuickSort(Data: Info returns Info)
  if size(Data) < 2 then Data
  // A function liml returns the lower bound of an array.
  else let Pivot := Data[liml(Data)];
          Low, Mid, High := for E in Data
                returns array of E when E < Pivot;
                        array of E when E = Pivot;
                        array of E when E > Pivot
            end for
      in QuickSort(Low) || Mid || QuickSort(High)
    end let
  end if
end function
```

The **case** expression looks as follows, where the *control expression* can select a *result expression list* by value, union tag or type signature:

case [**tag** | **type**] *control expression*
{ **of** *condition list* **then** *result expression list* }+
[**else** *result expression list*] **end case**

The **where** expression of Sisal 3.1 was reconsidered as compared to Sisal 90:

where *n-dimensional array A* **is** *name I* **in** *expression R* **end where**

The **where** expression returns an n-dimensional array of the same shape as the array A, where each element which corresponds to the array A element with the name I equals to the *expression R* result.

In Sisal 3.1, element selection and replacement expressions are almost the same as in Sisal 90: "*array [selection construction*[1] *]*" and "*array [selection construction :=*[2] *replacement construction]*". In addition to arithmetic, relational and Boolean vector operations of Sisal 90, Sisal 3.1 allows vector forms for any infix, prefix and postfix operations (including user defined ones). Sisal 3.1 also allows vector operations between streams and arrays that produce streams.

The Sisal loop expressions do not contradict the functional language semantics. Sisal 3.1 has three loop forms, however the paper considers only the **for** expression with a range generator, which has the following form:

for *range generator* [**repeat** *body*] **returns** *return statement* **end for**

The loop *body* defines a new scope and its names like the **let** expression. The **for** expression is parallel, when it has no "old N" names, a stream range sources in its loop *range generator* and sequential reductions in its *return statement*. The "old N" name equals to the value of the name N at the previous loop iteration.

---

[1] In Sisal 3.1 triplets, the symbol "!" is used instead of ":" symbol of Sisal 90.
[2] Here in Sisal 3.1, the symbols ":=" are used instead of "!" symbols of Sisal 90.

The one-dimensional *range generator* consists of a range or several ranges joined by **dot** keyword. A range is a triplet, array or stream. The joined ranges emit their values simultaneously until at least one of them can do it, while the others that cannot do it emit the error values.

The *return statement* consists of the reduction applications. Reductions are a special kind of functions that work with a sequence of values produced by loop iterations. There are some predefined reductions to obtain the last loop value, to compute a sum or product of loop values, to find the least or greatest loop value, to produce n-dimensional[3] ($n \geq 1$) array or stream of loop values and to catenate loop values that are arrays or streams.

3   The IR1 Internal Representation

Like their nodes, which express operations, IR1 graphs have ordered input and output ports. Typed edges of these graphs express informational relationships between ports. Each port can be a destination of no more than one edge. Conditional and loop expressions are represented via compound nodes which are nodes that additionally hold a sequence of IR1 graphs. Informational relationships between ports of these graphs and ports of the compound node are expressed implicitly by the kind of the compound node. As an example, consider Figure 1 that contains IR1-graphs, produced by our Sisal 3.1 front-end compiler for function *QuickSort* from Listing 1.1.

The compound node *Select*, which can directly represent the **if** expression of Sisal 3.1, has an arbitrary number of input ports and non-zero number of output ports. Let $N \geq 3$ be the number of its graphs. The input ports of all graphs are the same as the input ports of the compound node and directly receive values from them. All graphs except the first one have the same output ports as the output ports of the compound node. One of these $N - 1$ graphs is chosen to supply values of its output ports to the output ports of the compound node.

The choice is based on the first graph, which has different semantics as compared to its prototype from IF1. The first graph has $N - 2$ Boolean output ports (edges that end in these ports have Boolean type), which are sequentially checked until the *true* value is found at the output port with a number M. In that case, the graph with a number $M + 1$ is chosen. If no *true* value is found, then the last graph is chosen.

The compound node *Forall*, which can represent any one-dimensional **for** expression controlled by a range, has four graphs described in Table 1. Ports of these graphs can be divided in the following groups that consist of the same ports for each separate compound node *Forall*. A group C contains the constants imported to the compound node ports. A group R contains the result values exported from the compound node ports. A group L contains the new values of **old** names. A group L_2 contains the values which will not be required on the

---

[3] In Sisal 3.1, notation **array** $[n]$ and **stream** $[n]$ replaces array_nd and stream_nd notation of Sisal 90.

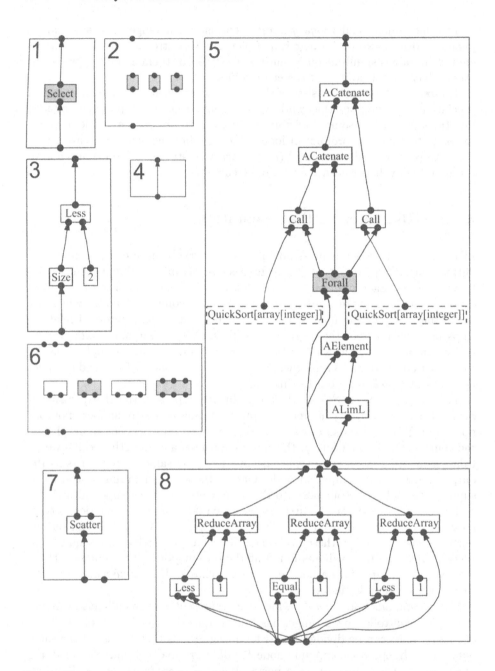

Fig. 1. IR1-graphs generated for "quick sort" function in Listing 1.1 (compound nodes and non-empty graphs are shaded): 1) the *QuickSort* graph; 2) the *Select* node graphs; 3) the condition; 4) the **then** branch; 5) the **else** branch (the graph layout was tweaked by hand to reduce its width); 6) the *Forall* node graphs; 7) the range generator; 8) the return statement

Table 1. Groups of ports for the compound node *Forall* and its graphs

Graph No.	Graph Name	Input port groups	Output port groups
	Forall	C	R
1	Initialization	C	L
2	Range generator	C	D
3	Loop body	L_{old}, D, C	L, L_2
4	Return statement	L_{old}, L, L_2, D, C	R

next loop iteration. A group L_{old} contains the values of **old** names from the iteration before. A group D contains the values of the loop range generator.

At the beginning, the output ports of the *initialization* graph are computed and their values are used as the values of the group L_{old} at the first iteration of the *loop body* graph. The *loop body* graph computes its output ports, for each instance of the group D, generated by the *range generator* graph. The *return statement* graph is computed after each loop iteration and after the last one, its output port values are used as the compound node results. Before the next iteration, the values from the group L are copied to the ports of the group L_{old}.

The *return statement* graph contains the reduction nodes that can only (and only they can) supply values to the output ports of this graph. These reduction nodes directly correspond to one-dimensional reductions of Sisal 3.1 and may depend on and recompute additional values every loop iteration.

The *range generator* graph also has the unique *Scatter* nodes that can only (and only they can) supply values to the output ports of this graph. The *Scatter* node has one input and two output ports. The input port has a type of an array or stream of a type T. The first output port has the type T and the second output port has the integer type. The *Scatter* node sequentially emits a new array or stream element with its index for every loop iteration. If there are several *Scatter* nodes, then they emit new values simultaneously until at least one of them can do it, while the others that cannot do it return the error values.

4 Decomposition of Case, Where and Vector Expressions

The conditional expression **case** is naturally decomposed into the conditional expression **if** with additional **elseif** branches, that is can be directly expressed by the IF1 language. Every selection list of the **case** expression is transformed into one **if** or **elseif** condition using logical disjunction and conjunction operations over the comparison operation results: equality ($=$), "less than or equal to" ($\leq$) and "greater than or equal to" ($\geq$). For expressions "**case tag**" and "**case type**", the infix operation **tag** (**tag** function of Sisal 90) and the expression "**type** [...]" are used, respectively.

The Sisal 3.1 **where** expression is decomposed into one-dimensional loops in the following way, where A, n, R and I names are taken from Section 2:

for $\overline{A_1}$[4] **in** A **returns array of**
  for $\overline{A_2}$ **in** $\overline{A_1}$ **returns array of** ...
    for I **in** $\overline{A_{n-1}}$ **returns array of** *expression* R **end for**
  ... **end for**
end for

All vector operations are decomposed into one-dimensional loops. An operation on multidimensional vectors is decomposed into a vector operation on vectors of lower dimensions.

Prefix and postfix operations on arrays $op\,(A)$ are decomposed into:

for $\overline{i}$ **in** A **returns array**($\mathrm{liml}(A)$) **of** $op\,(\overline{i})$ **end for**

Prefix and postfix operations on streams $op\,(S)$ are decomposed into:

for $\overline{i}$ **in** S **returns stream of** $op\,(\overline{i})$ **end for**

An infix operation op on two arrays A_1 and A_2 is decomposed into:

for $\overline{i_1}$ **in** A_1 **dot** $\overline{i_2}$ **in** A_2 **returns array of** $\overline{i_1}$ op $\overline{i_2}$ **end for**

An infix operation op on an array A and a stream S is decomposed into:

for $\overline{i_a}$ **in** A **dot** $\overline{i_s}$ **in** S **returns stream of** $\overline{i_a}$ op $\overline{i_s}$ **end for**

An infix operation op on an array A and a scalar value V is decomposed into:

for $\overline{i}$ **in** A **returns array**($\mathrm{liml}(A)$) **of** $\overline{i}$ op V **end for**

An infix operation op on a stream S and a scalar value V is decomposed into:

for $\overline{i}$ **in** S **returns stream of** $\overline{i}$ op V **end for**

5 Decomposition of the Multidimensional Loops

Let us consider the following n-ary m-dimensional loop, in which each reduction returns unary expression (for simplicity of further notation):

for D_1 **cross** D_2 **repeat** B
  returns RN_1 **of** RV_1 ; ...; RN_n **of** RV_n
end for

The name D_1 denotes the loop range generator part without the operator **cross** and multidimensional indices of the construction **at**, the name D_2 denotes the remaining part of the range generator, the name $RN_{i\in 1...n}$ denotes the reduction name with possible initial values, and the name RV_i denotes the reduction loop values. In this notation, a m-dimensional loop expression can be decomposed into the following two loop expressions of dimensions 1 and $m-1$, where names RN_i' and RN_i'' depend on the name RN_i as shown in Table 2:

---

[4] The overlined name denotes any unique name (the same in each code fragment).

for D_1 **repeat**
$\overline{x_1}$, ..., $\overline{x_n}$:= **for** D_2 **repeat** B
$\quad\quad\quad\quad\quad\quad\quad$ **returns** RN_1' **of** RV_1; ...; RN_n' **of** RV_n
$\quad\quad\quad\quad\quad$ **end for**
$\quad$ **returns** RN_1'' **of** $\overline{x_1}$; ...; RN_n'' **of** $\overline{x_n}$
end for

Table 2. Decomposition rules for multi-dimensional reductions, which show how to determine the names RN_i' and RN_i'', used in this section before, from the name RN_i

Value of the RN_i name	RN_i'	RN_i''
Equals to value, product, least, greatest, catenate, "catenate (...)" or user-defined reduction.	RN_i	value
Equals to "**array** $[k](i_1,\ldots,i_k)$", where:		
– part "$[k]$" is optional and equals to "$[m]$" by default;	$k > 1$ **array** $[k-1]$ $(i_2,\ldots,i_k)$	**array** (i_1)
– last indices of the part "$(i_1,\ldots,i_k)$" are optional like this whole part and equal to 1 if omitted.	$k = 1$ **array** $[1]$ $(i_2,\ldots,i_k)$	catenate (i_1)
Equals to "**stream** $[k]$", where part "$[k]$" is optional and equals to "$[m]$" by default.	$k > 1$ **stream** $[k-1]$ $k = 1$ **stream** $[1]$	**stream** catenate

If the range generator contains multidimensional indices "n **in** S **at** j_1, ..." before the operator **cross**, then the loop can be represented in the following way:

for D_3 n **in** S **at** j_1, D_4 **repeat** B
$\quad$ **returns** RN_1 **of** RV_1; ...; RN_n **of** RV_n
end for

The name D_3 denotes the range generator part without the operator **cross** and multidimensional indices of the construction **at**, the name S denotes the array or stream source of multidimensional indices, the name D_4 denotes the remaining part of the range generator. In this notation, a m-dimensional loop expression can also be decomposed into the following two loop expressions of dimensions 1 and $m - 1$:

for D_3 $\overline{n_1}$ **in** S **at** j_1 **repeat**
$\overline{x_1}$, ..., $\overline{x_n}$:= **for** n **in** $\overline{n_1}$ **at** D_4 **repeat** B
$\quad\quad\quad\quad\quad\quad\quad$ **returns** RN_1' **of** RV_1; ...; RN_n' **of** RV_n
$\quad\quad\quad\quad\quad$ **end for**
$\quad$ **returns** RN_1'' **of** $\overline{x_1}$; ...; RN_n'' **of** $\overline{x_n}$
end for

6   Decomposition of the Array Element Selection

Let us represent the element selection expression from the array A as "$A[$ *selection construction* $]$". If a selection construction does not have the **cross** (or comma) operator, then it can be represented as "D_1 **dot** D_2 **dot** ... **dot** D_m", where $m \geq 1$ and all expressions $D_1, \ldots, D_m$ are ranges (as required by the operator **dot** semantics). If $m = 1$ and the part D_1 is a singlet, then the array element selection operation can be represented directly in IR1 and does not require further decomposition, otherwise the array element selection operation can be decomposed into the following one-dimensional loop:

for x_1 **in** D_1 **dot** x_2 **in** D_2 **dot** ... x_m **in** D_m
    $\overline{A_1}$:= A [x_1, x_2, ..., x_m]
    returns array of $\overline{A_1}$
end for

The name x_i (here and below) denotes any unique name, if the part D_i does not have the form "*name N* **in** D_i", and denotes the name N otherwise. If the selection construction contains the operator **cross**, then it can be represented as "$S_1, S_2, \ldots, S_m$ **cross** C_1" or "D_1 **dot** D_2 **dot** ... **dot** D_m **cross** C_2", where $S_1, \ldots, S_m$ denote singlets, and the names C_1 (that does not begin with a singlet) and C_2 denote the remaining parts of the selection construction.

The array element selection operation beginning with a singlet can be decomposed into the following **let** expression:

let $\overline{A_1}$:= A [S_1, S_2, ..., S_m] **in** $\overline{A_1}$ [C_1] **end let**

The array element selection operation beginning with a range can be decomposed into the following one-dimensional loop:

for x_1 **in** D_1 **dot** x_2 **in** D_2 **dot** ... x_m **in** D_m **repeat**
    $\overline{A_1}$:= A [x_1, x_2, ..., x_m]
    returns array of $\overline{A_1}$ [C_2]
end for

The presented decomposition of the array element selection operation also explains an additional restriction, which is missed in Sisal 90 user's manual, for the selection construction triplets with omitted parts: they should be placed as the first operand of the selection construction or just after the **cross** operator. In the range D_1, the first and second omitted triplet parts are explicitly represented via "liml (A)" and "limh (A)", correspondingly. In the ranges $D_2, \ldots, D_m$, the triplet parts cannot be omitted because there is no corresponding univocal array dimension available whose lower and upper bounds can be taken. In summary, any array element selection operation was decomposed into the array element selection with simple indices.

7   Decomposition of the Array Element Replacement

This section continues to use the notation of selection construction introduced before. The array element replacement expression in a general form looks like "A [*selection construction* := *replacement construction* R]". As it will be shown below, any array element replacement expression can be decomposed into series of the array replacements that alter one element pointed by its index.

If the selection construction is a singlet list $S_1, \ldots, S_n$, then the *replacement construction* is allowed to be an expression list $E_1, \ldots, E_t$ and the array element replacement operation is elementary represented as a composition of the following one-element replacement operations:

$$A \ [\ S_1, \ \ldots, \ S_n \ := \ E_1 \ ] \ [\ S_1, \ \ldots, \ (\ S_n \ ) \ + \ 1 \ := \ E_2 \ ]$$
$$\ldots \ [\ S_1, \ \ldots, \ (\ S_n \ ) \ + \ (t-1) \ := \ E_t \ ]$$

Let us consider the case when the selection construction is not a singlet list and the *replacement construction* is an expression of type of the n-th dimension of the array A, where n is the number of the selection construction ranges and singlets. In this case, the array element replacement operation can be decomposed into nested one-dimensional loops obtained after the recursive application of the decompositions given below.

If the selection construction does not have the **cross** operator, the array element replacement operation can be presented as the one-dimensional loop:

for x_1 **in** D_1 **dot** x_2 **in** D_2 **dot** $\ldots$ x_m **in** D_m
  A := **old** A [$x_1, x_2, \ldots, x_m$:= R]
  returns value **of** A
end for

The array element replacement operation beginning with a singlet can be decomposed into the following **let** expression:

let $\overline{A_1}$:= A [$S_1, S_2, \ldots, S_m$] **in** $\overline{A_1}$ [C_1 := R] **end let**

The array element replacement operation beginning with a range can be decomposed into the following one-dimensional loop:

let $\overline{A_1}$:= A **in** **for** x_1 **in** D_1 **dot** x_2 **in** D_2 **dot** $\ldots$ x_m **in** D_m
    $\overline{A_2}$:= **old** $\overline{A_1}$ [$x_1, x_2, \ldots, x_m$];
    $\overline{A_3}$:= $\overline{A_2}$ [C_2 := R];
    $\overline{A_1}$:= **old** $\overline{A_1}$ [$x_1, x_2, \ldots, x_m$:= $\overline{A_3}$]
    returns value **of** $\overline{A_1}$
  end for
end let

Let us consider the case when the selection construction is not a singlet list and the *replacement construction* is an expression of type of a k-dimensional array of elements that have the type of the n-th dimension of the array A. In this case, k should be a sum of ranges in the selection construction minus the number of its **dot** operators. In this case, the array element replacement operation can also be decomposed into nested one-dimensional loops obtained after the recursive application of decompositions given below.

If the selection construction does not have the **cross** operator, the array element replacement operation can be presented as the one-dimensional loop:

let $\bar{i}$:= 1 **in for** x_1 **in** D_1 **dot** x_2 **in** D_2 **dot** ... x_m **in** D_m
$\quad A$:= **old** A [x_1, x_2, ..., x_m := (R) [$\bar{i}$]];
$\quad \bar{i}$:= **old** $\bar{i}$ + 1
$\quad$ **returns** value **of** A
$\quad$ **end for**
end let

The array element replacement operation beginning with a singlet can be decomposed into the same **let** expression as in the previous case when the *replacement construction* is an expression of type of the n-th dimension of the array A. The array element replacement operation beginning with a range can be decomposed into the following one-dimensional loop:

let $\overline{A_1}$:= A; $\bar{i}$:= 1
$\quad$ **in for** x_1 **in** D_1 **dot** x_2 **in** D_2 **dot** ... x_m **in** D_m
$\qquad \overline{A_2}$:= **old** $\overline{A_1}$ [x_1, x_2, ..., x_m];
$\qquad \overline{A_3}$:= $\overline{A_2}$ [C_2 := (R) [$\bar{i}$]];
$\qquad \overline{A_1}$:= **old** $\overline{A_1}$ [x_1, x_2, ..., x_m := $\overline{A_3}$];
$\qquad \bar{i}$:= **old** $\bar{i}$ + 1
$\qquad$ **returns** value **of** $\overline{A_1}$
$\quad$ **end for**
end let

8 Conclusion

The paper briefly presents the input language Sisal 3.1 and intermediate language IR1 of the functional programming system SFP intended to support supercomputing. During translation from Sisal 3.1 to the internal representation IR1, some complex Sisal 3.1 structures need to be reduced to more unified objects of the IR1 language. These transformations have been shown in terms of Sisal 3.1 by decomposition of complex language structures into more simple ones that can be directly represented by IR1. These transformations can help to better understand the translation strategy of front-end compiler from Sisal 3.1 into IR1. They can be used also as a basis for formal description of semantics of Sisal 3.1. For a general-purpose machine (without any special hardware support for the operations considered in this paper), the described transformations do not introduce unnecessary inefficiency and open additional optimization opportunities.

Acknowledgments. The authors are thankful to all colleagues taking part in the SFP project.

References

1. Backus, J.: Can programming be liberated from the von Neumann style? Commun. Commun. ACM. 21(8), 613–641 (1978)
2. Cann, D.: Retire Fortran? A debate rekindled. Commun. ACM. 35(8), 81–89 (1992)
3. Feo, J.T., Miller, P.J., Skedzielewski, S.K., Denton, S.M.: Sisal 90 user's guide. Lawrence Livermore National Laboratory, Draft 0.96, Livermore, CA (1995)
4. Stasenko, A.P., Sinyakov, A.I.: Basic means of the Sisal 3.1 language. A.P. Ershov Institute of Informatics Systems, Tech. Rep. N 132 (in Russian), Novosibirsk (2006)
5. Kasyanov, V.N., Stasenko, A.P., Gluhankov, M.P., Dortman, P.A., Pyjov, K.A., Sinyakov, A.I.: SFP – An interactive visual environment for supporting of functional programming and supercomputing. WSEAS Transactions on Computers, 5(9), 2063–2070 (2006)
6. Kasyanov, V.N., Biryukova, Y.V., Evstigneev, V.A.: A functional language Sisal 3.0. Supercomputing support and Internet-oriented technologies, Novosibirsk (in Russian) pp. 54–67 (2001)
7. Stasenko, A.P.: Internal representation of functional programming system Sisal 3.0. A.P. Ershov Institute of Informatics Systems, Tech. Rep. N 110 (in Russian), Novosibirsk (2004)
8. Skedzielewski, S.K., Glauert, J.: IF1 – An intermediate form for applicative languages, version 1.0. LLNL, Tech. Rep. M-170, Livermore, CA (1985)
9. Kasyanov, V.N., Lisitsyn, I.A.: Hierarchical graph models and visual processing. In: Proc. of Intern. Conf. on Software: Theory and Practice, 16th IFIP World Computer Congress, PHEI, Beijing, pp. 179–182 (2000)

Towards a Computing Model
for Open Distributed Systems

Achour Mostefaoui

IRISA, Université de Rennes 1, Campus de Beaulieu, 35042 Rennes, France
`achour@irisa.fr`

Abstract. This paper proposes an implementation of the data structure called bag or multiset used by descriptive programming languages (e.g. Gamma, Linda) over an open system. In this model, a succession of "chemical reactions" consumes the elements of the bag and produces new elements according to specific rules. This approach is particularly interesting as it suppresses all unneeded synchronization and reveals all the potential parallelism of a program. An efficient implementation of a bag provides an efficient implementation of the subsequent program. This paper defines a new communication and synchronization model adapted from workqueues used in parallel computing. The proposed model allows to benefit from the potential parallelism offered by this style of programming when only an approximate solution is needed.

Keywords: Bag data structure, Chemical reaction, Distributed programming, Fault-Tolerance, Open system, Parallel programming, Synchronization, Workqueue.

1 Introduction

Context. Most programming languages use sequential control. Even parallel executions are composed of sequential processes. A sequential control flow offers simplicity of the design, better fits the functioning of processors and moreover, benefits from many theoretical results (e.g. decidability and computability). This style of programming introduces unneeded control as it orders operations that are not semantically related (e.g. a loop that initializes an array to zero). Those constraints make the mapping of sequential programs on machines automatic and straightforward as it perfectly fits the von Neumann processing model. However, this leads to high interprocess synchronization. The consequence is that the unneeded control limits the potential parallelism of the program that may benefit from the continuously increasing power offered by platforms like parallel machines, local area networks and more recently peer-to-peer systems. Almost parallel programs are designed for an a priori given and generally fixed number of processes although this has nothing to do with the problem to solve. This motivated research of a programming model that abstracts this aspect.

A bag is a data structure (also called multiset [2], tuple space [5] or more recently JavaSpace [8]) is the basis to implement a parallel program on the model of a chemical reaction over the elements of the bag. The execution ends when the bag reaches a stable state. The following example taken from [2] represents a program that computes the

V. Malyshkin (Ed.): PaCT 2007, LNCS 4671, pp. 74–79, 2007.

maximum value of a set: max : $x, y \rightarrow y \Leftarrow x \leq y$. The right part ($x \leq y$) specifies the reaction condition whereas the left part specifies the action. Each time two elements x and y satisfy the reaction condition, they are replaced by the result of the action on then (the maximum, i.e. y). The parallelism is implicit as several pairs of distinct values can react simultaneously; notice also the nondeterminism concerning what values do react together. This style of programming is free from unnecessary synchronization. The number and relative speed of processes are totally absent from the program and may vary at runtime. The efficiency of the execution is mainly determined by the efficient implementation of the bag data structure and its accessing operation (insert data, pick data and look for data that could react).

In timesharing, each process is granted a quatum of time (neither too small nor too big). In our model, data represents this "energy" or "potential of computation" instead of time. If no data satisfies the reaction condition, the potential of the bag is null. The more there is reacting data the higher the potential of the bag. Any number of processes can execute the same program code each at its own speed. They only interact via the bag when they access it (each access gets/inserts a quantum of data). The finest grain depends on the arity of the reaction condition/action.

Contribution of the paper. This paper proposes a new approach to implement a bag. It has been pointed out by previous works that any implementation faces two main problems: (1) synchronization between the different processes through the basic operations on bags and (2) termination detection. To detect termination, it is necessary to test the reaction condition on all possible combinations of data. This means that if the reaction condition is n-ary then any subset of n elements should be eventually tested. Hence, no locality of accesses could be defined on the bag. The "data quantum" should be as small as possible n elements (n-uples) as considered by all existing implementations. This leads to frequent accesses and thus frequent synchronizations.

In this paper, a bag is implemented by a distributed data structure called MergeQueue that resembles the workqueue structure used in parallel programming. The MergeQueue is composed of blocks of equal size it is initialized to the values of the inital bag. When a process requests a block, it gets the block at the head of the MergeQueue and produces an output block not necessarily of the same size that is dispatched over several blocks at the tail of the MergeQueue. The insertion of the resulting data is done when its estimated potential of computing is lower than a threshold. The potential of computation being the ratio of n-uples that may react. Finally, we propose some parameters that allow tuning the system (size of a block, number of new blocks over which inserted data is dispatched, value of the potential computation below which a block is changed).

Related works. Since the publication of the first results on bag-transformation languages (e.g. Gamma and Linda), many implementations have been proposed. They are based on compilation [3], shared memory [6] or database [8]. Compilation-based implementations try to translate bag-based programs to classical programs by using derivation reintroducing the unnecessary synchronization. The concept of DSM is closely related to the classical imperative programming languages that use variables and control-driven executions. Consistency algorithms and cache coherence are based on the relation between successive read and write operations. Caching allows improving the efficiency of memory systems thanks to what is called the locality property. It is not hard to see that this locality property is in fact due to sequential programming. In a bag, data is totally anonymous. Grid computing is static compared to the chemical reaction paradigm. In term of data quantum, they have a very big quantum. Moreover, processes do not necessarily execute the same code and cannot be added on the fly transparently. The flow of data in well-controlled and the failures are detected and treated in a static way. Implementations that use databases are not in the scope of this work as the main goal of databases is to ensure persistence and consistency of data. The object oriented approach like JavaSpace has a main drawback that is the granularity of data (one object=one element) that may entail high synchronization time overhead. The most close work is the one on workqueues. However, the main difference, is that a workqueue is used mainly to communicate they are constituted of cells (insert/get a cell) in a strict fifo policy. The MergeQueue as proposed in this paper serves mainly to merge the blocks obtained by different processes. Moreover, the access operations are not as strict as for the workqueue (they are not necessarily atomic).

2   Computing Model

We consider a three-layer architecture: the underlying system is represented any distributed platform prone to failures and mobility (dynamic systems) and the upper-layer is represented by the processes that execute a bag-based program. The distributed data structure represents the medium layer.

System Model. The assumed underlying system offers the possibility to launch a program by assigning to it a group of processes that execute its reactions. We first consider a message-passing synchronous system (the duration of internal instructions and the communication delays are bounded).

Each application process is associated with a controller (a kind of daemon) that serves as an interface with the system. It gets a block, provides the process when requested with a given number of elements (according to the arity of the reaction condition), inserts in the block the result of the action and keeps an estimation of the potential of computing of the block. When the potential of computing is lower then a threshold, the controller inserts the block in the MergeQueue and gets a new one.

In Section 5, we consider a more general case where processes may crash and where there is no assumption on time. This represents a typical open asynchronous system prone to process failures where processes may arrive and leave and where the exact number of processes is not known.

Bag Transformation-Based Programming Language. As said in the Introduction, the bag transformation is defined by pairs (reaction condition, action). When the bag reaches a stable state the program ends. In the program max given in the Introduction, the reaction condition is of arity 2. The associated action takes two parameters and produces one value. This means that the size of the bag can only diminish. Let us consider a second program that sorts an array. The initial bag is composed of pairs of values (index, value). The final bag is composed of the same number of pairs, the same projection on the domain of indices and the same projection on the domain of values. This means that the program only permutes non sorted values. sort : $(i, v), (j, w) \rightarrow (i, w), (j, v) \Leftarrow (i < j) \wedge (v > w)$.

In a general case, the arity of the reaction condition is not necessarily two although small values of the arity imply less combinatorial. For example, the reaction condition of a program that computes the transitive closure of a graph is of arity 3. Note that the program that suppresses any two identical consecutive values from an array has a locality property due to data dependence. In such situation, the selection of pairs of values that may potentially interact is deterministic. This suggests to offer the possibility to use structured bags.

3 The Distributed MergeQueue

A MergeQueue is an abstract type close to the workqueue data structure. It is composed of a series of blocks of the same size. It offers two main atomic operations *get* and *insert*. No two processes can get the same block nor insert two blocks at the same place in the queue. When a process calls *get*, the block at the head of the queue is withdrawn from the queue and returned to the process. When a process inserts data in the MergeQueue, it is inserted at the tail of the queue but dispatched over several blocks (Figure 1). Initially, all the elements of the bag (for sake of simplicity, we consider a unique bag) are inserted in a contiguous way in the MergeQueue. A queue could be seen as a circular management of a physical memory. There is no interaction between processes except when they access the MergeQueue, thus the necessity to fix a reasonable size for a block of data which represents the quantum (the unity of data allocation). To respect the (weak) atomicity of the accesses, synchronization is necessary each time a process accesses the queue.

The management of the MergeQueue is done through locks put on blocks of data (block allocation) and slot reservation (data insertion). The synchronization needed between processes, is not necessarily mutual exclusion or consensus. The renaming agreement problem [1] seems to be more appropriate. The renaming problem differs from consensus in the agreement property. Consensus: all processes make the same decision. Renaming: no two processes make the same decision. It has been proved that consensus is harder to solve than renaming [1]. If the underlying system is message-passing, a queue can be implemented using active replication (partial or total replication). Each process (in the case of total replication) keeps a copy of the queue. Allocation of blocks of data and of free slots is done through ordered communication primitives (total order multicast) or explicit calls to agreement primitives (renaming, consensus).

The proposed approach does not ensure termination detection of a program as it is not sure that two different elements will be associated in the same block to be considered for reaction unless processes access "enough" blocks and the bag is shacked between the different accesses. The shaking of memory is not done on the whole memory, it is

Fig. 1. Management of the MergeQueue data structure

done locally (over a given number of blocks) each time a process inserts its output data (recall that the inserted data has a low potential of computing i.e. only few of its element can react). The inserted data is thus sliced and each part is inserted in a different block. This means that when a process obtains a free slot to insert its data; in fact, it gets as many slots from different blocks as the number of slices it has to insert. It is not hard to see that the more a block is thinly sliced during the insertion, the more processes need synchronization (the future block a process gets is a combination of the results of many processes) but the memory is better shacked. Conversely, the less a block is thinly sliced, the less processes need synchronization (the future block a process gets is a combination of the results of few processes) but the memory is less shacked.

4   About Termination

As stated before, the proposed implementation does not ensure termination this is why approximate computing is assumed (i.e. the produced result is only an approximation of the expected one). It can be advocated that many computations are such that the data they use is a result of physical measures (e.g. sensors), images, and sound, or the data is by itself not very precise. In such situations, it is not shocking if the obtained result is also an approximation. There are classical approximate computations (Runge-Kutta, Monte Carlo, probabilistic SAT, simulated annealing).

After the potential of computation of a considered block is beyond a threshold, the process inserts its resulting data in the bag and asks for a new block. For this, we define a metrics that associates with any set of data a numeric value numerical (its potential of computation) that could be defined as the ratio of the number of n-uples (n being the arity of the condition/action) that may interact over the total number of possible combinations. Obviously, if this number is null, no reaction is possible and the execution program is finished. In this paper, we consider the execution of a program as finished as soon as its potential of computation is beyond a threshold.

Each program is materialized by a non-fixed number of processes. A program is also composed of a process "sentinel" that does not need synchronization to access to the bag (read-only accesses). Its role consists of computing the potential of computation of the bag. As soon as this potential is beyond a threshold, the sentinel process sets a flag that will cause the other process to stop their execution. This sentinel process will be the only alive process when the program execution is finished. It will act as the frontal process with respect to the user. It is also possible to have a timer-based termination.

5   Open Systems

The approach proposed in this paper could be extended to encompass asynchronous distributed systems prone to process failures (local area network, open system). In such systems, agreement services are essential (consensus, total order multi/broad-cast, renaming, etc.). Moreover, there exist randomized solutions to distributed agreement problems cited above [4,7]. If we consider an open system, a process could be materialized by a group of f processes (active replication - they all do the same work) assuming that no more than a minority of those f processes disconnect/crash simultaneously without informing other processes. Each of the processes composing a group ask for a block. They do it through a consensus in order to get a same block. Each of them transforms the block and the insertion is also made through a consensus as the resulting multiset is not necessarily the same for all the processes of the group due to the non-determinism. If we consider that each group is alive then the system composed of the "macro-processes" (groups) is fault-free. The sentinel process also is implemented using a group of processes.

It is important to mention that there exist approximate agreement services. This means that the agreement property is weak. This is not a problem for some programs. For the program that computes the maximum value of an array, if the operation that allocates the block is not atomic, the resulting value is always the same. This is also the case for the program that computes the transitive closure of a graph. The problem that may appear is an increase of the potential of computation. Of course, if the atomicity is always violated, the program may be prevented from terminating even according to our new definition. If the atomicity violation seldom happens and the efficiency of the agreement services is greatly enhanced than this may be very interesting if allowed by the program. Some other programs may see wrong values inserted in the bag if atomicity is violated. For example, a program that computes the number of occurrences of each element of a bag. If the atomicity is violated, the number of occurrences of some values could be a little bit augmented/diminished. The proposed approach mainly targets open systems to offer them a computing model.

6   Concluding Remarks

This paper presented a data structure called MergeQueue. A bag is the basis of programming languages like Gamma which use the chemical reaction principal. This structure can serve as a starting point to offer a programming model to open systems. This paper also pointed out many research directions on different parameters that need to be fixed such as the size of a block, the number of new blocks over which an inserted block is dispatched, the value of the threshold for changing a block.

References

1. Attiya, H., Bar-Noy, A., Dolev, D., Peleg, D., Reischuk, R.: Renaming in an Asynchronous Environment. Journal of the ACM 37(3), 524–548 (1990)
2. Banatre, J.P., Fradet, P., Le Metayer, D.: Gamma and the chemical reaction model: Fifteen years after. In: Calude, C.S., Pun, G., Rozenberg, G., Salomaa, A. (eds.) Multiset Processing. LNCS, vol. 2235, pp. 17–44. Springer, Heidelberg (2001)
3. Chaudron, C., de Jong, E.: Towards a compositional method for coordinating Gamma programs. In: Hankin, C., Ciancarini, P. (eds.) COORDINATION 1996. LNCS, vol. 1061, pp. 107–123. Springer, Heidelberg (1996)
4. Eugster, P., Handurukande, S., Guerraoui, R., Kermarrec, A.M., Kouznetsov, P.: Lightweight probabilistic broadcast. In: Proc. DSN 2001 (July 2001)
5. Gelertner, D.: Generative communication in Linda. ACM TOPLAS 7(1), 80–112 (1985)
6. Gladitz, K., Kuchen, H.: Parallel implementqtion of the Gamma-operation on bags. In: Proc. ofthe PASCO Conference, Linz, Austria (1994)
7. Rabin, M.: Randomized Byzantine Generals. In: Proc. 24th IEEE Symposium on Foundations of Computer Science (FOCS'83), pp. 403–409, Tucson (AZ) (1983)
8. Sun Microsystems, JavaSpace Specification (March 1998) http://java.sun.com/products/jini/specs

Enhancing Online Computer Games for Grids

Jens Müller and Sergei Gorlatch

Westfälische Wilhelms-Universität Münster, Germany

Abstract. Massively multiplayer online games (MMOG) require large amounts of computational resources for providing a responsive and scalable gameplay for thousands of concurrently participating players. In current MMOG, large data-centers are dedicated to a particular game title. Such static hosting requires a huge upfront investment and carries the risk of false estimation of user demand. The concept of grid computing allows to use resources on-demand in a dynamic way, and is therefore a promising approach for MMOG services to overcome the limitations of static game provisioning. In this paper, we discuss different parallelization mechanisms for massively multiplayer gaming and grid architecture concepts suitable for on-demand game services. The work presented here provides both a state-of-the-art analysis and conceptual use case discussion: We outline the new European project *edutain@grid* which targets at scaling real-time interactive online applications and MMOG, including First Person Shooter (FPS) and Real-Time Strategy (RTS) games, in an on-demand manner using a distributed grid architecture. Finally, we describe our experimental online game Rokkatan and report experimental scalability results for this game on a multi-server grid architecture.[1]

1 Introduction

Online gaming has become a major worldwide trend and experienced a massive growth during the past years. According to the game search service *gamespy* [1], currently about 250.000 users are online playing *First Person Shooter (FPS)* games on more than 70.000 servers at any time of the day worldwide. The *Steam* platform reports 140.000 servers with more than 2.8 million individual users monthly for the games hosted on that platform [2]. In the area of *Massively Multiplayer Online Role-Playing Games (MMORPG)*, the number of players has doubled over the last three years and more than 12 million users are currently subscribed to different games [3].

While the number of players drastically increases, the basic concepts and technologies of hosting games on the Internet have not been changed since the beginning of online gaming. Most of the game servers have to be manually set up, started and administrated in a static way, which does not allow for automatic service adjustments with regard to the dynamic user demands.

---

[1] The work described in this paper is partially supported by the European Commission through the project *edutain@grid* (IST 034601).

V. Malyshkin (Ed.): PaCT 2007, LNCS 4671, pp. 80–95, 2007.

In this paper we discuss how the concept of grid computing developed in the academic and business area can be used in the realm of distributed interactive applications including online games. The term grid [4] originates from the conceptual analogy to the power grid, where computational power can be as easily and transparently obtained as electricity by inserting a plug into a power socket. Although there are already some commercial game-related grid systems like *Butterfly* [5] or the *BigWorld* system [6] available, these systems target the MMORPG genre and are barely suitable for running FPS or RTS games. A consistent grid approach for a broad class of real-time interactive applications including e-learning, interactive simulation and training is still missing.

This paper summarises our recent work on scalable network architectures for real-time games and discusses scalability dimensions of different online game genres. We present a novel concept of multi-server game world replication as a feasible approach to scale FPS and RTS games, which so far have been only played in small-scale game sessions. The *proxy-server architecture*, is described as an operational network architecture for our replication approach. We outline real-time computation and communication framework inside the *edutain@grid* architecture[7] for scaling a variety of interactive online application classes. Finally, we present a practical implementation of our approach within a novel real-time strategy game Rokkatan and report experimental scalability results.

2   Parallelisation Approaches to Scaling Online Games

Small-scale sessions of online games usually run on a single game server. This server runs a game-update loop in a periodic manner, in which it has to receive and process all user inputs, process user-independent parts of the game (compute artificial intelligence of NPCs, respawn items, etc.), and send the resulting new state to all game clients. The frequency of the game state update depends on the particular responsiveness requirements of an actual game and ranges from about 5 updates per second for RTS and RPG up to 35 updates per second in fast-paced FPS action games. The update frequency leaves the server a particular maximum time for processing a single loop (less than 30 ms in case of 35 updates per second): if the server is not able to finish the calculations in time and send the new state back to clients, then the users will immediately be disrupted in their game immersion due to this computational lag.

Because the server has to maintain the update rate of the periodic real-time state processing, there is a maximum amount of data which can be processed in time. When increasing the number of players, the demand for data processing is rising. However, the computation power of a server is constant, which makes the single-server architecture approach unable to support MMOGs.

2.1   Scalability Dimensions

In order to scale a game application, i.e., to increase particular characteristics like the number of players without violating the real-time constraints of the game update loop, the processing has to be parallelised. Before discussing different approaches to parallelisation, we summarize three main scalability dimensions identified in our previous work for different MMOG genres:

1. The overall number of participating users needs to be scalable in every massively multiplayer game. All these users are connected to a single game session and generally able to interact with each other.

2. The game world size needs to be scalable in particular in MMORPGs, where the world usually is very large. Scaling the game world size requires increasing of two resources: (1) processing power for processing more actively computer-controlled entities filling the world, and (2) main memory for storing an increasing amount of static terrain geometry and dynamic entities.

3. The player density has to be scalable especially in action-oriented Player-versus-Player (PvP) games like FPS. In contrast to the huge game world of MMORPG, these games are played in much smaller environments; users move their avatars where some action is going on, and thus dynamically create local player clusters with a high density. Player density has to be scalable in order to provide responsive gameplay for situations with a lot of action.

There have been different parallelisation approaches discussed in academia as well as implemented in commercial games to scale some of these dimensions for different types of genres. In the following, we briefly discuss the well-known zoning concept and our novel replication approach.

2.2 Game World Zoning

In the zoning parallelization approach, the game world is partitioned into independent zones which are processed in parallel on several servers. The game client has to change the server connection if the user moves his avatar into a different zone. Figure 1 illustrates an example of a game world with four zones.

The game world zoning is usually incorporated in MMORPGs. Regarding the scalability dimensions discussed above, this approach is very suitable for scaling the total number of users and the overall game world size, as long as the users scatter themselves regularly in the huge game world. However, the third dimension of player-density is not scalable, because a particular single zone is only maintained at a single server. If, as for example in an action-oriented FPS game,

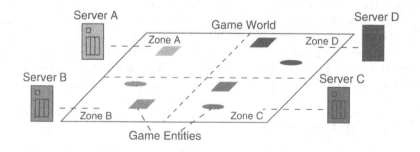

Fig. 1. Game World Zoning

a lot of players gather within a small area in a large fight, the corresponding zone server will become congested, similar to the single server in the conventional client-server architecture. Zoning is, therefore, a suitable and important approach for MMORPG, where users are encouraged to spread out, because due to advancing avatar level and proceeding quest lines only a particular subset of zones is interesting for a particular user. For action-oriented PvP games, however, zoning is not feasible because users are interested in fighting other players and therefore gather together, which dynamically increases the player density and congests a single zone.

2.3   Game World Replication

Our concept of game world replication [8] is an alternative parallelization approach for scaling the density of players in a real-time game session. In this approach, each server holds a complete copy of the game state as illustrated in Fig. 2 and the processing of entities is distributed among participating servers: Each server has to process its *active entities*, while *shadow entities* are maintained at remote servers. After each entity update, the corresponding server broadcasts a corresponding update message.

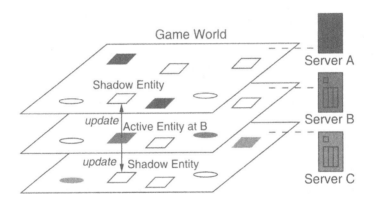

Fig. 2. Game World Replication

The replication concept allows to scale the density of players, because the processing amount available for a particular static region of the game world can be increased this way. If players cluster together in a big fight, then the processing of all the interactions and visibility checks is split up among all participating servers. We implement this approach in our *proxy-server architecture* [9] and demonstrate its feasibility in our scalable RTS game *Rokkatan* (Section 5) which can be played by several hundreds of users in a single session on a comparatively small game world.

3   Grid Computing for Online Games

A computational grid allows users to access resources (processing power, storage space, network bandwidth, etc.) in an on-demand fashion. Instead of buying resources and setting them up statically and privately inside of academic or business institutions, resources are shared over institutional boundaries by so-called virtual organisations. If a user asks for a particular resource (for example, an SMP server with at least eight CPUs running at 1.2 GHz or higher), then a grid middleware like the Globus toolkit [10] or Unicore [11] acts as a market broker between the user and resource providers for negotiating resource characteristics, usage time and prices. After successful negotiations, the user can start own computations on the remote server by running a binary copied over or using pre-installed services.

The main functional characteristics of grid systems are as follows:

- *Dynamicity*: instead of statically running services regardless of the actual user demand, a grid allows to automatically start and stop services with respect to the demand and provides resources in a just-in-time manner when they are actually needed by users.
- *Scalability*: in order to provide a high amount of computational power, the goal of modern grid middleware is to create a virtual cluster of several servers for a single performance-demanding application.
- *Checkpointing and Migration*: several grid infrastructures allow to store the state of running user applications, which can be used to periodically checkpoint the state of a long-time computation and restart it from the last state in case of a server crash or other failures. Additionally, this functionality allows to migrate a computation from one host to another, for example for load-balancing purposes.
- *Accounting and Billing*: users and service providers usually have their own personal account in the grid infrastructure which is used for authentication and billing purposes.

There exist grid systems and middleware which provide the basis for productive grid environments especially in the academic area, where physicians, meteorologists or geologists run distributed and collaborative simulations in an on-demand manner.

In the challenging area of online computer games, there have been some academic and commercial grid-related infrastructures developed and presented. Basically, existing approaches can be distinguished to follow one of the following two concepts:

Grids for Single-Server FPS
In the current state of the art of FPS game hosting, users rent servers at a flat rate from hosting companies on a monthly basis. Casual users which do not have control over such a server can only play on public servers and are not able to set up an Internet-based session for a closed group of users with their own rules. Grid systems for single-server FPS allow users to start FPS game sessions in an

on-demand manner for short durations. Instead of statically renting a server at a particular hoster, users specify the game and related characteristics like number of players, private/public game etc. and the grid system negotiates these requirements with several hosters participating in this infrastructure. After contracting with a particular hoster, the user can configure game-specific settings like the map being played on, the score or time limit to win. The system then schedules the start of a binary game server featuring the user-specific settings according to the booking. Such a grid system was discussed, for example, in [12]; we also presented a prototype of an infrastructure providing this functionality in [13]. Such a FPS grid system does not use the general grid concept to its full potential. Regarding the general features described in Section 3, only the dynamicity of the grid approach and potentially its accounting applies to the hosting of a particular subclass of online games. Such a single-server grid using the available game server binaries can neither scale a single game session nor migrate it onto a different host for overall load balancing. However, it still provides an improvement over the static server hosting and is a first partial demonstrator of what grids can provide for online game hosting.

Grids for Multi-Server MMORPG
The user demand for playing a particular MMORPG is dynamic in several dimensions, the most important are: (1) short-time variation of logged-in users depending on daytime and weekday, and (2) changing total playerbase. The first dimension reflects peak usage times of a constant total subscriber number, while the second dimension usually varies more slowly and reflects the game's overall lifecyle of release, growth, saturation and finally decrease, possibly restarted with the release of expansions. Following these varying user demands, the game provider has to ensure that sufficient computation resources are available. In order to provide the required flexibility regarding the setup of an MMORPG, different grid infrastructures have been proposed and commercially applied, as for example *Butterfly.net* [5] or *BigWorld* [6]. These infrastructures provide a server-side API to define game zones and instances and map them to actual server hosts at runtime. In comparison to grids for single-server FPS, these infrastructures provide more sophisticated functionality of the general grid concept (as summarized in Section 3) to online gaming: They enable dynamic game services, scale a single massively multiplayer session by providing zones and instances and incorporate accounting functionality. However, these grids are especially targetting MMORPGs and are barely usable for other online gaming genres for which the built-in zoning concept is not appropriate. Additionally, the servers used by a single MMORPG realm still reside at a particular hoster and there is no option to migrate sessions between data centers for load-balancing reasons and for enabling an open market of MMOG hosting.

Existing game-related grid infrastructures mainly target a specific MMOG genre. For optimizing the distribution of server processing power for overall online gaming, a comprehensive approach suitable for all classes of online games is required. The recently started *edutain@grid* project [7] targets at providing the grid concept not only to online gaming, but also to other online interactive multi-user applications like e-learning, training and simulation applications.

In the following, we outline the concept and use cases for a grid infrastructure which provides dynamicity and scalability for all major types of online games. Our main idea is to scale all the different scalability dimensions introduced in Section 2.1 by combining several scalability approaches suitable for the various game genres. The resulting architecture should be practically usable, i.e. the complexity and dynamicity of the multi-server parallelisation has to be hidden as much as possible from the game developer inside of a convenient API, without restricting optimization possibilities for a specific application implementation.

Our grid concept follows the familiar paradigm of game entities and game-loop-centric processing. In particular, a comprehensive infrastructure has to support zoning, replication and instancing of particular game world regions. The overall resulting concept is illustrated in Figure 3.

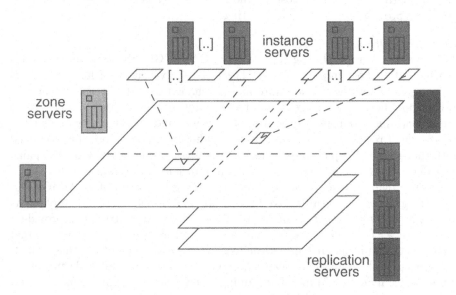

Fig. 3. Comprehensive Scalability Framework

The particular combination of zoning and instancing is already practically used by commercial MMORPGs. However, using replication in combination with zoning is a novel concept which allows to scale the density of players inside of a particular zone. Combining these different approaches allows to scale all three main scalability dimensions for a single application instance and, therefore, results in a parallelisation architecture generally suitable for scaling all classes of multiplayer games.

4   Dynamic Scaling of Game Environments

While the overall architecture illustrated in Figure 3 combines the different scalability approaches, an enclosing grid infrastructure is still required to provide server resources for the zones, instances and replicas in a dynamic manner. In the following, we illustrate two main use cases of dynamically mapping game world regions to servers, for particular user demand and behaviour.

In Player-vs-Player scenarios using several zones, it can be expected that users dynamically gather in a particular area and fight each other. The corresponding zone then should be replicated using several servers for scaling the density of users as illustrated for the bottom right zone in Fig. 4(a).

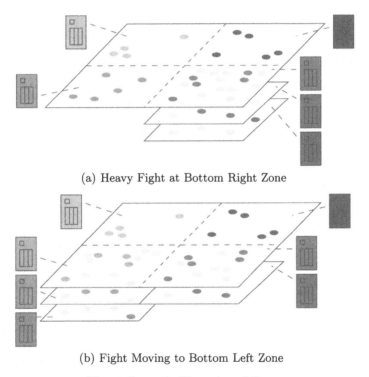

(a) Heavy Fight at Bottom Right Zone

(b) Fight Moving to Bottom Left Zone

Fig. 4. Dynamic Clustering of Users

In such a scenario of a fight with a high user density, it can be expected that users eventually move over to an adjacent zone. In Figure 4(b), the bottom right zone then becomes less frequented because users move over to the bottom left zone. This zone now has to be replicated in order to scale the density of users, while the replication degree of the previously frequented zone can be lowered due to decreasing load. Our concept of the comprehensive scalability framework supports dynamic adding and removing of replications, and the overall grid infrastructure has to dynamically reassign the replication servers to zones according to the user behaviour.

Increasing Instance Demand. As another example of how our concept of the overall scalability framework can be dynamically orchestrated by a grid infrastructure respecting the actual user demand, let us imagine that the users are distributed across several zones of the virtual world. Besides the zones, there are particular instanced areas which are only barely frequented in the beginning as illustrated in Fig. 5(a).

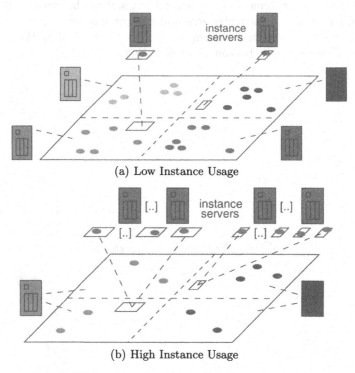

(a) Low Instance Usage

(b) High Instance Usage

Fig. 5. Changing demand for Instances

Especially in MMORPG, it is a common scenario that the instance utilization increases drastically during night time, because users pre-arrange groups to adventure collaboratively. As a result, many more instance servers are required as illustrated in Figure 5(b) while the general zoned game world might be less frequented. A grid infrastructure therefore has to be able to dynamically increase the number of instance servers and possibly combine zones to reassign zone servers to instances.

5   Case Study: Rokkatan

In this section, we present our demonstrator game Rokkatan, which belongs to the popular genre of real-time strategy (RTS) games. The development of Rokkatan pursued three major goals:

1. Evaluation of the proxy-server topology: Rokkatan serves as a detailed case-study of how to design and implement a sophisticated and scalable real-time game using the proxy-server approach. In particular, our goal was to detect potential difficulties in the usage of the eventual consistency model for server synchronisation and possible problems in providing the required responsiveness for a fast-paced real-time game.

2. Incorporation of the Game Scalability Model (GSM): The GSM [14] provides the possibility to be incorporated in a particular game implementation by measuring execution times for several basic tasks that have to be accomplished during a running game session. Based on these times, the model calculates a forecast of maximum player numbers without exhaustive tests. Such a mechanism, integrated into a real game implementation, helps to determine required server capabilities and provides hints for an efficient setup of servers and session rules.

3. Conceptual evaluation of a massively multiplayer RTS game design: Current large-scale game designs concentrate on Massively Multiplayer Online Role Playing Games (MMORPG) like *Everquest* or *World of Warcraft*, which provide a huge persistent world for the users to adventure in. However, other game genres like First Person Shooter or Real-time strategy games have rarely been adapted to massively multiplayer sessions so far. With Rokkatan, we propose a possible game design which extends current real-time strategy gaming to the massively multiplayer realm.

5.1   Rokkatan: The Game

In Rokkatan, each user has control over a single unit, his avatar, and belongs to a particular team. The number of teams playing in a single game session is set up arbitrarily upon session creation. After connecting to a running game session, the user chooses a team to join and the class and name of his avatar. Currently, there are two classes implemented in the game: the warrior, fighting within close range, and the archer who can shoot arrows at distant enemies.

Users of the same team coordinate themselves and move around to occupy flags scattered in the game environment. For each flag currently occupied, a team periodically gains score points. Each team has an initial amount of score points and the team with most points will win the session after a certain time of playing. Therefore, avatars of opposite teams have to fight for supremacy of flags. Such real-time fights, as depicted by the screenshots of Fig. 6 for a small duel and a large battle, play a major role in Rokkatan. Each avatar has a particular amount of health points which decreases when the avatar is hit by an enemy warrior or archer. If the health points of an avatar drop to zero, then he is "dead" for a short period of time, after which he respawns at the starting area of his team. Additionally, the team score points for an avatar which temporarily lost his life.

The game style of Rokkatan is comparable to RTS games like *Command and Conquer* or *Warcraft III*, with the main difference that not few users control large groups of avatars, but each avatar of the game is controlled by a single user. Therefore, it is necessary for all users of a single team to coordinate their

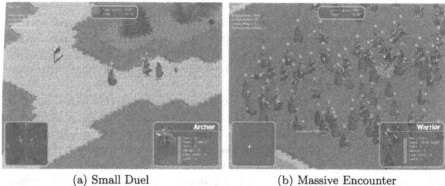

(a) Small Duel   (b) Massive Encounter

Fig. 6. Small Duel and Massive Encounter in Rokkatan

actions. Some avatars guard the occupied flags, while others try to conquer new areas of the game environment. This goal of occupying flags is comparable to tactical FPS games like *Battlefield 1942*, in which several flag points have to be captured in order to win the game session.

A Rokkatan game session takes place in a particular game environment, the game map, which is described in an easily editable text-file. At different locations in the map, potions are available, which can be picked up, carried by avatars and used later on. If the user decides to use such a potion, his avatar immediately regains health points, which makes potions very valuable when fighting enemies.

5.2   Processing of User Actions

There are two main types of user actions in Rokkatan: Movement commands and interaction commands. A movement command can be processed directly at the proxy a client is connected to, because this action only affects the state of the user's avatar. The proxy it is connected to is the only process allowed to alter this data for a particular client, such that the position change of the avatar resulting from a movement command can immediately be performed and acknowledged. Additionally, the proxy communicates this game state change to all other servers which update their local game state replicas accordingly.

The processing of interactions, however, can not be done solely by the local proxy of a particular client. The interaction command can affect either other avatars, e.g., by attacking an opponent, or the general game environment, e.g., by picking up a potion. Therefore, the state of the target game entity like an avatar or a potion has to be changed. In the general case, a remote proxy will be authoritative for the state of the interaction target, which requires sending the interaction to this remote proxy for evaluation. Fig. 7 depicts an example of user interaction processing in Rokkatan.

In Fig. 7, the user at client A issues an interaction affecting the avatar of client B, e.g., attacking the position of the avatar of B in the game environment. In step ①, client A submits the action to its proxy server which validates the

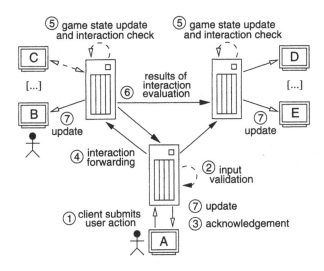

Fig. 7. Interaction Processing

received input in step ②. If the validation was successful, i.e., the state of the avatar allows to perform the attack, then the proxy sends an acknowledgement back to client A (step ③) and forwards the interaction to all other participating servers in step ④. The other proxies update their local game state, i.e., they update the avatar's state of the attacking client A in step ⑤. Additionally, each remote proxy checks whether a game element it is responsible for is affected by the attack of avatar A. In this example, the avatar of client B is hit by the attack. The local proxy of client B updates the state of its avatar by decrementing health points and informs all other proxies about this state change (step ⑥). Finally, in step ⑦, all proxies inform local clients which are directly affected by the interaction (client A and B). Additionally, all clients, whose avatar is located near to the interacting avatars, are notified about the interaction. For example, users at the clients D and E observe the interaction and the proxies inform the clients about it.

5.3 Rokkatan Implementation and Scalability Experiments

Rokkatan is implemented in C++ and uses the *Kyra sprite* engine and the Simple Directmedia Layer (SDL) for client graphics and sound. The game communication is based on our Game Proxy Architecture (GPA) library which we developed to make the usage of the proxy-server approach convenient for game developers. The library provides a simple API for clients and proxy servers to send and receive game messages at different levels of reliability. For the inter-proxy communication, game messages are sent using IP-Multicast. If proxies are not able to participate in the IP-Multicast group, the GPA automatically falls back to unicast message sending. This way, scalable multicast communication is used whenever possible and the unicast fallback ensures general functionality of game sessions in networks not supporting multicast.

While the concept of the proxy-server topology determines the general design of the Rokkatan implementation, some Rokkatan-specific issues had to be additionally addressed in order to ensure the scalability of the game. For these particular problems, we developed solutions and implemented them directly into the Rokkatan application. Although developed for Rokkatan, these solutions can be reused in other games using the proxy-server topology and thus provide an extension of the generic proxy architecture.

We ran numerous test sessions in order to studyy the scalability of the actual Rokkatan implementation using the proxy-server architecture and to verify our analytical model. Although we tested Rokkatan with various connection types of clients (modem, ISDN, DSL) in order to confirm the general functionality of Rokkatan under higher latencies, the scalability tests were conducted in the local area network of our department because a large number of hosts was required.

The Rokkatan client includes a special "bot" mode, which automatically participates in a game session. This client-side bot issues actions based on the current gaming situation and makes full usage of all possible game interactions like moving, attacking, occupation of flags and pickup of potions. It uses potions to recover health points and retrieves from fights when all stocked potions have been consumed. For a server, the bot-mode of a client is transparent and can not be distinguished from a human user.

The experiments were conducted for two test maps of different sizes (64x64 and 128x128 ground tiles). The dimensions of both maps are comparable to those of commercial real-time strategy games like *Warcraft 3*. It takes about 90 seconds for the smaller and 180 seconds for the larger test map to walk diagonally from the upper left to the lower right corner.

Our reference server host is a Pentium 4 1.7 GHz system with 640 MB RAM running Linux with kernel 2.6, of which we have several systems available.

For our tests, a total of 25 computers were used. Five of them act as proxy servers while the other hosts run the bot clients, of which several can be started on a single computer. For the experiments using both test maps, Fig. 8 shows the maximum number of clients which were able to play before servers became congested. Additionally, the plots show the maximum client numbers as predicted using the Game Scalability Model[14].

The scalability of a game session depends on the size of the game map. In the smaller map, the density of avatars increases faster than in the larger map, which leads to congestion much earlier. Fig. 8 demonstrates that the GSM forecasts are very near to the actually measured player numbers, with a maximum deviation of 5 %. The model's forecasts for larger session setups with more than five proxy servers (which we were not able to measure experimentally) show that more than 500 players are expected to be able to participate in a large session of Rokkatan.

The forecasts and actual measurements for the average bandwidth at a single proxy server are shown in Table 1 for the smaller test map; again, our measurements were done for up to five servers. With a maximum deviation of 7 %, the

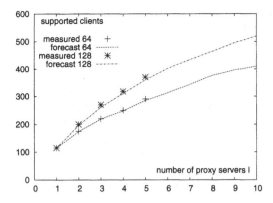

Fig. 8. Maximum Number of Players

Table 1. Estimated and measured bandwith at a single proxy server for a 64x64 map

Session	estimated	measured	deviation
1 pr., 115 cl.	150.7 kB/s	152.0 kB/s	2 %
2 pr., 170 cl.	213.9 kB/s	210.3 kB/s	2 %
3 pr., 220 cl.	245.3 kB/s	235.5 kB/s	5 %
4 pr., 250 cl.	237.0 kB/s	222.7 kB/s	7 %
5 pr., 290 cl.	243.7 kB/s	242.5 kB/s	1 %
6 pr., 310 cl.	257.1 kB/s	-	-
8 pr., 375 cl.	284.8 kB/s	-	-
10 pr., 410 cl.	291.2 kB/s	-	-

bandwidth predictions are quite accurate as well. Due to the dead reckoning used in Rokkatan, the amount of data sent to a single client is quite low, ranging from about one to ten kBytes per second depending on the game situation. However, the proxy servers fully synchronize their state at each tick in order to provide the required responsiveness for direct interactions. Overall, the bandwidth utilization at a single proxy is low enough to allow sessions with a large number of users when the servers are hosted at high capacity Internet connections.

6 Conclusion and Related Work

In this paper, we summarized the main scalability dimensions of online computer games and provided an overview of existing scalability approaches. The zoning concept [15,16], which is widely used by existing MMORPG, scales the total number of users and the game world size. For scaling the density of players, however, our replication concept using the *proxy-server architecture* [9] is more feasible. As a general result of this discussion, we outlined our approach of a comprehensive scalability framework which combines zoning, instancing and replication and is thus suitable to scale all contemporary genres of online games.

Besides scalability, three other functional characteristics of grids – dynamicity, migration and accounting – promise an enormous improvement over the currently usually static online game hosting. The current game-related grid infrastructures target specific game genres and do not provide the full benefits of grid computing to general online game hosting yet.

There has been a lot of work in the area of scalable network topologies dedicated to massively multiplayer gaming. Most of the presented architectures partition the game world into several zones. The authority for such zones, which commonly are used in MMORPG, is either assigned to single servers as in, or distributed dynamically in a decentralized way. However, in our Rokkatan game, due to the much smaller size of its map in comparison to an MMORPG environment, a map partitioning is not feasible. In the worst case, all avatars would be clustered within a single zone and the single responsible server would quickly become congested. The proxy-server approach performs much better in such a scenario with a high avatar density. Rokkatan shows the feasibility of the proxy architecture to host game sessions for hundreds of users in a small game environment at very high responsiveness of 25 updates per second.

In the area of game design for other MMOG genres besides role playing games, only little research has been done, although there are already commercial games of the FPS genre, suitable for a high number of participating players. Such games like *Joint Operations* or *Soeldner* take place in a huge area and simulate a small warfare, in which users have to coordinate themselves in a team. The single-server approach used by these games limits the player number, although the game design itself would support many more players in a session. The proxy approach is feasible for these fast-paced action games and will allow a much higher number of users.

With the development of Rokkatan, we showed the scalability of our proxy-server architecture for game designs requiring high responsiveness. The behaviour of the client bots in the experiments was sophisticated enough to make the test sessions comparable to human user sessions. There were always several large battles taking place, bots fought for supremacy of flags, used potions and tried to save themselves when being low on health points. This proves that, with a game map of adequate size, fluent and responsive game sessions involving several hundreds of users are possible in Rokkatan.

References

1. IGN Entertainment. Gamespy, http://www.gamespy.com/
2. Valve Corporation. Steam platform, http://www.steampowered.com/
3. Bruce Sterling Woodcock. Mmorpg chart, http://www.mmogchart.com/
4. Foster, I., Kesselmann, C. (eds.): The Grid: Blueprint for a New Computing Infrastructure. M. Kaufmann, Seattle (1998)
5. Butterfly.net, http://www.butterfly.net
6. BigWorld. Bigworld technology, http://www.bigworldtech.com/
7. edutain@grid project, http://www.edutain.eu/
8. Müller, J., Gorlatch, S.: Rokkatan: scaling an RTS game design to the massively multiplayer realm. ACM Computers in Entertainment 4(3), 11 (2006)

9. Müller, J., Fischer, S., Gorlatch, S., Mauve, M.: A proxy server-network for real-time computer games. In: Danelutto, M., Vanneschi, M., Laforenza, D. (eds.) Euro-Par 2004. LNCS, vol. 3149, pp. 606–613. Springer, Heidelberg (2004)
10. Globus Alliance. Globus toolkit, http://www.globus.org/toolkit/
11. Unicore Forum e.V. Unicore-grid, http://www.unicore.org
12. Shaikh, A., Sahu, S., Rosu, M., Shea, M., Saha, D.: Implementation of a service platform for online games. In: Proceedings of ACM Network and System Support for Games Workshop (NetGames), Portland, Oregon, USA (September 2004)
13. Müller, J., Schwerdt, R., Gorlatch, S.: Dynamic service provisioning for multiplayer online games. In: Cao, J., Nejdl, W., Xu, M. (eds.) APPT 2005. LNCS, vol. 3756, pp. 461–470. Springer, Heidelberg (2005)
14. Müller, J., Gorlatch, S.: GSM: a game scalability model for multiplayer real-time games. In: Infocom, I.E.E.E. (ed.) IEEE Infocom 2005, Miami, Florida, USA, March 2005, IEEE Communications Society (2005)
15. Cai, W., Xavier, P., Turner, S.J., Lee, B.S.: A scalable architecture for supporting interactive games on the internet. In: Proceedings of the 16th Workshop on Parallel and Distributed Simulation, pp. 60–67, IEEE, Washington, D.C. (May 2002)
16. Knutsson, B., Lu, H., Xu, W., Hopkins, B.: Peer-to-peer support for massively multiplayer games. In: IEEE Infocom 2004, Hong Kong, China, IEEE Communications Society (2004)

Optimized Parallel Approach for 3D Modelling of Forest Fire Behaviour

Gilbert Accary[1], Oleg Bessonov[2], Dominique Fougère[3],
Sofiane Meradji[3], and Dominique Morvan[4]

[1] Université Saint-Esprit de Kaslik, B.P. 446 Jounieh, Lebanon
[2] Institute for Problems in Mechanics of Russian Academy of Sciences,
101, Vernadsky ave., 119526 Moscow, Russia
[3] Laboratoire de Modélisation en Mécanique à Marseille, L3M–IMT, La Jetée,
Technopôle de Château-Gombert, 13451 Marseille Cedex 20, France
[4] Université de la Méditerranée, UNIMECA, 60, rue Joliot Curie,
13453 Marseille Cedex 13, France
gilbertaccary@usek.edu.lb, bess@ipmnet.ru, fougere@l3m.univ-mrs.fr,
sofiane@l3m.univ-mrs.fr, dominique.morvan@univmed.fr

Abstract. In this paper we present methods for parallelization of 3D CFD forest fire modelling code on Non-uniform memory computers in frame of the OpenMP environment. Mathematical model is presented first. Then, some peculiarities of this class of computers are considered, along with properties and limitations of the OpenMP model. Techniques for efficient parallelization are discussed, considering different types of data processing algorithms. Finally, performance results for the parallelized algorithm are presented and analyzed (for up to 16 processors).

1 Introduction

This work is carried out within the context of the European integrated fire management project (Fire Paradox) aiming to obtain a full-physical three-dimensional model of forest fire behaviour. The proposed approach accounts for the main physical phenomena involved in a forest fire by solving the conservation equations of physics applied to a medium composed of solid phases (vegetation) and gas mixture (combustion gases and the ambient air). The model consists in coupling the main mechanisms of decomposition (drying, pyrolysis, combustion) and of transfer (convection, diffusion, radiation, turbulence, etc.) taking place during forest fire propagation [1]. This multiphase complete physical approach already exists in 2D approximation [2] and consists in solving the described model in a vertical plane defined by the direction of fire propagation. The 3D extension of the existing model will enable to render 3D effects observed in real fires and to represent the real heterogeneous structure of the vegetation. The CFD code under development is currently at the stage of predicting turbulent gas flows and has been validated on several benchmarks of natural, forced, and mixed convection [3].

V. Malyshkin (Ed.): PaCT 2007, LNCS 4671, pp. 96–102, 2007.

The extended 3-dimensional formulation requires much more computational resources than the previous 2D model. The new model needs substantially bigger grids ($N_x \times N_y \times N_z$ vs. $N_x \times N_y$ grid points), more complicated discretizations (more terms in the equations), additional grid compression in problematic areas (because of non-flat fire interfaces), more robust and expensive algebraic solvers. As a result, the total computational complexity of the algorithm increases by two orders of magnitude or more.

In order to be able to perform precise computations in reasonable time, it is necessary to exploit efficiently all available resources and improve computational performance by combining the following considerations: efficient numerical method and procedure, robust algebraic solvers, optimization of the code for modern superscalar microprocessors with memory hierarchies, and parallelization of the algorithm for moderate number of processors. However, this last consideration remains the most efficient way for increasing the speed of computations.

The next important point is the choice of a parallel computer architecture and parallelization model for this work. Generally, distributed memory parallel computers (clusters) are used for large-scale computations. However, such parallel computers, used with the appropriate MPI message-passing model, result in very complex algorithms and require tight optimization of communication exchanges [4]. In addition, a model with relatively slow communication exchanges can't be efficiently used for many algorithms [5]. Finally, it is difficult to implement a portable code that would work on any parallel platform with required efficiency.

Thus, shared-memory computer architecture was chosen as a target for the new parallel code. An OpenMP parallelization model without explicit exchanges is used for the algorithm [6]. This model, which is the natural choice for shared-memory computers, is just an extension of high level languages (Fortran, C). With appropriate programming, the code may work on a parallel system with any number of processors. Consequently, the new code becomes portable and compatible with many parallel platforms.

However, implementation of the shared-memory paradigm encounters another difficulty: almost all modern shared-memory systems with moderate or high number of processors (4, 8, 16 and more) belong to the class of Non-uniform Memory Access (NuMA) computers. It means that every processor or group of processors (processor node) is directly connected only to its own (local) memory while an access to the non-local (remote) memory is performed through intermediate communication network. Due to such organization, remote accesses become much slower than local ones. This restriction requires a special approach for the organization of parallel algorithms in order to ensure that most or all accesses from every processor node occur within this node's local memory.

Thereby, in the presented paper we will describe the mathematical model and numerical method, strategy of OpenMP parallelization on NuMA computers, results of parallelization efficiency of the new 3D code, and summary with conclusions.

2   Mathematical Model and Numerical Method

We consider Newtonian fluid whose flow is governed by non-stationary Navier-Stokes equations in Boussinesq approximation. The model is also capable to handle the Low Mach number approximation in the context of perfect gas [3]. The set of equations consists of the continuity equation, the momentum equations in three spatial dimensions ($i = 1, 2, 3$) and the equations for energy and turbulent quantities. The generalized governing equation for all variables is expressed in the following conservative form:

$$\frac{\partial}{\partial t}(\rho\phi) + \frac{\partial}{\partial x_i}(\rho\phi u_i) = \frac{\partial}{\partial x_i}\left(\Gamma\left(\frac{\partial\phi}{\partial x_i}\right)\right) + S_\phi \quad \text{with} \quad \phi = 1, u_1, u_2, u_3, T, k, \epsilon$$

where ϕ represents the transported variable; ρ and u_i are respectively the local density and the i-th component of velocity; Γ – the effective diffusion coefficient; S_ϕ – the source term for the corresponding variable.

The Finite Volume discretization is applied to the non-uniform Cartesian staggered grid. Second-order discretizations are used, employing the quadratic upstream interpolation of advective terms with flux limiters.

The transport equations are solved by a fully implicit segregated method based on the SIMPLER algorithm [7]. The non-symmetric linear systems obtained from the discretized equations are solved by the BiCGStab iterative method, while the symmetric linear system of the pressure equation is solved by the Conjugate Gradient method (CG). The use of under-relaxation techniques, when necessary, allows better convergence and stability of the solution.

The code is applicable for simulation of flows in rectangular domains. Validation of the sequential version of the code has been performed for several common benchmarks (lid driven cavity, differentially heated cavity etc.).

3   OpenMP Parallelization on NuMA Computers

We will consider the strategy of OpenMP parallelization using the SGI Altix 350 shared memory system with non-uniform organization. It consists of 10 processor nodes, each with two Intel Itanium 2 processors (1.5 GHz, L3-cache 4 Mbyte) and 4 Gbyte of the local memory. Processor nodes are interconnected by the special NuMA-link interfaces through the high-speed switch that provides accesses to non-local (remote) memories. Logically, the considered system belongs to the shared-memory class, when every process may transparently access any memory location in a system. However, remote accesses are much slower than local ones. For example, the peak memory read rate (throughput) within a node is equal to 6.4 Gbyte/s, while the peak throughput of NuMA-links is two times less.

Direct measurements show that the speed of regular read accesses achieves 6.1 GByte/s for local memories, and only 2.4 GByte/s for remote locations. This speed is very important for many computational algorithms that perform processing of data in big 3-dimensional arrays. Performance of such memory-bound algorithms depends on the memory throughput almost linearly.

Therefore, it is necessary to ensure that all processes of a parallel program access only (or mostly) data located within a local memory. On the system level, it can be done by the special utility that affiliates (bounds) every process to its own processor. This binding is needed to avoid migration of processes between processors and to guarantee that every processor executes only one process. In a multi-user computer system, some discipline must be established in order to avoid interference of processes from different programs.

On the application level, it is important to organize an algorithm in such a way that every thread (branch) of a parallelized algorithm would process only (mostly) a corresponding piece of data. Additionally, these data must be distributed between processor node's memories by the appropriate way (in the beginning of the execution). If these requirement are not fulfilled, parallel performance may drop two times or more.

The same rules and restrictions apply to another types of NuMA computer systems. For example, systems built on AMD Opteron processors also use relatively slow interprocessor links. In these systems, processors are interconnected into a mesh that imposes an additional limitation: access to some particular memory location may pass through several intermediate (transit) processors if the target processor (who owns the required location) is not connected directly to the requesting one. Therefore, Opteron-based systems (with mesh topology) may become less flexible and less efficient for OpenMP parallelization, in comparison to switch-based systems (with star topology).

Generally, the OpenMP extension to a high level language (Fortran in our case) is very simple and complements this language by several comment-like directives. These directives instruct a compiler how to perform parallelization of a program. The most important and popular directive is "PARALLEL DO" which is usually applied to an outermost "do" statement (for nested loops) (see example on Fig. 1, left). In accordance with the number of processors requested, iterations of this loop are evenly distributed between branches (threads) of a program for execution in different processors. This corresponds to the geometric splitting of a processed data array (3-dimensional, as a rule) into sub-arrays by the last spatial dimension (Fig. 1, right).

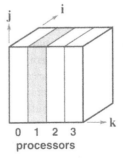

Fig. 1. Example of "PARALLEL DO" directive (left); geometric splitting of data array by this directive (right)

The OpenMP parallelization model is very convenient for "true" shared-memory computers with uniform memory. For these computers, it is possible to split a multidimensional computational domain by any spatial direction. For non-uniform systems, only splitting by the last direction ensures that necessary portions of data are fully located within the corresponding processor node's memory. In order to avoid remote memory accesses, algorithms must be rearranged. Some sorts of algorithms (for example, those with recursive dependences in all spatial directions) can't be parallelized easily and efficiently within the OpenMP model. On the other hand, algorithms of the "explicit" nature, that pass sequentially through data arrays and use small local data access patterns (stencils), may benefit from this model. Accesses to remote memory occur only within boundaries between subdomains in this case.

One-dimensional splitting of multidimensional arrays imposes another limitation on the OpenMP model for NuMA computers: subdomains become very "narrow" by this dimension, and, as a result, accesses to remote memory through boundaries become frequent enough (compared to the number of local accesses). Also, the last dimension may become not divisible by the number of processors that results in a bad load balance. These limitations restrict the degree of efficient parallelization by moderate number of processors (typically 8–16).

Unfortunately, OpenMP in the current state has no special tools or directives for NuMA parallelizations. Therefore, only indirect techniques (as described in the current paper) may by applied to customize parallelization methods for this sort of computers.

4   Parallelization Approach and Results

In the current implementation, the considered CFD code has the "explicit" nature, i.e. it doesn't employ direct implicit solvers. Most part of its computational time (about 80 %) is consumed by two Conjugate Gradient type solver routines – CG (for pressure) and BiCGStab (for transport equations). These routines process data arrays with 7-point local stencils and therefore perform remote memory accesses only when processing data near subdomain boundaries. As a result, these CG-type routines can be efficiently parallelized using the OpenMP model for NuMA. Another time-consuming routines also belong to the "explicit" class and can be parallelized without difficulties.

In order to ensure that data are correctly distributed within local memories of corresponding processor nodes, it is necessary to perform special initialization of all important data arrays. Neither the current OpenMP standard, nor the OpenMP-aware compiler used in this work (Intel Fortran 9.1) have any tools for explicit data distribution. To provide this distribution, a simple routine is used that initializes all arrays in nested loops with "PARALLEL DO" directives. This routine is called in the beginning of the code when memory pages for arrays are not yet allocated. Since this allocation occurs "by demand", it is necessary to issue the first request to any element of data from the same processor node, which will be used for further processing of this element. Therefore, parallel loops for initialization of data must be organized similarly to data-processing "do" loops with exactly the same splitting of outermost iterations between processors (Fig. 1).

Validation of the parallelized code and measurements of its parallelization efficiency were performed on the benchmark problem of natural convection in differently heated cavity [8]. We used the Boussinesq flow configuration with Rayleigh number $Ra = 10^6$ and grid size $60 \times 60 \times 60$. Performance results are presented on Fig. 2. In the table, results of relative acceleration (compared to the previous grade with half number of processors), absolute acceleration (compared to one processor) and parallelization efficiency are shown.

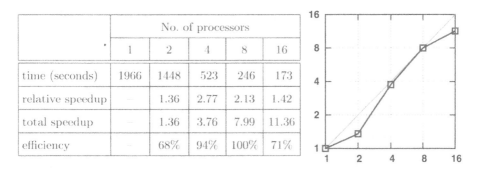

		No. of processors			
·	1	2	4	8	16
time (seconds)	1966	1448	523	246	173
relative speedup	–	1.36	2.77	2.13	1.42
total speedup	–	1.36	3.76	7.99	11.36
efficiency	–	68%	94%	100%	71%

Fig. 2. Parallelization results for the benchmark problem

Relative acceleration for two processors is not high because both processors compete for the same memory, and performance is limited by its throughput. On the other hand, for 4 and 8 processors we see a superlinear speedup owing to the help of a large 4 MByte L3-cache in each processor. As a result, total acceleration for 4 and 8 processors corresponds to the linear profile. For 16 processors, some negative effects are accumulated: load disbalance (60 is not divisible by 16) and influence of big boundaries (1 boundary grid point per 2 or 3 internal points). Due to these effects, parallelization efficiency drops. It follows that the reasonable degree of efficient parallelization for this configuration is 8, at most 16, that corresponds to the goal of the current work.

The presented parallel code is based on a serial code that was initially optimized for modern pipelined processors with memory hierarchies. Further optimization of the code will be devoted to the acceleration of algebraic solvers by applying efficient preconditioners. It was demonstrated that the explicit-class (local) Jacobi preconditioner can be easily parallelized. However, for more efficient implicit (global) line-Jacobi preconditioner, new parallelization technique must be developed with parallel solution of tri-diagonal linear system. This parallelization will be based on the previous work [4]. Another direction of the development of the current CFD code will consist in incorporation of the radiation transfer algorithm. This algorithm can't be parallelized by geometric manner and will need a special approach based on the concept of input data parallelism.

5   Conclusion

In this work we developed the strategy of OpenMP parallelization for NuMA computers and parallelization method for 3D CFD code for modelling of forest fire behaviour, taking into account restrictions and limited flexibility of the current state of the OpenMP environment. This new method allows to achieve good parallelization efficiency for moderate number of processors (up to 16). The obtained results correspond to the general goal of the work – to obtain a tool for performing precise 3D computations in reasonable time.

Acknowledgements. This work was supported by the European integrated fire management project (Fire Paradox) under the Sixth Framework Programme (Work Package WP2.2 "3D-modelling of fire behaviour and effects"), and by the Russian Foundation for Basic Research (project RFBR-05-08-18110).

References

1. Morvan, D., Dupuy, J.L.: Modeling of fire spread through a forest fuel bed using a multiphase formulation. Combust. Flame 127, 1981–1994 (2001)
2. Morvan, D., Dupuy, J.L.: Modeling the propagation of a wildfire through a Mediterranean shrub using a multiphase formulation. Combust. Flame 138, 199–210 (2004)
3. Le Quéré, P., et al.: Modelling of natural convection flows with large temperature differences: A Benchmark problem for Low Mach number solvers. Part 1. Reference solutions. ESAIM: Math. Modelling and Num. Analysis 39(3), 609–616 (2005)
4. Bessonov, O., Brailovskaya, V., Polezhaev, V., Roux, B.: Parallelization of the solution of 3D Navier-Stokes equations for fluid flow in a cavity with moving covers. In: Malyshkin, V. (ed.) PaCT 95. LNCS, vol. 964, pp. 385–399. Springer, Heidelberg (1995)
5. Bessonov, O., Fougère, D., Roux, B.: Parallel simulation of 3D incompressible flows and performance comparison for several MPP and cluster platforms. In: Malyshkin, V. (ed.) PaCT 2001. LNCS, vol. 2127, pp. 401–409. Springer, Heidelberg (2001)
6. Dagum, L., Menon, R.: OpenMP: an industry-standard API for shared-memory programming. IEEE Computational Science and Engineering 5(1), 46–55 (1998)
7. Moukalled, F., Darwish, M.: A unified formulation of the segregated class of algorithms for fluid flow at all speed. Numer. Heat Transfer, Part B 37, 103–139 (2000)
8. Bessonov, O., Brailovskaya, V., Nikitin, S., Polezhaev, V.: Three-dimensional natural convection in a cubical enclosure: a bench mark numerical solution. In: de Vahl Davis, G., Leonardi, E (eds.) CHT'97: Advances in Computational Heat Transfer. Proc. of Symposium, Cesme, Turkey. Begell House, Inc., New York, pp. 157–165 (1998)

A High-Level Toolkit for Development of Distributed Scientific Applications*

Alexander Afanasiev, Oleg Sukhoroslov, Mikhail Posypkin

Institute for Systems Analysis, Russian Academy of Sciences,
Prosp. 60-let Oktyabrya 9, 117312 Moscow, Russia
`{apa, os, posypkin}@isa.ru`

Abstract. The paper presents IARnet toolkit, a set of high-level tools and services simplifying integration of software resources into a distributed computing environment and development of distributed applications involving dynamic discovery and composition of resources. A case study of using IARnet for solving large scale discrete optimization problems is discussed.

Keywords: distributed computing, Grid, integration of software resources, middleware, information service, distributed workflow, discrete optimization.

1 Introduction

The Grid, emerged from the relatively narrow problem of wide-area access to high-performance computing resources, is transforming now into a general-purpose infrastructure for coordinated resource sharing within dynamic virtual organizations. Resources being "plugged" to Grid are no more limited to computing facilities, but include any resources that can be used in collaborative scientific applications: knowledge bases, software libraries and applications, instruments, etc. This extends the scope of Grid applications from high-performance computing to a wider class of complex problems which are decomposable into multiple subproblems being solved by existing resources. Next-generation Grid applications will involve dynamic composition and orchestration of various types of distributed resources and services forming an application workflow.

The widespread adoption of Grid computing among scientists is impeded by the difficulty of developing Grid services and implementing Grid-enabled applications. Among the several efforts targeting this problem most are focused on a simple unified API for various Grid middleware platforms [1, 2]. The presented in this paper IARnet toolkit differs from above approaches by providing a set of tools and services simplifying both deployment of existing software resources and remote access to deployed resources, as well as dynamic discovery and composition of resources into workflows. Despite its focus on integration of software applications IARnet has proven its usefulness in traditional high-performance computing, as demonstrated by the BNB-Grid application described in the end of this paper.

---

* Partially supported by the RFBR grant 05-07-90182-в and RAS Presidium Programme 15П.

V. Malyshkin (Ed.): PaCT 2007, LNCS 4671, pp. 103–110, 2007.

2 IARnet Toolkit

The IARnet toolkit, aimed at the integration of software resources rather than "raw" computational facilities and data storages, extends classical view on the Grid computing while conforming to the modern service-oriented architecture (SOA).

At the core of IARnet is the notion of *information-algorithmic resource (IAR)*, by which we generally mean any software component with certain specified capabilities aimed at solving a well-defined range of applied problems, such as special-purpose collections of applied computational algorithms, mathematical and simulation models, etc. Following this definition, IARnet provides a set of high-level tools for exposing, discovering and accessing IARs enabling development of distributed scientific applications. The IARnet architecture is composed of resource agents, services and IARnet API (Fig. 1).

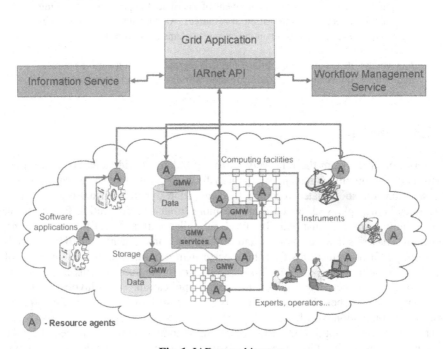

Fig. 1. IARnet architecture

Resource agents are software components acting as mediators between resources and client applications. An agent provides unified access to a resource in accordance with its type, integrates it into the system, and controls user's access to it. In terms of SOA, agents expose resources to applications as standard services.

IARnet services are general-purpose components which provide basic mechanisms required by applications, such as resource discovery. Current version of IARnet contains two services – Information Service and Workflow Management Service, which are described later in this paper. It is important to note that IARnet services are considered as special types of IARs, so they are implemented and accessed using the same tools as resources.

IARnet API defines a high-level application programming interface for development of applications on top of IARnet. Current version of IARnet API is implemented in Java and represents a library used by applications to discover and access resources and services. IARnet API is also used by resources and services for interactions between each other.

As shown in Fig. 1, unified access to "typical" Grid resources such as computing and data storage facilities can be provided for IARnet applications by special agents which interact with these resources indirectly via existing Grid middleware (GMW), basic Grid services, or simple Grid APIs.

2.1 Integration of Software Resources

The problem of resource integration can be stated as how to expose a given software resource as a remote-accessible service with standard interface expected by clients. This requires one to provide a remote access to a resource, as well as implement mapping between unified and implementation-specific interfaces. These two tasks are separated and accomplished by different components of IARnet.

One of the main goals of IARnet was to make the development of distributed applications easy for people unfamiliar with distributed programming and middleware. To abstract developers away from details of remote access the transport level of IARnet is completely hidden from them by IARnet API. This also means that agent and application developers don't have to manually generate or use any stubs.

Resource Agent. The different resource implementations providing same functionality are highly heterogeneous, so there's a strong need in unified interfaces for different types of IARs which hide this heterogeneity from user and provide transparent access to dynamic collections of resources. The basic functionality of resource agent conforms to adapter design pattern where agent implements mapping between the unified interface for a given resource type and the native interface of resource implementation. Each agent implements two interfaces: base general-purpose interface, which is used for operations such as resource type inspection, and an interface of the corresponding resource type. Current version of IARnet supports development of resource agents in Java and C++. As a rule, agent developer needs only to implement resource-specific interface by extending from base agent class.

Container. Resource agents don't provide remote access to resources. To ensure flexibility and extensibility of IARnet this task is isolated in another component called container. *Container* is a hosting environment for resource agents which provide remote access to agents by means of some middleware technology. IARnet supports multiple implementations of transport level, called middleware profiles. Current version of IARnet includes three middleware profiles based on CORBA (JacORB [3]), Web services (Apache Axis [4]) and Ice [5], accompanied with corresponding container implementations. Upon deployment of agent container returns a string reference which is used to access the resource from client applications as discussed in the next section.

Client API. An application developer uses IARnet API to access resources via *proxy* objects instantiated by resource references. Each proxy implements a standard interface Resource (Fig. 2) which corresponds to the base interface of resource agent and contains methods for inspection and invocation of resource operations.

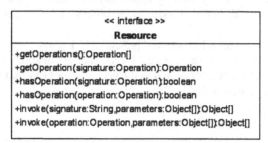

Fig. 2. Resource interface

2.2 Information Service

The Grid applications require ability to dynamically discover resources currently available in Grid and inspect their metadata. This functionality is provided in IARnet by Information Service (IS). While following the basic producer-aggregator-consumer architecture IS differs from widely deployed systems, such as MDS [6] and R-GMA [7], by exploring the use of Semantic Web technologies [8] in Grid along with Semantic Grid projects [9].

IS enables information producers to publish information about resource types and individual resources. The information models of resource type and resource are defined in the core IARnet ontology by means of Web Ontology Language (OWL). The core ontology can be further extended by domain-specific ontologies, e.g. mathematical resources. Standard RDF/XML format is used for information representation and exchange with clients. Information consumers can query IS by means of SPARQL language. There is also a simple interface for common queries, such as searching resources by type. For basic RDF/OWL operations and RDF data storage IS uses Jena RDF toolkit [10].

Among the other components IS includes a high-level Java API for constructing and exploring metadata conforming to the core IARnet ontology, which doesn't require from developer a knowledge of RDF/OWL. Recently developed Web interface allows users to explore metadata published in IS via Web browser.

2.3 Workflow Management Service

The composition and orchestration of Grid services is another hot topic targeted by many experimental projects. The focus on integration of software resources and solving of decomposable problems necessitate the support for workflow composition and execution in IARnet. This functionality is provided by the Workflow Management Service (WfMS).

Among the various workflow representation techniques we have chosen high-level Petri nets [11] as an approach based on a strict mathematical formalism and neutral with respect to middleware technologies in contrast to such languages as WS-BPEL. The use of high-level Petri nets for Grid workflows was first introduced in [12]. IARnet WfMS is built on top of Renew framework [13] which provides graphical Petri Net editor (Renew GUI) and simulator.

The workflow composition is carried out in Renew GUI. A user can annotate net transitions with invocations of IARnet resources and use typed tokens as arguments and return values for resource calls. Composed workflow can be deployed in WfMS as a new IARnet resource ready for remote execution. The workflow deployment and control of workflow execution is also carried out in Renew GUI by means of specially made plug-in. The deployed workflow instance is opened in a new window where user can examine its state during the execution. The user is also supplied with a string reference to the workflow instance which he can use later to reopen the instance window or to send it to the other users. Via the IARnet WfMS plug-in menu user can start, pause and resume the execution of workflow or terminate it.

Since all workflow instances are deployed as resources the other IARnet resources can use standard mechanisms for interaction with the workflow. This is especially useful for the implementation of asynchronous callbacks which are often required by Grid workflows. Each workflow resource has a standard operation which can be used by participating resources to send a callback. The received data is placed as a new token in a specified place in the net and then processed according to defined transitions.

The initial tests of IARnet WfMS showed promising results to be further proved by a real-world application.

3 BNB-Grid: Using IARnet for Solving Large Scale Discrete Optimization Problems

In a most general form the discrete optimization problem is formulated as follows: given a finite set G and a function $f : G \rightarrow R$ find $x^* \in G$ such that $f(x^*) \geq f(x)$ for all $x \in G$ (or $f(x^*) \leq f(x)$ for all $x \in G$). Many discrete optimization problems are NP-hard and their resolution requires significant computational resources. That is why this sort of problems is a traditional subject for parallel and distributed computing. The branch-and-bound method is one of the main approaches to solve discrete optimization problems. The approach is based on a tree-like decomposition of the search space. Since different branches can be processed almost independently the branch-and-bound method perfectly suits for implementing in parallel and distributed computing environments.

The BNB-Grid is a programming infrastructure for solving optimization problems with branch-and-bound method in a distributed computing environment. The distributed computing environment is characterized by the following issues:

1. computing nodes may have different architecture and significantly differ in performance;
2. a computing node may not be available all the time along the search: it may join or leave the system at an arbitrary moment;
3. computing nodes are connected via Internet or Intranet: links may be relatively slow and an access may be secured.

The approaches based on "Grid"-MPIs (MPICH-G2, PACX etc.) are unacceptable because of three reasons. First these versions of MPI do not efficiently cope with issue 2 listed above: there is no a reliable mechanism to handle occasional failure of one of computing nodes. Second MPI is not a best platform for shared-memory systems. Third, setting up a Grid-enabled version of MPI and its integration into a particular batch-system requires administrative privileges. That may not be feasible on a large system running in a production mode (like publicly available supercomputers). The completely distributed approach based on some Grid middle-ware like Condor or Globus Toolkit faces similar difficulties with administrative privileges. Second the comprehensive utilization of computing resources of a given node is difficult: for shared memory machines tools based on threading technologies are better and on HPC clusters the conventional MPI is the best solution.

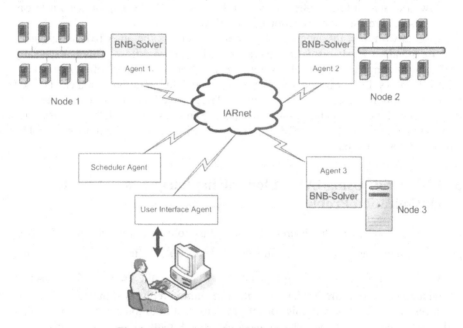

Fig. 3. The structure of the BNB-Grid application

The BNB-Grid approach is as follows. Inside each computing node the solver is implemented according to the best technology appropriate for this node. From the outside the computing node is visible as an IARnet resource (IAR). Different IARs cooperate via IARnet. This structure is depicted at the Fig. 1. A sample distributed system consists of three nodes: nodes 1 and 2 are multiprocessor systems while node 3 is a powerful workstation. Each computing node runs a BNB-Solver [14]: a branch-and-bound solver targeted at uni- and multi-processor systems. The BNB-Solver is represented in a system as an IAR through an agent (agents 1,2,3 in the case under consideration). Besides agents representing computing nodes there are also the scheduler agent and the user interface agent. The former manages work distribution among computing nodes. The latter handles the user input and allows the user to load problem type and data, manage the distributed environment and control the search process.

During the search computing nodes may join or leave the distributed system at arbitrary moments. It may happen because nodes are turned on and off or because of batch system running on HPC cluster introduces delays in starting the BNB-Solver application or terminates it before the computation is completed. To cope with this issue BNB-Grid backs up tasks sent to a computing node agent and if the computing node fails the tasks are rescheduled to other nodes.

Computational experiments were run on a system consisting of a central work-station at Institute for systems analysis of Russian academy of sciences and two HPC clusters: MVS 15000BM and MVS 6000IM located at Joint Supercomputer Center and Computational Center of Russian academy of sciences respectively. Both clusters contain CPU nodes of approximately same performances on the considered kind of problems.

The following knapsack problem instance was selected for experiments: $\sum_{i=1}^{30} 2x_i \rightarrow \max$, $\sum_{i=1}^{30} 2x_i \leq 31$, $x_i \in \{0,1\}, i = 1, 2, ..., 30$. This problem is known as a hard one: the number of vertices in the search tree is 601080389. Three configurations were tried. The average running times obtained from several runs are given in the Table 1.

Table 1. Running times for different configurations

#	Description:	Running time:
1	8 CPU MVS 15000 BM	5.57 minutes
2	8CPU MVS 6000 IM	6.03 minutes
3	8 CPU MVS 15000 BM + 8 CPU MVS 6000 IM	3.15 minutes

The simple stealing-based scheduling policy was used: when one node runs out of work the given number of subproblems is "stolen" from the other node. Experimental results show that even with this simple scheduling policy remarkable speedup could be obtained. However for some problems the speedup is much less than the theoretically estimated. This is the subject for future research to improve the scheduling policy.

7 Conclusions

The presented IARnet toolkit fills the gap between the low-level middleware technologies and the needs of application developers by providing high-level tools for development of distributed scientific applications. These tools allow developers to focus on a problem being solved instead of becoming an expert in middleware and Grid technologies. The distinctive feature of IARnet is a support for easy integration and deployment of software resources.

The availability of multiple transport level implementations allowed us to evaluate different middleware technologies, namely CORBA, Web services and Ice. Our experience indicates that Web services, which are being widely adopted by Grid projects, offer the poorest performance and suffer from immaturity issues. While the Ice technology provides consistent and powerful framework lacking deficiencies of both aged CORBA and immature Web services.

The next version of IARnet will be completely based on Ice to introduce the advanced functionality, such as secure communication, authentication, session management, flexible configuration and administration of a local resource pool. The future work on IARnet will also focus on integration with popular Grid middleware.

References

1. Allen, G., Davis, K., Goodale, T., Hutanu, A., Kaiser, H., Kielmann, T., Merzky, A., Van Nieuwpoort, R., Reinefeld, A., Schintke, F., Schuett, T., Seidel, E., Ullmer, B.: The Grid Application Toolkit: Towards Generic and Easy Application Programming Interfaces for the Grid. Proceedings of the IEEE 93(3), 534–550 (2005)
2. Goodale, T., Jha, S., Kaiser, H., Kielmann, T., Kleijer, P., von Laszewski, G., Lee, C., Merzky, A., Rajic, H., Shalf, J.: SAGA: A Simple API for Grid Applications, High-Level Application Programming on the Grid. Computational Methods in Science and Technology 12(1), 7–20 (2006)
3. JacORB, The free Java implementation of the OMG CORBA (2007) http://www.jacorb.org/
4. Apache Axis, The Apache SOAP Project (2007) http://ws.apache.org/axis/
5. Henning, M.: A New Approach to Object-Oriented Middleware. IEEE Internet Computing 8(1), 66–75 (2004)
6. Czajkowski, K., Fitzgerald, S., Foster, I., Kesselman, C.: Grid Information Services for Distributed Resource Sharing. In: Proceedings of the 10th IEEE International Symposium on High-Performance Distributed Computing (HPDC-10), IEEE Press, New York (2001)
7. Cooke, A., Gray, A., Ma, L., Nutt, W., Magowan, J., Taylor, P., Byrom, R., Field, L., Hicks, S., Leake, J.: R-GMA: An Information Integration System for Grid Monitoring. In: Proceedings of the 11th International Conference on Cooperative Information Systems (2003)
8. Berners-Lee, T., Hendler, J., Lassila, O.: The Semantic Web. Scientific Am. 34–43 (May 2001)
9. De Roure, D., Jennings, N.R., Shadbolt, N.R.: The Semantic Grid: Past, Present, and Future. Proceedings of the IEEE 93(3), 669–681 (2005)
10. Jena – A Semantic Web Framework for Java (2007) http://jena.sourceforge.net/
11. Jensen, K.: An introduction to the theoretical aspects of Coloured Petri Nets. In: de Bakker, J.W., de Roever, W.-P., Rozenberg, G. (eds.) A Decade of Concurrency. LNCS, vol. 803, pp. 230–272. Springer, Heidelberg (1994)
12. Hoheisel, A.: User Tools and Languages for Graph-based Grid Workflows. In: Workflow in Grid Systems (Special Issue of Concurrency and Computation: Practice and Experience), vol. 18(10), Wiley, Chichester (2006)
13. Kummer, O., Wienberg, F., Duvigneau, M., Schumacher, J., Köhler, M., Moldt, D., Rölke, H., Valk, R.: An extensible editor and simulation engine for Petri nets: Renew. In: Cortadella, J., Reisig, W. (eds.) ICATPN 2004. LNCS, vol. 3099, pp. 484–493. Springer, Heidelberg (2004)
14. Posypkin, M., Sigal, I.: Investigation of Algorithms for Parallel Computations in Knapsack-Type Discrete Optimization Problems. Computational Mathematics and Mathematical Physics 45(10), 1735–1743 (2005)

Orthogonal Organized Finite State Machine Application to Sensor Acquired Information

Brian J. d'Auriol, John Kim, Sungyoung Lee, and Young-Koo Lee

Department of Computer Engineering, Kyung Hee University, Korea
dauriol@acm.org, johnkim_korea@yahoo.ca, sylee@oslab.khu.ac.kr,
yklee@khu.ac.kr

Abstract. The application of the Orthogonal Organized Finite State Machine (OOFSM) to the representation of data acquired by sensor networks is proposed. The OOFSM was proposed in earlier work; it is succinctly reviewed here. The approach and representation of the OOFSM to sensor acquired data is formalized. The usefulness of this OOFSM application is illustrated by several case studies, specifically, gradients, contouring and discrete trajectory path determination. In addition, this paper informally discusses the OOFSM as a Cellular Automata.

1 Introduction

Finite State Machines (FSMs) have a long history of theoretical and practical developments. In brief simplicity, an FSM is characterized by a set of states and a set of transitions between these states, often together with definitions of the set of start and terminal states as well as perhaps with other attributes. The majority of FSMs in the literature do not consider the spatial relationships between states. In [1], an orthogonal arrangement of states is considered: this is termed an *Orthogonal Organized Finite State Machine (OOFSM)*. There are several advantages of such an organization including the definition of indexing and selection functions to select regions of interest as well as the state space discretization of continuous complex dynamic systems [1].

The intent of the OOFSM as developed in [1] is to realize a discretized representation of a continuous complex dynamic system. In particular, trajectories in the continuous system are represented by a sequence of labeled transitions between states in the OOFSM, these labels are in fact based on the index (metric) space. The goals of the original work include the understanding of the behavior of the regions that trajectories pass through. In the OOFSM representation, these regions can be identified by the indexing/selection functions. Ultimately, one of the aims is to predict trajectory evolutions towards cascading failure states.

Sensor networks are especially designed for data acquisition. Sensor networks can be wired or wireless, static or mobile, and may have other properties such as autonomic, low-power budgets and small physical size [2]. Sensors may be placed in a physical environment that is modeled by a dynamic system. In such cases, the sensors provide observations of the partial or full state space of the dynamic system.

V. Malyshkin (Ed.): PaCT 2007, LNCS 4671, pp. 111–118, 2007.
© Springer-Verlag Berlin Heidelberg 2007

The earlier work is extended in a new direction in this paper. First, we consider the problem of observable data given an OOFSM representation. In particular, we consider sensor network acquired data and treat these data points as observations. In this work, we generate the acquired data via simulation, although, empirically obtained data could also be used. Our objectives are: a) representing the observable data as a discrete labeled trajectory in an OOFSM, b) describing the discrete regions of interest and/or behavior associated with these discrete trajectories. We do not consider the problem of relating the observable data in the discrete space back to a continuous system in this paper.

This paper is organized as follows. The next section, Section 2, reviews the definition of OOFSM based on [3] and is provided here as the succinct formal definition of the OOFSM abstraction. Section 3 describes the approach and methodology used in this paper. Section 4 describes several applications of the OOFSM applied to sensor acquired data. The relationship with Cellular Automata is discussed in Section 5. Technological aspects are discussed in Section 6. Conclusions are given in Section 7.

2   Review [3]

Orthogonal Organized Finite State Machines (OOFSM) [1] represent a lattice partitioned, and therefore a discretized, state space of a dynamic system. Formally, it is defined by $M = (Y, \mathcal{L}, \overline{V}_Y)$. A lattice partitioning $\mathcal{L}$ applied to an n dimension state space $X = \{x_1, x_2, \ldots, x_n\}, x_i \in \mathbb{R}$ leads to a set of discretized states $\mathcal{L} : X \to Y$ where $Y = \{y_0, y_1, \ldots, y_{o-1}\}$ for some finite o. In general, $\mathcal{L}$ defines a set of partition boundaries $P = \{p_{i_j} | 1 \leq i \leq n, 0 \leq j \leq o - 1\}$ with $p_{i_j} \in \mathbb{R}^{n-1} = (b_l, b_u)_{i_j}, b_u > b_l$. Each p_{i_j} is aligned normal with the corresponding ith state variable; $\iota(b)$ denotes this value. A discrete direction vector field $\overline{v}_j = (\ldots, a_i, \ldots)$ where $a_i = \bigcup_k v_{j_{k_i}}$ is the union of a set of discrete direction vectors $\{v_{j_k} \mid k \geq 1\}$ in state y_j of Y; $a_i \in \{-1, 0, 1\}$. The intersection of a trajectory $e \in E$ with $p_j \in P$ for a fixed j derives v_j; the intersections of all $e \in E$ with $p_j \in P$ derives $\overline{v}_j$ for a fixed j. Lastly, the set $\overline{V}_R = \{\overline{v}_j \mid j \in R\}$ for region R defines a region field; $\overline{V}_Y$ denotes some general region field. A uniform region field has the same region field for each $y_j \in R$. For convenience, elements of Y may be interchangeably expressed in terms of the dimension of the system. Figure 1 illustrates an OOFSM for: $n = 2$, uniform unit $\mathcal{L}$ so that $o = 16$ and $P = \{p_{1_0}, p_{2_0}, p_{1_1}, p_{2_1}, \ldots p_{1_j}, p_{2_j}, \ldots p_{1_{15}}, p_{2_{15}}\}$ such that $p_{1_0} = (b_{l_{1(0,0)}}, b_{u_{1(0,0)}})$ where $\iota(b_{l_{1(0,0)}}) = 0$ and $\iota(b_{u_{1(0,0)}}) = 1$ (i.e., the values on the x_1 axis corresponding with the lower and upper boundaries of the 'vertical' partition pair comprising the 'left' and 'right' sides of state $y_{0,0}$ and so forth with $X = \{x_1, x_2\}$, and $\overline{V}_Y = \overline{V}_{R_1} \cup \overline{V}_{R_2}$ where $\overline{v}_{0,3} = (\{0\}, \{0\})$ defines the uniform region field $\overline{V}_{R_1}$ for $R_1 = \{y_{k,3} | 0 \leq k \leq 3\}$ and $\overline{v}_{0,0} = (\{0\}, \{1\})$ defines the uniform region field $\overline{V}_{R_2}$ for $R_2 = \{y_{k,l} | 0 \leq k \leq 3, 0 \leq l \leq 2\}$ (i.e., there are two uniform region fields with the first being null (terminal states) associated with the 'top row' and the second being 'up-wards only' associated with the remaining states).

3   Approach and Methodology

The initial inputs are obtained from a sensor network. Such a sensor network typically has many spatially distributed sensors that acquire data at specific times. In general, the data has two fundamental properties: *structure* and *value*. Its structure is derived from two possibilities, either the physical placement of the sensors determines physical coordinates (e.g. x,y,z coordinates, GPS coordinates, etc.) or the data itself has some *apriori* defined structure (e.g. vectors, tensors, etc.) Its value refers to the semantics of the actual measurement. Values have ranges (e.g. an interval in $\mathbb{R}$). These properties have been noted elsewhere in the literature, for example, in data visualization [4,5].

Let the set $D^* = \{D_1, D_2, \ldots\}$ denote a collection of temporal organized data values where D_i denotes all the sensor data at some ith time. And, $D = (d_1^s, d_2^s, \ldots, d_{m_1}^s, d_1^v, d_2^v, \ldots, d_{m_2}^v)$ where d_i^s, d_i^v denotes, respectively, structure and value components and each d_i^s, d_j^v such that $1 \leq i, j \leq m_1, m_2$ is in the, respectively, maximal measurement range of the associated sensor's data organization and data value.

If a dynamic system is known, than X and $\overline{V}_Y$ are also given. Given X, then $d_i \mapsto x_j$ for $1 \leq i \leq m$ and $j \in [1..n]$, that is, there are m observable states in an n dimensional state space, $m \leq n$.

For the case where there is no dynamic system or it is unknown, both X and $\overline{V}_Y$ need be determined from the sensor data. Let $\bar{X}$ denote the determined space (the shift of notation provides the semantics that no underlying dynamic system is involved). Consider the two cases:

1. $\bar{X}$ is determined from the data's structure: $d_i^s \mapsto x_i$ for $1 \leq i \leq m_1$, $n = m_1$. Here, the structure states are observable and the state space directly represents the organization of the data. $\mathcal{L}$ reflects the OOFSM structuring imposed on the organization of the sensors. Transitions through this space reflect ordered selections of the value elements. Let some arbitrary bijective function $f(D^*) \mapsto \overline{V}_R$, that is f applied to the sensor acquired data results in a set of state transitions. The choice for f is motivated by seeking *logical* orderings of the sensor data subject to the nearest neighbor connections mandated by the OOFSM.

2. $\bar{X}$ is determined from the data's value: $d_i^v \mapsto x_i$ for $1 \leq i \leq m_2$, $n = m_2$, that is, all states are considered to be observable. $\mathcal{L}$ reflects the discretization over the sensor measurements: in this paper we assume that the discretization results in well-behaved transitions, for example, to ensure nearest-neighbor state changes. In [1], a partial region field was discussed as a model for transitions determined by a finite sub-set of all possible trajectories in the underlying dynamic system. Similar here, we can say that $D \mapsto y_k$ for some kth state and $D^* \mapsto \overline{V}_R$ where the region field is a partial field. The larger D^*, the more state transitions may be defined and the more complete the region field becomes.

Now, Y has been determined. Each state in Y is labeled; a simple practical method is to select b_l from all P in $\mathbb{N}^m$ (e.g. $y_{0,0}, y_{1,0}$, etc. in Figure 1).

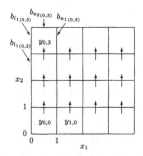

Fig. 1. Illustration of state space definitions, $n = 2$, $o = 16$ and uniform unit partition $\mathcal{L}$

	0	1	2	3	4	5	6	7	8	9	10
5	19.00	19.00	19.00	19.00	19.00	20.00	21.00	22.00	23.00	24.00	
4	18.00	18.00	18.00	18.00	18.00	19.00	20.00	21.00	22.00	23.00	
3	17.00	17.00	17.00	17.00	17.00	18.00	19.00	20.00	21.00	22.00	
2	16.00	16.00	16.00	16.00	16.00	17.00	18.00	19.00	20.00	21.00	
1	15.00	15.00	15.00	15.00	15.00	16.00	17.00	18.00	19.00	20.00	

Fig. 2. Temperature distribution in the corresponding OOFSM

4   Applications to Sensor Acquired Data

This section consists of simulated examples as case studies. The first two case studies are based on a simulation of 50 two-dimensional lattice-arranged temperature sensors constructed with each sensor's location placed such that the location represents the center of the state determined by $\mathcal{L} = \{$boundaries intersecting the axes at ordinal values$\}$. Hence, the data's structure consists of x,y coordinates and its value is a scalar in $\mathbb{R}$ (we ignore the operating ranges of sensors here). The third case study eliminates the structure and instead, considers the state system to be composed of discretized ranges over each sensor's value. This more closely represents the view-point adopted by observable states associated with a dynamic system.

4.1   Gradient

A temperature gradient is considered in this case study. The temperature values are distributed according to simple (linear) assumptions (since we are not interested here in simulation accuracy with thermo-models). Figure 2 shows the raw data temperature distribution in the corresponding OOFSM while Figure 3 shows a typical visualization of the temperature distribution in the OOFSM. These figures are generated by AVS/Express visualization software. Neither the raw data nor the visualization provide sufficient clarity regarding the possible bifurcation in the system; as shown dramatically in Figure 4. In this figure, the uniform vector fields corresponding to the transitions from low-values to high-values are plotted; hence two regions of behavior are identified.

4.2   Contouring

A temperature contour is considered in this case study. The distribution, shown in Figure 5, is somewhat modified from that used earlier (the change better clarifies the results). Figures 6 and 7 show typical visualizations of the data, the first

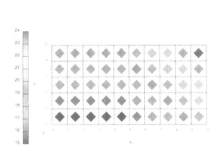

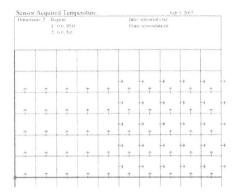

Fig. 3. Temperature visualization

Fig. 4. Uniform vector fields in the OOFSM

uses a standard scatter-to-uniform 2ed-order interpolator to fill-in data values in-between the sensor points, and the second graphs the contours based on the interpolated values. As before, AVS/Express software is used. The corresponding OOFSM in which the contours are represented by state transitions only to neighboring states of the same value is shown in Figure 8. The discontinuity in the trajectory path between states 6,2 and 7,1 containing the data value of 17 occurs due to the non-neighboring transitions, exactly in this case, corner-wise. A refined lattice partitioning would usually take care of this situation. Furthermore, we could allow the corner-wise transition to pass by the corresponding neighboring states (e.g. via state 6,1 or 7,2) Note that there were many such corner-wise transitions in the previous case study.

4.3 Temperature System

Let the lattice partitioning impose a discretization over the ranges of sensor acquired temperatures. Since each sensor uniquely monitors its environment, each sensor provides an independent temperature measurement. For each such measurement, the discretization reflects a single dimension of the overall state space; hence, the number of temperature dimensions equals the number of sensors. Such high dimensional state systems are very common in dynamic systems.

For this discussion, we assume two sensors, hence a two-dimensional state space. Let us choose a partitioning such that each state is unit temperature as illustrated in Figure 9. This figure shows a hypothetical trajectory as might be determined by a sequence of temperature measures over time.

5   Cellular Automata Discussion

There is a close relationship between the OOFSM described in this paper and cellular automata (CA). In [6], four features are identified to characterize a CA: geometry, cell neighborhoods, cell states and local transition rules for cell

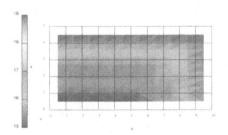

Fig. 5. Temperature distribution in the corresponding OOFSM

Fig. 6. Temperature visualization, standard 2ed-order interpolation from the scatter data

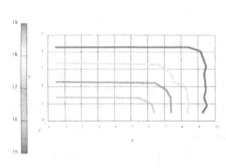

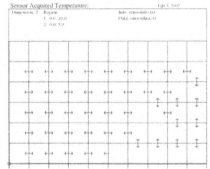

Fig. 7. Temperature visualization showing contouring

Fig. 8. Uniform vector fields in the OOFSM

state changes. The orthogonal structure of the OOFSM, i.e. as given by $\mathcal{L}$, corresponds with an n-dimension CA of the orthogonal neighborhood type. The neighborhood is defined by all the transitions into a given cell state, that is, all the states in the OOFSM with at least one discrete direction vector defining a transition from that cell state to the current cell state. For example, in Figure 1, the neighborhood of $y_{i,j}$ is $y_{i,j-1}$ for $0 \leq i \leq 3, 1 \leq j \leq 3$. Cell states and the local transition rules are contextually defined by the applications. In this paper, the cell states reflect properties of the sensor acquired data. The local transition rule is a cell-centric interpretation of the *factors* that determines the discrete direction vectors defining the neighborhood. This refers to $f(D^*)$ for Case 1 and D^* for Case 2 of Section 3. This completes the informal description of the OOFSM as a CA.

An example for the Gradient application discussed in Section 4.1 is given. Recall, the sensor data is D^* with temperature d_1^v and that f defines transitions from low to high temperature values. Let $t_k = d_1^v$ for the kth cell state (a matter of convenience). Then, the local rule may be defined as $\max_{y_k \in \overline{Y}}(t_k) < t_j$ where $\overline{Y}$ denotes the set of states of the neighborhood. For the particular temperature

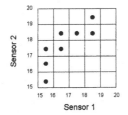

Fig. 9. Two temperature sensor state space, a hypothetical trajectory is shown

values given in Figure 2, a specific local rule could be: select any neighbor and add one to its state. The interpretation of local rule here suggests that the local rule is *representation-driven* and not compute-driven. The state values are already known, but the local rule is not. The process is to infer the local rule from the known parameters.

6 Technological Aspects

Some brief comments about the concurrency inherent in the application of the OOFSM to sensor acquired data are made in this section. A full treatment of the concurrency inherent in the OOFSM, the related CA and associated processes is beyond the scope of this paper.

Consider the computations needed for to determine $\overline{Y}$. For Case 1 of Section 3, without loss of generality, $\overline{Y}$ is computable by considering two states which share a surface. Each such pairing is independent of another (assuming that concurrent updates are handled in concept by appropriate semaphore locks). Hence, there is a high degree of inherent fine-grained parallelism. For example, in the Gradient application, Section 4.1, the pairings are: $(y_{i,j}, y_{i+1,j})$, $(y_{i,j}, y_{i-1,j})$, $(y_{i,j}, y_{i,j+1})$ and $(y_{i,j}, y_{i,j-1})$. For Case 2 of Section 3, $\overline{Y}$ is computable by considering the time sequences in D^*. When D^* is known (as for example when the data is stored at a centralized database), then there is inherent fine-grained parallelism between D_i and D_{i+1}. However, when D^* is available as a real-time stream, then the process itself is inherently sequential due to the streaming. Each $\overline{v}_k$ is local to the state k and may be stored locally in a distributed-memory multicomputer. The issues of partitioning and mapping fine-grained parallelism onto multicomputers have been well investigated (see for example [7]); past experience suggests that further performance analysis is needed.

7 Conclusion

The Orthogonal Organized Finite State Machine (OOFSM)was proposed in earlier work as a mathematical model that supported representation and visualization of dynamic systems. In this paper, its use is broadened by considering the OOFSM representation of data acquired by sensors. The usefulness of this

OOFSM application is illustrated by several case studies. Specifically, gradients, contouring and discrete trajectory path determination were studied. In addition, this paper informally discusses the OOFSM as a Cellular Automata.

This paper concentrated on the ideas behind these novel application areas of the OOFSM. Clearly, enhanced simulations and experimental results are needed to provide realistic data sets which in turn would be used in realistic evaluations of our approach. This constitutes the bulk of our intended future work.

Acknowledgements

This research was supported by the MIC (Ministry of Information and Communication), Korea, under the ITFSIP (IT Foreign Specialist Inviting Program) supervised by the IITA (Institute of Information Technology Advancement).

References

1. d'Auriol, B.J.: A finite state machine model to support the visualization of cmplex dynamic systems. In: Proceedings of The, International Conference on Modeling, Simulation and Visualization Methods (MSV'06), pp. 304–310. CSREA Press, Las Vegas (2006)
2. Chong, C.-Y., Kumar, S.P.: Sensor networks: Evolution, opportunities, and challenges 9(8), 1247–1256 (2003)
3. d'Auriol, B.J., Carswell, P., Gecsi, K.: A transdimension visualization model for complex dynamic system visualizations. In: Proceedings of The 2006 International Conference on Modeling, Simulation and Visualization Methods (MSV'06), pp. 318–324. CSREA Press, Las Vegas (2006)
4. Brodlie, K., Carpenter, L.A., Earnshaw, R.A., Gallop, R., Hubbolt, R., Mumford, A.M., Osland, C.D., Quarendon, P. (eds.): Scientific Visualization: Techniques and Applications. Springer, Heidelberg (1992)
5. Ware, C.: Information Visualization Perception for Design, 2nd edn. Morgan Kaufmann, San Francisco (2004)
6. Sarkar, P.: A brief history of cellular automata. ACM Computing Surveys 32(1), 80–107 (2000)
7. d'Auriol, B.J., Bhavsar, V.C.: Generic program concurrent modules for systolic computations. In: Arabnia, H. (ed.) Proc. of the 1999 International Conference on Parallel and Distributed Processing Techniques and Applications (PDPTA'99), pp. 2012–2018. Las Vegas, Nevada, USA (1999)

Parallel Broadband Finite Element Time Domain Algorithm Implemented to Dispersive Electromagnetic Problem*

Boguslaw Butrylo

Bialystok Technical University,
Wiejska 45D, 15-351 Bialystok, Poland
bogb@pb.edu.pl

Abstract. The numerical analysis of some broadband electromagnetic fields and frequency-dependent materials using a time domain method is the main subject of this paper. The spatial and time-dependent distribution of the electromagnetic field is approximated by the finite element method. The parallel form of the algorithm valid for some linear materials, and the formulation of the FE code for a dispersive electromagnetic problem are presented and compared. The complex forms of these algorithms have an effect on the memory and computational costs of the distributed formulation. The properties of the algorithm are estimated using high performance cluster of workstations.

1 Introduction

Investigation of time-variable electromagnetic fields using high performance computer systems is a useful tool for computer aided analysis and designing of broad spectrum of electromagnetic systems (e.g. some microwave circuits, wireless communication networks, medical equipments) [1,2,3,4]. A typical problem in computational electromagnetic (CEM) includes analysis of some broadband electromagnetic waveforms and their interaction with some solid structures.

Ideally any CEM algorithm should model time-dependent electromagnetic phenomena accurately and efficiently. The analysis of the propagated nonharmonic electromagnetic waves is possible owing to direct integration of partial differential equations in time domain. In general case, the size of the model relative to the wavelength of the electromagnetic wave, as well as the implemented schemes of numerical integration lead to a definition of a hard computational problem. The CEM algorithm for broadband problems should also have enough flexibility to represent complex properties of any material structure (including geometry and material properties). Unfortunately these expectations tend to be mutually exclusive. Depending on the aim of the analysis a compromise must be find.

---

* The work has been performed under the Project HPC-EUROPA (RII3-CT-2003-506079), with the support of the European Community - Research Infrastructure Action under the FP6 *Structuring the European Research Area* Programme.

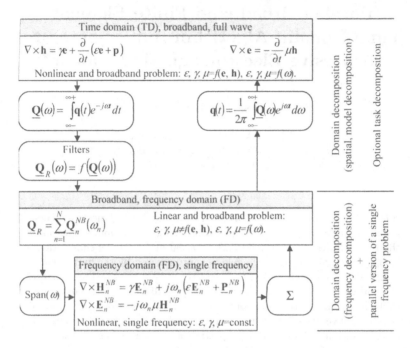

Fig. 1. Dependency of the formulations of a CEM problem, including problem formulation and form of the parallel algorithm. The $\mathbf{q}$ indicates the field quantity $\mathbf{q} \in \{\mathbf{e}, \mathbf{h}, \mathbf{p}\}$.

The CEM methods have evolved to more accurate and real-time algorithms based on either frequency-domain (FD) or time-domain (TD) formulation of the problem (Fig. 1). The direct integration of the Maxwell's equations in time domain is more suitable for complex analysis than any frequency domain formulation. The numerical complexity of the algorithm increases, but the formulation of time-domain algorithm is suitable for parallel analysis of electromagnetic problems in either shared or distributed memory computer system [1,4,5]. Both the domain decomposition and task decomposition can be implemented in a parallel version of the CEM-TD algorithm.

According to the Fourier's theory, the time domain representation of any complex electromagnetic waveform is equivalent to the related frequency domain form. Analysis of the broadband EM phenomena forces definition of a multiplicative frequency domain algorithm [5]. In this way, any full wave electromagnetic problem must be reduced to a set of single-frequency problems. Unfortunately, direct implementation of this scheme in numerical analysis of a large-scale EM problem is not efficient. The size of the analyzed electromagnetic problem, and infinite spectrum of some real signals are the main constraints. The split-step frequency domain approach provides a powerful tool for analysis of some linear electromagnetic problems with a simple, reduced spectrum of the waveform, and significantly reduced model of dispersity. The real spectrum of dispersive material is sampled in frequency domain. The parallel implementation of the single-frequency CEM algorithm can be developed with domain decomposition and/or task decomposition paradigm [1,6].

The objective of this paper is a finite element time domain (FE-TD) method in a parallel version. The effect of medium dispersion is incorporated in the presented algorithm. Two forms of the parallel finite element-time domain algorithm for linear and dispersive materials are presented and discussed. The efficiency of these algorithms is analyzed. The memory cost and performance of the FE-TD formulations for dispersive materials are presented. The properties of the algorithm are validated using a cluster of workstations system.

2   Problem Formulation

The common form of the wave equation is derived from the time-dependent Maxwell's equations [7]. It describes the physical state of the analyzed system, assuming linear and dispersionless properties of material structures

$$\nabla \times \frac{1}{\mu} \nabla \times \mathbf{E} + \gamma \frac{\partial \mathbf{E}}{\partial t} + \mathbf{f}(t) + \epsilon \frac{\partial^2 \mathbf{E}}{\partial t^2} = 0, \tag{1}$$

where $\mathbf{f}(t)$ denotes imposed currents, γ, ϵ, μ represent electrical conductivity, permittivity and permeability of the medium respectively. The distribution of the field is expressed by the vector of electric field intensity $\mathbf{e} = \mathbf{e}(x, y, z, t) = E_x \cdot \mathbf{1}_x + E_y \cdot \mathbf{1}_y + E_z \cdot \mathbf{1}_z$, defined in the four dimensional continuum. This form of the constitutive equation is valid for a narrow-band analysis of the electromagnetic filed or a problem where, the properties of the media do not depend on the frequency of the electromagnetic wave (Fig. 1).

Some widely implemented material structures have dispersive properties (e.g. non-ideal dielectrics, composites, fiber-wires, biological tissues). An induced high frequency polarization of molecules and particles changes the resultant spatial distribution of electric flux density in this system, $\mathbf{D}(\omega) = \epsilon_0 \epsilon_\infty \mathbf{E}(\omega) + \epsilon_0 \chi(\omega) \mathbf{E}(\omega)$, where ϵ_0 is permittivity of free space, ϵ_∞ is the infinite frequency relative permittivity, and $\chi(t)$ is the electric susceptibility. Therefore, the time-dependent distribution of electric field in the broadband formulation, assuming dispersity of some materials, is stated by equation

$$\nabla \times \frac{1}{\mu} \nabla \times \mathbf{E} + \gamma \frac{\partial \mathbf{E}}{\partial t} + \epsilon_0 \epsilon_\infty \frac{\partial^2 \mathbf{E}}{\partial t^2} + \epsilon_0 \frac{\partial^2}{\partial t^2} \left(\int_0^t \chi(t - \tau) \mathbf{E}(t) \, d\tau \right) = 0, \tag{2}$$

where $\chi(t) = \mathcal{F}^{-1}\{\chi(\omega)\}$ is a time domain form of frequency dependent susceptibility. In this formulation, the dispersity of the model is described by the empirical, multipole resonance Lorentz model of susceptibility [7,8,9]

$$\chi(t) = \mathcal{F}^{-1} \left\{ \sum_{p=1}^{P} \frac{\Delta \epsilon_p \omega_{a,p}^2}{\omega_{o,p}^2 + j\omega\nu_p - \omega^2} \right\} = \sum_{p=1}^{P} \frac{\Delta \epsilon_p \omega_{a,p}^2}{\omega_{d,p}^2} e^{\frac{-t\nu_p}{2}} \sin(\omega_{d,p} t) \cdot u(t), \tag{3}$$

where P is the order of the model, $\Delta \epsilon_p$ is a decrement of permittivity for p-th pole, $\omega_{a,p}$ - plasma frequency, $\omega_{o,p}$ - resonant frequency, ν_p - damping frequency, $\omega_{d,p} = \sqrt{\omega_{o,p}^2 - 0,25\nu_p^2}$, and $u(t)$ is the unitary step function.

The equation (2), after implementation of Galerkin method, is solved with the finite element (FE) algorithm. The geometry of the model is discretized using the first order tetrahedral, edge elements [1]. In this formulation of the FE method, the distribution of electric field is approximated by circulation of electric field along any edge of the model. Therefore, the total number of degrees of freedom (N_{DOF}) is equal to number of edges in the model (N_E).

The convolution of susceptibility and time-dependent distribution of electric field in the model is approximated by the PLRC (Piecewise Linear Recursive Convolution) method [8,9]. The second order derivative of the convolution is calculated using unconditionally stable Euler-backward scheme. The approximated form of the wave equation (1) or (2) is integrated in time domain using the unconditionally stable, second order accurate Newmark-beta method [4,9]. Therefore the final form of matrix equation is given by

$$
\mathbf{A} \cdot \mathbf{E}_{n+1} = \left(2 \sum_{m=1}^{M} \mathbf{T}_{\infty,m} - \frac{\Delta t^2}{2} \mathbf{S} \right) \cdot \mathbf{E}_n -
$$

$$
- \left(\sum_{m=1}^{M} \mathbf{T}_{\infty,m} - \frac{\Delta t}{2} \mathbf{R} - \frac{\Delta t^2}{2} \mathbf{S} \right) \cdot \mathbf{E}_{n-1} +
$$

$$
+ \sum_{m=1}^{M} \sum_{p=1}^{P} \left(2 - e^{-\varphi \Delta t} \right) \cdot \mathbf{T}_{0,m} \mathbf{C}_{p,n} - \mathbf{T}_{0,m} \mathbf{C}_{p,n-1}, \tag{4}
$$

where the $\mathbf{A}$ matrix is a linear combination of $\mathbf{T}_{\infty,m}$, $\mathbf{R}_\sigma$, and $\mathbf{S}$ matrices

$$
\mathbf{A} = \sum_{m=1}^{M} \int_V \epsilon_{\infty,m} \mathbf{U}_i \mathbf{U}_j dV + \frac{\Delta t}{2} \int_V \sigma \mathbf{U}_i \mathbf{U}_j dV +
$$

$$
+ \frac{\Delta t^2}{4} \int_V \frac{1}{\mu} \left(\nabla \times \mathbf{U}_i \right) \left(\nabla \times \mathbf{U}_j \right) dV. \tag{5}
$$

Dispersity of any material in the model changes the form of the matrix equation. A supplementary matrix associated with dispersity of the model is added in the PLRC form

$$
\mathbf{A}_d = \mathbf{A} + \sum_{m=1}^{M} \sum_{p=1}^{P_m} \mathbf{T}_{0,m} \frac{\Delta \epsilon_p \omega_{a,p}^2}{\Delta t \kappa_p^2 \omega_{d,p}} \left(\Delta t \kappa_p - 1 + e^{-\kappa_p \Delta t} \right). \tag{6}
$$

These additional components change the form of the resultant matrix. Simultaneously, the stability and convergence of the algorithm can drastically degrade. The temporary value of convolution is expressed by equation

$$
\mathbf{c}_{p,n+1} = e^{-\kappa_p \Delta t} \mathbf{c}_{p,n} + \sum_{p=1}^{P} \mathbf{E}_{n+1} \frac{\Delta \epsilon_p \omega_{a,p}^2}{\Delta t \kappa_p^2 \omega_{d,p}} \left(\Delta t \kappa_p - 1 + e^{-\kappa_p \Delta t} \right) +
$$

$$
+ \sum_{p=1}^{P} \mathbf{E}_n \frac{\Delta \epsilon_p \omega_{a,p}^2}{\Delta t \kappa_p^2 \omega_{d,p}} \left(1 - \Delta t \kappa_p e^{-\kappa_p \Delta t} - e^{-\kappa_p \Delta t} \right). \tag{7}
$$

3   Distributed Formulation of the Problem

Concerning parallelization of the time-domain algorithm, a common 1D domain decomposition paradigm is used. The set of edges in the FEM model is decomposed into non-overlapping sub-domains. Depending on degrees of freedom in the FE model and implemented model of dispersion, the algorithm can be flexible matched to a multi-computer platform [1,4].

The distributed FETD algorithm is elaborated by *explicit* parallelization of the sequential code. The own, parallel implementation of preconditioned conjugate gradient (PCG) algorithm is used to solve the matrix equation (4) [10]. Since the resultant matrices $\mathbf{A}$, $\mathbf{R}$, $\mathbf{S}$, $\mathbf{T}_{\infty,n}$, and $\mathbf{T}_{0,n}$ are sparse, they full representation in the computer memory are squeezed with the CRS (Compressed Row Storage) algorithm. However, these matrices remain the largest data structures in the algorithm, and they are homogeneously decomposed between processing units PE. The size of common matrices $\mathbf{A}$, $\mathbf{T}$, $\mathbf{R}$, $\mathbf{S}$ for the linear problem, as well as $\mathbf{T}_{\infty,n}$, $\mathbf{T}_{0,n}$ in dispersive formulation, makes data transfers between computing units non-efficient or even impossible. These data structures are included into the critical section of the algorithm (Fig. 2). The critical section of the common FE-TD algorithm gathers the operations with some distributed parts of matrices. The spatial decomposition of the matrices on either distributed or shared memory environment is the general constraint of the presented algorithm. The critical section of the algorithm consists of tasks, where one of the operands is a part of local sub-matrix.

The implemented model of electromagnetic dispersion shapes the final form of the distributed FE-TD algorithm. Dispersity of materials and broadband analysis of EM field yield the complex formulation of the FE-TD algorithm (Fig. 3). The broadband formulation of the electromagnetic phenomena requires to solve the large scale matrix equation and step-by-step calculation of convolution between time-dependent distribution of electric field and the complex-form time dependent susceptibility (2). Two coupled sets of unknowns are defined. The first one, typical for a common, linear version of the algorithm (1), consists of three vectors of electromagnetic field in the successive time steps $\{\mathbf{E}_{n-2}, \mathbf{E}_{n-1}, \mathbf{E}_n\}$, $dim\,(\mathbf{E}_n) = N_{DOF}$. The time variable vectors of convolutions form the set of extraordinary variables, $\{\mathbf{C}_{1,n-1}, \mathbf{C}_{1,n}, \cdots, \mathbf{C}_{p,n-1}, \mathbf{C}_{p,n}, \cdots, \mathbf{C}_{P,n-1}, \mathbf{C}_{P,n}\}$, $dim\,(\mathbf{C}_{p,n}) = N_{DOF}$. The vectors of calculated electromagnetic field, as well as the vectors of convolution $\{\mathbf{C}_{1,n}, \cdots, \mathbf{C}_{p,n-1}\}$ are duplicated in the computing nodes. As some consequences, the computational cost of the algorithm drastically increases. If the number of the matrix-vector multiplications in the linear problem is stated by equation $N^l_{M\times v} = 3 + N_{PCG}$ the FE dispersive problem requires $N^{nl}_{M\times v} = 3 + N_{PCG} + \sum_{m=1}^{M} P_m$ multiplications in each time step. The M denotes number of dispersive materials, and P_m - the order of dispersity for the m-th material. The N_{PCG} means the number of iterations in the implemented iterative matrix solver (e.g. preconditioned conjugate gradient algorithm).

Finally, the structure of the distributed algorithm must be changed, since some new bottlenecks are determined, and calculation of coupled unknowns $\{\mathbf{E}_{n-2}, \mathbf{E}_{n-1}, \mathbf{E}_n\}$ and $\{\mathbf{C}_{1,n-1}, \cdots, \mathbf{C}_{P,n}\}$ must be interlaced. The distributed

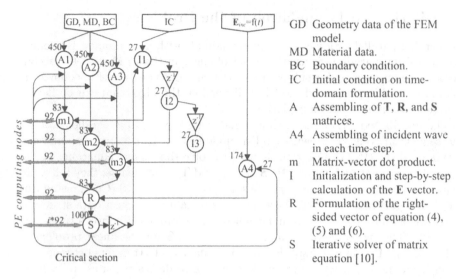

Fig. 2. Graph of the finite element time domain algorithm for a linear narrow-band EM problem. Weight coefficients of threads (*nodes on the graph*) and relations between threads (*thin arrows*) are estimated for a medium sized FEM model $N_{DOF} = 337620$. Wide, gray, horizontal arrows indicate data transfers between processing units.

In the figure legend:

GD Geometry data of the FEM model.
MD Material data.
BC Boundary condition.
IC Initial condition on time-domain formulation.
A   Assembling of **T**, **R**, and **S** matrices.
A4 Assembling of incident wave in each time-step.
m   Matrix-vector dot product.
I   Initialization and step-by-step calculation of the **E** vector.
R   Formulation of the right-sided vector of equation (4), (5) and (6).
S   Iterative solver of matrix equation [10].

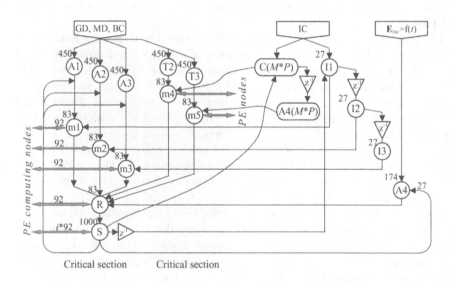

Fig. 3. Graph of the FE-TD algorithm for a dispersive, broadband EM problem. The C denotes initialization and step-by-step calculation of the $(M \cdot P_m)$ convolution vectors, and $A4$ is the assembling task for the dispersive components of the **A** matrix.

version of the algorithm must bring together memory cost and distributed structure of data structures of the extended formulation and the computational cost of some extraordinary subroutines.

4   Numerical Performance

The algorithms mentioned above are tested using NEC Xeon EM64T Cluster with $N_{PE} = 64$ computing nodes connected by the Infiniband network. The distributed processing is supported by the MPI 2.0 standard. The final form of the code is tuned and optimized with the aim to get the best performances on this platform.

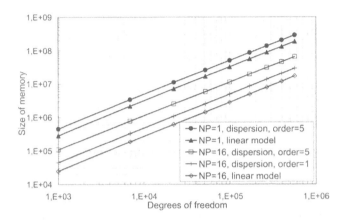

Fig. 4. Comparison of the memory cost for linear and dispersive algorithms

The total memory cost depends on the number of computing units in the cluster, and assumed dispersity of the model (Fig. 4). The number of computing units N_{PE} can be matched to the size of the model, but some extraordinary data structures enlarge the memory cost of the distributed algorithm. The dispersive form of the EM problem introduces some new data structures, therefore its relative scalability is quite worse than the linear formulation. Increasing the number of dispersive materials and the order of dispersity in the analyzed CEM problem either the size of the FE model must be reduced or the number of computing units in the COW should be enlarging.

Some improvements of computing time are found when the number of computing units is less then 48 (Fig. 5). If $N_{PE} > 48$, the speedup of the algorithm degrades, since communication cost of the distributed solver exceeds profits of parallel processing. The speedup of the elaborated algorithms depends on the bandwidth of communication network in the multi-computer, memory distributed system. Therefore, the calculated speedups increase linearly with respect to number of processing units for some small and medium size COW systems. The speedup curves are saturated, when the communication network could not cope with some indispensable data transfers.

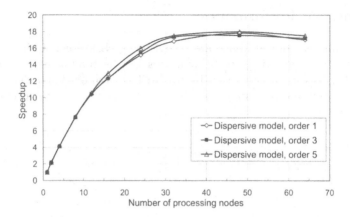

Fig. 5. Speedup of the FE algorithm as a function of the order of dispersity

5 Conclusions

Implementation of dispersive materials has an effect on memory cost and overall performance of the distributed analysis. The number of interlaced and coupled distributed tasks in the dispersive EM problem is larger than in the linear one. The throughput of the network and the latency of the communication constitute the limits of efficiency of the presented algorithms. The interdependences between decomposed data structures demand the simultaneous, step-by-step processing of the electromagnetic field and the convolution vectors. It should be stressed that, the distributed subtasks in the presented time domain linear and dispersive algorithms are tightly coupled. Therefore, the implemented model of communication is constrained by the mathematical formulation of the EM problem. The consistency of numerical solution of electromagnetic phenomena requires implementing some blocking communication commands, including the point-to-point communication and broadcast commands. An alternative pattern of communication with non-blocking commands has to be implemented with some predefined barrier points in the algorithm. The locations of these synchronization points are extorted by the causality of the leapfrog form of the time domain algorithm (i.e. $\mathbf{E}_0 \rightharpoonup \mathbf{C}_0 \rightharpoonup \mathbf{E}_1 \rightharpoonup \mathbf{C}_1 \rightharpoonup \cdots$). They do not depend on the properties of implemented distributed-memory platform.

Therefore, the dispersity of the EM model enlarges the memory as well as computational cost of the FE-TD algorithm. The presented formulation of the finite element time domain method for dispersive materials results in an I/O bound algorithm.

References

1. Vollaire, C., Nicolas, L., Nicolas, A.: Parallel computing for the finite element method. The European Physical Journal Applied Physics 1, 305–314 (1998)
2. Buyya, R.: High Performance Cluster Computing, vol. 2. Prentice Hall PTR, New Jersey (1999)

3. Christopoulos, Ch.: Multi-scale modeling in time-domain electromagnetics. International Journal of Electronics and Communications 57(2), 100–110 (2003)
4. Butrylo, B., Musy, F., Nicolas, L., Parrussel, R., Scorretti, R., Vollaire, C.: A survey of parallel solvers for the finite element method in computational electromagnetics. Compel 23(2), 531–546 (2004)
5. Navsariwala, U., Gedney, S.: An Efficient Implementation of the Finite-Element Time Domain Algorithm on Parallel Computers Using a Finite-Element Tearing and Interconnecting Algorithm. Microwave and Optical Technology Letters 16(4) (1997)
6. Vollaire, C., Nicolas, L., Nicolas, A.: Finite Element and Absorbing Boundary Conditions for scattering problems on a parallel distributed memory computer. IEEE Transactions on Magnetics 33(2), 1448–1451 (1997)
7. Monk, R.: Finite Element Methods for Maxwell's Equations. Oxford University Press, Oxford (2003)
8. Edelvik, F., Strand, B.: Frequency dispersive materials for 3-D hybrid solvers in time domain. IEEE Transactions on Antennas and Propagation 51(6), 1199–1205 (2003)
9. Maradei, F.: A frequency-dependent WETD formulation for dispersive materials. IEEE Transactions on Magnetics 37(5), 3303–3306 (2001)
10. Butrylo, B., Nicolas, A., Nicolas, L., Vollaire, C.: Performance of Preconditioners for the Distributed Vector Finite Element Time Domain Algorithm. IEEE Transactions on Magnetics 41(5), 1716–1719 (2005)

Strategies for Development of a Parallel Program for Protoplanetary Disc Simulation*

Sergei Kireev[1], Elvira Kuksheva[2], Aleksey Snytnikov[1],
Nikolay Snytnikov[1], and Vitaly Vshivkov[1]

[1] ICMMG SB RAS, Novosibirsk, Russia
kireev@ssd.sscc.ru
[2] BIC SB RAS, Novosibirsk, Russia

Abstract. Protoplanetary disc simulation must be done first, with high precision, and second, with high speed. Some strategies to reach these goals are presented in the paper. They include: the reduction of the 3D protoplanetary disc model to quasi-3D, the use of fundamental Poisson equation solution, the simulation in the natural (cylindrical) coordinate system and computation domain decomposition. The domain decomposition strategy is shown to reach the simulation goals the best.

1 Introduction

The origin and evolution of protoplanetary discs have been widely studied in recent time (for a review see e.g. [1]). The problem of organic matter genesis in the Solar System is a matter of special interest. In [2] the protoplanetary disc is considered as a catalytic chemical reactor for the synthesis of primary organic compounds.

N-body interaction in self-consistent gravitational field is one of the most important problems in the study of physical processes in protoplanetary discs [6]. The mathematical model of the interaction consists of the two equations: Vlasov-Liouville collisionless kinetic equation and Poisson equation. Numerical solution of Vlasov-Liouville equation is carried out by the Particle-in-Cell (PIC) method [4,5].

The bottleneck of the numerical experiments is the solution of 3D Poisson equation at each timestep. Moreover, it is necessary to trace the individual movement of a large number of particles [7]. Finally, the 3D grid arrays of density, potential and gravitational forces must be stored in the RAM.

The spatial resolution (that is, the computation grid size) must be high enough to study the nonlinear processes such as formation of clumps [6]. The clumps are thought to be probable planet embryos and their size is much lower than

* The present work was supported by Subprogram 18-2 of RAS Presidium Program "Biosphere origin and evolution", Subprogram $\varPi$-04 of RAS Presidium Program "Stars and galaxies origin and evolution", RFBR (grant 05-01-00665), SB RAS Program on Supercomputers, Grant of Rosobrazovanie, contracts PH$\varPi$.2.2.1.1.3653 and PH$\varPi$.2.2.1.1.1969.

the computation domain size. Thus the formation of clumps would be simulated incorrectly with low spatial resolution (on a coarse grid).

The above listed difficulties were partially removed by reducing the 3D model of the disc to a quasi-3D one [8,9,10]. In the quasi-3D model the matter has no vertical velocity, but the gravitational field distribution must still be considered three-dimensional, that is why the model is called quasi-3D, not just 2D.

The quasi-3D model is probably valid in the case of the protoplanetary disc, its thickness being by one order of magnitude less than its radius. Another stipulation for the quasi-3D model of the disc is the presence of a large body in the centre of the disc [12]. Thus the quasi-3D model is suitable to study the later stages of the protoplanetary disc evolution. On the other hand, there are problems that cannot be solved with the quasi-3D model. For example the reconstruction of the observable spectral emission diagram (SED) of the protoplanetary disc [3] can be done only by means of the full 3D simulation.

On the basis of the PIC method we have designed a number of numerical implementations of mathematical model of protoplanetary disc that differ by the Poisson equation solver [7,8,12,11]. It is necessary due to the following two reasons:

- the problem lacks an analytical solution in a wide range of initial parameters and the comparison of numerical experiments with different programs could be used for the verification of the numerical solution,
- the designed parallel algorithms may work differently with various parameters of the numerical experiment such as the number of particles and the number of grid nodes.

In the present paper we consider various strategies of parallel implementation of the protoplanetary disc model depending on the features of the model. In section 2 the considered protoplanetary disc model is presented and its numerical implementation is briefly discussed. Then in section 3 the goals of parallel implementation of the protoplanetary disc model are listed (section 3.2) and the general method for reaching these goals is proposed (section 3.3). In further sections the different strategies for implementation of the protoplanetary disc model are presented.

All the numerical experiments were conducted with the supercomputer MVS-1000M based on Alpha21264 processor in both Siberian Supercomputer Center (Novosibirsk) and Joint Supercomputer Centre (Moscow). MPI library is used to perform the interprocessor communications.

2   Protoplanetary Disc Model

2.1   Basic Equations

The dynamics of the dust component of a protoplanetary disc is described by Vlasov-Liouville kinetic equation. The gravitational field is determined by Poisson equation. These equations have the following form:

$$\begin{cases} \dfrac{\partial f}{\partial t} + v\nabla f + a\dfrac{\partial f}{\partial v} = 0 \\[2ex] \Delta\Phi = 4\pi G\rho, \end{cases} \tag{1}$$

where $f(t, r, v)$ is the time-dependent one-particle distribution function along coordinates and velocities, $a = -\nabla\Phi$ is the acceleration of unit mass particle. G is the gravitational constant, Φ is the gravitational potential. Here we employ the collisionless approximation of the mean self-consistent field. The detailed description of the model could be found in [7,8,9,10].

The full-scale model of the protoplanetary disc also includes gas dynamics, radiation, chemical reactions, coagulation of dust particles etc. But the present paper is focussed on the two presented equations since their solution is the bottleneck for parallel implementation.

2.2   Numerical Implementation of the Model

Protoplanetary disc simulation involves solution of the complex system of equations: Vlasov-Liouville kinetic equation and Poisson equation. Vlasov-Liouville equation is widely [4] solved by the Particle-in-Cell method [5].

There are a lot of Poisson equation solvers (they can be found in [14]). However for our model we have special requirements and restrictions. First of all, we need to solve 3D dimensional Poisson equation on very fine grids. The fastest techniques based on circular reduction (e.g. FACR, DCR) could not be used on fine grids due to intrinsic numerical instability. Second, numerical method must be easily parallelized. And finally, Poisson equation must be solved at every timestep of the computational experiment. Thus the iterative methods are worth using since they can capitalize on the potential from the previous timestep into account.

The parallel programs that we have designed differ by the Poisson equation solver in the first place. The following methods were employed:

- 3D Fast Fourier Transform (in the program with domain decomposition),
- Fast Fourier Transform with Successive Over-Relaxation (3D program in cylindrical coordinates and quasi-3D program)
- and the solver based on the fundamental solution of Poisson equation.

In sequential program FFT is the fastest if the Poisson equation is solved once, FFT with SOR is faster than mere FFT when there is a number of timesteps in a sequence. Solver based on the fundamental solution is the slowest from the three but it is parallelized the best.

3   Parallel Implementation of the Protoplanetary Disc Model

3.1   Necessity of Parallelization

The computational resources required for the solution of the present problem could be estimated, for example, in the following way.

The most interesting area in the simulation of the Solar System genesis is situated inside the Mars orbit, its radius being 40 times smaller than the full radius of the system (the radius of Pluto orbit). If 10 grid nodes are set at the length of Mars orbit, which is at least necessary, then the total grid size is 400 nodes along radial direction in the cylindrical coordinate system. In such a way we get an estimate of 400^3 nodes for the 3D grid.

For the noise level to be less than 10% it is necessary to have more than 100 particles for a grid cell. Thus we get 6.4 billion particles, which is about 300 Gb RAM (3 coordinates and 3 velocities for each particle in double precision).

Modern workstations are capable of numerical experiments with the maximal number of grid nodes 128^3 and the number of particles not more than 10 million. And even this requires from two up to seven days [12].

Thus the parallel implementation of the mathematical model (1) is absolutely necessary for simulation of the protoplanetary disc.

3.2 Goals of Parallelization

Goals for parallel implementation of the mathematical model of the protoplanetary disc are the following:

- Conduct the numerical experiments with both the number of grid nodes and number of particles high enough to provide the desired precision of the computation. Computational experiments of such a large size are usually impossible for single processor workstations.
- Conduct a set numerical experiments (possibly including dozens of experiments with different initial parameters) at a reasonable time. From our point of view, this reasonable time for a set of numerical experiments aimed at validation of a hypothesis should not exceed one month.

In such a way high values of speedup are not relevant for a parallel program implementing the mathematical model of a protoplanetary disc. Moreover, the concept of speedup itself should be refined. If it is considered as a sign of quality of the parallel implementation of a mathematical model, it should be corrected. The speedup is usually defined as a ratio of the computation time on a single processor to the computation time on a multiprocessor system. But the problem is that the single processor computations might be of no interest for a physicist.

The main requirement to the parallel program implementing the model of the protoplanetary disc is the ability to distribute the computation uniformly between the maximal number of processors. It is necessary to achieve the high precision of computation by means of using large amounts of RAM, and to achieve the high speed of computation by means of using a large number of processors. To provide the ability to distribute the computation it is necessary to have:

- uniform workload of processors
- minimal amount of interprocessor communications.

3.3   Strategies of Parallelization

It should be taken into account that different parallel implementations may result in different computation times depending on the parameters of the numerical methods. That is why we consider various parallelization strategies.

Special numerical methods should be selected for the parallel implementation of a mathematical model. That is, the methods that could be naturally divided into an arbitrary number of equal independent parts. It is one of the key ideas of the assembly technology for parallel program synthesis [15]. This requirement is satisfied by the PIC method for Vlasov-Liouville equation and Fourier Transform method for Poisson equation.

The Discrete Fourier Transform reduces the 3D Poisson equation: (in cylindrical coordinate system)

$$\frac{1}{r}\frac{\partial}{\partial r}\left(r\frac{\partial \Phi}{\partial r}\right) + \frac{1}{r^2}\frac{\partial^2 \Phi}{\partial \varphi^2} + \frac{\partial^2 \Phi}{\partial z^2} = 4\pi G\rho \tag{2}$$

to a set of independent 2D equations of potential harmonics (here denoted as $H_k(r, z)$):

$$\frac{1}{r}\frac{\partial}{\partial r}\left(r\frac{\partial H}{\partial r}\right) + \frac{1}{r^2}\sin\frac{\pi k}{N_\varphi}H + \frac{\partial^2 H}{\partial z^2} = 4\pi GR,$$

$$k = 0, ..., N_\varphi - 1$$

$$H_k(r, z) = \sum_{k=0}^{k=N_\varphi-1} \Phi(r, \varphi, z)\cos\frac{\pi k\varphi}{N_\varphi} \qquad R_k(r, z) = \sum_{k=0}^{k=N_\varphi-1} \rho(r, \varphi, z)\cos\frac{\pi k\varphi}{N_\varphi} \tag{3}$$

So it was quite natural to use this feature to parallelize the solution of Poisson equation by assigning groups of harmonics to processors.

The PIC method [5] reduces the solution of Vlasov-Liouville kinetic equation to the solution of movement equations for separate particles. Since the computation of coordinates and velocities of a particle does not depend on other particles, then the PIC method is the natural method for the parallel solution of Vlasov-Liouville equation.

In such a way the possibility of parallelization must be present in the very structure of the employed mathematical methods, as it is seen in formulae 3.

4   Parallel Program for Quasi-3D Disc Model

A parallel implementation of the 3D disc model would require interprocessor communications involving 3D arrays. The easiest way to implement a parallel model of the protoplanetary disc is to reduce the 3D model to quasi-3D. In quasi-3D model the vertical motion in the disc is neglected, however, the gravitational field must be considered three-dimensional.

Poisson equation is solved on a grid in cylindrical coordinate system in order to take disc symmetry into account and rule out the non-physical structures appearing in Cartesian coordinates. The details of the Poisson equation solver are given in [8,13]. First, the FFT is applied along the angular coordinate and then each harmonic of the potential is evaluated by the Successive Over-Relaxation method.

The considered Poisson equation solver succeeds to completely avoid the data exchange during the iteration stage. This is because equations for potential harmonics do not depend on each other. After iteration stage the potential should be gathered from all the processors for further computation. Therefore it is possible to divide the computation domain into completely independent subdomains along angular wavenumbers.

Particles are also uniformly distributed between the processors with no dependency of their spatial location. Since a particle might fly to any point of the disc in the course of simulation every PE should possess the potential values for the whole disc surface.

At each timestep data exchange is performed twice. First, after the convergence has been reached the potential harmonics in the disc plain are gathered for inverse Fourier transformation. Then the partial density fields, computed in each PE, are added up and sent to all processors.

These all-to-all communications are only possible because the model is quasi-3D: 2D arrays are sent from one processor to another instead of 3D arrays in the case of a full 3D model.

The 2D equation systems for potential harmonics require different number of iterations for convergence, as figure 1 shows. Here the number of iterations depends on the conditionality of the equation system matrix. It means that the processors would have different workload when provided with the same number of harmonics. Thus, initially equal workload can not be provided for all the processors. There are two ways to solve this problem: first, to use faster

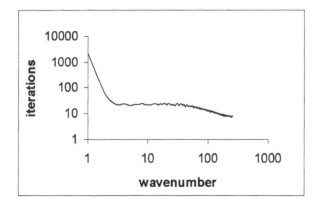

Fig. 1. Number of SOR iterations depending on wavenumber

methods when the convergence rate is slow, and second, to use dynamic load balancing. Dynamic load balancing here means to move some harmonics from the overloaded processor.

As a result of the reduction of the 3D model to the quasi-3D one we obtain a parallel program that is quite easy to implement and also capable of production of reasonable physical results. Nevertheless, in the quasi-3D model the processor workload is non-uniform and the speedup is not very high: 5 on 32 processors for grid size $400 \times 512 \times 200$ nodes with 20 million particles. The worktime for one timestep of simulation is 25 seconds on one processor for the given model size. The speedup is low because of the restictions of the Poisson equation solver. Thus a new solver should be introduced to increase the speedup.

5   Parallel Program Based on the Fundamental Solution of Poisson Equation

Poisson equation has its fundamental solution in the form:

$$\Phi(\boldsymbol{\tau}) = \int \frac{\rho(\tau')}{|\boldsymbol{R}|} d\tau' \tag{4}$$

where $|\boldsymbol{R}| = |\boldsymbol{\tau} - \boldsymbol{\tau}'|$, $\Phi(\boldsymbol{\tau})$ is the potential that is to be computed at the point $\boldsymbol{\tau}$. Let the two-dimensional computation domain be defined by the radius R_N in polar coordinates. Then a uniform 2D grid is introduced for the potential Φ with grid steps h_r and h_φ:

$$\begin{cases} r_i = h_r \cdot i, & i = 0, 1, , N_r, & h_r = \frac{R_N}{N_r} \\ \varphi_j = h_\varphi \cdot j, & j = 0, 1, , N_\varphi, & h_\varphi = \frac{2 \cdot \pi}{N_\varphi} \end{cases} \tag{5}$$

In the nodes of the defined grid the integral in (4) is replaced by the sum:

$$\Phi_{i',j'} = \sum_i \sum_j \frac{M_{i,j}}{R_{i,j,i',j'}} \tag{6}$$

$\Phi_{i',j'}$ is evaluated by summation of point mass potentials, the masses are set in the centres of the grid cells. In such a way masses form their own grid that is shifted relatively to the potential grid and $R_{i,j,i',j'}$ - is the distance from the node (i', j') of the Φ grid to the node (i, j) of the mass grid.

The evaluation of potential by the formula (6) could be easily divided between processors, for example, as follows:

$$\Phi_{i',j'} = \sum_{i=N_r/N_{proc}*rank}^{i=N_r/N_{proc}*(rank+1)} \sum_j \frac{M_{i,j}}{R_{i,j,i',j'}} \tag{7}$$

here N_{proc} is the number of processors, $rank$ is the rank of current processor ($rank = 0, ..., N_{proc} - 1$). The present method makes processor workload completely uniform, and consequently the speedup of the parallel program is high: see table 1.

Table 1. Worktime for different number of processors for a grid with $N_r = 400$, $N_\varphi = 400$ nodes

Number of processors	Worktime, minutes
1	75
12	5.55
25	2.63
50	1.36
100	0.75
200	0.49

Unfortunately for small number of processors the evaluation of potential with formula (7) is much slower than with the method described in the section 4. Moreover, both described programs are capable of simulation of the protoplanetary disc dynamics only for some restricted set of problems.

6   3D Parallel Program in Cylindrical Coordinate System

As it was mentioned in section 3.1, there are problems requiring full 3D simulation. Thus a numerical model was implemented with the matter posessing vertical component of the velocity [12].

Poisson equation is solved by a combination of the FFT applied to the angular coordinate and the SOR applied to the separate potential harmonics as in section 4. As it was mentioned above in section 4, one of the difficulties here is the non-uniform workload of the processors due to different computation time for different harmonics. This difficulty is present in 3D case as well as in quasi-3D, despite these model have lots of differences, for example in boundary conditions, density distribution etc.

Thus it is necessary to design an algorithm for distribution of harmonics to make processor workload close to uniform. Taking into account that dynamic load balancing might have negative effect due to the increase of interprocessor communications, we have decided to make static load setting. This load setting algorithm is based on the experimental data about the computation time for each harmonic:

- A separate processor is assigned for the evaluation of the harmonic with wavenumber $m = 0$.
- Each processor (except the above mentioned one) has harmonics with both low and high wavenumbers. Each harmonic was evaluated by one processor

This simple algorithm provided processor workload close to uniform. In table 2 the computation time is given for different parts of Poisson equation solver. The part of the solver that is parallelized is the evaluation of harmonics assigned to a processor. But as it is seen from table 2 that the most time-consuming parts are the FFTs for density and potential and also the gathering of evaluated

Table 2. Computation time (in seconds) for different parts of Poisson equation solver at a timestep for one processor

Number of processors	FFT for density	Evaluation of harmonics	Gathering of harmonics	FFT for potential	Total time
10	0.3	0.7	0.65	0.4	2.05

harmonics (data transmission between processors) since they work with 3D data arrays.

It should be noticed that the difficulty with long computation of the FFTs arises only in 3D case because Fourier Transform has to be applied to the whole 3D arrays of density and potential. It means that further improvement of the parallel program implementing 3D model of protoplanetary disc is only possible by means of decomposition of computation domain.

7   3D Parallel Program Based on Decomposition of the Computation Domain

Domain decomposition is applied to fulfil the requirements to the parallel implementation of the protoplanetary disc model given in 3.2. Moreover, the particles belonging to one subdomain are distributed between the processors each holding grid arrays for the subdomain.

The decomposition is done in the straightforward way - by dividing the computation domain into equal parts along one of the coordinate planes as shown in figure 2. In this case each layer has only two adjacent layers. As a result, the exchanging of particles with adjacent layers is very simple.

Due to the features of protoplanetary disc simulation most particles are situated near the disc plane. The disc is rotating around the axis parallel to Z and passing through the centre of the disc. This is why the planes dividing the computation domain go along YZ plane. Thus we avoid the initially non-uniform distribution of particles between processors, which may happen if the domain was divided along XY plane. In the present implementation the computation domain is divided into layers of nearly equal thickness with partial overlay of boundaries.

Poisson equation is solved in Cartesian coordinate system on a uniform grid. Such a simple grid enables us to employ a sufficiently fast solver - 3D Fast Fourier Transform. To discretize the second derivatives in Poisson equation a 27-point stencil is used. The FFT on a multiprocessor system is performed by the free FFTW library.

To provide the uniform distribution of particles between processors every layer is assigned to a group of processors as shown in figure 3. The grid values in the whole layer (potential, density etc.) are stored in all the processors of the group and the particles of the layer are uniformly distributed between the processors of the group. Each group has a head processor. The division of processors into groups is static and takes into account the distribution of particles in the whole

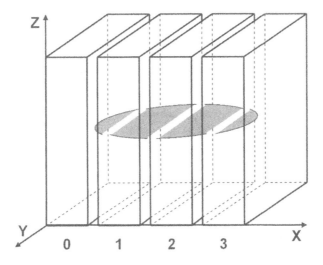

Fig. 2. Decomposition of the 3D computation domain

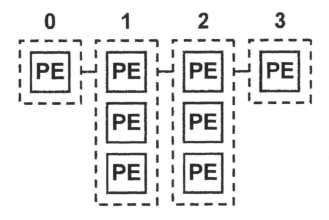

Fig. 3. Assignment of subdomains to groups of processors

computation domain. In the course of computation the particles fly from one layer to another, and they should be transmitted from one group of processors to another. The algorithm of selection of sender and receiver processors keeps the uniform distribution of particles between processors of a group.

Figure 4 shows that when a subdomain is worked up by a group of processors (line "c") worktime is a bit longer than when each subdomain is worked up by one processor (line "b"). But in the first case it is possible to compute the model of a larger size and this is the main goal of parallel implementation of protoplanetary disc model, as it was stated in section 3.2.

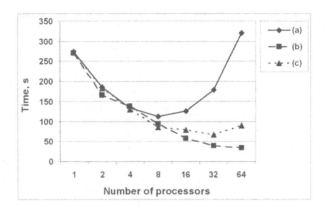

Fig. 4. Worktime for the program with domain decomposition. "a" - no domain decomposition, "b" - one processor for each subdomain, "c" - a group of processors for each subdomain.

The 2D distribution of density, potential etc., obtained by either quasi-3D or fully 3D programs are nearly identical in the cases when quasi-3D model is correct. So the fully 3D model in necessary to trace the vertical movement.

8   Summary

The program for the quasi-3D model may be thought to be a prototype for a full parallel implementation of the protoplanetary disc model. The program based on fundamental solution achieves good results as a parallel implementation of the disc model (good speedup) due to the ultimate simplification of the model. The 3D model in cylindrical coordinate system definitely shows all the difficulties of the full 3D implementation of the protoplanetary disc model. The domain decomposition program satisfies the requirements for the protoplanetary disc model the best: it is full 3D, it has virtually no limits for grid size and number of particles and it can reasonably reduce the computation time by increasing the number of processors.

References

1. Woolfson, M.M.: The Origin and Evolution of the Solar System. IoP Publishing, Bristol (2000)
2. Snytnikov, V.N., Dudnikova, G.I., Gleaves, J.T., Nikitin, S.A., Parmon, V.N., Stoyanovsky, V.O., Vshivkov, V.A., Yablonsky, G.S., Zakharenko, V.S.: Space chemical reactor of protoplanetary disk. Adv. Space Res. 30(6), 1461–1467 (2002)
3. D'Alessio, P., Calvet, N., Hartmann, L., Lizano, S., Canto, J.: Accretion disks around young objects. II. Tests of well-mixed models with ISM dust. Astrophysical Journal 527, 893–909 (1999)

4. Hockney, R.W., Eastwood, J.W.: Computer Simulation Using Particles. IOP Publishing, Bristol (1988)
5. Grigoryev Yu, N., Vshivkov, V.A., Fedoruk, M.P.: Numerical Particle-in-Cell Methods. Theory and Applications. VSP (2002)
6. Nikitin, S.A., Snytnikov, V.N., Vshivkov, V.A.: Ion-acoustic type instability in protoplanetary disk. Plasma in the Laboratory and in the Universe. In: AIP Conf. Proc. vol. 703, pp. 280–283 (2004)
7. Snytnikov, V.N., Vshivkov, V.A., Neupokoev, E.V., Nikitin, S.A., Parmon, V.N., Snytnikov, A.V.: Three-Dimensional Numerical Simulation of a Nonstationary Gravitating N-Body System with Gas. Astronomy Letters 30(2), 124–138 (2004)
8. Kuksheva, E.A., Malyshkin, V.E., Nikitin, S.A., Snytnikov, A.V., Snytnikov, V.N., Vshivkov, V.A.: Numerical Simulation of Self-Organisation in Gravitationally Unstable Media on Supercomputers. In: Malyshkin, V. (ed.) PaCT 2003. LNCS, vol. 2763, pp. 354–368. Springer, Heidelberg (2003)
9. Kuksheva, E.A., Malyshkin, V.E., Nikitin, S.A., Snytnikov, V.N., Vshivkov, V.A.: Supercomputer Simulation of Self-Gravitating Media. Future Generation Computer Systems 21, 749–757 (2005)
10. Snytnykov, A.: Parallel gravitational solver for protoplanetary disc simulation. Science and Technology, 2003. In: Proceedings KORUS 2003. The 7th Korea-Russia International Symposium, vol. 2, pp. 390–395 (2003)
11. Kuksheva, E.A., Snytnikov, V.N.: Parallel implementation of the fundamental solution for Poisson equation. Vychislitel'nye technologii (in Russian) 10(4), 63–71 (2005)
12. Vshivkov, V.A., Snytnikov, N.V., Snytnikov, V.N.: Simulation of three-dimensional dynamics of matter in gravitational field with the use of multiprocessor computer. Vychislitel'nye technologii (in Russian) 11(2), 15–27 (2006)
13. Snytnikov, A.V., Vshivkov, V.A.: A Multigrid Parallel Program for Protoplanetary Disc Simulation. In: Malyshkin, V. (ed.) PaCT 2005. LNCS, vol. 3606, pp. 457–467. Springer, Heidelberg (2005)
14. Demmel, J.W.: Applied Numerical Linear Algebra. SIAM (1997)
15. Kraeva, M.A., Malyshkin, V.E.: Assembly Technology for Parallel Realization of Numerical Models on MIMD-multicomputers. Future Generation Computer Systems 17(6), 755–765 (2001)

Generation of SMACA and Its Application in Web Services

Anirban Kundu, Ruma Dutta, and Debajyoti Mukhopadhyay

Web Intelligence & Distributed Computing Research Lab, Techno India Group
(West Bengal University of Technology)
EM 4/1, Sector V, Salt Lake, Calcutta 700091, India
{anik76in, rumadutta2006, debajyoti.mukhopadhyay}@gmail.com

Abstract. Web Search Engine uses forward indexing and inverted indexing as a part of its functional design. This indexing mechanism helps retrieving data from the database based on user query. In this paper, an efficient solution to handle the indexing problem is proposed with the introduction of Nonlinear Single Cycle Multiple Attractor Cellular Automata (SMACA). This work simultaneously shows generation of SMACA by using specific rule sequence. Searching mechanism is done with linear time complexity.

1 Introduction

Most people today can hardly imagine life without the Internet [3,4]. It provides access to information, news, email, shopping, and entertainment. World Wide Web (WWW) has brought a huge information at door-step of every user. The World Wide Web Worm (WWWW) was one of the first Web Search Engines which was basically a storage of huge volume of information. To handle these informations, proper indexing has been done in several ways [1,2]. This work reports an efficient scheme for designing an n-bit Single Cycle Multiple Attractor Cellular Automata (SMACA) [8,11] for handling the forward indexing and inverted indexing in a fast and inexpensive way. It is built around nonlinear scheme. Generated SMACAs have been used for information storage which requires special attention considering the huge volume of data in Web to be dealt with by the Search Engines [5,6]. The major contributions of this paper can be summarized as follows: (1) Design of an n-bit SMACA; (2) Usage of SMACA in forward indexing; (3) Usage of SMACA for replacing inverted indexing; (4) Searching mechanism using SMACA.

2 Cellular Automata (CA) Preliminaries

An n cell CA consists of n cells (Figure 1(a)) with local interactions [7]. It evolves in discrete time and space. The next state function of three neighbourhood CA cell (Figure 1(b)) can be represented as a rule as defined in Table 1 [9]. First row of Table 1 represents $2^3 = 8$ possible present states of 3 neighbours of ith

V. Malyshkin (Ed.): PaCT 2007, LNCS 4671, pp. 140–152, 2007.

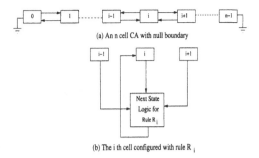

(a) An n cell CA with null boundary

(b) The i th cell configured with rule R $_i$

Fig. 1. Local Interaction between Cellular Automata Cells

Table 1. Truth Table of sample rules of a CA cell showing the next state logic for the Minterms of a 3 variable boolean function -The 8 minterms having decimal values $0, 1, 2, 3, 4, 5, 6, 7$ are referred to as Rule Minterms (RMTs)

Note : Set of Minterms $T = \{7, 6, 5, 4, 3, 2, 1, 0\}$ represented as $\{T(7), T(6), T(5), T(4), T(3), T(2), T(1), T(0)\}$ ($T(m) = m$, m = 0 to 7) in the text, are noted simply as q.

Present states of 3-neighbours	111	110	101	100	011	010	001	000	Rule
$(i-1), i,$ and $(i+1)$ of ith cells	(7)	(6)	(5)	(4)	(3)	(2)	(1)	(0)	Number
(Minterms of a 3 variable boolean function)	T(7)	T(6)	T(5)	T(4)	T(3)	T(2)	T(1)	T(0)	
	0	1	0	1	1	0	1	0	90
	1	0	0	1	0	1	1	0	150
Next state of ith cell	0	1	1	1	1	0	0	0	120
	0	0	0	0	1	1	0	0	12
	1	1	0	1	0	0	1	0	210

cell - (i-1), i, (i+1) cells. Each of the 8 entries (3 bit binary string) represents a minterm of a 3 variable boolean function for a 3 neighbourhood CA cell. In subsequent discussions, each of the 8 entries in Table 1 is referred to as a Rule Min Term (RMT). The decimal equivalent of 8 minterms are 0, 1, 2, 3, 4, 5, 6, 7 noted within () below the three bit string. Each of the next five rows of Table 1 shows the next state (0 or 1) of ith cell. Hence there can be $2^8 = 256$ possible bit strings. The decimal counterpart of such an 8 bit combination is referred to as a CA rule [9,10]. The rule of a CA cell can be derived from Table 1 of the ith cell.

2.1   Definitions

Definition 1: Reachable state - A state having 1 or more predecessors is a reachable state.

Definition 2: Non-reachable state - A state having no predecessor (that is, r=0) is termed as non-reachable.

Definition 3: Transient state - A non-cyclic state of a non-group CA is referred to as a transient state. Definition 4: Attractor Cycle - The set of states in a cycle is referred to as an attractor cycle.

Definition 5: Self-Loop Attractor(SLA) - A single cycle attractor state with self-loop is referred to as SLA.

Definition 6: Rule Vector(RV) - The sequence of rules $< R_0 R_1 \cdots R_i \cdots R_{n+1} >$, where i^{th} cell is configured with rule R_i.

3 Generation of SMACA and Its Application in Indexing

Synthesis of SMACA demands formation of a rule vector with group and non-group rules in specific sequence. The method to identify such a sequence is described in the following discussions. A scheme is outlined here to identify the sequence of rules in the rule vector that makes the CA a SMACA. The rule vector of an n-cell CA is denoted as $<R_0, R_1, \cdots, R_i, R_{i+1}, \cdots, R_{n-1}>$, where i^{th} cell is configured with R_i. A non-linear [12,13] SMACA consists of 2^n number of states where n is the size of SMACA. The structure of a non-linear SMACA has attractors (self-loop or single length cycle), non-reachable states, and transient states. The attractors form unique classes (basins). All other states reach the attractor basins after certain time steps. To classify a set of k classes, (k-1) number of attaractors are used, each identifying a single class. Consider, k=4 for a particular situation, i.e., four attractors are required. To manage this situation, '00', '01', '10' & '11' may be considered as attractors for classification of distinct states into 4 categories. Instead of using four attractors, three attractors may be used. So, we may consider '00', '01', '10' as attractors and the 4th attractor need not be specified. If we put concerned states over these three attractors, remaining states can be considered under the unspecified (4th) attractor. To get an illustrative idea, follow [10,11]. Figure 2 shows an arbitrary example of Non-linear SMACA with its irregular structure. States 1 & 9 are attractors. States 3, 5, 7, 11, 13 & 15 are transient states. All other states are Non-reachable states.

It is found through exhaustive experimentation that there are fifteen such classes for all the rules which can be used to form SMACA in a specific sequence. These classes are denoted as {I, II, III, IV, V, VI, VII, VIII, IX, X, XI, XII, XIII, XIV and XV} in Table 2. Table 3 dictates the rule of $(i + 1)^{th}$ cell from the class of ith cell. The table is formed in such a way that SMACA is formed if and only if the relationship between R_i and R_{i+1} is maintained. Since the design is concerned with null boundary CA, there are $2^{2^2} = 16$ effective rules for the left most (R_0) as well as the right most (R_{n-1}) cells. The RMTs 4, 5, 6 & 7 can be treated as don't care for R_0 as the present state of left neighbor of cell 1 is always 0. So, there are only 4 effective RMTs (0, 1, 2, & 3) for R_0. Similarly, the RMTs 1, 3, 5 & 7 are don't care RMTs for R_{n-1}. The effective RMTs for R_{n-1} are 0, 2, 4 & 6. R_0 and R_{n-1} are listed in Table 4 & Table 5 respectively.

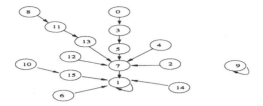

Fig. 2. Structure of a SMACA with Rule Vector (RV) <4 102 53 85>

Table 2. SMACA Class Table

Class	Rules
I	0, 16, 32, 48, 64, 80, 96, 112, 128, 144, 160, 176, 192, 208, 224, 240
II	1, 17, 33, 49, 65, 81, 97, 113, 129, 145, 161, 177, 193, 209, 225, 241
III	2, 18, 34, 50, 66, 82, 98, 114, 130, 146, 162, 178, 194, 210, 226, 242
IV	4, 20, 36, 52, 68, 84, 100, 116, 132, 148, 164, 180, 196, 212, 228, 244
V	5, 21, 37, 53, 69, 85, 101, 117, 133, 149, 165, 181, 197, 213, 229, 245
VI	6, 22, 38, 54, 70, 86, 102, 118, 134, 150, 166, 182, 198, 214, 230, 246
VII	7, 23, 39, 55, 71, 87, 103, 119, 135, 151, 167, 183, 199, 215, 231, 247
VIII	8, 24, 40, 56, 72, 88, 104, 120, 136, 152, 168, 184, 200, 216, 232, 248
IX	9, 25, 41, 57, 73, 89, 105, 121, 137, 153, 169, 185, 201, 217, 233, 249
X	10, 26, 42, 58, 74, 90, 106, 122, 138, 154, 170, 186, 202, 218, 234, 250
XI	11, 27, 43, 59, 75, 91, 107, 123, 139, 155, 171, 187, 203, 219, 235, 251
XII	12, 28, 44, 60, 76, 92, 108, 124, 140, 156, 172, 188, 204, 220, 236, 252
XIII	13, 29, 45, 61, 77, 93, 109, 125, 141, 157, 173, 189, 205, 221, 237, 253
XIV	14, 30, 46, 62, 78, 94, 110, 126, 142, 158, 174, 190, 206, 222, 238, 254
XV	15, 31, 47, 63, 79, 95, 111, 127, 143, 159, 175, 191, 207, 223, 239, 255

3.1 Synthesis of SMACA

The synthesis algorithm generates the rule vector R = $< R_0, R_1, \cdots, R_{n-1} >$ for an n-cell SMACA, where R_i is the rule with which the ith CA cell is to be configured. The characterization of SMACA points to the fact that the design of SMACA for any arbitrary n boils down to:

I. Form the classes of rules - that is, formation of Table 2 to Table 5, and
II. Find the class of $(i + 1)^{th}$ cell rule depending on the rule of ith cell and its class.

Task I : Construction of Table 2 to Table 5 involves one time cost.
Task II : The class of $(i + 1)^{th}$ cell rule is determined from the rule R_i and its class. Based on the rule class table (Table 2 to Table 5), we sequentially assign a rule R_{i+1} to the $(i + 1)^{th}$ CA cell (i = 1, 2, $\cdots$, (n-1)) to form the rule vector R = $< R_0, R_1, \cdots, R_i, \cdots, R_{n-1} >$. The R_0 is selected randomly from Table 4 and R_{n-1} from Table 5. Based on Task II, Algorithm 1 is further designed.

Table 3. Relationship of R_i and R_{i+1}

Class of R_i	R_{i+1}
I	0-2, 4-18, 20-34, 36-50, 52-66, 68-82, 84-98, 100-114, 116-130, 132-146, 148-162, 164-178, 180-194, 196-210, 212-226, 228-242, 244-255
II	20, 22, 25, 28, 29, 30, 38, 40-41, 44-46, 52, 54, 56-57, 60-62, 69, 71, 75, 77, 79, 84-87, 89, 91-95, 101-111, 116-127, 135, 138-139, 142-143, 148-151, 153-159, 166-175, 180-191, 197, 199, 202-203, 205-207, 212-215, 217-223, 229-239, 244-255
III	0-2, 4-6, 8-10, 12-14, 16-18, 20-22, 24-26, 28-30, 32-34, 36-38, 40-42, 44-46, 52, 54, 56-57, 60-62, 64-66, 68-70, 72-74, 76-77, 80-82, 84-86, 88-89, 92-93, 96-98, 100-102, 104-106, 108-109, 116, 118, 120-121, 124-125, 128-130, 132-134, 136-138, 140, 142, 144-146, 148-150, 152-154, 156, 158, 160-162, 164, 166, 168-170, 172, 174, 180, 182, 184-185, 188, 190, 192-194, 196-197, 200, 202, 208-210, 212-213, 224-226, 232, 234
IV	0-2, 4-18, 20-34, 36-50, 52-66, 68-82, 84-98, 100-114, 116-130, 132-146, 148-162, 164-178, 180-194, 196-210, 212-226, 228-242, 244-255
V	0-2, 4-6, 8-10, 12-14, 16-18, 20-22, 24-26, 28-29, 32-34, 36-38, 40-42, 44, 46, 64-66, 68-74, 76-82, 84-96, 98, 100-111, 116-119, 122-130, 132-134, 136-145, 148-162, 164-175, 181, 183-194, 196-209, 212-224, 226, 228-239, 244-255
VI	0-14, 16-26, 28-30, 32-38, 40-46, 48-50, 52-54, 56-58, 60-62, 64-77, 80-89, 92-93, 96-102, 104-109, 112-113, 116-117, 120-121, 124-125, 128-140, 142, 144-154, 156, 158, 160-164, 166, 168-172, 174, 176, 178, 180, 182, 184, 186, 188, 190, 192-203, 208-215, 224-227, 232-235
VII	0-2, 4-6, 8-10, 12-14, 16-18, 20-22, 24-26, 28-30, 32-34, 36-38, 40-42, 44-46, 64-77, 80-82, 84-86, 88-89, 92-93, 96-107, 128-140, 142, 144-155, 160-162, 164, 166, 168-170, 174, 192-203, 208-215, 224-227, 232-235
VIII	0-2, 4-18, 20-34, 36-50, 52-66, 68-82, 84-98, 100-114, 116-130, 132-146, 148-162, 164-178, 180-194, 196-210, 212-226, 228-242, 244-255
IX	20-23, 28-31, 40-47, 52-63, 65, 67, 69, 71, 73, 75, 77, 79, 81, 83-87, 89, 91-95, 97, 99, 101-111, 113, 115-127, 130-131, 134-135, 138-139, 142-143, 146-151, 153-159, 162-163, 166-175, 178-191, 193-195, 197-199, 201-203, 205-207, 209-215, 217-223, 225-227, 229-239, 241-255
X	0-2, 4-6, 8-10, 12-14, 16-18, 20-21, 24-26, 28-29, 32-34, 36-38, 40, 42, 44, 46, 64-66, 68-74, 76-82, 84-98, 100-106, 108-111, 116-119, 121-134, 136-146, 148-150, 152-162, 164-175, 181-194, 196-209, 212-224, 226, 228-239, 244-255
XI	65, 67, 69, 71, 73, 75, 77, 79, 84-87, 89, 91-95, 97-99, 101-103, 105-107, 109-111, 116-127, 130-131, 134-135, 138-139, 142-143, 145-147, 149-151, 153-155, 157-159, 166-175, 180-191, 193-195, 197-199, 201-203, 205-207, 209-215, 217-223, 225-227, 229-239, 244-255
XII	0-2, 4-17, 20-21, 24-32, 34, 36-40, 42, 44-47, 64-66, 68-82, 84-96, 98, 100-104, 106, 108-112, 114, 116-120, 122, 124-130, 132-145, 148-149, 152-162, 164-177, 180-181, 184-194, 196-210, 212-226, 228-242, 244-255
XIII	0-47, 64-255
XIV	0-47, 64-255
XV	0-47, 64-255

For the formation of SMACA, the synthesis scheme is achieved through Algorithm 1.

Algorithm 1. *SMACA Synthesis*
Input : n (CA size), Tables (2, 3, 4 & 5)
Output : A SMACA - that is, rule vector $R = < R_0, R_1, \cdots, R_{n-1} >$
Step 1 : Pick up the first rule R_0 randomly from Table 4, and set the class of R_1
$C :=$ Class of R_1 ($C \in \{I, II, III, IV, VII, VIII, XI, XIII, XIV, XV\}$ of Table 4)
Step 2 : For i := 1 to n-2; repeat Step 3 and Step 4

Table 4. First Rule Table (R_0)

Rules for R_0	Class of R_1
0	I
1	II
2	III
4	IV
7	VII
8	VIII
11	XI
13	XIII
14	XIV
15	XV

Table 5. Last Rule Table (R_{n-1})

Rule Class for R_{n-1}	Rules for R_{n-1}
I	0, 4, 16, 21, 64, 69, 84, 85
II	69, 84, 85
III	0, 4, 64
IV	0, 4, 16, 21, 64, 69, 84, 85
V	0, 4, 64, 69, 84, 85
VI	0, 1, 4, 16, 64
VI	0, 4, 64
VIII	0, 4, 16, 21, 64, 69, 84, 85
IX	21, 69, 81, 84, 85
X	0, 4, 64, 69, 84, 85
XI	69, 84, 85
XII	0, 4, 64, 69, 84, 85
XIII	0, 1, 4, 64, 69, 81, 84, 85
XIV	0, 1, 4, 64, 69, 81, 84, 85
XV	0, 1, 4, 64, 69, 81, 84, 85

Step 3 : From Table 2 pick up a rule as R_i arbitrarily for Class C
Step 4 : Find Class C for the next cell rule using Table 3
Step 5 : From Table 5 pick up a rule as R_{n-1}
Step 6 : Form the rule vector $R = < R_0, R_1, \cdots, R_{n-1} >$
Step 7 : Stop

The complexity of Algorithm 1 is O(n).

Example 1 : Synthesis of 4-cell SMACA:
Consider, rule 2 is selected as R_0. Therefore, the class (obtained from Table 4) of next cell rule is III. From class III of Table 2, rule 178 is selected randomly as R_1. Since, rule 178 is of class III; so, from Table 3, the next state value can be easily found by selecting a random value as r_{i+1}^{th} rule. Say, rule 44 is selected as R_2. From Table 2, rule 44 is of class XII. The class of last cell is, therefore,

XII. Rule 64 is selected randomly for R_3 from Table 5. Therefore, the SMACA is R $= < 2, 178, 44, 64 >$.

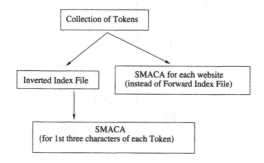

Fig. 3. Pictorial Representation of Our Approach

Definition 7: Token - Minimum term by which one or more dictionary words can be managed while creating/modifying database of Search Engine. For example, "traverse" is a token managing "traversal", "traverses", "traversed", etc..

Definition 8: Key/State value - A unique number is assigned to every Web-page for representing the Web-pages as states of SMACA. This is known as Key/State value.

Definition 9: Conflict - Traversal from one state to another within a SMACA depends on its RMT (as shown in Table 1 for Rule 90, 150, etc.). While generating a state of SMACA, if any mismatch happens, one or many bit position of the current state will not reach the next predefined state(0/1) as per the RMT table of concerned rule vector. This situation is known as Conflict.

Non-linear SMACA is used (generated by Algorithm 1) for replacing forward indexing, and inverted indexing. Tokens are generated in conventional manner like other Web Search Engines.

   Mainly four algorithms are used to accomplish our objective in four steps.

   These steps are as follows:

(a) generation of SMACA for each Website;
(b) generation of inverted indexed file;
(c) replacing inverted indexed file by SMACA;
(d) searching mechanism.

   Figure 3 depicts pictorial represention of our current research work. It is clearly shown in the figure that step (a) and step (b) are done concurrently to reduce the generation time of Search Engine.

   The next four algorithms will describe our new approach step by step:

Algorithm 2. *SMACA Generation for Forward Indexing*
Input : A set of tokens of Web-pages of a Website
Output : Set of SMACAs
Step 1 : Generate key values of Web-pages

Step 2 : Assign key values of Web-pages as self-loop attractors of the SMACA
Step 3 : Generate key values of tokens
Step 4 : Assign key values of tokens as non-reachable state, or, transient state of the SMACA
Step 5 : If conflict occurs goto Step 3
Step 6 : Generated SMACA
Step 7 : Stop

Definition 10: Website Identification Number (WSID) - Unique identification number has been alloted to each Website. This is known as WSID.

Algorithm 3. *Inverted Indexed File Generation*
Input : Token
Output : Inverted indexed file
Step 1 : Generate WSID
Step 2 : Search for token whether it already exists in inverted indexed file
Step 3 : If successful, link the WSID with the token
Step 4 : Else, make a new entry in inverted indexed file and link the WSID with the token
Step 5 : Stop

Definition 11: SMACA-ID - Unique identification number has been alloted to each generated SMACA. This is known as SMACA-ID.

Question: Why do first three characters of token take into consideration while generating SMACA-ID?

Answer: After vigorous searching through WWW, it has been found that a token of any Web-page consists of a minimum of three characters. Less than three character words are generally the "stop-words". That's why, we have taken first three characters of token into consideration for generating SMACA-ID. For example, "sachin" and "sacrifice" both tokens have same first three characters "sac". So, Algorithm 4 generates a SMACA-ID for a specific SMACA within which both the tokens reside as the states. WSIDs of the Websites, within which the related tokens appear, will be assigned as attractors of that particular SMACA.

Algorithm 4. *SMACA Generation from Inverted Indexed File*
Input : Inverted Indexed File
Output : Set of SMACAs equivalent to inverted indexed file
Step 1 : For each combination of first three characters of token, generate SMACA-ID from the input file
Step 2 : Assign WSIDs for which first three characters of related token appear, as attractors of SMACA
Step 3 : For each token matching first three characters, generate key value
Step 4 : For each token, concatenate WSIDs and generated key value of token as a state value
Step 5 : Assign each state value as a non-reachable or transient state of SMACA
Step 6 : If conflict occurs goto Step 2

Step 7 : Store generated SMACAs with corresponding SMACA-ID
Step 8 : Stop

Algorithm 5. *Users Search*
Input : Users' query
Output : Desired Web-pages
Step 1 : When query is submitted tokens are generated for the words in query
Step 2 : First three characters of each token are extracted
Step 3 : These three characters are encoded and SMACA-IDs are generated
Step 4 : With these generated SMACA-IDs, the Searcher searches the corresponding SMACA (replacing inverted indexed file) from the storage
Step 5 : State values are generated from the tokens
Step 6 : Applying these SMACAs with the state values, the corresponding WSIDs are found
Step 7 : The Searcher searches for the SMACAs (replacing forward indexing) for these WSIDs
Step 8 : Applying these SMACAs with the state values previously generated by tokens, the corresponding Web-page for each Website (attractor) is found
Step 9 : These Web-pages are extracted from the repository and displayed to the user
Step 10 : Stop

4   Experimental Results

This section reports a detailed study on nonlinear Cellular Automata based designing on Storage of Hypertext data while building a Web Search Engine. Our experiment shows that it will take less storage space and less time while searching through Internet / Intranet.

For experimental purpose, we have considered a huge number of Websites within which we have shown the details of four Websites and only four Webpages of each Website as a sample study.

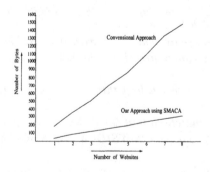

Fig. 4. Space required for Forward Indexing

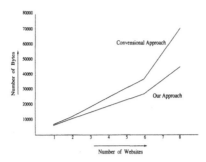

Fig. 5. Space required for Inverted Indexing

List of Websites & corresponding Web-pages with details are given below:

(1) AceWebTech
http://www.acewebtech.com/index.htm (35 bytes) (No. of tokens = 129)
http://www.acewebtech.com/webservices/website_maintenance .htm (62 bytes)
(No. of tokens = 222)
http://www.acewebtech.com/pofile.htm (36 bytes) (No. of tokens = 279)
http://www.acewebtech.com/webservices/services.htm (50 bytes) (No. of tokens
= 260)
To store all these 4 Web-pages we need a CA of size = 13 with four(4) number
of attractors.

In Forward Indexing:
Total space required in conventional way = (35+62+36+50) bytes = 183 bytes.
Maximum space required in our approach = (13x3) bytes = 39 bytes.

(2) AnimalSafari
http://www.animalsafari.com/index.htm (37 bytes) (No. of tokens = 183)
http://www.animalsafari.com/html/Admissions.htm (47 bytes) (No. of tokens
= 241)
http://www.animalsafari.com/html/Attractions.htm (48 bytes) (No. of tokens
= 3)
http://www.animalsafari.com/html/Park_Lore.htm (46 bytes) (No. of tokens =
277)
To store all these 4 Web-pages we need a CA of size = 13 with four(4) number
of attractors.

In Forward Indexing:
Total space required in conventional way = (37+47+48+46) bytes = 178 bytes.
Maximum space required in our approach = (13x3) bytes = 39 bytes.

(3) Maps of India
http://www.mapsofindia.com/outsourcing-to-india/history-of-outsourcing.html
(75 bytes) (No. of tokens = 498)

Table 6. Experimental Results on Time required for Searching

Search Samples	No. Of Website (Time in Seconds)			
	1	2	6	8
Ace	0.016	0.016	0.016	0.019
Ace + reliable	0.016	0.016	0.018	0.019
Ace + reliable +forum	0.016	0.016	0.018	0.018
Ace + reliable + forum + Flash	0.016	0.016	0.018	0.018
Hyena		0.023	0.025	0.037
Hyena + Encyclopedia		0.024	0.024	0.035
Hyena + Encyclopedia + Unfortunately		0.023	0.024	0.038
Hyena + Encyclopedia + Unfortunately + mancaus		0.023	0.024	0.038
Hyena + Encyclopedia + Unfortunately + mancaus + Ace		0.025	0.024	0.040
Kanniyakumari			0.036	0.053
Peninsular			0.030	0.032
choice				0.018
Encyclopedia + Kanniyakumari				0.039
Encyclopedia + Kanniyakumari + Wolfram				0.039

http://www.mapsofindia.com/reference-maps/geography.html (56 bytes) (No. of tokens = 302)

http://www.mapsofindia.com/maps/india/india.html (48 bytes) (No. of tokens = 2388)

http://www.mapsofindia.com/stateprofiles/index.html (51 bytes) (No. of tokens = 259)

To store all these 4 Web-pages we need a CA of size = 15 with four(4) number of attractors.

In Forward Indexing:
Total space required in conventional way = (75+56+48+51) bytes = 230 bytes.
Maximum space required in our approach = (15x3) bytes = 45 bytes.

(4) Tourism of India

http://www.tourism-of-india.com/adventure-tours-to-india.html (61 bytes) (No. of tokens = 133)

http://www.tourism-of-india.com/festival-tours-of-india.html (60 bytes) (No. of tokens = 158)

http://www.tourism-of-india.com/historical-places-in-india.html (63 bytes) (No. of tokens = 525)

http://www.tourism-of-india.com/kolkata.html (44 bytes) (No. of tokens = 585)

To store all these 4 Web-pages we need a CA of size = 14 with four(4) number of attractors.

In Forward Indexing:
Total space required in conventional way = (61+60+63+44) bytes = 228 bytes.
Maximum space required in our approach = (14x3) bytes = 42 bytes.

In Inverted Indexing:

Total space required for all the four Websites in conventional way = 35797 bytes.

Maximum space required for all the four Websites in our approach = 23765 bytes.

The space required for Forward Indexing and Inverted Indexing are shown in Figure 4 & Figure 5 respectively.

The time required for Searching is shown in Table 6 with some examples.

5   Conclusion

In a general Search Engine, forward indexing and inverted indexing files are used for searching. A new methodology is discussed here to minimize storage requirement by using non-linear SMACA while building forward and / or inverted indexed file. This approach processes users' query in linear time complexity while searching the Web through a Search Engine. Using Cellular Automata in storing Search Engine indexing data is a tricky approach that has been successfully implemented in this work offering better results in form of space efficiency.

References

1. Brin, S., Page, L.: The Anatomy of a Large-Scale Hypertextual Web Search Engine. In: Proceedings of the Seventh International World Wide Web Conference, Brisbane, Australia (April 1998)
2. Arasu, A., Cho, J., Garcia-Molina, H., Paepcke, A., Raghavan, S.: Searching the Web, ACM Transactions on Internet Technology, vol. 1(1) (August 2001)
3. Flake, G.W., Lawrence, S., Giles, C.L., Coetzee, F.M.: Self Organization and Identification of Web Communities. IEEE Computer 35(3), 66–71 (2000)
4. Glover, E.J., Tsioutsiouliklis, K., Lawrence, S., Pennock, D.M., Flake, G.W.: Using Web Structure for Classifying and Describing Web Pages. In: WWW2002, pp. 7–11. Honolulu, Hawaii, USA (May 2002)
5. Chakrabarti, S., Dom, B.E., Kumar, R., Raghavan, P., Rajagopalan, S., Tomkins, A., Gibson, D., Kleinberg, J.: Mining the Web's Link Structure. IEEE Computer 1999, 60–67 (1999)
6. Mukhopadhyay, D., Singh, S.R.: Algorithm for Automatic Web-Page Clustering using Link Structures. In: Proceedings of the IEEE INDICON 2004, Conference, IIT Kharagpur, India, pp. 472–477 (December 20-22, 2004)
7. Neumann, J.V.: The Theory of Self-Reproducing Automata. In: Burks, A.W. (ed.) University of Illinois Press, Urbana and London (1966)
8. Sipper, M.: Co-evolving Non-Uniform Cellular Automata to Perform Computations. Physica D 92, 193–208 (1996)
9. Wolfram, S.: Theory and Application of Cellular Automata. World Scientific, Singapore (1986)
10. Chaudhuri, P.P., Chowdhury, D.R., Nandi, S., Chatterjee, S.: Additive Cellular Automata. In: Theory and Applications, vol. 1, IEEE Computer Society Press, Los Alamitos (1997)

11. Maji, P., Shaw, C., Ganguly, N., Sikdar, B.K., Chaudhuri, P.P.: Theory and Application of Cellular Automata For Pattern Classification. Fundamenta Informaticae 58, 321–354 (2003)
12. Das, S., Kundu, A., Sikdar, B.K.: Nonlinear CA Based Design of Test Set Generator Targeting Pseudo-Random Pattern Resistant Faults. In: Asian Test Symposium, pp. 196–201 (2004)
13. Das, S., Kundu, A., Sen, S., Sikdar, B.K., Chaudhuri, P.P.: Non-Linear Celluar Automata Based PRPG Design (Without Prohibited Pattern Set). In: Linear Time Complexity, Asian Test Symposium, pp. 78–83 (2003)

Enhancing Fault-Tolerance of Large-Scale MPI Scientific Applications

G. Rodríguez, P. González, M.J. Martín, and J. Touriño

Computer Architecture Group, Dep. Electronics and Systems
University of A Coruña, Spain
{grodriguez,pglez,mariam,juan}@udc.es

Abstract. The running times of large-scale computational science and engineering parallel applications, executed on clusters or Grid platforms, are usually longer than the mean-time-between-failures (MTBF). Therefore, hardware failures must be tolerated to ensure that not all computation done is lost on machine failures. Checkpointing and rollback recovery are very useful techniques to implement fault-tolerant applications. Although extensive research has been carried out in this field, there are few available tools to help parallel programmers to enhance their applications with fault tolerance support. This work presents an experience to endow with fault tolerance two large MPI scientific applications: an air quality simulation model and a crack growth analysis. A fault tolerant solution has been implemented by means of a checkpointing and recovery tool, the CPPC framework. Detailed experimental results are presented to show the practical usefulness and low overhead of this checkpointing approach.

Keywords: Fault tolerance, checkpointing, parallel applications, MPI.

1   Introduction

Checkpointing has become a widely used technique to provide fault tolerance by periodically saving the computation state to stable storage, so that this state can be restored in case of execution failure.

One of the most remarkable properties of general checkpointing techniques is *granularity*. Checkpointing can be performed from two different granularity levels: *data segment level* and *variable level*. On data segment level the entire application state is saved (data segment, stack segment and execution context), recovering it when necessary. Most of fault-tolerance tools present in the bibliography [1,2,3,4,5] perform data segment level checkpointing. This approach presents a general advantage: its transparency from the user's point of view, since the application is seen as a black box. However, saving the application state entirely leads to lack of portability, as a number of non-portable structures will be saved along with application data (as application stack or heap).

A variable level approach saves only restart-relevant state to stable storage. Many fault tolerant solutions implement variable level checkpointing by manually determining the data to be saved, and inserting code to save that data on

V. Malyshkin (Ed.): PaCT 2007, LNCS 4671, pp. 153–161, 2007.

disk and to restart the computation after failure. The code becomes as portable as the original application and, provided that checkpoints are saved in a portable format, the application can be restarted on different platforms. Unfortunately, this method requires a data-flow analysis, which can be a tedious and error-prone task to be performed by the user. Thus, a recent approach [6], developed by the authors, tries to automatize a variable level checkpointing of message-passing parallel applications by means of a checkpointing library and a compiler that instruments MPI code.

The purpose of this work is to develop fault tolerant solutions for two different computationally intensive MPI codes, an air quality model [7] and a crack growth analysis [8]. A variable level checkpointing approach is followed, implemented through the use of our checkpointing and recovery tool, *CPPC*.

The structure of this paper is as follows. Section 2 introduces the problem of endowing parallel applications with fault tolerance, and gives an overview of the CPPC tool and how it solves the major issues. Section 3 describes the applications used for the tests. Experimental results about the use of the CPPC tool are presented in Section 4. Finally, Section 5 concludes the paper.

2   Checkpointing and Recovery of Parallel Applications: The CPPC Tool

There are several issues to be solved in implementing checkpointing solutions for parallel applications, such as consistency, portability, memory requirements, or transparency. CPPC is a checkpointing infrastructure that implements scalable, efficient and portable checkpointing mechanisms. This section details various aspects of CPPC's design associated with major issues.

2.1   Global Consistency

Consistency is a key issue when dealing with the checkpoint of a parallel program using the message-passing paradigm. The state of a parallel application is defined as the set of all its processes states. There are two situations that require actions to be performed in order to achieve a correct restart: existence of *in-transit* messages (sent but not received), and existence of *ghost* messages (received but not sent) in the set of processes states stored.

Checkpoint consistency has been well-studied in the last decade [9]. Approaches to the consistent recovery can be categorized into different protocols: uncoordinated, coordinated and communication-induced checkpointing; and message logging.

In uncoordinated checkpoint protocols the checkpoint of each process is executed independently of the other processes, leading to the so called *domino* effect (process may be forced to rollback up to the beginning of the execution). Thus, these protocols are not used in practice. In coordinated checkpoint protocols, all processes coordinate their checkpoints so that the global system state composed of the set of all process checkpoints is coherent. Communication-induced checkpoint tries to take advantage of uncoordinated and coordinated checkpoint techniques. Based on the uncoordinated approach, it detects risk of inconsistent state, and forces processes to checkpoint. While this approach seems to be very interesting theoretically, in practice it turns out to be quite inefficient.

Message logging saves messages with checkpoint files in order to replay them for the recovery. The main disadvantage of log-based recovery is its high storage overhead.

CPPC achieves global consistency by using spatial coordination, rather than temporal coordination. Checkpoints are thus taken at the same relative code points by all the processes (assuming SPMD codes). To avoid problems caused by messages between processes, checkpoint directives must be inserted at points where it is guaranteed that there are no in-transit, nor ghost messages. These points are called *safe points*. For an automatic identification of safe points, a static analysis of interprocess message flow is needed. This automatization is currently under development.

2.2 Portability

The availability of the application to be executed across multiple platforms plays an important role in current trends towards new computing infrastructures, such as heterogeneous clusters and Grid systems.

A state file is said to be portable if it can be used to restart the computation on an architecture (or OS) different from that where the file was generated on. This means that state files should not contain hard machine-dependent state, which should be recovered at restart time using special protocols.

The solution used in CPPC is to recover non-portable state by means of the re-execution of the code responsible for creating such opaque state in the original execution. Hence, the new code will be just as portable as the original code was. Moreover, in CPPC the effective data writing will be performed by a selected writing plugin implementation, using its own format. This enables the restart on different architectures, as long as a portable dumping format is used for program variables. Currently, a writing plugin based on HDF5 is provided. HDF5 [10] is a general purpose library and file format for storing scientific data in a portable way. The CPPC HDF5 plugin allows the generated checkpoint files to be used across multiple platforms. CPPC-generated HDF5 files are much like binary files, except that all data are tagged to make conversions possible when restarting on different platforms.

2.3 Memory Requirements

The solution of large large scientific problems may need the use of massive computational resources, both in terms of CPU effort and memory requirements. Thus, many scientific applications are developed to be run on a large number of processors. The checkpointing of this kind of applications would lead to a great amount of stored state, the cost being so high as to become impractical.

CPPC reduces the amount of data to be saved by including in its compiler a live variable analysis in order to identify those variable values that are only needed upon restart. Besides, the HDF5 library can accommodate data in a variety of ways, including a compressed format based on the ZLib library [11]. This, or other compression algorithms, can be included in a writing plugin without recompiling the CPPC library. A multithreaded dumping option [12] is also provided by the CPPC tool to improve performance when working with large datasets. A new thread handles checkpoint file creation while the application continues normal execution.

2.4   Transparency

This property is measured in terms of user effort to insert checkpoint support into the application. On the one hand, data segment level approaches are completely transparent to programmers, as they do not need much information about the applications being treated. On the other hand, variable level strategies have to get some metadata about the application in order to operate correctly, and they usually get it from the programmer.

The CPPC tool appears to the user as a compiler tool and a runtime library which help achieve the goal of inserting fault tolerance into a parallel application in an almost transparent way. The library provides checkpoint-support routines, and the compiler tool seeks to automatize the use of the library. The user must insert only one compiler directive into the original application (the cppc checkpoint pragma) to mark points in the code where the relevant state will be dumped to stable storage in a checkpoint file. The compiler performs a source-to-source transformation, automatically identifying both the variables to be dumped to the checkpoint file and the non-portable code to be re-executed upon restart; and it also inserts the necessary calls to functions of the CPPC library, as well as flow control code needed to recover the non-portable state.

3   The Applications

In this section, two large-scale scientific applications are described: an air quality model and a crack growth simulation. Both applications were found to be good candidates for using the CPPC tool. Originally, none of them provided fault-tolerance. However, being long running critical applications, both would benefit from this feature.

The STEM-II Model. Due to the increasing sources of air pollutants, the development of tools to control and prevent the pollutants' accumulation has become a high priority. Coal-fired electrical power plants constitute one of the most significant sources of air pollutants, thus its study is a key issue in pollution control specifications. The STEM-II model [13] is used to know in advance how the meteorological conditions, obtained from a meteorological prediction model, would affect the emissions of pollutants by the power plant of As Pontes (A Coruña, Spain) in order to fulfill EU regulations.

Air quality models can be mathematically described as time-dependent, 3D partial differential equations. The underlying equation used is the atmospheric-diffusion equation. The numerical solution of this equation consists of the integration of a system of coupled non-linear ordinary differential equations. STEM-II solves this system using a finite element method (FEM).

The sequential program consists mainly of four nested loops, a temporal loop (loop_t) and a loop for each dimension of the simulated space (loop_x, loop_y and loop_z). The main modules of the code are: horizontal transport, vertical transport and chemical reactions, and I/O module. The model requires as input data the initial pollutant concentrations, topological data, emissions from the power plant and meteorological data. The initial pollutant concentrations and topological data are read only once, at the beginning of the simulation. The meteorological data and the emissions from the power plant are time-dependent and must be read each 60 iterations, that is, each new hour of simulation. The output consists of spatially and temporally gaseous and aqueous concentrations of each modeled specie, reaction rates, in and out fluxes, amount deposited and ionic concentrations of hydrometeor particles. As this model is computationally intensive, it has been parallelized using MPI [7].

Crack Growth Analysis Using Dual BEM (DBEM). Cracks are present in all structures, usually as a result of localised damage in service, and may grow by processes such as fatigue, stress-corrosion or creep. The growth of the crack leads to a decrease in the structural strength. Thus, fracture occurs, leading to the failure of the structure.

The Boundary Element Method (BEM) has been acknowledged as an alternative to FEM in fracture mechanic analysis. BEM reduces the dimensionality of the problem under analysis through the discretization of the boundary domain only.

Despite the reduction of dimensionality using BEMs instead of FEMs, the crack growth analysis leads to a large number of discretized equations that grow at every step when the crack growth is evaluated. Analysis of real structural integrity problems may need the use of large computational resources, both in terms of CPU and memory requirements.

The boundary element code to assemble the linear equations is essentially a triple-nested DO loop. The external loop is over the collocation nodes, the middle loop is over the boundary elements, and the internal loop is over the Gauss points. Coarse grain parallelization can be achieved by distributing collocation nodes among processors [8].

Although assembling the linear equations is a key task in the simulation process, the bottleneck of the crack growth analysis is the solution of the resultant dense linear system. The traditional method for the solution of a dense linear system would be the application of the Gauss elimination method. However, as the problem size increases the use of iterative methods is demanded. This application uses the GMRES iterative method, regarded as the most robust of the Krylov subspace iterative methods.

Table 1. Applications' summary

Tested application	Programming Language	Number of files	Lines of Code	running on 4 nodes	
				Memory requirements	Disk quota
STEM	F77	149	9609	180MB	560MB
DBEM	F77	45	13164	370MB	170MB

4 Experimental Results

In this section, the results of applying the CPPC tool to the large-scale applications described in the previous section are presented. Results include checkpointing overhead, restart overhead, portability and checkpoint file size. Tests were performed on a cluster of Intel Xeon 1.8 Ghz nodes, 1GB RAM, connected through an SCI network.

Table 1 summarizes the two tested applications: the air quality simulation model (from now on referred to as STEM) and the crack growth simulation (DBEM).

CPPC treats the applications as black boxes, and automates the insertion of checkpoint-support routines provided by the CPPC library, identifying the variables to be dumped and the non-portable code to be re-executed upon restart, and inserting flow control code. The `cppc checkpoint` is the only directive not yet automated, and thus the programmer must find a safe point in the original code for the checkpointing file dumping. Safe points can be easily found in both codes, since they follow the SPMD paradigm. This point has been found at the end of the outer loop (`loop_t`) in the STEM code. In these experiments it executes 1440 iterations of the outer loop, which corresponds to 24 hours of real-time simulation. In the DBEM code, the checkpoint directive has been placed at the beginning of the main loop in the GMRES solver. In these experiments DBEM performs a crack growth simulation on a mesh of 496 collocation nodes, which involves the solution of a dense linear system of 1494 equations.

Figure 1 shows the execution times for both applications. Results are shown for the original execution, execution with CPPC checkpointing instrumentation, and two executions including different checkpoint frequencies. CPPC instrumentation includes calls to CPPC library routines, such as CPPC initialization or variable registration routines, and flow control code. As can be seen in the figure, the overhead introduced by the CPPC instrumentation remains under 5% for both applications.

The overhead of a single checkpoint file dumping depends on the amount of data to be stored and the format used for the data storage. Results shown in Figure 1 were obtained using HDF5 format. Early tests were carried out with one checkpoint file dumping each 60 iterations (labeled as "1/60" in the figure). Then, more tests were performed increasing the checkpoint frequency up to one checkpoint each ten iterations (labeled as "1/10"). Increasing the checkpoint frequency did not noticeably vary the total execution time, since

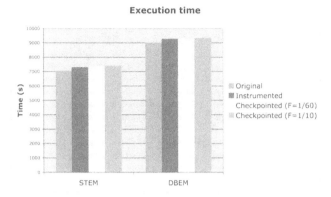

Fig. 1. Execution times in failure-free tests

once the instrumentation overhead is introduced, the multithreaded technique hides the overhead of the data dumping step.

These results have been obtained assuming no failures during the execution. In other case, the restart time should be also considered in the total execution time. Restart overhead is less important than checkpointing overhead. The application is expected to be restarted only in case of failure and, in long running applications, it will be always better than to re-execute the application from the beginning. Results for restart execution times can be seen in Figure 2. The total restart time is divided in two sections: overhead due to the checkpoint file read and overhead due to state recovery. Results labeled as "native" correspond to those obtained when restarting an application from checkpoint files generated in the same platform. In order to perform also a portability test, these applications were executed on an HP Superdome located at the Galician Supercomputing Center (Intel Itanium 2 nodes at 1.5Ghz, 3GB RAM, connected through Infiniband) with its proprietary Fortran compiler and MPI implementation. Checkpoint files created in this platform were used to restart the applications on the SCI cluster, thus allowing the comparison of restart times using both native and imported files (native and cross-platform results, respectively, in Figure 2). Reading time increases if data transformations are needed, since they will take place at application restart. Results have shown that the overhead introduced is low enough to be negligible, even in the cross-platform case.

As pointed out in Section 2, when dealing with large-scale applications, checkpointing could lead to a great amount of state stored. Hence, techniques to reduce the checkpoint file size are of capital importance. Table 2 compares CPPC generated file sizes to those obtained using a segment level approach. As can be seen, CPPC achieves very important size reductions by performing a live variable analysis (the number of live variables registered by CPPC are shown in the table). Table 2 also shows chekpoint file generation time (dumping time) when using the CPPC tool. Results of dumping time with and without the multithreading

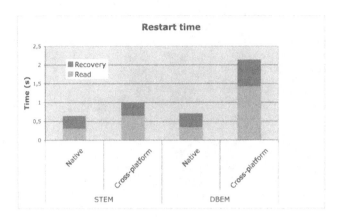

Fig. 2. Restart overhead

Table 2. Checkpoint file generation results

Tested application	Segment level ckpt-file size	CPPC ckpt-file size	registered variables	dumping time (s) absolute	multithread
STEM	187 MB	121 MB	156	0.42	0.18
DBEM	290 MB	145 MB	178	0.91	0.52

option demonstrate that the checkpoint file generation has a minimal influence on the performance of long running applications.

5   Conclusions

Currently, there are several solutions available that deal with checkpointing of parallel applications. However, most of them implement data segment level approaches, which present serious drawbacks for real scientific applications, such as memory requirements or portability. Thus, development of new tools to provide variable level solutions with a high level of transparency from the user's point of view becomes a great challenge.

In this paper a variable level checkpointing tool, CPPC, has been tested with two large-scale scientific applications. CPPC resolves major issues in implementing scalable, efficient and portable checkpointing by using a variable level, non-coordinated, non-logging, portable approach. Experimental results have demonstrated the efficacy of this approach, in terms of execution times, checkpointing overhead, memory requirements, portability and usability.

CPPC version 0.5 can be downloaded at http://cppc.des.udc.es.

Acknowledgments. This work has been supported by the Ministry of Education and Science of Spain (ref: TIN-2004-07797-C02 and FPU grant AP-2004-2685),

Galician Government (ref: PGIDIT04TIC105004PR) and CYTED Program (ref: 506PI0293). We gratefully thank CESGA (Galician Supercomputing Center) for providing access to the HP Superdome computer.

References

1. Bosilca, G., Bouteiller, A., Cappello, F., Djilali, S., Fedak, G., Germain, C., Herault, T., Lemarinier, P., Lodygensky, O., Magniette, F., Neri, V., Selikhov, A.: MPICH-V: Toward a scalable fault tolerant MPI for volatile nodes. In: Proceedings of the 2002 ACM/IEEE Supercomputing Conference, pp. 1–18 (2002)
2. Louca, S., Neophytou, N., Lachanas, A., Evripidou, P.: MPI-FT: Portable fault tolerance scheme for MPI. Parallel Processing Letters 10(4), 371–382 (2000)
3. Agbaria, A., Friedman, R.: Starfish: Fault-tolerant dynamic MPI programs on clusters of workstations. In: 8th IEEE International Symposium on High Performance Distributed Computing, pp. 167–176 (1999)
4. Rao, S., Alvisi, L., Vin, H.: Egida: An extensible toolkit for low-overhead fault tolerance. In: 29th International Symposium on Fault-Tolerant Computing (FTCS-29), pp. 48–55 (1999)
5. Bronevetsky, G., Marques, D., Pingali, K., Stodghill, P.: Automated application-level checkpointing of MPI programs. In: ACM SIGPLAN Symposium on Principles and Practices of Parallel Programming (PPOPP), pp. 84–94 (2003)
6. Rodríguez, G., Martín, M., González, P., Touriño, J.: Controller/precompiler for portable checkpointing. IEICE Transactions on Information and Systems E89-D(2), 408–417 (2006)
7. Martín, M., Singh, D., Mouriño, J., Rivera, F., Doallo, R., Bruguera, J.: High performance air pollution modeling for a power plant environment. Parallel Computing 29(11-12), 1763–1790 (2003)
8. González, P., Cabaleiro, J.C., Pena, T.F., Rivera, F.F.: Dual BEM for crack growth analysis in distributed-memory multiprocessors. Advances in Engineering Software 31(12), 921–927 (2000)
9. Elnozahy, E., Alvisi, L., Wang, Y., Johnson, D.: A survey of rollback-recovery protocols in message-passing systems. ACM Computing Surveys 34(3), 375–408 (2002)
10. National Center for Supercomputing Applications: HDF5: File Format Specification [last accessed May 2007] http://hdf.ncsa.uiuc.edu/HDF5
11. Gailly, J., Adler, M.: Zlib home page [last accessed May 2007] http://www.zlib.net
12. Li, K., Naughton, J.F., Plank, J.S.: Low-latency concurrent checkpointing for parallel programs. IEEE Transactions on Parallel and Distributed Systems 5(8), 874–879 (1994)
13. Carmichael, G., Peters, L., Saylor, R.: The STEM-II regional scale acid deposition and photochemical oxidant model - I. An overview of model development and applications. Atmospheric Environment 25A(10), 2077–2105 (1991)

Study of 3D Dynamics of Gravitating Systems Using Supercomputers: Methods and Applications[*]

Nikolay Snytnikov[1], Vitaly Vshivkov[1], and Valery Snytnikov[2]

[1] Institute of Computational Mathematics and
Mathematical Geophysics SB RAS,
630090, prosp. Lavrentieva, 6, Novosibirsk, Russia
{nik,vsh}@ssd.sscc.ru
http://www.ssd.sscc.ru
[2] Boreskov Institute of Catalysis SB RAS,
630090, prosp. Lavrentieva, 5, Novosibirsk, Russia
snyt@catalysis.nsk.su

Abstract. We describe parallel numerical code for solving problems of stellar dynamics. The code is based on numerical solving of Poisson and Vlasov equations in cylindrical coordinates using particle-in-cells method. The code is designed for use on supercomputers with distributed memory. We consider different possible strategies of parallelization according to initial technical parameters of numerical methods and physical conditions of the model. We present results of numerical simulations for the following problems of stellar dynamics: investigation of influence of central potential on the vertical motions of thin gravitating disk; stability of uniform sphere with anisotropic distribution of velocity; numerical approximation of equilibrium states of gravitating systems.

1 Introduction

Problems of stellar dynamics — investigation of stellar systems formation, their equilibrium and stability, appearance of spirals and bars — require to solve N-body problem in self-consistent gravitational field [1]. Its mathematical model consists of collisionless Vlasov equation for distribution function of matter (hereinafter, DF) and Poisson equation for gravitational potential. Numerical solving is based on particle-in-cells method [2] (also called particle-mesh).

Complexity of this numerical model is conditioned by three-dimensions and non-stationarity of the problem. It's required to compute individual motions of huge number of particles, to solve 3D Poisson equation and to store 3D mesh functions of potential, gravitational forces and density of matter as 3D arrays in computer's RAM. At the same time the number of particles and nodes of

---

[*] The present work was supported by Grant of Rosobrazovanie, contract RNP.2.2.1.1.1969; Grant of Rosobrazovanie, contract RNP.2.2.1.1.3653.

V. Malyshkin (Ed.): PaCT 2007, LNCS 4671, pp. 162–173, 2007.

the mesh should be sufficient to provide reliability of the simulation results[1]. That's why numerical simulations for considered class of problems are close to computer's capabilities. Hence there is a strong requirement to develop effective parallel algorithms and to employ supercomputers.

Mentioned difficulties can be partially overcome with the help of quasi-3D model [3], special approximation of 3D model, which neglects vertical motions of the matter (however it's still needed to solve 3D Poisson equation). This approximation is especially useful to overcome problem with storing 3D data, because on each time step only values of mesh functions in plane $z = 0$ (where matter has non-zero density) are needed. It seems, that quasi-3D approximation is suitable in the presence of massive central gravitational field and initial DF in the form of thin disk, that is the case of circumstellar disk model. However for the large class of problems, such as investigation of globular clusters and systems with distinct vertical motions of matter or non-uniform vertical structure, completely 3D model msut be studied.

In the present paper we describe parallel numerical algorithms for investigation of 3D dynamics of gravitating systems. We consider possible approaches to the parallelization of numerical methods according to their technical parameters (number of mesh nodes and particles) and initial physical conditions of the problem. With the help of implemented parallel code we are able to perform numerical simulations for important problems of stellar dynamics. We present some applications:

- investigation of influence of central potential on the vertical motions of thin gravitating disk,
- stability of uniform sphere with anisotropic distribution of velocity,
- approach to study equilibrium states of gravitating systems.

2 Mathematical Model of 3D Dynamics of Gravitating Systems

The foundation of numerical model of 3D dynamics of gravitating systems is collisionless Vlasov equation for DF and Poisson equation for self-consistent gravitational potential [1].

Collisionless Vlasov equation has the following form:

$$\frac{\partial f}{\partial t} + \mathbf{u}\frac{\partial f}{\partial \mathbf{r}} - \nabla\Phi\frac{\partial f}{\partial \mathbf{u}} = 0, \tag{1}$$

where $f(t, \mathbf{r}, \mathbf{u})$ is time-dependent DF of coordinates $\mathbf{r}$ and velocities $\mathbf{u}$. Gravitational potential satisfies Poisson equation, which has the following form in chosen cylindrical coordinates:

$$\frac{1}{r}\frac{\partial}{\partial r}\left(r\frac{\partial\Phi}{\partial r}\right) + \frac{1}{r^2}\frac{\partial^2\Phi}{\partial\phi^2} + \frac{\partial^2\Phi}{\partial z^2} = 4\pi G\rho. \tag{2}$$

---

[1] E.g. there are very few supercomputers in the world allowing to carry out experiments with the number of particles equal to number of stars in Galaxy $\sim 10^{11}$.

System is completed with equation for density of matter:

$$\rho(t, \mathbf{r}) = \int\limits_{\mathbf{u}} f(t, \mathbf{r}, \mathbf{u}) d\mathbf{u}. \tag{3}$$

To obtain non-dimensional parameters there are chosen distance R_0, mass M_0 and gravitational constant G. R_0 and M_0 could be either radius of galaxy and its mass or typical dimension of circumstellar disk and mass of protostar. Corresponding values of velocity V_0, time t_0 and potential Φ_0 could be noted in the following way:

$$V_0 = \sqrt{\frac{GM_0}{R_0}}, \quad t_0 = \frac{R_0}{V_0}, \quad \Phi_0 = V_0^2.$$

Important criterion of accuracy of obtained solution is verification of conservation laws: mass, momentum, angular momentum, energy.

3   Numerical Methods

In this section we briefly describe used numerical methods for solving system (1) – (3). More detailed description can be found in [4].

3.1   Vlasov Equation

Vlasov equation (1) for DF $f(t, \mathbf{r}, \mathbf{u})$ is solved with the help of particle-in-cells method [2]. Space cylindrical domain is divided by mesh into cells. The mesh then is used during solving Poisson equation (2). In the initial moment particles are put in cells in such way, that their number in cell corresponds to the density of matter in cell. Equations of motion for separate particle are:

$$\frac{d\mathbf{v}_i}{dt} = -\frac{\nabla\Phi}{m_i}, \quad \frac{d\mathbf{r}_i}{dt} = \mathbf{v}_i, \tag{4}$$

where $\mathbf{v}_i, \mathbf{r}_i$ – velocity and coordinates of particle with number i. Particles, which have coordinate $\mathbf{r}$ and located in volume $V(\mathbf{r})$, determine DF $f(t, \mathbf{r}, \mathbf{u})$ and density $\rho(\mathbf{r}) = \frac{1}{V(\mathbf{r})} \sum m_j$.

   Then density function $\rho(t, \mathbf{r})$ is restored using multilinear interpolation of particles' masses into the nodes of the mesh.

3.2   Poisson Equation

Potential function, solution of Poisson equation, is approximated on an introduced mesh with the help of finite-difference methods using seven-spot pattern. Boundary conditions for gravitational potential are defined as:

$$\Phi|_\Gamma = -\frac{M_{disk}}{\sqrt{r^2 + z^2}}. \tag{5}$$

It corresponds to the case when total mass of the matter is located at the center of the system. Such an approximation of boundary conditions helps to avoid direct summation of potential produced by particles for each boundary node of the mesh.

Obtained system of linear equations (SLE) is solved with FFT applied to the azimuthal coordinate. As a result we obtain K_{max} independent SLE for complex functions of wave harmonics of potential, where K_{max} is number of azimuthal nodes of the mesh. Then each system is solved using relaxation method applied to radial coordinate and sweeping procedure applied to vertical axis. After that mesh function of potential is restored using FFT applied to known values of potential harmonics.

The solving method was chosen for the two reasons. First, it's known to be effective for the Laplace equation [3] (which, in fact, is used in quasi-3D model instead of Poisson equation). The second reason is the possibility of parallelization, since SLE for complex functions of wave harmonics can be treated completely separate. However, there are some difficulties, which are related to ill-conditioning of the system [4]. The most ill-conditioned system is the one corresponding to the harmonics with wave number 0. The use of simple relaxation method is related to the fact that initial approximation for the next time step can be taken from previous one.

Finally restoring of mesh functions for forces is done using leap-frog finite-difference method.

4   Parallelization Techniques

For numerical experiments and study non-stationary 3D dynamics of gravitating matter it's required to integrate system (1) – (3) on a large time scales. At the same time sufficiently small spatial step must be provided in order to investigate non-linear structures such as spirals, rings, bending instabilities, which are much smaller than computational domain; hence, fine meshes must be applied.

In spite of its reliability described numerical model is rather time- and memory-consuming. Modern PC can process numerical simulations with the following technical parameters: number of mesh nodes is 128^3, and number of particles not more than 10^7. It's needed from 2 up to 7 days to complete one numerical experiment[2]. The only way to employ meshes with greater number of particles is to develop and implement effective parallel algorithms for solving both Poisson and Vlasov equations.

The main challenge for parallelization is concerned with some restrictions from physical point of view: density modification in one point of space implies an

---

[2] Maximum numbers of mesh nodes and particles can be estimated in the following way. 5 3D arrays are used for 3 forces, density and potential, 3 3D arrays are needed for harmonics storing and temporary data. So it's needed about 400 Mb of RAM to store 128^3 double-precision 3D arrays. Since each particle has 3 space coordinates and 3 velocities it's needed about 500 Mb to store arrays for 10^7 particles. Amount of RAM in modern PC rarely exceeds 1 Gb.

instant response in modification of gravitational potential in other space points. In other words, it does not matter, how to decompose the computational domain, or what procedures are parallelized; at each time step it's needed to exchange 3D data with values of density and potential between processors. It can be optimized, for example, with some techniques of apriori estimations what computational subdomains have density equal to zero and so on. But such techniques are heuristics and can not be applied for general problem.

In the following sections we describe implemented parallel algorithms which are suitable for a large class of initial physical conditions. Possible directions of further development are also discussed.

4.1   Poisson Equation

Parallelization of solving Poisson equation is based on an independence of solving systems of linear equations (SLE) for complex functions of wave harmonics of potential. SLEs are divided into groups and assigned to corresponding processors.

It's known [3] that implementation of similar parallel algorithm for solving Laplace equation has a difficulty: different time is needed for solving different SLE due to ill-conditioning of SLE for wave harmonics with small numbers; it may leads to non-uniform loading of processors. The same problem was observed during development of solving methods for Poisson equation. Fig. 1 shows distributions for logarithm of time needed for solving SLE for the first time step (a), and for mean time of thousand time steps (b). Almost all time is taken by SLE for harmonics with wave number 0, which is the most ill-conditioned. Then computation time is distributed with the obvious rule — the most time is needed for solving SLE for harmonics with wave numbers close to zero (Fig. 1, (b)). Based

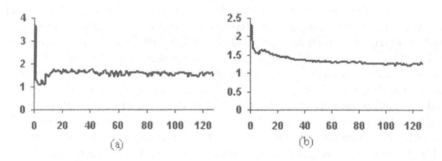

Fig. 1. Logarithm of solving time for SLE (vertical axis) depending on wave number of harmonics (horizontal axes) is represented: **(a)** on the first time step, **(b)** average for thousand time steps

on this experimental data, we have implemented the algorithm of distribution harmonics between processors in the following way:

– SLE for harmonics with wave number 0 is assigned to the separate processor with number $procRank = 0$,

– Processor with number $procRank > 0$ solves group of SLEs with numbers $m = procRank + i*(procNb-1)$, where $procNb$ is total number of processors (less than total number of harmonics), i –integer.

Tabl. 1 shows timing distribution for separate procedures of Poisson equation solving algorithm. This algorithm takes 3D array for mesh function of density as input and returns 3D array for potential as output (storing harmonics values for using them on the next time step). Solving harmonics' SLE is parallelized procedure and its speed-up factor is about 34 with 40 employed processors. So there is no need to apply more complex technique such as algorithm of dynamic load-balancing as in [3]. At the same time total speed-up factor of Poisson equation

Table 1. Typical distribution of computation time for separate procedures of solving algorithm of Poisson equation for one of the processors on 10-th time step. Number of SLE is 256, dimension of SLE is 212×146.

Number of processors	FFT for density, sec	Harmonics' SLE solving, sec	Gathering of harmonics, sec	FFT for potential, sec	Total time, sec
1	0.3	6.8	—	0.4	7.5
10	0.3	0.7	0.65	0.4	2.05
40	0.3	0.2	0.42	0.4	1.32

solving is about 3.7 with employed 10 processors and 5.7 with 40. The reason of such a weak speed-up factor is that bottlenecks are non-parallelized parts: FFT applied to 3D mesh functions, and gathering of harmonics. These parts can not be parallelized with the help of standard tools, because of increasing of interprocessor communications.

The possible optimization of FFT is domain decomposition technique. It's needed to apply FFT for 3D mesh functions defined only on subdomain nodes. However optimization possibilities of harmonics' gathering procedure have fundamental restriction imposed by physical statement of problem which was mentioned at the beginning of the section 4.

4.2   Vlasov Equation

Since computation of DF (coordinates and velocities for each particle) on the next time step requires only computed mesh function of gravitational potential and does not depend on coordinates of other particles, it is a source of natural parallelism. There could be applied two different strategies of parallelization.

First strategy is based on domain decomposition technique: each processor is treated its own space subdomain; computation of particles' coordinates, which are located in a subdomain, is assigned to corresponding processor. The obvious advantage of this algorithm is the theoretical opportunity of arbitrary number of mesh nodes, because it's needed to store 3D arrays only for mesh functions defined in its subdomain. On the other hand it requires to transfer some particles between processors at each timestep, because particles change coordinates and subdomains during evolution. Also it's needed to take into account possible localization of density (and, hence, huge number of particles) in small subdomains, re-dividing domain and reassigning new subdomains to processors.

Second strategy, implemented for the present moment, consists of the following: particles are distributed on processors in correspondance to their numbers without taking into account their coordinates. Then each processor computes coordinates of its particles on the next time step. The advantage of this algorithm is that it does not require redistribution of particles during solving. At the same time there is a restriction for the number of nodes of the mesh (not more than $256 \times 512 \times 256$) due to the storing 3D arrays for the whole domain. But for meshes of average size (the most typical one is $256 \times 256 \times 256$) this algorithm is the most efficient. This strategy is limited only to collisionless models, since taking into account possible collisions of particles implies interactions between processors and exchanging data with each other.

4.3 Performance Measuring

Testing of implemented parallel algorithm was done on MVS-1000 in Siberian Supercomputer Center and on MVS-1500 in Moscow Joint Supercomputer Center. The greatest number of mesh nodes was $256 \times 512 \times 256$ and number of particles 10^9 with 200 processors. Fig. 2 shows speed-up factor for typical simulations with mesh nodes $212 \times 256 \times 146$ and number of particles 10^8. It's shown an estimation of computation time for sequential simulation (number of processors equal to 1), since simulation requirs more than 5 Gb of RAM. The ratio of solving Poisson equation and Vlasov equation was 30% and 70% correspondingly for the simulation with 40 processors.

The greatest speed-up factor was obtained on 20 processors and decreased with increasing of number of processors because of the discussed problems with the parallelization of Poisson equation.

It's necessary to mention that with increasing number of particles it's recommended to increase number of processors. E.g., for simulations involving 4×10^8 it's natural to use from 40 up to 80 processors.

5   Applications

In this section we describe results of numerical simulations on supercomputers.

First of all it is interesting to investigate the reliability of quasi-3D model, which is widely used for simulations of circumstellar disk [3]. A typical feature of circumstellar disk is a massive central body. In the subsection 5.1 we describe results of study of influence of central body on the vertical motions of thin disk.

Second series of numerical experiments (presented in subsection 5.2) are devoted to the investigation of equilibrium and stability of gravitating systems, the one of the fundamental problems of stellar dynamics [1,5]. Analytical solving of given class of problem has obvious restriction: it's needed to simplify a problem

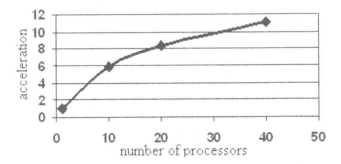

Fig. 2. Speed-up factor depending on number of processors. Technical parameters: $212 \times 256 \times 146$ mesh nodes, 10^8 particles.

and to consider only special class of systems, e.g., which have spherical or axis symmetry, constant density and so on. The real DF of stellar systems are more complex, and it seems that they can be restored only with numerical simulations. Besides, it's needed to restore DF with good accuracy, that implies employing huge number of particles.

With the help of implemented parallel code it's possible to numerically investigate equilibrium DF in the most general way without restrictions for the form of distribution functions, which were typical for earlier attempts [6]. We propose an approach for investigation of different kinds of equilibrium distributions with the help of solving non-stationary problem, that requires to observe the evolution of the gravitating system during a lot of rotations. Starting from given distribution, orbits of particles are intermixed during their evolution, so the whole system moves to stationary state. Obtained function is considered as equilibrium.

5.1 Influence of Central Body on the Vertical Motions of Thin Disk

The following axisymmetric function of surface density is used for initial state:

$$z = 0, \sigma(r) = \begin{cases} \sigma_0 \sqrt{1 - \left(\frac{r}{R_0}\right)^2}, & r \le R_0, \\ 0, & r > R_0; \end{cases}$$

$$z \neq 0, f(t, \mathbf{r}, \mathbf{u}) = 0.$$

(6)

where σ_0 is derived from the condition that the total mass of disk is equal to M_0.

Initial velocities of particles correspond to the circular rotation around origin. Dispersions of radial and vertical velocities c_r and c_z are set in accordance with Gauss distribution.

The following parameters are constants: sum of masses of the disk and central body $M_{disk} + M_{cb} = 7.0$, value of initial dispersion of radial velocity $c_r = 0.12$. As variable parameters we take initial value of vertical dispersion c_z in the range $0.0001 \div 1.0$ and ratio k_M in the range $k_M = \frac{M_{cb}}{M_{disk}} = 0.0 \div 6.0$.

In the case of $k_M \leq 1.5$ at earlier stage of evolution there are observed clusterization accompanied by bending of the disk (non-symmetric distribution of matter w.r.t. the plane $z = 0$). At later stages a lot of matter are thrown from the plane of the disk.

In the case of massive central body $k_M \geq 2.0$, and small vertical dispersion $0.0001 \leq c_z \leq 0.2$, at the first stage there are observed spirals (Fig.3 a,b). Then disk evolves to the quasi-stationary state (Fig.3 b). Strong non-symmetries of DF is not observed. More of that, at later stages of evolution disk has almost constant height. Further increasing of k_M leads to increasing of stability of the disk both in vertical and radial directions.

So, employing quasi-3D model is suitable for simulations with initial distributions of matter in the form of thin disk and in presence of massive central body, that is the case of circumstellar disk.

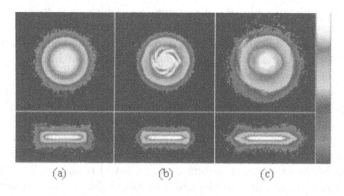

Fig. 3. Logarithm of surface density for the points of time $t = 1.0$ (a), $t = 4.0$ (b) $t = 15.0$ (c) in the planes $z = 0$ (upper) and $y = 0$ (lower). Computation parameters: $k_M = 4.0$, $c_z = 0.01$.

5.2   Approach to the Investigation of the Equilibrium States of Gravitating System

Stability of uniform sphere with anisotropic distribution of velocities.
Good demonstration of reliability of the implemented numerical model for investigation of equilibrium states is Einstein's model. In the initial step matter has the form of sphere with the uniform density. Each particle has a circular rotation around origin with arbitrary direction. Total angular momentum of the system is equal to zero. It's one of the models with analytically proved properties of equilibrium and stability [1].

Numerical simulations with this initial distribution showed the same result. The evolution of the system was observing during the several rotations of particles around the origin and no fluctuations of density were noticed.

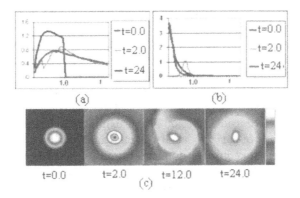

Fig. 4. Diagrams of rotation curve (a) and surface density for the points of time $t = 0.0$, $t = 2.0$ and $t = 24.0$. Initial parameters: $M_0 = 1.0$, $c_r = 0.5$, $c_z = 0.09$, $c_\phi = 0$.

Evolution of thin disk with exponential surface of density. Let us consider approach proposed in the section 5 in the case of evolving thin disk with exponential density surface, which is usually used for approximation of surface density of real galaxies [7]:

$$\sigma(r) = \begin{cases} \sigma_0 e^{-\frac{r}{L}}, \, r \leq R_0, \\ 0, \, r > R_0; \end{cases} \tag{7}$$

where σ_0 is derived from the condition that total mass is equal to M_0, L is a parameter of density scale. Initial velocities of matter are chosen in accordance

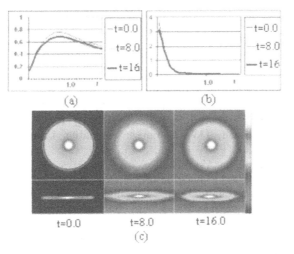

Fig. 5. Diagrams of rotation curve (a) and surface density for the points of time $t = 0.0$, $t = 12.0$ and $t = 18.4$. Initial distribution – approximation of the equilibrium distribution function, $M_0 = 0.83$.

with Gauss distribution with given dispersions c_r, c_z, c_ϕ and mean values corresponding to the rotation around origin.

Numerical simulations showed that the distribution function defined in such a way is not an equilibrium one. At the same time after sufficiently great number of rotations the system evolves to the equilibrium state (Fig. 4), with the ellipsoid in central region, which rotates with constant angular velocity. On the Fig. 4 there are shown diagrams of rotation curve and surface density.

Then, obtained distribution function is approximated with the help of axisymmetric mesh functions of surface density, azimuthal velocity, and dispersions of velocities. At that we take into account matter only in central region of the domain ($r < 3R_0$). This approximation is suitable because total mass of excluded matter is less than 20% and it has a weak impact on the dynamics of matter in central region. As it is shown on the Fig. 5 the obtained approximation is close to equilibrium state.

6 Conclusion

We have implemented parallel numerical code, based on particle-in-cells method and designed to study 3D dynamics of gravitating systems. Parallel implementation is effective for simulations with number of mesh nodes less than $212 \times 256 \times 146$ and number of particles $\sim 10^8$. To use finer mesh we discussed possible strategy based on domain decomposition technique.

Using parallel code we are able to study a large class of gravitational physics problems, that is demonstrated with apllications: investigation of central body influence to the vertical dynamics of thin disk and study equilibrium and stability of gravitating system. To provide fine accuracy and large time scales for numerical simulations, there is a fundamental requirement to use supercomputers.

References

1. Fridman, A.M., Polyachenko, V.L.: Ravnovesie i ustoychivost' gravitiruyushchikh sistem. (Moscow: Nauka; revised English ed. 1984 Physics of gravitating Systems, Vol.1: Equilibrium and Stability), Springer, Heidelberg (1976)
2. Hockney, R.W., Eastwood, J.W.: Computer Simulation Using Particles, p. 540. McGraw-Hill, New York (1981)
3. Kuksheva, E.A., Malyshkin, V.E., Nikitin, S.A., Snytnikov, A.V., Snytnikov, V.N., Vshivkov, V.A.: Numerical Simulation of Self-Organisation in Gravitationally Unstable Media on Supercomputers. In: Malyshkin, V. (ed.) PaCT 2003. LNCS, vol. 2763, pp. 354–368. Springer, Heidelberg (2003)
4. Vshivkov, V.A., Snytnikov, V.N., Snytnikov, N.V.: Simulation of three-dimensional dynamics of matter in gravitational field with the use of multiprocessor computer. Computational Technologies (in Russian) 11(2), 15–27 (2006)

5. King, I.R.: Introduction to Classical Stellar Dynamics (in Russian), p. 214. URSS, Moscow (2002)
6. Barnes, J., Goodman, J., Hut, P.: Dynamical instabilities in spherical stellar systems. The Astrophysical Journal 300, 112–131 (1986)
7. Morozov, A.G., Khoperskov, A.V.: Physics of the disks (In Russian) http://www.astronet.ru:8101/db/msg/1169400

Transient Mechanical Wave Propagation in Semi-infinite Porous Media Using a Finite Element Approach with Domain Decomposition Technology

Andrey Terekhov[1], Arnaud Mesgouez[2], and Gaelle Lefeuve-Mesgouez[2]

[1] Institute of Computational Mathematic and Mathematical Geophysics,
Prospect Akademika Lavrentjeva, 6, Novosibirsk, 630090, Russia
[2] UMR Climate, Soil and Environment, University of Avignon, France,
Faculté des Sciences, 33 rue Louis Pasteur, F-84000 Avignon,
Phone: +33(0)490144463; Fax: +33(0)490144409
arnaud.mesgouez@univ-avignon.fr

Abstract. In this paper, the authors propose a numerical investigation in the time domain of the mechanical wave propagation due to an impulsional load on a semi-infinite soil. The ground is modelled as a porous saturated viscoelastic medium involving the complete Biot theory. An accurate and efficient Finite Element Method using a matrix-free technique is used. Two parallel algorithms are used: Geometrical Domain Decomposition (GDD) and Algebraic Decomposition (AD). Numerical results show that GDD algorithm has the best time. Physical numerical results present the displacements of the fluid and solid particles over the surface and in depth.

1 Introduction

The study of the mechanical wave propagation in porous media is a subject of great interest in diverse scientific fields ranging from environmental engineering or vibration isolation to geomechanics. At the macroscopic scale, the medium is considered as a two-phase continuum. The Biot theory is known as the reference theory to deal with the macroscopic mechanical wave propagation phenomenon, see Biot [1] or Coussy [2] for instance.

Theoretical works are restricted to simple geometries. Consequently, they have to be completed by numerical approaches such as Finite Element or Boundary Element Methods, allowing the study of more complex problems to better represent the ground. The difficult study of transient regimes in geomechanics has been treated numerically by several authors but only for specific cases, Zienkiewicz and Shiomi [3], Simon et al. [4] and Gajo et al. [5] for example. In particular, in many cases, the tortuosity and the physical damping parameters are not taken into account.

Moreover, even with an efficient and optimized finite element code, only a restricted range of problems can be treated. As a matter of fact, solution of

V. Malyshkin (Ed.): PaCT 2007, LNCS 4671, pp. 174–183, 2007.

practical problems (for instance, realistic 3D geometries, and problems with short pulse load needing fine meshes for representing well the high frequencies) usually requires millions of degrees of freedom. This is often virtually out of capabilities of contemporary sequential computers either because of lack of memory or abundantly long computation time. In all these cases, parallel programming techniques may be a good solution to overcome the computational complexity.

In this paper, the authors propose a parallelized version of a finite element C++ code specifically developed at the Climate Soil and Environment Laboratory to study transient wave propagation. This approach includes the whole Biot theory with all the couplings which represent the interactions between the solid and fluid phases. The sequential version has previously been presented at ICCS 2005, Mesgouez et al. [6].

Two parallelization techniques have been achieved: the first one uses an algebraic grid partitioning and the second one a Geometrical Domain Decomposition. MPI standard library is used to exchange data between processors. Numerical results, obtained for a two-dimensional problem, include the analysis of speed-up and efficiency on several super computers.

2   Mechanical and Numerical Works

2.1   Spatial Scales and Macroscopic Approach

When we focus our attention on the description of a porous medium, the first question to be put is that of the spatial scale of analysis: indeed, two approaches are conceivable. The first one is situated at the microscopic scale. The characteristic length size is the dimension of the pore. In this configuration, the solid matrix is partially or completely filled with one or several viscous fluids. One geometric point is thus located in one of the different identifiable solid or fluid phases. Mechanical equations of each phase and mixture with compatible interface conditions are written. They correspond to those of linear elasticity in the solid and to the equations of Stokes in the fluid. This approach deals with problems like interface modelling or description of microscopic geological structures. Homogenization is then obtained through asymptotic developments or averaging procedures and leads to a macroscopic description of the porous medium, see Terada and al. [8] or Coussy et al. [9] for instance. We obtain thus the famous set of macroscopic mechanical equations for a representative elementary volume. In this macroscopic spatial description, the porous medium is seen as a two-phase continuum. This scale, we study here, is well adapted to most of practical geomechanical problems.

Writing u_i and U_i respectively the macroscopic solid and fluid displacements components, Biot's equations can be written with usual notations as follows:

$$\sigma_{ij,j} = (1 - \phi)\rho_s \ddot{u}_i + \phi\rho_f \ddot{U}_i \tag{1}$$

$$p_{,i} = -\tfrac{\phi}{K}(\dot{U}_i - \dot{u}_i) + \rho_f(a - 1)\ddot{u}_i - a\rho_f \ddot{U}_i \tag{2}$$

$$\sigma_{ij} = \lambda_{0v}\varepsilon_{kk}\delta_{ij} + 2\mu_v\varepsilon_{ij} - \beta p\delta_{ij} \tag{3}$$

$$-\phi\left(U_{k,k} - u_{k,k}\right) = \beta u_{k,k} + \tfrac{1}{M}p. \tag{4}$$

σ_{ij} are the total Cauchy stress tensor components and p is the pore pressure. The soil's characteristics are: λ_{0v} and μ_v (drained viscoelastic equivalent Lamé constants), ρ_s and ρ_f (solid grains and fluid densities), ϕ (porosity), K (hydraulic permeability representing the viscous coupling), a (tortuosity standing for the mass coupling), M and β (Biot coefficients including the elastic coupling). In this problem, the unknowns to be determined are the solid and fluid components of displacements.

2.2   Finite Element Formulation and Numerical Resolution

To determine the solid and fluid displacements in the ground, we develop a numerical code based on the finite element method for the space integration, coupled to a finite difference method for the time integration. The main steps are:

- some boundary and initial conditions are associated to the previous partial differential system. Some modifications on the field equations are done in order to lead to a Cauchy's problem.
- integral forms are obtained using the weighted residual method. They are then spatially and analytically discretized and lead to a time differential system. The global differential system to be solved can be written as

$$[M]\frac{d}{dt}\{W^{(G)}\} + [K]\{W^{(G)}\} = \{F^{(G)}\}. \tag{5}$$

$[M]$ and $[K]$ are respectively the global mass and stiffness matrices. $\{W^{(G)}\}$ and $\{F^{(G)}\}$ are the global vectors of unknowns and solicitation. With the developed technique, the mass matrix is diagonal and can be easily inverted.
- the backward finite difference method modified with an upward time parameter is used to obtain an approximate solution of the problem.

2.3   Structure of the Code and Parallelization

The sequential code called FAFEMO (Fast Adaptive Finite Element Modular Object), developed to solve the previous problem, constitutes an efficient code to deal with transient 2D problems and small 3D ones. The use of a matrix free technique, not necessary for small cases, becomes interesting for huge 3D configurations. An expert multigrid system is also used to optimize the problem size and yields a modification of the global matrices at each time step. The two previous techniques lead to a high performance level both for the storage and the CPU costs. The C++ code is organized in three classes connected by a single heritage: *element*, *elementary matrices* and *building-resolution* classes.

More informations on the finite element formulation and the sequential version of FAFEMO can be found in reference [10].

For huge problems, the elementary vectors have to be calculated and assembled for each time step since they are too expensive in terms of Input/Output cost to be stored. In order to treat 3D problems and to perform intensive 2D parametric studies, we propose and compare two parallel algorithms to reduce the time calculation.

The Unix/Linux *gprof* tool draws a time profile of the sequential code. For a two-dimensional application, the elapsed time is divided as presented in Table 1, for each of the three classes.

Table 1. Time profile of the 2D sequential code

reading of the data files and *element* class	*elementary matrices* class	*building-resolution* class
7.45%	90.60%	1.95%

The part which is the largest consumer of elapsed time clearly appears to be the *elementary matrices* class. This can be explained as the elementary matrices have to be calculated for each time step. Besides, as we use a matrix free technique with a diagonal mass matrix, the resolution part is more efficient and needs little computational time. Moreover, the process of construction of the elementary matrices and vectors $[K_e]$, $[M_e]$ and $\{f_e\}$ is iterative and independent element by element. This independent and time-consuming loop can thus be divided into several processors by distributing the n elements between p quasi-equitable parts. A good load balancing is thus obtained.

2.4 Algebraic Decomposition (Grid Partitioning)

Firstly we propose grid partitioning based on algebraic decomposition which is performed randomly without any geometric factors. Several advantages are:

– unlike the domain decomposition method, this technique does not need any particular interface management. This is particularly important when an expert multigrid system is activated, or when the geometry is changed.
– moreover, when the size of the grid is modified, the algebraic distribution of the elements leads to an equitable load balancing between processors at each time step.
– another advantage of this approach is that the implementation is as close to the original sequential solver as possible.

The main disadvantage of Algebraic Decomposition is that this algorithm does not take into account information concerning geometrical properties of the domain and all the information has to be communicated to a master processor.

The parallelization of the FAFEMO code corresponds to a SPMD programming model with in this configuration an algebraic distribution of the different finite elements of the grid. MPI standard library is used to exchange data concerning the elementary matrices between master and slave processors. The architecture of the parallelized version of the code is summarized on figure 1.

You can find more information and some numerical results obtained by the authors on Algebraic Decomposition in [7] .

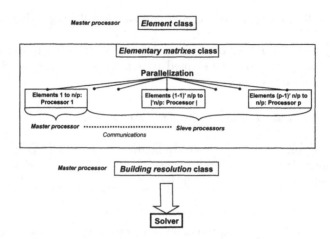

Fig. 1. Structure of the parallelized version of the C++ finite element code

2.5 Domain Decomposition

One of the most widespread parallel algorithms for solving problems with finite elements method is the method of Domain Decomposition, which main advantage is the use of information about geometrical form of area. Communication operations are used only between neighboring domains. Therefore, the number of communications is smaller than when we use algebraic decomposition. Moreover, global memory can be distributed between processors because we know precisely how much memory each processor needs. Thus, in this case, we can store the elementary matrices and vectors.

In the following, we propose to use DD technique. The main idea is to divide area into several nonintersecting domains.

First, we convert the mesh into graph-format (see Metis documentation [11]). Then, we use freeware soft for graph partitioning (Chaco [12], Metis [11]). These programs realize graph partitioning algorithms, for instance: linear, internal-KL, multilevel-KL, spectral. They associate each vertex of the graph with the number of the domain it belongs to. In our problem, each vertex of the graph corresponds to a node of an element. Before executing the FAFEMO program, we create the communication map, which describes communication messages between domains. For instance, figure 2 presents a simple part of the mesh. Two numbers are associated to each node of the mesh: the first number is the global number of the node, the second number is the number of the domain. Let's consider some cases with various numbering elements:

1. If the nodes of one element belongs to the same domain, we do not need to exchange information between domains.
2. For an element presenting two identical domain numbers, for example (10, a), (11, b), (12, b), processor "a" needs to transfer data to processor "b" and processor "b" needs to transfer data to processor "a".

3. For an element with nodes belonging to three different domains, for instance (11, a), (12, b), (13, c), processor "a" needs to transfer data to processors "b" and "c", etc.

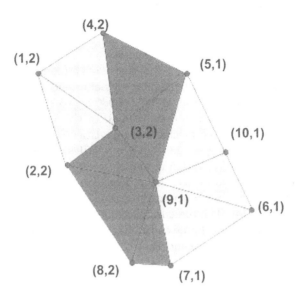

Fig. 2. Example of grid with marked nodes

Thus, in figure 2, the dark grey part represents data to be exchanged between the neighboring domains. High efficiency of the given algorithm is reached because exchanges only occur between neighboring domains.

3 Results

In this section, numerical results are presented for 2D problems involving 25,617 (Test 1) and 100,620 (Test 2) nodes to estimate the performance of the parallelized version of the FAFEMO+DD code. Two supercomputers were used:

1. Supercomputer Zeus (IBM sp4) is installed at the National Computer Center of Higher Education (CINES, Montpellier, France). This cluster is based on IBM Power4 1.3 GHz. Each node has 32 processors. The total number of nodes is 9. These nodes are connected by Switch Hight Performance (HPS).
2. Supercomputer MBC15000-MB is installed at the Joint Supercomputer Center (Moscow, Russia). It is a cluster based on PowerPC 970+ 2.2 GHz with 4 GB Shared RAM. Nodes are connected by high speed Myrinet 2000 network (2Gb/S) and two GigabitEthernet. The peak performance of this supercomputer equals 8.13 Teraflops. Total amount of the RAM equals 1848 GBytes.

3.1   Test 1

In this paragraph, we consider the solution of equations (1-4) for the dimensionless 2D geometry presented in figure 3. The applied solicitation is a vertical impulse of very short duration which dimensionless value is 0.2 (corresponding to 2 ms). The grid is selected according to the studied points and the duration of the study. The boundary is then modelled with Dirichlet conditions, imposing a zero displacement for each of the two phases.

The space (Ω) is of dimensionless radial size $r = 3.5$ (corresponding to 70 m). It is built in a grid with 50,626 triangular elements and 25,617 nodes with 8 degrees of freedom, which is on the whole 204,936 degrees of freedom. One side of the space grid triangle has a step $dx = 0.03$. In the following, we give only dimensionless values; the three mechanical quantities chosen for this problem are: $\mu = 10^{10}$ Pa, $\rho_s = 2,600$ kg m^{-3} and $\eta =0.01$ s, from which we deduce reference length and time: $l_{ref} =19.5$ m and $t_{ref} = 0.01$ s.

The characteristics of the ground have been chosen from a bibliographical study. The papers used are in particular those of Gajo et al. [5], Akbar et al. [13] and Dvorkin and Nur [14]. The dimensionless mechanical values are as follows: drained viscoelastic equivalent Lamé constants $\lambda_{0v}^* = 0.556$ and $\mu_v^* = 0.833$; first Biot coefficient $M^* = 0.5267$; second Biot coefficient $\beta =0.72$; density of solid grains $\rho_s^* =1$; density of fluid component $\rho_f^* = 0.3846$; hydraulic permeability coefficient $K^* = 0.65$; porosity $\phi = 0.4$; tortuosity coefficient $a = 1.2$; damping coefficient $\eta^* = 0.1$.

The equations (1-4) are solved using Backward Step Method for Cauchy's problem and Finite Element Method for spatial approximation. The time step is 0.002 and the study duration is 3.

Figures 6-8 present speed-up, efficiency, elapsed time obtained on the two supercomputers. For the MBC-15000MB, speed-up is a linear function whereas for IBM supercomputer Zeus the non linear part can be explained by architecture of processors. We assume that all frequently used data are put in cache memory which leads to a non linear increasing speed-up and an increasing efficiency. Moreover, the chosen scale magnifies the irregularities of the curve. This

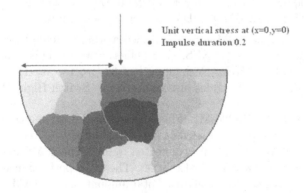

- Unit vertical stress at (x=0,y=0)
- Impulse duration 0.2

Fig. 3. Example of geometry

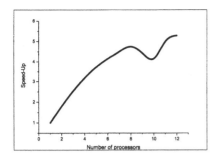

Fig. 4. Test 1. Speed-up on MBC-15000MB obtained with AD

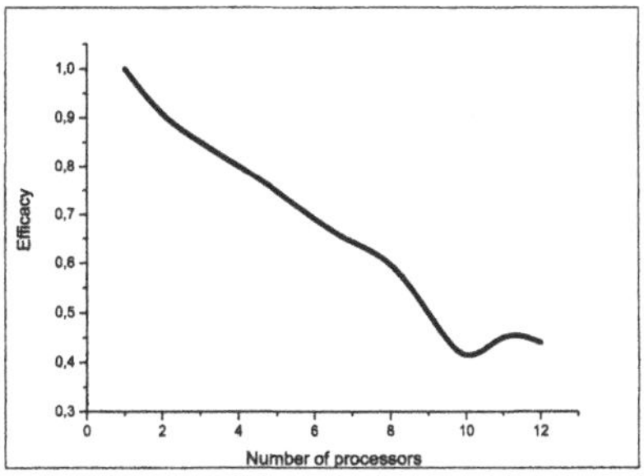

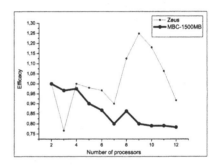

Fig. 5. Test 1. Efficiency on MBC-15000MB obtained with AD

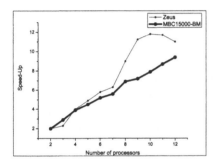

Fig. 6. Test 1. Speed-up on MBC-15000MB and Zeus obtained with GDD

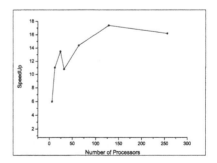

Fig. 7. Test 1. Efficiency on MBC-15000MB and Zeus obtained with GDD

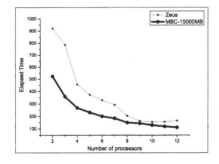

Fig. 8. Test 1. Elapsed time in seconds on MBC-15000MB and Zeus obtained with GDD

Fig. 9. Test 2. Speed-up on MBC-15000MB obtained with GDD

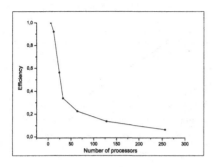

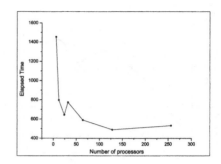

Fig. 10. Test 2. Efficiency on MBC-15000MB obtained with GDD

Fig. 11. Test 2. Elapsed time in seconds on MBC-15000MB obtained with GDD

picture shows better results for Geometrical Domain Decomposition than the ones obtained by Algebraic Decomposition method, see figure 4-5.

3.2 Test 2

For this test, we use the same physical and numerical parameters as in Test 1, but we change the numbers of nodes and elements: number of elements equals 100, 620 and number of nodes 199, 142. Figures 9-11 present the speed-up, efficiency and elapsed time for large numbers of processors. We can say that results are not good because the grid is too small for the use of many processors. If we calculate the number of nodes per processor, we obtain about 5000 − 1000 nodes. We use GID generator which does not allow to create very large grids for supercomputers. In further work, we will introduce huger grids using parallel mesh generator. Some physical parameters studies using FAFEMO code can be found in [10].

4   Conclusion

A parallelized finite element code has been presented to study wave propagation phenomena in poroviscoelastic grounds. In fact, the applications are wider and can concern for instance porous bones or foams. Besides, the code can treat all propagation wave phenomena: a version studying electromagnetic wave propagation has been developed in the same way.

Two parallel algorithms were compared and has shown that Domain Decomposition Method gives better results for huge problems.

References

1. Biot, M.A.: Theory of propagation of elastic waves in a fluid-saturated porous solid. I- Low-frequency range. The Journal of the Acoustical Society of America 28(2), 168–178 (1956)

2. Coussy, O.: Mécanique des milieux poreux. Ed. Technip, Paris (1991)
3. Zienkiewicz, O.C., Shiomi, T.: Dynamic behaviour of saturated porous media: the generalized Biot formulation and its numerical solution. International Journal for Numerical and Analytical Methods in Geomechanics 8, 71–96 (1984)
4. Simon, B.R., Wu, J.S.S., Zienkiewicz, O.C., Paul, D.K.: Evaluation of u-w and u-π finite element methods for the dynamic response of saturated porous media using one-dimensional models. Int. J. Numer. Anal. Methods Geomech 10, 461–482 (1986)
5. Gajo, A., Saetta, A., Vitaliani, R.: Evaluation of three and two field finite element methods for the dynamic response of saturated soil. Int. J. Numer. Anal. Methods Geomech 37, 1231–1247 (1994)
6. Mesgouez, A., Lefeuve-Mesgouez, G., Chambarel, A.: Simulation of transient mechanical wave propagation in heterogeneous soils. In: Sunderam, V.S., van Albada, G.D., Sloot, P.M.A., Dongarra, J.J. (eds.) ICCS 2005. LNCS, vol. 3514, pp. 647–654. Springer, Heidelberg (2005)
7. Mesgouez, A., Lefeuve-Mesgouez, G., Chambarel, A., Fougere, D.: Numerical modeling of poroviscoelastic grounds in the time domain using a parallel approach. In: Alexandrov, V.N., van Albada, G.D., Sloot, P.M.A., Dongarra, J.J. (eds.) ICCS 2006. LNCS, vol. 3992, pp. 50–57. Springer, Heidelberg (2006)
8. Terada, K., Ito, T., Kikuchi, N.: Characterization of the mechanical behaviors of solid-fluid mixture by the homogenization method. Comput. Methods Appl. Mech. Eng. 153, 223–257 (1998)
9. Coussy, O., Dormieux, L., Detournay, E.: From Mixture theory to Biot's approach for porous media. Int. J. Solids Struct. 35, 4619–4635 (1998)
10. Mesgouez, A., Lefeuve-Mesgouez, G., Chambarel, A.: Transient mechanical wave propagation in semi-infinite porous media using a finite element approach. Soil Dyn. Earth. Eng. 25, 421–430 (2005)
11. http://www-users.cs.umn.edu/~karypis/metis
12. Hendrickson, B., Leland, R.: The Chaco User's Guide: Version 2.0. Tech Report SAND94-2692 (1994)
13. Akbar, N., Dvorkin, J., Nur, A.: Relating P-wave attenuation to permeability. Geophysics 58(1), 20–29 (1993)
14. Dvorkin, J., Nur, A.: Dynamic poroelasticity: a unified model with the squirt and the Biot mechanisms. Geophysics 58(4), 524–533 (1993)

The Location of the Gene Regions Under Selective Pressure: Plato Algorithm Parallelization

Yuri Vyatkin[1], Konstantin Gunbin[1],
Alexey Snytnikov[2], and Dmitry Afonnikov[1]

[1] Institure of Cytology and Genetics SB RAS
Lavrentyev aven., 10, 630090, Novosibirsk, Russia
{vyatkin,genkvg,ada}@bionet.nsc.ru
[2] Institute of Computational Mathematics and Mathematical Geophysics SB RAS
Lavrentyev aven., 6, 630090, Novosibirsk, Russia
snytav@ssd.sscc.ru

Abstract. The number of sequenced genes is dramatically increasing with that of international genomic projects. The gene sequence information proved to be helpful in predictions of protein structure, protein function and mutations targeted at improving the biological and biotechnological properties of proteins. Processing of the immense information stored in the databases demands high-throughput computational approaches. Here, we performed a parallelization of the algorithm for analysis of nucleotide substitutions in gene sequences from different organisms previously implemented in the PLATO program. The results demonstrated that the parallelization of the algorithm provides linear speedup of the PLATO program.

Keywords: gene evolution, maximum likelihood, algorithm, parallel computing.

1 Introduction

Gene sequence information is accumulating at an accelerating pace at genomic centers worldwide. The incremental number of sequenced genes stored in the databases in now over 60 millions for more than 165,000 organisms (http://www.ncbi.nlm.nih.gov/Genbank/). Analysis of the sequences provides clues to prediction of the function of genes, their evolutionary features, structure of the proteins they encode, also mutation effect on their structure.

An important problem in comparative analysis of genomic sequences from different organisms is detection of genes or their parts that possess specific modes of nucleotide substitutions with significant deviations in the evolutionary parameters resulted from selective forces due to their specific origin, structure, or function. Therefore, the obtained information is helpful in detecting genes of functional importance. Grassly and Holmes [1] have proposed a method for the

V. Malyshkin (Ed.): PaCT 2007, LNCS 4671, pp. 184–187, 2007.

detection of gene regions evolving anomalously using the likelihood approach implemented in the PLATO program (http://evolve.zps.ox.ac.uk/software/Plato/main.html). Due to use of computation of the likelihood and the Monte Carlo sampling to estimate statistical significance of likelihood deviation, the original program was time- and labor-consuming. This became critical in large scale evolutionary analyses. In this work, we perform parallelization of the PLATO algorithm and apply the modified program to analysis of gene sequences of the myostatin family [2].

2   Methods and Algorithms

The PLATO algorithm is based on the likelihood approach [3]. With this method, the occurrence probability of a sequence, in a given evolutionary model, defined by parameters such as phylogenetic tree topology, nucleotide substitution rate and probability, is estimated. It is assumed that nucleotides mutate independently, thus the likelihood of the sequence is the product of the likelihood for each nucleotide site, and their logarithms are summed up. To identify the anomalously evolving regions, the function was calculated for a window scanning along a sequence:

$$Q = \frac{\sum_{i=sp}^{i<(sp+s)} \ln L_i}{s} \bigg/ \frac{\sum_{i=1}^{i<sp} \ln L_i + \sum_{i=(sp+s)}^{i=n} \ln L_i}{n-s} . \tag{1}$$

For the sequence of the length n and the sliding window of the length s starting from the site sp the logarithmic likelihoods, L_i, for each site i are summed over the region within the window; the sum is divided by the length of the region. The denominator contains the average likelihood for the nucleotide sites except the s region. Thus, the value Q is a measure of the mean likelihood for the particular window relative to the mean likelihood for the rest of the sequence. The gene regions with high Qs correspond to the regions with the least likelihoods and are most likely subject to anomalous evolution (due to natural selection, genetic recombination etc.). Authors used Monte Carlo simulation to estimate statistical significance of the Q parameter using Z-score technique [1].

Work with the PLATO program requires laborious calculations to estimate likelihood function in sequence sites. PLATO calculates the Q value for the window s from 5 nucleotides to $n/2$ in length, for all windows starting form the sp position along the sequence ($1 \le sp \le n - s + 1$). The Q values for each position and window length form the matrix. The calculation of the matrix is the most time consuming part of the algorithm. In our parallel implementation, the matrix element calculation was equally distributed among the processors as jobs. This distribution is done automatically, depending on how many processors are accessible to the program. Thus, each processor contains a piece of the resulting matrix after finishing its job. The pieces are assembled into the matrix, which is then sent to all the processors so that each contains a full copy of the similarity matrix for the sequences being analyzed by the sliding window. Parallelization is done using the MPI library.

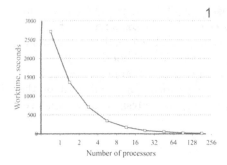

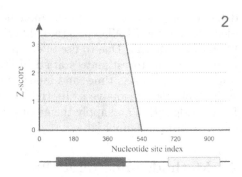

Fig. 1. Performance of the PLATO parallel version. The number of processors used for PLATO implementation on the myostatin gene family is plotted along the X axis. Calculation time (sec) is plotted along the Y axis.

Fig. 2. Results of the PLATO algorithm analysis of the myostatin family genes. The X axis corresponds to the nucleotide site number at the position of myostatin. The Z-score calculated using PLATO is plotted along the X axis. The functionality of the myostatin sequence is shown in the graph: *LAP*, black, *TGF-b*, grey rectangles.

Aligned nucleotide sequences of related genes from several organisms, also phylogenetic tree topology, are PLATO input. PLATO outputs a list of gene regions whose evolutionary mode was anomalous as opposed to the rest of the gene.

Here, we analyse the evolutionary features of the genes of the myostatin family. The myostatins are negative regulators of skeletal muscle development and regarded as good drug targets. There was reason expect that therapeutics that modulate skeletal muscle growth would be useful for disease conditions such as muscular dystrophy, sarcopenia, cachexia, even diabetes [2]. The myostatins are secreted from the cell in the non-active dimer form, noncovalently bound at their N-ends containing the so-called *LAP* (Latency Associated Peptide) domains. For conversion to the active form, proteins are activated by detachment of the *TGF-b* (functional domain) and LAP from each other, which occurs through site-specific proteolysis of the *LAP* domain [4]. The domains *TGF-b* and *LAP* accomplish different functions. Using the PLATO program, we analyse here the evolutionary modes of the myostatin gene regions to compare their evolutionary features.

Multiple alignment of myostatins contains 44 sequences 1002 nucleotides in length. The PHYML program was utilized to reconstruct the phylogenetic tree [5].

3   Results

The original PLATO version did not allow to analyse the myostatin family because work with such long sequences was unstable. Before proceeding to parallelization, the code was improved. The parallel version of PLATO is more stable and calculation time under multiprocessor mode is significantly reduced.

Calculations using the parallel version of PLATO ran at PC-clusters with different numbers of CPUs. The program was developed and bug-fixed on MVS-1000 at the Siberian Supercomputer Center in Novosibirsk (128 Alpha 21264 processors), most calculations were done on MVS-15000 at the Joint Supercomputer Center in Moscow (900 PowerPC 970FX processors). The more processors were employed per task, the less time it took to complete the calculations (Fig. 1); for example, 256 processors did the job in 15 seconds (for comparison, one processor did it in 45 minutes). The tests have shown the linear speedup of the program relative to the number of processors.

Analysis of sequences in the myostatin family genes carried out using the modified PLATO program demonstrated that the Q value Z-score is greater than the value of 3 for the N-end LAP domain, and it is 0 for the TGF-b domain (Fig. 2). The significant deviation of the Q parameter in the region of the LAP domain may be due to the positive selective pressure, as previously reported [6], [7].

Acknowledgments. This work was supported by the program Promotion of Scientific Potential in Higher Education Institutions of Russian Federal Agency on Education, project 2.1.1.4935, program 10002-251 /P-25 /155-270 /200404-082 "Biosphere Origin and Evolution" of the Presidium of the Russ. Acad. Sci., CRDF grant RUX0-008-NO-061, and grants 05-04-49141-a, 05-07-98012-p from Russian Foundation of the Basic Research.

References

1. Grassly, N.C., Holmes, E.C.: A likelihood method for the detection of selection and recombination using nucleotide sequences. Molecular Biololy Evolution 14(3), 239–247 (1997)
2. Tsuchida, K.: Activins, myostatin and related TGF-beta family members as novel therapeutic targets for endocrine, metabolic and immune disorders. Current Drug Targets – Immune, Endocrine, Metabolic Disorders 4(2), 157–166 (2004)
3. Felsenstein, J.: Evolutionary trees from DNA sequences: a maximum likelihood approach. Journal of Molecular Evolution 17(6), 368–376 (1981)
4. Lee, S.J.: Regulation of muscle mass by myostatin. Annual Reviev Cellellular Development Bioliology 20, 61–86 (2004)
5. Guindon, S., Lethiec, F., Duroux, P., Gascuel, O.: PHYML Online: a web server for fast maximum likelihood-based phylogenetic inference. Nucleic Acid Research 33 (Web Server issue), W557–W559 (2005)
6. Tellgren, A., Berglund, A.C., Savolainen, P., Janis, C.M., Liberles, D.A.: Myostatin rapid sequence evolution in ruminants predates domestication. Molecular Phylogenetics Evolution 33(3), 782–790 (2004)
7. Kerr, T., Roalson, E.H., Rodgers, B.D.: Phylogenetic analysis of the myostatin gene sub-family and the differential expression of a novel member in zebrafish. Evolution Development 7(5), 390–400 (2005)

Object Serialization and Remote Exception Pattern for Distributed C++/MPI Application

Karol Bańczyk, Tomasz Boiński, and Henryk Krawczyk

Gdańsk University of Technology, Faculty of Electronics, Telecommunication and Informatics, ul. Gabriela Narutowicza 11/12, 80-952 Gdańsk
{aban,tobo,hkrawk}@eti.pg.gda.pl

Abstract. MPI is commonly used standard in development of scientific applications. It focuses on interlanguage operability and is not very well object oriented. The paper proposes a general pattern enabling design of distributed and object oriented applications. It also presents its sample implementations and performance tests.

Keywords: MPI, object serialization, remote exception handling.

1 Introduction

MPI[1] is a widely accepted standard for message passing in scientific applications. It focuses on interlanguage compatibility (FORTRAN, C, C++) rather than on leveraging a single language constructs. Nevertheless, in many C++ applications a more object oriented, MPI based network interface (later referred to as connector) would be desireable. Although bindings for C++ were introduced to MPI [1], more sophisticated features are often needed for practical use.

This work focuses on object serialization and remote exception handling. The former is a mechanism for converting objects between their in-memory representations and a stream of bytes. The latter allows us to transmit exceptions occurring in a remote server process to the calling client process. Some example applications are also shown.

The paper consists of five sections: Section 2 define design goals; Section 3 presents the proposed pattern; Sections 4 and 5 provide sample implementations and Section 6 discusses certain experimental results.

2 Design Goals

The connector should provide methods for collective and for point-to-point communication as well the possibility to receive exceptions that occurred remotely. A remote exception should be handled in the same way as any local exception. An application satisfying those features could be implemented without any new communication layer. Most of the design goals could be achieved using either the SR language [5] or its Java based ancestor, JR [6] [4], or else MPI wrappers for Java (like mpiJava [10]).

V. Malyshkin (Ed.): PaCT 2007, LNCS 4671, pp. 188–193, 2007.
© Springer-Verlag Berlin Heidelberg 2007

It is risky to write a sophisticated program in a language, such as SR, which has small community around it and few available libraries. Java serialization mechanisms has negative impact on overall performance (which is confirmed by the below mentioned results). Similarly, the mpiJava, as a wrapper around C, introduces additional overhead. So we decided to create the C++ application and implement simplified versions of suitable Java oriented mechanisms.

3   Architecture of Application Pattern

The assumed architecture is depicted in Fig. 1. with two lower layers: Object Lifecycle Management (OLM) and Object Serialization (OS), both inspired by Java's mechanisms, i.e. reflection and serialization. The former enables class identification and memory management for objects. The letter provides methods for writing and reading objects to/from a stream of integers.

Serialization, though inspired by Java[8], is a simple solution. Per class implementation is needed for each serializable object, no security issues are considered and the serialized stream contains no matadata. This solution requires more development time, but reduced serialization time. Similarly, in Java a per class implementation is also needed, if performance issues are a concern.

The connector transmits serializable Message objects between the nodes. It uses MPI as its underlying network communication library but also Object Serialization with Object Lifecycle Management for converting object messages to/from byte sequences required by MPI.

Every exception occurring during handling procedures is caught by the communication layer, transmitted through the network to the appropriate node and thrown the next time that node invokes a method on the communication layer.

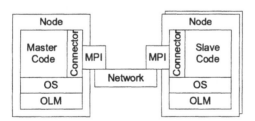

Fig. 1. Application architecture pattern

4   Implementation

4.1   Basic Classes

In the proposition each serializable class has to be subclass of the IntSerializableObject class and has to implement writeToInts and readFromInts methods. A special Exception class was also defined. Unfortunately, it is impossible to transmit the original exception object itself. The C++ specification [7] states that the memory for the temporary copy of the exception being thrown is allocated in an unspecified way thus allowing each compiler implementation to do it differently. This conflicts with the idea of ObjectFactory and could lead to uncontrollable memory leaks if not handled properly. Both the abovementioned Message class and Exception class needs to be serializable.

Some sublasses of Message are defined: SimpleMessage used for wrapping requests and responses; CarrierMessage employed in transmitting any number of different objects of the IntSerializableObject type in one communication attempt; and ExceptionMessage used for wrapping and transmitting exceptions.

Any of given classes can be further subclassed by any number of more specialized ones to better suite the given solution.

4.2 Serialization

Here is and example ofserialization algorithm: two objects, containing fields f1 and f2, wrapped into CarierMessage, will be serialized in the following way:

1. CarrierMessage class Id is written so that Object Factory will be able to recreate it;
2. CarrierMessage's writeToInts method is invoked in such a way that:
   (a) the object's Id is written so that recipient can deduct meaning of this message, i.e. if it is a message with results or a control message,
   (b) number of contained objects is written (here 2),
   (c) for each of the objects its class Id is written and its writetoInts method is invoked; this method stores Id and fields of that object.

Then, the message is being send and after receiving the serialized object it is recreated as follow:

1. Class Id is read and used for recreating the object, CarrierMessage in this case;
2. CarrierMessage readFromInts method is executed; this method:
   (a) restores value of it's Id,
   (b) reads number of contained objects,
   (c) each contained object is being recreated and it's readFromInts method is employed.

4.3 Remote Exceptions

Exceptions were added to MPI C++ bindings. However, they only apply to MPI communication operations so a more general solution for user aplication exceptions is needed.

Fig. 2 presents the algorithm for remote exception handling. When an exception on a remote node occurs and cannot be handled locally on that node, it is caught and wrapped into an ExceptionMessage object. That object is serializable and thus can be transmitted through the network. After that it is deserialized and thrown again on the target node. Later, on a proper solution for the problem, it can be transmitted to the node where the exception originated.

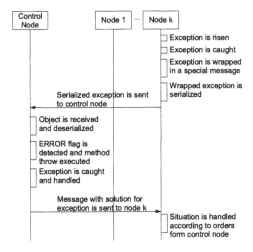

Fig. 2. Remote exception handling algorithm

5   Application Examples

5.1   Assertions

Assertions are a well-known method for finding bugs in software[2]. If a condition is not fulfilled on a single node the standard C++ assert macro silently terminates, leaving the other nodes completely unaware of that fact.

We created our own version called xassert. When the assertion fails on one node, the process throws an Exception. It reaches the master node and causes a standard fatal error handling procedure that can, for example, send all the slaves a termination message and gracefully shut down the whole system.

5.2   Exceptions Thrown in a Slave Node

We developed a master-slave applications designed to solve timetabling problem [3]. Exceptions thrown within slave nodes may sometimes be handled locally, like buffer overflow errors, otherwise have to be passed to master. When, for example, a slave node cannot generate random individuals for given input data, an exception needs to be passed to the master node, where the user is notified about the problem and can apply the solution for it. This approach can be used in any type of client/server approach.

6   Test Results

This section shows the results proving serialization's efficiency. All presented tests were performed on a 10 node cluster. Each node consists of 4 Intel Xeon CPU 2.80GHz and has 4GB of RAM. The nodes are connected via gigabit ethernet network. Measured latency was around 100 microseconds.

6.1 Serialization's Overhead

Table 1. compares time (in microseconds) of preparation of MPI message buffer with serialized objects by means of the proposed serialization mechanisms to writing to a raw integer buffer. For this test we have created a serializable class containing a vector of integers of agiven length. No actual sending is performed.

Table 1. Serialization time in microseconds

Vector size	With serialization	Without serialization	With/Without ser.
1	1.62	0.20	8.10
10	2.74	0.21	13.05
100	4.84	0.40	12.10
1000	10.46	1.37	7.64
		Average:	10.22

The average serialization is 10.22 times slower than writing data directly to integer vector. Nevertheless, it is by one level of magnitude shorter than the latency time, and it simplifies and structurizes the code, which makes the performance loss is acceptable.

6.2 Comparison to Java

Java offers very good methods of serialization and remote exception handling. These methods, however, introduce additional overhead both in terms of needed time and size of the result. For this test, a simplified connector was implemented in Java. Also two realizations of serialization were provided: normal (standard java.util.ArrayList class with standard serialization) and optimized (using com.sosnoski.util.array.IntArray [9], an array optimized for storing integers and custom read and write methods).

Table 2. Java and C++ serialization comparison

Vector size	Standard Java	Optimized Java	C++
10	32.00	25.00	2.74
100	107.00	16.00	4.84
1000	1180.00	43.00	10.46

The results are presented in Table 2. (in microseconds). Java serialization is slower than the proposed C++ implementation, especially when using standard Java classes. Although simpler to code, optimized Java serialization is 4 to 10 times slower than C++ implementation. Additionally, C++ application in general has smaller memory requirements.

7 Conclusions

The object serialization presented in the paper proved to be efficient and simple for implementation. All types of objects are being serialized in the same manner thanks to usage of integers as a common way of representing data. It allowed us to transport a wide range of objects between nodes. The presented solution provides full transparency both from object's and application's point of view. In all those aspects it is similar to Java solutions yet faster and simpler.

The proposed remote exception handling, is simple but requires forming a special Message objects for each type of exception sent. Those, however, can be coded once and included into a library for future reuse.

In addition to design goals, introduction of a Connector makes applications, built with this patter in mind, extendable. Communication performance and reliability tuning becomes very easy as only changes to Connector needs to be done.

References

1. Message Passing Interface Forum: MPI-2: Extensions to Message-Passing Interface. Message Passing Interface Forum (1997)
2. Andrew, H., David, T.: The Pragmatic Programmer: From Journeyman to Master. Addison Wesley Longman, Redwood City (2000)
3. Bańczyk, K., Boiński, T., Krawczyk, H.: Parallelisation of genetic algorithms for solving university timetabling problems. In: PARELEC 2006, pp. 325–330. IEEE Computer Society, Los Alamitos (2006)
4. Chan, H.N., et al.: An Exception Handling Mechanism for the Concurrent Invocation Statement. In: Cunha, J.C., Medeiros, P.D. (eds.) Euro-Par 2005. LNCS, vol. 3648, pp. 699–709. Springer, Heidelberg (2005)
5. SR Language: http://www.cs.arizona.edu/sr/
6. JR Language: http://www.cs.ucdavis.edu/~olsson/research/jr/
7. National Committee for Information Technology Standards: International Standard ISO/IEC 14882, Programming Language - C++ Approved by NCITS as an American National Standard, http://www.ncits.org/standards/pr14882.htm
8. Java Serialization Specification, version 1.5: http://java.sun.com/j2se/1.5.0/docs/guide/serialization/spec/serialTOC.html
9. Sosnoski, D.: Type-Specific Collections Library. http://www.sosnoski.com/opensrc/tclib/index.html
10. mpiJava: http://www.hpjava.org/mpiJava.html

Improving Job Scheduling Performance with Dynamic Replication Strategy in Data Grids

Nguyen Dang Nhan[1], Soon Wook Hwang[1], and Sang Boem Lim[2]

[1] Korea Institute of Science and Technology Information,
Daejeon, Republic of Korea
{ndnhan, hwang}@kisti.re.kr
[2] Konkuk University,
Seoul, Republic of Korea
sblim@konkuk.ac.kr

Abstract. Dealing with a large amount of data in Data Grids makes the requirement for efficient data access more critical. In this paper, we proposed a new approach to replication problem by organizing the data into several data categories that it belongs to. This organizing will help improving placement strategy of data replication. We studied our approach in combination with scheduling issue and evaluating it through simulation. The result shows that our strategy has improved the scheduling performance by 30%.

1 Introduction

Data Grid is an integrating architecture that allows the connection of hundreds of geographically distributed computers and storage resources located in different part of the world to facilitate sharing of data and resources [4]. Dealing with large amount of data that are geographically spread causes many challenges to Data Grid. One of them is how the scheduling efficiently work with the amount of data and the impact of replication to the scheduling performance.

1.1 Motivation

Replication and scheduling problem has been studied separately for a long time. However those of Data Grid have just recently received attention from researchers. Effective job scheduling in Data Grid has its own complicated characteristics since it deals with a large amount of data input in the dynamic environment of Grid. The decision of where and when to execute a job is made by considering the job requirement and current status of The Grid, here are computational, storage and network resources. In Data grid, the performance is greatly influenced by the data's locality [5]. A good scheduling strategy will allow shorter access to required data, therefore reduces the data access time. Vice versa, replication strategy that allows placing data in a wisely manner will offer a faster access to files require by grid jobs, hence increases the job execution.

V. Malyshkin (Ed.): PaCT 2007, LNCS 4671, pp. 194–199, 2007.

1.2   Related Works

There are some recent works that address the problem of scheduling and/or replication of Data Grid, and their combination. The importance of data locality in job scheduling problem was first proposed by Ranganathan and Foster [5]. The authors propose Data Grid architecture and evaluate the scheduling performance in combination with replication. Even though the architecture and algorithms are simple, results of this study show the importance of data locality in job scheduling.

In OptorSim [1,2], data replication is combined with job scheduling in a two-stage optimization mechanism. Our proposed architecture, however, is the combination of the two mentioned above. Some more recent works by Chakrabati, et al. [6] or Tang Ming et al. [7] improved the previous works by integrating the scheduling and replication strategy to improve the scheduling performance.

Having analyzed these works, the author found two shortcomings. The first one is the relationship among data and between the data and job using them. Instead of relying on the grid capability, we approach the problem from the job and data property. The second issue is that the important role of Dataset Scheduler was not fully recognized.

This paper is organized as followed: Section 2 describes the scheduling issue, section 3 goes in detail the replication strategy, of which the simulation results are presented in Section 4. Section 5 summarizes the paper.

2   Scheduling Strategy

Scheduling strategy is relied on the estimation of completion time of a job:

$$ETTC_{j,i} = \max\{DT_{f(j),i}, QT_{j,i}\} + EET_{j,i} \ . \tag{1}$$

This estimation equation is similar to what was introduced in [7]. In the real case, the work of obtaining $QT_{j,i}$ - queuing time in site i - is quite simple. Suppose that j-1 is the last job in site i's queue. We can realize that $QT_{j,i} = ETTC_{j-1,i}$. Resource broker can communicate with local scheduler to obtain $ETTC_{i-1,j}$. Data transferring time $DT_{f(j),i}$ can also be estimated by the Grid status information as described in [7].

3   Dynamic Replication

We assume that Data Grid is used for some fields of study, such as Physics, Biology, Chemistry, Meteorology, etc. These fields can be divided into sub-fields, for example biology can be divided to cell biology, molecular of biology, cell technology, etc. Data in Data Grid must belong to one of these fields. The reason behind this assumption is that data in one field rarely or never be used in other fields. By doing so, we can form a hierarchical tree of data category, on which we define the relationship between data in same category and relationship between nearby categories. Our idea is to gather the data that are "related" to each other into the small region so that the job that uses such data will be executed within that region in order to lower data transfer cost. Considering current data and scenario, we can just define a flat category system, including a set of category. Data in one category can only be used with data in the same one.

With the above assumption, we define an strategy called Dynamic Data Replication Strategy (DR) to solve the replication question (which data to be replicated and where to place the replica) in following sections.

3.1 Replica Decision

In order to decide which file needs to be replicated, we use a metric call average number of access of a file as indicated in [7]. In replication mechanism, each replication server maintains data accesses record. When it is time to replicate data, all replication servers send the access records to the central replication manager. The manager will aggregate and create a summarized access record for every unique file identifier (FID). Each item $NOA(f)$ on the record indicates the times that a file with unique ID f is accessed on the whole grid system. Once the average number of accesses is calculated, if a replica is accessed more than the average, it needs to be replicated.

- Compute average number of access:

$$\overline{NOA} = \sum_{\forall f} NOA(f)/N \ . \tag{2}$$

N: number of distinguished data file (number of FID) in Grid system. $NOA(f)$: number of access of file f
- For every file f that satisfies:

$$\frac{NOA(f)}{NOR(f)} \times |f| > \overline{NOA} \times \overline{|f|} \ . \tag{3}$$

($NOR(f)$: number of replicas of file f on the whole grid system; $|f|$ is average file size of all files in the system)
create new replica for f at site chosen by Replication Placement Strategy.

3.2 Replica Placement

As described above, our strategy is to place replicated files that belong to the same category close to each other so that job of the same category will be executed nearby. Then, the cost of transferring files will be reduced. We call this strategy Dynamic Replication Placement (DP).

To measure how close a replica is to the data in the same category, we define a new concept: Dis(i.e. Distance).

- Distance is measured from site D to site $D1$ for a file f (of category C) is defined as time to transfer all files that belong to C on $D1$ to D: If D is the same as $D1$, then $Dis(f, D1) = 0$. Else:

$$Dis(f_D, D_1) = \pm \left(\sum_{f_i \in D_1, f_i \in C} |f_i| \right) / BW_{D,D_1} . \tag{4}$$

$Dis(fD, D1)$ carries sign $+(-)$ when $D1$ does (does not) contain a replica of f. It means the further the distance of the two replicas of one file, the better it is. However, they are close enough to other files of the same category.
- Similarly, distance for a replica f (of category C) on site D to all files of C is time to transfer all files belongs to category C on the Grid system to D:

$$Dis(f_D) = \sum_{\forall D_i} Dis(f_D, D_i) . \tag{5}$$

Lower $Dis(f_D)$ indicates that f_D is closer to other files in the same category.

To choose a site to place a new replica, $Dis(f, D)$ for each site in the Grid system is evaluated. Site with lowest $Dis(f, D)$ will be chosen to store the replica. We use Least Recently Used (LRU) [2] as replacement strategy for its efficiency.

4   Performance Studies

In order to evaluate the performance of the replication strategy, the OptorSim simulation tool and The EU Data Grid configuration are used. The grid job is submitted to the RB for every 2.5 seconds. Each computing node has a processing speed of 0.1 second/GB. The initial file distribution among the grid sites is random. Each node has 0 or 1 Storage Element of size 15GB to 100GB.

4.1   Replica Placement Strategy Evaluation

The replica placement strategy is tested to measure its performance against the random placement strategy. In this test, we use the calculation equation in Section 3.1 to decide which replica to be replicated. The site to place the newly created replica was chosen randomly (RP) or by the strategy that is described in Section 3.2 (DP). The scheduling strategies set up for this test were the Random scheduling (RS) and Combined-cost Scheduling (CCS) as in [2]. For each combination of methods and parameters, the mean job execution time was measured (Figure 1(a)). The DP is outperformed that with random placement.

4.2   Dynamic Replication Strategy Evaluation

The whole replication strategy is evaluated with the OptorSim's LFU (Least Frequently Used) and LRU (Least Recently Used) replication. Once again, the OptorSim's CCS scheduling strategy is used.

The simulation result (Figure 1(b)) shows that by combining Dynamic Replication Strategy (DR) with LRU (as a replacement strategy), the performance is significantly increased by 30%.

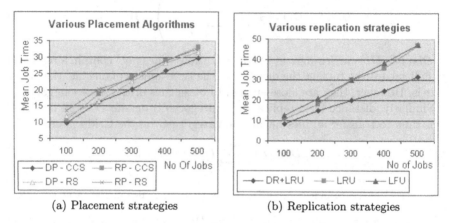

(a) Placement strategies   (b) Replication strategies

Fig. 1. Job performance when using various (a) placement algorithms (b) replication strategies

5   Conclusion

In this paper, we found a new approach to the replication problem in Data Grid and combining it with job scheduling strategies. The simulation result showed that our replication placement strategy overcomes the random placement strategy. Also, the dynamic replicating algorithm made an improvement and could be used with OptorSim's replication optimization. In the future work, we will improve the replication strategy. Meanwhile, the scheduling component needs to be completed for integrating with replication mechanism to perform a whole system simulation.

References

1. William, H.B., et al.: OptorSim - A Grid Simulator for Studying Dynamic Data Replication Strategies. Int. J. of High Perf. Comput. Appl. 17(4), 403–416 (2003)
2. Cameron, D.G., et al.: Evaluating Scheduling and Replica Optimisation Strategies in OptorSim. In: Proc. of 4th Int. Workshop on Grid Comput (Grid 2003), IEEE-CS Press, Los Alamitos (2003)
3. Ranganathan, K., Foster, I.: Decoupling computation and data scheduling in distributed data-intensive applications. In: Proc. of the 11th IEEE Symposium on High Performance Distributed Computing (HPDC) (July 2002)
4. Lamehamedi, H., et al.: Simulation of Dynamic Data Replication Strategies in Data Grids. In: Proc. of 12th Heterogeneous Comput. Workshop (HCW2003), April 2003, IEEE-CS Press, Los Alamitos (2003)

5. Ranganathan, K., Foster, I.: Simulation Studies of Computation and Data Scheduling Algorithms for Data Grids. J. of Grid Computing 1(1), 53–62 (2003)
6. Chakrabarti, A., Dheepak, R.A., Sengupta, S.: Integration of Scheduling and Replication in Data Grids. In: Bougé, L., Prasanna, V.K. (eds.) HiPC 2004. LNCS, vol. 3296, pp. 375–385. Springer, Heidelberg (2004)
7. Tang, M., et al.: The impact of data replication on job scheduling performance in the Data Grid. Future Generation Computing System 22(3), 254–268 (2006)

Address-Free All-to-All Routing in Sparse Torus

Risto Honkanen[1], Ville Leppänen[2], and Martti Penttonen[1]

[1] Department of Computer Science
University of Kuopio
P.O.Box 1627, 70211 Kuopio, Finland
{honkanen,penttonen}@cs.uku.fi
[2] Department of Computer Science
University of Turku
Lemminkäisenkatu 14a, 20520 Turku, Finland
ville.leppanen@it.utu.fi

Abstract. In this work we present a simple network design for all-to-all routing and study deflection routing on it. We present a time-scheduled routing algorithm where packets are routed address-free. We show that a total exchange relation, where every processor has a packet to route to every other processor, can be routed with routing cost of $1/2 + o(1)$ time units per packet.

The network consists of an n-sided d-dimensional torus, where the n^{d-1} processor (or input/output) nodes are sparsely but regularly situated among $n^d - n^{d-1}$ deflection routing nodes, having d input and d output links. The finite-state routing nodes change their states by a fixed, preprogrammed pattern.

Keywords: network, routing, hot-potato, torus, sparse.

1 Introduction

Routing algorithms have many applications in computation and in data communication. Our work is motivated by situations, where there is need to transfer a lot of messages between a large number of sources and destinations. Such settings appear in the Internet and telecommunication network routing switches, but also in implementing shared memory abstraction on top of distributed memory modules. In the latter case, a large number of processors can send each other messages, on almost every step of computation.

In this paper we focus on describing a large-scale routing switch based on a sparse (optical) torus. We claim that the sparse torus is truly scalable, efficient and offers a high bandwidth. In the 2-dimensional case, our switch resembles a crossbar of n vertical and n horizontal wires, but has only connections of a constant length. An $n \times n$ crossbar can deal with n packets at a time whereas our 2-D sparse torus moves n^2 packets at a time. In [1,2], the architectural approach is very similar but the main focus is on link load instead of overall routing time.

By [10], in 3-dimensional world, the distance of processors grows at least by the cubic root of the number of processors. 2- and 3-dimensional *meshes* and

V. Malyshkin (Ed.): PaCT 2007, LNCS 4671, pp. 200–205, 2007.
© Springer-Verlag Berlin Heidelberg 2007

tori are such architectures. Note, however, that higher dimensional structures may still be useful at the design level, because it may be possible to embed them in a 2- or 3-dimensional structure. If the routing network has the *diameter* (or average routing distance) ϕ, then obviously a packet needs time $\Omega(\phi)$ to get to the target. However, if the network can move $\Omega(p\phi)$ packets in each step, where p is the number of sources and destinations, it may be possible to route ph packets in time $O(h)$ for some $h > \phi$. Hence, it may be possible to achieve a constant time cost per packet. We present such a cost-optimal solution for the d-dimensional torus. Other architectural solutions satisfying the above have been presented; see [1,2,5,8,9], for example.

The condition that the network must be able to move at least ϕ packets per processor, assuming that nodes have a constant degree, implies that at most $O(1/\phi)$'th of the nodes can be processors. Such an architecture is called *sparse* or *sparsely populated*. It may seem waste to have ϕ routers per processor, but it is the price for the ability to inject a packet at every step. Note, however, that the routers can be very simple components in comparison with processors. Of course, "dense" (or fully populated) architectures may work, if only a sparse rate of packet injection is needed.

2   Sparse Torus $ST(n, d)$

A d-dimensional n-sided *sparse torus* $ST(n, d)$ consists of n^d nodes. Among these, n^{d-1} are processors that are located "sparsely", and the rest are routers.

Definition 1. *Layer j of the sparse torus $ST(n, d)$ is the set*

$$L_{d,n}(j) = \{(x_1, x_2, \ldots, x_d)| \sum_{i=1}^{d} x_i = j\}.$$

Nodes in layers $0, n, \ldots, (d-1)n$ are called processors *and other nodes are* routers.

In $ST(6, 2)$ of Figure 1, there are two processor layers having six processors altogether. In $ST(4, 3)$, there are three layers with one, twelve and three processors.

Router nodes $R_{x_1, x_2, \ldots, x_d}$ are located at positions $(x_1, x_2, \ldots x_d)$ such that $\sum_{i=1}^{d} x_i \not\equiv 0 \bmod n$ and $0 \le x_i \le n - 1$. The d outputs of a node at location $(x_1, x_2, \ldots x_d)$ (processor or router) are connected to the routers or processors at locations $(x_1 + 1 \bmod n, x_2, \ldots, x_d)$, $(x_1, x_2 + 1 \bmod n, x_3, \ldots, x_d)$, $\ldots$, and $(x_1, x_2, \ldots, x_{d-1}, x_d + 1 \bmod n)$. All connections are *unidirectional*. In Figure 1, directions are to the "right", "up", and "away". We assume that each deflection node and processor is capable of receiving (along incoming link) and sending (along outgoing link) one message per link in one time unit.

Consider *projection* $\pi_i((x_1, \ldots, x_d)) = (x_1, \ldots, x_{i-1}, x_{i+1}, \ldots, x_d)$ of $\{0, 1, \ldots, n-1\}^d$ to $\{0, 1, \ldots, n-1\}^{d-1}$. As an immediate corollary we get

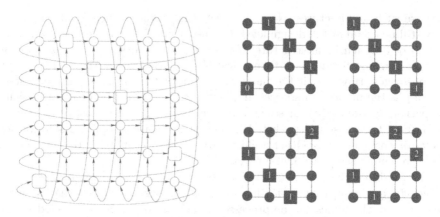

Fig. 1. Left picture: A 6-processor 6×6 sparse optical torus $ST(6,2)$. Circles are router nodes. Right picture: $ST(4,3)$ in slices.

Lemma 1. *For $ST(n,d)$,*

   (i) The number of processors is n^{d-1}.

   (ii) Processors, when projected to the surfaces of $ST(n,d)$, cover the whole surface. I.e., for all i, $\{\pi_i((x_1,\ldots,x_d))|x_1 + \ldots + x_d \equiv 0 \pmod{n}\} = \{0,1,\ldots,n-1\}^{d-1}$.

(iii) Average distance from processors to the origin $(0,0,\ldots,0)$ is $d(n-1)/2$

Proof is easy.

By lemma 1 we can now estimate how fast it might be possible to route packets. Each packet sent by any of the n^{d-1} processors needs $d(n-1)/2$ moves in the torus, on the average. On the other hand, each of the n^d routers can forward d packets. Hence, if there are no collisions, on the average we need

$$\frac{n^{d-1} \times d(n-1)/2}{dn^d} = \frac{(n-1)}{2n} \approx 1/2$$

routing steps per packet. Indeed, it is possible to achieve this bound, but in order to prove it we need to know more about the structure of the $ST(n,d)$.

Lemma 2. *(i) $|L_{d,n}(0)| = 1$,*

(ii) $|L_{d,n}(k)| = \binom{k+d-1}{d-1} - \sum_{i=1}^{\lfloor k/n \rfloor} \binom{d-1+i}{d-1} \times |L_{d,n}(k - i \cdot n)|$ when $0 < k \le d(n-1)$.

(iii) $|L_{d,n}(k)| = 0$ when $k < 0$ or $k > d(n-1)$.

Proof of (i) and (iii) is obvious, and (ii) bases on a recursive argument.

In $ST(n,2)$, there is one processor at the origin and $n-1$ processors at the distance n from the origin and the distance from a processor to another is $n-1$. In higher dimensional cases, the numbers of processors at different levels, and also the distance from processor to processor vary. In $ST(8,4)$, for example, the sizes of processor levels are 1, 161, 315, and 35, and the distance from a processor to another can be 8, 16, or 24. Due to this irregularity it is not obvious how to route packets efficiently.

3   Scheduled Routing of h-Relations

A routing strategy used to resolve the output port contention problem in packet-switched interconnection networks is the *hot-potato* or *deflection* routing strategy. In the hot-potato routing all entering packets must leave at the next step – i.e. packets cannot be buffered as in the store-and-forward routing strategy. In general, in each node the out-degree must be at least the in-degree, and the output port contention must be resolved somehow. If there are multiple packets preferring the same output port, the routing strategy must select at most one for each out-going link. See [4] or [7] for definitions and a survey of hot-potato routing techniques and results.

In Section 2, we reasoned that on a d-dimensional sparse torus it may be possible to achieve the routing cost $\approx 1/2$ per packet. The question is, whether this routing cost indeed can be achieved and how.

In deflection routing, packets move so that the coordinate sum increases by 1 (mod n) at every moment. In $ST(n,d)$, processors are located at distances mod n. Therefore, packets sent at different moments (mod n) cannot collide. It is enough to avoid collisions between packets sent at the same moment (mod n).

Consider a *path pattern* $\Pi = \ll \Delta_1, \Delta_2, \ldots, \Delta_d \gg$, where $\sum_{i=1}^d \Delta_i \equiv 0 \bmod n$, $0 \le \sum_{i=1}^d \Delta_i < dn$, and $0 \le \Delta_i < n$ for $1 \le i \le d$. From each processor node, such a path pattern leads to another processor node. In fact, a path pattern forms a permutation of processor nodes. Moreover, consider the *rotation* operator $\rho(\Pi) = \ll \Delta_n, \Delta_1, \ldots, \Delta_{n-1} \gg$. Then $\rho(\Pi), \rho^2(\Pi), \ldots, \rho^{d-1}(\Pi)$ also are path patterns. Note, however, that not all rotations of a path pattern are different. E.g. if $\Pi = \ll 1, 4, 1, 4 \gg$, then path patterns Π and $\rho^2(\Pi)$ form the same permutation, similarly $\rho(\Pi)$ and $\rho^3(\Pi)$.

An important observation is that if one packet is sent to the first dimension by Π, another packet to the second dimension by $\rho(\Pi)$ etc, these packets always turn at the same time and do not collide.

Now, the basic idea of scheduled routing in the d-dimensional case should be obvious. First consider all processors at layer $L_{d,n}((d-1)n)$ and the corresponding path patterns $\ll \Delta_1, \Delta_2, \ldots, \Delta_d \gg$, for which $\sum_{i=1}^d \Delta_i = (d-1)n$ and $0 \le \Delta_i < n$. Divide the path patterns to groups, where patterns are rotations of each other, and route the whole group at the same time to the (at most) d dimensions. The same is repeated for all layers.

As in the 2-dimensional case, in n consecutive steps we can start routing packets along n different cyclic path patterns. Each cyclic path pattern forms a wave, and waves do not interact. Also, as explained previously, no conflicts appear within waves.

As routing packets in layer $L_{d,n}(kn)$ takes kn steps, the processors can not use time moments $n, 2n, 3n, \ldots (k-1)n$ time units later. A new sending can be started kn time units later. However, n successive time moments are indepent of each other, and there can be n sending processes running in parallel. Figure 2 shows a schedule for ST(3,4).

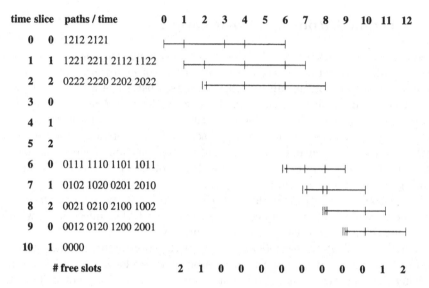

time slice		paths / time	0	1	2	3	4	5	6	7	8	9	10	11	12
0	0	1212 2121													
1	1	1221 2211 2112 1122													
2	2	0222 2220 2202 2022													
3	0															
4	1															
5	2															
6	0	0111 1110 1101 1011													
7	1	0102 1020 0201 2010													
8	2	0021 0210 2100 1002													
9	0	0012 0120 1200 2001													
10	1	0000													
# free slots			2	1	0	0	0	0	0	0	0	0	1	2	

Fig. 2. Schedule for ST(3,4). Altogether $3^3 = 27$ packets are sent, 10 to distance 6, 16 to distance 3, and 1 to distance 0. In each group of rotated paths, we show the schedule for the first one starting with dimension 1. Thus, 1221 starts with the dimension 1, 2211 with the dimension 4, 2112 with the dimension 2, and 1122 with the dimension 3. Note that the packets sent at moments 0, 1, 2 prevent sending at moments 3, 4 and 5, because the time slice is not free. At moment 12 all packets have reached the target. Hence, the cost per packet is $12/27 < 1/2$.

In the following Theorem, we consider a *total exchange p*-relation, where every processor sends exactly one packet to every other processor.

Theorem 1. *The scheduled routing protocol routes any total exchange relation on $ST(n,d)$, for $d \geq 3$, in time $p/2 + o(1)$, where $p = n^{(d-1)}$. Hence the cost per packet is approximately $1/2$.*

Proof is nontrivial but omitted due to page limit.

In $ST(n,2)$ it is easy to schedule the routers so that they move simultaneously to the crossing state and back to the direct state. It would be interesting to know, if the same is possible for the $ST(n,d)$, too, and at what cost.

In this work we have studied only the total exchange operation. However, by a general result [6], a h-relation with large h can be implemented with $(h/p)(1 + o(1))$ total exchange operations, with high probability. Obviously, if processors have h packets to random addresses and h grows high, the routing relation approaches to a multiple total exchange relation, and the routing cost tends towards 0.5 time per packet.

4   Conclusions

We presented a routing architecture, sparse d-dimensional (optical) torus, studied its routing properties, and described deflection algorithms for routing packets efficiently on it. We believe that the simple, regular structure and efficient communication are important benefits of the architecture. The architecture suits especially for on-line routing situation where steady high bandwidth is more important than the actual latency. We also believe that the presented routing algorithms based on greedy principle are useful and realistic.

References

1. Azizoglu, M.C., Egecioglu, Ö.: Lower Bounds on Communication Loads and Optimal Placements in Torus Networks. IEEE Trans. Comput 49(3), 259–266 (2000)
2. Blaum, M., Bruk, J., Pifarre, G.D., Santz, J.L.C.: On Optimal Placements of Processors in Tori Networks. In: Proceedings, Eighth IEEE Symposium on Parallel and Distributed Processing, pp. 552–555. IEEE Computer Society Press, Los Alamitos (1996)
3. Goldberg, L.A., Matias, Y., Rao, S.: An Optical Simulation of Shared Memory. In: SPAA'94, 6th Annual Symposium on Parallel Algorithms and Architectures, Cape May, New Jersey, pp. 257–267 (June 1994)
4. Honkanen, R., Leppänen, V., Penttonen, M.: Hot-Potato Routing Algorithms for Sparse Optical Torus. In: Proceedings, International Conference of Parallel Parallel Processing, ICPP' 2001, pp. 302–307 (2001)
5. Leppänen, V., Penttonen, M.: Work-Optimal Simulation of PRAM Models on Meshes. Nordic Journal on Computing 2(1), 51–69 (1995)
6. Suel, S.T., Tsantilas, T.: Efficient Communication Using Total-Exchange. In: em 9th International Parallel Processing Symposium IPPS'1995 (1995)
7. Schuster, A.: Bounds and Analysis Techniques for Greedy Hot-Potato Routing, ch. 11, pp. 283–354. Kluwer Academic Publishers, Boston (1997)
8. Sibeyn, J.: Solving Fundamental Problems on Sparse-Meshes. IEEE Trans. Parallel Distrib. Syst. 11(12), 1324–1332 (2000)
9. Valiant, L.G.: General Purpose Parallel Architectures. In: Algorithms and Complexity, Handbook of Theoretical Computer Science, vol. A, pp. 943–971 (1990)
10. Vitányi, P.M.B.: Locality, Communication, and Interconnect Length in Multicomputers. SIAM Journal on Computing 17(4), 659–672 (1988)

On the Parallel Technologies of Conjugate and Semi-conjugate Gradient Methods for Solving Very Large Sparse SLAEs*

Valery P. Ilin and Dasha V. Knysh

[1] Head of Laboratory, Institute of Computational
Mathematics and Mathematical Geophysics, SBRAS,
Novosibirsk, Lavrentiev ave.,6, (383) 330-60-62
ilin@sscc.ru
[2] PhD student, Novosibirsk State University,
Novosibirsk, Pirogova str, 2, 8-913-754-56-15

Abstract. The parallel technologies of iterative solving the symmetric and nonsymmetric systems of linear algebraic equations (SLAEs) with very large sparse matrices by means of conjugate and semi-conjugate gradient iterative methods are described. The performance computing for various matrix formats (diagonal, compressed sparse row/column), at the different degrees of freedom of SLAEs, are analysed. The results of experimental measurements under OPENMP, MPI and hybrid systems are presented and discussed.

Introduction

The goal of this paper consists in experimental investigation and performance measurements for parallel implementation technologies of iterative solving the systems of linear algebraic equations (SLAEs) with very large sparse matrices, symmetric or non-symmetric, which arise in grid approximations of multi-dimensional boundary value problems (BVPs) for mathematical modeling, see [1], [2] for example. These topics have been considered by many authors, and corresponding literature is presented in [3].

We focus our attention on two algorithms in Krylov subspaces: classical conjugate gradient (CG) method for symmetric positive definite (s.p.d.) SLAE and non-conventional left semi-conjugate gradient (LSCG, see [4]) method for solving non-symmetric system. In the last case, we suppose that the original matrix A has s.p.d. own symmetric part $A^s = (A + A^t)/2$, i.e. the real parts of eigenvalues of A are positive.

The estimations of computational resources, in terms of the number of arithmetic operations and memory volume, necessary for obtaining required accuracy of iterative solution, and efficiency of parallelezation are presented, under the simple assumptions on computing model, as well as results of numerical experiments for the representative set of test problems. We consider the systems of

---

* This work was supported by RFBR grant N 05-01-10487.

V. Malyshkin (Ed.): PaCT 2007, LNCS 4671, pp. 206–214, 2007.
© Springer-Verlag Berlin Heidelberg 2007

seven-diagonal equations, provided by exponential type finite volume approach on the structured mesh, for 3-D Dirichlet BVP for convection-diffusion partial differential equation (PDE) in unit cube computational domain, which was described in [5].

Parallelezation of iterative processes is made by means of domain decomposition techniques, see [6] and references citied there. Realization of algorithms and computations are fulfilled in the framework of OPEN MP and MPI systems at the platforms with shared and distributed memory. The influence of different matrix formats is analyzed for the set of embedded grids. For the simplicity, we do not use any preconditioning procedure.

This paper is organized as follows. Into section 2, a short description of iterative methods and their peculiarities are introduced. The third section is devoted to discussion of program implementation and parallel technologies in the code development. In the last section we give and analyze the results of comparative performance measurements at the clusters, on the base of Itanium-2 processors.

1 Conjugate and Semi-conjugate Iterative Methods

Let us consider the system of linear algebraic equations (SLAEs)

$$Au = f, \quad u = \{u_i\}, \quad f = \{f_i\} \in R^N, \quad A = \{a_{i,j}\} \in R^{N,N}, \tag{1}$$

with real, square, non-singular and symmetric or non-symmetric matrix A which is positive definite, in the sense,

$$(Au, u) \geq \delta(u, u), \quad \delta > 0, \quad \forall u \in R^N. \tag{2}$$

The last means positiveness of real parts of eigenvalues of matrix A and positive definitness of symmetric part of matrix A: $A^s = (A + A^t)/2$, A^t is the trasposed matrix.

For solving SLAE(1), some conjugate direction method is applied, see [1]–[2]:

$$r^0 = g - Au, \quad p^0 = r^0; \quad n = 0, 1, \dots : \\ u^{n+1} = u^n + \alpha_n p^n, \quad r^{n+1} = r^n - \alpha_n A p^n, \tag{3}$$

which has variational or/and orthogonal properties in Krylov subspaces

$$\mathcal{K}_{n+1}(r^0, A) = span\{p^0, p^1, \dots, p^n\} = span\{p^0, Ap^0, \dots, A^n p^0\}. \tag{4}$$

For symmetric A, we use the classical conjugate gradient (CG) method defined by the formulas

$$p^{n+1} = r^{n+1} + \beta_n p^n, \quad \alpha_n = (r^n, r^n)/(Ap^n, p^n), \quad \beta_n = (r^{n+1}, r^{n+1})/(r^n, r^n). \tag{5}$$

This algorithm provides the residual and direction vectors with the following orthogonal properties:

$$(r^n, r^k) = \rho_n \delta_{n,k}, \quad \rho_n = (r^n, r^n), \quad (Ap^n, p^k) = \sigma_n \delta_{n,k}, \\ \sigma_n = (Ap^n, p^n), \quad (r^n, p^k) = 0, \text{ for } k \neq n, \tag{6}$$

where $\delta_{n,k}$ is Kroneker symbol. Also, CG method is minimizing the functional $(A^{-1}r^n, r^n)$ in Krylov subspace, and for error reducing: $(A^{-1}r^n, r^n)/(A^{-1}r^0, r^0) \leq \varepsilon$ the following estimation of necessary iteration number is valid –

$$n(\varepsilon) \leq ln\frac{1 + \sqrt{1 - \varepsilon^2}}{\varepsilon}/ln\gamma + 1, \quad \gamma = (\sqrt{æ} - 1)/(1 + \sqrt{æ}), \qquad (7)$$

where $æ = \|A\|_2 \cdot \|A^{-1}\|_2$ being the spectral condition number of matrix A.

If matrix A is non-symmetric, two-terms recursions (5) with orthogonal properties (6) are not valid, and direction vectors p^n, in general, can be found from the "long" recursions

$$p^{n+1} = r^{n+1} + \sum_{k=0}^{n} \beta_{n,k} p^k = p^{n+1,l} + \sum_{k=l}^{n} \beta_{n,k} p^k, \quad l = 0, 1, ..., n,$$
$$p^{n+1,0} = r^{n+1}, \quad p^{n+1,l} = p^{n+1,l-1} + \beta_{n,l-1} p^{l-1}, \quad p^{n+1} = p^{n+1,n}. \qquad (8)$$

Let us define the coefficients $\alpha_n, \beta_{n,k}$ in (3), (8) from the condition that direction vectors being left semi-A-orthogonal (left semi-conjugate), see [4]:

$$(Ap^n, p^k) = 0, \quad k = 0, 1, ..., n - 1. \qquad (9)$$

Then the residual vectors satisfy to orthogonal properties (6), α_n are defined by (5), as in CG method, and for coefficients $\beta_{n,k}$ the following formula is applicable:

$$\beta_{n,k} = -(p^k, Ap^{n,k})/(p^k, Ap^k), \quad k = 0, 1, ..., n - 1. \qquad (10)$$

So, the formulaes (2), (3),(6), (8), (10) define left semi-conjugate gradient (LSCG) method as generalization of CG algorithm for non-symmetric case. Inplementation of each LSCG iteration needs only one matrix-vector multiplication, similar to CG algorithm. However, LSCG method has not any variational property and the estimation of type (7) for $n(\varepsilon)$ can not be obtained. In a similar way the right semi-conjugate gradient (RSCG) method could be derived.

It is evident from (8) that realization of long recursions in LSCG method for solving non-symmetric SLAE requires to store at n-th iteration the direction vectors $p^0, p^1, ..., p^{n-1}$ and to compute $n^2/2$ additional vector-vector operations in total. For this reason, it increases considerably the computational complexity of algorithm, in compare to CG. There are two approaches which provide the decreasing of necessary memory and the number of arithmetic operations.

The first one is based on using restarts after given number m_r of iterations. It means that at each iterations $n = n_q = \left[\frac{n}{m_r}\right] \cdot q$, $q = 1, 2, ...$ ([a] is the integer part of value a) the residuals vectors are calculated not by recurrent relations (3), but from original equation directly:

$$r^{n_q} = f - Au^{n_q}. \qquad (11)$$

The rest iterations are implemented in convential form (3), (8).

The second approach applies the truncated semi-orthogonalization of direction vectors p^k: for given integer m_0 and $n > m_0$ we save the last m_0 vectors only and use reduced recurion

$$p^{n+1} = r^{n+1} + \sum_{k=n-m_0}^{n} \beta_{n,k} p^k = p^{n+1,n},$$
$$p^{n+1,n-m_0} = r^{n+1}, \quad p^{n+1,l} = p^{n+1,l-1} + \beta_{n,l-1} p^{l-1}, \quad l = n - m_0 + 1, ..., n. \tag{12}$$

Also, it is possible to generalize, or to combine formally these two aproaches: for given integers m_r and m_0 we can define $m = min\{m_0, m_r\}$ and compute direction vectors by formulaes (12), under changing symbol m_0 into m.

It should be remarked that restart and truncated orthogonalization approaches decrease the iterative convergence, because of reducing the dimension of Krylov subspaces in both case.

2   The Parallel Technologies of Algorithms Implementation

In the Table 1 we give the values of memory P and the total number of arithmetic operations Q which are necessary for implementation of CG and LSCG methods. It is supposed here that the total number of nonzero matrix entries $S \gg 1$, as well as $n \gg 1$, $N \gg 1$.

Table 1. The volumes of necessary resources for CG and LSCG methods

	CG	LSCG
P	$4N + S$	$4N + S + mN$
Q	$2(5N + S)n$	$2(5N + S + mN)n$

We remark here that in both method only one matrix-vector product is needed at each iteration, and for stopping criteria we check the condition

$$\|r^n\| = (r^n, r^n)^{1/2} \leq \|f\| \varepsilon, \tag{13}$$

where $\varepsilon \ll 1$ is the given tolerance.

We consider the parallelezation of algorithms for solving SLAEs which arise in approximation of 3-D boundary value problems at the parallelepiped reqular mesh

$$\begin{aligned} x_{i+1} &= x_i + h_i^x, \quad i = 0, 1, ..., I, \\ y_{j+1} &= y_j + h_j^y, \quad j = 0, 1, ..., J, \\ z_{k+1} &= z_k + h_k^z, \quad k = 0, 1, ..., K. \end{aligned} \tag{14}$$

For simplicity, the computational domain is supposed to be cube $\Omega = [x_0, x_{I+1}] \times [y_0, y_{J+1}] \times [z_0, z_{K+1}]$, and the matrix A is seven-diagonal one, which is defined from the set of equations at the regular seven-point grid stencil:

$$(Au)_{i,j,k} = p^0_{i,j,k} u_{i,j,k} - p^1_{i,j,k} u_{i-1,j,k} - p^2_{i,j,k} u_{i,j-1,k} -$$
$$-p^3_{i,j,k} u_{i+1,j,k} - p^4_{i,j,k} u_{i,j+1,k} - p^5_{i,j,k} u_{i,j,k-1} - p^6_{i,j,k} u_{i,j,k+1}, \qquad (15)$$
$$i = 1, ..., I; \quad j = 1, ..., J; \quad k = 1, ..., K.$$

So, in convential algebraic representation vector u has dimension $N = IJK$:

$$u = \{u_{i,j,k} = u_s, \ \ s = s(i,j,k)\}. \qquad (16)$$

The quality of parallelezation will be estimated by the speedup and efficiency coefficient

$$R = T_1/T_q, \quad E = R/q, \qquad (17)$$

where T_q is the time of solving the problem at q-processor computer (in our case, it will be implementation time of one iteration). This value is assembled from CPU time (implementation of arithmetic operation) and communication time (data exchanges between different processors):

$$T = T_a + T_c, \quad T_a = Q\tau_a, \quad T_c = \sum_{t=1}^{M}(\tau_0 + \tau_c V_t). \qquad (18)$$

Here we use the simplest computational model, i.e. τ_a is the realization time of an average arithmetic operation, τ_c is transfer time for one value, M is the number of communications, τ_0 is delay time for one exchange, and V_t is the number of exchanged values in t-th array communication. Usually, $\tau_a \ll \tau_c \ll \tau_0$, but in modern computers with multi-level memory and vectorization possibilities the real times T_a, T_c and T can differ from (18) significantly.

For parallelezation of iterative alorithms, we shall use the simplest 1-D domain decomposition technique: computational domain Ω is divided into strips $\Omega_t = \{I_t \leq i < I_{t+1}, \ t = 1, ..., q\}$ which are corresponding to "own" processors.

The main operations in CG and LSCG methods are matrix-vector multiplication, vector- vector inner product and linear combinations of vectors. The performance of the first operation depends on the sparse matrix storage formats, and we compare the efficiency of parallelezation for three types of storage. In the first format, matrix A is represented by the values of it's diagonal entries $p^0_{i,j,k}, p^1_{i,j,k}, ..., p^6_{i,j,k}$, the zero values including (DS – diagonal storage). The second and the third formats are general compressed row storage (CRS) and compressed column storage (CCS), see [2]. If the matrix A is symmetric, we only store the upper triangular portion of the matrix.

3   Results of Numerical Experiments

We demonstrate the performance of described methods and technologies in application for solving symmetric and non-symmetric SLAEs which are obtained by exponential type finite volume approximation of the Dirichlet boundary value problem for diffusion-convection equation [5]

$$\frac{\partial^2 u}{\partial x^2} + \frac{\partial^2 u}{\partial y^2} + \frac{\partial^2 u}{\partial z^2} + p\frac{\partial u}{\partial x} + q\frac{\partial u}{\partial y} + r\frac{\partial u}{\partial z} = f(x,y,z), \quad (x,y,z) \in \Omega, \tag{19}$$

$$u|_\Gamma = g(x,y,z),$$

in unit cube at the set of cubic grids with the meshsteps

$$h = 1/(N+1), \quad N = I = J = K = 32, 64, 128.$$

The functions f and g from (19) are choosed under condition that exact solution $u(x,y,z) = 1$. The initial guess for iterations was $u^0 = 0$, and tolerance value $\varepsilon = 10^{-4}$ in all experiments. The computations were done in standard double precision, at the cluster with Itanium-2 processors. The code was realized in FORTRAN 90.

For illustration of the numerical efficiency of considered methods we present in each cell of Table 2 three values: number of iterations, CPU time (sec) for one processor and resulting error of obtained solution. Here we use convection coefficients $a = p = q = r = 0, 4, 8, 16$, restart parameters (for non-symmetric cases only) $m = m_r = m_0 = 8, 32, 200$, and three different grids with total numbers of nodes $32^3, 64^3, 128^3$. In the following, we use CG method for $a = 0$ (symmetric case) and LSCG method for $a = 4, 8, 16$.

Table 2. The characteristics of CG and LSCG methods

a	0	4			8			16		
m	∞	8	32	200	8	32	200	8	32	200
	53	177	102	80	135	113	84	101	122	89
$I = 32$	0.043	0.34	0.50	0.89	0.26	0.54	0.97	0.19	0.60	1.09
	1.1E-4	1.2E-4	5.2E-4	3.7E-4	1.0E-3	3.7E-4	4.8E-4	5.6E-4	2.3E-4	2.4E-4
	105	549	185	152	409	188	162	270	211	173
$I = 64$	1.58	19.6	15.8	52.6	14.9	15.5	59.2	9.7	17.6	66.6
	1.9E-4	3.9E-3	1.6E-3	7.3E-4	2.9E-3	8.4E-4	7.4E-4	1.9E-3	1.3E-3	6.7E-4
	204	1797	581	369	1349	462	400	854	366	407
$I = 128$	20.7	527.7	420.1	126.6	396	324	148	251	256	148
	4.8E-4	1.1E-2	4.6E-3	2.2E-3	8.6E-3	3.7E-3	1.8E-3	5.9E-3	2.6E-3	1.9E-3

Next two tables present the results of performance measurements for CG method with using DS matrix format at three different grids. Table 3 includes CPU times for separate using OMP and MPI. For OMP the integer t means the number of threads defined at the node. The application of OpenMP is based on using PARALLEL DO Directive for each loop in the CG code and static definition of the number of threads, with equal execution of CHUNK=N/OMP_NUM_THREADS.

The cases MPIa and MPIb for the number of nodes $t = 2, 4$ are corresponding to loading the processors from the different nodes or from the same node, respectivaly.

In the Table 4, we give the similar experiment data for hybrid use of OpenMP and MPI possiblilities. Here s means the number of nodes and t is the number of defined threads for each node, so the total number of processors is $s \cdot t$.

Table 3. CPU times for different OpenMP and MPI specifications (CG method, DS format)

t	1	2			4		
	OMP	OMP	MPIa	MPIb	OMP	MPIa	MPIb
64	1.50	1.15	1.04	0.92	0.28	0.32	0.58
128	20.1	18.0	12.5	11.9	17.8	11.8	8.97
256	357	316	260.1	171.63	299	255.5	105.2

Table 4. The results of CG performance measurements: combine use of the OpenMP and MPI, DS format

s	2			4		
t	1	2	4	1	2	4
64	0.53	0.23	0.13	0.32	0.26	0.24
128	8.28	6.87	6.34	4.78	4.03	3.5
256	127	105	100	68.9	57.6	56.0

In each cell of the Table 5, 6 three CPU times are given: for $t = 1, 2$ and 4 OpenMP threads respectivaly (one cluster node was used only). Here, we compare the results of using CSR and CSC formats for $a = 0, 4$, in implementation of CG($a = 0$) and LSCG($a = 4$) with $m = 8, 32, 200$. Three values in each cell of these Tables, frov the top to bottom, are corresponding to $m = 1, 2, 4$ respectivaly.

Table 5. CPU times for CG and LSCG, CSR format, OpenMP, $t = 1, 2, 4$

a	0	4		
m	∞	8	32	200
	0.14	0.66	0.63	0.96
32	0.078	0.64	0.88	1.60
	0.055	0.42	0.63	1.26
	2.43	28.8	17.8	53.7
64	1.39	19.8	14.3	47.1
	0.84	15.3	11.8	39.6
	40.8	755.1	465.9	1285.0
128	25.3	581.6	406.6	1216.1
	19.1	516.1	382.8	1175.9

Table 7 demonstrates performance of CG method ($a = 0$) under hybrid OpenMP and MPI using for CSR format for numbers $s = 1, 2, 4$ and $t = 1, 2, 4$.

In the Tables 8, 9, we present the values of CPU times for solving SLAEs with CSR format for the grids $N = 64, 128$ by the CG method ($a = p = s = r = 0$) and LSCG algorithm ($a = 4, m = 8$), under MPI system at the numbers of processors $s = 1, 2, 4, 8$. Here the first columns contain into the bracket the corresponding numbers of iterations.

Table 6. CPU times for CG and LSCG, CSC format, OpenMP, $t = 1, 2, 4$

a	0	4		
m	∞	8	32	200
	0.093	0.59	0.59	0.92
32	0.125	0.59	0.97	1.78
	0.117	0.59	0.75	1.36
	2.04	24.6	15.6	47.1
64	1.95	22.5	15.5	48.4
	1.91	19.6	13.2	40.9
	35.0	701.5	449.2	1272.3
128	34.3	660.1	416.2	1169.0
	32.6	637.5	415.0	1161.2

Table 7. CPU times for CG, CSR, OpenMP+MPI

s	1	2			4		
t	1	1	2	4	1	2	4
64	2.43	1.70	1.36	1.14	1.66	1.56	1.49
128	40.8	31.6	25.1	21.4	29.1	25.0	23.5
256	636.0	501.4	387.4	337.4	448.6	390.1	367.4

Table 8. CPU times for CG method, MPI, CSR format

s	1	2	4	8
64(105)	2.74	2.07	0.78	0.33
128(204)	43.89	29.12	14.77	7.4

Table 9. CPU times for LSCG method ($m = 8, a = 4$), MPI, CSR format

s	1	2	4	8
64(549)	30.52	18.99	8.56	3.75
128(1797)	871.18	622.73	313.77	166.73

In conclusion, we can make the following derivation about the results of numerical experiments.

- The number of iterations in CG and LSCG methods without preconditioning are several times bigger, in compare with incomplete factorization algorithms, presented in [5] for similar test problems. But implementation of considered in this paper methods is reasonable at the multi-processor computers because parallelezation of preconditioned algorithms presents a "bottle neck" in computational algebra.
- Using the diagonal format provides the more high performance then general compressed sparse formats. So, the first one is more preferable for simple computational domains. But for real life BVPs, the parallelezation of matrix

operation in solving SLAEs with universal compessed formats is an important question for investigation.

- Performance of conjugate gradient method is approximately the same for CSR and CSC formats, but the last one is more preferable for the fine grids (bigger degree of freedom (d.o.f.), or dimension of SLAE). It is true for different numbers of threads in OpenMP ($t = 1, 2, 4$).
- Increasing the number of processors provides reducing CPU times, although speedup is small enough for OpenMP and hybrid OpenMP-MPI programming. These "negative" results were obtained for both considered algorithms, for different orders of SLAEs, different matrix formats, and for various numbers of computer nodes, processes and threads. But using MPI system demonstrates very good speedup, sometime even super linear one (efficiency coefficient $E > 1$).
- The unification of cluster resources is the unique approach now for solving very large SLAE, i.e. tens and hundred millions of d.o.f. with huge computational complexity. I.e., the speedup is not the unique reason for using multi-processor computing.
- The further research should be continued for code optimization and development of technologies for parallelezation of iterative algorithms with different matrix storage: multi-dimension domain decomposition techniques, loop unrolling, using various compiler options and OpenMP directives, creating special library of tools to solve large SLAEs, etc.

References

1. Il'in, V.P.: Iterative Incomplete Factorization Methods. World Sci. Pub. Co., Singapore (1992)
2. Saad, Y.: Iterative methods for sparse linear systems. PWS Publishing, New York (1996)
3. Dongarra, J.J., Duff, I.S., Sorensen, D.C., Van der Vorst, H.A.: Solving Linear Systems on Vector and Shared Memory Computers. SIAM, Philadelphia (1991)
4. Juan, J.Y., Golub, G.H., Plemmons, R.J., Cecilio, A.B.: Semi-conjugate direction methods for real positive definite systems.–Techn. Rep. SCCM Pc 02-02, Stenford Univ. (2003)
5. Andreeva, M.Y., Il'in, V.P., Itskovich, E.A.: Two solvers for nonsymmetric SLAE Bulletin of the Novosibirs Computing Center. Num. Anal. 12(12), 1–16 (2004)
6. Il'in, V.P.: On the strategies of parallelization in mathematical modeling. Programming N 1, 41–46 (1999)

TRES-CORE: Content-Based Retrieval Based on the Balanced Tree in Peer to Peer Systems*

Hai Jin and Jie Xu

Cluster and Grid Computing Lab
School of Computer Science and Technology
Huazhong University of Science and Technology, 430074, Wuhan, China
{hjin, jiexu}@hust.edu.cn

Abstract. Most existing Peer to Peer (P2P) systems support name-based retrieval and have provided very limited support for the full-text search of document contents. In this paper, we present a scheme (TRES-CORE) to support content-based retrieval. First, we propose a tree structure to organize data objects in vector-format in the P2P system, which is height-balanced so that the time complexity of search can be decreased. Second, we give a simple strategy for the placement of tree's nodes, which can guarantee both load balancing and fault tolerance. Then an efficient policy for the query is given. Besides theoretical analysis that can prove the correctness of our scheme, a simulation-based study is carried out to evaluate its performance under various scenarios finally. In this study, it shows that using this content-based retrieval scheme (TRES-CORE) is more accurate and more efficient than some other schemes in the P2P system.

1 Introduction

Peer to Peer (P2P) systems have wide applications in many fields in recent years, such as file sharing, distributed computing and so on. Information retrieval is the key technology for file sharing. However, traditional approaches have either been centralized or used flooding to ensure the accuracy of results returned and most of them only provide name-based retrieval, that is, the user can not search a data object unless he knows its name. They lack support for content-based retrieval.

Current P2P retrieval technologies can be classified into three types. First, a centralized index is maintained at a server, and all queries are directed to this server. However, a centralized search engine is not suitable to be scalable, which can not perform the efficient retrieval in the P2P system and it is also a single point of failure, such as Napster [1]. Second, a distributed index is employed. The query will be flooded across the network to some other peers. But, network traffic

---

* This work is supported by National Science Foundation of China (NSFC) under grant No.60433040 and by China CNGI Projects under grant No.CNGI-04-12-2A, CNGI-04-12-1D.

V. Malyshkin (Ed.): PaCT 2007, LNCS 4671, pp. 215–229, 2007.

generated by these flooding queries becomes un-scalable in large environments and it will lead to the poor network utilization. An example of this approach is the Gnutella system [2]. The third approach is the Distributed Hash Table (DHT) based scheme where the peer and the data object are structurally organized by a hash function. A query can get the result in $O(\log N)$ hops and it can generate fewer traffic in comparison with flooding-based mechanisms. Whereas, it can only support exact match queries and incurs the overhead maintaining the structure. Chord [3], Can [4], Pastry [5] and Tapestry [6] are examples of this approach.

In this paper, we explore the content-based retrieval scheme in P2P systems. First, traditional information retrieval techniques [7][8] are used to extract feature vectors from data objects. Using feature vectors of all data objects, a balanced search tree structure is formed. Then based on this search tree, we give an efficient retrieval scheme. And the time complexity of searching is $O(\log_B N)$ because the tree is height-balanced where B is the balancing factor of the tree. Our simulation results show using our content-based retrieval scheme(TRES-CORE) can increase recall and reduce the network traffic, that is, it can improve the efficiency of query routing.

The rest of this paper is organized as follows. In section 2, we present related works to our work. Section 3 explains basic ideas of our information retrieval scheme. Section 4 discusses some improvements to the basic design in order to provide load balancing, fault tolerance and efficiency. Experimental results are presented in section 5, and the last section gives conclusions and future works of our work.

2 Related Work

There are also some of today's works in the P2P information retrieval focusing on the content-based search. We describe them as follows.

A Hierarchical Summary Structure is proposed in [9], which employs three levels of summarization, naming as unit level, peer level and super level. However, in each level summary, how it is organized is not explained. And this is a key problem, which is able to result in the liner time complexity for the search if it is not organized well. Furthermore, it is another problem that how the feature vector of super peers and ordinary peers is generated accurately, which can effect the recall for the retrieval operation.

PlantP [10] presents a distributed content-based search algorithm in P2P systems. An inverted (word-to-document) index of the data objects that the peer wishes to share is created in each peer, and this index is summarized in a compact form. Then the summary is diffused throughout the network. Using these summaries, any peer can query and retrieve matching information from the collective information store of system. However, it is suitable for the multi-keyword-based retrieval but not for content-based retrieval using an inverted index.

The basic idea behind EZSearch [11] is in the following. Peers are partitioned into clusters. Each cluster contains peers having similar contents and manages a subspace of indices or an index zone. For a query, the simplest solution is to scan all the clusters, which, however, would incur a linear search time. Alternatively, similar to using search trees for the logarithmic runtime search, the Zigzag hierarchy [12] originally devised for the streaming multimedia is built on top of these clusters such that the search scope will be reduced by some factor if the query is forwarded from a high layer of the hierarchy to a lower layer. However, this method is suitable for the environment that each peer only shares a single category of data, which is unrealistic in P2P systems.

In pSearch [13], documents in the network are organized around their vector representations (based on modern document ranking algorithms) such that the search space for a given query is organized around related document. And it is designed for the structured overlay network.

There are also some other content-based retrieval schemes [14][15] that are built on the hybrid P2P systems. In such a network, Ultra Peers act as directory service providers. These directory peers that provide regional directory services construct and use the content models of neighboring peers to determine how to route query messages through the network. Leaf peers that provide information use content-based retrieval to decide which data objects to retrieve for queries. However, how best to relay the query among the Ultra Peers is an open problem. In these schemes, an Ultra Peer represents a neighboring Ultra Peer by the terms in the queries it has satisfied in the past. This approach can improve the efficiency of local query routing, but still makes it difficult to find relevant information in a large network.

In most of the prior researches, peers are clustered by the similar content. The problem of this kind of approach is that it is able to decrease the recall because some matching data objects are not in any peer of target clusters. Therefore, rather than clustering peers based on their contents, a height-balanced hierarchical tree(doc-tree) is employed to cluster data objects sharing in the P2P system. Then, a content-based retrieval scheme(TRES-CORE) based on this doc-tree is presented, which can resolve all of the flaws describing above.

3   TRES-CORE Scheme

In this section, we firstly give the data model for our scheme. Then we introduce the definition of doc-tree and give the theoretical foundation for building it. In the following, we describe how to construct a doc-tree. At last, we present a retrieval algorithm based on this tree.

3.1   Model

In our model, we consider a P2P system where each peer has a set of data objects to share with other peers in the system. These data objects are described based on the vector space model used in the information retrieval theory [7][8]. Each data object and each query are abstractly represented as a vector, where each dimension is associated with a distinct term (word). The vector space would have k dimensions if there were k distinct terms. The value of each component of the vector represents the importance of that word (typically referred to as the weight of the word) to that data object or the query. Such as, the data object x can be represented as a k-dimensional vector $\vec{d^x} = \{d_1^x, d_2^x, \cdots, d_k^x\}$, where each dimension reflects the term associated with x and the weight d_i^x reflects the significance of each term representing the semantic of x. Then, given a query vector $\vec{q} = \{q_1, q_2, \cdots, q_k\}$ to search a set of similar data objects from all of the data objects sharing in the P2P system, we rank the relevancies of data objects to that query by measuring the similarity between the query's vector and each of the candidate data objects' vectors. The similarity between the vector x and the vector y is generally measured as the cosine of the angle between them, using the following equation:$simdist = \dfrac{\vec{x} \cdot \vec{y}}{\| \vec{x} \|_2 \| \vec{y} \|_2}$, where $\vec{x} \cdot \vec{y}$ is the dot product between x and y and $\| \bullet \|_2$ is the Euclidean vector norm. The larger $simdist(\vec{x} \cdot \vec{y})$ is, the more semantically similar are x and y to each other. If $simdist(\vec{d} \cdot \vec{q})$ is larger than a predefined threshold θ, we say that $\vec{d}$ and $\vec{q}$ are similar and $\vec{d}$ is the data object that the query $\vec{q}$ wants to get.

3.2   Definitions and Properties of Doc-Tree

We use the concept similar to that proposed in BIRCH [16] for merging sub-nodes incrementally based on the node feature NF to derive a strategy to group similar data objects. In this paper, the node is only referred to the node in the doc-tree, but not be referred to the peer in the network.

Definition 1. $NF(N) = (m, \vec{\mu^N}, \vec{\delta^N})$ *is defined as the feature value of node* N, *where m is the number of data objects maintained by this node. If there are m data points $\{\vec{d^1}, \vec{d^2}, \cdots, \vec{d^m}\}$ in node N, the j-th mean and variance of node N are defined as:*

$$\mu_j^N = \frac{1}{m} \sum_{i=1}^{m} d_j^i, \quad \delta_j^N = \frac{1}{m} \sum_{i=1}^{m} (d_j^i - \mu_j^N)^2, \quad j = 1 \ldots k.$$

Definition 2. *The intra-distance of a node is a triple $D = < NDP, \mu, \sigma >$, where $NDP = \{d_i | d_i \in R\}$ is a population of nearest distances, μ and σ are the mean and standard deviation of NDP. Each d_i in NDP is the smallest distance from each sub-node to other sub-nodes in the node.*

A doc-tree is a height-balanced tree with a parameter B just like the B+ tree [17][18] and CF tree [16]. Data objects are organized in a multi-layer hierarchy of clusters recursively defined as follows (where H is the number of layers, B is a balancing factor):

- Layer 0 contains all data objects;
- Data objects in layer $j < H - 1$ are partitioned into clusters of sizes in $[1, B]$, Layer $H - 1$ has only one cluster which has a size in $[2, B]$.

Each node contains $[1, B]$ entries except the root node containing $[2, B]$ entries. The form of entries is $(NF_i, child_i), i = 1, 2, \cdots, B$, in which $child_i$ is a pointer to its i-th child node, and NF_i is the feature vector of sub-node represented by this child. That is, a node represents a cluster made up of all the sub-nodes represented by its entries. Furthermore, all entries in a node must satisfy the following threshold condition: let $D_N =< NDP, \mu, \sigma >$ be the intra-distance of node N. Given a lower limit $L_L = \mu - \sigma$ and an upper limit $U_L = \mu + \sigma$, the node N must satisfy: $L_L \leq d_i \leq U_L$ for $\forall d_i \in NDP$.

And each node in the tree maintains several data structures described in the Table1.

Table 1. Data Structure of Node N

Notation	Definition
$parent$	the pointer to the parent node (null for root)
n	the number of sub-nodes
m	the number of data objects
$(NF_i, chilid_i), i = 1, 2, \cdots, k$	$child_i$ is a pointer to its i-th child node
	NF_i is the NF of sub-node represented by this child
$D =< NDP, \mu, \sigma >$	the intra-distance of node N

Theorem 1. *Assume that there are n sub-nodes in node N and NF vectors of its sub-nodes N_i are $NF_i = (m_i, \vec{\mu^i}, \vec{\delta^i})$, $i = 1, 2, \cdots, n$. Then the NF vector of node N is $NF = (m, \vec{\mu}, \vec{\delta})$, in which $m = \sum_{i=1}^{n} m_i$ and the j-th mean and variance of node N is defined as:*

$$\mu_j = \frac{\sum_{i=1}^{n} m_i \mu_j^i}{\sum_{i=1}^{n} m_i}, \delta_j = \frac{\sum_{i=1}^{n} m_i \delta_j^i + \sum_{i=1}^{n} m_i (\mu_j^i - \mu_j)^2}{\sum_{i=1}^{n} m_i}.$$

Proof. Assume that there are m data objects $\{\vec{d^1}, \vec{d^2}, \cdots, \vec{d^m}\}$ in node N. According to Definition1, the j-th mean and variance of node N are $\mu_j = \frac{1}{m} \sum_{i=1}^{m} d_j^i$, $\delta_j = \frac{1}{m} \sum_{i=1}^{m} (d_j^i - \mu_j)^2$.

Assume that there are n sub-nodes in node N and NF vectors of its sub-nodes N_i are $NF_i = (m_i, \mu^i, \delta^i)$, $i = 1, 2, \cdots, n$ and each sub-node maintains m_i data objects. Hence, $m = \sum_{i=1}^{n} m_i$. According to Definition1, the j-th mean and variance of node N_i is $\mu_j^i = \frac{1}{m_i} \sum_{i=1}^{m_i} d_j^i$, $\delta_j^i = \frac{1}{m_i} \sum_{i=1}^{m_i} (d_j^i - \mu_j^i)^2$, $i = 1.2. \cdots, n$.

Therefore, $\sum_{i=1}^{m_i} d_j^i = m_i \mu_j^i$,

$$\sum_{i=1}^{m_i} (d_j^i)^2 = m_i \delta_j^i + 2\mu_j^i \sum_{i=1}^{m_i} d_j^i - m_i (\mu_j^i)^2$$
$$= m_i \delta_j^i + 2m_i (\mu_j^i)^2 - m_i (\mu_j^i)^2$$
$$= m_i \delta_j^i + m_i (\mu_j^i)^2,$$

$$\mu_j = \frac{1}{m} \sum_{i=1}^{m} d_j^i = \frac{\sum_{i=1}^{n} \sum_{k=1}^{m_i} d_j^k}{\sum_{i=1}^{n} m_i} = \frac{\sum_{i=1}^{n} m_i \mu_j^i}{\sum_{i=1}^{n} m_i},$$

$$\delta_j = \frac{1}{m} \sum_{i=1}^{m} (d_j^i - \mu_j)^2 = \frac{\sum_{i=1}^{n} \sum_{k=1}^{m_i} (d_j^k - \mu_j)^2}{\sum_{i=1}^{n} m_i}$$
$$= \frac{\sum_{i=1}^{n} \sum_{k=1}^{m_i} (d_j^k)^2 - 2\mu_j \sum_{i=1}^{n} \sum_{k=1}^{m_i} d_j^k + \sum_{i=1}^{n} m_i (\mu_j)^2}{\sum_{i=1}^{n} m_i}$$
$$= \frac{\sum_{i=1}^{n} [m_i \delta_j^i + m_i (\mu_j^i)^2] - 2\mu_j \sum_{i=1}^{n} m_i \mu_j^i + \sum_{i=1}^{n} m_i (\mu_j)^2}{\sum_{i=1}^{n} m_i}$$

$$= \frac{\sum_{i=1}^{n} m_i \delta_j^i + \sum_{i=1}^{n} m_i (\mu_j^i)^2 - 2\mu_j \sum_{i=1}^{n} m_i \mu_j^i + \sum_{i=1}^{n} m_i (\mu_j)^2}{\sum_{i=1}^{n} m_i}$$

$$= \frac{\sum_{i=1}^{n} m_i \delta_j^i + \sum_{i=1}^{n} m_i (\mu_j^i - \mu_j)^2}{\sum_{i=1}^{n} m_i}.$$

So, from the above description, the theorem holds. $\qquad \square$

Theorem 2. *Assume that there are n sub-nodes in node N and its NF vector is $NF = (m, \overrightarrow{\mu}, \overrightarrow{\delta})$ and NF vectors of its sub-nodes N_i are $NF_i = (m_i, \overrightarrow{\mu^i}, \overrightarrow{\delta^i})$, $i = 1, 2, \cdots, n$. A new node $NF_{n+1} = (m_{n+1}, \overrightarrow{\mu^{n+1}}, \overrightarrow{\delta^{n+1}})$ wants to join node N. Then the new NF vector of node N is $NF' = (m', \overrightarrow{\mu'}, \overrightarrow{\delta'})$, in which $m' = m + m_{n+1}$ and the j-th mean and variance of node N is modified: $\mu_j' = \frac{m\mu_j + m_{n+1}\mu_j^{n+1}}{m + m_{n+1}}$, $\delta_j' = \frac{m\delta_j + m(\mu_j)^2 + m_{n+1}\delta_j^{n+1} + m_{n+1}(\mu_j^{n+1})^2 - (m+m_{n+1})(\mu_j')^2}{m + m_{n+1}}$.*

Proof. According to the definition of NF vector, we can get $m' = m + m_{n+1}$. Assume that there are m data objects $\{\overrightarrow{d^1}, \overrightarrow{d^2}, \cdots, \overrightarrow{d^m}\}$ in node N. According to Definition1, the j-th mean and variance of node N is $\mu_j = \frac{1}{m} \sum_{i=1}^{m} d_j^i$, $\delta_j = \frac{1}{m} \sum_{i=1}^{m} (d_j^i - \mu_j)^2$.

Therefore, $\sum_{i=1}^{m} d_j^i = m\mu_j, \sum_{i=1}^{m} (d_j^i)^2 == m\delta_j + m(\mu_j)^2$.

After inserting a new node $NF_{n+1} = (m_{n+1}, \overrightarrow{\mu^{n+1}}, \overrightarrow{\delta^{n+1}})$ which maintains m_{n+1} data objects into node N and $\sum_{i=m+1}^{m+m_{n+1}} d_j^i = m_{n+1}\mu_j^{n+1}, \sum_{i=m+1}^{m+m_{n+1}} (d_j^i)^2 = m_{n+1}\delta_j^{n+1} + m_{n+1}(\mu_j^{n+1})^2$, the j-th mean and variance of node N is

$$\mu_j' = \frac{\sum_{i=1}^{m} d_j^i + \sum_{i=m+1}^{m+m_{n+1}} d_j^i}{m + m_{n+1}} = \frac{m\mu_j + m_{n+1}\mu_j^{n+1}}{m + m_{n+1}},$$

$$\delta_j' = \frac{\sum_{i=1}^{m+m_{n+1}} (d_j^i - \mu_j')^2}{m + m_{n+1}} = \frac{\sum_{i=1}^{m+m_{n+1}} (d_j^i)^2 - \sum_{i=1}^{m+m_{n+1}} d_j^i \mu_j' + (m+m_{n+1})(\mu_j')^2}{m + m_{n+1}}$$

$$= \frac{m\delta_j + m(\mu_j)^2 + m_{n+1}\delta_j^{n+1} + m_{n+1}(\mu_j^{n+1})^2 - (m+m_{n+1})(\mu_j')^2}{m + m_{n+1}}.$$

So, from the above description, the theorem holds. $\qquad \square$

Theorem 3. *Assume that there are n sub-nodes in node N and its NF vector is $NF = (m, \overrightarrow{\mu}, \overrightarrow{\delta})$ and NF vectors of its sub-nodes N_i are $NF_i = (m_i, \overrightarrow{\mu^i}, \overrightarrow{\delta^i})$, $i = 1, 2, \cdots, n$. A sub-node $NF_{n+1} = (m_{n+1}, \overrightarrow{\mu^{n+1}}, \overrightarrow{\delta^{n+1}})$ wants to leave from node N. Then the new NF vector of node N is $NF' = (m', \overrightarrow{\mu'}, \overrightarrow{\delta'})$, in which $m' = m - m_{n+1}$ and the j-th mean and variance of node N is modified: $\mu_j' = \frac{m\mu_j - m_{n+1}\mu_j^{n+1}}{m - m_{n+1}}$, $\delta_j' = \frac{m\delta_j + m(\mu_j)^2 - m_{n+1}\delta_j^{n+1} - m_{n+1}(\mu_j^{n+1})^2 - (m-m_{n+1})(\mu_j')^2}{m - m_{n+1}}$.*

The theorem's proof is similar to that for Theroem 2 so that we omit it here.

Corollary 1. *Assume that a data object $\overrightarrow{d^i} = (d_1, d_2, \cdots, d_d)$ will join node N whose NF vector is $NF = (m, \overrightarrow{\mu}, \overrightarrow{\delta})$. Then the new NF vector of node N is $NF' = (m', \overrightarrow{\mu'}, \overrightarrow{\delta'})$, in which $m' = m + 1$ and the j-th mean and variance of node N is defined as $\mu_j' = \frac{m\mu_j + d_j}{m+1}$, $\delta_j' = \frac{m\delta_j + m(\mu_j)^2 + d_j^2 - (m+1)(\mu_j')^2}{m+1}$.*

According to Theorem 2, we can get Corollary 1.

Corollary 2. *Assume that a data object* $\vec{d^i} = (d_1, d_2, \cdots, d_d)$ *leaves from node* N *whose NF vector is $NF = (m, \vec{\mu}, \vec{\delta})$. Then the new NF vector of node N is $NF' = (m', \vec{\mu'}, \vec{\delta'})$, in which $m' = m - 1$ and the j-th mean and variance of node N is defined as $\mu'_j = \frac{m\mu_j - d_j}{m-1}$, $\delta'_j = \frac{m\delta_j + m(\mu_j)^2 - d_j{}^2 - (m-1)(\mu'_j)^2}{m-1}$.*

According to Theorem 3, we can get Corollary 2.

Corollary 1 and Corollary 2 are the basis for constructing the doc-tree. Corollary 1 are applied to join a node for the doc-tree and Corollary 2 is applied to delete a node for the doc-tree.

Definition 3. *$Dis(N, M)$ is defined as the distance measure between node N and node M. The following formula is used: $Dis(N, M) = \|\overrightarrow{\mu^N} - \overrightarrow{\mu^m}\|$. $Dis(N, M)$ is small when $\overrightarrow{\mu^N}$ and $\overrightarrow{\mu^M}$ are close. That is, the similar two nodes are, the smaller the value $Dis(N, M)$ is. It is applied to join a node for the doc-tree.*

3.3 Construction of a Hierarchical Tree

We now present the algorithm for constructing a hierarchical tree, which include two operations: adding a data object to the hierarchical tree and deleting a data object from the hierarchical tree. The sensitivity of input ordering is one of the major issues in incremental hierarchical clustering [19]. In order to overcome it, the algorithm must enjoy two properties: homogeneity and monotonicity. A homogeneous node is a set of sub-nodes satisfying the threshold condition. A hierarchy of nodes satisfies the monotonicity property if the intra-distance of a node is always smaller than the intra-distance of its parent[20].

A data object joins

Our approach to incorporating a new data object S into a cluster hierarchy incrementally proceeds as below:

Step 1. Identify the appropriate location: Starting from the root, it recursively descends the hierarchical tree by choosing a sub-node according to the smallest value of the distance measure(Definition 3) until the new data object can reach a leaf node. At the same time, it is to modify the information on the path from the root to the leaf, that is, after inserting a data object into the hierarchical tree, we must update the NF information for each node on the path from the root to the new leaf node according to Corollary 1.

Step 2. Assuming the leaf node that the new object S wants to insert is N and d is the smallest distance from the data object to the other data object in node N(see Fig.1):

   a) if $m < B$ and for each d_i s.t. $L_L \le d_i \le U_L$, then $INSERT(S, N)$
   b) if $m == B$ and $L_L \le d_i \le U_L$ or$\ni$ d_i s.t. $d_i < L_L$, then $SPLIT(N + S)$
   c) otherwise, $NEWNODE(S)$.

Node splitting is done by choosing the farthest pair of entries as seeds, and redistributing the remaining entries based on the closest criteria.

Step 3. After inserting a new data object into a leaf node, we must update the information for each non-leaf node on the path to the leaf node. In the absence of a split, nothing is modified for non-leaf nodes. A leaf node split requires us to insert a new non-leaf entry into the parent node. If the parent has space for this entry, we only add an entry to reflect the addition in the parent node. Otherwise, we have to split the parent as well, and so on up to the root.

However, one of the problems is that a node is stranded at an upper level cluster. Hence,

Step 4. Employ the standard in Step 2 and Theorem 1 to eliminate the inhomogeneous clusters at the upper level if the information of non-leaf node is changed.

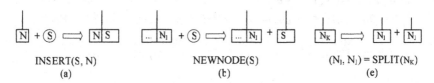

INSERT(S, N)   NEWNODE(S) $(N_I, N_J) = SPLIT(N_K)$
(a)   (b)   (e)

Fig. 1. Node operations

A data object leaves
If a data object is found not to exist in the P2P system during a searching process, the entry in the leaf node maintaining the data object will be omitted and NF vectors of the nodes on the path from root to the leaf node will be changed according to Corollary 2 and employ the standard in Step 2 and Theorem 1 to maintain the homogeneity for each modified node.

The placement of tree nodes
Which server is each node in the tree placed on when a doc-tree is constructing? A root node can be created by and placed on the server who joins the P2P system firstly. The existence and address of the root node are assumed to be either well-known, or disseminated in an application-specific manner in the P2P system. Assume when a server P publishes a new data object to the system, a node N_a is created in the hierarchical tree. Then, the owner of N_a is P or the owner of N_a's parent and all the nodes in the tree are placed on their owner. Each node has a single owner, and may be replicated at servers other than the owner. The information about a node may also be cached by other servers. We also describe the placement scheme in section 4.

3.4   Query Processing

Let $q = \{\overrightarrow{Q}, \theta, id_q\}$ be the query feature vector. id_q is a pseudorandom number, uniquely identifying each query. $simdist(\overrightarrow{\mu}, \overrightarrow{Q})$ is the distance measure between the query and a node whose mean is $\overrightarrow{\mu}$. The search algorithm needs to return data objects such that $simdist(\overrightarrow{d}, \overrightarrow{Q}) \geq \theta$.

Assume a peer P initiates a search to find similar data objects to its query. First, the features of this query are extracted and used to calculate the distance between the query and the tree node. The query will forward the root node and the query also forward tree nodes maintained in the peer if $simdist(\overrightarrow{\mu}, \overrightarrow{Q}) \geq \theta$.If the query reaches a tree node, all the nodes maintained by the peer maintaining this node are checked whether they satisfy the matching criteria. Hence, the peer is labeled by id_q such that the query is not propagated if it reaches this peer again. If there is no existing the node such that $simdist(\overrightarrow{\mu}, \overrightarrow{Q}) \geq \theta$ or $\theta == 0$, the node which $simdist(\overrightarrow{\mu}, \overrightarrow{Q})$ is largest is selected to transmit the query. Until a leaf node reaches, the address of data object will send back to the query peer if $simdist(\overrightarrow{d}, \overrightarrow{Q}) \geq \theta$, $\overrightarrow{d}$ is the feature vector representing the data object maintained by the leaf node. During each searching processing, the query only passes through the server at most one time. The doc-tree is a balanced tree and the number of data objects M is in direct proportion to the number of servers N in the system so the time complexity for the searching is $O(log_B N)$.

Example: Assume server 1 in Fig.2. initiates a search to find similar data objects to its query $q = \{\overrightarrow{Q}, \theta, id_q\}$. First, this query is routed to server 5 maintaining the root node $n1$. And at the same time, it is also routed to server 4 because the distance between $\overrightarrow{Q}$ and the node $n5$ maintained by server 4 is larger than θ. Furthermore, the data object $d4$ in server 4 satisfies the matching criteria. Therefore, server 4 will reply the requester server 1 about the address of $d4$. And, node $n8$ maintained by server 4 is also larger than θ. So the server 4 will reply the server 1 about the address of $d8$, which is a matching result. Then server 4 is labeled to have been visited so that this query passes through it next time will be ignored. Also, the query reaching the root is routed to server 3 because the node $n3$ in server 3 also satisfies the matching criteria and then server 3 is labeled to have been visited. The query continues to route to server 2 and server 4 because both $n7$ and $n8$ in them satisfy the matching criteria. Because server 4 has been labeled, the query routed to it will be ignored. Server 2 will reply the requester server 1 about the address of $d6$ because it satisfies the matching criteria.

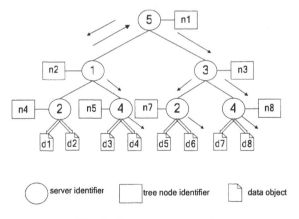

Fig. 2. The query processing

4   Extension to the TRES-CORE Scheme

TRES-CORE described above is only a basic scheme. Many other problems must be considered, such as fault tolerance, load balancing and the efficiency. We will discuss them in this section.

4.1   Load Balancing

All of the tree nodes in the doc-tree must be placed on different servers in order to achieve load balancing among the servers in the system.

From [21], we can know there are a kind of servers in the network who provide very high quality connections, stay consistently connected and allocate large amounts of disk space. We call these peers as strong peers and the others are called as weak peers. Generally, in order to maintain load balancing in the system, the overhead for the computing, the communication and the key data are taken on by strong peers. And the overhead of storage is taken on by weak peers.

Nodes in the doc-tree can also be classified into two categories: non-leaf nodes and leaf nodes. The visiting frequency of non-leaf nodes is high so that they need strong consistency and the frequency of node splitting is low. However, the visiting frequency of leaf nodes is low and the frequency of node splitting is high. Therefore, non-leaf nodes are placed on strong peers and leaf nodes are placed on weak peers.

So, the placement of tree nodes can be modified as following. Assume when a server P publishes a new data object to the system, a node N_a is created in the hierarchical tree. Then, the owner of N_a is P if P is a strong peer or N_a is a leaf node. Otherwise, the owner of N_a is the owner of N_a's parent and all the nodes in the tree are placed on their owner.

4.2   Fault Tolerance

At the same time, in order to guarantee fault tolerance of the doc-tree, each tree nodes must replicate in several servers. Assume that a server P publishes a new data object to the system.

(1) If the new data object is placed on a node N, node N will be replicated on the server P;

(2) If a leaf node N is on the server, all the nodes from the root to the node N are replicated on the server.

Each node is replicated several copies so that all the copies must be modified when a node is changed in order to maintain the consistency.

4.3   Improvement of the Efficiency

The change of doc-tree is very frequent if there are too many data objects. Therefore, in order to improve the efficiency for building the doc-tree, we can employ some classic clustering algorithms [22] to cluster all the data objects sharing in every server in advance. After that, the centroid of each cluster can be regarded as a data object to join the doc-tree. During the searching process, a cluster's centroid which is most similar to the query can be found and then the query will route to this cluster for the result. That is, clustering locally in advance can reduce the burden of building the doc-tree in a large-scale data environment and improve the speed of searching.

5   Simulation

In this section, we provide a brief description of each experiment and the results obtained. We conduct simulation experiments to prove our algorithms are effective and efficient.

5.1   Experiment Setup

For content-based retrieval in P2P systems, both the retrieval accuracy and the efficiency of query routing are important. So we measure the performance using three accepted metrics: *recall*, *msg* and *efficiency*, which are defined as follows:

$$recall = \frac{|\{\forall \vec{d}, simdist(\vec{d}, \vec{q}) > \theta, \vec{d} \in results\}|}{|\{\forall \vec{d}, simdist(\vec{d}, \vec{q}) > \theta, \vec{d} \in dataset\}|},$$

$$msg = \sum_{i=1}^{|P|} message(p_i), efficiency = \frac{recall}{msg}.$$

The metric *recall* captures the fraction of relevant documents a search and retrieval algorithm is able to identify and present to the user, which measures the retrieval accuracy. The metric *msg* shows the number of query messages generated for a query. The metric *efficiency* measures the efficiency of query routing.

We simulate our system with a certain number N of peers. The method that each peer joins the system is the same as that for Gnutella. Then Data objects are assigned to peers in the following manner. First, L sets of the mean vector and the variance vector are generated randomly. The dimension of these vectors is D and the range of each dimension is shown in Table 2. Each set represents a kind of data objects. In the following, we randomly assign S different classes to each peer. Then one data point is generated according to the normal distribution for each chosen class in every peer. After building the system and the doc-tree, each peer initiates 20 queries. We take the average for the number of query messages generated and recall accordingly. Table 2 gives some simulation parameters and their values.

5.2   Experiment Results

In this section, we compare TRES-CORE with the random BFS [23], one of the methods in the Gnutella network. We explore how the performances are affected by:

(1) different number of peers in the P2P systems;
(2) different balancing factor B of the doc-tree.

Table 2. Parameters and Settings

Algorithm	Average routing latency	Latency stretch
N	1000-10000	Number of peers in the system
θ	0.9	Query range threshold
L	100	Number of classes in the system
S	50	Number of classes in each peer
Mean	[0,1]	Range of mean
Var	[0.05,0.5]	Range of variance
D	200	Number of dimension
TTL	7	Time to live for each query for BFS
M	4	The maximal number of neighbor
B	2-10	Balancing factor of the doc-tree

Fig.3. depicts the recall against the number of peers for BFS and TRES-CORE with $B = 2$, $B = 5$ and $B = 10$ respectively. When the size of network increases, the recall of our scheme continues to remain at a higher range, while the recall for BFS drops when the size of network grows. And in our scheme, the smaller B is, the bigger the metric recall is. We conclude that our algorithm is insensitive to the change of network size, that is, our mechanism is more scalable.

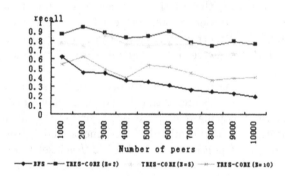

Fig. 3. Recall against the number of peers

Fig.4(a). shows the number of query messages against the number of peers for BFS and TRES-CORE with $B = 2$. We vary the number of peers from 1000 to 10000 in the network to observe changes in the number of query messages generated when a peer initiates a search. From Fig.4(a), the TRES-CORE method shows a much slower increase in the number of query messages than the BFS method. Fig.4(b). shows the number of query messages against the number of peers for TRES-CORE with different balancing factors. From it, we can know that the bigger B is, the smaller the number of query messages is. Therefore, we can conclude that the TRES-CORE method can generate much less network traffic.

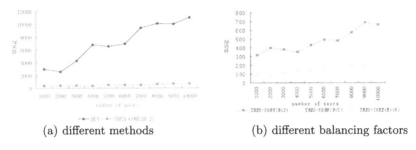

(a) different methods   (b) different balancing factors

Fig. 4. Number of query messages against the number of peers

Fig.5. depicts the query efficiency against the number of peers for BFS and TRES-CORE with $B = 2$, $B = 5$ and $B = 10$, respectively. The TRES-CORE always outperforms BFS although query efficiencies of all of them decrease when the size of network increases. From it, we can also know that the query efficiency will increase with the increase of the balancing factor B. However, if B is too large ($B = 10$), the query efficiency will decrease.

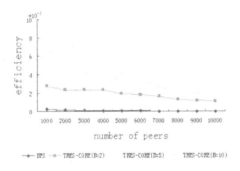

Fig. 5. Query efficiency against the number of peers

6   Conclusion and Future Work

In this paper, we propose a new scheme TRES-CORE for P2P content-based information retrieval, along with various optimization techniques to improve system efficiency and the quality of search results. We made the following contributions: (1) we propose a height-balanced tree structure doc-tree to organize data objects in vector-format in the P2P system which can reduce the time complexity of searching; (2) we give a simple strategy for the placement of tree's nodes, which can guarantee both load balancing and fault tolerance; (3) TRES-CORE can be used to support content-based retrieval. Simulation results show TRES-CORE is an accurate and efficient scheme. In the future, we will study how to maintain the consistency of several copies in a large scale environment and the cache scheme in the P2P system. We also plan to construct a P2P system that gets physically neighboring peers into a cluster. Then, TRES-CORE is employed in each cluster, which is the more suitable environment.

References

1. Napstry. http://www.napstry.com/
2. Gnutella. http://www.gnutellaforums.com/
3. Stoica, I., Morris, R., Karger, D., et al.: Chord: A Scalable Peer-to-Peer Lookup Service for Internet Applications. In: Govindan. (ed.) Proc. of the ACM SIGCOMM, pp. 149–160. ACM Press, San Diego (2001)
4. Ratnasamy, S., Francis, P., Handley, M., et al.: A Scalable Content-Addressable Network. In: Govindan. (ed.) Proc. of the ACM SIGCOMM, pp. 161–172. ACM Press, San Diego (2001)
5. Rowstron, A., Druschel, P.: Pastry: Scalable, Distributed Object Location and Routing for Large-scale Peer-to-Peer Systems. In: Guerraoui, R. (ed.) Middleware 2001. LNCS, vol. 2218, pp. 329–350. Springer, Heidelberg (2001)
6. Zhao, B.Y., Huang, L., Stribling, J., Rhea, S.C., Joseph, A.D., Kubiatowicz, J.: Tapestry: A Resilient Global-Scale Overlay for Service Deployment. IEEE Journal on Selected Areas in Communications 22, 41–53 (2004)
7. Michael, W.B., Zlatko, D., Elizabeth, R.J.: Matrices, Vector Spaces, and Information Retrieval. SIAM Review 2, 335–362 (1999)
8. Deerwester, S.C., Dumais, S.T., Landauer, T.K., Furnas, G.W., Harshman, R.A.: Indexing by Latent Semantic Analysis. Journal of the American Society for Information Science 6, 391–407 (1990)
9. Shen, H.T., Shu, Y.F., Yu, B.: Efficient Content-Based Text Search in P2P Network. IEEE Transaction on Knowledge and Data Engineering (TKDE) (Special Issue on P2P Data Management) 7, 813–826 (2004)
10. Cuenca-Acuna, F.M., Nguyen, T.D.: Text-Based Content Search and Retrieval in Ad Hoc P2P Communities. Technical Report DCS-TR-483, Department of Computer Science, Rutgers University (2002)
11. Tran, D.A.: A Hierarchical Semantic Overlay Approach to P2P Similarity Search. In: Proceedings of USENIX Annual Technical Conference, pp. 355–358 (2005)
12. Tran, D.A., Hua, K.A., Do, T.T.: Zigzag: An Efficient Peer-to-Peer Scheme for Media Streaming. In: Proc. of the IEEE INFOCOM 2003. IEEE Computer and Communications Societies, New York, pp. 1283–1293 (2003)
13. Tang, C., Xu, Z., Mahalingam, M.: pSearch: Information Retrieval in Structured Overlays. ACM SIGCOMM Computer Communication Review 1, 89–94 (2003)
14. Renda, M.E., Callan, J.: The Robustness of Content-Based Search in Hierarchical Peer to Peer Network. In: Proceedings of the thirteenth ACM international conference on Informa-tion and knowledge managemen (2004)
15. Liu, J., Callan, J.: Content-Based Retrieval in Hybrid Peer-to-Peer Networks. In: Proceedings of the twelfth international conference on Information and knowledge management, pp. 562–570 (2003)
16. Zhang, T., Ramakrishnan, R., Livny, M.: BIRCH: A New Data Clustering Algorithm and Its Applications. Data Mining and Knowledge Discovery 2, 141–182 (1997)
17. Forouzan, B.A., Gilberg, R.F.: Data Structures: A Pseudocode Approach with C++. Brooks/Cole Pub. Co. (2000)

18. Fisher, D.H., Xu, L., Zard, N.: Ordering Effects in Clustering. In: Proceedings of the 9th International Conferenceon Machine Learning (1992)
19. Widyantoro, D., Yen, J.: An Incremental Approach to Building a Cluster Hierarchy. In: Proceedings of the 2002 IEEE International Conference on Data Mining, pp. 705–708 (2002)
20. Wilcox-O'Hearn, B.: Experiences Deploying a Large-Scale Emergent Network. In: Proceedings of the First International Workshop on Peer-to-Peer Systems, pp. 104–110 (2002)
21. Comer, D.: The Ubiquitous Btree. ACM Computing Surveys 2, 121–137 (1979)
22. Jain, A.K., Murty, M.N., Flynn, P.J.: Data Clustering: A Review. ACM Computing Sur-veys 31, 265–322 (1999)
23. Kalogeraki, V., Gunopulos, D., Zeinalipour-Yazti, D.: A Local Search Mechanism for Peer-to-Peer Networks. In: Proc. of the 11th Int'l Conf. on Information and Knowledge Management, pp. 300–307. ACM Press, New York (2002)

Efficient Race Verification for Debugging Programs with OpenMP Directives

Young-Joo Kim, Mun-Hye Kang, Ok-Kyoon Ha, and Yong-Kee Jun

Information Science, Gyeongsang National University
Jinju, 660-701 South Korea
{akates,munhye,okkyoon,jun}@gnu.ac.kr
http://is.gsnu.ac.kr

Abstract. Races must be detected for debugging parallel programs with OpenMP directives because they may cause unintended nondeterministic results of programs. The previous tool that detects races does not verify the existence of races in programs with no internal nondeterminism because the tool regards nested sibling threads as ordered threads and has the possibility of ignoring accesses involved in races in program models with synchronization such as critical section. This paper suggests an efficient tool that verifies the existence of races with optimal performance by applying race detection engines for labeling and detection protocol. The labeling scheme generates a unique identifier for each parallel thread created during a program execution, and the protocol scheme detects at least one race if any. This tool verifies the existence of races over 250 times faster in average than the previous tool even in the case that the maximum parallelism increases with the fixed number of total accesses using a set of synthetic programs without synchronization such as critical section.

Keywords: OpenMP directive, races, verification, labeling scheme, protocol scheme.

1 Introduction

Races [11] of a serious error in OpenMP programs with directives occur when two more parallel threads access to at least a write access of each shared variable without proper inter-thread coordination. Races must be detected for debugging parallel programs because they may cause unintended nondeterministic results. On-the-fly detection technique [4,10] which detects races by monitoring accesses of each shared variable during a program execution is efficient in the aspect of space complexity because it may remove the unnecessary information while monitoring an execution.

Intel Thread Checker [6,7,13], the previous tool for detecting on-the-fly races in programs with OpenMP directives, sequentially executes parallel threads and detect races by checking data dependency during an execution of program with no internal nondeterminism [4]. The tool however regards nested sibling threads

V. Malyshkin (Ed.): PaCT 2007, LNCS 4671, pp. 230–239, 2007.

as ordered threads and has the possibility of ignoring accesses involved in races in program models with synchronization such as critical section. So this tool does not verify the existence of races in programs with no internal nondeterminism

This paper suggests an efficient tool that verifies the existence of races with optimal performance by applying race detection engines for labeling and detection protocol. The labeling scheme generates a unique identifier in each parallel thread created during a program execution, and the protocol scheme detects at least one race if any. Target program model is C programs with OpenMP directives, which may include the parallel directives "#pragma omp parallel for" and the synchronization directives "#pragma omp critical." To verify the existence of races with optimal performance, we classify program models into two types based on the existence of synchronization.

We use a computer based on linux on a dual 64bit Intel Xeon processor for experimentation of the suggested tool, and use Intel C/C++ compiler [5] installed for compiling the target programs. We use a set of synthetic programs with activity management models that execute jobs in each thread independently usually with different kinds of data structures. This tool verifies the existence of races over 250 times faster in average than the previous tool even in the case that the maximum parallelism increases with the fixed number of total accesses.

Section 2 illustrates data races that occur in programs with OpenMP directives, and indicates the problems of the previous tool. Section 3 designs and implements the efficient race-verification. Section 4 shows the experimentation results on the efficiencies of the previous tool and the suggested tool. The last section includes conclusions and future work.

2   Background

This section illustrates OpenMP programs with directives and races to occur in the programs and explains about the operation principle and problems of the previous tool for detecting races.

2.1   The Data Race in OpenMP Program

OpenMP programs [2,12] are an industry-standard program model for shared memory parallel programs written in C/C++ and Fortran 77/90 and These consist of compiler directives,library routines, and environment variables. The directives extend the Fortran or C sequential programs and provide support for the sharing and privatization of data. The library routines and environment variables provide the functionality to control the run-time execution environment. The sequential programs can be transformed easily into parallel programs because of providing compiler directives of OpenMP. These directives [12] consist of parallel directives, work-sharing directives, data-environment directives, and synchronization directives.

An execution of parallel programs with no internal nondeterminism [4] is represented by a directed acyclie graph called POEG (Partial Order Execution

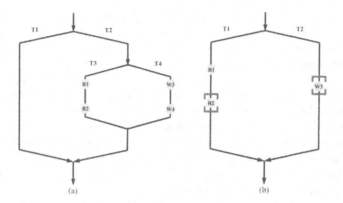

Fig. 1. POEG for program model with nested parallelism and critical section

Graph) [3]. In this Fig. 1, a vertex of POEG means a fork or join operation for parallel threads, and an arc started from a vertex represents a thread started from the vertex. The access r and w drawn with small disks upon the arcs represent a read and a write access which access a shared variable. A number attached to each access indicates an observed order, and an arc segment delimited by symbol $\sqcap$ and $\sqcup$ means a critical section protected by lock variable. With POEG, we can easily understand a partial order of happens-before relationship of accesses that occurred in an execution instance of parallel programs. Two accesses is ordered relationship if a path exists in two accesses and two accesses are concurrent relationship if not. Fig. 1(a) is to represent programs with nested parallelism as POEG. In this Figure, $r1$ has the ordered relationship with $r2$ because the path exists in the accesses. $r1$ has the concurrent relationship with $w3$ because the path does not exist in the accesses.

We call it *races* when it includes at least one write access of two concurrent accesses without proper inter-thread coordination and represent races as e_i-e_j. Fig. 1(a) has four races: $\{r1$-$w3, r1$-$w4, r2$-$w3, r2$-$w4\}$. Fig. 1(b) is to represent programs with synchronization as POEG. This figure has only one race: $\{r1$-$w3\}$. $r2$ in thread $T1$ is concurrent with $w3$ thread $T2$ but $r2$ and $w3$ are not involved in a race because $r2$ and $w3$ are protected by the same lock. Races must be detected for debugging the programs because of causing unintended nondeterministic results.

2.2   The Previous Tool

On-the-fly detection technique [4,10] which detects races monitoring accesses of each shared variable during a program execution is efficient in the aspect of space for detecting races because it removes the unnecessary information while the technique collects information for accesses. The previous tool that detects races on-the-fly in OpenMP programs with directives are Thread Checker of

Intel corporation is a unique tool. The errors detected by Thread Checker are deadlock, race, logical error, and so on. This paper applies only to races.

The projection technique [13] of Thread Checker [6,7,13] for OpenMP programs uses sequential execution information obtained during the compilation of program and checks data dependency [1,13] on-the-fly to detect races. This technique is applied only to relaxed sequential OpenMP programs [13] which consist of only OpenMP directives for parallelism. Thread Checker detects races as follows. First, when the programs written in OpenMP directives are compiled, a part of this tool integrated in the compiler traces the information related to OpenMP directives and shared variables into an exclusive database. Second, OpenMP directives are ignored when the compiled program is executed sequentially. Third, the tool uses the traced information in any storage to check data dependency of accesses to shared variables whenever OpenMP directives is executed. Last, the tool reports the accesses as races if it satisfies a anti, a flow, and an output data dependency [1] except an input data dependency.

Thread Checker does not detect races in the program model with nested parallelism of Fig. 1(a) but four races exist in this program: $\{r1\text{-}w3, r1\text{-}w4, r2\text{-}w3, r2\text{-}w4\}$. four accesses that exist in nested threads have an ordered relationship because Thread Checker regards nested sibling threads as ordered threads. Also, Thread Checker does not detect races in the program model with synchronization of Fig. 1(b) but one race exists in this program: $\{r1\text{-}w3\}$. Because Thread Checker has the possibility of ignoring accesses involved in races, $r1$ is removed by $r2$. Therefore, Thread Checker does not verify the existence of races in programs with nested parallelism or synchronization.

3   Efficient Race Verification

This section explains the race detection technique which uses the efficient race verification tool. This tool uses the labeling scheme and the protocol scheme for race verification and analyzes race detection engines according to OpenMP programs models.

3.1   The Verification Schemes

This tool uses labeling schemes [8,14] and protocol schemes [4,10]. The labeling schemes create a logical concurrency of created threads during a program execution and the logical concurrency is a unique identifier of each thread. The protocol schemes detect races by comparing current access with previous accesses that are saved in *access history* of shared data structure every time accesses occur in a thread. Access history consists of concurrent accesses in set of accesses to occur in a program execution. It is possible to verify the existence of races if the labeling and protocol schemes are applied. This tool provides the configuration for efficient verification of the existence of races with optimal performance by applying race detection engines which classify the labeling and the protocol schemes according to program models. These program models are distinguished with no synchronization and synchronization.

First, we explain the labeling scheme. In the program models for no synchronization, Nest-Region (NR) labeling [8,14] scheme is used. This scheme does not have the bottleneck problem proportionate to the number of maximum parallelism because of using a private structure and creating the concurrency information. So this scheme has the most superior performance in the aspect of time and space. And in the program models for synchronization, Nest-Region (NR) Labeling which applies Lock Cover [4] scheme are used. Next, we explain the protocol scheme. In the program models for no-synchronization, Mellor-Crummey protocol [10] scheme is used. This scheme has high efficiency in the aspect of space because of keeping the access history to save only three accesses: the most late-write access, the most left-read access, and right-read access. And in the program models for synchronization, Dinning protocol [4] scheme is used. This scheme has the most superior performance in the aspect of time and space in the program model with synchronization such as critical section because of removing all accesses within access history after checking races when a write access in a thread without critical section occurs.

3.2 The Efficient Tool

A source program written in directives of OpenMP program is transformed into a instrumented program which libraries for monitoring are inserted where the libraries consist of labeling and protocol engines. The labeling engines create "Label log" including fork/join information of threads and lock/unlock information of critical section during a program execution. The detection engine which takes the information created by labeling engine creates "Detect log" including the detected races for each shared variable.

The labeling engine consists of *Foker*, *Joiner*, and *Locker* of a library type. Forker module creates the label information for threads created by the directive like "#pragma omp parallel for," Joiner module creates new label information according to joins of parallel threads by the join directives and implicit join operation, and Locker module creates to remove lock information by the directive like "#pragma omp critical." In the program with synchronization, lock information is created in the beginning of the critical section and is removed in termination of the critical section. The detection engine consists of *MellDetector* for the programs without synchronization and *DiScDetector* for the programs with synchronization. MellDetector applies the protocol scheme of Mellor-Crummey which creates access history for each shared variable and reports races by analyzing label information of accesses. DiScDetector applies the protocol scheme of Dinning which initializes the structure for saving lock variables and creates access history for each shared variable and reports races by analyzing label and lock information of accesses.

Fig. 2 is to show that labeling and protocol engines are applied to target program. *InitLabel* of line 2 creates label information for the most top parent and initializes the structure for label. *InitDetection* of line 3 allocates the memory for access history of each shared variable. "#pragma omp parallel for" of line

```
1:      main () { ···
2:         InitLabel(···);
3:         InitDetection(···);
4:         ···
5:      #pragma omp parallel for shared(x)private(y,z,i)
6:         for (i=0 ; i < 100 ; i++) {
7:         Forker(···); ···
8:            y = x + i;
9:         ReadChecker(···); ···
10:     #pragma omp critical(L1) {
11:        LockAdder(···);
12:           x = z + i;
13:        WriteChecker(···); ··· }
14:        LockRemover(···); ··· }
15:        Joiner(···); ··· }
```

Fig. 2. Labeling Engine and Detection Engine in OpenMP

5 parallelize threads and variable x is shared variable by shared(x) and variable y, z, and i are private variable by private(y,z,i). *Forker* of line 7 uses label information of parent thread and creates label information of current thread. *ReadChecker* of line 9, construction factor of detection engine, compares current read access with previous write accesses and reports races after checking concurrency relationship and then determines whether current access is updated in access history.

Line 10 of source code is set to critical section by lock variable $L1$ using the directive of "#pragma omp critical." *LockAdder* of line 16 adds the information for lock variable defined by line 11 into current thread's label information. *WriteChecker* of line 13, construction factor of detection engine, compares current write access with previous read and write accesses and reports races after checking concurrency relationship. If races is reported, *WriterChecker* removes the label and lock information of accesses which is saved in access history and the information for current write access is added in access history. The critical section defined by line 10 is terminated in line 13, and *LockRemover* of line 14 removes the lock information created by *LockAdder* in thread's label information. *Joiner* of line 15 creates the label information of the joined thread using the parent thread's label information and the current thread's label information.

4 Experimentation

The section measures the required time for verifying the existence of races using synthetic programs written for proving the efficient race verification, and we analyze the previous tool and the suggested tool using the measured result.

Table 1. The Detected Races

	A-113			Race Verification	Previous Tool
1		$r1$ [$w3$] [$r2$]		$r1$-$w3$	-
2	[$r1$]	$r2$ [$w4$] [$r3$]		$r2$-$w4$	-
3	[$r1$ $w2$]	[$r3$] [$w5$] $r4$		$w2$-$r4$, $r1$-$w5$, $r3$-$w5$, $r4$-$w5$, $w2$-$w5$	$w2$-$r4$

4.1 Synthetic Programs

We use synthetic programs for experimenting the efficiency and the possibility of race verification in the previous tool and the suggested tool. OpenMP programs with directives based on C language have a parallel computing program model [15] and an activity management program model [15] based on parallel threads. Parallel Computing Program divides single computation job into several parallel jobs and these jobs have data structure and variables of the same kind. Activity Management Program creates parent and child threads that have the allocated jobs in a program and these jobs have the different kind of data structure.

In race detection, dependency for tool's efficiency is graphed considering the number of accesses and maximum parallelism, and Accesses occurred in various locations of source code and threads is executed independently so that the synthetic programs based on activity management program models than parallel computing program models are effective and general program in the experiment. Also, For race verification analysis, synthetic programs is written considering synchronization and nested parallelism, and for the efficient analysis, synthetic programs is written considering critical section, maximum parallelism, and the number of total accesses in the programs without synchronization and nested parallelism where maximum parallelism is increased as two exponents and the number of accesses per thread creates one hundred, two hundred, and three hundred and odd threads create read accesses and even threads create write accesses in the programs.

4.2 Race Verification and Its Efficiency

We measure the required time in race verification using synthetic programs. The system based on linux which is used for the experimentation is the computer with 64bit Intel Xeon Dual CPU and has Intel C/C++ compiler [5] for OpenMP

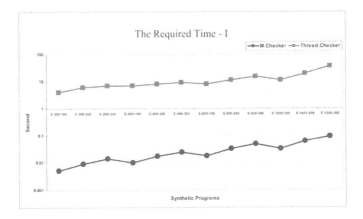

Fig. 3. The Required Time according to Total Accesses

programs with directives. For the previous tool, Thread Checker 3.0 is installed and for the suggested tool, the libraries for verifying the existence of races are installed in this system. These libraries are implemented by C language. Two tool experiment in the same system environment.

Table 1 is the result which verifies the existence of races using the suggested tool and the previous tool in the synthetic programs with synchronization and nested parallelism. Symbol "[ ]" means lock. In Table 1, the previous tool does not verify the existence of races in the first and second programs but the suggested tool does. For the efficiency of these tools, we measure the required time for race detection using synthetic programs. We knew empirically this fact that the race detection technique of Intel Thread Checker has practical performance in the aspect of required time and space in the programs based on parallel computing program models, because this tool does not monitor the accesses if accesses having the same date structure occur repetitively. For example, Intel Thread Checker recognizes as one access and detects races. So parallel computing program models excludes in this experimentation. Fig. 3 shows the result which measures the required time for race detection in synthetic programs. These synthetic programs are increased to two exponents for maximum parallelism and the number of accesses per thread: {E-200-100, E-200-200, E-200-300, E-400-100, E-400,200, E-400-300, E-800-100, E-800-200, E-800-300, E-1600-100, E-1600-200, E-1600-300}. The top line is to show time variation for the previous tool, Intel Thread Checker. The bottom line is to show time variation for the suggested tool according to these synthetic programs. As the result of Fig. 3, the time variation of two tools increased progressively according to the number of total accesses but the suggested tool is averagely over 250 times faster than the previous tool.

Fig. 4 is to measure the required time in detecting races with synthetic programs. These synthetic programs fixed the number of total accesses to 4000 and

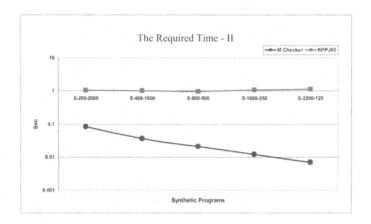

Fig. 4. The Required Time according to Maximum Parallelism

increased to two exponents for maximum parallelism: {E-200-2000, E-400-1000, E-800-500, E-1600-250, E-3200-125}. The top line is to show time variation for the previous tool [9] which has been developed in our laboratory, the bottom line is to show time variation for the suggested tool according to these synthetic programs. As the result of Fig. 4, there is scarcely the time variation of the previous tool [9] although maximum parallelism is increased but the detection time of the suggested tool is reduced as the increase of maximum parallelism occurs. Therefore, the suggested tool is more efficient than the previous tools in detecting races

5   Conclusions

Races must be detected for debugging parallel programs with OpenMP directives because they may cause unintended nondeterministic results of programs. The previous tool that detects races does not verify the existence of races in programs with no internal nondeterminism because the tool regards nested sibling threads as ordered threads and has the possibility of ignoring accesses involved in races in program models with synchronization such as critical section. This paper suggests an efficient tool that verifies the existence of races with optimal performance by applying race detection engines for labeling and detection protocol. The labeling scheme generates a unique identifier for each parallel thread created during a program execution, and the protocol scheme detects at least one race if any. This tool verifies the existence of races over 250 times faster in average than the previous tool even in the case that the maximum parallelism increases with the fixed number of total accesses using a set of synthetic programs without synchronization such as critical section. We are going to make the integrated environment for detecting races in the future.

References

1. Banerjee, U., Bliss, B., Ma, Z., Petersen, P.: A Theory of Data Race Detection. In: Proc. of Workshop on Parallel and Distributed Systems: Testing and Debugging (PADTAD), pp. 69–78, ACM, Portland, USA (July 2006)
2. Dagum, L., Menon, R.: OpenMP: An Industry-Standard API for Shared Memory Programming. Computational Science and Engineering 5(1), 46–55 (1998)
3. Dinning, A., Schonberg, E.: An Empirical Comparison of Monitoring Algorithms for Access Anomaly Detection. In: 2nd Symp. on Principles and Practice of Parallel Programming, ACM, pp. 1–10 (March 1990)
4. Dinning, A., Schonberg, E.: Detecting Access Anomalies in Programs with Critical Sections. In: 2nd Wrokshop on Parallel and Distributed Debugging, pp. 85–96, ACM (May 1991)
5. Intel Co.: Intel C++ Compiler 8.1 for Windows: Getting Started Guide (2004)
6. Intel Corp.: Getting Started with the Intel Thread Checker, 2200 Mission College Blvd., Santa Clara, CA 95052-8119, USA (2004)
7. Intel Corp.: Intel Thread Checker for Windows 3.0 Release Notes, 2200 Mission College Blvd., Santa Clara, CA 95052-8119, USA (2005)
8. Jun, Y., Koh, K.: On-the-fly Detection of Access Anomalies in Nested Parallel Loops. In: 3rd ACM/ONR Workshop on Parallel and Distributed Debugging, pp. 107–117, ACM (May 1993)
9. Kim, Y., Park, M., Park, S., Jun, Y.: A Practical Tool for Detecting Races in OpenMP Programs. In: Malyshkin, V. (ed.) PaCT 2005. LNCS, vol. 3606, pp. 321–330. Springer, Heidelberg (2005)
10. Mellor-Crummey, J.M.: 'On-the-fly Detection of Data Races for Programs with Nested Fork-Join Parallelism. Supercomputing, pp. 24–33, ACM/IEEE (November 1991)
11. Netzer, R.H.B., Miller, B.P.: What Are Race Conditions? Some Issues and Formalizations. Letters on Prog. Lang. and Systems 1(1), 74–88 (1992)
12. OpenMP Architecture Review Board: OpenMP Fortran Application Program Interface, Ver. 2.0 (November 2000)
13. Petersen, P., Shah, S.: OpenMP Support in the Intel Thread Checker. In: Voss, M.J. (ed.) WOMPAT 2003. LNCS, vol. 2716, pp. 1–12. Springer, Heidelberg (2003)
14. Park, S., Park, M., Jun, Y.: A Comparision of Scalable Labeling Schemes for Detecting Races in OpenMP Programs. In: Eigenmann, R., Voss, M.J. (eds.) WOMPAT 2001. LNCS, vol. 2104, pp. 66–80. Springer, Heidelberg (2001)
15. Rinard, M.: Analysis of Multithreaded Programs. In: Cousot, P. (ed.) SAS 2001. LNCS, vol. 2126, pp. 1–19. Springer, Heidelberg (2001)

Adaptive Scheduling and Resource Assessment in GRID

V. Krasnotcshekov and A. Vakhitov

Chair of Software Engineering,
Department of Mathematics and Mechanics,
Saint Petersburg State University,
198504 Russia Saint Petersburg Universitetsky pr., 28
av38@yandex.ru, venia_k@mail.ru

Abstract. The problems of scheduling computations in GRID and optimal usage of GRID resources from client side are considered. The general cost functional for GRID scheduling is defined. The cost function is then used to define some scheduling policy based on Simutaneous Perturbation Stochastic Optimization Algorithm, which is used because of it's fast convergence in multidimensional noisy systems. The technique proposed is being implemented for brokering in GPE4GTK environment to compare it with other techniques.

1 Introduction

Last years GRID technologies grow rapidly. People start to use GRID on commercial basis for not only scientific, but also industrial purpose. To succeed in this, high quality (and high efficiency) control of computational process is needed. This means new resource allocation and management facilities. Standards for resource management in GRID do exist; however, there are not many products which match the standards perfectly.

Here we consider two problems of control and optimization of the GRID: scheduling of GRID Single Program Multiple Data computation. Second: how to solve some problem having GRID as a black-box computational device.

SPMD computing is used in variety of fields [1]. Good discussion about SPMD tasks is provided in [2]. The results about SPMD computing and adaptive techniques now start to appear. Earlier, the comparatively simple strategies were used [3]. Later, several different problems of adaptive learning class in scheduling field appeared. Firstly, the distributed computing runtime can adopt the number of client computers used by any task [4, 2]. Research proposed here can be generalized with techniques from [4]. Here we address only problem of optimal execution of the one SPMD task; in [4, 2] it is assumed that there are several concurrent.

Some authors propose to adapt to the imbalance by changing the "`relative power'" on each step when imbalance is more than some threshold. In our opinion, this is not often needed. If the system performs in average well, then there is no need to change the work given to target systems on each step.

V. Malyshkin (Ed.): PaCT 2007, LNCS 4671, pp. 240–244, 2007.

2 Scheduling of Computations

2.1 Cost Function Definition

In usual GRID system there exist *resources of sequential use,* which serve as atomic containment of GRID, and some *resource broker*, which is given the right to manage them (to make scheduling). Typical scheduling of some long-running computation has two main steps:

- Distribution of computations to resources of sequential use contained in the GRID system;
- Synchronization of the results.

We suppose that the cost function of a scheduler looks like:

$$F(\alpha) = \sum_{i=1}^{N(\alpha)} (Z_i(\alpha) + L_i(\alpha)) + G(C, T) \tag{1}$$

$\alpha -$ is a vector of problem being solved, with all parameters and requirements;

$Z_i(\alpha) -$ time for loading some sub-task and unloading the results from itch computational device (resource);

$L_i(\alpha)$ – idle time of i-th resource, or time between the i-th finishes its computations and the whole computation is finished;

$N(\alpha)$ – determines number of resources, which can be used in these computations on current step;

C – cost;

T – time for computations;

$G(C,T)$ – If the task is not finished in time T, then monetary losses are equal to cost C and it is included to the cost function as G(C,T).

2.2 Cost Function Motivation

The best scheduler is supposed to give minimal value for $F(\alpha)$ among all the possible balancers. However, the best scheduler for every computation α obviously cannot be found. Different strategies succeed in different cases, so the problem of minimization in mean should be taken into account.

The cost function proposed is very general. It serves to determine how efficiently the task is computed. It includes the main resource wastement components: waiting, communication, and also penalty. Next, we will explain some derivation based on this cost function with specific scheduling approach.

The problem of brokering computations between resources which are given to the process can be easily adapted to cost functional (1). Brokering usually is defined by some policy. In systems like Grid Programming Environment [5] brokering is done without any feedback after the atomic task is completed. So, the problem of search for of reliable task distribution between resources of sequential use without feedback is of interest. We propose to formalize a problem by considering a policy based on ratios for every device. Let us denote $|\alpha|$ as number of atomic sub-tasks. Then ratio for each resource i from 1 to $N(\alpha)$ is $p^{(i)}=|\alpha_i|/|\alpha|$. The scheduling policy then is defined by a vector of ratios.

We propose to use algorithms of SPSA class for the optimization of the scheduling [6,7].

Consider problem described in [8]. Let the task be consisting of a large set of primitive calculations $\{o_1,...,o_N\}$. It will be grouped into sequential portions, which will correspond to distribution-synchronization steps of the balancing, and each portion will be divided into blocks given to each computational resource.

Then, we can approximately say that time of calculations of some task on one system S can be seen as an integral of some function $Op(k)$ (time to complete k-th computation) over some segment.

$$t(i, s_{ij}, p_i^{(j)}) = \sum_{k=s_{ij}}^{s_{ij}+p_i^{(j)}b} Op(k) \approx \int_{s_{ij}}^{s_{ij}+p_i^{(j)}b} Op(x)dx, \qquad (2)$$

where b is the size of task. Parameter i denotes the step of iterative ratios adjustment, $p_i^{(j)}$ are as before.

We will not go deeper into the design of the controller for GRID in this extended abstract. We should say only, that SPSA deals with approximation of the function t (tracking in close model of [2], Pic. 1 (b)). Controller uses this approximation to build next estimator division of a portion into blocks.

3   Resources Assessment Problem

3.1   Problem Description

When customer of GRID system prepares a task for processing the main question is the cost of distributed resources and the time witch is necessary for calculation. Obviously, resources have to be allocated according to priority. Such priority can depend on requested time and suggested price. Thus appraise task is estimation of optimal cost of required resources.

It is possible request to calculate several small tasks and consider reaction of system, thus, determine optimal cost and time for solving the whole task. The author's approach to resources assessment is based on that idea.

Suppose that the task consists of a lot of small independent subtasks $\gamma = \{\gamma_1, \gamma_2, ...\gamma_L\}$. The question: is it optimal to send the whole task for processing in GRID or it is better to send one by one small tasks. Evidently, that long task can be marked with low priority and process long time, however, sending small task, which marked with high priority, it is possible to get the solution faster. Thus, optimization - means to determining optimal block of subtasks, witch is sending to distributed system. Moreover, it is necessary to adapt to changes of system capacity. Methods of stochastic optimizations (SPSA)[1,2] are good in such problem area, because of sufficient uncertainty of the system and fast convergence needed.

3.2 Problem Statement

Suppose that we need to solve the task $\gamma = \{\gamma_1, \gamma_2, ... \gamma_L\}$, where L - is comparatively big, and $S(\gamma_i) \simeq S(\gamma_j) \forall i, j \in [1, L]$. One step of algorithm sends some collection of $\{\gamma_i\}$ with range r elements of task γ (*block*) to the GRID. Here $S(\gamma_i)$ - "capacity" of calculations for element γ_i from task γ. Let choose $N < L$. N -number of blocks, composed with elements γ_i from task γ, witch are sending before algorithm changes the range of block r.

$$F(\gamma, r, k, N) = \frac{L}{Nr}\left(W(\gamma, r) + \sum_{i=1}^{N} T(\gamma, r, (kN+i)) \right)$$

where r is a range of block (number of γ_i which are being sent simultaneously to computation system), $W(\cdot)$ - expenses for load of block with r subtasks (r is constant and not dependent on the range of block value); $T(\gamma, r, i)$ - time for processing of block witch consists of r subtasks from γ starting with γ_i.

3.3 SPSA Algorithm

Algorithm performs following steps:

- Step 1. Choose start value of estimation of block range $\hat{r}_0$;
- Step 2. Generate Δ_n;
- Step 3. Before each step calculate $r_n = \hat{r}_{n-1} + \beta \Delta_n$;
- Step 4. After each step calculate new value $\hat{r}_n = \hat{r}_{n-1} - (\alpha/\beta)\Delta_n F(\gamma, r_n, n, N)$;
- Step 5. Increase n;
- Step 6. Go to step 2 or stop algorithm, in case when during several sequential iteration estimation changes very low.

Δ_n - Bernoulli sequences of independent random value equal to ± 1. α, β - fitted value.

Algorithm is very simple, and, at the same time, allows quick adaptation even with noise in system. Moreover, on each step it is required only one noise calculation of cost function.

4 Conclusion

Two different tasks for optimization of the calculation in GRID were considered above. The aim of both tasks is to increase controllability and efficiency of GRID.

Implementation of suggested algorithms is in process, and modeling can't give the exact results, because building of GRID system is very complex.

Authors are members of research project on GRID in SPRINT Lab of SPbSU with Intel collaboration. Our main software is GPE4GTK tool [4]. In this project the goals are to investigate dispatching and resources optimization problems together with development of tools to make GRID software adoption easier on arbitrary system. The model of programming for GPE is very high-level, based on standard BPEL workflow definition. The whole GRID runs on Java platform, so it works in similar way on the platforms supported by JRE.

In the project group we have several SPMD tasks implemented. We start to investigate better scheduling using the cost function discussed and its derivations. Our main future work is to propose better algorithm for the broker of GPE.

References

1. Nakano, A.: High performance computing and simulations (Spring '07) online: http://cacs.usc.edu/education/cs653.html
2. Weissman, J.: Prophet: automated scheduling of SPMD programs in worksation networks. Concurrency: Practice and Experience 11(6), 301–321 (1999)
3. Cermele, M., Colajanni, M., Necci, G.: Dynamic load balancing of distributed SPMD computations with explicit message-passing. In: Proceedings of the IEEE Workshop on Heterogeneous Computing, pp. 2–16 (1997)
4. He, Y., Hsu, W., Leiserson, C.: Provably efficient adaptive scheduling for parallel jobs. In: Proceedings of the 12th Workshop on Job Scheduling Strategies for Parallel Processing (2006)
5. Lukichev, A., Odintsov, I., Petrov, D., et al.: Grid Programming Environment Reference Documentation. http://gpe4gtk.sourceforge.net
6. Granichin, O.: Linear regression and filtering under nonstandard assumptions (Arbitrary noise). IEEE Transactions on Automatic Control 49, 1830–1835 (2001)
7. Spall, J.C., Cristion, J.A.: Model-Free Control of Nonlinear Stochastic Systems with Discrete-Time Measurements. IEEE Transactions on Automatic Control 43, 1198–1210 (1998)
8. Vakhitov, A.T.: Methods of Load Balancing for Multiprocessor Systems. In: Granichin, O. (ed.) Stochastic Optimization in Informatics, Vol. 2. Saint Petersburg (in russian) (2006) http://www.math.spbu.ru/user/gran/sb2/vakhitov.pdf

Dynamic Load Balancing of *Black-Box* Applications with a Resource Selection Mechanism on Heterogeneous Resources of the Grid

Valeria V. Krzhizhanovskaya[1,2] and Vladimir V. Korkhov[1,2]

[1] University of Amsterdam, Faculty of Science, Section Computational Science
[2] St. Petersburg State Polytechnic University, Russia
{valeria,vkorkhov}@science.uva.nl

Abstract. In this paper we address the critical issues of efficient resource management and high-performance parallel distributed computing on the Grid by introducing a new hierarchical approach that combines a user-level job scheduling with a dynamic load balancing technique that automatically adapts a *black-box* distributed or parallel application to the heterogeneous resources. The algorithm developed dynamically selects the resources best suited for a particular task or parallel process of the executed application, and optimizes the load balance based on the dynamically measured resource parameters and estimated requirements of the application. We describe the proposed algorithm for automated load balancing, paying attention to the influence of resource heterogeneity metrics, demonstrate the speedup achieved with this technique for different types of applications and resources, and propose a way to extend the approach to a wider class of applications.

Keywords: dynamic load balancing, resource management, high-performance computing, Grid, heterogeneous resources, parallel distributed application.

1 Introduction and Motivation

Grid-based problem-solving environments (PSEs) play an increasingly more important role in a broad range of applications stemming from fundamental and applied sciences, engineering, industry, medicine and economy. In [1,2] we provide an extensive overview of the Grid-aware problem-solving environments and virtual laboratories for complex applications. A great number of noticeable advances were achieved as a result of joint efforts of the multidisciplinary research society, such as the development of widely acknowledged standards in methodologies, formats and protocols used within the environments [11]. Another manifesting development concerns the move from specific one-application PSEs to the high-level generic environments that provide services, tools and resources to formulate and solve a problem using standardized methods, modules, workflows and resource managers [1]. Our research in this field has started from porting a Virtual Reactor problem-solving environment to the Grid [1-5], pioneering the move of fully integrated simulators from a single PC via computer clusters with a remote user interface [5] to fully distributed heterogeneous

V. Malyshkin (Ed.): PaCT 2007, LNCS 4671, pp. 245–260, 2007.
© Springer-Verlag Berlin Heidelberg 2007

Grid systems [2,3]. A detailed description of the Virtual Reactor application and our "gridification" activities can be found in [1-5].

We have implemented and tested several approaches, and adapted an existing interactive distributed application to the peculiarities of the Grid, thanks to the complementary projects developing Grid middleware, tools and portals [3,9,10]. However a few things shadow the overall optimistic picture of the major advances in Grid usability as observed in our extensive experiments with different Grid implementations. Among the most prominent and as yet unsolved problems we experienced are efficient resource management at the application and system levels, and optimization of the workload allocation for parallel and distributed applications on highly diverse and dynamically changing Grid resources. These two intertwined fundamental issues hindering the progress of Grid computing have pulled the forces of a vast computer society that strive to extrapolate an efficient high-performance computing on the Grid from a single demo test-case to a ubiquitous reality. A huge number of algorithms, approaches and tools have been developed to bring Grid resource management and job scheduling issues to a more advanced level of efficiency and, even more importantly, usability (see for instance [12-21]). In addition to that, an excessive number of load balancing techniques have been implemented and tested since the times when heterogeneous cluster computing emerged. We could not find a recent book providing a good overview of the state-of-the-art in load balancing, and a list of relevant papers would take at least several pages, so we will give references only to those intimately related to the technique we propose hereunder.

In a seemingly successful research field teeming with various solutions at hand, when things came to practice it turned out to be impossible to find a tool/library for automatic load balancing of a parallel distributed application on heterogeneous resources of the Grid. The first-priority consideration we had in mind was instrumenting our Virtual Reactor application with a library that would require minimal intrusion into the code and that would adapt the parallel codes previously developed for homogeneous computer clusters to the heterogeneous and dynamically changing Grid resources. Another goal was finding the means to enable "smart" resource selection and efficient utilization for the whole problem-solving environment, i.e. distributing the PSE disparate modules wisely, according to their individual requirements. The stumbling-block is that these *application requirements are not known beforehand* in most real-life complex applications, where only the key developers can embrace the complexity and dependencies of the PSE components. And even the code designers aware of the numerical methods' particularities can not predict the exact application requirements, which differ in each new computational experiment, depending on initial conditions, combination of real-life processes to be simulated, numerical schemes chosen, computational parameters, etc. This uncertainty prompted us to use the term *black-box* applications in the title of this article; we certainly do not mean that the user does not know what application he is running and of what avail. Our extensive benchmarking and performance assessment of the Virtual Reactor application clearly showed that even within one solver different trends can exist in the application requirements and parallel efficiency, depending on the problem type and computational parameters, therefore distinct resource management and optimization strategies shall be applied, and automated procedures for load balancing are needed to successfully solve complex simulation problems on the Grid [6-8].

A countless number of parallel and distributed applications have been developed for traditional (i.e. static homogeneous) parallel computers or cluster systems. Porting such applications from homogeneous computing environments to dynamic heterogeneous computing and networking resources poses a challenge to keep up a high level of application efficiency. To assure efficient utilization of Grid resources, special methods for workload distribution control should be applied. *An adequate workload optimization method should take into account* two aspects:

- (1) The **application characteristics**, such as the amount of data transferred between the processes, logical network topology, amount of floating point operations, memory requirements, hard disk or other I/O activity, etc.
- (2) The **resource characteristics**, like computational power and memory of the worker nodes, network links bandwidth, disk I/O speed, and the level of heterogeneity of the resources randomly assigned to the application by the Grid resource broker.

The method should be (a) self-adapting and flexible with respect to the type of application, (b) computationally inexpensive not to induce a large overhead on the application performance, and (c) should not require significant modifications in the code. On top of that, the load balancing shall be (d) dynamic and fully automated since we want to hide the "ugly" features of the Grid from innocent users.

2 Background: Automated Load Balancing on the Grid

The issue of load balancing in Grid environments is addressed by a number of research groups. Generally studies on load balancing consider distribution of processes to computational resources on the system/library level with no modifications in the application code [22,23]. Less often, load balancing code is included into the application source-code to improve performance in specific cases [24,25]. Some research projects concern load balancing techniques that use source code transformations to speedup the execution of the application [26]. We employ an application-centric approach where the balancing decisions are taken by the application itself. This is dictated by two arguments: first, the immaturity (or the lack of "intelligence") of the middleware or system-level resource managers; and second, the complexity of the problem-solving environments such as our Virtual Reactor, which has a number of communicating modules, some of which are parallel programs. An important feature of our approach is that although it is application-centric, the algorithm that estimates available resources and suggests the optimal load balancing of a parallel job is generic and can be employed in any parallel application to be executed on heterogeneous resources by instrumenting it with the load-balancing library.

A detailed description of global load optimization approaches for heterogeneous resources and adaptive mesh refinement applications can be found for instance in [29,30,31]. We shall note however, that in [29] and [31] no network links heterogeneity was considered and only static resource estimation (initialization) was performed in [29] and [30]. These two issues are the major challenges of Grid high-performance computing: 1) the heterogeneity of the network links can be two orders of magnitude higher that that of the processing power; and 2) Grid resources are inherently dynamic. Developing our algorithm, we tried to address specifically these two issues. The approaches discussed in [29] and [31] are only valid for batch sequential applications (specifically for the queuing systems and computer cluster schedulers), whereas our effort is directed towards *parallel* programs utilizing heterogeneous resources.

A number of semi-automatic load balancing methods have been developed (e.g. diffusion self-balancing mechanism, genetic networks load regulation, simulated annealing technique, bidding approaches, multiparameter optimization, numerous heuristics, etc.), but all of them suffer one or another serious limitation, most noticeably the lack of flexibility, high overheads, or inability to take into consideration the specific features of the application. Moreover, all of them lack the higher-level functionality, such as the resource selection mechanism and job scheduling. In our view, this is an essential step to be made in order to make Grid computing efficient and user-friendly. Although some tools are already available for "smart" system-level process-resource matching and job scheduling on the Grid, none of them is automatic yet, and none is coupled with a mechanism evaluating the application requirements. We aim to bridge this gap by building a hierarchical approach that combines a user-level job scheduling [32,33] with a dynamic load balancing technique that automatically adapts a *black-box* distributed or parallel application to the heterogeneous Grid resources.

To summarize, the existing algorithms and tools provide only a partial solution. Our target is to combine the best achievements and to design a flexible tool for automated load balancing on the Grid. In this paper we present the results of the ongoing work in this direction. In Section 3 we introduce the basic ideas and steps of a generalized automated load balancing technique for a *black-box* application on the Grid. Section 4 presents the results of implementation of the load balancing algorithm, describes a synthetic test application developed for experiments, and shows the trends of the load balancing speedup and the influence of the resource heterogeneity level. Section 5 concludes the paper with discussion and future plans.

3 Generalized Automated Load Balancing with Resource Selection

Based on our previous experience [6-8], we developed a load balancing technique that takes into account the heterogeneity and the dynamics of the Grid resources, estimates the initially unknown application requirements, and provides the resource selection and most optimal mapping of the parallel processes to the available resources. In the most general case we consider that the resources have been randomly assigned to the application by a Grid resource broker via the User-Level Scheduler [32,33], or that the application can request the desirable resources with a set of parameters. An important feature of the proposed mechanism is that all the functionality described below is implemented as an external library, and the application is instrumented by linking to this library. As we mentioned in the introduction, this is a work in progress: The technique described below has not been fully implemented yet. A part of coupling the parallel load balancer with the user-level job scheduler is under development now. It will be published with additional details after deployment and testing.

3.1 The Basic Algorithm of the Automated Load Balancing

The load balancing meta-algorithm includes 8 basic Steps. Below we provide a descriptive explanation of each Step, mentioning special cases to be considered at each stage. We shall note that this is a conceptual description, rather than a mathematically strict algorithm. An exact formulation of the core load balancing heuristic is provided in the next subsection.

Step 1.   Benchmarking resources: Measuring the computational power and memory available on the worker nodes, network links bandwidth, hard disk capacity and I/O speed. In a more generic sense of "resources", some other metrics can be added characterizing the equipment and tools associated with a particular Grid node. These can be various parameters of databases, storages, sensors, scanners, and other attached devices.

Step 2.   Ranking resources: The priority of ranking parameters shall be dependent on the type of application. For traditional parallel computing solvers, which we consider as test-case applications in present work, the first ranking parameter shall be computational power (CPU) of the processor, the second parameter being the network bandwidth to this processor. For memory-critical applications, memory shall be the top-priority metric. For a large emerging class of multimedia streaming applications, the network bandwidth and the disk I/O speed would be the key parameters. In most cases memory ranking is an essential complimentary operation, since available memory can be a constraining factor defining if the resource can be used by the application or not. The same goes for the free disk space parameter that can constrain the streaming applications that damp data on hard disks.

Step 3.   Checking the level of heterogeneity: This parameter is often not considered in the load balancing heuristics; however it plays a crucial role in the choice of load balancing approach to be taken. The first and most obvious argument is that if the resources happen to be almost homogeneous, for traditional parallel applications no additional load rebalancing is required (and parallel tasks are distributed in equal chunks). In subsection 3.2, we discuss how the levels of heterogeneity affect the weighting factors used for calculating the workload per processor. We introduce the heterogeneity metrics and pay special attention to the way it influences the load balancing performance for our parallel computing test-case application.

Step 4.   Testing application components and their interconnections: For that, run a small subset of the routine operations on the resources given. For a majority of traditional computational applications, the best is to perform one or a few time steps, iterations or events (depending on the type of simulation) in order to ensure that no time is wasted just for the testing, and the simulation is already running, though not in the most optimal way yet. This Step will measure the application performance on a given set of resources and collect the data needed to calculate the application requirements.

Step 5.   Estimating the application requirements: The idea is to *quantitatively* estimate the requirements of the application based on the results of resource benchmarking (Step 1) and measurements of the application response (Step 4). For our parallel computing test-case application, the requirements to be calculated are the communication to computation ratio and the minimally required memory per node. An extensive description of the theoretical background and details of the corresponding heuristic can be found in [6-8]. In the next subsection we give an excerpt completing this meta-algorithm.

Step 6. Matching resources I. Constraining factors: This is the first stage of checking the suitability of the available resources to the given application. It is based on the analysis of the results of Steps 2 and 5. In our computational application example, memory can be the constraining factor: In case of sufficient memory on allocated processors, the load balancing can be performed further, taking into account all the other factors. In the unfavourable case of insufficient memory on some of the processors, they must be disregarded from the parallel computation or replaced by other, better suited processors. This shall be done on the level of job scheduling and resource allocation, within the framework of a combined approach coupling the application-centered load balancing with a system-level resource management. For this, we consider the User-Level Scheduler [32,33] as a feasible application-level intermediate resource managing approach.

Step 7. Matching resources II. Selecting resources: This is the second stage requiring a hierarchical approach we are developing. It provides the means to select the best-suited resources for each of the PSE components. This Step consists of 3 basic functionalities: finding an optimal number of processors for each application component, the actual resource matching, and rejecting some of the resources and requesting some others -depending on the approach taken and resource availability. The resource matching procedure (to be distinguished from process *mapping*) shall take into account the application requirements derived in Step 5 and can be implemented using some standard multi-parameter optimization method. In our parallel computing test-case, selecting resources might look fairly simple: we always want the fastest processors with the fastest links between them. But with the severe heterogeneity of Grid resources, this is not so trivial anymore. What is better, fast worker nodes connected by the slow links or slower processors with the fast links? The answer is strongly dependent on the application characteristics: the communication-bound applications will achieve a better performance on faster links even with slower processors, and the computation-intensive application will not care about the network bandwidth. Another open question to be answered is how many worker nodes shall be assigned to a parallel solver. Again, the answer will be different depending on the solver characteristics: For a majority of "pleasingly" parallel applications (employing the resource farming concept), the more processors the better, so the actual number of processors to be allocated is an issue of availability and competition with the other PSE components. On the other hand, for a wide class of "normal" parallel applications (characterized by a speedup saturation with a growing number of parallel processors), an optimal number of processors can be estimated based on the measured resource parameters and the application fractional communication overhead.

Step 8. Load balancing: After selecting the best suited set of resources, we need to perform the actual optimization of the workload distribution within the parallel modules, in order words *mapping* the processes onto the allocated resources. This Step is based on the heuristic developed earlier [6-8], which includes a technique to calculate the weighting factors for each processor depending on the resource characteristics and application requirements established in Step 5. In Section 3.2 we summarize the methodology, introduce some corrections in the theoretical formulation and discuss the role of the heterogeneity function.

In case of dynamic resources where performance is influenced by other factors (which is generally the case on the Grid), a periodic re-estimation of resource parameters and load re-distribution shall be performed. This leads to repeating all the meta-algorithm Steps except of Step 4 and Step 5. In most cases this can be done by running the application with a few consecutive time steps or iterations (see comments to Step 4). NB: if the selected resources did not change much, Steps 6 and 7 can be omitted not to incur unnecessary overhead.

If the application is dynamically changing (for instance due to adaptive meshes, moving interfaces or different combinations of physical processes modeled at different simulation stages) then the application requirements must be periodically re-estimated even on a static set of resources. In this case, the periodic re-estimation loop stars from Step 4, with the same remark on skipping Steps 6 and 7 if the application change is not dramatic.

Periodic re-estimations shall be performed frequently during the runtime of the application to correct the load imbalance with a reasonably short delay. The minimally required frequency of rebalancing can be estimated and dynamically tuned by calculating the relative imbalance introduced during the controlled period of time.

In the next subsection we provide a strict formulation of the most important aspects essential for understanding the experimental results shown in Section 4. A scrupulous mathematical description of all the conditions, metrics and algorithms in a complete meta-algorithm we save for another paper.

3.2 Adaptive Load Balancing on Heterogeneous Resources: Theoretical Approach

In [6,7] we proposed a methodology for adaptive load balancing of parallel applications on heterogeneous resources, extending it to *dynamic* load balancing and introducing the heterogeneity metrics in [8]. In this section we give a theoretical description of the basic concepts and parameters mentioned in the meta-algorithm, and concentrate on the two most important issues: (1) estimating the application requirements (Step 4 and Step 5) and (2) the actual load balancing of parallel or distributed *black-box* applications on heterogeneous Grid resources (Step 8). The load balancing Step aims at optimizing the load distribution among the resources already selected in previous Steps (after performing the check against the restricting factors such as the memory deficiency). Therefore the theory is given under the assumption that the resources are "fixed" for a single load-balancing loop, and that using *all* these resources provides a reasonably good performance result (e.g. parallel speedup for traditional parallel computing applications). Another prerequisite is that the application is already implemented as a parallel (or distributed) program, and is able to distribute the workload by chunks of controllable size. Saying this we kept in mind the Master-Worker model, but the technique is applicable to other communication logical topologies, given that the measurements are carried out along the links used within the application. The load balancing procedure we describe is implemented as an external library, and after linking with the application provides a recommendation on how much work shall be done by each of the assigned processors to ensure the fastest possible execution time –taking into account the specific parameters of the resources and the estimated application requirements [6-8]. We designed the algorithm in such a way that the knowledge of these resource and application characteristics would give an instant solution to the workload distribution, thus making the procedure very lightweight and suitable for dynamic load balancing at runtime.

The main generic parameters that define a parallel application performance are:

- An application parameter $f_c = N_{comm}/N_{calc}$, where N_{comm} is the total amount of application communications, i.e. data to be exchanged (measured in bit) and N_{calc} is the total amount of computations to be performed (measured in Flop);
- The resource parameters $\mu_i = p_i/n_i$, where p_i is the available performance of the ith processor (measured in Flop/s) and n_i is the network bandwidth to this node (measured in bit/s).

The resource characteristics p_i and n_i we obtain in Step 1 after benchmarking the resources, but the application parameters N_{comm} and N_{calc} are not known beforehand in real-life applications. The target is to experimentally determine the value of the application parameter f_c that provides the best workload distribution, i.e. minimal runtime of the application mapped to the resources characterized by a parameter set $\mu = \{\mu_i\}$.

A natural way to do that is to run through the range of possible values of f_c with a discrete step, calculating a corresponding load distribution and performing one time step/iteration with a new load distribution. Measuring the execution time of this iteration and comparing it for different values of f_c, we find an optimal value f_c^*, which provides the minimal execution time. This idea is implemented in Step 5 and will be illustrated in the Results section (4.2). A detailed algorithm is described in [8]. There we suggested estimating the range of possible values of the application parameter f_c as following: The minimal value is $f_c^{min} = 0$, which corresponds to the case when no communications occur between the parallel processes of the application. The maximal possible value was calculated as $f_c^{max} = \max(n_i)/\min(p_i)$. Experimenting with this rough upper bound evaluation, we found that in many cases it gives a too high value of f_c^{max}, unnecessarily extending the search range and thus reducing the efficiency of the load balancing procedure. Another approach to search for the optimal value f_c^* can be borrowed from the optimization theory, for instance using an adaptive 1-dimensional non-linear constrained optimization method with a correction for small stochastic perturbations in resource performance [34]. This approach can reduce the number of the load balancing loops needed to find the best load distribution.

To calculate the amount of the work per processor in the load balancing Step 8, we assign a weight-factor to each processor according to its processing power and network connection. A similar approach was applied in [25] and in [27] for heterogeneous computer clusters, but the mechanism for adaptive calculation of the weights - taking into account the application requirements- was not developed there. Moreover, the tools developed for cluster systems can not be used in Grid environments without modifications since static resource benchmarking is not suitable for dynamic Grid resources.

The weighting factor w_i determines the final workload to be assigned to each of N processors: $W_i = w_i\,W$, where W is the total workload. The weighting factor w_i shall reflect both the capacity of resources according to the estimated infrastructure parameters μ_i and the application parameter f_c. In [8] we derived an expression for processor weights analogous to that used by other authors [25,27]. Extensive experimentation and analysis of this expression revealed that the optimal balance for computation-intensive applications running on fast network links is not computed correctly. To correct this, we modified the equation for weights calculation, deriving it from the first principles of equalizing the time spent by each processor. In the simplified model of communication that can suite as the first approximation of real communication topologies, the weights can be calculated as follows:

$$w_i = q_i \left/ \sum_{i=1}^{N} q_i \right. ; \quad q_i = p_i/(1 + \varphi f_c \mu_i) \tag{1}$$

Here q_i is the dimensional weight calculated from the resource parameters p_i and μ_i, and from the guessed application parameter f_c. φ is the heterogeneity metrics of the network links that can be expressed as a standard deviation of the set of normalized dimensionless resource parameters:

$$\varphi = \sqrt{\frac{1}{N-1} \sum_{i=1}^{N} (1 - n_i/n_{avg})^2}, \quad n_{avg} = \frac{1}{N} \sum_{i=1}^{N} n_i \tag{2}$$

The purpose of this heterogeneity metrics is to ensure that if the network links are homogeneous, i.e. $n_i = n_{avg}$, then the weighting is done only according to the processors capacity. In this case $\varphi = 0$, and the last term in the denominator of Eq.(1) is nullified, thus providing that the weights w_i are linearly proportional to the processing power p_i. Then we can see that in the infrastructure of heterogeneous processors connected by homogeneous network links the value of application parameter f_c does not affect the load distribution, which is exactly the case in the Master-Worker lock-step synchronous communication model. Generally speaking, in other communication models this can be different, so a bit more sophistication is needed in order to design a generic algorithm that would suit well the majority of logical topology models.

To evaluate the efficiency of the workload distribution we introduce the load balancing speedup $\Theta = T_{non-balanced}/T_{balanced} \cdot 100\%$, where $T_{non-balanced}$ is the execution time of the parallel application without the load balancing (even distribution of the prosesses), and $T_{balanced}$ is the execution time after load balancing on the same set of resources. This metric is used to estimate the application parameter f_c^* that provides the best performance on given resources, that is the largest value of speedup Θ in a given range of f_c. In a non-trivial case we expect to find a maximum of Θ and thus an optimal f_c^* for some workload distribution, which means that the application requirements fit best the resources in this particular workload distribution. The case of $f_c^* = 0$ while $\varphi \neq 0$ means that the application is totally computation dominated, i.e. there is no communication between different processes, and the optimal workload distribution will be proportional only to the computational power of the processors.

While deriving Eq. (1), we considered a simple case when memory requirements only put a Boolean constraint to the allocation of processes on the resources: either there is enough memory to run the application or not. But memory can be one of the determining factors of the application performance and play a role in the load balancing process. This is the case for applications that are able to control memory requirements according to the available resources. In this case there will be additional parameters analogous to f_c and μ_i, but the idea and the load balancing mechanism remain the same. Similar considerations shall be applied for the other types of applications. For instance, in a widely used class of applications performing sequential computing with hard disk intensive operations, the network link bandwidth parameter n_i shall be replaced with the disk I/O speed for finding an optimal load distribution in "farming" computations on the Grid.

4 Performance Results

In this section we provide some details on implementing the load balancing algorithm and show the results illustrating the load balancing technique for our computational application case-study and demonstrating the speedup achieved with this technique for different types of applications and resources. The adaptive load balancing technique we propose was first applied while deploying the Virtual Reactor parallel components on heterogeneous Grid resources [3]. Several simulation types have been extensively tested on various sets of resources, demonstrating how the algorithm works. However one application can obviously provide only a limited freedom for experiments. To be able to examine the behavior of an *arbitrary* parallel application (characterized by various values of the application parameter f_c and various interprocess communication topologies) on *arbitrary* sets of heterogeneous resources, we developed a synthetic parallel application that allowed us to model different combinations and to compare the best theoretically achievable performance results with those given by our workload-balancing approach.

4.1 Synthetic Application and Experimental Setup

To evaluate the performance of the proposed load balancing technique for generic cases, we developed a "synthetic" application modeling different types of parallel applications mapped to the resources of various capacity and levels of heterogeneity. From a technical point of view, this synthetic application is an MPI program running on a homogeneous computer cluster system. Flexible configuration capabilities allow tuning the communication-computation ratio f_c within the application, and designing the communication logical topology (i.e. the patterns of interconnections between the processes). The latter gives the possibility to model different connectivity schemes, e.g. Master-Worker, Mesh, Ring, Hypercube etc. The value of the application parameter f_c is controlled by changing the total amount of calculations to be performed and the total amount of data to be sent between the nodes. The underlying heterogeneous resources are modeled by imposing extra load on the selected processors or links, thus reducing their capacity available for the application.

The load balancing algorithm was implemented as an external library using the MPI message passing interface, and the synthetic application (also an MPI program) has been instrumented with this library as any other application would be. We use this experimental setup to examine how a specific parallel application defined by a combination of communication/computation ratio f_c and communication logical topology will behave on different types of heterogeneous resources, and what types of applications can show the best performance on a given set of resources. To validate the synthetic simulator, we modeled and analyzed the performance of the Virtual Reactor solvers on sets of resources similar to those used in our previous experiments on the RIDgrid [7,8]. The experiments were carried out on the DAS-2 computer cluster [35], using MPICH-P4 implementation of MPI.

4.2 Load Balancing Speedup for Different Applications

In this section we illustrate the idea of searching through the space of possible values of the application parameter f_c in order to find the actual application requirement F_c (see Step 5 of the meta-algorithm and the detailed description of the procedure in Section 3.2). Figure 1 presents the results of load balancing of our synthetic application with the Master-Worker non-lockstep asynchronous communication logical topology (when a Worker node can immediately start calculation while the Master continues sending data to the other Workers). We show a load balancing speedup for 5 applications with different pre-defined values of F_c (0.1 – 0.5) on the same set of heterogeneous resources. The value of f_c^* corresponding to the maximal speedup assures the best application performance. We can see that the best speedup in all cases is achieved with f_c^* close to the real application F_c, thus proving the validity of our approach. Another observation is that the applications characterized by a higher communication to computation ratio F_c, achieve a higher balancing speedup, which means that the communication-intensive applications benefit more from the proposed load balancing technique. It is also worth noticing that the distribution of the workload proportional only to the processor performance ($f_c=0$) also gives a significant increase of the performance (180 % in case of F_c =0.5), but introduction of the

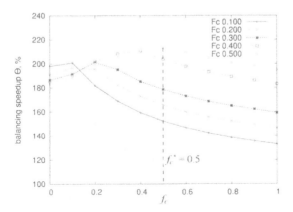

Fig. 1. Dependency of the load balancing speedup Θ on the "guessed" application parameter f_c for 5 synthetic applications with different values of F_c

dependency on application and resource parameters adds another 35 % percent to the balancing speedup in this case (up to 217 %). In experiments with a higher level of resource heterogeneity, this additional speedup contributed up to 150 %.

4.3 Load Balancing for Master-Worker Model: Heuristic Versus Analytically Derived Load Distribution

To test our load balancing algorithm, we analytically derived the best workload distribution parameters for some specific communication logical topologies of parallel applications, and compared the speedup achieved with our heuristic algorithm with that provided by the theoretical method. Here we present the analytically derived weights and the performance comparison for a widely used Master-Worker non-lockstep asynchronous communication model. The values of the weighting factors defining the *best* (most optimal) load distribution have been derived from the principle of equalizing the time spent by each processor working on the application, following the same idea used for derivation of eq. (1). Omitting the mathematical details, we present the final recurrence relation for calculating the weights:

$$q_N = \left(1 + \sum_{i=2}^{N}\prod_{k=i}^{N}\frac{\tau_k + T_k}{T_{k-1}}\right)^{-1}, \quad q_{i-1} = q_i\,\frac{\tau_i + T_i}{T_{i-1}} \text{ for } i = N...2; \quad w_i = q_i\Big/\sum_{i=1}^{N}q_i \qquad (3)$$

where $\tau_i = N_{comm}/n_i$ is the time for sending the total amount of application communications N_{comm} from the Master to the ith Worker node over the network link with the measured bandwidth n_i; and $T_i = N_{calc}/p_i$ is the time for performing the total amount of application's calculations N_{calc} by the ith processor with the processing power of p_i.

We have tested our synthetic applications with different communication to computation ratios F_c on different sets of resources, with the two different load distributions: theoretical and heuristic. In Fig. 2 we present an example of comparison of the execution times achieved with these load balancing strategies on a set of highly heterogeneous

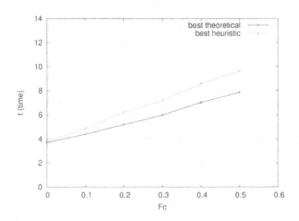

Fig. 2. Comparison of the execution times for different weighting: the best theoretical distribution versus the generic heuristic load balancing

resources. We can see that the heuristic time is only about 5-15 percent higher than the best possible for these applications (the larger difference attributed to the very communication-intensive test). Considering that our approach is generic and suits any type of communication topology, this overhead is a relatively small impediment.

4.4 Influence of the Resource Heterogeneity on the Load Balancing Efficiency

Thorough testing of the different applications on different sets of resources showed a strong influence of the level of resource heterogeneity on the results achieved. We performed a series of targeted experiments varying the resource heterogeneity both in the processor power and the network links bandwidth. As a sample of these tests, in Fig. 3 we show the dependency of the load balancing speedup on the processing power heterogeneity metrics, analogous to that of the networks links heterogeneity introduced by Eq. (2). As we see, the speedup grows superlinearly with the heterogeneity level, thus indicating that our approach is especially beneficial on strongly heterogeneous resources, such as the Grid resources.

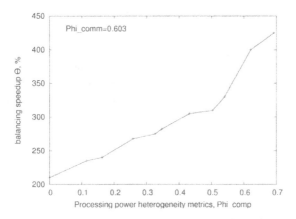

Fig. 3. Dependency of the load balancing speedup Θ on the resource heterogeneity metrics φ

5 Conclusions and Future Work

We introduced a new hierarchical approach that combines user-level job scheduling with dynamic load balancing technique that automatically adapts a *black-box* distributed or parallel application to the heterogeneous resources. The proposed algorithm dynamically selects the resources best suited for a particular task or parallel process of the application, and optimizes the load balance based on the dynamically measured resource parameters and estimated requirements of the application. We studied the performance of this load balancing approach by developing a synthetic application with flexible user-defined application parameters and logical network topologies, on artificially designed heterogeneous resources with a controlled level of heterogeneity. Some of the conclusions from our methodological experiments are as follows:

- The proposed algorithm adequately finds the application requirements;
- Based on that, our approach adapts the application to the set of heterogeneous resources with a very high load balancing speedup (up to 450 %);
- The novelty of our load balancing approach –dependency of the load distribution on the application and resource parameters– adds up to 150 % to the balancing speedup compared to the balancing that takes into account only the processors' performance;
- Analysis of the speedup achieved for different types of applications and resources indicates that the communication-intensive applications benefit most from the proposed load balancing technique.
- The speedup from applying our approach grows superlinearly with the increase of the resources' heterogeneity level, thus showing that it is especially useful for the severely heterogeneous Grid resources.
- Comparison of the performance of our heuristic load balancing with the performance achieved with the analytically derived weights, showed a relatively small discrepancy of 5-15 %, with a larger difference attributed to the very communication-intensive applications. This overhead is a relatively small impediment, considering that our approach is generic and suits any type of communication topology.

The results presented here were obtained for traditional parallel computing applications with the most widespread communication model: a Master-Worker scheme in a non-lockstep asynchronous mode. At present, we test other connectivity schemes, such as the different Master-Worker modes, as well as Mesh, Ring and Hypercube topologies. Another direction of our work is implementation and testing of hierarchical coupling of user-level job scheduling with the load balancing algorithm presented. The User-Level Scheduler [32,33] will provide a combined resource management strategy connecting the application-level resource selection mechanism to the system-level job management. In addition to that, it can support resource usage optimization and fault tolerance [23], as a desirable functionality increasing the usability of the Grid. We also plan to extend our approach to a wider class of applications, including memory-critical applications, multimedia streaming applications, and a widely used class of applications performing sequential computing with hard disk intensive operations.

Acknowledgments. The authors would like to thank Peter Sloot for fruitful discussions of this paper. The research was conducted with financial support from the Dutch National Science Foundation NWO and the Russian Foundation for Basic Research under projects # 047.016.007 and 047.016.018, and with partial support from the Virtual Laboratory for e-Science Bsik project.

References

1. Krzhizhanovskaya, V.V., Korkhov, V.V.: Problem-Solving Environments for Simulation and Optimization on Heterogeneous Distributed Computational Resources of the Grid. In: Proceedings of the Third International Conference on Parallel Computations and Control Problems PACO'2006, Moscow, Russia, pp. 917–932. Trapeznikov Institute of Control Sciences RAS, Moscow (2006)

2. Krzhizhanovskaya, V.V., Sloot, P.M.A., Gorbachev, Y.E.: Grid-based Simulation of Industrial Thin-Film Production. Simulation: Transactions of the Society for Modeling and Simulation International 81(1), 77–85 (2005)
3. Krzhizhanovskaya, V.V., Korkhov, V.V., Tirado-Ramos, A., Groen, D.J., Shoshmina, I.V., Valuev, I.A., Morozov, I.V., Malyshkin, N.V., Gorbachev, Y.E., Sloot, P.M.A.: Computational Engineering on the Grid: Crafting a Distributed Virtual Reactor. In: Second IEEE International Conference on e-Science and Grid Computing (e-Science'06), p. 101 (2006)
4. Krzhizhanovskaya, V.V., et al.: A 3D Virtual Reactor for Simulation of Silicon-Based Film Production. In: Proceedings of the ASME/JSME PVP Conference. ASME PVP-vol. 491(2), pp. 59–68, PVP2004-3120 (2004)
5. Krzhizhanovskaya, V.V., Zatevakhin, M.A., Ignatiev, A.A., Gorbachev, Y.E., Sloot, P.M.A.: Distributed Simulation of Silicon-Based Film Growth. In: Wyrzykowski, R., Dongarra, J.J., Paprzycki, M., Waśniewski, J. (eds.) PPAM 2001. LNCS, vol. 2328, pp. 879–888. Springer, Heidelberg (2002)
6. Korkhov, V.V., Krzhizhanovskaya, V.V.: Workload Balancing in Heterogeneous Grid Environment: A Virtual Reactor Case Study. In: Proceedings of the Second International Conference Distributed Computing and Grid Technologies in Science and Education, pp. 103–113. Publ: JINR, Dubna, D11-2006-167 (2006)
7. Korkhov, V.V., Krzhizhanovskaya, V.V.: Benchmarking and Adaptive Load Balancing of the Virtual Reactor Application on the Russian-Dutch Grid. In: Alexandrov, V.N., van Albada, G.D., Sloot, P.M.A., Dongarra, J.J. (eds.) ICCS 2006. LNCS, vol. 3991, pp. 530–538. Springer, Heidelberg (2006)
8. Korkhov, V.V., Krzhizhanovskaya, V.V., Sloot, P.M.A.: A Grid Based Virtual Reactor: Parallel performance and adaptive load balancing. Revised version submitted to the Journal of Parallel and Distributed Computing (2007)
9. CrossGrid EU Science project: http://www.eu-CrossGrid.org
10. Nimrod-G: http://www.csse.monash.edu.au/~davida/nimrod/
11. Fox, G.: Grid Computing environments. IEEE Computers in Science and Engineering 10, 68–72 (2003)
12. Nabrzyski, J., Schopf, J.M., Weglarz, J. (eds.): Grid Resource Management: State of the Art and Future Trends. Kluwer Academic Publishers, Boston (2004)
13. Foster, I., Kesselman, C. (eds.): The Grid 2: Blueprint for a New Computing Infrastructure. Morgan Kaufmann, Seattle (2003)
14. Buyya, R., Cortes, T., Jin, H.: Single System Image. The International Journal of High Performance Computing Applications 15(2), 124–135 (2001)
15. Maghraoui, K.E., Desell, T.J., Szymanski, B.K., Varela, C.A.: The Internet Operating System: Middleware for Adaptive Distributed Computting. The International Journal of High Performance Computing Applications 20(4), 467–480 (2006)
16. Sonmez, O.O., Gursoy, A.: A Novel Economic-Based Scheduling Heuristic for Computational Grids. The International Journal of High Performance Computing Applications 21(1), 21–29 (2007)
17. Boyera, W.F., Hura, G.S.: Non-evolutionary algorithm for scheduling dependent tasks in distributed heterogeneous computing environments. J. Parallel Distrib. Comput. 65, 1035–1046 (2005)
18. Collins, D.E., George, A.D.: Parallel and Sequential Job Scheduling in Heterogeneous Clusters: A Simulation Study Using Software in the Loop. SIMULATION 77, 169–184 (2001)
19. Schoneveld, A., de Ronde, J.F., Sloot, P.M.A.: On the Complexity of Task Allocation. Complexity 3, 52–60 (1997)

20. de Ronde, J.F., Schoneveld, A., Sloot, P.M.A.: Load Balancing by Redundant Decomposition and Mapping. Future Generation Computer Systems 12(5), 391–407 (1997)
21. Karatza, H.D., Hilzer, R.C.: Parallel Job Scheduling in Homogeneous Distributed Systems. SIMULATION 79(5-6), 287–298 (2003)
22. Barak, A., Wheeler, R.G., Guday, S.: The MOSIX Distributed Operating System. LNCS, vol. 672. Springer, Heidelberg (1993)
23. Overeinder, B.J., Sloot, P.M.A., Heederik, R.N., Hertzberger, L.O.: A Dynamic Load Balancing System for Parallel Cluster Computing. Future Generation Computer Systems 12(1), 101–115 (1996)
24. Shao, G., et al.: Master/Slave Computing on the Grid. In: Proceedings of Heterogeneous Computing Workshop, pp. 3–16. IEEE Computer Society Press, Los Alamitos (2000)
25. Sinha, S., Parashar, M.: Adaptive Runtime Partitioning of AMR Applications on Heterogeneous Clusters. In: Proceedings of 3rd IEEE Intl. Conference on Cluster Computing, pp. 435–442 (2001)
26. David, R., et al.: Source Code Transformations Strategies to Load-Balance Grid Applications. In: Parashar, M. (ed.) GRID 2002. LNCS, vol. 2536, pp. 82–87. Springer, Heidelberg (2002)
27. Teresco, J.D., et al.: Resource-Aware Scientific Computation on a Heterogeneous Cluster. Computing in Science & Engineering 7(2), 40–50 (2005)
28. Kufrin, R.: PerfSuite: An Accessible, Open Source Performance Analysis Environment for Linux. In: 6th International Conference on Linux Clusters, Chapel Hill, NC (2005)
29. Lu, C., Lau, S.-M.: An Adaptive Load Balancing Algorithm forHeterogeneous Distributed Systems with Multiple Task Classes. In: International Conference on Distributed Computing Systems (1996)
30. Lan, Z., Taylor, V.E., Bryan, G.: Dynamic Load Balancing of SAMR Applications on Distributed Systems. In: Proceedings of the 2001 ACM/IEEE conference on Supercomputing (2001)
31. Zhang, Y., Hakozaki, K., Kameda, H., Shimizu, K.: A performance comparison of adaptive and static load balancing in heterogeneous distributed systems. In: The 28th Annual Simulation Symposium, p. 332 (1995)
32. Germain-Renaud, C., Loomis, C., Moscicki, J.T., Texier, R.: Scheduling for Responsive Grids. Grid Computing Journal (Special Issue on EGEE User Forum) (2006)
33. Moscicki, J.T., Bubak, M., Lee, H.-C., Muraru, A., Sloot, P.: Quality of Service on the Grid with User Level Scheduling. In: Cracow Grid Workshop Proceedings (2006)
34. Calvin, J.M.: A One-Dimensional Optimization Algorithm and Its Convergence Rate under the Wiener Measure. Journal of Complexity N 17, 306–344 (2001)
35. http://www.cs.vu.nl/das2/

A Novel Algorithm of Optimal Matrix Partitioning for Parallel Dense Factorization on Heterogeneous Processors

Alexey Lastovetsky and Ravi Reddy

School of Computer Science and Informatics, University College Dublin, Belfield,
Dublin 4, Ireland
{alexey.lastovetsky,manumachu.reddy}@ucd.ie

Abstract. In this paper, we present a novel algorithm of optimal matrix partitioning for parallel dense matrix factorization on heterogeneous processors based on their constant performance model. We prove the correctness of the algorithm and estimate its complexity. We demonstrate that this algorithm better suits extensions to more complicated, non-constant, performance models of heterogeneous processors than traditional algorithms.

1 Introduction

The paper presents a novel algorithm of optimal matrix partitioning for parallel dense matrix factorization on heterogeneous processors based on their constant performance model. We prove the correctness of the algorithm and estimate its complexity. We demonstrate that this algorithm better suits extensions to more complicated, non-constant, performance models of heterogeneous processors, such as a model presented in [1,2], than traditional algorithms.

A number of matrix distribution strategies for parallel dense matrix factorization in heterogeneous environments have been designed and implemented. Arapov *et al.*, [3] propose a distribution strategy for 1D parallel Cholesky factorization. They consider the Cholesky factorization to be an irregular problem and distribute data amongst the processors of the executing parallel machine in accordance with their relative speeds. The distribution strategy divides the matrix into a number of column panels such that the width of each column panel is proportional to the speed of the processor. This strategy is developed into a more general 2D distribution strategy in [4]. Beaumont *et al.*, [5-6] employ a dynamic programming algorithm (DP) to partition the matrix in parallel 1D LU decomposition. When processor speeds are accurately known and guaranteed not to change during program execution, the dynamic programming algorithm provides the best possible load balancing of the processors. A static group block distribution strategy [7-8] is used in parallel 1D LU decomposition to partition the matrix into groups (or *generalized blocks* in terms of [4]), all of which have the same number of blocks. The number of blocks per group (size of the group) and the distribution of the blocks in the group over the processors are fixed and are determined based on speeds of the processors, which are represented by a single constant number. All these aforementioned distribution strategies are based on a performance model,

V. Malyshkin (Ed.): PaCT 2007, LNCS 4671, pp. 261–275, 2007.

which represents the speed of each processor by a constant positive number and computations are distributed amongst the processors such that their volume is proportional to this speed of the processor. The number characterizing the performance of the processor is typically its relative speed demonstrated during the execution of the code solving locally the core computational task of some given size.

We present in this paper a novel matrix partitioning algorithm for 1D LU decomposition called the Reverse algorithm. Like the DP algorithm, the Reverse algorithm always returns an optimal solution. The complexity of the Reverse algorithm is a bit worse than that of the DP algorithm, but the algorithm has one important advantage. It better suits extensions to more complicated, non-constant, performance models of heterogeneous processors, such as the functional performance model [1,2], than traditional algorithms.

The rest of the paper is organized as follows. In Section 2, we present the homogeneous LU factorization algorithm that is used for our heterogeneous modification. In section 3, we outline two existing heterogeneous modifications of this algorithm using the constant model of heterogeneous processors before presenting our original modification, the Reverse algorithm. This section also presents the correctness of the algorithm and its complexity. Finally we present experimental results on a local network of heterogeneous processors to demonstrate why the proposed algorithm better suits extensions to the functional performance model of heterogeneous processors than the traditional algorithms.

2 LU Factorization on Homogeneous Multiprocessors

Before we present our matrix partitioning algorithm, we describe the LU Factorization algorithm of a dense $(n \times b) \times (n \times b)$ matrix A, one step of which is shown in Figure 1, where n is the number of blocks of size $b \times b$, optimal values of b depending on the memory hierarchy and on the communication-to-computation ratio of the target computer [9,10].

The LU factorization applies a sequence of Gaussian eliminations to form $A = P \times L \times U$, where A, L, and U are dense $(n \times b) \times (n \times b)$ matrices. P is a permutation matrix which is stored in a vector of size $n \times b$, L is unit lower triangular (lower triangular with 1's on the main diagonal), and U is upper triangular.

At the k-th step of the computation $(k=1,2,...)$, it is assumed that the $m \times m$ submatrix of $A^{(k)}$ $(m = ((n - (k-1)) \times b)$ is to be partitioned as follows:

$$\begin{pmatrix} A_{11} & A_{12} \\ A_{21} & A_{22} \end{pmatrix} = P \begin{pmatrix} L_{11} & 0 \\ L_{21} & L_{22} \end{pmatrix} \begin{pmatrix} U_{11} & U_{12} \\ 0 & U_{22} \end{pmatrix}$$

$$= P \begin{pmatrix} L_{11}U_{11} & L_{11}U_{12} \\ L_{21}U_{11} & L_{21}U_{12} + L_{22}U_{22} \end{pmatrix}$$

where the block A_{11} is $b \times b$, A_{12} is $b \times (m-b)$, A_{21} is $(m-b) \times b$, and A_{22} is $(m-b) \times (m-b)$. L_{11} is unit lower triangular matrix, and U_{11} is an upper triangular matrix.

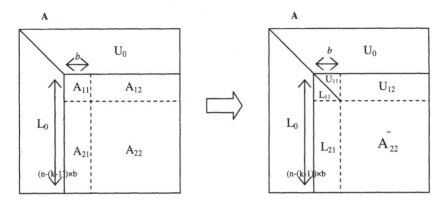

Fig. 1. One step of the LU factorization algorithm of a dense matrix A of size (n×b)×(n×b)

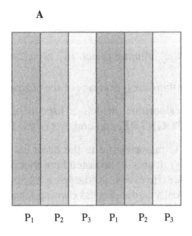

P_1 P_2 P_3 P_1 P_2 P_3

Fig. 2. Column-oriented CYCLIC distribution of six column blocks on a one-dimensional array of three homogeneous processors

At first, a sequence of Gaussian eliminations is performed on the first $m×b$ panel of $A^{(k)}$ (i.e., A_{11} and A_{21}). Once this is completed, the matrices L_{11}, L_{21}, and U_{11} are known and we can rearrange the block equations

$$U_{12} \leftarrow \left(L_{11}\right)^{-1} A_{12},$$

$$\tilde{A}_{22} \leftarrow A_{22} - L_{21}U_{12} = L_{22}U_{22}.$$

The LU factorization can be done by recursively applying the steps outlined above to the $(m-b)×(m-b)$ matrix $\tilde{A}_{22}$. Figure 1 shows how the column panel, L_{11} and L_{21}, and the row panel, U_{11} and U_{12}, are computed and how the trailing submatrix A_{22} is updated. In the figure, the regions L_0, U_0, L_{11}, U_{11}, L_{21}, and U_{12} represent data for which the corresponding computations are completed. Later row interchanges will be applied to L_0 and L_{21}.

Now we present a parallel algorithm that computes the above steps on a one-dimensional arrangement of p homogeneous processors. The algorithm can be summarized as follows:

1. A CYCLIC(b) distribution of columns is used to distribute the matrix A over a one-dimensional arrangement of p homogeneous processors as shown in Figure 2. The cyclic distribution assigns columns of blocks with numbers $1,2,\ldots,n$ to processors $1,2,\ldots,p,1,2,\ldots,p,1,2,\ldots$, respectively, for a p-processor linear array ($n \gg p$), until all n columns of blocks are assigned.
2. The algorithm consists of n steps. At each step ($k=1,2,\ldots$),

- The processor owning the pivot column block of the size $((n-(k-1))\times b)\times b$ (i.e., A_{11} and A_{21}) factors it;
- All processors apply row interchanges to the left and the right of the current column block k;
- The processor owning L_{11} broadcasts it to the rest of the processors, which convert the row panel A_{12} to U_{12};
- The processor owning the column panel L_{21} broadcasts it to the rest of the processors;
- All the processors update their local portions of the matrix, A_{22}, in parallel.

The implementation of the algorithm, which is used in the paper, is based on the ScaLAPACK [10] routine, **PDGETRF**, and consists of the following steps:

1. **PDGETF2:** Apply the LU factorization to the pivot column panel of size $((n-(k-1))\times b)\times b$ (i.e., A_{11} and A_{21}). It should be noted here that only the routine **PDSWAP** employs all the processes involved in the parallel execution. The rest of the routines are performed locally at the process owning the pivot column panel.

- [Repeat b times ($i = 1,\ldots,b$)]

• **PDAMAX:** find the (absolute) maximum element of the i-th column and its location
• **PDSWAP:** interchange the i-th row with the row that holds the maximum
• **PDSCAL:** scale the i-th column of the matrix
• **PDGER:** update the trailing submatrix

- The process owning the pivot column panel broadcasts the same pivot information to all the other processes.

2. **PDLASWP:** All processes apply row interchanges to the left and the right of the current panel.
3. **PDTRSM:** L_{11} is broadcast to the other processes, which convert the row panel A_{12} to U_{12};
4. **PDGEMM:** The column panel L_{21} is broadcast to all the other processes. Then, all processes update their local portions of the matrix, A_{22}.

Because the largest fraction of the work takes place in the update of A_{22}, therefore, to obtain maximum parallelism all processors should participate in its update. Since A_{22} reduces in size as the computation progresses, a cyclic distribution is used to ensure that at any stage A_{22} is evenly distributed over all processors, thus obtaining their balanced load.

3 LU Factorization on Heterogeneous Platforms with a Constant Performance Model of Processors

Heterogeneous parallel algorithms of LU factorization on heterogeneous platforms are obtained by modification of the homogeneous algorithm presented in Section 2. The modification is in the distribution of column panels of matrix A over the linear array of processors. As the processors are heterogeneous having different speeds, the optimal distribution that aims at balancing the updates at all steps of the parallel LU factorization will not be fully cyclic. So, the problem of LU factorization of a matrix on a heterogeneous platform is reduced to the problem of distribution of column panels of the matrix over heterogeneous processors of the platform.

Traditionally the distribution problem is formulated as follows: Given a dense $(n \times b) \times (n \times b)$ matrix A, how can we assign n columns of size $n \times b$ of the matrix A to p $(n \gg p)$ heterogeneous processors P_1, P_2, ..., P_p of relative speeds $S = \{s_1, s_2, ..., s_p\}$, $\sum_{i=1}^{p} s_i = 1$, so that the workload at each step of the parallel LU factorization is best balanced? The relative speed s_i of processor P_i is obtained by normalization of its (absolute) speed a_i , understood as the number of column panels updated by the processor per one time unit, $s_i = \dfrac{a_i}{\sum_{i=1}^{p} a_i}$. While a_i will increase with each next step of the LU factorization (because the height of updated column panels will decrease as the LU factorization progresses, resulting in a larger number of column panels updated by the processor per time unit), the relative speeds s_i are assumed to be constant. The optimal solution sought is the one that minimizes $\max_i \dfrac{n_i^{(k)}}{s_i}$ for each step of the LU factorization ($\sum_{i=1}^{p} n_i^{(k)} = n^{(k)}$), where $n^{(k)}$ is the total number of column panels updated at the step k and $n_i^{(k)}$ denotes the number of column panels allocated to processor P_i.

The motivation behind that formulation is the following. Strictly speaking, the optimal solution should minimize the total execution time of the LU factorization, which is given by $\sum_{k=1}^{n} \max_{i=1}^{p} \dfrac{n_i^{(k)}}{a_i^{(k)}}$, where $a_i^{(k)}$ is the speed of processor P_i at step k of the LU factorization and $n_i^{(k)}$ is the number of column panels updated by processor P_i at this step. However, if a solution minimizes $\max_{i=1}^{p} \dfrac{n_i^{(k)}}{a_i^{(k)}}$ for each k, it will also minimize $\sum_{k=1}^{n} \max_{i=1}^{p} \dfrac{n_i^{(k)}}{a_i^{(k)}}$. Because

$$\max_{i=1}^{p} \frac{n_i^{(k)}}{a_i^{(k)}} = \max_{i=1}^{p} \frac{n_i^{(k)}}{s_i \times \sum_{i=1}^{p} a_i^{(k)}} = \frac{1}{\sum_{i=1}^{p} a_i^{(k)}} \times \max_{i=1}^{p} \frac{n_i^{(k)}}{s_i} \text{ , then for}$$

any given k the problem of minimization of $\displaystyle\sum_{k=1}^{n} \max_{i=1}^{p} \frac{n_i^{(k)}}{a_i^{(k)}}$ will be equivalent

to the problem of minimization of $\max_{i=1}^{p} \dfrac{n_i^{(k)}}{s_i}$. Therefore, if we are lucky and

there exists an allocation that minimizes $\max_{i=1}^{p} \dfrac{n_i^{(k)}}{s_i}$ for each step k of the LU

factorization, then the allocation will be globally optimal, minimizing

$\displaystyle\sum_{k=1}^{n} \max_{i=1}^{p} \dfrac{n_i^{(k)}}{a_i^{(k)}}$. Fortunately, such an allocation does exist [5,6].

Now we briefly outline two existing approaches to solve the above distribution problem, which are the Group Block (GB) distribution algorithm [7] and the Dynamic Programming (DP) distribution algorithm [5,6].

The GB algorithm. This algorithm partitions the matrix into groups (or *generalized blocks* in terms of [4]), all of which have the same number of column panels. The number of column panels per group (the size of the group) and the distribution of the column panels within the group over the processors are fixed and determined based on relative speeds of the processors. The relative speeds are obtained by running the DGEMM routine that locally updates some particular dense rectangular matrix. The inputs to the algorithm are p, the number of heterogeneous processors in the one-dimensional arrangement, b, the block size, n, the size of the matrix in number of

blocks of size $b \times b$ or the number of column panels, and $S = \{s_1, s_2, ..., s_p\}$ ($\sum_{i=1}^{p} s_i = 1$), the relative speeds of the processors. The outputs are g, the size of

the group, and d, an integer array of size p, the i-th element of which contains the number of column panels in the group assigned to processor i. The algorithm can be summarized as follows:

1. The size of the group g is calculated as $\lfloor 1/\min(s_i) \rfloor$ ($1 \leq i \leq p$). If $g/p < 2$, then $g = \lfloor 2/\min(s_i) \rfloor$. This condition is imposed to ensure there is sufficient number of blocks in the group.

2. The group is partitioned so that the number of column panels d_i assigned to

   processor i in the group will minimize $\max_i \dfrac{d_i}{s_i}$ (see [5] for a simple algorithm

   performing this partitioning).

3. In the group, processors are reordered to start from the slowest processors to the fastest processors for load balance purposes.

The complexity of this algorithm is $O(p \times \log_2 p)$. At the same time, the algorithm does not guarantee that the returned solution will be optimal.

The DP algorithm. Dynamic programming is used to distribute column panels of the matrix over the processors. The relative speeds of the processors are obtained by running the DGEMM routine that locally updates some particular dense rectangular matrix. The inputs to the algorithm are p, the number of heterogeneous processors in the one-dimensional arrangement, b, the block size, n, the size of the matrix in number of blocks of size $b \times b$ or the number of column panels, and $S = \{s_1, s_2, ...,$ $s_p\}$ ($\sum_{i=1}^{p} s_i = 1$), the relative speeds of the processors. The outputs are c, an integer array of size p, the i-th element of which contains the number of column panels assigned to processor i, and d, an integer array of size n, the i-th element of which contains the processor to which the column panel i is assigned. The algorithm can be summarized as follows:

```
(c₁,...,cₚ)=(0,...,0);
(d₁,...,dₙ)=(0,...,0);
for(k=1; k≤n; k=k+1)  {

        Cost_min=∞;
        for(i=1; i<=p; i=i+1)  {
            Cost=(cᵢ+1)/sᵢ;
            if (Cost < Cost_min) {Cost_min=Cost; j=i;}
        }
        d_{n-k+1}=j;
        cⱼ=cⱼ+1;

}
```

The complexity of the DP algorithm is O($p \times n$). The algorithm returns the optimal allocation of the column panels to the heterogeneous processors [6]. The fact that the DP algorithm always returns the optimal solution is not trivial. Indeed, at each iteration of the algorithm the column panel k is allocated to one of the processors, namely, to a processor, minimizing the cost of the allocation. At the same time, there may be several processors with the same, minimal, cost of allocation. The algorithm randomly selects one of them. It is not obvious that allocation of the column panel to any of these processors will result in a globally optimal allocation. But, fortunately, for this particular distribution problem this is proved to be true.

In this paper, we propose another algorithm solving this distribution problem, a Reverse distribution algorithm. Like the DP algorithm, the Reverse algorithm always returns the optimal allocation. The complexity of the Reverse algorithm, $O(p \times n \times \log_2 p)$, is a bit worse than that of the DP algorithm, but the algorithm has one important advantage. It better suits extensions to more complicated, non-constant, performance models of heterogeneous processors (such as the functional model [1, 2]) than both the DP and GB algorithms.

The Reverse algorithm. This algorithm generates the optimal distribution $(n_1^{(k)},\ldots,n_p^{(k)})$ of $n\times b$ column panels of the dense $(n\times b)\times(n\times b)$ matrix over p heterogeneous processors for each step k of the parallel LU factorization $(\sum_{i=1}^{p} n_i^{(k)} = n-k+1,\ k=1,\ldots,n)$ and then allocates the column panels to the processors by comparing these distributions. In other words, the algorithm extracts the optimal allocation of the column panels from a sequence of optimal distributions of the panels for successive steps of the parallel LU factorization. The inputs to the algorithm are p, the number of heterogeneous processors in the one-dimensional arrangement, b, the block size, n, the size of the matrix in number of blocks of size $b\times b$ or the number of column panels, and $S=\{s_1, s_2, \ldots, s_p\}(\sum_{i=1}^{p} s_i = 1)$, the relative speeds of the processors. The output is d, an integer array of size n, the i-th element of which contains the processor to which the column panel i is assigned. The algorithm can be summarized as follows:

$(d_1,\ldots,d_n)=(0,\ldots,0);$
$w=0;$
$(n_1,\ldots,n_p)=\text{HSP}(p, n, S);$
for $(k=1; k<n; k=k+1)$ {
    $(n_1',\ldots,n_p') = \text{HSP}(p, n-k, S);$
    if $(w==0)$
    then if $((\exists! j \in [1, p])(n_j == n_j' +1) \wedge (\forall i \neq j)(n_i == n_i'))$
        then $\{d_k=j;\ (n_1,\ldots,n_p) = (n_1',\ldots,n_p');\}$
        else $w=1;$
    else if $((\exists i \in [1, p])(n_i < n_i'))$
        then $w=w+1;$
        else {
          for $(i=1; i\leq p; i=i+1)$
            for $(\Delta = n_i - n_i';\ \Delta\neq 0;\ \Delta=\Delta-1, w=w-1)$
              $d_{k-w}=i;$
          $(n_1,\ldots,n_p) = (n_1',\ldots,n_p');$
          $w=0;$
        }
}
If $((\exists i \in [1, p])(n_i == 1))$
then $d_n=i;$

Here, HSP(p, n, S) returns the optimal distribution of n column panels over p heterogeneous processors of the relative speeds $S=\{s_1, s_2, ..., s_p\}$ by applying the algorithm for optimal distribution of independent chunks of computations from [5]

Table 1. Reverse Algorithm with three processors P_1, P_2, P_3

Step of the algorithm (k)	Distributions at step k			Allocation made
	P_1	P_2	P_3	
	6	2	2	
1	5	2	2	P_1
2	4	2	2	P_1
3	3	2	2	P_1
4	1	3	2	No allocation
5	1	3	1	No allocation
6	1	2	1	P_1, P_1, P_3
7	1	1	1	P_2
8	0	1	1	P_1
9	0	0	1	P_2
10				P_3

(HSP stands for Heterogeneous Set Partitioning). Thus, first we find the optimal distributions of column panels for the first and second steps of the parallel LU factorization. If the distributions differ only for one processor, then we assign the first column panel to this processor. The reason is that this assignment guarantees a transfer from the best workload balance at the first step of the LU factorization to the best workload balance at its second step. If the distributions differ for more than one processor, we postpone allocation of the first column panel and find the optimal distribution for the third step of the LU factorization and compare it with the distribution for the first step. If the number of panel columns distributed to each processor for the third step does not exceed that for the first step, we allocate the first and second column panels so that the distribution for each next step is obtained from the distribution for the immediate previous step by addition of one more column panel to one of the processors. If not, we delay allocation of the first two column panels and find the optimal distribution for the fourth step and so on.

In Table 1, we demonstrate the algorithm for $n=10$. The first column represents the step k of the algorithm. The second column shows the distributions obtained during each step by HSP. The entry "Allocation made" denotes the rank of the processor to which the column panel k is assigned. At steps $k=4$ and $k=5$, the algorithm does not make any assignments. At $k=6$, processor P_1 is allocated column panels (4, 5) and

Table 2. Distribution algorithms and their complexities

Distribution Algorithm	Complexity
GB	$O(p \times \log_2 p)$
DP	$O(p \times n)$
Reverse	$O(p \times n \times \log_2 p)$

processor P_2 is allocated column panel 6. The output d in this case would be $(P_1P_1P_1P_1P_1P_3P_2P_1P_2P_3)$.

Proposition 1. The Reverse algorithm returns the optimal allocation.

Proof of Proposition 1. If the algorithm assigns the column panel k at each iteration of the algorithm, then the resulting allocation will be optimal by design. Indeed, in this case the distribution of column panels over the processors will be produced by the HSP and hence optimal for each step of the LU factorization.

Consider the situation when the algorithm assigns a group of w ($w>1$) column panels beginning from the column panel k. In that case, the algorithm first produces a sequence of $(w+1)$ distributions $(n_1^{(k)}, \ldots, n_p^{(k)})$, $(n_1^{(k+1)}, \ldots, n_p^{(k+1)})$, ..., $(n_1^{(k+w)}, \ldots, n_p^{(k+w)})$ such that

- the distributions are optimal for steps k, $k+1$, ..., $k+w$ of the LU factorization respectively, and
- $(n_1^{(k)}, \ldots, n_p^{(k)}) > (n_1^{(k+i)}, \ldots, n_p^{(k+i)})$ is only true for $i=w$ (by definition, $(a_1, \ldots, a_p) > (b_1, \ldots, b_p)$ if and only if $(\forall i)(a_i \geq b_i) \wedge (\exists i)(a_i > b_i)$).

Lemma 1. Let $(n_1, \ldots, n_p)$ and $(n_1', \ldots, n_p')$ be optimal distributions such that

$$n = \sum_{i=1}^{p} n_i > \sum_{i=1}^{p} n_i' = n', \quad (\exists i)(n_i < n_i') \quad \text{and} \quad (\forall j)(\max_{i=1}^{p} \frac{n_i}{s_i} \leq \frac{n_j + 1}{s_j}).$$

Then, $\max_{i=1}^{p} \dfrac{n_i}{s_i} = \max_{i=1}^{p} \dfrac{n_i'}{s_i}$.

Proof of Lemma 1. As $n > n'$ and $(n_1, \ldots, n_p)$ and $(n_1', \ldots, n_p')$ are both optimal distributions, then $\max_{i=1}^{p} \dfrac{n_i}{s_i} \geq \max_{i=1}^{p} \dfrac{n_i'}{s_i}$. On the other hand, there exists $j \in [1, p]$ such that $n_j < n_j'$, which implies $n_j + 1 \leq n_j'$. Therefore, $\max_{i=1}^{p} \dfrac{n_i'}{s_i} \geq \dfrac{n_j'}{s_j} \geq \dfrac{n_j + 1}{s_j}$. As we assumed that $(\forall j)(\max_{i=1}^{p} \dfrac{n_i}{s_i} \leq \dfrac{n_j + 1}{s_j})$, then

$$\max_{i=1}^{P} \frac{n_i}{s_i} \le \frac{n_j + 1}{s_j} \le \frac{n_j^{'}}{s_j} \le \max_{i=1}^{P} \frac{n_i^{'}}{s_i}. \quad \text{Thus, from} \max_{i=1}^{P} \frac{n_i}{s_i} \ge \max_{i=1}^{P} \frac{n_i^{'}}{s_i}$$

and $\max_{i=1}^{P} \dfrac{n_i}{s_i} \le \max_{i=1}^{P} \dfrac{n_i^{'}}{s_i}$ we conclude that $\max_{i=1}^{P} \dfrac{n_i}{s_i} = \max_{i=1}^{P} \dfrac{n_i^{'}}{s_i}.$ □

We can apply Lemma 1 to the pair $(n_1^{(k)}, \ldots, n_p^{(k)})$ and $(n_1^{(k+l)}, \ldots, n_p^{(k+l)})$ for any

$l \in [1, w-1]$ .Indeed, $\sum_{i=1}^{P} n_i^{(k)} > \sum_{i=1}^{P} n_i^{(k+l)}$ and $(\exists i)(n_i^{(k)} < n_i^{(k+l)})$. Finally,

the HSP guarantees that $(\forall j)(\max_{i=1}^{P} \dfrac{n_i^{(k)}}{s_i} \le \dfrac{n_j^{(k)} + 1}{s_j})$ (see [5,6]). Therefore,

$$\max_{i=1}^{P} \frac{n_i^{(k)}}{s_i} = \max_{i=1}^{P} \frac{n_i^{(k+1)}}{s_i} = \ldots = \max_{i=1}^{P} \frac{n_i^{(k+w-1)}}{s_i}. \quad \text{In particular, this means}$$

that for any $(m_1, \ldots, m_p)$ such that $\min_{j=k}^{k+w-1} n_i^{(j)} \le m_i \le \max_{j=k}^{k+w-1} n_i^{(j)}$

$(i = 1, \ldots, p)$, we will have $\max_{i=1}^{P} \dfrac{m_i}{s_i} = \max_{i=1}^{P} \dfrac{n_i^{(k)}}{s_i}$. The allocations made in

the end by the Reverse algorithm for the column panels k, k+1,...,k+w-1 result in a new sequence of distributions for steps k, k+1,...,k+w-1 of the LU factorization such that each next distribution differs from the previous one for exactly one processor. Each distribution $(m_1, \ldots, m_p)$ in this new sequence satisfies the inequality

$\min_{j=k}^{k+w-1} n_i^{(j)} \le m_i \le \max_{j=k}^{k+w-1} n_i^{(j)}$ $(i = 1, \ldots, p)$. Therefore, all they will have

the same cost $\max_{i=1}^{P} \dfrac{n_i^{(k)}}{s_i}$, which is the cost of the optimal distribution for these

steps of the LU factorization found by the HSP. Hence, each distribution in this sequence will be optimal for the corresponding step of the LU factorization. □

Proposition 2. The complexity of the Reverse algorithm is $O(p \times n \times \log_2 p)$.

Proof. At each iteration of this algorithm, we apply the HSP, which is of complexity $O(p \times \log_2 p)$ [5]. Testing the condition $(\exists! j \in [1, p])(n_j == n_j^{'} + 1) \wedge (\forall i \ne j)(n_i == n_i^{'})$ is of complexity $O(p)$. Testing the condition $(\exists i \in [1, p])(n_i < n_i^{'})$ is also of complexity $O(p)$. Finally, the total number of iterations of the inner loop of the nest of loops

```
for (i=1; i≤p; i=i+1)
    for ( Δ = n_i - n_i' ; Δ≠0; Δ=Δ-1, w=w-1)
        d_{k-w}=i;
```

Table 3. Specifications of sixteen Linux computers of a heterogeneous network

Processor	GHz CPU	RAM (mBytes)	Cache (kBytes)	Absolute speed (MFlops)
hcl01	3.6 Xeon	256	2048	246
hcl02	3.6 Xeon	256	2048	226
hcl03	3.4 Xeon	1024	1024	258
hcl04	3.4 Xeon	1024	1024	258
hcl05	3.4 Xeon	1024	1024	260
hcl06	3.4 Xeon	1024	1024	258
hcl07	3.4 Xeon	256	1024	257
hcl08	3.4 Xeon	256	1024	257
hcl09	1.8 AMD Opteron	1024	1024	386
hcl10	1.8 AMD Opteron	1024	1024	347
hcl11	3.2 P4	512	1024	518
hcl12	3.4 P4	512	1024	258
hcl13	2.9 Celeron	1024	256	397
hcl14	3.4 Xeon	1024	1024	558
hcl15	2.8 Xeon	1024	1024	472
hcl16	3.6 Xeon	1024	2048	609

during the execution of the algorithm cannot exceed the total number of allocations of column panels, n. Thus, the overall complexity of the algorithm is upper-bounded by $n \times O(p \times \log_2 p) + n \times O(p) + n \times O(p) + p \times n \times O(1) = O(p \times n \times \log_2 p)$. Table 2 presents the complexities of the algorithms employing the constant performance model of heterogeneous processors.

4   Experimental Results

A small heterogeneous local network of sixteen different Linux workstations shown in Table 3 is used in the experiments. The network is based on 2 Gbit Ethernet with a switch enabling parallel communications between the computers.

The absolute speed of a processor is obtained by running the DGEMM routine that is used in our application to locally update a dense non-square matrix of size $n_1 \times n_2$. DGEMM is a level-3 BLAS routine [11] supplied by Automatically Tuned Linear Algebra Software (ATLAS) [12]. ATLAS is a package that generates efficient code for basic linear algebra operations. The total number of computations involved in updating $A_{22} = A_{22} - L_{21} \times U_{12}$ of the rectangular $n_1 \times n_2$ matrix A_{22}, where L_{21} is a matrix of the size $n_1 \times b$ and U_{12} is a matrix of the size $b \times n_2$, is $2 \times b \times n_1 \times n_2$. The block size b used in the experiments is 32, which is typical for cache-based workstations [9,10].

Figure 3 shows the first set of experiments. For the range of problem sizes used in these experiments, the speed of the processor is a constant function of the problem size. These experiments demonstrate the optimality of the Reverse and the DP

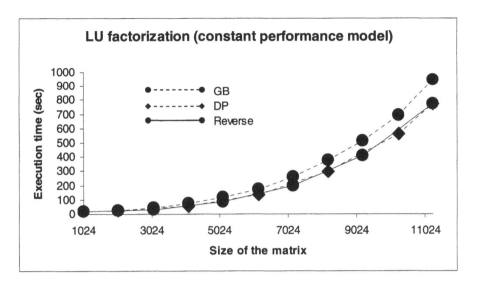

Fig. 3. Execution times of the Reverse, DP, and GB distribution strategies for LU decomposition of a dense square matrix

algorithms over the GB algorithm when the speed of the processor is a constant function of the problem size. The figure shows the execution times of the LU factorization application using these algorithms. The single number speeds of the processors used for these experiments are obtained by running the DGEMM routine to update a dense non-square matrix of size 5120×320. These speeds are shown in the last column of Table 3. The ratio of speeds of the most powerful computer *hcl16* and the least powerful computer *hcl01* is 609/226 ≈ 2.7.

Tables 4 and 5 show the second set of experiments showing the execution times of the different strategies presented in this paper along with their extensions using the functional model of heterogeneous processors [1, 2]. The strategies FDP, FGB, and FR are extensions of the DP, GB, and the Reverse algorithms respectively using the functional model of heterogeneous processors.

We consider two cases for comparison in the range (1024, 25600) of matrix sizes. The GB and DP algorithms uses single number speeds. For the first case the single number speeds are obtained by running the DGEMM routine to update a dense non-square matrix of size 16384×1024. This case covers the range of small sized matrices. The results for this case are shown in Table 4. For the second case the single number speeds are obtained by running the DGEMM routine to update a dense non-square matrix of size 20480×1440. This case covers the range of large sized matrices. The results for this case are shown in Table 5. The ratios of speeds of the most powerful computer *hcl16* and the least powerful computer *hcl01* in these cases are (531/131 = 4.4) and (579/64 = 9) respectively.

It can be seen that the FR algorithm, which is an extension of the Reverse algorithm and employing the functional model of heterogeneous processors performs well for all sizes of matrices. The Reverse and the DP algorithms perform better than the GB algorithm when the speed of the processor is represented by a constant

Table 4. Execution times (in seconds) of the LU factorization using different data distribution algorithms

Size of the matrix	FR	FDP	FGB	Reverse/DP	GB
1024	**15**	17	18	16	20
5120	**86**	155	119	103	138
10240	**564**	1228	690	668	919
15360	**2244**	3584	2918	2665	2829
20480	**7014**	10801	8908	9014	9188
25360	**14279**	22418	19505	27204	27508

Table 5. Execution times (in seconds) of the LU factorization using different data distribution algorithms

Size of the matrix	FR	FDP	FGB	Reverse/DP	GB
1024	**15**	17	18	18	18
5120	**86**	155	119	109	155
10240	**564**	1228	690	711	926
15360	**2244**	3584	2918	2863	3018
20480	**7014**	10801	8908	9054	9213
25360	**14279**	22418	19505	26784	26983

function of the problem size. The main reason is that the GB algorithm imposes additional restrictions on the mapping of the columns to the processors. These restrictions are that the matrix is partitioned into groups, all of which have the same number of blocks. The number of columns per group (size of the group) and the distribution of the columns in the group over the processors are fixed. The Reverse and the DP algorithms impose no such limitations on the mapping.

5   Conclusions and Future Work

In this paper, we presented a novel algorithm of optimal matrix partitioning for parallel dense matrix factorization on heterogeneous processors based on their constant performance model. We prove the correctness of the algorithm and estimate its complexity. We demonstrate that this algorithm better suits extensions to more complicated, non-constant, performance models of heterogeneous processors than traditional algorithms.

Acknowledgement

This work was supported by the Science Foundation Ireland (SFI).

References

[1] Lastovetsky, A., Reddy, R.: Data Partitioning with a Realistic Performance Model of Networks of Heterogeneous Computers. In: Proceedings of 18th International Parallel and Distributed Processing Symposium (IPDPS'04), IEEE Computer Society Press, Los Alamitos (2004)

[2] Lastovetsky, A., Reddy, R.: Data Partitioning with a Functional Performance Model of Heterogeneous Processors. International Journal of High Performance Computing Applications 21, 76–90 (2007)

[3] Arapov, D., Kalinov, A., Lastovetsky, A., Ledovskih, I.: Experiments with mpC: Efficient Solving Regular Problems on Heterogeneous Networks of Computers via Irregularization. In: Ferreira, A., Rolim, J.D.P., Teng, S.-H. (eds.) IRREGULAR 1998. LNCS, vol. 1457, pp. 332–343. Springer, Heidelberg (1998)

[4] Kalinov, A., Lastovetsky, A.: Heterogeneous Distribution of Computations Solving Linear Algebra Problems on Networks of Heterogeneous Computers. Journal of Parallel and Distributed Computing 61, 520–535 (2001)

[5] Beaumont, O., Boudet, V., Petitet, A., Rastello, F., Robert, Y.: A Proposal for a Heterogeneous Cluster ScaLAPACK (Dense Linear Solvers). IEEE Transactions on Computers 50, 1052–1070 (2001)

[6] Boulet, P., Dongarra, J., Rastello, F., Robert, Y., Vivien, F.: Algorithmic issues on heterogeneous computing platforms. Parallel Processing Letters 9, 197–213 (1999)

[7] Barbosa, J., Tavares, J., Padilha, A.J.: Linear Algebra Algorithms in a Heterogeneous Cluster of Personal Computers. In: 9th Heterogeneous Computing Workshop (HCW 2000), pp. 147–159 (2000)

[8] Barbosa, J., Morais, C.N., Padilha, A.J.: Simulation of Data Distribution Strategies for LU Factorization on Heterogeneous Machines. In: Proceedings of 17th International Parallel and Distributed Processing Symposium (IPDPS 2003), IEEE Computer Society Press, Los Alamitos (2003)

[9] Choi, J., Dongarra, J., Ostrouchov, L.S., Petitet, A.P., Walker, D.W., Whaley, R.C.: The Design and Implementation of the ScaLAPACK LU, QR, and Cholesky Factorization Routines. Scientific Programming 5, 173–184 (1996)

[10] Blackford, L., Choi, J., Cleary, A., D'Azevedo, E., Demmel, J., Dhillon, I., Dongarra, J., Hammarling, S., Henry, G., Petitet, A., Stanley, K., Walker, D., Whaley, R.: ScaLAPACK User's Guide. SIAM (1997)

[11] Dongarra, J., Croz, J.D., Duff, I.S., Hammarling, S.: A set of level-3 basic linear algebra subprograms. ACM Transactions on Mathematical Software 16, 1–17 (1990)

[12] Whaley, R.C., Petitet, A., Dongarra, J.: Automated empirical optimizations of software and the atlas project. Technical report, Department of Computer Sciences, University of Tennessee, Knoxville (2000)

Parallel Pseudorandom Number Generator for Large-Scale Monte Carlo Simulations[*]

Mikhail Marchenko

Institute of Computational Mathematics and Mathematical Geophysics SB RAS,
Prospekt Lavrentieva 6, 630090, Novosibirsk, Russia
Tel.: (383)330-77-21; Fax: (383) 330-87-83
mam@osmf.sscc.ru

Abstract. A parallel random number generator is given to perform large-scale distributed Monte Carlo simulations. The generator's quality was verified using statistically rigorous tests. Also special problems with known solutions were used for the testing. The description of program system MONC for large-scale distributed Monte Carlo simulations is also given.

1 Introduction

Assume that while solving equations of mathematical physics one wants to estimate some functional φ. To implement a Monte Carlo technique one writes the following stochastic representation

$$\varphi \approx \mathrm{E}\zeta = \mathrm{E}\zeta(\omega).$$

Here ω is a sample trajectory of stochastic process, ζ is called a stochastic estimator. Note that the above mentioned relationship gives the fair approximation. It means that the stochastic estimator has nonzero deterministic error. Then one evaluates the value of $\mathrm{E}\zeta$ using the sample average

$$\varphi \approx \bar{\zeta} = \frac{1}{N} \sum_{n=1}^{N} \zeta_n.$$

Here N is quite large number of independent samples ζ_n.

When M independent processors are used and independent trials are distributed over the processors, the time complexity of statistical modeling is obviously reduced by M times, because the combined complexity of the final summation and averaging is negligible. Naturally, there should exist a possibility for handling samples of different volumes on different processors with the use of statistically optimal averaging of the results based on the formula

---

[*] The work was supported by RFBR grants No. 06-01-00586 and No. 06-01-00046, President grant No. 4774.2006.1 of "Leading scientific schools" program, INTAS grant No. 05-109-5267 and SB RAS Lavrientiev's grant.

V. Malyshkin (Ed.): PaCT 2007, LNCS 4671, pp. 276–282, 2007.

$$\bar{\zeta} = \sum_{m=1}^{M} n_m \bar{\zeta}_m \Big/ \sum_{m=1}^{M} n_m,$$

where n_m is the sample volume on the m-th processor and $\bar{\zeta}_m$ is the corresponding average.

When M is large, the corresponding sample of the underlying pseudorandom numbers is also large. Therefore, the use of long period sequences of pseudorandom numbers is expedient if a simple method for splitting the sequences into M subsequences of required length is available (see description of the bf-generator in Sect. 3). Such modified algorithms for generating pseudorandom numbers require approximately modified statistical testing (see Sect. 5). To obtain a global estimate of the solution in the C metric, the groups of trajectories originating from different points of the phase space can be simulated on different processors. In so doing, it is expedient to use the same pseudorandom numbers at different points (possibly, on different processors). These numbers should be distributed between individual trajectories by means of a special deterministic procedure (see description of the lf-generator in Sect. 3).

Note that there does not exist any ideal algorithm for parallel realization of a stochastic ensemble of N_0 interacting particles. However, for such an ensemble, the asymptotic determinate error of estimators for the functionals under study is $C_1 N_0^{-1}$ and the probabilistic error is $C_2 N_0^{-0.5}$. Therefore, to reduce the probabilistic error, such an ensemble should be simulated independently on different processors $(C_2/C_1)^2 N_0$ times, the resulting estimates for the functionals should be averaged.

2 Generating Pseudorandom Numbers on Single Computer

Typically, a pseudorandom variable ξ with a given distribution is modeled by transforming one or several values of a pseudorandom numbers distributed uniformly over the interval $(0, 1)$. That is, the following formula is used

$$\xi = f(\alpha_1, \alpha_2, \ldots).$$

A sequence of "sampled" values of α is generally obtained by applying number-theoretic algorithms. Among them, the most frequently used is the residue method (also called the *congruential generator*) formulated as follows:

$$u_0 = 1, \ u_n \equiv u_{n-1} A \ (\text{mod } 2^r), \qquad \alpha_n = u_n 2^{-r}, \qquad n = 1, 2, \ldots,$$

Here, r typically denotes the number of bits used in the computer to represent a number and A is a sufficiently large number relatively prime with respect to 2^r. We call A the generator factor. The quantities α_n are called *pseudorandom numbers*. They are verified by statistical testing, by analytical studies, and by using them in solving typical problems (see, for example, [1], [2], [6]). For the above mentioned generator the period of the sequence $\{\alpha_n\}$ equals to 2^{r-2}.

3 Generating Pseudorandom Numbers in Parallel

The solutions to various problems may be correlated by using pseudorandom numbers as follows. The sequence $\{u_n\}$ is splitted into subsequences of length m that start with the numbers u_{km}, $k = 0, 1, \ldots$ called the initial values of the subsequences. Each subsequence is used to construct the corresponding sample trajectories of the process to be modeled (i.e., its separate trials). The value of m should be such that m pseudorandom numbers would be sufficient to construct a trajectory. In the residue method, the initial values u_{km}, $k = 0, 1, 2, \ldots$ of the subsequences are obviously calculated as follows

$$u_{(k+1)m} = u_{km} A_m \ (\mathrm{mod}\ 2^r), \qquad k = 0, 1, 2, \ldots,$$

Here the factor A_m in the auxiliary generator of leaps of length m is calculated as

$$A_m \equiv A^m (\mathrm{mod}\ 2^r)$$

Thus, the k-th trajectory is simulated using the subsequence in the residue method that starts from

$$\alpha_{km} = u_{km} \, 2^{-r}$$

We call this method the **lf-generator** ('lf' means 'little frog'). Clearly, the value of m for the lf-generator should be chosen in such way that its divisors include each n corresponding to successful n-dimensional uniformity tests (see Sect. 5).

In contrast to the straightforward distribution of pseudorandom numbers in the order of their generation, the lf-generator ensures a small change in simulated results under small variation of the parameters of the problem. Accordingly, the lf-generator is more amenable to the testing based on solution of typical problems than the conventional generator. Moreover, the lf-generator is better suited to the important multidimensional uniformity tests in estimation problems for multidimensional integrals (see Sect. 5).

The modified generator considered above can obviously be used to distribute pseudorandom numbers over individual processors, but the leaps should be considerably longer to do this. More precisely, m should be replaced by $\mu = mN$, where N is the number of trajectories that are actually simulated on an individual processor. This "large-scale" generator is called the **bf-generator** ('bf' means 'big frog').

It is recommended to use both the lf- and bf-generators while performing distributed Monte Carlo simulations. Modifying the expression for lf-generator we find that the initial values of the subsequences can be calculated as

$$u_{j+lm} = u_{j+(l-1)m} A_m \ (\mathrm{mod}\ 2^r), \qquad j = 1, 2, \ldots, M, \ l = 1, 2, \ldots,$$

where u_j are the initial values of the subsequences for the bf-generator.

4 Choice of Parameters for the Parallel Generator

As a source generator, we used one of the congruential generators tested in [1]. Its parameters are

$$r = 128, \ A \equiv 5^{100109} \ (\mathrm{mod}\ 2^{128}).$$

i.e., the corresponding period is

$$L = 2^{126} \approx 10^{38}.$$

Different values of the factor A are given in [1]. For the first billion numbers (starting with $u_0 = 1$), standard statistical tests were successfully performed in [1]. Analytical studies of the n-dimensional distributions were additionally performed in [1] for the method of residues. It was shown in [5] that these distributions are concentrated on sets of planes, i.e., on manifolds of lower dimension. On the other hand, it was shown in [1] for the generator considered here that these manifolds densely fill the corresponding n-dimensional hypercubes, but this shortcoming can be disregarded. A FORTRAN code for the congruential generator with above mentioned parameters is presented in [3].

We used the following value of the leap length in the bf-generator:

$$\mu = 10^{26} \approx 2^{86}.$$

This value is more than sufficient to have enough pseudorandom numbers for computations on each processor. The suggested bf-generator makes it possible to distribute the original sequence evenly between processors: 10^{26} pseudorandom numbers for about $10^{12} \approx 2^{40}$ processors. Both the factor for the bf-generator and a FORTRAN code for its computation are presented in [3]. The corresponding initial values $u_0 = 1$, $u_\mu = A_\mu$, $u_{2\mu} = A_{2\mu}, \ldots$ of the subsequences for the bf-generator are also given in [3].

5   Statistical Test of Parallel Generator

We examined the constructed bf-generator by performing n-dimensional uniformity tests (see [2] for a sample of 10^{10} numbers, which was obtained by joining the first 10^9 numbers from the first ten subsequences. Each of them used no more than 10^9 pseudorandom numbers. The resulting statistical estimates were averaged as indicated in the Introduction. The multidimensional distributions were checked for uniformity for $n = 1, 2, \ldots, 7$ by using the criterion χ^2, with partition along each axis into one hundred parts for $n = 2$ and 3 and into ten parts for $n = 4, \ldots, 7$. We denote by $k(n)$ the number of degrees of freedom of the distribution χ^2 corresponding to n. In this way, the number of classes (i.e., the number of elementary cubes), which equals $k(n) + 1$, was 10^{2n} at $n = 2$ and 3 and 10^n for $n = 4, \ldots, 7$. The number of classes used for $n = 1$ was chosen to maximize the efficiency of the criterion according to the formula (see [2])

$$k(1) + 1 \sim 4\sqrt[5]{2}(R/d_\alpha)^{2/5},$$

where R is the sample size, and the constant $d_\alpha = O(1)$ can be set equal to two for practical purposes. In this case, $R = 10^{10}$ and $k(l) + 1 \approx 34800$ according to above mentioned formula. We denote by $\tilde{\chi}^2_{k(n)}$ the sampled value of the criterion:

$$\tilde{\chi}^2_{k(n)} = \frac{1}{r_n} \sum_{i=1}^{k(n)+1} (r_i^{(n)} - r_n)^2,$$

where $r_n = R(n)/(k(n) + 1)$ is the theoretical frequency of finding a number in a class, $R(n)$ is the sample volume corresponding to n, and $\{r_i^{(n)}\}$ are the sampled frequencies obtained. In analyzing the results of the statistical test of the constructed bf-generator, we used the fact that the quantity

$$\tilde{\eta}_n = (\tilde{\chi}^2_{k(n)} - k(n))/\sqrt{2k(n)}$$

corresponding to genuine random numbers is a standard normal random variable to a high accuracy for the values of $k(n)$ involved; i.e., it satisfies the relations

$$P(|\tilde{\eta}_n| > 1) \approx 0,32, \ P(|\tilde{\eta}_n| > 2) \approx 0,05, \ P(|\tilde{\eta}_n| > 3) \approx 0,003.$$

The numerical results obtained are shown in table. Thus, the values of $k(n)$ are irrelevant, and the test is passed.

Table 1. Results of statistical test of multidimensional uniformity for bf-generator

Parameters	$n=1$	$n=2$	$n=3$	$n=4$	$n=5$	$n=6$	$n=7$
$R(n)$	10^{10}	$5 \cdot 10^9$	$\approx 3,3 \cdot 10^9$	$2,5 \cdot 10^9$	$2 \cdot 10^9$	$\approx 1,67 \cdot 10^9$	$\approx 1,43 \cdot 10^9$
$k(n)$	34799	9999	999999	9999	99999	999999	9999999
$\tilde{\eta}_n$	$0,215$	$0,622$	$1,472$	$-0,76$	$0,913$	$-0,448$	$1,104$

The least common multiple of the numbers n in the table is 420. Therefore, it is expedient to set $m = 420 \cdot s$ for the lf-generator, where s is such a number that m pseudorandom numbers are practically sufficient to construct a trial.

Let us point out that a comparison between numerical results obtained by solving specific diffusion problems with the use of the generator suggested here and those obtained with the use of the well known congruential generator with $r = 40$ and $r = 128$ was presented in [6]. It was shown that these generators are statistically equivalent for the problems considered. In addition, the computations performed in that study for a problem with a known exact solution have shown that the modified generator provides a statistical estimate that is in satisfactory agreement with the exact solution. Essentially, this is one more successful test of the modified generator suggested in this paper.

6 Review of System MONC

In conclusion, let us briefly describe the program system named MONC (MONC corresponds to 'Monte Carlo') for the large-scale distributed Monte Carlo simulations [4]. This system is based on the use of above mentioned 128-bit generator and bf-generator. It uses ordinary networked PCs to create powerful computational cluster.

MONC is more convenient to use than the existing competitors: it allows user to perform distributed Monte Carlo simulations in easy way. For example, it doesn't require user to insert MPI calls into the computational program. This

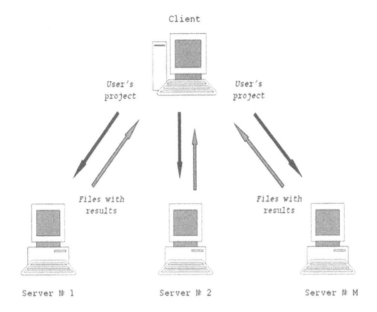

Fig. 1. Principle of MONC operation

make programming for MONC an easy operation. It means that the user have the possibility to concentrate on his Monte Carlo algorithm, not thinking about its parallel implementation.

MONC copies user's program and all other necessary data (all this data is called *User's project*) to remote servers, starts the execution of the program, follow the execution on servers, stops execution, copies results and averages them. It is very easy to start the execution of the project once again after the occasional fault such as electrical power fault, etc.

The idea of MONC corresponds to the philosophy of the use of GRID infrastructure. It makes MONC the desirable instrument for the specialists in Monte carlo simulations.

The principle of MONC is given on the Fig. 1. Here files with results represent the calculated values of ζ_n (see Introduction).

References

1. Dyadkin, I.G., Hamilton, K.G.: A study of 128-bit multipliers for congruential pseudorandom number generators. Comput. Phys. Comm. 125, 239–258 (2000)
2. Kendall, M.G., Stuart, A.: The Advanced Theory of Statistics, Griffin, London, vol. 2, 1961, Translated under the title Statisticheskie vyvody i svyazi, Moscow, Nauka (1973)
3. Marchenko, M.A.: Parallel 128-bit congruential pseudorandom generator: a manuscript is given on the web site, http://osmf.sscc.ru/ mam/ generator_eng.htm

4. Marchenko, M.A., Mikhailov, G.A.: Distributed computations in Monte Carlo method. Automation and Remote Control 5 (to be published 2007)
5. Marsaglia, G.: Random numbers fall mainly in the planes. Proc. Nat. Acad. Sci. 61, 23–25 (1968)
6. Mikhailov, G.A., Marchenko, M.A.: Parallel Realization of Statistical Simulation and Random Number Generators. Russ. J. Numer. Analys. Math. Modelling. 17(1), 113–124 (2002)

Dynamic Job Scheduling on the Grid Environment Using the Great Deluge Algorithm

Paul McMullan and Barry McCollum

School of Electronics, Electrical Engineering and Computer Science,
Queen's University of Belfast, Northern Ireland
Tel.: +44(0)28 90974653
p.p.mcmullan@qub.ac.uk

Abstract. The utilization of the computational Grid processor network has become a common method for researchers and scientists without access to local processor clusters to avail of the benefits of parallel processing for compute-intensive applications. As a result, this demand requires effective and efficient dynamic allocation of available resources. Although static scheduling and allocation techniques have proved effective, the dynamic nature of the Grid requires innovative techniques for reacting to change and maintaining stability for users. The dynamic scheduling process requires quite powerful optimization techniques, which can themselves lack the performance required in reaction time for achieving an effective schedule solution. Often there is a trade-off between solution quality and speed in achieving a solution. This paper presents an extension of a technique used in optimization and scheduling which can provide the means of achieving this balance and improves on similar approaches currently published.

Keywords: Grid, Job Scheduling, Great Deluge, Simulated Annealing, Network, Parallel Processing.

1 Introduction

A compute-intensive application can benefit in terms of completion time through distribution to many processors, each of which completes an allocated task in a parallel or pipelined fashion with respect to the overall goal of the computation. Unfortunately distributed processor systems are not available to the majority of those in need of greater computation power. Computational Grids are a relatively new development in addressing this problem. They allow the sharing of geographically distributed networked resources to create a dynamic and scalable cluster-based multi-processor system. This requires the integration of a task scheduling system, to allocate a set of tasks or applications for different users to available remote computing resources and minimise the completion time [1,2,3]. Current scheduling systems are limited by the time constraints required for remapping resources in a dynamic environment such as the Grid. The most effective scheduling algorithms generally require an impractical amount of time in which to produce a solution [4]. This paper

V. Malyshkin (Ed.): PaCT 2007, LNCS 4671, pp. 283–292, 2007.

introduces a new directed search algorithm based on the Great Deluge [5] which uses a relatively simple set of neighbourhood search heuristics to produce good quality schedules quickly.

2 The Scheduling Problem

As demand for the Grid increases over the next few years, effective scheduling algorithms are required to address new concerns within the grid environment. The computational resources available using the Grid are provided for researchers on a "first come first served" basis. As such, resources can be limited, requiring very efficient protocols for maximising the usage of available resources, in terms of load balancing and maintaining a fair allocation of resources for all users. Additionally, the network can be quite dynamic, with "nodes" added and removed continually, increasing the unpredictability of the network. Any scheduling system controlling task allocation must take this into account and be able to maintain efficiency as much as possible.

2.1 Scheduling Algorithms

The scheduling of computational processes and sub-tasks to available resources in an efficient manner is recognised as a hard problem that has been tackled for many years by researchers in the areas of distributed processor parallelisation and Artificial Intelligence [1]. Multi-processor systems and local "Cluster" networks have been the target of this research for several decades. However, with the emergent demand being placed on the resources of the Computation Grid, further considerations and complications not previously faced by traditional load balancing and task allocation methodologies must be addressed.

As the Grid expands and its use increases, the rather simple scheduling algorithms currently used for scheduling work on compute resources become more and more inadequate. A number of heuristic scheduling algorithms have been proposed in the last number of years to address the increasing complexity of resource allocation for computational networks [2]. List Scheduling heuristics utilises a set of priorities which are assigned to available processors, taking into account relationships between tasks. Each task is selected in order of its priority and scheduled to a processor based on the minimisation of a predefined cost function. Clustering algorithms merge task clusters onto a bounded number of processors and order the tasks within each processor. These are mainly effective for homogenous clusters and do not lend themselves readily to changes in resource availability or bandwidth conditions. Several solutions which provide task scheduling for heterogeneous systems have been proposed [3]. Although more applicable to the grid environment in terms of target resources, the consideration and influence of dynamic resource characteristics is again limited.

More current research into guided search techniques has provided useful tools to address the problem of dynamic remapping of resources using re-scheduling and repair mechanisms. Neighbourhood search techniques use a single- or multi-objective function to drive the scheduler towards an optimum schedule solution, including objective goals such as minimisation of communication time and total task completion time while maximising throughput. The most popular of these are in the area of Genetic Algorithms [4], using an evolutionary-based "selection of the fittest" approach to obtaining an optimal scheduling solution from an evolving population of possible solutions. One of the biggest drawbacks of this technique is the time required to obtain an acceptable solution, as it must maintain a dynamic population of candidate solutions throughout the search process. This problem is common to most of the more complex search techniques.

A more practical approach is with the use of Simulated Annealing, an extension to the simple Hill-climbing algorithm which uses a simple neighbourhood search to improve an initial schedule solution. Simulated annealing [6] accepts worse solutions (to avoid getting caught in local optima) with a probability: $P = e^{-\Delta P/T}$, where $\Delta P = f(s^*) - f(s)$ and the parameter T represents the temperature, analogous to the temperature in the process of annealing. The temperature is reduced according to a cooling rate which allows a wider exploration of the solution space at the beginning, avoiding getting trapped in a local optimum. Applied to grid scheduling, this technique has provided the balance between search time and measured results [7] [8].

2.2 Great Deluge Algorithm

The Great Deluge (also known as Degraded Ceiling) was introduced by Dueck [5] as an alternative to Simulated Annealing. This uses a Boundary condition rather than a probability measure with which to accept worse solutions. The Boundary is initially set slightly higher than the initial solution cost, and reduced gradually through the improvement process. New solutions are only accepted if they improve on the current cost evaluation or are within the boundary value. This has been applied successfully in other NP-hard solution space applications such as timetabling [9] and Telecommunications [10], and has proved more effective in obtaining a better quality solution within experimental time constraints. [11] describes a modification of the Great Deluge algorithm for Multi-criteria decision making.

Given this, it is proposed to build on the prediction models already employed in [7] to compare the results from an extended Great Deluge scheduler (described in the next section) against Simulated Annealing. A simple Hill-climbing approach is included to provide an idea of the scale of improvement in the new approach. The application used within the experiment is a compute-intensive bin-packing algorithm (SPAL) used in the optimisation of office and teaching space planning based on pedagogic and resource constraints for an expanding or new-build educational institution [12]. It was originally adapted for the GrADS (Grid Application Development Software) [13] and has been analysed to build a predictive performance model in which to estimate the computation time during experimentation. The simulator will also use the Globus Metacomputing Directory Service (MDS) [14] with the Network Weather Service (NWS) [15] to obtain resource availability information and processor load, memory and communication for each machine.

2.3 Extended Great Deluge with Reheat

The standard Great Deluge algorithm has been extended to allow a reheat, similar to that employed with simulated annealing in timetabling [16]. The aim of this approach is to both improve the speed at which an optimal solution can be found and at the same time utilise the benefits of this technique in avoiding the trap of local optima. In order to reduce the amount of time taken, relatively simple neighbourhood moves are employed.

Generally, the Great Deluge or Simulated Annealing processes will terminate when a lack of improvement has been observed for a specified amount of time, as the most optimal solution will have been reached. Rather than terminating, the Extended GD will employ the reheat to widen the boundary condition to allow worse moves to be applied to the current solution. Cooling will continue and the boundary will be reduced at a rate according to the remaining length of the run. The algorithm for the Extended Great Deluge is presented in Figure 1.

The initial solution construction is handled with an Adaptive (Squeaky-Wheel) ordering heuristic [17] technique. This utilises a weighted order list of the events to be scheduled based on the individual penalties incurred during each iteration of construction. The adaptive heuristic does not attempt to improve the solution itself, but simply continues until a feasible solution is found.

```
Choose virtual machine size
Set the initial schedule s using a construction heuristic – random
    selection from machines of chosen size;
Calculate initial cost function f(s) based on Performance Model
Set Initial Boundary Level B₀ = f(s)
Set initial decay Rate ΔB based on Cooling Parameter
While stopping criteria not met do
Apply neighbourhood Heuristic S* on S
      Calculate f(s*)
        If f(s*) <= f(s) or (f(s*) <= B Then
         Accept s = s*
        Lower Boundary B = B - ΔB
        If no improvement in given time T Then
         Reset Boundary Level B₀ = f(s)
          Set new decay rate ΔB based on Secondary
             Cooling Parameter
```

Fig. 1. Extended Great Deluge Algorithm

The first parameter used within the Extended Great Deluge is the initial decay rate, which will dictate how fast the Boundary is reduced and ultimately the condition for accepting worse moves is narrowed. The approach outlined in this paper uses a Decay Rate proportional to 50% of the entire run. This will force the algorithm to attempt to reach the optimal solution by, at the very most, half-way through the process. Generally, a continuous lack of improvement will occur before this is reached, at which time the re-heat mechanism is activated. The 'wait' parameter which dictates when to activate the re-heat mechanism due to lack of improvement can be specified in terms of percentage or number of total moves in the process. Through experimentation with a number of data set instances a general value for this parameter can be established. Figure 2 illustrates the process of initial decay, 'wait' time and subsequent re-heat.

After reheat the Boundary ceiling is once again set to be greater than the current best evaluation by a similar percentage to that applied in the initial boundary setting. The subsequent decay is set to a 'quicker' rate than with the initial decay, in order to increase the speed of the exploration of neighbouring solutions for improvement. The general setting chosen for the algorithm outlined is set to 25% of the remaining time, with the improvement wait time remaining unchanged.

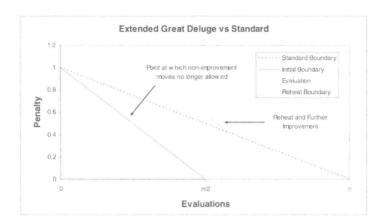

Fig. 2. Boundary behaviour of extended algorithm compared to Standard Great Deluge

The neighbourhood structures employed in the process are deliberately kept simple, to avoid the scheduler repeatedly getting stuck in local optima. Neighbourhood heuristics are deliberately kept simple to maximise performance of the algorithm and include adding / removing selected resources and swapping the order of tasks and resources.

3   Experimentation and Results

The SPAL application is intended to provide decision support and advice on projected plans for expansion or reduction of estate, changes to activities (in this case an educational institution) or cost / income requirements. The application will analyse all existing and historical data and provide an exhaustive set of projections and validations to justify and support major strategic change-decisions in the planning process. Initial 'quality' criteria and targets are introduced to the application, which then undertakes analysis of existing statistics, processes and models within the institution. This forms the basis for a required projection model which is used to then begin the process of creating valid projections for schedules, space and resource requirements and curriculum activity. Figure 3 illustrates the process from initial requirement specification to termination.

The process is detailed as follows:

Phase A – Analysis of existing data:

1. Estate planning requirements – analysis of existing plans, direct / indirect costs
2. General Constraints and Utilisation Targets – analysis of historical timetabling trends and schedule patterns

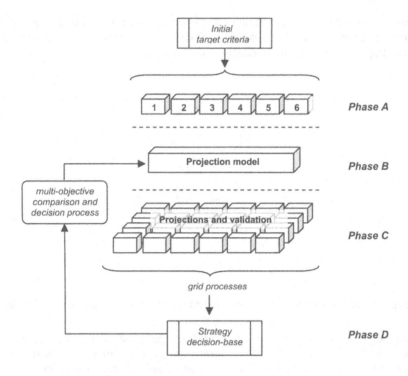

Fig. 3. Processes involved in SPAL analyser

3. Staffing and resource requirements – plans, inventory, human resource details and costs
4. Curriculum expansion – analysis of existing curriculum and enrolment patterns
5. General FTE (Full-Time Equivalent) statistics, pro-rata income and costs
6. Research, Commercial and Administration activities, including resource usage, costs and income

Phase B – Projection Model

7. Profiling of delivery and estate requirements based on expansion of student numbers, extended curriculum, increased / reduced estate, cost projections or projected cost reductions

Phase C – Projections and Validation of Assumptions

8. Creation and validation of scenarios based on initial requirements, including timetable and allocation, estate projections and curriculum structures

Phase D – Decision Process

9. Multi-objective decision process based on overall set criteria, including full comparison to set targets and trade-off with measures of quality between dominant pareto-front solutions

10. Feedback of decisions to projection model (step 7) - analysis repeats for given process time

The quality measurement used for the final strategy model or feedback to further iterations of the process is a multi-objective trade-off between a number of pareto points. [18] provides further explanation of the multi-objective process and its applications.

The experiments were run using the dynamic information obtained using MDS and NWS and the Performance Model to estimate execution time and hence provide a basis for driving the Great Deluge algorithm in optimising the schedule solution. A set of 8 benchmark data instances and constraints were used in the SPAL application, each of which have a differing level of complexity based on the amount of constraints involved. A total of 10 iterations were used for each instance (listed in order of difficulty), with average computation times presented in Figure 4. This is compared against two similar runs – one with standard Hill Climbing, the other using Simulated Annealing. In order to provide accurate comparison between techniques, the same random seed was used for each method, therefore the solution quality measurements did not differ between each. A standard cluster size of 10 virtual machines was used.

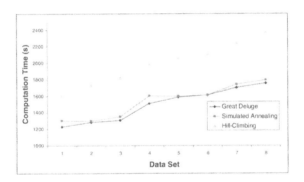

Fig. 4. Great Deluge vs Simulated Annealing and Hill Climbing

As can be seen, the Great Deluge generally performs better over Simulated Annealing, although in several cases there is very little difference between each. The most obvious occurrence of this is in Data Sets 2 and 8, where the ratio between amount of constraints and the size of problem is almost 1:1 for both, which may explain the lack of significant improvement. The experiments were also run using different cluster sizes of virtual machine to determine the effects of a decrease or increase in predicted communication load. In general, the Great Deluge algorithm achieved better results than Simulated Annealing. With more, smaller sized resources the difference between the two are greater for the smaller data sets (1 - 3), therefore the Great Deluge is most effective when potential resource usage and communication is higher.

Figure 5a gives a breakdown of the first (least complex) data set, with runs over 2, 4, 8 and 16 processors. As can be seen, the amount of improvement over different cluster sizes depends on the characteristics of the data set. The eighth data set used is one which represents a much more complex set of requirements and data model. The difference actually decreases as extra processors are introduced, as shown in Figure 5b. The main reason for this stems from the fact that the smaller data sets are generally less constrained by their nature, with a much larger potential search space. Therefore an increased amount of potential solutions with which to compare in order to maintain our pareto set of non-dominated solutions requires more inter-processor communication. As cluster size increases, communication requirements also increase and potential gains can be reduced accordingly.

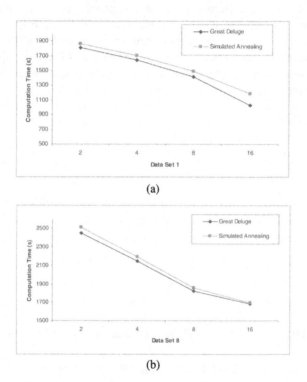

(a)

(b)

Fig. 5. Performance of Methods for differing cluster sizes

4 Conclusions and Future Work

In this paper, we set out to improve on current research into task scheduling for distributed applications running on the Computational Grid. The work extends current investigations into using directed searches to achieve a schedule of resource allocation, optimising on computation and communication time. Measurements are based on a predictive performance model of computation on the grid, but show that the current approach improves on previous similar techniques in this area. Although

Simulated Annealing is more effective than standard hill climbing algorithms in escaping from local optima, the Great Deluge is more successful given the limited time in which an effective scheduling solution must be achieved. Investigation will continue to directly compare the results from the scheduling algorithm against other reported benchmark results in the current literature. A full appraisal of the performance model will also be performed to determine how close the simulated results are to real distributed applications on the Grid. There are also many parameters used within the Great Deluge algorithm, such as cooling / reheat frequency. Full analysis of the limits of these parameters and how they affect solution quality will be carried out.

References

[1] Fernandez-Baca, D.: Allocating Modules to Processors in a Distributed System. IEEE Transactions on Software Engineering 15(11), 1427–1436 (1989)

[2] Tracy, D., et al.: A Comparison of eleven Static Heuristics for Mapping a Class of Independent Tasks onto Heterogeneous Distributed Computing Systems. Journal of Parallel and Distributed Computing 61, 810–837 (2001)

[3] Liu, L., Zhan, J., Lian, L.: A Runtime Scheduling Approach with Respect to Job Parallelism for Computational Grid. In: Proc. Of 3rd International Conference of Grid and Cooperative Computing (2004)

[4] Mika, M., et al.: A Metaheuristic Approach to Scheduling Workflow Jobs on a Grid. In: Grid Resource Management: State of the Art and Future Trends, Kluwer Academic Publishers, Boston (2003)

[5] Dueck, G.: Threshold Accepting: A General Purpose Optimization Algorithm Appearing Superior to Simulated Annealing. J. Computational Physics 90, 161–175 (1990)

[6] Kirkpatrick, S., Gellat, J.C.D., Vecci, M.P.: Optimization by Simulated Annealing. Science 220, 671–680 (1983)

[7] Yarkhan, A., Dongarra, J.: Experiments with Scheduling Using Simulated Annealing in a Grid Environment. In: Parashar, M. (ed.) GRID 2002. LNCS, vol. 2536, pp. 232–242. Springer, Heidelberg (2002)

[8] Fidanova, S.: Simulated Annealing for Grid Scheduling Problem. In: IEEE John Vincent Atanasoft International Symposium on Modern Computing (JVA '06), pp. 41–45 (2006)

[9] McMullan, P.: An Extended Implementation of the Great Deluge Algorithm for Course Timetabling. In: International Conference on Computational Science (ICCS 2007). LNCS, Springer, Heidelberg (to appear)

[10] Kendall, G., Mohamad, M.: Channel Assignment in Cellular Communication Using a Great Deluge Hyper-Heuristic. In: Proc. of IEEE International Conference on Network (ICON'04), pp. 769–773 (2004)

[11] Petrovic, S., Burke, E.K.: University Timetabling, Handbook of Scheduling: Algorithms, Models and Performance Analysis, ch. 45. CRC Press, Boca Raton (2004)

[12] McMullan, P., Roche, T.: An Intelligent Space Allocation and Planning Tool for Educational Requirements. Technical Report, RTS-TR-2005-2 (2005)

[13] Berman, F., et al.: The GrADS Project: Software Support for high-level Grid application development. Int. Journal of High Performance Computing Applications 15(4), 327–344 (2001)

[14] Foster, I., Kesselman, C.: The Globus Toolkit. In: Foster, I., Kesselmanm, C. (eds.) The Grid: Blueprint for a New Computing Infrastructure, ch. 11, Morgan Kaufmann, San Francisco (1999)

[15] Wolski, R., Spring, N., Hayes, J.: The Network Weather Service: a Distributed Resource Performance Forecasting System for Metacomputing. Future Generation Computing Systems 15(5-6), 757–768 (1999)

[16] Burke, E.K., Newall, J.P.: Solving Examination Timetabling Problems through Adaptation of Heuristic Orderings, Technical Report, Nottingham (2002)

[17] Abramson, D., Krishnamoorthy, M., Dang, H.: Simulated Annealing Cooling Schedules for the School Timetabling Problem. Asia-Pacific Journal of Operation Research 16, 1–22 (1999)

[18] Marler, R.T., Arora, J.S.: Survey of multi-objective optimization methods for engineering. Journal Structural and Multidisciplinary Optimization 26(6), 369–395 (2004)

Parallelism Granules Aggregation with the T-System

Alexander Moskovsky, Vladimir Roganov, and Sergei Abramov

Program System Institute Russian Academy of Science,
Pereslavl-Zalessky, 152020, Yaroslavl Region, Russia
moskov@lcc.chem.msu.ru, var@pereslavl.ru,
abram@botik.ru
http://www.botik.ru/PSI

Abstract. T-system is a tool for parallel computing developed at the PSI RAS. The most recent implementation is available on both Linux and Windows platforms. The paper is dedicated to one of important T-system aspects — ability to change parallelism granule size at runtime. The technique is available, primarily, for recursive programs, but it's possible to extent it to non-recursive ones as well. In the latter case, we employ C++ template "traits" for program transformation. The technique is shown to reduce overhead incurred by runtime support library dramatically.

Keywords: T-system, OpenTS, parallel programming, C++, computational clusters, parallel computing.

1 Introduction

The building of snow castle is a favorite winter-time game of Russian children. One has to use large snowballs to build one (or two, or three) walls and, may be, a tower. Then the castle is ready to protect it's builders from others in snowball game. If weather is appropriate (just below zero Celsius plus a major snowfall), snow castles mushroom along recreation areas in residential city blocks. One, who ever seen a snow castle know, that it's constructed of large snowballs, not small ones, the size is to be like ones to build a snowman, or even larger. It's just too boring to build snow castle out of small snowballs, while small ones can be used to fill gaps between major ones, level walls and correct imperfectness. And it's not possible to build a snow castle treating snowflakes individually.

As well, the proper choice of granule size is very important for the parallel computation to be effective. If the granules are too large, there may be not enough granules to load all available CPUs. With large granules the cost of scheduling error is larger too: cohesion, caused by assigning tasks to wrong CPU, will last longer. At the same time, if granules are too small, the overhead incurred by runtime system may be too large. In this paper we describe the granule size control techniques, applicable for the context of the T-system approach. In T-system, a potential granule is called "T-Function" and is, actually, a C-functions

V. Malyshkin (Ed.): PaCT 2007, LNCS 4671, pp. 293–302, 2007.

that can be computed in parallel. That creates a possible conflict of goals: the "functions" in C/C++ program are to structure source code and make program easier to read, while in T-system they serve as granules of parallelism, which size should be large enough to pay back runtime system overhead. So, the dynamic granules size — aggregation of multiple function calls in single granule — may be very important to improve ease of parallel programming with the T-system.

2   Related Work

The ability to dynamically adjust size and number of parallelism granules can be enabled by either well-defined program structure or rigorous approach, based on functional programming and graph reduction. The Open MP [1] may be considered as the most widely used implementation of the first approach: number of threads created is in particular section is defined equal to number of CPUs available. However, Open MP is mostly applied to loop parallelization, when loop iterations have approximately equal CPU instructions. In more sophisticated cases, graph partitioning is widely used in high-performance scientific calculations involving meshes [2].

Much more general approaches exist in the realm of parallel functional programming. "Task inlining" [3], "lazy task creation" [4] and "leapfrogging" [5] has been devised almost two decades ago for Mul-T [3] and Multilisp[6]. In principle, all these techniques are applicable in context of any futures-based system, like it has been recently shown for Java-based system in [7]. A lot of work has been done on granularity control in Glasgow Parallel Haskell both in terms of CPU and memory resources [8,9]. However, the application of these approaches in high-performance computing requires very tight limits on overhead, added by the mechanism. For the parallel programming environment to be useful, it should not only provide good speedup when running parallel programs, but allow low-level optimization as well. It's well known, that good optimizing compiler may improve speed of application by 100-300% and this requires only applying some optimization switches during compilation. For the majority of platforms, good optimizing compilers are available for C/C++ and Fortran, but not other programming languages. It may also important to allow compiler apply loop optimization techniques, like loop unrolling, vectorization, skewing etc [10], to load CPU pipelines and multiple execution units. The T-system design addresses these issues: we use C++ as a basic language, and allow low-level optimization in parallelism granules, at the same time, C++ inlining, in principle, should allow compiler to optimize loops including "aggregated" granules (see below).

In this paper we focus on implementation of granules aggregation in the context of T-system [11]. T-system provides programming model, which extends C++ language to express parallelism, and runtime support library to enable program execution on multi-cores, SMPs, computational clusters. The T-system enables writing much more compact programs model than traditional Message-passing interface (MPI) libraries. There are many C++ extensions available, designed to provide high-level programming tools [12]. It's interesting to note, that even original C++ design goals was to support parallelism, but it has been decided later to rely on libraries with that aspect [13]. Rather novel approach relies upon C++ templates to "extend" C++ language for parallelism [14,15,16]. Due to size limitations of this manuscript, we would like to refrain from comprehensive overview of C++ language extensions. However, we must notice distinctive features of T-system approach:

- "Functional-based" approach to parallelisation (see below)
- Mutliple assigment support for global variables (in T++ language, see below)
- Custom ligtweight thread library (in Open TS)
- Distributed garbage collector

The ability to aggregate granules, specified by a programmer is a distinctive feature as well. Combined with the availability on both Windows and Linux Platform makes T-system convenient tool to a wide community of potential users.

3 OpenTS: T-System Implementation

Open TS is the most recent full-scale implementation of T-system approach [11]. OpenTS provides a T++ — a language for parallel programming, which is a seamless extension of C++ language with only 7 keywords:

- **tfun** — a function attribute which should be placed just before the function declaration. A function with the "tfun" attribute is named "T-function", and runtime support system can compute such functions is parallel — in separate threads of execution.
- **tval** — a variable type attribute which enables variables to contain a non-ready value. The variable can be cast to the "original" C++-type variable, which makes the thread of execution suspend until the value becomes ready.
- **tptr** — a T++ analogue of C++ pointers which can hold references to a non-ready value.
- **tout** — a function parameter attribute used to specify parameters whose values are produced by the function. This is a T++ analog of the "by-reference" parameter passing in C++.
- **tdrop** — a T++ -specific macro which makes a variable value ready. It may be very helpful in optimization when it's necessary to make non-ready values ready before the producer function finishes.
- **tct** — an explicit T-context specification. This keyword is used for specification of additional attributes of T-entities.

Generally, Open C++ [17] reflection is used for conversion of the T++ programs to C++ with calls to Open TS runtime support library. The simplest sample program — Fibonacci numbers calculation is presented below.

```
tfun int fib(int n)
{
    if (n<2) return 1;
    return (fib(n-1)+fib(n-2));
}
tfun int main (int argc, char *argv[])
{
    int n = atoi(argv[1]);
    printf("Fibonacci %d is %d\n",n,(int)fib(n));
    return 0;
}
```

Casting (int)fib(n) is necessary to make main thread to wait for other threads to complete. Open TS runtime support library relies on MPI for communication in cluster environment, while addtional options are available (PVM, and TCP/IP when MPI is not applicable). Open TS features custom lightweight thread library, which is capable to make up to millions of context switches on a modest CPU. Another important Open TS capability is automatic garbage collection of non-ready values. By the end of 2006, the Windows port has been finished. The "cross-platform" version is available for download at URL http:// www.opents.net.

4   Granule Aggregation in Recursive Programs

Sometimes, even bantamweight threads are too heavy: the program may be most naturally expressed in terms of functions which take only few CPU instructions to compute. The Fibonacci example above is program of that kind: most of CPU time is spent on thread and non-ready values management by the runtime system, not on summation of integers. One may require programmer to coarsen parallelism grains supplied to system — the simplest solution. Consider the following modification of original Fibonacci code:

```
int cfib (int n) {
    return n < 2 ? n : cfib(n-1) + cfib(n-2);
}

tfun int fib (unsigned n)
{
  if (n < 32) {
    return cfib(n);
  } else {
    return fib(n-1) + fib(n-2);
  }
}

tfun int main (int argc, char* argv[])
```

```
{
  int n;
  if (argc < 2) {
  fprintf(stderr,"Usage: %s <number>\n", argv[0]);
    return -1;
  }
  n = atoi(argv[1]);
  printf("fib(%d) = %d\n", n, (int)fib(n));
  return 0;
}
```

The whole source is obscured a bit, moreover, the summation is replicated in two pieces of program — making in harder to support. The alternative for OpenTS is an implementation of technique, similar to "inline" of MultiLisp [6]. In that case, when a user program is calling a T-function "fib", runtime system may decide don't create any new T-threads, but, instead, evaluate a function, calling it's as ordinary C-function. That reduces parallelism: the runtime system will not be able to make some threads run in parallel. At the same time, it removes much overhead from runtime execution, since there is no need to create extra task object, schedule it and so forth. The benefit in terms of execution time reduction on one CPU is observable for Fibonacci:

Table 1. Exectuion times for calculating 41-st Fibonacci number

Program	Number of threads	Execution time
Fib(41)	535828592	7108.952 sec
Fib(41)-aggregate	8192	5.603 sec
Fib-cilk-5.4.3	n/a	19.7 sec

Here and below, measurements hes been done on dual Athlon MP 1800+ system with 1Gbyte of RAM, only one CPU was used. Program has been built with GNU C++ compiler version 3.2.2 and -O3 optimization flag. Here we applied a simple heuristic: calls, with recursion level deeper than the threshold (namely, 17), are implemented as C-call, not thread-creating calls. For comparison, we present also running time for calculation of the 41-st Fibonacci number with Cilk version 5.4.3, which is approximately 19 seconds. The Cilk [20] is a multi-threading programming environment for symmetric multi-processors (SMPs) and multi-core processors, which won HPC Challenge class 2 (most productivity) [21] award on Supercomputing conference [22] in the year 2006.

The recursion depth heuristic can be applied for a more sophisticated program: calculating the π number with the numerical integration method (it's concept similar to **sum-tree** test of [4]):

```
#include <math.h>
#include <stdio.h>
#include <stdlib.h>
```

```
tfun double isum(double begin,
                         double finish,
                         double d) {
    double dl = finish - begin;
    double mid = (begin + finish) / 2;
    if (fabs(dl) > d)
        return isum(begin, mid, d) +
                     isum(mid, finish, d);
    return (double)f(mid) * dl;
}
tfun double f(double x) {
    return 4/(1+x*x);
}
tfun int main(int argc, char* argv[ ]) {
    unsigned long h;
    double a, b, d, sum;

    if (argc < 2) {return 0;}
    a = 0; b = 1; h = atol(argv[1]);
    d = fabs(b - a) / h;
    sum = isum(a, b, d);
    printf("PI is approximately %15.15lf\n", sum);
    return 0;
}
```

One may notice, that only minor changes were necessary to make this program to run in parallel with the Open TS. Without granules aggregation, the overhead, introduced by the T-system would be very large, comparing it with few CPU instructions, which are necessary to calculate the "isum" function. To make this program efficient in that case, it would be necessary to create a loop inside the "isum" function, calculating the "f" multiple times. The T-system runtime with support of recursive granule aggregation is much more forgiving: it even allows placing "tfun" keyword for "f" function which is not practical to calculate in parallel on either cluster or SMP system. Consider the run time measurements: Only subtle differences are observable, one the scale of hundredth of second.

Table 2. Exectuion times for calculating π, 100000000 points

Program	Number of threads	Execution time
Pi — no aggregation	402653184	5589.667
Pi (tfun f)	8192	11.670 sec
Pi (no tfun)	8192	11.543 sec
Pi — C version	1	8.774 sec

C version is produced, removing all T++ keywords from the source code by preprocessor, which result in sequential program.

5 Granules Aggregation in "Map" Parallel Programming Template

The "Map" high-level function is widely known concept in functional programming [19]. The "Map" takes two arguments: input set and function, which has to be applied to each element of the input set, producing the output set. Since the operation on elements of the input set are independent from each over, parallelization of "Map" is straightforward. In C++, the high-level function can be implemented with the help of template functions. In C++ Standard Template Library(STL) it's a "transform" template, taking input, output iterators and function. In many cases, "Map" may be substitute for "for" loops. It is also may be beneficial to use "Map" instead of loop, since loop parallelization in plain T++ requires at least two loops instead of one: C++ code:

```
int do_something(int);
...
int res[NMAX]
for (int i=0;i<NMAX;++i)
    res[i]=do_something(x[i]);
```

The equivalent T++ code looks like: T++ code:

```
tfun int do_something(int x);
...
tval int tres[i];
for (int i=0;i<NMAX;++i)
    tres[i]=do_something(x[i]);
for (int i=0;i<NMAX;++i)
    res[i]=tres[i]
```

We have implemented the "Map" template with the C++ language and T-Sim C++ template library. It is based on "futures" [6] approach to parallelization, thus it's compatible with OpenTS in many aspects. Details of this library will be presented elsewhere. For the sake of implementation simplicity, user should supply the "functoid" [18] object to the template. The "Map" based code for an example above may look like the following:

```
int do_something(int);
...
Functoid<do_something> f;
MapD(x,x+NMAX,res,f);
```

The condition of speedup on parallel machine for this program is that the function do_something must constitute large enough chunk of work. But, in general case, it may not be sufficient to pay back amount of time, spent by runtime support library on handling the task and data transmission. That general case may be the simplest for the programmer to implement. However, our "Map" template is capable aggregating individual operations, producing larger grains and reducing the runtime overhead. Currently, programmer should supply an extra parameter to the template, "trait" for granule aggregation. Consider the following fragment for aggregation by the compile-time specified number:

```
MapA<FixedAggregation<100> >(x,x+NMAX,res,f);
```

The "Map" template produces granules by splitting large "transform" into lesser ones, which constitutes library-supplied grains of parallelism. It should be noted, that, since aggregation is done at compile time, individual `do_something` calls may be inlined by compiler inside the granule loop. This enables all toolset of optimizations, that are available for loops in modern C++ compilers.

6   Future Work

It's clear, that for the T-system, runtime overhead may be incurred not only from the task and thread management, but from the variable mechanism as well. Consider the following naive program to calculate N-th prime number:

```
// n -- desired prime number
// j -- current number
// i -- number of primes found <=j
tfun long nprimes (int n, long j, tval long i) {
    tval long tmp;
    tval long ni;
    tmp = nprimes (n,++j,ni); // start the

    bool is = is_prime(++j); //verify, if the number is prime

    if (n==i) return j; // Runtime environment should cancel
                        // subsequent "nprimes" calls started,
    else {
        if (is) {
            ni = ++i;  // increment the number of primes found
            return tmp; // return the result of subsequent calls
        }
        else {
            ni = i; // no change, connect non-ready
            return tmp;
        }
    }
}
```

For this program to be executed effectively in parallel, runtime system should provide "lazy" task evaluation strategy, as well as an ability to cancel tasks, which result are not necessary. The first is existing, and the latter is a prospective feature of OpenTS. In principle, the overhead of thread management may be kept low with the help of "inlining" technique [3]. However, management of non-ready variables ni and tmp may claim more CPU cycles than useful is_prime, especially, in OpenTS, where grabage collector is present. One of future work directions may be investigation of dynamic specialization mechanism for non-ready variables.

7 Conclusion

Implemntation of granules aggregation technique improves a lot ease of use for parallel programming tool. "The program mer takes on the burden of identifying what can be computed safely in parallel, leaving the decision of exactly how the division will take place to the run-time system." [3] The runtime support library may vary the "weight" of tasks in wide limits, so it capable to adapt program to wide variety of parallel computers that exist today: multi-core, SMPs, computational clusters with different kind of interconnects. At the same time, programmer may write very simple code, separating the computation code from the code, managing computational process (scheduling, aggregation and so forth). However, development of adaptive mechanisms, capable to measure individual granule weight and aggregate them accordingly, is a subject of future work, as well as attempt to provide lightweight non-ready variables.

Acknowledgments. This work is supported by Russian Foundation of Basic Research grant N 050708005ofi_a and basic research program of Presidium of Russian Academy of Science "Development of basics for implementation of distributed scientific informational-computational environment on GRID technologies".

References

1. Chandra, R., Menon, R., Dagum, L., Kohr, D., Maydan, D., McDonald, J.: Parallel Programming in OpenMP. Morgan Kaufmann, San Francisco (2000)
2. Schloegel, K., Karypis, G., Kumar, V.: Graph Partitioning for High-Performance Scientific Simulations. In: Dongarra, J., et al. (eds.) Sourcebook of parallel computing, Morgan Kaufmann, San Francisco (2003)
3. Kranz, D., Halstead, R., Mohr, E.: Mul-T, A High-Performance Parallel Lisp ACM SIGPLAN '89 Conference on Programming Language Design and Implementation, Portland, OR, pp. 81–90 (June 1989)
4. Mohr, E., Kranz, D., Halstead, R.: Lazy Task Creation: A Technique for Increasing the Granularity of Parallel Programs IEEE Trans. Parallel Distrib. Syst. 2(3), 264–280 (1991)
5. Wagner, D., Calder, B.: Leapfrogging: a portable technique for implementing efficient futures Proceedings of the fourth ACM SIGPLAN symposium on Principles and practice of parallel programming
6. Halstead, R.: MULTILISP: a language for concurrent symbolic computation. ACM Transactions on Programming Languages and Systems (TOPLAS) 7(4), 501–538 (1985)

7. Zhang, L., Krintz, C., Soman, S.: Efficient Support of Fine-grained Futures in Java International Conference on Parallel and Distributed Computing Systems (PDCS), Dallas, TX (November 2006)
8. Loidl, H-W., Trinder, P.W., Butz, C.: Tuning Task Granularity and Data Locality of Data Parallel GpH Programs. Parallel Processing Letters 11(4), 471–486 (2001)
9. Loidl, H.-W.: Granularity in Large-Scale Parallel Functional Programming PhD. Thesis. University of Glasgow (March 1998) Available online, http://www.dcs.gla.ac.uk/~hwloidl/publications/PhD.ps.gz
10. Alt, M.: Coding Considerations Practical Methods to Maximum Efficiency for Intel Itanium Architecture Intel Corp. (2004)
11. Abramov, S., Adamovich, A.I., Inyukhin, A., Moskovsky, A., Roganov, V., Shevchuk, E., Yu, S., Vodomerov, A.: OpenTS: An Outline of Dynamic Parallelization Approach. In: Malyshkin, V. (ed.) PaCT 2005. LNCS, vol. 3606, pp. 303–312. Springer, Heidelberg (2005)
12. Talia, D.: Advances in Programming Languages for Parallel Computing in Annual Review of Scalable Computing, Yuen C. K., pp. 28–58 (2000)
13. Stroustrup, B.: The Design and Evolution of C++ Addison-Wesley (2004) (in Russian translation: Piter, St.Petersburg 2007)
14. Intel Thread Building Blocks, Intel Corp. http://www.intel.com/cd/software/products/asmo-na/eng/294797.htm
15. An, P., et al.: An Adaptive, Generic Parallel C++ Library Wkshp. In: Dietz, H.G. (ed.) LCPC 2001. LNCS, vol. 2624, pp. 193–208. Springer, Heidelberg (2003)
16. Bischof, H., Gorlatch, S., Leshchinskiy, R.: DatTel: A Data-parallel C++ Template Library. In: HLPP 2003 Second International Workshop on High-Level Parallel Programming and Applications, June 15-17, 2003, Paris, France (2003)
17. Chiba, S.: A Metaobject Protocol for C++. In: Proceedings of the ACM Conference on Object-Oriented Programming Systems, Languages, and Applications (OOPSLA), pp. 285–299 (October 1995)
18. McNamara, B., Smaragdakis, Y.: Functional Programming in C++. In: The 2000 International Conference on Functional Programming (ICFP), September 2000, Montreal, Canada, pp. 18–20 (2000)
19. Abelson, H., Sussman, G.J.: Structure and Interpretation of Computer Programs. MIT Press, Cambridge (1996)
20. Randall, K.H.: Cilk: Efficient Multithreaded Computing. Ph. D. Thesis, MIT Department of Electrical Engineering and Computer Science (June 1998)
21. Luszczek, P., Bailey, D., Dongarra, J., Kepner, J., Lucas, R., Rabenseifner, R., Takahashi, D.: The HPC Challenge (HPCC) Benchmark Suite SC06 Conference Tutorial, IEEE, US, Tampa, Florida (November 12, 2006)
22. Kuszmaul, B.: A Cilk Response to the HPC Challenge (Class 2) SC06 Conference, IEEE, USA, Tampa, Florida (November 13-16, 2006)

Toward a Distributed Implementation of OpenMP Using CAPE

Éric Renault

GET / INT – CNRS UMR 5157 SAMOVAR
91011 Évry, France
`eric.renault@int-evry.fr`

Abstract. Traditionally, checkpointing techniques have been used to secure the execution of sequential and parallel programs. This article shows that checkpointing techniques can also be used to automatically generate a parallel program from a sequential program, this program being executed on any kind of distributed parallel system. The article also presents how this new technique have been included inside the usual compilation chain to provide a distributed implementation of OpenMP. Finally, some performance measurements are discussed.

1 Introduction

Radical changes in the way of taking up parallel computing has operated during the past years, with the introduction of cluster computing [1], grid computing [2], peer-to-peer computing [3]... However, if platforms have evolved, development tools remain the same. For example, HPF [4], PVM [5], MPI [6] and more recently OpenMP [7] have been the main tools to specify parallel code in programs (especially when supercomputers were the main issue for parallel computing), and they are still used in programs for cluster and grid architectures.

Many works [8,9] have been done in order to automatically extract parallel opportunities from sequential programs in order to avoid developers from having to deal with a specific parallel library, but most methods have difficulties to identify these parallel opportunities outside nested loops. Recent research in this field [10,11], based on pattern-maching techniques, allows to substitute part of a sequential program by an equivalent parallel subprogram. However, this promising technique must be associated an as-large-as-possible database of sequential algorithm models and the parallel implementation for any target architectures for each of them.

At the same time, the number of problems that can be solved using parallel machines is getting larger everyday, and applications which require weeks (or months, or even more...) calculation time are more and more common. Thus, checkpointing techniques [12,13,14] have been developed to generate snapshots of applications in order to be able to resume the execution from these snapshots in case of problem instead of restarting the execution from the beginning. Solutions have been developed to resume the execution from a checkpoint on the same

V. Malyshkin (Ed.): PaCT 2007, LNCS 4671, pp. 303–312, 2007.

node or on another node, or to migrate a program in execution from one node to another, this program being composed of a single process or a set of processes executing in parallel.

This article adresses a different problem. Instead of securing a parallel application using checkpointing techniques, checkpointing techniques are used to introduce parallel computing inside sequential programs, i.e. to allow the parallel execution of parts of a program for which it is known these parts can be executed concurrently. This technique is called CAPE which stands for Checkpointing Aided Parallel Execution. It is important to note that CAPE does not detect if parts of a program can be executed in parallel. We consider it is the job of the developer (or another piece of software) to indicate what can be executed in parallel. CAPE consists in transforming an original sequential program into a parallel program to be executed on a distributed parallel system. As OpenMP already provides a set of compilation directives to specify parallel opportunities, we decided to use the same in order to avoid users from learning yet another API. As a result, our method provides a distributed implementation of OpenMP in a very simple manner.

The article is organized as follows. First, we present CAPE, our method to make a parallel program from a sequential program. Then, we show that the result of the execution of the generated parallel program is equivalent to the execution of the original sequential program. The next section presents how we have developed a distributed implementation of OpenMP on top of CAPE. Section 5 provides performance results we have measured on one of our clusters and the last section draws a comparison between CAPE and other existing solutions.

2   CAPE

CAPE, which stands for Checkpointing Aided Parallel Execution, consists in modifying a sequential program (for which parts are recognized as being executable in parallel) so that instead of executing each part the one after the other one on a single node, parts are automatically spread over a set of nodes to be executed in parallel. Lots of work have been done to distribute processes over a set of nodes. Thus, in the following, we consider that another application (like Globus [15,16], Condor [17,18] or XtremWeb [19,20]) is available to start processes on remote nodes and return the result of the remote execution on the original node. Conveniently, this application is called the "dispatcher".

The behaviour of the dispatcher is as follows. The set of available nodes is managed so that each time a process has to be restarted on a remote node, the next node in the set is removed and associated to the process; when the process finishes, results are made available and the node returns to the set of available nodes, ready to run another process. Also note that in the following, it is considered that intermediate files (like images or delta files) are stored on a shared filesystem that can be created with NFS typically. Considering that filesystems are independent is not a key issue as it just requires to copy some files from one location to another.

The main purpose of CAPE consists in managing process images. In the following, the image of a process is the set of information that needs to be saved in order to be able to restart the execution of the process at the location in the program where the snapshot was taken without any loss of information. CAPE is based on a set of six primitives:

- `create` (`filename`) stores in file `filename` the image of the current process. There are two ways to return from this function: the first one is after the creation of file `filename` in the calling process; the second one is after resuming the execution from the image stored in file `filename`. This function is very similar to the `fork` system call. The calling process is similar to the parent process with `fork` and the process resuming the execution from the image is similar to the child process with `fork`. However, `create` allows to resume the execution from the image more than once; there is no such equivalence with the `fork` system call. The value returned by this function has a similar meaning as those of the `fork` system call. In case of error, the function returns `-1`. In case of success, the returned value is `0` if the current execution is the result of resuming its execution from the image and a strictly positive value in the other case. Unlike the `fork` system call, this value is not the PID of the process resuming the execution from the image stored in the file and has no specific meaning.
- `diff` (`first, second, delta`) stores in file `delta` the list of modifications to perform on file `first` in order to obtain file `second`.
- `merge` (`base, delta`) applies on file `base` the list of modifications from file `delta`.
- `restart` (`filename`) resumes the execution of the process which image was previously stored in file `filename`. Note that, in case of success, this function does not return as the image of the target process has been changed. The way processes are restarted from images depends upon the checkpointer. For example, `ckpt` version 1.3 [12] requires an extra executable file (called `restart`) to load the content of the snapshot before resuming the execution. With `ckpt` version 1.4, the snapshot generated by `ckpt` is an executable file and can be restarted direclty.
- `copy` (`source, target`) copies the content of file `source` to file `target`.
- `wait_for` (`filename`) waits for any merges required to update file `filename` to complete.

The description of the primitives highlights that the size of images is one of the key issues for an efficient implementation with CAPE: the smaller, the better. There is no real limitation on the size of images; the absolute limitation is the size of the virtual address space like any other processes.

Let P_1 and P_2 be two parts of a sequential program that can be executed concurrently. Fig. 1 presents the typical code one should write using OpenMP and Fig. 2 presents the code to substitute to run P_1 and P_2 in parallel with CAPE. Error cases (especially when saving the current process image) are not represented.

```
# pragma omp parallel sections
{
        # pragma omp section
        P₁
        # pragma omp section
        P₂
}
```

Fig. 1. Example of OpenMP code for parallel sections

```
parent = create ( original )
if ( parent )
        copy ( original, target )
        ask the dispatcher to restart ( original )
                on a distant node
        P₁
        parent = create ( after₁ )
        if ( parent )
                diff ( original, after₁, delta₁ )
                merge ( target, delta₁ )
                wait_for ( target )
                restart ( target )
else
        P₂
        parent = create ( after₂ )
        if ( parent )
                diff ( original, after₂, delta₂ )
                merge ( target, delta₂ )
```

Fig. 2. General template for CAPE

The first step consists in creating an "original" image used to resume the execution on a distant node, calculate the delta for each part executed in parallel and build the "target" image to resume the sequential execution at the end.

The second step consists in executing parts and generating deltas. Thus, the local node asks the dispatcher to resume the execution of the "original" image on a distant node. Parts are executed, two "after" images are generated to produce two "delta" files; then, these "delta" files are merged to the "target" image; all these operations are executed concurrently. The main difficulty here is to make sure that both the current frame in the execution stack and the set of processor registers are consistent. However, this can be easily achieved using a good checkpointer.

The last step consists in making sure all "delta" files have been included in the "target" image and then restarting the "target" image in the original process.

3   Proof of Concept

In order to prove that our solution is correct, one must show that when executing P_1 and P_2, modified or not by CAPE, the result is the same. That is, the set of updated variables (and the associated values) from the original program is the same for both executions. Two assumptions have to be made.

The first assumption is that the implementation of functions related to image management do not involve onboard effects on the running program. In fact, functions dedicated to image management shall be understood as a transparent set of services provided to the application, and executing a program with or without CAPE must provide the same result. This assumption is not irrealistic as some checkpointers can be dynamicly linked to a program and creating an image or resuming the execution from an image can be performed from outside the program, thus having the program unchanged.

The second assumption is that P_1 and P_2 satisfy Bernstein's conditions. Let I_i be the set of variables read when executing part P_i and O_i be the set of variables written when executing part P_i. Note that in this context, a "variable" shall be understood in the most general way, i.e. as a "memory location". According to Bernstein's conditions, both P_1 and P_2 can be executed concurrently if and only if the following condition is satisfied: $I_1 \cap O_2 = O_1 \cap I_2 = O_1 \cap O_2 = \emptyset$. This assumption means that no variable must be shared by the different parts except for reading only. In this case, "delta" files generated by CAPE refers to different memory location. When the "target" image is being built, there is no conflict between "delta" files and the result is the same as when the program is executed sequentially. This limitation is acceptable for many applications. However, others are requesting the use of shared variables. Fortunately, taking them into account is not a key issue as several solutions have been developed already. For example, each shared variable can be encapsulated using a mutual exclusion mechanism; this way, a single value for the shared variable is seen and updated by all threads, and optimizations like the use of caches can allow to get better performance. For the reconstruction of the "target" image, shared variables should be dealt with differently in order not to take their value from "delta" files but from the mutual exclusion area.

4   Distributed Implementation of OpenMP Using CAPE

In order to validate the concepts associated with CAPE, we are developing a distributed implementation of OpenMP. The current implementation is based on top of ckpt version 1.3 [12]. It has been necessary to slightly patch the original version of ckpt so as to be able to make the difference between the execution following the storage of the image of the current process in a file and the execution which is the result of resuming the execution from an image. No other checkpointer has been tried yet. However, we believe it shall be easy to implement this solution on top of any checkpointer as long as functions presented in Sec. 2 are implemented.

dompcc (the Distributed OpenMP compiler we developed) is built on top of gcc version 3.2.2. It consists in adding an extra stage in the usual compilation chain for C programs. As shown on Fig. 3, the extra compilation stage (sc, which stands for Specific Compiler) has been added after the C preprocessor (cpp) and before the stage of compilation itself (cc).

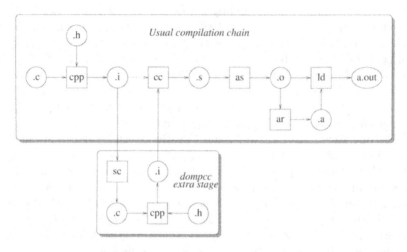

Fig. 3. The compilation chain for dompcc

Including the extra compilation stage at this location in the compilation chain allows to take benefits of the result of the C preprocessor (file inclusions, macros, conditionals) and thus to work on a complete C program free of lines beginning with a pound sign (except lines beginning by # pragma omp used to identify OpenMP directives). After transforming the original program using sc, the generated .c file is processed by the C preprocessor again in order to return in the usual compilation chain at the stage where the usual compilation chain was rerouted.

It is important to note that, as dompcc is based on gcc, options of gcc are available for dompcc. For example, if this implementation has to be included in a larger application, it is possible to use dompcc instead of gcc for compilation. This way, paths to header files and libraries are set correctly and others if any for larger applications can be added conveniently. Once compiled, the executable file is autonomous and can be run directly.

At present, not all OpenMP constructs have been implemented and only the **parallel sections** and **parallel for** constructs are available. The decision to focus on these two constructs first is based on the fact that they represent the main cases for parallel applications. However, considering there is no technology lock for the implementation of the other constructs, we expect to be able to provide them very soon.

5   Performances

The performance have been measured on a platform composed of a set of eight Pentium-III running at 800 MHz with 1.2 GB of memory on each node and operated by Linux RedHat version 3.2.2-5 (using Linux kernel 2.4.20-8). The interconnexion network on this platform is Ethernet 100 Mbit/s or Myrinet 2000. However, as our implementation is intended to run on any distributed parallel system, we used only the Ethernet network so as to be as generic as possible.

In order to measure performance of OpenMP over CAPE, we used a matrix-matrix product. The size of matrices is given as the number of elements ("Me" for millions of elements) for each matrix (i.e. 840×840, 1680×1680, 2520×2520 and 3360×3360 respectively). Matrices are dense and each value in the result matrix is the sum of the scalar products of the corresponding lines and rows. Note that one optimization have been implemented for both CAPE and MPI matrix-matrix product: the grain of parallelism is not a single column but a set of columns (ie. the total number of columns divided by the number of processes).

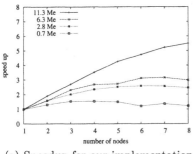

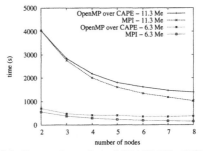

(a) Speedup for our implementation   (b) Comparison OpenMP/CAPE - MPI

Fig. 4. Performance evaluation

Fig. 4(a) presents the speedup for various matrix size. Performance measurements show that the larger the size of the matrix, the higher the speedup. In fact, as the complexity of the matrix-matrix product is $O(n^3)$, the larger the matrices, the less important both the network latency to transfer images (which complexity is $O(n^2)$) and the time to determine the set of updated variables (which complexity is also $O(n^2)$). As a result, performance measurements show that, with the current implementation, this technique is well-adapted to coarse-grain parallel loops. Moreover, performance show that the larger the size of the grain of parallelism, the better the speed up.

The comparison with an equivalent MPI program is interesting. Fig. 4(b) presents execution times for matrix-matrix products with both CAPE and MPI. The MPI program was written for the experiment and satisfies the same requirements as for CAPE (for the complexity essentially). Performance measurements have been done on the same platform with similar experimental conditions (especially average load for CPUs). MPI is mpich version 1.2.5.10 with driver ch_p4. Fig. 4(b) shows that, even if the execution time with MPI is always faster than the execution time with CAPE, the difference between the execution of the MPI program and the program automatically generated by CAPE from the sequential version is not very large. Moreover, both OpenMP over CAPE and MPI implementations are providing a linear speed up.

In fact, at present, the main part of the overhead when using CAPE is in the image management. According to Fig. 2, every time an image is generated, it is written on the disk; then, "after" images are compared to the "original" image and the difference is also stored on the disk. A significant improvement could be achieved while using an incremental checkpointer that would directly generates "delta" files instead of "after" images, avoiding at the same time the cost to evaluate the difference with the "original" image.

6   Related Works

Other works have presented solutions to provide a distributed implementation of OpenMP [21]. Considering that OpenMP has been designed for shared-memory parallel architectures, the first solution consisted in executing OpenMP programs on top of a distributed shared memory based machine [22]. More recently, other solutions have emerged, all aiming at transforming OpenMP code to other parallel libraries, like Global Arrays [23] or MPI [24].

The execution of OpenMP programs on top of a distributed shared memory is quite straightforward as no specific development is required except making sure the distributed shared memory behaves the same way as a real shared memory. Unfortunately, at present, distributed shared memory systems have scalability issues and several projects (like XtremOS [25]) are aiming at providing large-scale distributed shared memory or single-system images.

Implementing OpenMP directives on top of a pre-existing message-passing library involves lots of problems regarding the management of variables. For example, the determination of the list of variables updated by a thread may be very complex. This is obvious when variables are specified using either the private or the shared directive, but it becomes harder when no directive is provided or when a variable is accessed through indirections (eg. through a pointer).

The implementation with CAPE allows OpenMP programs to be better scalable as traffic and connectivity between nodes is limited. Moreover, there is no limitations on the detection of memory areas that have been updated as they are automatically taken into account.

7   Conclusion

This article presented how to transform a sequential program into a parallel program using checkpointing techniques. We showed that CAPE is consistent, i.e. executing a program tranformed using CAPE and executing the same program sequentially provides the same result. Moreover, CAPE provides three main advantages. First, there is no need to learn yet another parallel programming environment or methodology as the specification of parallel opportunities in sequential programs is performed using OpenMP directives. Second, CAPE inherently introduces safety in the execution of programs as tools for checkpointing are used to run concurrent parts of programs in parallel. Third, more than one node is used only when necessary, i.e. when a part of the program requires only one node to execute (for example if this part is intrinsincly sequential), only one node is used for execution. As performance measurements show, the only drawback of the current implementation is that the checkpointer we used for experiments generates very large images. We are investigating to significantly reduce the overhead involved by the management of these images.

Then, we presented the distributed implementation of OpenMP we have developed using CAPE. Performance measurements show that it is interesting to execute coarse-grain parallel applications and that the larger the size of the grain, the higher the speed up. Performance measurements also showed that the execution time for large matrices with our implementation is quite similar to the execution time when using MPI. Investigations show that the difference between both execution times is mainly due to the overhead involved by the management of images and we proposed a solution to investigate in order to bypass the problem.

References

1. Buyya, R.: High Performance Cluster Computing: Architectures and Systems, vol. 1. Prentice-Hall, Englewood Cliffs (1999)
2. Foster, I., Kesselman, C., Tuecke, S.: The Anatomy of the Grid: Enabling Scalable Virtual Organizations. The International Journal of High Performance Computing Applications 15(3), 200–222 (2001)
3. Leuf, B.: Peer to Peer. In: Collaboration and Sharing over the Internet, Addison-Wesley, London (2002)
4. Loveman, D.B.: High Performance Fortran. IEEE Parallel & Distributed Technology: Systems & Applications 1(1), 25–42 (1993)
5. Geist, A., Beguelin, A., Dongarra, J., Jiang, W., Manchek, R., Sunderam, V.S.: Parallel Virtual Machine: A Users' Guide and Tutorial for Network Parallel Computing (Scientific and Engineering Computation). Scientific and Engineering Computation Series. MIT Press, Cambridge (1994)
6. Snir, M., Otto, S., Huss-Lederman, S., Walker, D., Dongarra, J.: MPI: The Complete Reference (The MPI Core), 2nd edn. Scientific and Engineering Computation Series. MIT Press, Cambridge (1998)
7. OpenMP Architecture Review Board: OpenMP Application Program Interface, Version 2.5 Public Draft (November 2004)
8. Allen, J.R., Callahan, D., Kennedy, K.: Automatic Decomposition of Scientific Programs for Parallel Execution. In: Proceedings of the 14th ACM SIGACT-SIGPLAN symposium on Principles of programming languages, Munich, West Germany, pp. 63–76. ACM Press, New York (1987)

9. Feautrier, P.: Automatic parallelization in the polytope model. In: The Data Parallel Programming Model: Foundations, HPF Realization, and Scientific Applications. In: Perrin, G.-R., Darte, A. (eds.) The Data Parallel Programming Model. LNCS, vol. 1132, pp. 79–103. Springer, Heidelberg (1996)

10. Barthou, D., Feautrier, P., Redon, X.: On the Equivalence of Two Systems of Affine Recurrence Equations. In: Monien, B., Feldmann, R.L. (eds.) Euro-Par 2002. LNCS, vol. 2400, pp. 309–313. Springer, Heidelberg (2002)

11. Alias, C., Barthou, D.: On the Recognition of Algorithm Templates. In: Knoop, J., Zimmermann, W. (eds.) Proceedings of the 2nd International Workshop on Compiler Optimization meets Compiler Verification, Warsaw, Poland, pp. 51–65 (April 2003)

12. Web page: Ckpt (2005) http://www.cs.wisc.edu/~zandy/ckpt/

13. Osman, S., Subhraveti, D., Su, G., Nieh, J.: The Design and Implementation of Zap: A System for Migrating Computing Environments. In: Proceedings of the 5th USENIX Symposium on Operating Systems Design and Implementation, Boston, MA, pp. 361–376 (December 2002)

14. Plank, J.S.: An Overview of Checkpointing in Uniprocessor and Distributed Systems, Focusing on Implementation and Performance. Technical Report UT-CS-97-372, Department of Computer Science, University of Tennessee (July 1997)

15. Foster, I., Kesselman, C.: Globus: A Metacomputing Infrastructure Toolkit. The International Journal of Supercomputer Applications and High Performance Computing 11(2), 115–128 (1997)

16. Web page: Globus (2007) http://www.globus.org/

17. Litzkow, M., Livny, M., Mutka, M.: Condor - A Hunter of Idle Workstations. In: The 8th International Conference on Distributed Computing Systems, San Jose, CA, pp. 104–111. IEEE Computer Society Press, Los Alamitos (1988)

18. Web page: Condor (2007) http://www.cs.wisc.edu/condor/

19. Fedak, G., Germain, C., Néri, V., Cappello, F.: XtremWeb: A Generic Global Computing System. In: Buyya, R., Mohay, G., Roe, P. (eds.) Proceedings First IEEE/ACM International Symposium on Cluster Computing and the Grid, Brisbane, Australia, pp. 582–587. IEEE Computer Society Press, Los Alamitos (2001)

20. Web page: XTremWeb (2006) http://www.xtremweb.org/

21. Merlin, J.: Distributed OpenMP: extensions to OpenMP for SMP clusters. In: 2nd European Workshop on OpenMP (EWOMP'00), Edinburgh, UK (September 2000)

22. Karlsson, S., Lee, S.W., Brorsson, M., Sartaj, S., Prasanna, V.K., Uday, S.: A fully compliant OpenMP implementation on software distributed shared memory. In: Sahni, S.K., Prasanna, V.K., Shukla, U. (eds.) HiPC 2002. LNCS, vol. 2552, pp. 195–206. Springer, Heidelberg (2002)

23. Huang, L., Chapman, B., Liu, Z.: Towards a more efficient implementation of OpenMP for clusters via translation to global arrays. Parallel Computing 31(10-12), 1114–1139 (2005)

24. Basumallik, A., Eigenmann, R.: Towards automatic translation of OpenMP to MPI. In: Proceedings of the 19th annual international conference on Supercomputing, Cambridge, MA, pp. 189–198. ACM Press, New York (2005)

25. Consortium, X.: Linux-XOS specification. XtreemOS Integrated Project Deliverable D2.1.1 (November 2006)

Multicriteria Scheduling Strategies in Scalable Computing Systems

Victor Toporkov

Computer Science Department, Moscow Power Engineering Institute,
ul. Krasnokazarmennaya 14, Moscow, 111250 Russia
Phone: +7(495)3627145; Fax: +7(495)3625506
ToporkovVV@mpei.ru

Abstract. An approach to generation and optimization of scheduling and resource allocation strategies in scalable computing systems is proposed. The approach allows the decomposition of the problem of multicriteria strategy synthesis for the totality of parameterized models of programs with the use of partial and vector quality criteria including, for instance, a cost function and load balancing factors.

Keywords: scheduling, resource allocation, strategy, scalability, quality criteria.

1 Introduction

The need for special resource management mechanisms in distributed computing systems arose a long time ago and is well-recognized [1]. In some cases, complex sets of interrelated tasks (jobs) require co-scheduling [2] and resource co-allocation [3] in several processing nodes. Each node may be in an autonomous administrative domain and be represented by a multi-processor unit managed by a local batch system, e.g. CODINE, LL, LSF, NQE, Condor, PBS etc. Analysis of the resource co-allocation problem in distributed systems, including Grid, has shown that efficient management of job processing can be implemented on the basis of strategies that include combinations of different scheduling algorithms and heuristics [4, 5], various factors and critera (management policies, workload etc.) [3, 6]. In a number of papers [3-7], the authors conclude that it is necessary to use multifactor and multicriteria strategies. However, in practice only one of the possible resource allocation algorithms is used, and the set of criteria is convolved into a scalar productivity function [3]. In [6], a method for strategy generation in real-time computer systems is proposed.

In this paper, the method proposed before in [6] is developed and refined as follows. The problem of multicriteria strategy synthesis is considered for different parameterized graphs of programs. In the case of a single program model, it may occur that a schedule does not exist. One possible reason is that there are no free processors because of failures in the system. Therefore, it is impossible to resolve the collisions of parallel tasks [7] that compete for the same processor node. Hence, it is necessary to have strategies for program models with different levels of parallelism and task details.

V. Malyshkin (Ed.): PaCT 2007, LNCS 4671, pp. 313–317, 2007.

2 Assumptions and Statement of the Problem

By T_0^*, we denote the set of program models. Each of these models is associated with some totality of partially ordered tasks $T = \{T_1, T_2, ..., T_n\}$. The relation of the partial order on T is specified by a directed acyclic graph whose set of vertices corresponds to tasks of processing and memory access in subset $P \subseteq T$ and to tasks of data exchange in subset $D \subseteq T$. The set of arcs of the graph represents the informational and logical relations between the tasks. Fig. 1 shows some examples of information graphs in models with different degrees of parallelism and task details.

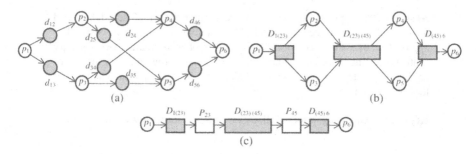

Fig. 1. Information graphs of programs with different degrees of parallelism and task details

The nonshaded vertices correspond to data processing, and the shaded ones correspond to data transmission. The graph of the program is parameterized by a priori estimates, namely, the running time t_{ij}^0 of task $T_i \in T$, $i = 1, ..., n$, on the j th type of processor resource, $j = 1, ..., J$; the amount v_{ij} of computations etc. The parameters of processing tasks are given in Table 1, which corresponds to the graphs shown in Figs. 1a and 1b. When task aggregating, as shown in Fig. 1b and 1c, the values of the corresponding parameters of subtasks are summarized. The duration of all of the data exchanges for the graph in Fig. 1a is equal to one time unit, while data exchanges $D_{1(23)}$ and $D_{(45)6}$ in the graphs in Figs. 1b and 1c need two time units and data exchange $D_{(23)(45)}$ needs four time units. In the resource allocation for tasks in T on a time interval $[0, t^*]$ a resource type is determined by the allocation u_i. We have $u_i = j$ if task $p_i \in P$ is assigned to a so-called basic processor resource whose level is bounded and depends on the parallelizing degree, the cost of the j th type resource, and some other factors [6]. If there occurs a collision of parallel tasks [7] in P, which compete for the same resource of type j, then, taking into account the architecture scalability, we introduce a resource of type $j^\circ \in \{1, ..., J\}$ (whose characteristics are not worse than those of the basic resource) and assign $u_i = j^\circ$. We represent a variant of admissible resource allocation in a quality criterion $w(r)$ by a vector $r = (t_1,...,t_n,u_1,...,u_n)$, and t_i is the running time of task $T_i \in T$. We estimate the efficiency of the resource allocation by the vector $W(r) = (w_1(r),...,w_L(r))$, where $w_l(r)$, $l = 1,...,L$, is a partial criterion.

Table 1. Estimates of parameters of tasks

Parameters	Processing tasks					
	p_1	p_2	p_3	p_4	p_5	p_6
Running time on the processor 1	2	3	1	2	1	2
Running time on the processor 2	4	6	2	4	2	4
Running time on the processor 3	6	9	3	6	3	6
Running time on the processor 4	8	12	4	8	4	8
Amount of computations	20	30	10	20	10	20

An example of the efficiency criterion is a cost function of the form

$$CF = \sum_{i=1}^{n} c_i(t_i,u_i) = \sum_{i=1}^{n} \left\lceil v_{ij} / t_{ij} \right\rceil, \ t_{ij} \geq t_{ij}^0, \tag{1}$$

where t_{ij} is the time of execution of task p_i on a processor of the j th type, n is the number of processing tasks, and $\lceil \cdot \rceil$ denotes the smallest integer not less than a given number.

Suppose that the active (binding) constraints

$$t_g^* - t_g \geq 0, \ t_h^* - \sum_h t_h \geq 0, \ g, \ h \in \{1,...,n\}, \tag{2}$$

are specified for individual tasks and jobs of the program, where t_g, t_h are the execution times for tasks T_g, $T_h \in T_i$ and t_g^*, t_h^* are limiting times of execution of task T_g and a job that includes the task T_h.

Let S be a strategy, i.e., a set of alternatives such that each alternative $r \in S$ corresponds to an admissible resource allocation under the constraints (2). The vector criterion $W(r)$ generates a binary relation F (e.g., the Pareto-relation) for comparison of alternatives on S. We refer to the set of alternatives optimal with respect to F as an F-optimal strategy of resource allocation. It is required to find an F-optimal strategy for all models of the set T_0^*.

3 Strategy Synthesis by the Totality of Criteria and Models

When searching for the F-optimal strategy on the basis of the parallel scheme [7], the synthesis may be decomposed by the totality of basic schemes, each one providing a conditionally optimal strategy by the corresponding partial criterion $w_l(r)$.

Example 1. Suppose conditionally optimal strategies of process allocation should be constructed by the basic scheme [7] for the information graph in Fig. 1a. The limiting time $t^* = 20$ is specified for the execution of all these tasks. Let the vector criterion include the cost function CF (1) and the loading factors $UP_j, j = 1,...,4$, of the basic processors. The collisions between competing tasks are resolved at the expense of nonallocated basic processors such that their inclusion in the set of resources is accompanied by the minimal value of the penalty cost function on the analogy of (1), where $v_{ij} = v_{ij^\circ}$, $t_{ij} = t^0_{ij^\circ}$, $j^\circ \in \{1,...,J\}$. Strategies are constructed for the upper and lower bounds of the maximal interval of the variation of t_i. Strategies conditionally optimal by criteria CF, UP_1, UP_2, UP_3, and UP_4 are represented in Table 2 by the variants No. 1-3; 4-7; 8 and 9; 10 and 11; and 12-14, respectively. The collisions between tasks p_4 and p_5 in variants 2, 13 are resolved by allocating task p_4 to a processor of type 3 and task p_5 to a processor of type 4.

Table 2. Scheduling strategies for the graph in Fig. 1a

No.	Running time						Allocation						Criterion				
	t_1	t_2	t_3	t_4	t_5	t_6	u_1	u_2	u_3	u_4	u_5	u_6	CF	UP_1	UP_2	UP_3	UP_4
1	2	3	3	2	2	10	1	1	3	1	2	4	41	0,35	0,10	0,15	0,50
2	2	3	3	10	10	2	1	1	3	3	4	1	37	0,35	0	0,65	0,50
3	10	3	3	2	2	2	4	1	3	1	2	1	41	0,35	0,10	0,15	0,50
4	2	3	3	2	2	10	1	1	3	1	2	1	41	0,85	0,10	0,15	0
5	2	3	3	10	10	2	1	1	3	4	1	1	38	0,85	0	0,15	0,50
6	2	11	11	2	2	2	1	4	1	1	2	1	39	0,85	0,10	0	0,55
7	10	3	3	2	2	2	1	1	3	1	2	1	41	0,85	0,10	0,15	0
8	2	11	11	2	2	2	1	4	2	1	2	1	39	0,30	0,65	0	0,55
9	10	3	3	2	2	2	2	1	2	1	2	1	41	0,35	0,75	0	0
10	2	11	11	2	2	2	1	3	4	1	2	1	41	0,30	0,10	0,55	0,55
11	10	3	3	2	2	2	3	1	3	1	2	1	41	0,35	0,10	0,60	0
12	2	3	3	2	2	10	1	1	3	1	2	4	41	0,35	0,10	0,15	0,50
13	2	3	3	10	10	2	1	1	3	3	4	1	39	0,35	0	0,65	0,50
14	10	3	3	2	2	2	4	1	3	1	2	1	41	0,35	0,10	0,15	0,50

Applying a family of parallel schemes, we synthesize strategies conditionally optimal by the corresponding partial criterion $w_l(r)$ for all models from T_0^*.

Example 2. Consider the models which are presented by the graphs in Figs. 1a and 1c. For the graph in Fig. 1a, the initial conditions are the same as in Example 1. For the graph in Fig. 1c, the strategy is constructed on the whole interval of t_i variation. We must construct the F-optimal strategy, where F is the union of G_l, $l = 1,...,L$, and G_l is generated by one of the criteria CF, $UP_1,...,UP_4$. The results of the resource allocation for the graph in Fig. 1c are presented in Table 3 by the variants No. 1-6.

The F-optimal strategy coincides with the strategy presented in Tables 2 and 3 up to the equivalence relation.

Table 3. Scheduling strategies for the graph in Fig. 1c

No.	Running time				Allocation				Criterion				
	t_1	t_{23}	t_{45}	t_6	u_1	u_{23}	u_{45}	u_6	CF	UP_1	UP_2	UP_3	UP_4
1	2	8	6	4	1	1	1	1	25	1	0	0	0
2	4	8	3	5	1	1	1	1	24	1	0	0	0
3	6	4	6	4	1	1	1	1	24	1	0	0	0
4	8	4	3	5	1	1	1	1	27	1	0	0	0
5	10	4	3	3	1	1	1	1	29	1	0	0	0
6	11	4	3	2	1	1	1	1	32	1	0	0	0

4 Conclusions

In this paper, we propose the approach for the problem of multicriteria scheduling strategy synthesis in computing systems with a scalable architecture.

First, this approach allows us to obtain a strategy, which is conditionally optimal by a partial criterion. Second, the strategy synthesis may be decomposed by the totality of partial criteria. Finally, the general decomposition allows us to generate scheduling strategies by a vector criterion for different models of the same program.

Acknowledgments. This work was supported by the Russian Foundation for Basic Research, grant no. 06-01-00027.

References

1. Casavant, T.L., Kuhl, J.G.: A Taxonomy of Scheduling in General-Purpose Distributed Computing Systems. IEEE Trans. on Software Eng. 14(2), 141–154 (1988)
2. Ioannidou, M.A., Karatza, H.D.: Multi-site Scheduling with Multiple Job Reservations and Forecasting Methods. In: Guo, M., Yang, L.T., Di Martino, B., Zima, H.P., Dongarra, J., Tang, F. (eds.) ISPA 2006. LNCS, vol. 4330, pp. 894–903. Springer, Heidelberg (2006)
3. Kurowski, K., Nabrzyski, J., Oleksiak, A., et al.: Multicriteria Aspects of Grid Resource Management. In: Nabrzyski, J., Schopf, J.M., Weglarz, J. (eds.) Grid Resource Management. State of the Art and Future Trends, pp. 271–293. Kluwer Acad. Publ., Boston (2003)
4. Zhang, Y., Franke, H., Morreira, J.E., et al.: An Integrated Approach to Parallel Scheduling Using Gang-Scheduling, Backfilling, and Migration. IEEE Trans. on Parallel and Distributed Systems 14(3), 236–247 (2003)
5. Hanzich, M., Gine, F., Hernandez, P., et al.: CISNE: A New Integral Approach for Scheduling Parallel Applications on Non-dedicated Clusters. In: Cunha, J.C., Medeiros, P.D. (eds.) Euro-Par 2005. LNCS, vol. 3648, pp. 220–230. Springer, Heidelberg (2005)
6. Toporkov, V.V.: Optimization of Resource Allocation in Hard-Real-Time Environment. J. of Computer and Systems Sciences Int. 43(1), 383–393 (2004)
7. Toporkov, V.V.: Decomposition Schemes for Synthesis of Scheduling Strategies in Scalable Systems. J. of Computer and Systems Sciences Int. 45(1), 77–88 (2006)

Latencies of Conflicting Writes on Contemporary Multicore Architectures

Josef Weidendorfer, Michael Ott, Tobias Klug, and Carsten Trinitis

Technische Universität München
Lehrstuhl für Rechnertechnik und Rechnerorganisation / Parallelrechnerarchitektur
Boltzmannstraße 3, 85748 Garching bei München
{weidendo,ottmi,klug,trinitic}@in.tum.de

Abstract. This paper provides a detailed investigation of latency penalties caused by repeated memory writes to nearby memory cells from different threads in parallel programs. When such writes map to the same corresponding cache lines in multiple processors, one can observe the so called *false sharing* effect. This effect can unnecessarily hamper parallel code due to the line granularity based cache hierarchy, which is common on contemporary processor architectures. In this contribution, a benchmark allowing for quantitative estimates about the consequences of the false sharing effect, is presented. Results show that multicore architectures with shared cache can reduce unwanted effects of false sharing.

Keywords: Multicore, CMP, False Sharing, Cache.

1   Introduction

Within the scope of MMI (Munich Multicore Initiative)[1], which was founded by Lehrstuhl für Rechnertechnik und Rechnerorganisation / Parallelrechnerarchitektur (Prof. Dr. A. Bode) at Technische Universität München, there is research going on about positive effects of shared caches in the latest multicore architectures. These are found for example in recent Intel processors based on the Intel Core microarchitecture. The processors consist of two or four cores, using shared cache memory for two cores, respectively [1].

Multicore architectures provide a large number of design alternatives with regard to cache hierarchies. Within this context, an interesting topic is the effect of shared or distributed cache memory on the performance of parallel programs. In general, shared cache memory has an advantage if cores need to access the same data, or, if a parallel application requires a lot of synchronization and communication effort.

This paper deals with an effect which can increase synchronization efforts for parallel applications due to inefficient programming: *false sharing*. False sharing occurs if two threads running on two different processors repeatedly access independent data which are physically located at addresses close to each other.

---

[1] http://mmi.in.tum.de

V. Malyshkin (Ed.): PaCT 2007, LNCS 4671, pp. 318–327, 2007.

Although the data accesses are independent, the hardware might need to perform synchronization, as cache architectures work on blocks of data (a typical granularity in contemporary architectures being 64 bytes). This effect can significantly slow down program execution [2]. However, the detection of false sharing requires detailed analysis with appropriate programming tools, thus, optimizations aiming at preventing false sharing effects are often omitted.

The next section will explain in detail under which circumstances *false sharing* effects can occur. Section 3 deals with related work, section 4 describes a benchmark program capable of making negative *false sharing* effects visible and detecting advantages of contemporary processor architectures related to false sharing. Finally, results obtained on several processor architectures are presented in section 5, and section 6 gives an outlook on future investigations regarding shared caches on multicore architectures.

2   False Sharing

On shared memory based multiprocessor systems, threads in a parallel program exchange data via commonly used main memory addresses.

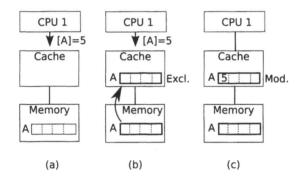

Fig. 1. Write Access to Memory in a Write Back Cache

Due to the memory wall problem (i.e. the difference in access speed between main memory and CPUs), caches, holding a copy of a memory block in buffers which are closer to the CPU are utilized. On the one hand, caches are faster than memory, on the other hand, their capacity comprises only a portion of that of main memory. In order to avoid unnecessary load on the memory bus, caches are often designed as *write back*-caches: When writing data to main memory, the corresponding block is fetched from main memory into the appropriate cache line. Then the block is marked for exclusive use by the CPU – this corresponds to the *exclusive* state in the MESI [3,4] cache coherency protocol. From now, the copy can be modified in the cache, see fig. 1, (a - c). The state switches to *modified*, without requiring a bus transaction. The new value is not written back

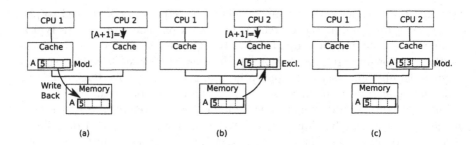

Fig. 2. Two CPUs writing to the same Cache Line

into main memory, under the assumption that the CPU will subsequently write to this memory block, thus avoiding time consuming bus transactions.

It is now assumed that the second CPU writes data to a neighboring cell in main memory (which belongs to the same memory block). Since this scenario is not regarded as real communication between two CPUs, the common use of the same memory block is referred to as *false sharing*. For the write access to succeed, the memory block must first be loaded into the second CPU's local cache. Prior to this, however, a time consuming write back from the first CPU's local cache is required in order to update the data in main memory (see fig. 2, (a)). Then, the memory block (which is now valid) can be loaded into the second CPU's cache and modified as required (see fig. 2, (b) and (c)).

False sharing occurs as an undesired event. Normally, variables being used by two CPUs but not required for data exchange would be written to separate memory blocks. This means that each CPU works with its own cache copy, making the caches' write back strategy work: No bus transactions are required after the data has been loaded into the cache. Contrary to that, in case of false sharing the memory block has to be written back and reloaded with each write transaction, i.e. two undesired full memory transactions are required.

The scenario described above assumes that each CPU has its own separate cache memory. Even if two cache levels are used, and the second level cache is implemented as a shared cache, false sharing occurs if the first level cache is implemented as a write back cache separately for each CPU, as is the case with Intel's Core 2 Duo architecture. However, due to the low latency, writing back from level 2 cache can be intercepted by the other CPU core, which means that a bus transaction might not be required.

3   Related Work

Several scientific papers dealing with *false sharing* have been published. In [5], several definitions of *false sharing* and its consequences are introduced and investigated with regard to their applicability. The authors conclude that a quantitative evaluation of the consequences of *false sharing* is extremely difficult, as it depends on several different parameters, such as cache line size, data layout, application specific data access patterns, coherency protocol overhead, etc. When an application is adapted to a specific processor architecture to avoid *false sharing*, side effects affecting the memory system usually occur. Therefore, it is extremely difficult to separate and measure *false sharing* effects from other effects mentioned above.

In [6], Desikan et al. introduce a method called *Sharing Speculation*, in which data is loaded speculatively: When the processor wants to load some data, which resides in a cache line marked as invalid, the data is sent to the processor but marked as speculative.

At the same time, cache coherency operations are started in order to make the cache line valid. As soon as the cache line has been updated, the cache controller checks if the data has been modified. If it has not been modified, *false sharing* has occurred, and the processor is informed that the speculation was successful. If the data has been modified, the cache sends the correct value to the processor, which needs to make sure that a valid state is restored.

In [7], Liu and King introduce the concept of *Sectored Caches*. Each cache line is split into sub-blocks representing the elementary coherency units. The advantage of this concept is that in case of *false sharing*, the cache line does not need to be marked as invalid, as long as the corresponding sub-blocks are coherent. The authors present an extension of the MESI-protocol using *sectored caches*. By simulating representative benchmark scenarios, it is shown that 30 to 80 per cent of all cache misses caused by *false sharing* could be avoided. A similar concept is used by Kadiyala et al. in [8]. In addition, their approach allows to dynamically adapt the size of the sub-blocks.

The publications mentioned above either deal with evaluating *false sharing* or propose mechanisms to reduce its effects. However, none of the papers has investigated the effects on multicore processors with shared caches.

4   Benchmark

For the investigation of the *false sharing* problem, a synthetic benchmark which artificially causes *false sharing*, has been developed: First, an array whose size can be specified by a parameter is stored on the heap. The array's base address is aligned to an address that can be divided by 64, which ensures that this base address corresponds to the starting address of a cache line. By the use of OpenMP directives, two threads are generated. Via sched_setaffinity() system calls, it is ensured that these threads are bound to separate processor cores. Thus, cache thrashing by moving threads can be avoided. Both threads then execute in three phases, iterating through the previously allocated array (see fig. 3). The number of iterations can also be specified by a parameter. For the investigations carried out for this paper, the number of iterations was chosen such that the benchmark lasts for about 10 seconds. More specifically, the three phases work as follows:

- In the first phase the *false sharing* scenario is simulated: Both threads are using the previously allocated memory area. In each iteration, each thread

writes one word into the array, respectively. Thread #0 always writes to
the first word in a cache line, thread #1 writes to the second word in the
same cache line. After each iteration, the target address is incremented by
64 Bytes, which corresponds to the cache line length in contemporary x86
processors. If the memory address exceeds the ending address of the allocated
memory space, it is reset to its base address. As long as the array's size
exceeds 64 Bytes, it is ensured that each iteration accesses another cache
line. The number of iterations should be chosen such that cache lines are
accessed multiple times.

- In the second phase, a scenario with no *false sharing* is simulated: The array
  is divided such that each thread is assigned half of it. Then, each thread
  executes the same memory access as in phase 1 on its own memory region.
  By ensuring that both threads work on separate memory regions, it is guaranteed that one thread never accesses a cache line which resides in the other
  processor core's cache.
- In phase 3, the overhead caused by the loop run and the computation of
  the memory addresses is measured. The same loop as in phases 1 and 2 is
  executed, with one minor difference: No memory access to the array takes
  place inside the loop.

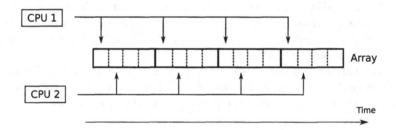

Fig. 3. Access to the Array in the Benchmark Program

Upon entering and upon leaving a phase, each thread reads its CPU's time-
stamp counter by calling **rdtsc**. From the difference between those two values,
an average value for both threads is calculated. The three phases are executed
100 times, respectively. Upon each execution, three time stamps are saved, yielding a minimum, a maximum, and an average value for each phase over all 100
executions. These values are then divided by the number of iterations, which
finally gives minimum-, maximum-, and average values for the required clock
cycles for a single iteration. This allows for a comparison of the measurements
for CPUs with different clock rates. In addition, the overhead measurement in
phase 3 gives some hints with regard to the real costs of a pure memory access.

As described in section 2, a false sharing event causes a write back of the
corresponding cache line. The number of such events are additionally measured
using hardware performance counters (e.g. for the Intel Core architecture this
event is called L1D_M_EVICT).

Critical Evaluation of the Benchmark Test

The basic idea of the benchmark is to enforce *false sharing* with each write access to the array. This means that both processors write alternately to a memory block in the array. In order to guarantee this, the processors would have to be synchronized. Since x86 synchronization primitives are carried out via the memory bus, this would cause an overhead tampering the benchmark results significantly. Therefore, synchronization is avoided, which can lead to variations in the results. These variations can be derived from finding minima and maxima over 100 test series. As it is shown in section 5, the average value is stable and close to the maximum. Furthermore, the data derived from hardware performance counters allows one to verify whether the number of witnessed cache line evictions (i.e. false sharing events) corresponds to the number of write accesses. Thus, even without synchronization, the benchmark can be regarded as representative.

5 Results

Memory access latencies cannot explicitly be measured on modern superscalar processor architectures, as the instructions following the write access are immediately executed, and the write access is performed simultaneously in the background. One way to implicitly measure the latencies is to repeatedly execute memory accesses and thereby completely utilize the memory subsystem. Then, the latency of the slowest transaction in the memory subsystem can be determined in the critical path. In this case, a transaction is part of the critical path, if its completion is required for starting the next transaction.

By provoking *false sharing*, the cache coherency protocol's latency times (see fig. 2) determine the duration of a complete memory access. This is denoted as normalized clock cycles in the test series. The pure loop overhead in the

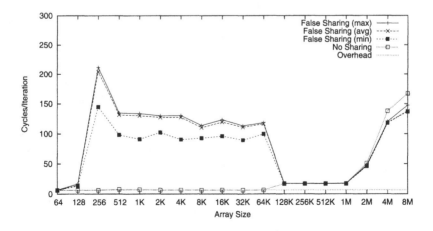

Fig. 4. Intel Core Duo T2600 with shared L2-Cache

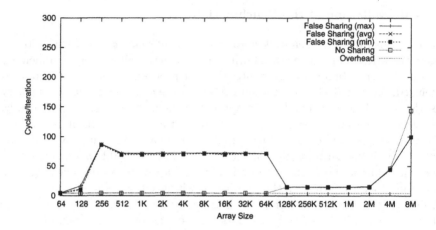

Fig. 5. Intel Xeon 5300 with shared L2-Cache

benchmark has no influence here, as it is completely overlapped by the higher latency of the memory subsystem.

The following systems were used as a test environment:

- Intel Core Duo T2600, 2.16 GHz, 667 MHz FSB, 2 MB shared L2-cache, 1 processor (2 cores), 1 GB DDR2 667 MHz
- Intel Xeon 5300 (preliminary), 2.40 GHz, 1066 MHz FSB, 2x4 MB shared L2-cache (for 2 cores, respectively), 2 processors (8 cores), 8 GB DDR2 667 MHz
- AMD Opteron 275, 2.20 GHz, Hypertransport 1000 MHz, 2x1 MB distributed L2-Cache, 2 processors (4 cores), 4 GB DDR1 400 MHz

Figures 4 and 5 show the results for Intel CPUs with shared L2 cache, respectively. Due to the very low latency times for array sizes up to 128 Bytes, it is assumed that hardly any coherency transactions are carried out, and the write accesses are not always visible from outside. This assumption is also supported by the hardware performance counter measurements: Only on array sizes larger than 256 Bytes the number of cache line evictions matches the number of write accesses. This phenomenon can only be explained by the existence of a local write buffer above the L1 cache. When the latency increases rapidly at 256 Bytes, the write buffer is full, and its contents become visible from outside, requiring cache coherency protocol execution. With further increasing array size, the frequency of memory accesses to the same address is reduced, which seems to hide the actual costs of such an access. From an array size of 128KB, the obtained value drops to the latency of an L2 read access. This can be explained by the fact that the array no longer fits into the L1 cache (i.e. the write back is no longer in the critical path, but instead has been carried out before by an eviction of the modified cache line). *False sharing* no longer occurs. From array sizes of 1 MB (Core Duo) or 2 MB (Xeon) the array no longer fits into the L2 cache, and the obtained latency is that of a read transaction from main memory.

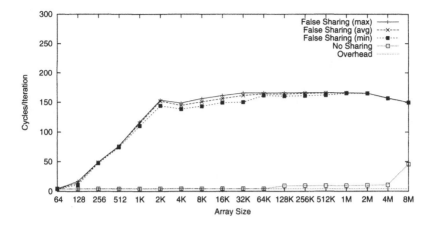

Fig. 6. Intel Xeon 5300 with separate L2-Cache

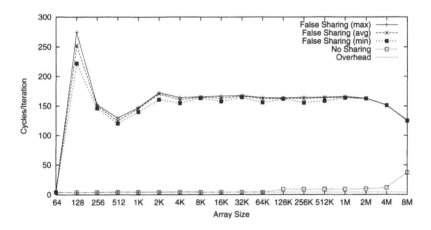

Fig. 7. Intel Xeon 5300 on separate CPUs

Figures 6 and 7 show the measurement results for the Intel Xeon 5300. In the first case, the threads are bound to two cores located on the same processor with separate L2 caches. In the second case, the threads are executed on two separate processors. One would expect similar results for both cases, which holds true for array sizes from 2KB. Latencies obtained here correspond to those of main memory accesses. Thus, it can be assumed that cache coherency is realized by writing data to main memory. As long as the array size does not exceed the L2 cache's capacity, *false sharing* occurs frequently. The effects which can be observed up to an array size of 2KB are subject to future research.

Figure 8 shows the results for the AMD Opteron 275, with two cores on one processor with separate caches. For the measurements whose results can be seen in fig. 9, one core on two identical processors was used, respectively. Although

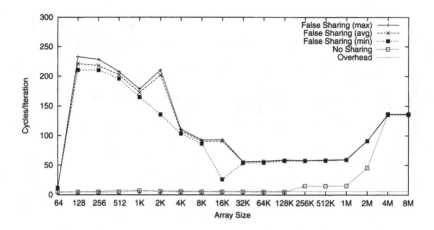

Fig. 8. AMD Opteron X2 275 with separate L2-Cache

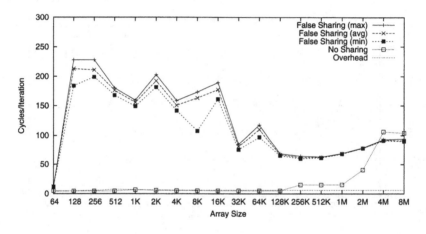

Fig. 9. AMD Opteron X2 275 on separate CPUs

some variations can be observed in fig. 9, both experiments show similar characteristics. The variations probably occur due to side affects caused by the NUMA
architecture. When directly comparing the results to the ones in figures 6 and 7,
it can be observed that for Opteron processors, the latencies drop continuously
after an initial peak, until they eventually become stable for array sizes from
32KB. The level obtained for these array sizes is significantly lower than that
for Intel CPUs. The difference can be explained by the use of the MOESI [9] coherency protocol in AMD CPUs. In contrast to the standard MESI protocol (as
being used by Intel processors), MOESI allows for direct exchange of cache lines
between two processors. This also yields advantages with regard to execution
times.

6 Conclusions and Outlook

In this paper, *false sharing* was investigated for contemporary multicore architectures. It could be shown that for processors with shared L2 cache, less performance is lost by this effect. As long as the working set exceeds the L1 cache's capacity, *false sharing* is completely avoided. For processors with distributed L2 caches, the performance loss can be reduced by the MOESI coherency protocol.

The benchmark introduced in this paper shows overlapping effects. Thus, the further improvement as well as the development of additional benchmarks, allowing for separate investigation of these effects, will be subject to further research. In the long term, it is planned to develop a tool that enables the user to make assumptions about advantages and disadvantages of multicore architectures with different caches or cache hierarchies.

References

1. Intel Corporation: Intel 64 and IA-32 Architectures: Software Developer's Manual, Denver, CO, USA (2006)
2. Torrellas, J., Lam, H.S., Hennessy, J.L.: False sharing and spatial locality in multi-processor caches. IEEE Trans. Comput. 43(6), 651–663 (1994)
3. Papamarcos, M.S., Patel, J.H.: A low-overhead coherence solution for multiprocessors with private cache memories. In: ISCA '98: 25 years of the international symposia on Computer architecture (selected papers), pp. 284–290. ACM Press, New York (1998)
4. Archibald, J., Baer, J.-L.: Cache coherence protocols: evaluation using a multiprocessor simulation model. ACM Trans. Comput. Syst. 4(4), 273–298 (1986)
5. Bolosky, W.J., Scott, M.L.: False sharing and its effect on shared memory performance. In: Proc. of the USENIX Symposium on Experiences with Distributed and Multiprocessor Systems (SEDMS IV), San Diego, CA, pp. 57–71 (1993)
6. Desikan, R., Burger, D., Keckler, S.W.: Sharing speculation: A mechanism for low-latency access to falsely shared data. Technical Report CS-TR-03-05, The University of Texas at Austin, Department of Computer Sciences, Friday, 11 August, 106 16:16:41 GMT (2003)
7. Liu, K.C., King, C.T.: On the effectiveness of sectored caches in reducing false sharing misses. In: International Conference on Parallel and Distributed Systems (ICPADS '97), December 11-13, 1997, Seoul, Korea, Proceedings, pp. 352–359 (1997)
8. Kadiyala, M., Bhuyan, L.N.: A dynamic cache sub-block design to reduce false sharing. In: ICCD '95: Proceedings of the 1995 International Conference on Computer Design, Washington, DC, USA, p. 313. IEEE Computer Society Press, Los Alamitos (1995)
9. Sweazey, P., Smith, A.J.: A class of compatible cache consistency protocols and their support by the ieee futurebus. In: ISCA '86: Proceedings of the 13th annual international symposium on Computer architecture, pp. 414–423. IEEE Computer Society Press, Los Alamitos (1986)

A Novel Self-Similar (S^2) Traffic Filter to Enhance E-Business Success by Improving Internet Communication Channel Fault Tolerance

Allan K.Y. Wong[1], Wilfred W.K. Lin[2], Tharam S. Dillon[2], and Jackei H.K. Wong[1]

[1] Department of Computing, Hong Kong Polytechnic University, Hong Kong S.A.R.
[2] Faculty of Information Technology, University of Technology Sydney, Australia
csalwong@comp.polyu.edu.hk, wilfred@it.uts.edu.au,
tharam@it.uts.edu.au, jwong@purapharm.com

Abstract. Internet traffic patterns can cause serious buffer overflow in electronic business (e-business) systems. This leads to widespread retransmission that prolongs the service roundtrip time (RTT). As a result customers are unhappy and avoid returning to do more business. The previous Real-Time Traffic Pattern Detector (RTPD) was proposed to improve Internet channel fault tolerance. With RTPD support time-critical applications can identify the traffic patterns and invoke the corresponding measures to neutralize their ill effects in a dynamic manner. The extant RTPD, however, cannot detect self-similar traffic. This inspired the development of the novel self-similarity (S^2) filter proposed in this paper, which makes the RTPD capability more complete. The "RTPD + S^2" package is the *enhanced* RTPD or ERTPD package. The test results indicate that the addition of the S^2 mechanism can indeed contribute to improved e-business communication channels over the Internet.

Keywords: S^2 filter, e-business, Internet traffic, ERTPD, dynamic buffer size tuning.

1 Introduction

Electronic business (e-business) includes both PC-based e-commerce and mobile business (m-business) on the mobile Internet [1]. No matter what form that an e-business setup assumes it still fits the general framework of Internet-based distributed computing. E-businesses are intrinsically time-critical because they should deliver their service within a reasonable time. This requires fast service response, which results from fault-tolerant communication channels. For example, only with fast service response can an e-business galvanize consumers within their short attention spans [2].

In the distributed computing framework, which includes mobile (wireless) and tethered (wireline) activities, customers and e-businesses (e.g. e-shops) interact in a client/server relationship. Wireless interactions involve client mobility, and the

V. Malyshkin (Ed.): PaCT 2007, LNCS 4671, pp. 328–339, 2007.
© Springer-Verlag Berlin Heidelberg 2007

communication cell in which a client/server interaction is conducted is the smart space [3] (Figure 1). A mobile client continues to interact with the same server (e.g. e-shop) while moving from one smart space to another. In contrast, wireline interactions are cable-based.

Figure 1 shows the essence of an e-shop operation, which is typical of those that sell shoes in Mainland China. The basic elements are: a virtual e-showroom, its own shoe manufacturing facility, a remote order service (ROS), and a list of collaborators that can supply the goods. For example, if the right shoes are not found in the e-shop's virtual showroom, the client simply provides the detailed specification so that the e-shop can either custom-make it or locate it from its collaborators. A key to success for e-shops is a fast service response that makes customers happy and willingly return for more business. Part of the fast response requirement is good communication channel fault tolerance.

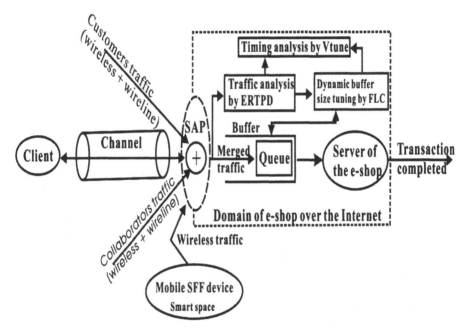

Fig. 1. Client/server interaction of an e-shop

Service response (i.e. service roundtrip time (RTT) in the client/server interaction) can be delayed seriously by widespread retransmission. If the communication channel in Figure 1 has the error probability ρ, the average number of trials (ANT) to get a successful transmission is $ANT = \sum_{j=1}^{\infty} jP_j \approx \frac{1}{(1-\rho)}$, where P_j the probability of success at the jth trial. One factor that enlarges ρ and prolongs ANT is e-shop buffer overflow. The overflow is caused by the unpredictable nature of the incoming request streams (in the form of IAT (inter-arrival times)), which merge (i.e. represented by

$\oplus$ in Figure 1) at the service access point (SAP) [4]. A sudden burst of short IATs would surge the queue length to overflow its buffer easily. Self-similar traffic usually associates with this kind of short bursts [5]. Post-mortem/off-line analyses confirm that Internet traffic patterns can be short-range dependence (SRD) (e.g. Markovian) or long-range dependence (LRD) (e.g. self-similar or heavy-tailed) [6]. One way to eliminate buffer overflow is to effectively make the buffer length always cover the queue length [7]. This strategy is called dynamic buffer tuning [8], which should be statistical [9]. To work effectively, dynamic buffer tuning needs RTPD support because it needs to detect the current traffic pattern and reconfigure to ward off its traffic ill effects on the fly [10]. This results in better channel fault tolerance and shorter client/server service response for e-business.

The only tool published in the literature for on-line traffic pattern detection and analysis is the *real-time traffic pattern detector* (RTPD) [11]. It differentiates SRD from LRD but cannot confirm if a LRD pattern is self-similar or heavy-tailed. The S^2 filter proposed in this paper augments the RTPD so that self-similar traffic patterns can be correctly identified spontaneously. It works by the "*continuous aggregate based (CAB)*" mechanism, and the "RTPD $+ S^2$" combination is the *enhanced RTPD* or ERTPD.

2 Related Work

The Internet's sheer size and heterogeneity naturally involve different protocols for client/server interactions [12]. As a result the Internet traffic follows the power laws [13], and over time the traffic pattern change suddenly, for example, back and forth between LRD and SRD [14]. Using the Hurst (H) effect as the yardstick [15], LRD is in the $0.5 < H < 1$ range and $0 < H < 0.5$ for SRD [6]. The RTPD core is the based on the traditional R/S (*rescaled adjusted statistics*) approach for off-line applications. Basically it is the "$M^3 RT + R/S + filtration$" package, but R/S is now enhanced (explained later). The $M^3 RT$ module is a *micro Convergence Algorithm* (CA) or MCA implementation [16]. It is micro because it exists as a logical object, which can be invoked for service anytime and anywhere by message passing. MCA predicts the mean of any waveform quickly and accurately in a dynamic fashion. In effect, the "$M^3 RT / MCA + R/S$" is the enhanced R/S (i.e. E-R/S) mechanism. The *filtration* process activates the right filter to identify the exact traffic pattern. For example, the *modified QQ-plot filter* identifies "heavy-tailedness". The novel S^2 filter enables the filtration process to successfully identify self-similarity. The traditional R/S is actually the following expressions,

$$R/S = \frac{\max\{W_i : i = 1, 2, ..., k\} - \min\{W_i : i = 1, 2, ..., k\}}{\sqrt{\operatorname{var}(X)}}$$, which normally caters

to off-line operations, where $W_i = \sum_{m=1}^{i} (X_m - \overline{X})$ for $i = 1, 2, ... k$ and $\overline{X}$ the mean by $\overline{X} = \frac{1}{k} \sum_{i=1}^{k} X_i$. The best value for k has to be found by trial and error. This uncertainty is a serious drawback in practice because the R/S accuracy and speed depend on k. The R/S ratio is the rescaled range of the stochastic process X over the interval k. X is the discrete process $\{X_i : i = 1,2,...k\}$. The log-log plot $\frac{R}{S} \approx (\frac{k}{2})^H$ yields H [6].

$$M_i = \frac{M_{i-1} + \sum_{j=1}^{j=F-1} m_j^i}{F} \dots\dots (2.1); M_0 = m_{j=0}^{i=1} \dots\dots (2.2); i \geq 1$$

The CA operation is based on the *Central Limit Theorem*. It is represented by the equations: (2.1) and (2.2). The estimated mean M_i in the ith prediction cycle works with the chosen (fixed) F (*flush limit*) number of data points. The cycle time therefore depends on the delay for collecting the F data points. It was confirmed that M_i has the fastest convergence for F=14 [16]. The other parameters include: a) M_{i-1} is the feedback of the last predicted mean to the current M_i prediction cycle, b) m_j^i is the jth data item sampled in the current i^{th} M_i cycle for $j = 1,2,3,....,(F-1)$, and c) M_0 is the first data sample when the MCA had first started. In the E-R/S framework M_i replaces $\overline{X}$; that is $W_i = \sum_{m=1}^{i} (X_m - M_i)$. This makes E-R/S suitable for real-time applications because the number of data items (e.g. IAT) to calculate W_i is now predictable (i.e. $F = 14$).

When ERTPD is in action the following elements, E-R/S, M^3RT and the invoked filter, are running in parallel. The overall ERTPD execution time depends on the module that has the longest execution. Repeated measurements confirmed that S^2 has the longest computation time. For example, under certain conditions the *Intel's VTune Performance Analyzer* [17] recorded the following average execution times in clock cycles: 981 for E-R/S, 250 for M^3RT , 520 for the *modified QQ-plot filter* and 1455 for S^2 . This means that the overall ERTPD execution time depends on S^2 .

3 The Self-Similarity (S^2) Filter

The S^2 filter identifies self-similar patterns on the fly. In fact, LRD traffic has at least two fractal elements: heavy-tailed and self-similar. The self-similar nature of many fractal point processes comes from the heavy-tailed distributions, for example the FRP (Fractal Renewal Process) IAT distribution. The heavy-tailed property, however, is not a necessary condition for self-similarity because at least the FSNDPP (Fractal-Shot-Noise-Driven Poisson Process) has no heavy-tailed property at all. The theoretical foundation for the novel S^2 filter is the "*asymptotically second-order self-similarity*" concept, which is called hereafter the *statistical* $2^{nd} OSS$ (or simply $S2^{nd} OSS$). This concept associates with a sufficiently large *aggregate at any level l or lag l* in a stochastic process X. If $X^m = \{X_l^m : l \geq 1\}$ is an aggregate in X of size m , $S2^{nd} OSS$ for a large enough m means that the associated *autocorrelation function* (ACF) $r^m(l)$ (i.e. for X^m) is proportional to $l^{-(2-2H)}$.

$S2^{nd} OSS$ is LRD, then its ACF is non-summable, $r^m(l) = \sum_{l-1}^{\infty} r^m = \infty$ .The condition " $r^m(l) \propto l^{-(2-2H)}$ for a large m " is mathematically the *slowly decaying variance* property. For a $2^{nd} OSS$ process X and $0.5 < H < 1$ the value relationship $\beta = 2 - 2H$ holds [6].

The equations (3.1) and (3.2) summarize the $S2^{nd} OSS$ property and they hold even for the weaker condition in equation (3.3). The *slowly decaying variance* property is conspicuous from the log-log plot for (3.4). $\log(Var(X^m))$ versus $\log(m)$ yields a straight line with slope $-\beta$; $H = 1 - (\beta/2)$. The working principle of the S^2 filter is to find β for X^m

$Var(X^m) = \dfrac{1}{m^{(2-2H)}} Var(X)$	Equation (3.1)
$r^m(l) = r(k)$	Equation (3.2)
$\lim_{m \to \infty} r^m(l) = r(k)$	Equation (3.3)
$\log(Var(X^m)) = \log(Var(X)) - \beta \log(m)$	Equation (3.4)

S^2 works with the initial aggregate size m (e.g. $m = 30$). If the sampled data points do not show stationarity, then another m data points are added so that the next round of stationarity testing will be based on the $2m$ data points. This process is called the "*continuous aggregate based (CAB)*" mechanism. The stationarity (or Gaussianity) test, which continues until it is confirmed, is based on the "*kurtosis and skewness (KS)*" technique. The kurtosis and skewness values together indicate if an aggregate is stationary. The R/S and S^2 elements in the ERTPD mechanism works for stationary conditions only. The normal bell/Gaussian curve represents an ideal stationary process. It has kurtosis and skewness equal to 3 and 0 respectively. The ideal [3,0] pair is difficult to obtain statistically, but previous empirical experience [PRDC05] show that stationarity can be established with chosen thresholds, for example [$\pm 6, \pm 3$]. Skewness measures a distribution's symmetry. The distribution skews to the right for positive skewness and to the left for a negative one. Higher positive kurtosis than 3 means a more "peaked" distribution. A negative kurtosis means a "flatter" one. Skewness is $\dfrac{\sum_{i=1}^{N}\left(x_i - \bar{x}\right)^3}{(N-1)\,sd^3}$, where $\bar{x}$ is the mean, sd the standard deviation value and N the number of data points in the aggregate. Kurtosis is

$$\frac{\sum_{i=1}^{N}\left(x_i - \bar{x}\right)^4}{(N-1)\,sd^4}.$$

4 Experimental Results

Simulations were designed to verify that the S^2 filter does indeed:

a)   Detect self-similar Internet traffic patterns correctly on the fly
b)   Enhance communication channel fault tolerance.

For the verification of point (b) the S^2 filter is combined with the FLC (Fuzzy Logic Controller) dynamic buffer tuner [18]. The argument is that if the S^2 can reduce the perturbations in the FLC control process consistently, then it contributes to the improvement of the channel fault tolerance because the chance for buffer overflow and thus widespread retransmission, is lessened.

The setup for the experiment is similar to Figure 1. The "traffic analysis by ERTPD" box traces the traffic pattern that produces the dynamic buffer tuning result. The FLC supported by the ERTPD mechanism, which includes S^2, tunes the buffer size on the fly to eliminate buffer overflow due to traffic ill effects. The traffic between the client and the SAP is either a simulated or pre-collected IAT traffic trace. The self-similar patterns were simulated by the Kramer tool [19]. The VTune tool [17] was used to measure the S^2 execution times under different conditions. The timing analysis with VTune is important for evaluating the S^2 fitness in time-critical applications in general.

Table 1 shows one set of results produced by the S^2 filter. The filter identifies the self-similar traffic patterns correctly with at least 90% confidence (i.e. the threshold Th_{R^2} was set at 90%). The data segment made up of the first five aggregates is basically monofractal because of their very similar H values. The aggregates, 6 and 7

Table 1. The S^2 filter identifies self-similar traffic correctly

Aggregate number	β slope	H (Hurst value), $H = (1 - \dfrac{\beta}{2})$	R^2 (coefficient of determination)	Aggregates in sequence
1	0.6583	0.671	0.956 (95.6%)	1
2	0.6809	0.660	0.975 (97.5%)	2
3	0.6425	0.679	0.977 (97.7%)	3
4	0.6473	0.677	0.972 (97.2%)	4
5	0.4685	0.766	0.959 (95.9%)	5
6	0.3762	0.812	0.885 (88.5%) (less than Th_{R^2})	6 (rejected)
7	0.1978	0.901	0.605 (60.5%)	7 (rejected)

Table 2. S^2 results for the Sony trace in light of stationarity, SRD and LRD

For basic aggregate size of m = 32	
Total no. of continuous aggregates	2548
Stationarity (%), SRD and LRD patterns intertwined	2446 (96.00%)
SRD (%)	1983 (81.07%)
LRD (%)	439 (17.95%)

Table 3. S^2 results for the Sony trace (for SRD and LRD differentiation)

Differentiation between self-similar and heavy-tailed traffic patterns	
Total number of LRD aggregates (Table 2)	439
Self-similar (SS) (%)	337 (76.77%)
Heavy-tailed (HT) (%)	375 (85.42%)
Both self-similar and heavy-tailed (%)	289 (65.83%)
$P(SS\|HT)$; both self-similar and heavy-tailed (overlapped)	77.07%
$P(SS\|\overline{HT})$; self-similar but not heavy-tailed	75.00%

are rejected because they do not satisfy the Th_{R^2} threshold. The collection of every aggregate (from 1 to 7) follows these steps: a) start with the basic aggregate size of $m=30$ data points; b) carry out the Gaussianity test with the KS technique; and c) if

Gaussinaity does not exist then collect $m=30$ more data points. If Gaussianity is confirmed then β is computed. In fact, the experimental results for different real-life Internet traffic traces indicate that the Internet traffic pattern definitely changes over time. This empirical fact is demonstrated here by the Sony trace [20], and the relevant results show that SRD and LRD data segments intertwine/interleave in the Sony trace as shown in Table 2. The basic aggregate size for the experiments with the Sony trace was m = 32. The percentages of SRD and LRD segments are 81.07% and 17.95% respectively. Table 3 shows that the percentages for self-similar and heavy-tailed patterns for the LRD segments are respectively 76.77% and 85.42%. Of the 439 LRD segments 289 (i.e. 65.83%) show both self-similar and heavy-tailed characteristics. This is possible because self-similarity usually comes from heavy-tailed-ness, even though the latter is not a necessary condition for the former.

4.1 Results with the FLC Dynamic Buffer Tuner

Dynamic buffer tuners were used successfully to shorten the service response time in different e-business setups [18]. Practically, improved tuner accuracy means shorter client/server roundtrip time (RTT). The FLC tuner was used as the test bed because so far it is the most efficient in the field [18]. Figure 2 shows the FLC design (i.e. FLC[4x4]) for the experiments. Its essence includes the following:

a) It uses the rate of change of the server queue length, $\dfrac{dQ}{dt}$ for derivative control.

b) It uses the "queue length over buffer length (QOB)" ratio for proportional control.

c) The dot marks the QOB reference (i.e. QOB_R) of 0.8, and X marks the inert "*don't care*" state.

d) The control decisions, which depend on the current QOB and dQ/dt values, include: Addition (buffer elongation) or "+", Subtraction (buffer shrinkage) or "-", and "*don't care*".

e) The linguistic variables for the FLC are as follows:

i) For QOB: ML for *Much Less* than QOB_R, L for *Less* than QOB_R, G for *Greater* than QOB_R, and MG for *Much Greater* than QOB_R.

ii) For the current dQ/dt : NL for *Negative* and *Larger* than the given threshold, NS for *Negative* and *Smaller* than the given threshold, PS for *Positive* and *Smaller* than the given threshold, and PL for *Positive* and *Larger* than the given threshold.

With the linguistic variables fuzzy rules for dynamic buffer tuning can be formulated such as follows (L_{new} and L_{old} denote the adjusted buffer length and the old buffer length respectively; ICM is the buffer adjustment):

Rule 1: If (QOB is MG) AND (dQ/dt is PL) Then Action is "+"(Addition) AND L_{new} = L_{old} + ICM
Rule 2: If (QOB is ML) AND (dQ/dt is NL) Then Action is "-"(Subtraction) AND L_{new} = L_{old} - ICM
Rule 3: If (QOB is L) AND (dQ/dt is NS) Then Action is "X"(Don't care) AND L_{new} = L_{old}

QOB		dQ/dt			
		NL	NS	PS	PL
0.7	ML	-	-	-	-
0.8	L	-	X	X	+
0.9	G	-	X	X	+
	MG	+	+	+	+

Fig. 2. The FLC[4x4] design

In the verification experiments the $\frac{dQ}{dt}$ control was adaptively tuned by a gradient percentage (GP) to produce the minimum mean deviation from QOB_R in the dynamic buffer tuning process. The tuning is adapted according to the traffic pattern identified by the novel ERTPD mechanism on the fly. The mean deviation (MD) is the average deviation from QOB_R in different experiments for the same type of request traffic (e.g. self-similar or Poisson). The GP/MD calibration, which represents our accumulated real-time traffic analysis experience over time, was used for the experiments as shown in Figure 3. The MD is scaled for the plot and 0.05 means five percent. In our experience the deviation from QOB_R for some self-similar traffic conditions under raw FLC control (without ERTPD support) can be as high as 35%. With the ERPTD presence the worst case observed was around 10%. If the ERTPD has detected self-similar traffic, the FLC selects $GP = 8\%$ to minimize MD. This selection yields MD=0.03, which is similar to the Poisson condition ($GP = 5\%$ should be used). A higher MD means increased chance for buffer overflow, widespread retransmission, large ANT, long service response time and unhappy e-business customers. Therefore, it is worthwhile to adapt the GP value to gain a lower MD for improved channel fault tolerance.

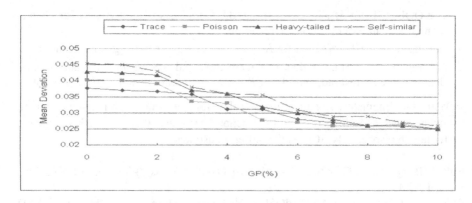

Fig. 3. The calibrated MD versus GP relationship

Figure 4 compares the FLC and "ERTPD + FLC" performance for a self-similar traffic trace simulated by the Kramer tool [19]. It shows that the latter consistently produces a much lower MD. The higher deviation by the raw FLC is around 8% and that for the ERTPD and FLC together (i.e. ERTPD-FLC plot) is only 4%.This is a significant contribution because it lowers the chance of buffer overflow and prevents wastage of memory in the dynamic buffer tuning process. As a fringe benefit the unused buffer memory can be recycled for other tasks in the system for better throughput.

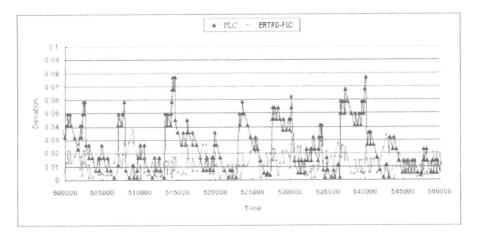

Fig. 4. FLC versus "ERTPD + FLC[4x4]" for a self-similar trace

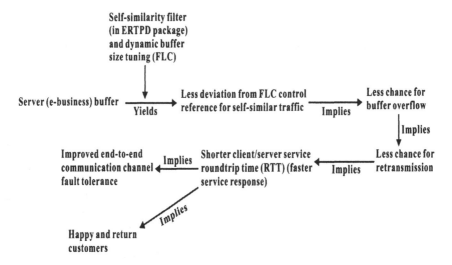

Fig. 5. Summary of positive effects of the S^2 filter at different stages

Figure 5 summarizes the positive effects of the S^2 filter in e-business from different angles. It enables the dynamic buffer size tuner (e.g. FLC) to detect the self-similar traffic conditions and use the detected result to fine-tune the control process. As a result, the deviation from the control reference, namely, QOB_R is lessened. This is translated into less chance for server buffer overflow and thus less retransmission that would prolong the client/server service roundtrip time (RTT). This leads to enhanced fault tolerance for the end-to-end communication channels and faster service response, which makes customers happy and return for more business.

5 Conclusion

The novel self-similarity (S^2) filter should enhance e-business success by improving Internet communication channel fault tolerance. It normally works as part of the ERTPD package in the form of a traffic filter to be invoked at the right moment. The results from different experiments indicate that S^2 can indeed identify self-similar traffic correctly. For example, the FLC dynamic buffer tuner with S^2 support consistently produced less deviation from the chosen QOB_R references for self-similar traffic conditions. As a result e-businesses with ERTPD support should have shorter service response time on average because the chance for buffer overflow to occur is lessened by S^2. The next planned step in the research is to validate ERTPD and S^2 with sizeable e-shops over the open mobile Internet.

Acknowledgment

The authors thank the Hong Kong Polytechnic University for supporting this research with the ZW93 grant.

References

1. Thomas, S.F., Gillenson, M.L.: Mobile Commerce: What It Is and What It Could Be. Communications ACM 46(12), 33–34 (2003)
2. Venkatesh, V., Ramesh, V., Massey, A.P.: Understanding Usability in Mobile Commerce. Communications of the ACM 46(12), 53–56 (2003)
3. Garlan, D., Siewiorek, D.P., Smailagic, A., Steenkiste, P.: Project Aura: Toward Distraction-free Pervasive Computing. IEEE Pervasive Computing 1(2), 22–31 (2002)
4. Wong, A.K.Y., Lin, W.W.K., Ip, M.T.W., Dillon, T.S.: Genetic Algorithm and PID Control Together for Dynamic Anticipative Marginal Buffer Management: An Effective Approach to Enhance Dependability and Performance for Distributed Mobile Object-Based Real-time Computing over the Internet. Journal of Parallel and Distributed Computing (JPDC) 62, 1433–1453 (2002)

5. Wu, R.S.L., Wong, A.K.Y., Dillon, T.S.: RDCT: A Novel Reconfigurable Dynamic Cache Size Tuner to Shorten Information Retrieval Time over the Internet International Journal of Computer Systems. Science & Engineering 19(6), 363–372 (2004)
6. Molnar, S., Dang, T.D., Vidacs, A.: Heavy-Tailedness, Long-Range Dependence and Self-Similarity in Data Traffic. In: Proc. of the 7th Int'l Conference on Telecommunication Systems, Modelling and Analysis, Nashville, USA, pp. 18–21 (1999)
7. Wong, A.K.Y., Dillon, T.S.: A Fault-Tolerant Data Communication Setup to Improve Reliability and Performance for Internet-Based Distributed Applications. In: Proc. of the 1999 Pacific Rim International Symposium on Dependable Computing (PRDC'99), Hong Kong (SAR), pp. 268–275 (December 1999)
8. Wong, A.K.Y., Dillon, T.S., Ip, M.T.W., Lin, W.W.K., Wong, B.: A Collaboration Model for Better Reliability and Performance for Object-Based Distributed Applications over the Internet. International Journal of Computer Applications in Technology, 16, 78–86 (2002)
9. Paxson, V., Floyd, S.: Wide-Area Traffic: The Failure of Poisson Modeling. IEEE/ACM Transactions on Networking 3(3), 226–244 (1995)
10. Lin, W.W.K., Wong, A.K.Y., Dillon, T.S.: A Novel Fuzzy-PID Dynamic Buffer Tuning Model to Eliminate Overflow and Shorten the End-to-End Roundtrip Time for TCP Channels. In: Cao, J., Yang, L.T., Guo, M., Lau, F. (eds.) ISPA 2004. LNCS, vol. 3358, pp. 783–787. Springer, Heidelberg (2004), http://www.springerlink.com/index/VF155CH38XFLLB4H
11. Lin, W.W.K., Wu, R.S.L., Wong, A.K.Y., Dillon, T.S.: A Novel Real-Time Traffic Pattern Detector for Internet Applications. In: Proc. of the Australasian Telecommunication Networks and Applications Conference, Sydney, Australia (ATNAC'04), pp. 224–227 (December 2004)
12. Lewandowski, S.M.: Frameworks for Component-based Client/Server Computing. ACM Computing Surveys 30(1), 3–27 (1998)
13. Medina, A., Matta, I., Byers, J.: On the Origin of Power Laws in Internet Topologies. ACM SIGCOMM 30(2), 18–28 (2000)
14. Willinger, W., Paxson, V., Hiedi, R.H., Taqqu, M.S.: Long-Range Dependence and Data Network Traffic. In: Doukhan, P., et al. (eds.) Theory and Applications of Long-Range Dependence, Birkhauser, pp. 373–408 (2003)
15. Taqqu, M.S.: Fractional Brownian Motion and Long-Range Dependence. In: Doukhan, P., et al. (eds.) Theory and Applications of Long-Range Dependence, pp. 5–38. Birkhauser (2003)
16. Wong, A.K.Y., Wong, J.H.C.: A Convergence Algorithm for Enhancing the Performance of Distributed Applications Running on Sizeable Networks. The International Journal of Computer Systems, Science & Engineering 16(4), 229–236 (2001)
17. Intel's VTune Performance Analyzer, http://ww.intel.com/support/performancetools/vtune/v5
18. Lin, W.W.K., Wong, A.K.Y., Dillon, T.S.: Application of Soft Computing Techniques to Adaptive User Buffer Overflow Control on the Internet. IEEE Transactions of Systems, Man and Cybernetics, Part C (2005)
19. Generator of Self-Similar Network Traffic, http://wwwcsif.cs.ucdavis.edu/~kramer/code/trf_gen1.html
20. WongTrace, http://www4.comp.polyu.edu.hk/~cswklin/traces_wonghokleung/

Accelerating the Singular Value Decomposition of Rectangular Matrices with the CSX600 and the Integrable SVD

Yusaku Yamamoto[1], Takeshi Fukaya[1], Takashi Uneyama[2], Masami Takata[3], Kinji Kimura[4], Masashi Iwasaki[5], and Yoshimasa Nakamura[2]

[1] Nagoya University, Nagoya, 464-8603, Japan
`yamamoto@na.cse.nagoya-u.ac.jp`
Tel.: +81-52-789-5380; Fax: +81-52-789-4656
[2] Kyoto University, Kyoto, 606-8501, Japan
[3] Nara Women's University, Nara, 630-8506, Japan
[4] Niigata University, Niigata, 950-2181, Japan
[5] Kyoto Prefectural University, 606-8522, Japan

Abstract. We propose an approach to speed up the singular value decomposition (SVD) of very large rectangular matrices using the CSX600 floating point coprocessor. The CSX600-based acceleration board we use offers 50GFLOPS of sustained performance, which is many times greater than that provided by standard microprocessors. However, this performance can be achieved only when a vendor-supplied matrix-matrix multiplication routine is used and the matrix size is sufficiently large. In this paper, we optimize two of the major components of rectangular SVD, namely, QR decomposition of the input matrix and back-transformation of the left singular vectors by matrix Q, so that large-size matrix multiplications can be used efficiently. In addition, we use the Integrable SVD algorithm to compute the SVD of an intermediate bidiagonal matrix. This helps to further speed up the computation and reduce the memory requirements. As a result, we achieved up to 3.5 times speedup over the Intel Math Kernel Library running on an 3.2GHz Xeon processor when computing the SVD of a 100,000 × 4000 matrix.

1 Introduction

We consider the problem of computing the singular value decomposition $A = U\Sigma V^T$ of a large thin rectangular matrix A. Such problem arises in many applications including signal processing, image processing, information retrieval and electronic structure calculation. The matrix size can be very large in some applications. For example, the filter diagonalization method [10] for large-scale electronic structure calculation requires computing the SVD of matrices with thousands of columns and up to millions of rows repeatedly.

Recently, the use of dedicated floating point coprocessors like ClearSpeed's CSX600 [2] and the GRAPE-DR processor [5] has attracted much attention as a means to solve such large problems. These processors integrate dozens or

V. Malyshkin (Ed.): PaCT 2007, LNCS 4671, pp. 340–345, 2007.

even hundreds of floating point units and deliver performance that is order of magnitudes larger than standard microprocessors. For example, the ClearSpeed Advance board with two CSX600 processors claims 50GFLOPS of sustained performance [2]. This is several times faster than the speed provided by popular Intel Xeon processors.

However, it is not straightforward to fully exploit the performance of floating point coprocessors in intricate matrix computations such as the SVD. In fact, in the case of the CSX600 processor, the performance mentioned above can be obtained only when a vendor-supplied matrix-matrix multiplication routine (BLAS routine DGEMM [4]) is used and the matrix size is sufficiently large. This is mainly because the host processor and the coprocessor are connected via the PCI-X bus and the overhead of data transfer between them is substantial.

In this paper, we propose an approach to speed up the computation of SVD of very large rectangular matrices. To this end, we reorganize two of the main components of rectangular SVD algorithm, namely, QR decomposition of the input matrix A and back-transformation of the left singular vectors by matrix Q, so that large-size matrix multiplications can be used efficiently. In addition, we employ the Integrable SVD (I-SVD) algorithm [6], a fast and memory-efficient algorithm developed by some of the authors, to compute the SVD of an intermediate bidiagonal matrix. Thanks to these optimizations, our implementation running on the ClearSpeed Advance board achieves 3.5 times speedup over the Intel Math Kernel Library running on a 3.2GHz Xeon processor when computing the SVD of a $100,000 \times 4000$ matrix.

The rest of this paper is structured as follows: in section 2, we explain the standard algorithm for rectangular SVD and show how it can be optimized to use the CSX600 efficiently. Performance results are presented in section 3. Finally, section 4 gives some concluding remarks.

2   The Rectangular SVD Algorithm and Its Optimization for the CSX600

Let A be an $m \times n$ rectangular matrix and assume that $m \gg n$. The standard algorithm for the SVD of A consists of the following five steps [4]:

(a) **QR decomposition of A:** $A = QR$, where Q is an $m \times n$ matrix with ortho-normal columns and R is an $n \times n$ upper triangular matrix.
(b) **Bidiagonalization of R:** $R = U_1 B V_1^T$.
(c) **Singular value decomposition of B:** $B = U_2 \Sigma V_2^T$.
(d) **Back-transformation by U_1 and V_1:** $U' = U_1 U_2$, $V = V_1 V_2$.
(e) **Back-transformation by Q:** $U = QU'$.

By performing these steps, we obtain the singular value decomposition $A = U \Sigma V^T$. Among the steps, we especially focus on steps (a) and (e) since they involve $O(mn^2)$ work, while the others involve only $O(n^2)$ to $O(n^3)$ work. In addition, we decided to use our new I-SVD algorithm [6] in step (c) since the popular QR algorithm is too slow when n exceeds 1,000 and the divide-and-conquer (DC) method as implemented in LAPACK [1] requires as much as $4n^2$ words of extra work space, thereby limiting the size of the problem that can be solved. As for steps (b) and (d), we decided to use the LAPACK routines. In the following subsections, we explain our implementation of steps (a), (e) and (c) in more detail.

2.1   QR Decomposition and Back-Transformation by Q

To exploit the performance of the CSX600 in the QR decomposition and back-transformation by matrix Q, we have to reorganize the algorithm so that most of the computational work is done in the form of matrix multiplication. Furthermore, since the current implementation of DGEMM on the CSX600 works only when all the three sizes M, N, and K are greater than 448, we must make sure that this condition is satisfied.

The QR decomposition routine implemented in LAPACK uses a blocked algorithm [4]. It partitions the matrix A into panels of width L, computes the QR decomposition of each panel using Householder transformations, aggregates the transformations as a compact-WY representation [8], and updates the areas right to the panel using the compact-WY representation. In this approach, the update operation, which accounts for most of the work, can be done with the DGEMM. However, to use the CSX600, we need $L \geq 448$. In that case, the QR decomposition of the panel, for which the CSX600 cannot be used, takes long time and spoils the overall performance.

An alternative approach is the recursive QR decomposition proposed by Elmroth and Gustavson [3]. In this algorithm, we partition A into two panels and proceed in the same way as in the blocked algorithm. However, to compute the QR decomposition of each panel, we again partition the panel into two smaller panels and apply the blocked algorithm. This is repeated recursively. This algorithm can perform most of the work in the form of DGEMM, though the size of matrix multiplication becomes smaller as the level of recursion becomes deeper. Hence it is more suited for the CSX600 and we adopt it as the algorithm for step (a).

One of the shortcomings of the recursive QR algorithm is that it requires more computational work than the blocked algorithm; the former needs $3mn^2$ work, while the latter needs only $2mn^2$ work when $L \ll n$. To mitigate this, we seek to minimize the computational work in step (e) by looking into the operation $U = QU'$ in more detail.

To do this, we extend the $m \times n$ matrix Q to an $m \times m$ matrix $\bar{Q}$ by adding columns of zeros and extend the $n \times n$ matrix U' to an $m \times n$ matrix $\bar{U}'$ by adding rows of zeros. In the blocked QR decomposition, the matrix $\bar{Q}$ is expressed as a product of $p = n/L$ compact-WY representations as follows:

$$\bar{Q} = (I - Y_p T_p Y_p^T) \cdots (I - Y_2 T_2 Y_2^T)(I - Y_1 T_1 Y_1^T). \tag{1}$$

On the other hand, in the recursive QR algorithm, $\bar{Q}$ is expressed as a single compact-WY representation:

$$\bar{Q} = I - YTY^T. \tag{2}$$

If we don't exploit the zero structure of $\bar{U}'$, the work to compute $U = \bar{Q}\bar{U}'$ is about $4mn^2$ whether we use eq. (1) or (2). However, since $\bar{U}'$ has nonzero elements only in the leading $n \times n$ block, most of the operations in the computation of $Y_1^T\bar{U}'$ and $Y^T\bar{U}'$ can be omitted. The amount of work saved by this is larger for the recursive algorithm; it is $2mn^2$ for the recursive QR, while it is $2mnL$ for the blocked QR. This effect more than compensates for the increase of work in the QR decomposition phase. Hence we can regard the recursive algorithm as the best one both from the utilization of DGEMM and from the amount of computational work.

2.2 SVD of the Intermediate Bidiagonal Matrix

In step (c), the standard algorithm is the QR algorithm or the divide-and-conquer method. The QR algorithm requires $O(n^3)$ work when computing all the singular values and singular vectors of an $n \times n$ matrix. This is too costly when n is large, since the coefficient behind O is much larger compared with those in steps (b) and (d). The DC method is much faster and its execution time is usually smaller than the time for step (b). However, the DC method as implemented in LAPACK requires as much as $4n^2$ words of extra work space. This limits the size of the problem that can be solved.

In our implementation, we use the Integrable SVD algorithm [6] developed by some of the authors. The I-SVD algorithm is based on the fact that the solution of the Lotka-Volterra equation approaches the singular values of a bidiagonal matrix specified by the initial conditions as time goes to infinity. This property still holds after some appropriate discretization, and we can formulate a new algorithm to compute the singular values. The singular values thus computed can be shown to have small relative errors even if their magnitude is small. This enables us to compute the singular vectors using the twisted factorization [7]. Note that we also use the Lotka-Volterra based algorithm in the twisted factorization to improve accuracy and numerical stability [9]. The computational work to compute one singular vector is $O(n)$, since each singular vector can be computed independently and no reorthogonalization among the singular vectors is needed.

In our context, the algorithm is attractive since it can compute the full SVD of a bidiagonal matrix in $O(n^2)$ time using only $O(n)$ extra work space. Thus it is superior to the QR and DC algorithms in terms of speed and memory efficiency. For details of the I-SVD algorithm, the readers are referred to [6] and [9].

3   Performance Results

We implemented the rectangular SVD algorithm using FORTRAN based on the ideas described in the previous section. More precisely, we use the recursive QR algorithm in step (a) and adopt the improvement to reduce the work in the multiplication by Q in step (e). For these two routines, we use the DGEMM routine on the CSX600 board whenever the matrix size is sufficiently large. In step (c), we use the I-SVD algorithm. Since most of the computation in the I-SVD is done with the level-1 BLAS [4], or simple vector-vector operations, we decided to perform this part on the host processor. Also, steps (b) and (d) are executed on the host processor using appropriate LAPACK routines, because these steps occupy only a fraction of the total work when $m \ll n$.

As test matrices, we used random matrices whose elements follow a uniform random variable in $[0, 1]$. The matrix size m was varied from 12,500 to 100,000, while n was varied from 1000 to 4000. As a test machine, we use a Xeon (3.2GHz) machine with 8G bytes of memory and the CSX600 acceleration board.

Now we compare the performance of our program with the Intel Math Kernel Library (MKL), which is known to be the fastest implementation of LAPACK on the Xeon processor. Note that the current version of MKL cannot benefit from the CSX600 board, since it uses the blocked QR algorithm not designed for a large block size (see subsection 2.1).

Fig. 1 shows the execution time of MKL on the Xeon processor and the execution time of our program on the Xeon processor with and without the CSX600 board. As can be seen from the graph, the MKL routine, which uses the DC method for the bidiagonal SVD, requires about 2850 seconds. Our program is a little faster, because the improvements described in section 2 is effective also for the Xeon processor. When the CSX600 board is used, the execution time of our program is reduced to only 808 seconds, which is 3.5 times faster than MKL.

Fig. 2 shows the speedup obtained by our program with the CSX600 over MKL. The speedup becomes greater as m increases, and also becomes greater as n increases as long as $m \ll n$ holds. From this result, we can expect that the effect of using the CSX600 increases for larger problems.

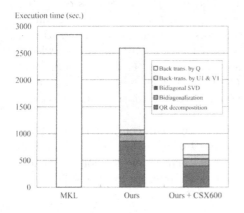

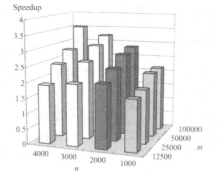

Fig. 1. Comparison of execution times: Intel MKL on Xeon, our code on Xeon and our code on Xeon with CSX600

Fig. 2. Speedup obtained by our code with CSX600 over MKL

4 Conclusion

In this paper, we proposed an approach to speed up the computation of singular value decomposition of very large rectangular matrices using the CSX600 floating point coprocessor. By reorganizing two major components of rectangular SVD, namely, QR decomposition of the input matrix and back-transformation of the left singular vectors by matrix Q to use large-size matrix multiplications efficiently, we were able to exploit the high-performance DGEMM routine on the CSX600. In addition, we used our fast and memory-efficient I-SVD algorithm to compute the SVD of an intermediate bidiagonal matrix. As a result of these optimizations, we achieved 3.5 times speedup over Intel MKL running on 3.2GHz Xeon when computing the SVD of a 100,000 by 4000 matrix. Future work includes further accelerating the program by porting routines other than DGEMM to the CSX600 using the C^n language [2].

References

1. Anderson, E., Bai, Z., Bischof, C., Demmel, J., Dongarra, J., Croz, J.D., Greenbaum, A., Hammarling, S., McKenney, A., Ostrouchov, S., Sorensen, D.: LAPACK User's Guide. SIAM, Philadelphia (1992)
2. ClearSpeed Technology Inc. http://www.clearspeed.com/
3. Elmroth, E., Gustavson, F.: Applying Recursion to Serial and Parallel QR Factorization Leads to Better Performance. IBM Journal of Research and Development 44, 605 (2000)
4. Golub, G.H., Van Loan, C.F.: Matrix Computations, 3rd edn. Johns Hopkins University Press, Baltimore (1996)
5. GRAPE-DR Project. http://grape-dr.adm.s.u-tokyo.ac.jp/
6. Iwasaki, M., Nakamura, Y.: Accurate Computation of Singular Values in terms of Shifted Integrable Schemes. Japan J. Indust. Appl. Math. 1, 239–259 (2006)
7. Parlett, B.N., Dhillon, I.: Fernando's Solution to Wilkinson's problem: An Application of Double Factorization. Linear Algebra Appl. 267, 247–279 (1997)
8. Schreiber, R., Van Loan, C.F.: A Storage-Efficient WY Representation for Products of Householder Transformations. SIAM J. Sci. Stat. Comput. 10, 53–57 (1989)
9. Takata, M., Kimura, K., Iwasaki, M., Nakamura, Y.: Performance of a New Singular Value Decomposition Scheme for Large Scale Matrices. In: Proceedings of The IASTED International Conference on Parallel and Distributed Computing and Networks, pp. 304–309 (2006)
10. Toledo, S., Rabani, E.: Very Large Electronic Structure Calculations using an Out-of-Core Filter-Diagonalization Method. J. Comput. Phys. 180, 256–269 (2002)

Parallel Dynamic SPT Update Algorithm in OSPF

Yuanbo Zhu, Mingwei Xu, and Qian Wu

Computer Science Department, Tsinghua University,
Beijing 100084, China
{zhuyb,xmw,wuqian}@csnet1.cs.tsinghua.edu.cn

Abstract. Shortest-Path-Tree (SPT) computation, as the main load in OSPF protocol, contributes to the slow convergence time in intra-domain routing. With the increasing interest for upcoming routers of multi-core based process-ing board, efficient parallel routing algorithms are required to take this advan-tage to speedup SPT computation in order to meet the needs for fast failure re-covery applications such as VoIP. However, currently available parallel SPT algorithms are all based on static method, which re-computes the entire tree for each link change. In this paper, we explore parallel algorithms for dynamic SPT update, a more efficient method, which only updates the affected nodes by mak-ing use of the previous SPT We first analyze characters of dynamic method to show how they affect parallel design; then we give our parallel dynamic SPT algorithm framework, which uses: (1) parallel distance-updating mode, to get a near liner speedup (assuming perfect load balance) and (2) group-removal schema, to reduce communication cost. Further, to provide load balance, we give a task distribution algorithm called RR_DFS, which makes use of the to-pology information of the previous SPT. Complexity analysis and simulation result are also presented

1 Introduction

The Shortest-Path-Tree (SPT) computation is a fundamental and critical issue for high performance routing in the interior network. In Open-Shortest-Path-First (OSPF) [1], which is a widely deployed intra-domain routing protocol, each router computes a SPT based on the network topology with itself as the root, and generates route table using the computed SPT in the routing area SPT computation, also known as the sin-gle source shortest path problem, can be constructed by Dijkstra algorithm [2] in $O(n^2 + m)$ time, where n is the number of nodes (routers) and m is the number of edges (links). This complexity seriously limits the scalability of OSPF.

Traditionally, there are two ways to reduce the SPT computation in OSPF: *(1)* limit the number of routers in the routing area (less than 200 [1]); and *(2)* limit the compu-tation frequency---link changes do not cause immediate computation but wait for SPT_hold time (30 seconds) to collect enough link changes to start another SPT com-putation. These two ways work well for the intra-domain routing environment in the past days. However, as for (1), the growing use of traffic engineering requires, *a lar-ger routing size*, in order to increase redundancy to allow routing optimization; as for

V. Malyshkin (Ed.): PaCT 2007, LNCS 4671, pp. 346–359, 2007.

(2), long SPT_hold time seriously delays convergence time (response to link changes) and *reducing SPT_hold* is claimed [9][10][11][12] to achieve faster intra-domain convergence to meet the needs for fast failure recovery applications such as VoIP. Both trends---to increase network size and to reduce SPT_hold time---bring new challenges for intra-domain routing algorithm and call for a SPT computation of more efficiency.

In this paper, we explore the parallel algorithm for SPT computation. Our work is also motivated by the increasing interest for upcoming routers with multi-core and multi-NPU based processing board which calls for parallel algorithms in routing. Though there has been a lot of parallel SPT algorithms [3][4][5][6], however, they are all based on the inefficient static method, without taking advantage of the alternative and yet more efficient method in OSPF.---- the dynamic update. Dynamic SPT update method works in an incremental fashion by using the information of the previous SPT. Since it only updates the affected nodes instead of re-compute the whole tree, it is more efficient than the static method and begins to be deployed in commercial routers [13]. However, its performance bottleneck still exists (especially in some worse cases) despite lots of improvement work [14][15][16][17], and we believe that an exploration of parallel algorithms based on dynamic method is a meaningful work for the next generation routers of multi-core and multi-NPU. To the best of our knowledge, this is the first time to explore the parallel algorithm for dynamic SPT computation ([8] gave parallel algorithms in dynamic settings only for all-pairs shortest path, but not for the single-source SPT problem used in OSPF, which is what we focus on in this paper).

We work in the following three steps: First, we analyze the characters of dynamic SPT update method and discuss how they affect the parallel design; then we give an algorithm framework for the parallel dynamic method. This framework provides parallel computation and communication fashions, but it does not include specific task distribution algorithm. In fact, it allows different task distribution algorithms to provide different load balance performances. On the assumption of perfect load balance, we give the computation and communication complexity analysis; further, we consider the load balance problem. We propose a task distribution algorithm called RR_DFS. It makes use of previous SPT information and provides, to some extend, load balance while with little extra cost involved.

The rest of the paper is organized as follows: section 2 gives background knowledge for both parallel SPT static algorithms and dynamic SPT update method; section 3 discusses some issues on parallel design of dynamic algorithm; in section 4 we give our parallel algorithm framework, with complexity analysis followed in section 5; section 6 presents our task distribution algorithm; and simulation results is shown in section 7; finally, we make conclusions in section 8.

2 Background

2.1 Parallel SPT Algorithms in Static Method

Parallel algorithms for single-source SPT can be classified into 2 modes: parallel distance updating (PDU) and parallel sub-region computation (PSC).

- **PDU:** see [3][4], each processor is given the entire graph and responsible for a set of nodes. First, a node with local minimum distance is selected in parallel and communication is performed to get a global minimum, then the distances of other nodes are updated in parallel before another selection begins.
- **PSC:** see [5][6], the entire network is partitioned into p sub regions, each being assigned to a processor. SPT computation is done independently and communication is needed only between processors who share the same nodes (called border nodes) to get border nodes' distance values.

Combination of the two can be found in [7].

2.2 Dynamic SPT Update Algorithms

The main idea of dynamic SPT update algorithm is to make use of the previous tree and only update affected nodes caused by topology change. Topology changes include node changes and link weight changes. For node changes, adding/removing a node usually involves "leaf" information, e.g. a new node Y is added to node X, then previous SPT is still correct by only appending Y to X; as removing nodes can be reduced to the case of link change (weight increases to infinite), so we focus on the cases of link change:

1) SPT_inc: weight increase, and changed link $\in$ old SPT

2) nSPT_inc: weight increase, and changed link $\notin$ old SPT

3) SPT_dec: weight decrease, and changed link $\in$ old SPT

4) nSPT_dec: weight decrease, and changed link $\notin$ old SPT

For a link change, the algorithm first determines, again, whether computation is needed. E.g. in case nSPT_inc, the old SPT is still correct and no nodes need to be updated. Otherwise, it starts computation from the end node of the changed link as the root, identifying some directly affected nodes and adding nodes into a queue. Then it follows iteration for selection.

In iteration, a node in the queue is selected and declared settled with its path and distance changed in the SPT. The settled nodes are removed from the queue and their adjacent nodes become affected nodes by being added into queue, or by being updated by new distance value if it is already in the queue. The algorithm continues the iteration until the queue is empty.

3 Parallel Analysis

We discuss some issues on parallel design by analyzing three characters that make dynamic method different from the static, and show how they affect the parallel design.

- **Dynamic topology that participates in computation**

The nodes that participate in computation (active nodes) in static method can be predicted; in fact they are all nodes in network. However, in dynamic algorithm, active nodes are affected nodes which are identified step by step until algorithm ends.

This indetermination makes PSC model which is based on region decomposition difficult to implement, because region decomposition needs network topology information in advance in order to deploy a proper decomposition on the whole graph. On the other hand, PDU model can be applied in this dynamic environment easily. In fact, identifying a new node means simply assigning it to a processor.

■ **Flexible Iteration Times**

The number of iterations in dynamic model can be much smaller than the static. The reason is twofold. (1): there are less active nodes in dynamic model. (2): In static algorithms, iteration times equal to the number of active nodes, while in the dynamic, iteration times is flexible, and can be much smaller than the number of active nodes if we use a *group-removal* schema.

Now we explain *group-removal* schema in (2). In dynamic algorithm [16], a node selected by the minimum distance increase and all its descendent nodes that are reachable in the existing SPT are settled. Since a group (the selected node and its descendent) instead of one (only the selected node) is settled in iteration, we call it group-removal; the *correctness* of group-removal is promised in dynamic method due to its use of previous SPT information and the proof can be found in [16]. Since in PDU mode, the number of communications equals to the number of iterations. Thus, PDU mode can benefit much less communication by group-removal schema.

■ **Great Load Changes in Interation**

Since a group of nodes are settled and removed from the queue, this load change is much greater than in static algorithms where in iteration only one node is removed. Great load change may lead to load imbalance among processors. Since the node selection requires a global synchronization among processors, such work imbalance among processors will result in idle time and thus lead to a longer running time. Therefore, an efficient task distribution algorithm for nodes assignment should be a crucial issue.

4 Parallel SPT Update Algorithm Framework

Based on above analysis, we give our parallel algorithm framework: each processor maintains the whole network topology and works in PDU model using *group removal* schema. The description is shown below.

Parallel dynamic SPT update algorithm framework:

Phase 1: **Initialization**:

Identify directly affected nodes, and assign them to processors by adding into the local queues in parallel.

Phase 2: **Iteration:** Repeat 2.1 ~ 2.5 until all local queues are empty

2.1 **Select** local node with the *minimum distance increment.*

2.2 **Send / receive** local selected nodes to / from other processors, select the global node with the minimum distance increment.

2.3 The selected global node *and all its descendents* are settled and **updated in the new SPT** in each processor

2.4 **Remove** the settled nodes from local queues in parallel

2.5 **Update local queues** in parallel. For new nodes, assign them to processors, and add them into the local queues.

Here, we assume the nodes have been assigned to processors, that is to say, specific task distribution algorithm is not included in the framework and the task distribution algorithm will be discussed in section 6.

Node selection (2.1) and distance update (2.5) are doing in parallel in PDU mode; the *group removal* schema will remove (in 2.3) the selected node (with the minimum distance increment in 2.2) and all its descendents.

■   **Example**

We give an example for the *SPT_inc* case. In Fig 1, the weight of link from node B to C increases from 2 to 7. We assume that there are 2 processors and the task distribution result is as shown in Table 1.

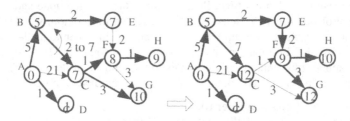

Fig. 1. An example of the algorithm

Since the changed link belongs to previous SPT and its weight increases, computation is needed to update SPT. Algorithm starts from node C as root and identifies all its descendent nodes C, F, H, G to be affected. Assume that the task distribution result is as shown in Table 1. Local queue for processor 1 and 2 are shown in Table 2. E.g. for node F, it may be updated by following the old path C with distance increased by 5 or choose another path. Because node E can offer F distance 9 which means that the

Table 1. Task distribution

Processor ID	Task nodes
Processor 1	C, F
Processor 2	H, G

Table 2. Parallel algorithm in the first iteration

	Processor 1	Processor 2
1. Init local queue	(C, B, 5), (F, E, 1)	(H, F, 5), (G, C, 5)
2.1 select local minimum	(F, E, 1)	(G, C, 5)
2.2 communicate for global minimum	(F, E, 1)	
2.3 settle E and its descent F in SPT	(F, E, 1), (H, F, 5)	(F, E, 1), (H, F, 5)
2.4 remove E , F	(C, B, 5)	(G, C, 5)
2.5 update queue	(C, B, 5)	(G, F, 2)

distance increase is 1 based on the old distance 8, therefore, the potential path for node F in new SPT is node E and the corresponding distance increase is 1.

In the following iteration, each processor selects a node with minimum increase from local queue and communicates with others. In the example, node F is selected the global minimum and each processor modifies its SPT by changing the path of F to be E and increase the distance of F by 1. Besides, node E, the descents of F, is also settled with its distance increased by the same value 1 and path unchanged. Thus, nodes F and E are updated in the new SPT in each processor. Then the settled nodes F and E will be removed from the local queue respectively. In the updating process of 2.5, the settle of node F provides node G with a smaller distance increase, thus G changes it potential path to be node F and distance increase to be 1. Then the iteration continues until the local queues are all empty.

5 Complexity

In this section, we first discuss the three components of the execution time: computation time, communication time and idle time. Then we give the total complexity and speedup, and analyze factors that affect them

Here we give some definitions. Let K be the number of iterations, N be the number of affected nodes, E be the number of edges whose sources correspond to affected nodes, and p be the number of processors.

5.1 Computation Time

The dynamic SPT update algorithm has four operations.

a) *adding and removing* (phase 1 and 2.3, 2.5);
b) *selecting* the node with the minimum distance (2.1, 2.2, 2.3);
c) *modifying* the SPT;
d) *updating* distance values for the local queue (2.5, 2.2, 2.3).

The operation *a* takes $2N$ time, because each affected node will be added and removed only once. The operation *b* takes $K*N$ time, because there are K iterations and in each iteration the up-bound of the queue size is N. The operation *c* takes N time, because each affected node will be modified in the new SPT. The operation *d* takes E time, because each affected edge will lead to one update operation for the source node. Therefore, the total computation time needed in the dynamic algorithm is

$$T_{total} = 2N + K*N + N + E \qquad (1)$$

In our parallel algorithm framework, operation *a*, *b*, and *d* are all doing in parallel, only operation *c* is doing serially, see section 4, thus, the parallel part takes

$$T_{parallel} = 2N + N*K + E \qquad (2)$$

The unparallel or serial part takes

$$T_{serial} = N \qquad (3)$$

Therefore, the ideal speedup the parallel algorithm can get is (without considering the communication cost)

$$Speedup_1 = \frac{T_{total}}{T_{parallel} / p + T_{serial}} = \frac{(2N + N \cdot K + E) + N}{(2N + N \cdot K + E) / p + N} \tag{4}$$

Since the significant operations are due to the selecting (operation b which takes $K*N$ time) and the updating (operation d which takes E time) operations, both of which are implemented in parallel, the parallel algorithm can get approximate linear ideal speedup.

The extra computation cost for the parallel algorithm is the global minimum selecting from p processors, with the cost of p, it follows that the computation time for each processor is

$$T_{comp} = E / p + K((N + 2) / p + p) + N \tag{5}$$

5.2 Communication Time

In each iteration, a *send/receive* communication is executed. It means sending the local minimum to other processors and receiving the local minimums from other processors. The goal of this commutation is twofold. First, it allows the selecting of a global minimum thus to make the algorithm proceed correctly. Second, with the selected global minimum, each processor can modify its existing SPT dependently.

Note that in most parallel routing table computation algorithms, communications usually involve two parts: the communication for computation and the communication for synchronization of the global route table after computation both of which are inevitable and mean extra cost. Here, in our framework, we put the two together into one: the communication for computation also works as the synchronizing of the route table, that is to say, when communication is performed during computation it finishes the synchronizing of the route table at the same time.

Since the number of selection or communications equals to the number of iterations, the following three numbers have the same value in the algorithm:

1) Iterations times
2) Selections times
3) Communications times

For one communication, only a *send / receive* operation is needed. That means we use broadcast for the send operation and waiting for all other processors for the receive operation. Thus the communication time for each processor is

$$T_{comm} = K \tag{6}$$

5.3 Idle Time

Idle time exists due to load imbalance among processors. Since a global synchronization communication is needed in 2.2 to allow the algorithm to proceed. The processors with fewer loads will wait at 2.2 for the busy processors to come to send messages. For the case of perfect load balance, the idle time is zero in each processor.

In our framework, load balance is provided by the task distribution algorithm which deals with how to assign nodes to processors. For simple, in the following complexity analysis, we assume the load is perfect balance among processors and the idle time is

$$T_{idle} = 0 \qquad (7)$$

5.4 Complexity Analysis

Based on (5) (6) (7), the execution time in each processor is

$$T_p = T_{comp} + T_{comm} + T_{idle}$$
$$= t_c \cdot (E / p + K((N + 2) / p + p)) + t_s \cdot K \qquad (8)$$

where t_c is the average time for one computation operation and t_s is the average time for one communication operation. The speedup of the algorithm follows (with considering the communication cost)

$$Speedup_2 = \frac{T}{T_p} = \frac{t_c((2N + N \cdot K + E) + N)}{t_c((2N + N \cdot K + E) / p + N) + t_s K} \qquad (9)$$

Next, we will further analyze the complexity and speedup by taking the link change probability into consideration.

Note that the complexity in (8) and the speedup in (9) we get are for the cases in which computation is executed or computation time is not zero when the link changes. However, as we have mentioned in section 2, not all the link changes will cause computation. In fact, for the nSPT_inc case in table 1, neither computation nor communication is needed, the execution time for this case is

$$T_{nSPT\_inc} = 0 \qquad (10)$$

For the other cases in table 1, the computation and communication time is as we have analyzed above, the execution time for them is

$$T_{SPT\_inc} = T_{SPT\_dec} = T_{nSPT\_dec} = T \qquad (11)$$

Now we give the probability of the four link change cases.

For a graph with n nodes and m edges, there are m links in total and $n-1$ links that belong to the SPT. We assume the link change is random, that is to say, all the links have an equal probability to change, therefore, the probability of the changed link belongs to the previous SPT is

$$P_{SPT} = \frac{n-1}{m} \qquad (12)$$

And the probability of the link does not belong to previous SPT is

$$P_{nSPT} = 1 - \frac{n-1}{m} \qquad (13)$$

Assume that for a link change, the probability for increase and decrease are equal, the probability for the four cases are

$$P_{SPT\_inc} = \frac{n-1}{2m} \tag{14}$$

$$P_{SPT\_dec} = \frac{n-1}{2m} \tag{15}$$

$$P_{nSPT\_inc} = \frac{1}{2} - \frac{n-1}{2m} \tag{16}$$

$$P_{nSPT\_dec} = \frac{1}{2} - \frac{n-1}{2m} \tag{17}$$

Therefore, for the serial algorithm, the computation complexity *for each link change* is:

$$T' = 0 * P_{nSPT\_inc} + T (P_{SPT\_inc} + P_{SPT\_dec} + P_{nSPT\_dec})$$
$$= (\frac{1}{2} - \frac{n-1}{2m}) * (t_c((2N + N \cdot K + E) + N)) \tag{18}$$

And for the parallel algorithm, in each processor, the computation complexity *for each link change* is:

$$T_P' = 0 * P_{nSPT\_inc} + T_p (P_{SPT\_inc} + P_{SPT\_dec} + P_{nSPT\_dec})$$
$$= (\frac{1}{2} - \frac{n-1}{2m}) * (t_c \cdot (E / p + K((N + 2) / p + p)) + t_s \cdot K) \tag{19}$$

And the speedup *for each link change* is

$$Speedup_3 = \frac{T'}{T_P'} = \frac{t_c((2N + N \cdot K + E) + N)}{t_c((2N + N \cdot K + E) / p + N) + t_s K} \tag{20}$$

Now we give the factor that affect the complexity (or the execution time) and the speedup of the parallel algorithm.

According to (19), the factors that affect the complexity include:

a) **N, K, E,** which depends on the network topology and the link change

b) average degree **D,** which depends on the network density

c) number of processors **p**

d) radio of **ts/tc**, which depends on machine parameters for the parallel implement.

e) the **load balance performance,** which depends on the task distribution algorithm.

According to (20), the factors that affect the speedup include: *a, c, d* and *e* which have been explained above.

Since *N, K, E* and *D* are all fixed due to the network topology and the link changes; the way left to improve the performance of the parallel algorithm includes: providing more processors (less than the number of nodes); an efficient communication mechanism and an efficient task distribution algorithm.

6 Task Distribution Algorithm

In this section, we give a task distribution algorithm to provide load balance. It uses the topology information of the previous SPT and make the nodes removed in each iteration be distributed evenly among processors.

The idea of our algorithm is based on this observation: each iteration, the nodes removed from queue are the selected node and all its descendants (we call it branch) in the existing SPT. If such changes are distributed onto different processors, queue sizes will change evenly among processors. That is to say, it is better for nodes in a branch to be shared by different processors than to be assigned to only one processor.

If we define the nodes assigned on one processor have relativity, the objective of our task distribution algorithm is to reduce the relativity of nodes in one branch as much as possible. This can be achieved by using Round-Robin distribution to each node in the Deep-First-Search (DFS), which at the same time performs the function of searching for affected nodes. The algorithm which we call Round Robin in DFS (RR_DFS) is described as follows:

Modified DFS for task distribution:
1.1RR_DFS (node v)
1.2{ Assign v to Processor ID = p;
1.3 add v into local queue of Processor ID = p;
1.4 $p = (p + 1)$ % Processor_number;
1.5 While (DFS find first child v != NULL)
1.6 { RR_DFS(node v);
1.7 DFS Get Next Child v; }
1.8 }

An example is given for the RR_DFS algorithm in Fig 2. (only links that belong to the SPT are shown) When the weight of link between node P and node A increases, processors begin DFS process, starting at node A as root to search for affected nodes. Assume that the nodes in the same level of the DFS have been arraied by their ID (such as router-id). The affected nodes got by DFS process in Initialization phase and the result of task distribution algorithm are shown in Fig. 2.

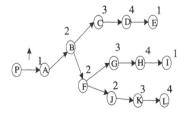

Processor_ID	Task nodes
1	A, E, I
2	B, F, J
3	C, G, K
4	D, H, L

Fig. 2. An example of the RR_DFS algorithm

If, in the following iteration, node C is selected to be the global minimum, node C together with its descendant node D and node E are removed from queue in processor 3, 4 and 1 separately, which means that the changed load (node C, D, E) is shared by processor 3, 4, 1.

RR_DFS algorithm can not promise perfect load balance among processors, but it provides, to some extend, load balance and its cost is very small. The cost for the DFS process to search for affected nodes lies on 1.3, and the extra cost for the task distribution lies on 1.2 and 1.4. Since they are all O(1) for one operation, the total complexity for the task distribution algorithm is the same as the complexity for searching for affected nodes, that is O(N).

7 Simulation

Now we investigate the efficiency of our parallel dynamic SPT update algorithm. The specific task distribution algorithm we use is the RR_DFS algorithm.

■ **Simulation Setup**

Network Generation
Networks in the simulations are generated using Random Topology Generator (RTG) [18] software. Fig.3 shows a randomly generated network topology of nodes size N=200 and average degree D=5.

In the following simulation, we investigate how the performance change with

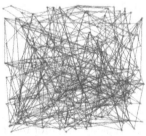

1) network size (denoted by node size N): we fix the average degree D = 10 and use node size between 50 ~ 500.
2) network density (denoted by average degree D), we fix the node size N = 200, and use average degree between 3 ~ 200 (all mesh).

Fig. 3. A randomly generated network

Event Generation
For a specific network topology, we test L continuous link changes and L is between 100~500. Changed links are chosen randomly and works in the way of first link down (weight increases to infinity) and then link up (weight recovers its old value).

Tasks assigned to processors are implemented as threads which use message passing as their communications.

A. Computation Complexity
During the simulation, we keep record of the number of computation operations in each processor and take the max number among the p processors to denote the computation complexity in the parallel algorithm.

Since most of the computation is doing in parallel, the speedup of the computation does not change much with the network size and density, see Fig. 4.(a) and (b). For small network size, e.g. N=50 the speedup is not significant since the number of affected nodes is small and can not keep all processors busy.

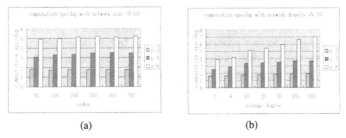

Fig. 4. Computation complexity

B. Communication Times

We record the number of communications each processor performs during the simulation. For L times link changes and C times communications involved, we use C/L to denote the average communication times for a single link change.

Network Size

Communication times for a single link event do not change much with network size, see Fig. 5.(a). This is because of the *group removal* schema. Though the affected nodes number increases with the network size, however, by using *group removal* schema, the size of removed group (including the selected nodes and all its descendants) increases, thus making the communication times do not show much increase.

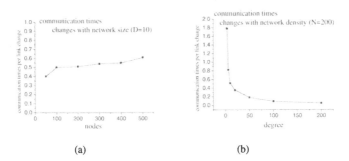

Fig. 5. Communication times

Network Density

The communication times for a single link change event become smaller as the network density increases, see Fig. 5.(b). This is because that not all link changes will cause computation, as we discuss in section 2. In the nSPT_inc case, each processor judges that the old SPT is still correct and ends the algorithm with no communication. Since for a fixed node size, as the network density increases, the probability of the nSPT_inc case increases, so the average communica-tion times for a single link change becomes smaller.

C. Load Balance Performance

To investigate the performance of load balance in our task distribution algorithm RR_DFS, we implement the frame-work using two task distribution algorithms:

RR_DFS and a random distribution algorithm. The random distribution algorithm can be described as: divide the nodes on the whole network into p groups randomly and each group is assigned to one processor before the Initialization phase. Performance comparison of the two task distribution algorithms are showed in Fig. 6.(a).

Since the RR_DFS algorithm takes the characteristic of the load change into consideration, the load change can be shared among different processors, making the queue size in each processor decrease averagely, thus a smaller running time can be got using RR_DFS than random distribution algorithm for most cases, see Fig. 6.(a).

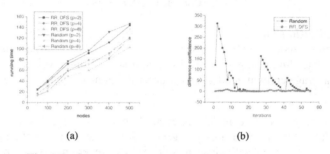

(a)   (b)

Fig. 6. Performance for two task distribution algorithms

Furthermore, we give a detail comparison of the load balance performance between the two task distribution algo-rithms. We maintain the network node size to be N = 200, average degree D = 10 and processor number p = 2, and we compare the metric *difference coefficient* in each iteration before the communication starts in the algorithms. The *difference coefficient* is defined to be the deviation of the queue size of p processors. Comparison result is showed Fig. 6.(b). The smaller *difference coefficient* value for the RR_DFS algorithm indicates that the working load among processors is more balanced than the Random distribution algorithm.

8 Conclusion

We explore the parallel algorithm for dynamic SPT update in this paper. Based on the three characters of the dynamic algorithms: dynamic topology in computation; flexible iteration times; great load changes in iteration, we give our parallel algorithm framework which: works in PDU mode to get near linear speedup and use *group-removal* schema to reduce communication. Simulation results show that the communication cost can be limited to a small number and does not change much with network size and decreases with network density. To further provide load balance, we propose a task distribution algorithm called RR_DFS. It makes use of the previous SPT information and shows a good load balance performance compared with the random distribution in our simulation.

The parallel algorithm present in this paper is for single link change. For multiple link changes, the algorithm can work by simply dealing with one link change after another. Though in real-life environment, single link change occupies most cases, it is still worthwhile to explore an efficient parallel dynamic algorithm for multiple link changes, and this is where our further work lies.

Acknowledgements

This research is supported by the National Natural Science Foundation of China (No. 90604024), the Key Project of Chinese Ministry of Education.(No.106012), and National 863 project of China (No. 2005AA121510).

References

1. Moy, J.: OSPF version 2, Internet Draft, RFC 2178 (1997)
2. Dijkstra, E.: A note two problems in connection with graphs. Numerical Math 1 (1959)
3. Paige, R., Kruskal, C.: Parallel algorithms for shortest paths problems. In: Proc. 1989 Intl. Conf. on Parallel Processing, pp. 14–19 (1989)
4. Brodal, G.S., Traff, J.L., Zaroliagis, C.D.: A parallel priority queue with constant time operations. Journal of Parallel and Distributed Computing 49(1), 4–21 (1998)
5. Cohen, E.: Efficient parallel shortest-paths in digraphs with a separator decomposition. J. Algorithms 21, 331–357 (1996)
6. Klein, P., Rao, S., Rauch, M., Subramanian, S.: Faster Shortest-path algorithms for planar graphs. In: Proceedings of the 26th Symposium on Theory of Computation (STOC), pp. 27–37 (1994)
7. Traff, J.L., Zaroliagis, C.D.: A simple parallel algorithm for the single-source shortest pathproblem on planar digraphs. Journal of Parallel and Distributed Computing 60(9), 1103–1124 (2000)
8. Subramanian, S.: Parallel and Dynamic Shortest-Path Algorithms for Sparse Graphs, PhD Thesis, Brown University (1995)
9. Basu, A., Riecke, J.G.: Stability issues in OSPF. In: Proceedings of ACM SIGCOMM (2001)
10. Francois, P., Filsfils, C., Bonaventure, O., Evans, J.: Achieving Sub-Second IGP Convergence in Large IP Networks. ACM SIGCOMM Computer Communication Review (2005)
11. Shaikh, A., Greenberg, A.: Experience in Black-box OSPF Measurement. In: Proc. ACM SIGCOMM Internet Measurement Workshop (IMW) (2001)
12. Alattinoglu, C., Jacobson, V., Yu, H.: Towards Milli-Second IGP Convergence, draft-alaettinoglu-ISISconvergence-00.txt (2000)
13. OSPF Incremental SPF, Cisco IOS Software Release 12.0 s, [Online]. Available: http://www.cisco.com
14. Ramalingam, G., Reps, T.W.: An Incremental Algorithm for a Generalization of the Shortest-Path Problem. Journal of Algorithms 21(2), 267–305 (1996)
15. Narvaez, P., Siu, K.-Y., Tzeng, H.-Y.: New Dynamic Algorithms for Shortest Path Tree Computation. IEEE Transactions on Networking 8(6) (December 2000)
16. Narvaez, P., Siu, K.-Y., Tzeng, H.-Y.: New dynamic SPT algorithm based on a ball-andstring model. IEEE/ACM Transactions on Networking 9, 706–718 (2001)
17. Xiao, B., Cao, J., Zhuqe, Q., Shao, Z., Sha, E.: Dynamic Update of Shortest Path Tree in OSPF. In: Interna-tional Symposium on Parallel Architectures, Algorithms and Networks (ISPAN'04) (2004)
18. Wei, L.: Random topology generator (RTG). Univ. of Southern California, Los Angeles, CA. [Online]. Available: http://lasr.cs.ucla.edu/save/topo.html

Pedestrian and Crowd Dynamics Simulation: Testing SCA on Paradigmatic Cases of Emerging Coordination in Negative Interaction Conditions

Stefania Bandini, Mizar Luca Federici, Sara Manzoni, and Giuseppe Vizzari

Complex Systems and Artificial Intelligence Research Center
University of Milan–Bicocca, Italy
tel.: +39-02-64487865
{bandini,federici,manzoni,vizzari}@disco.unimib.it

Abstract. The paper presents a set of theoretical experiments performed to evaluate Situated Cellular Agent (SCA) approach within pedestrian dynamics research context. SCA is a modeling and simulation approach based on Multi Agent Systems principles that derives from Cellular Automata. In particular, we focus on two emerging phenomena (freezing by heating and lane formation phenomena) that have been empirically observed and already modeled by analytical particle-based models and Cellular Automata–based models.

Keywords: Multi-Agent System, Crowd Simulation, Paradigmatic Cases, Lane Formation, Freezing by Heating, Situated Cellular Agents.

1 Introduction

The research context of this paper refers to bottom–up approaches to Pedestrian Dynamics that is, *the study of potentially complex dynamics that pedestrians produce as the result of (simple) local interactions occurring within a shared, limited, partially known spatial environment* [1]. The suitability of bottom–up approach to study these phenomena is supported by several years of studies and empirical observations in human sciences (e.g. sociology, psychology).

Available models for pedestrian dynamics can be classified into two main classes: many–particle models (e.g. Helbing's Social Force Model [5] is the most known) and approaches based on discrete dynamical systems. The first approach considers individuals as particles subjected to forces, space is continuous and single positions are defined by coordinates. Within the last class, Cellular Automata (CA) demonstrated to be particularly adequate for this type of context. According to CA peculiarities the spatial environment can be represented as a regular grid of cells, whose state can include the representation of the presence of individuals (or other environmental obstacles). Pedestrian movement is represented by synchronous CA state transition rules (e.g. an occupied cell becomes empty and, synchronously, an adjacent empty cell becomes occupied) and the dynamics of the system result from local interactions between CA cells. According to CA

V. Malyshkin (Ed.): PaCT 2007, LNCS 4671, pp. 360–369, 2007.

approach, several research groups have worldwide developed models for pedestrian dynamics both to reproduce specific phenomena (e.g. Lane Formation, that refers to the spontaneous formation of pedestrian lanes with same direction [18]), or specific scenarios (e.g. evacuation dynamics from public spaces like classrooms [7], underground stations [8]), and more general modeling approaches able to reproduce several phenomena and situations.

The success of CA-based approaches derives mainly from the fact that CA are simpler to understand and to be used by experts of several application contexts than the analytical models. However, like the analytical approaches, they suffer the limitation of considering individuals as homogeneous entities and generally do not provide a support to dynamism and flexibility of represented situations, while sometimes it is preferred to represent behavioral rules at individual scale. Multi Agent System (MAS) approach to pedestrian (and crowd) modeling [9,10,11], have been recently suggested and experimented since a MAS can represent a potentially heterogeneous system of agents in a partially known environment. Within MAS–based approaches, Situated Cellular Agents (SCA) [19] defines spatially situated agents in an environment endowed of an explicit structure that qualifies their perceptions, interactions and action abilities. The structure of SCA environment influences agents' actions and perception abilities. SCA has been presented as an extension of CA [3], and has been experimented in several contexts (among which the modeling of groups of pedestrians [11,12]).

In particular, in this paper we present a set of experiments that have been performed in order to evaluate SCA approach within pedestrian dynamics context. After a brief overview of SCA approach and its possible adoption in modeling crowding situations, we will describe and report main results of an experimental work we performed in order to reproduce Freezing by Heating and Lane Formation (in Section 3). The latter have been empirically observed and previously modeled as collective phenomena resulting from the local interaction induced by limited spatial resources for pedestrian movements in structured and densely populated environments [4].

2   SCA Model and Crowd Simulation

2.1   Situated Cellular Agent Model

Situated Cellular Agent model is a specific class of Multilayered Multi-Agent Situated System (MMASS) [13] providing a single layered spatial structure for agents environment and some limitations to the field emission mechanism.

A *Situated Cellular Agent* system is defined by the triple $\langle Space, F, A \rangle$ where *Space* indicates the environment where the set A of agents is situated, acts autonomously and interacts through the propagation of the set F of fields and through local *reaction*.

Space is defined by SCA as an undirected and unlabeled graph of sites. Every *site* $p \in P$ (where P is the set of sites of the layer) can contain at most one agent and is defined by the 3–tuple

$$\langle a_p, F_p, P_p \rangle$$

where $a_p \in A \cup \{\bot\}$ is the agent situated in p, $F_p \subset F$ is the set of fields active in p and $P_p \subset P$ is the set of sites adjacent to p.

A SCA agent is defined by the 3–tuple $< s, p, \tau >$ where τ is the *agent type*, $s \in \Sigma_\tau$ denotes the *agent state* and can assume one of the values specified by its type (see below for Σ_τ definition), and $p \in P$ is the site of the *Space* where the agent is situated. Agent *type* comprises agent state, perceptive capabilities and behavior. In fact an agent type τ is defined by the 3–tuple $\langle \Sigma_\tau, Perception_\tau, Action_\tau \rangle$. Σ_τ defines the set of states that agents of type τ can assume; $Perception_\tau$ is a function associating to each agent state a vector of pairs representing the *receptiveness coefficient* and *sensitivity thresholds* for that kind of field while $Action_\tau$ represents instead the behavioral specification for agents of type τ. Agent behavior can be specified using a language that defines four primitives. The $emit(s, f, p)$ primitive allows an agent to *start the diffusion of field f* on p, that is the site it is placed on; $react(s, a_{p_1}, a_{p_2}, \ldots, a_{p_n}, s')$ is the primitive that allows the specification of a *coordinated change of state* among adjacent agents; $transport(p, q)$ is the primitive that allows to *define agent movement* from site p to site q (that must be adjacent and vacant); $trigger(s, s')$ is the function that, like the *reaction* primitive, specifies that an agent must *change its state* when it perceives a particular condition in its local context (i.e. its own site and the adjacent ones), but it does not require a coordination with other agents.

Each SCA agent is provided with a set of sensors that allows its interaction with the environment and other agents. At the same time, agents can constitute the source of given fields acting within a SCA space (e.g. noise emitted by a talking agent). Formally, a field type t is defined by $\langle W_t, Diffusion_t, Compare_t, Compose_t \rangle$ where W_t denotes the set of values that fields of type t can assume; $Diffusion_t$ is the diffusion function of the field computing the value of a field on a given space site taking into account in which site and with which value it has been generated. $Compose_t$ expresses how fields of the same type have to be combined while $Compare_t$ is the function that compares values of the same field type. This function is used in order to verify whether an agent can perceive a field value by comparing it with the sensitivity threshold after it has been modulated by the receptiveness coefficient.

2.2   SCA–Based Model of Pedestrian Crowds: Overview

In order to adopt SCA approach in the crowding context, we defined the spatial abstraction in which the simulated entities are situated as a non–directed graph of *sites*, where graph nodes represent available space locations for pedestrians and graph edges define the adjacency relations among them (and agents' suitable movement directions).

We represented as SCA agents of different types both Pedestrians and relevant elements of the spatial structure that may interact with pedestrians and influence their movement (i.e. *active elements of the environment*). Agent type defines the set of suitable states, perceptive capabilities and behavioral abilities of agents.

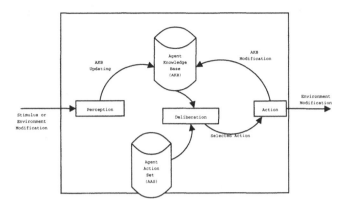

Fig. 1. A schematic representation of the internal architecture of SCA agents

Figure 1 shows a schematic representation of agent internal architecture. The architecture comprises two knowledge containers (i.e. *Agent Knowledge Base* and *Agent Action Set*) and three tasks that define the agent actual behavior (i.e. *Perception, Deliberation, and Action*). The Agent Action Set (AAS) contains the set of actions that are allowed to the agent in terms of L*MASS primitives [14] (i.e. agent abilities), while the Agent Knowledge Base (AKB) contains the internal representation of agent state and of its local environment (e.g. set of fields active in its site, set of empty sites in its surrounding). AAS is defined according to the agent type and cannot change during agent execution, while the AKB updating can be caused by the execution of trigger or react actions or by a change in the agent environment (e.g. an adjacent site becomes empty, a new field reaches the agent site or the agent moves to another site). *Perception* is a function that associates a set of influences with the set of possible actions. When a stimulus reaches the site where the agent is situated or some changes occur in the local environment (e.g. an adjacent site becomes empty), the perception module updates the AKB. Thus, *action* module applies a L*MASS primitive, in order to produce an action. The phase between perception and execution is *deliberation* that is, the component of an agent responsible of selecting an action to be executed from the set of activated actions (i.e. conflict resolution among activated actions). The SCA model does not specify a standard way to perform these tasks. In the following sections we give more details about their specifications in the presented experiments.

In our experiments we adopted a synchronous–parallel execution method, where at every step each agent selects the action to be performed (at fixed environment configuration), in order to take actions at the same time. This solution required the introduction of a conflict resolution strategy in the case of more than one agent choosing the same destination site.

3   Experimenting SCA on Phenomena Emerging from Negative Interaction for Space Sharing

This section presents an analysis of SCA expressive power in reproducing known and well-studied interaction situations in crowds (i.e. *Freezing by Heating* and *Lane Formation*). The latter have been observed within systems of human actors that interact to share a limited spatial environment in situations like the walking through a corridor, or the evacuation of a room. Freezing by Heating is a global slowdown of the system due to the high density rate of pedestrians, while Lane Formation is the spontaneous formation of two pedestrian flows with opposite walking directions.

In the following sections we describe the scenarios we modelled in order to check the ability of SCA to reproduce Freezing by Heating and Lane Formation. In the first scenario we model an evacuation situation where a given number of agents tries to leave a room through a single exit. Lane formation has been studied in an environment similar to a narrow passage populated by pedestrians moving towards one of two large opposite exits.

3.1   Freezing by Heating

Freezing by heating is a phenomenon that occurs in situations of high density of pedestrians and it consists in an extreme slowing down of the flow of pedestrians that can end in a complete stall situation. The immobility (freezing) is caused by the "will" (heating) of all the pedestrians to move towards a specific destination. The attempt of each pedestrian to move is the cause of the mutual hampering of the pedestrians.

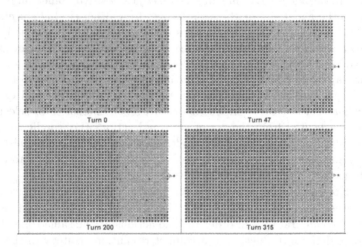

Fig. 2. The figure shows the screenshots of the simulation output with a population density of 40 percent (620 agents). Clear circles represent the agents-pedestrian that move towards the exit (situated on the right-side of the room).

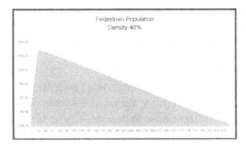

Fig. 3. The figure shows the number of still pedestrians for each simulation step (with a pedestrian population density of 40 percent). Freezing by heating phenomenon can be observed at about step 50.

The scenario of the simulation campaign is constituted by a population of pedestrian that attempt to exit a room endowed with only one exit that doesn't allow a huge volume of flow. The modeling of this scenario with SCA is quite simple (see Figure 2). Space has been modeled with a grid of 31x51 sites (a regular non oriented graph of Moore neighborhood) where each node represents a square area of 45 cm (this is the space occupied by a still person, in accord to literature). The exit is represented by a still agent that occupies a site reachable only from three adjacent sites.

The agent of type *exit* has a unique state and constantly emits a field perceived as attractive by the agents *pedestrians*. The exit field is spread through the environment with a diffusion function that makes the intensity of the field decreasing in relation to the distance from the source. Each pedestrian is represented by an agent, of a specific type, that locally behaves according to its state and to the intensity of the exit field (in case of multiple adjacent sites presenting the same intensity value, the agent will choose randomly its destination). When the agent reaches the exit, it exits the simulation.

The simulation campaign has been performed for a population density of 20, 40 and 60 percent, that means respectively 310, 620 and 930 agents distributed on 1550 sites/nodes. For each density value have been performed 10 experiments. At each step of the simulation we measured the number of *still pedestrians* that is, agents that are not able to move.

Figure 3 shows the average (measured on 10 experiments on a population density of 40 percent) of still pedestrians per step. The graphic allows to understand better what happens in the simulations. The population of pedestrians is directed towards the exit, some of the pedestrians find it difficult to move since the very firsts steps. Immobility increases constantly till it reaches a peak, generally around the step 40-45 (for all the densities). During these steps the percentage of agents that remain still for more than one step is very high (from 80 percent for simulations of density 20 percent to 91 percent in simulation where density is 60 percent). After few steps the peak of immobility decreases, slowly the situation becomes more dynamic and pedestrians can exit the room. The last agent, in average, leaves the room at step 460 (density 20 percent), 913 (density

40 percent) and 1363 (density 60 percent). The experimentation campaign has verified the phenomenon of the freezing by heating [7][5].

3.2   Lane Formation

Lane formation refers to the self–organization of pedestrians into separate flows. It has been empirically observed in scenarios like streets or corridor–like passages that are walkable in both directions. When density is high, pedestrians start to move more difficultly since they share a limited spatial environment. Pedestrian lanes form as the result of local behaviors and interactions of single agents that pursue their individual goals but also attempt to avoid collisions.

As in the previous experimentation, the simulation scenario consists of a regular grid of sites representing available locations for pedestrians, and two types of agents: Pedestrians and Exits. Both types of agents emit a presence field, and pedestrians are attracted by exits according to their individual goals (i.e. one of the two exits). In order to maintain constant the population density, pedestrians that exit the corridor are reinserted into the simulation. Figure 4 shows two screenshots where lane formation phenomena, obtained by simulation, can be observed in corridors of different size.

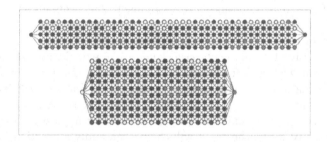

Fig. 4. Screenshots show lane formation phenomenon obtained in simulations in two different corridor topologies. Clear agents move towards the exit on the left, while dark agents are directed to the right exit.

We studied and implemented several behavioral models based on the combination of basic pedestrian behaviors. At each simulation step, each pedestrian perceives its local environment through presence fields of active elements of the environment (i.e. exits) and of other pedestrians. If possible, pedestrians move towards an empty adjacent site that presents the highest value of the field diffused by agent-exit (i.e. that value represents the next best destination). Otherwise, they remain still for at most a given number of steps, and then look for any adjacent empty site. Moreover, to represent the natural tendency of pedestrians to keep a certain distance between each other [5], each agent emits a presence field that is perceived as repulsive by other pedestrians. Presence fields of agents that move towards the same direction are interpreted as less repulsive than those emitted by agents that move in the opposite one. Finally, agents of opposite directions, under some conditions, are allowed to exchange their positions when the site occupied by an agent is the next best destination for the other, and vice versa.

The average speed of a pedestrian that walks in normal situation (neither in panic nor in danger) is indicated by the literature to be about 1,3 meters per second ([15]). In order to compare our results with the ones presented in the literature [18][16][5] we thus defined pedestrian speed in our simulation as one step each 0,3 seconds. This value has been derived by the minimum time required to walk along the whole corridor (i.e. 30 nodes representing 45 square centimeters each) moving one site each simulation step.

The mean speed of pedestrians in relation to population density is shown in Figure 5, where we reported with dotted lines also the results of reference works by Blue and Adler [18] and [16]. Simulations have been performed with densities from 10 to 90 percent.

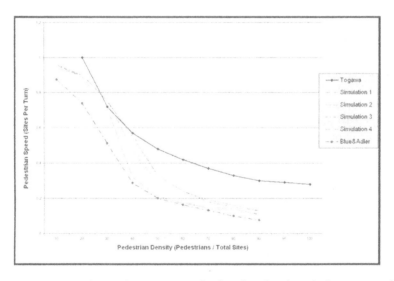

Fig. 5. The graphic shows the mean speed of pedestrian in relation to population density where, reported with dotted lines, also the results of reference works of Blue and Adler and Togawa are displayed

Curves of our simulations are between the two reference curves with some minor variations in relationship to different simulation settings. At higher densities the curve reaches values more close to Blue and Adler results, also in terms of speed values of pedestrians. A qualitative comparison with results reported in [5] confirmed as well the validity of our approach, although our results have been obtained by a different behavioral model.

4   Concluding Remarks and Future Works

We presented some experiments performed to verify whether SCA can replicate freezing by heating and lane formation phenomena. These results suggest SCA as a suitable tool for the modelling and simulation of evacuation scenarios and pedestrian dynamics. Results obtained by this MAS–based approach can be compared to the ones of more traditional approaches. These result encouraged us in considering MAS as a promising modeling tool that can be considered more flexible and more easily applicable to different scenarios. Moreover, in relation to the consideration about emergence and MAS we believe that the obtained phenomena fits the examined constraints and can though be defined "emergent" to the extent that they are not previously codified in the agents behavior, but result from local interactions of the agents. Lanes and groups moreover can be considered as entities that exert an effect on the behavior of the agent, that means that it is present a downward causality that is also considered as characteristic of self organizing systems. To the definition " emergent" we anyway prefer to use "resultant" as, in our opinion, it expresses in a less ambiguous way the real nature of the observed dynamics.

These experiments allowed us to propose some SCA model extensions to improve environment representation and agent behavior. In relation to Spatial Geography we suggest the introduction of a spatial description of sites; that might affect agent behavior as well as field diffusion. We suggest to introduce in the agent description a concept of direction, that could improve the realism of simulations and to adopt a weighted graph, in order to describe the environment with a more expressive ability allowing a more fine modulation of agent behavior and field diffusion. With *Directional Fields* (field that diffuse only in a specific direction) could be possible to introduce the concept of "sight" for the agents that would bring different way to perceive and influence other agents. Future activities will concern the extension of SCA formal specification and execution environment according to the suggestions stated above.

References

1. Schreckenberg, M., Sharma, S.: Pedestrian and Evacuation Dynamics. Springer, Heidelberg (2002)
2. Bandini, S., Federici, M.L., Manzoni, S., Vizzari, G.: Towards a methodology for situated cellular agent based crowd simulations. In: Dikenelli, O., Gleizes, M.-P., Ricci, A. (eds.) ESAW 2005. LNCS (LNAI), vol. 3963, Springer, Heidelberg (2006)
3. Bandini, S., Manzoni, S., Simone, C.: Enhancing cellular spaces by multilayered multi agent situated systems. In: Bandini, S., Chopard, B., Tomassini, M. (eds.) ACRI 2002. LNCS, vol. 2493, pp. 156–167. Springer, Heidelberg (2002)
4. Ferber, J.: Multi-Agent Systems. Addison-Wesley, Harlow (UK) (1999)
5. Helbing, D.: A fluid-dynamic model for the movement of pedestrians. Complex Systems 6, 391–415 (1992)
6. Blue, V.J., Adler, J.: Cellular automata microsimulation for modeling bidirectional pedestrian walkways. Trasportation Research Part B 35, 293–312 (2001)

7. Klupfel, H.: A Cellular Automaton Model for Crowd Movement and Egress Simulation. PhD thesis, Universitat Duisburg-Essen (2003) http://www.ub.uni-duisburg.de/ETD-db/theses/available/duett-08012003-092540/
8. Morishita, S., Shiraishi, T.: Evaluation of billboards based on pedestrian flow in the concourse of the station. In: El Yacoubi, S., Chopard, B., Bandini, S. (eds.) ACRI 2006. LNCS, vol. 4173, pp. 716–719. Springer, Heidelberg (2006)
9. Batty, M., Couclelis, H., Eichen, M.: Urban systems as cellular automata. 24 (1997)
10. Torrens, P.: Cellular automata and multi-agent systems as planning support tools. Planning Support Systems in Practice, 205–222 (2002)
11. Bandini, S., Manzoni, S., Vizzari, G.: Multi-agent approach to localization problems: the case of multilayered multi agent situated system. Web Intelligence and Agent Systems: An International Journal 2, 155–166 (2004)
12. Bandini, S., Manzoni, S., Vizzari, G.: SCA: a model to simulate crowding dynamics. Special Issues on Cellular Automata. IEICE Transactions on Information and Systems E87-D, 669–676 (2004)
13. Bandini, S., Manzoni, S., Simone, C.: Dealing with space in multi-agent system: a model for situated MAS. In: Castelfranchi, C., Johnson, L. (eds.) Proceedings of the 1st International Joint Conference on Autonomous Agents and MultiAgent Systems (AAMAS 2002), July 15-19, 2002, pp. 1183–1190. ACM Press, New York (2002)
14. Bandini, S., Manzoni, S., Pavesi, G., Simone, C.: L*MASS: A language for situated multi-agent systems. In: Esposito, F. (ed.) AI*IA 2001: Advances in Artificial Intelligence. LNCS (LNAI), vol. 2175, pp. 249–254. Springer, Heidelberg (2001)
15. Schadschneider, A.: Cellular automaton approach to pedestrian dynamics -theory (Pedestrian and Evacuation Dynamics) 75–86 (2001)
16. Still, G.K.: Crowd Dynamics. PhD thesis, University of Warwick, Warwick (2000) http://www.crowddynamics.com/
17. Helbing, D., Farkas, J.I., Molnàr, P., Vicsek, T.: Simulation of Pedestrian Crowds in Normal and Evacuation Situations. In: Proccedings of PED01, Pedestrian and Evacuation Dynamics, pp. 21–58. Springer, Heidelberg (2002)
18. Blue, V.J., Adler, J.L.: Cellular automata microsimulation for modeling bidirectional pedestrian walkways. Trasportation Research Part B 35, 293–312 (2001)
19. Bandini, S., Manzoni, S., Simone, C.: Situated Cellular Agents in Non-uniform Spaces. In: Malyshkin, V. (ed.) PaCT 2003. LNCS, vol. 2763, pp. 10–19. Springer, Heidelberg (2003)

Coarse-Grained Parallelization of Cellular-Automata Simulation Algorithms*

Olga Bandman

Supercomputer Software Department
ICM&MG, Siberian Branch, Russian Academy of Sciences
Pr. Lavrentieva, 6, Novosibirsk, 630090, Russia
bandman@ssd.sscc.ru

Abstract. Simulating spatial dynamics in physics by Cellular Automata (CA) requires very large computation power, and, hence, CA simulation algorithms are to be implemented on multiprocessors. The preconceived opinion, that no much effort is required to obtain highly efficient coarse grained parallel CA algorithm, is not always true. In fact, a great variety of CA modifications coming into practical use need appropriate, sometimes sophisticated, methods of CA algorithms parallel implementation. Proceeding from the above a general approach to CA parallelization, based on domain decomposition correctness conditions, is formulated. Starting from the correctness conditions particular parallelization methods are developed for the main classes of CA simulation models: synchronous CA with multi-cell updating rules, asynchronous probabilistic CA, and CA compositions. Examples and experimental results are given for each case.

1 Introduction

A Cellular Automaton (CA) is nowadays an object of growing interest as a mathematical model for spatial dynamics simulation. In some fundamental works [1,2] CA is expected to become a complement to partial differential equations due to its capability of simulating nonlinear and discontinuous processes. Particularly, CA may be helpful when there is no other way of representing a phenomenon to be simulated. By now a great variety of CA are known whose evolution simulate spatial dynamics of natural phenomena, which together with methods and tools for using them, are integrated under a unique concept referred to as *fine-grained parallelism*. The origin of fine-grained parallelism lays in classical CA theory. Classical CA have Boolean alphabet, deterministic one-cell updating transition functions, and synchronous mode of operation. They are capable to simulate diffusion, wave propagation, phase transitions, spatial self-organization [2,3], etc. A more complicated class of CA called Lattice-Gas models [4] is used in hydrodynamics. In chemistry [5] and microelectronics [6] asynchronous probabilistic

* Supported by 1)Presidium of Russian Academy of Sciences, Basic Research Program N 14.16 (2006), 2) Siberian Branch of Russian Academy of Sciences, Interdisciplinary Project 29 (2006).

V. Malyshkin (Ed.): PaCT 2007, LNCS 4671, pp. 370–384, 2007.

CA (sometimes referred to as Monte-Carlo methods) are used for simulating real atoms and molecules moving and interacting.

It is clear that CA simulation of processes on micro-level requires very large CA (up to $10^{10} - 10^{12}$ cells) and many (up to 10^5) iterative steps to obtain a wanted information. Hence, parallel implementation on a multiprocessor system is essential, and methods for CA algorithms parallelization have been developed and studied. Intrinsic fine-grained parallelism and the results of a number of case studies has created an illusion that domain decomposition methods always provide highly efficient parallel programs requiring no much effort [7,8,9] . In fact, the above is true only for classical CA . As for its numerous modifications yet known and intensively emerging, the problem may be more complicated. For example, domain decomposition method is to be modified for CA with multi-cell updating rules [10,12], the similar should be done when hybrid reaction-diffusion CA [11] is used. In case of asynchronous CA the operation mode is to be changed in order to achieve high efficiency of parallel implementation. At the same time, pursuing high efficiency it is possible to break the equality of the initial CA evolution and that of a decomposed CA. It follows therefrom that the problem is to be revised. In the paper an attempt to make such a revision is done based on *correctness conditions* which aim to guarantee the equality of initial CA evolution to that of its parallelized version. In fact, correctness conditions should provide conservation of transition rules of CA elementary automata involved in the interaction between processes. But, bearing in mind that CA mimics kinetics of real or virtual ("stylized") particles, correctness conditions may also be regarded as conservation laws corresponding to the real process under simulation.

The paper aims to formulate correctness conditions for domain decomposition methods of CA parallelization, and to show how parallel algorithms should be developed for the most known types of CA simulation models. In the second section correctness conditions are formulated. The following three sections are devoted to domain decomposition algorithms of synchronous, asynchronous and hybrid CA decomposition algorithms which are illustrated by the examples from series of simulations of flow propagation through porous media of different type.

2   Correctness Conditions for CA Domain Decomposition

2.1   Formal Definitions

Cellular Automaton is defined by four terms, $\aleph = \langle A, M, \Theta, \rho \rangle$ [12], which have the following meaning: A is a state alphabet, M is a naming set, Θ is a local operator, ρ is a mode of functioning. The alphabet may be any set of numbers, symbols, vectors or matrices. The naming set used in CA-simulation comprises coordinate vectors of discrete space points (i, j, k), which are for short denoted by a single symbol m. Two particular sets A and M define a class of *cellular arrays* $A \times M$, whose each representative $\Omega = \{(a, m) : a \in A, m \in M\}$ is a set of pairs called *cells*. Each cell corresponds to an elementary automaton, named $m \in M$ in a state $a \in A$. On M naming functions $\phi(m) : M \to M$ are defined, whose values associate with a cell m a number of its neighboring cells, forming a *local configuration*

$$Q(m) = \{(u_0, m), ..., (u_k, \phi_k(m)), ..., (u_q, \phi_q(m))\}, \tag{1}$$

where $U_Q(m) = \{u_0, u_1, ..., u_q\}$ is a *state set* of $Q(m)$, and

$$T_Q(m) = \{m, \phi_1(m), ..., \phi_k(m), ...\phi_q(m)\} \tag{2}$$

is the *underlying template* for $Q(m)$.

Two local configurations

$$Q(m) = \{(u_0, m), (u_1, \phi_1(m))..., (u_q, \phi_q(m))\},$$
$$S(m) = \{(v_0, \psi_0(m), (v_1, \psi_1(m), ...,)(v_s, \psi_s(m))\},$$

being composed into a substitution of the form

$$\Theta(m) : S(m) \rightarrow Q(m), \tag{3}$$

constitute a *local operator*, where $S(m)$ and $Q(m)$ are referred to *as a basic*, and a *next state* local configurations of Θ, respectively, m being called a *main cell* of Θ.

The next states $u_k \in U_Q$, $k = 0, ..., q$, are values of corresponding *transition function*

$$u_k = f_k(v_0, ..., v_s), \qquad k = 0, 1, ..., q. \tag{4}$$

Local operator Θ is applicable to a cell $m \in M$, if $T_S(m) \subseteq M$ and $v_k \in A$ for all $k = 0, ..., s$. Application of Θ to a cell $m \in M$ consists of two actions: 1) computing next states (4), and 2)updating cells of $Q(m)$ assigning the obtained values to their states.

A subset $M' \subseteq M$ referred to as a *main naming set* is defined, such that application of Θ to all $m \in M'$ comprises *an iteration* performing a global transition

$$\Theta(M') : \Omega(t) \rightarrow \Omega(t+1), \tag{5}$$

The sequence

$$\Sigma(\Omega) = (\Omega, \Omega(1), ..., \Omega(t), \Omega(t+1), ..., \Omega(\hat{t})), \tag{6}$$

obtained during iterative operation of the CA is called *the evolution*, t being the iteration number. CA evolution is the result of the simulation task, representing the process under simulation. If the process converges to a stable global state, then CA evolution has a termination, i.e. there exists such a $t = \hat{t}$, that $\Omega(\hat{t}) = \Omega(\hat{t}+1) = \Omega(\hat{t}+2) = ...$ If it is not so, then the evolution is infinite, exhibits oscillatory or chaotic behavior [2].

The mode $\rho \in \{\alpha, \beta, ..., \sigma\}$ of CA operation determines the order of cells to be chosen for local operator applications during the iteration. Synchronous (denoted as σ) and asynchronous (denoted as α) modes are the basic ones. Accordingly, a synchronous CA is denoted as $\aleph_\sigma$ and an asynchronous one - as $\aleph_\alpha$.

In synchronous CA cell-states of $\Omega(t)$ are updated only after all next states for all $m \in M$ are computed. Theoretically, it may be done in all cells simultaneously or at any order, which manifests the *cellular parallelism*. In fact, when a conventional sequential computer is used, such a cellular parallelism is imitated by delaying cell updating until all next states are obtained. So, really the cellular parallelism is a *virtual parallelism*, which cannot be for the benefit in conventional computers.

Asynchronous mode of operation suggests no simultaneous operation (neither real nor virtual). Intrinsic parallelism of $\aleph_\alpha$ is exhibited by the arbitrary order of cells to be chosen for application of $\Theta(m)$, the updating of cell states of $Q(m)$ being done immediately after $\Theta(m)$ is applied. So, each global transition $\Omega(t) \to \Omega(t+1)$ consists of $|M'|$ sequential acts of cell updating, being referred to as *global state transition sequences*. Due to random order of those acts the number of all possible transition sequences is qual to the number of transpositions in M, which is $\mu = |M|!$. The important property of asynchronous mode of operation is that the state values used by transition functions (4) may belong both to $\Omega(t)$ and to $\Omega(t+1)$. It is the reason why two CA - $\aleph_\sigma$ and $\aleph_\alpha$ with equal $\langle A, M, \Theta \rangle$ starting from the same Ω may have quite different evolutions. Although, some exotic "very good" CA are known, whose evolutions and attractors are invariant whatever mode of operation is used [12].

2.2   Correctness Conditions of CA Algorithms

A CA $\aleph_\varrho = \langle A, M, \Theta \rangle$ is considered to be a CA-algorithm, if its operation satisfies the following correctness conditions.

1. Noncontradictoriness. *Only one updating of a cell is allowed at one time step.*

Noncontradictoriness is a CA-version of *safeness* - a main property of parallel systems correct behavior. [12]. The sufficient condition of noncontradictoriness is as follows [12].

$$T_Q(m_k) \cap T_Q(m_l) = \emptyset \qquad \forall (m_k, m_l) \in M. \tag{7}$$

It guarantees the absence of conflicts, which are situations when two transition functions $f_g(m)$ and $f_h(\phi_l(m))$ are attempting to change the state of one and the same cell simultaneously. From (7) it follows, that for classical synchronous CA with $|Q(m)| = 1$ it is always satisfied. It is not so, if CA is a model of a process where some cells are to be changed simultaneously, i.e. $|Q(m)| > 1$. In this case a bit of cellular parallelism is to be sacrificed for noncontradictoriness by means of sequentializing the computation procedure as follows.

1) The main naming set M' is partitioned into b, $b \leq |T_Q|$, *stage-subsets*, $\{M'_0, ..., M'_b\}$, such that

$$M'_g \cap M'_h = \emptyset, \quad \forall (g, h) \in 1, ..., b, \qquad \bigcup_{g=0}^{p} M'_g = M', \tag{8}$$

and for any M'_g, $g = 1, ..., b$, the condition (7) holds.

2) The iteration is divided into p stages. At each g-th stage Θ is applied synchronously to all cells $m \in M'_g$.

Such mode of operation is called a *multi-stage synchronous* mode with multi-cell updating and denoted as $\aleph_\beta$. As for asynchronous CA, they always satisfy noncontradictoriness conditions, because $\Theta(m)$ is applied to a single cell at each time-step.

Equality of cells. *At each iteration $\Theta(m)$ should be applied to all cells $m \in M'$, to any cell $m \in M'$ being applied only once.* Equality of cells is a CA-version of *liveness condition* for parallel processes [12]. It provides all cells to have equal rights to participate in the CA operation process. Synchronous classical CA satisfy this property by the definition of synchronicity. When multi-stage synchronous mode is used the equality of cells is provided by condition (8). In asynchronous CA cells equality is the consequence of binomial probability distribution law.

2.3   Correctness Conditions of CA Decomposition

Inherent cellular parallelism of CA models predetermines domain decomposition to be a basic principle for CA parallelization. In terms of CA this principle is read as follows. CA $\aleph_\varrho = \langle A, M, \Theta \rangle$ is represented by a composition of n ones, such that

1) $\aleph_\varrho^{(k)} = \langle A, M_k, \Theta \rangle$, $k = 1, ..., n$;
2) each domain M_k is a compact part of M;
3) domains do not intersect, i.e.

$$\bigcup_{k=1}^{n} M_k = M, \qquad M_k \cap M_l = \emptyset, \qquad \text{for all} \quad k, l \in \{1, ..., n\}; \qquad (9)$$

4) all domains have equal cardinalities, $|M_1| = |M_2| = ... = |M_n|$.
5) It is convenient to assign cell names in the domains in such a way, that $(i, j) \in M_k$ is equal to $(i(mod N_i), j(mod N_j)) \in M$, where $N_i \times N_j$ is the size of Ω.

Since the result of CA simulation is its evolution, the main condition of coarse-grained parallelization is the equality of evolutions, i.e. *the evolution of n operating in parallel CA $\aleph_\varrho^{(k)} = \langle A, M_k, \Theta \rangle$, $k = 1, ..., n$; should be equal to that of a non-decomposed $\aleph_\varrho = \langle A, M, \Theta \rangle$* i.e.

$$\Sigma(\Omega) = \Sigma \left(\bigcup_{k=1}^{n} \Omega_k \right) \qquad \forall \Omega = \bigcup_{k=1}^{n} \Omega_{k.}, \qquad (10)$$

The condition being laid down, the problem is to organize the parallel operation in such a way that the condition is satisfied, i.e. make each domain to interact with the adjacent ones by exchanging data that are needed to be used in one of them for computing next-states in the other. To be more formal, let's denote as (M_l, M_r) a pair of adjacent domains. Being applied to a cell $m_l \in M_l$,

$\Theta(m_l)$ has to interact with the cells from $S(m_l)$, some of which, are allocated in M_r forming a *border area* of M_r denoted by Υ_r. The similar border area Υ_l comprises cells from M_l which are to be used by $\Theta(m_r)$.

$$\Upsilon_r = \bigcup_{m_l \in M_l} (T_S(m_l) \cap M_r), \quad \Upsilon_l = \bigcup_{m_r \in M_r} (T_S(m_r) \cap M_l). \tag{11}$$

To provide interactions between the domains two sets of cells $(\Upsilon_l', \Upsilon_r')$, whose cells are in one-to-one correspondence with those of (Υ_r, Υ_l), should be appended to the borders of (M_l, M_r), respectively, forming the extended naming sets $\hat{M}_l$, and $\hat{M}_r$.

The procedure of data exchange consists of copying cell states of $m_l \in \Upsilon_l$ into its counterpart $\Upsilon_r' \subseteq \hat{M}_r$, and copying cell states of Υ_r into $\Upsilon_l' \subseteq \hat{M}_l$. Modes of the exchange procedure depend on the mode of $\aleph_\varrho$, but in all cases correctness properties is achieved by obeying the following *data exchange rules*.

1. At any iteration each cell state $m_l \in \Upsilon_l$ should be copied into the corresponding cell of its counterpart Υ_r'.

2. Between two acts of copying the state of $m_l \in \Upsilon_l$ into Υ_r', the cell m_l should be updated, and only once.

3. No cell in an appended area $m' \in \Upsilon_l'$ is allowed to be updated by $\Theta(m_l)$.

The first two rules provide the condition of cells equality in the adjacent border areas. The third ascertains that noncontradictoriness condition is not violated in border areas.

From the above rules the method for allocating the a CA $\aleph_\rho = \langle A, M, \Theta \rangle$ to be run on n processors is as follows.

Step 1. Cut the cellular array into n compact equal parts with naming sets $\{M_k : k = 1, ..., n\}$ satisfying (9).

Step 2. Determine the border areas $\Upsilon_l \subseteq M_k$ and their counterparts $\Upsilon_r' \subseteq M_k$ according to (11) for all the borders of each domain.

Step 3. Develop the data exchange procedure according to the above four rules and to the mode of operation of $\aleph_\rho$.

It is the last step which constitutes the problem of parallelization, because the differential peculiarities of CA simulation models require special techniques to obey the above four data exchanging rules. For the most widely used CA-models the techniques are presented in the next section,

3 Parallelization of CA Algorithms

3.1 Synchronous CA Parallelization

The most simple for parallelization are synchronous CA-models with a single cell updating, $|Q(m)| = 1$. For them the procedure of data exchanging is trivial: at each iteration the border areas of adjacent domains are copied into their counterparts. It is easily seen that the procedure obeys all four data exchange rules. MPI tools, which are mainly used for performing data exchange, allow to make the transfer of data during the internal cells next states computation. Hence, the efficiency of parallel implementation is close upon 100%. It decreases only when the size of the domains is so small, that internal computation time does not exceed the time of data transferring [15]. The most known and well studied CA-models of this type belong to Lattice-Gas hydrodynamics [4]. The peculiarity of Lattice-Gas CA is in the fact that each iteration consists of two sequential stages (propagation and collision of particles). Since intercell communication occurs only at the propagation stage, the exchange of data may be done during the collision stage, which makes data exchange no time consuming procedure. Parallel implementation efficiency is thoroughly investigated in [14], where it is shown that degradation of the parallelization efficiency may occur due to small domain size and due to communication system problems.

As for synchronous CA-models with multi-cell updating ($|Q(m)| = q, q > 1$), the procedure of data exchange is more complicated, because noncontradictoriness conditions (7,8) require the following two statements to be taken into account.

- In each k-th domain the main naming set $M'_k \subseteq M_k$ is partitioned into p stage-subsets $\{M'_g : g = 1, ..., q\}$.
- Belonging to different stage-subsets M'_g, $g = 1, ..., q$ the main cells of $\Theta(m_l)$ $m_l \in M'_l$ occur at different distances from the domain border. Hence, border areas differ from stage to stage, $\Upsilon_l(g) \neq \Upsilon_l(h)$.

Based on the above statements data exchanging procedure is as follows.

1) In all domains the stage subarrays $M'_g \subset M_k$, $g = 1.,,,.q$, are defined according to (9).

2) The iteration is divided into q stages. At each g-th stage Θ is applied to the cells of M'_g of all the domains.

3) For each g-th stage subarray, $g = 1, ..., q$, border areas $\Upsilon_l(g) \subseteq M_l$ and $\Upsilon_r(g) \subseteq M_r$ should be determined according to (11) for all borders pairs of adjacent domains (M_l, M_r), $l, r = 1.,,,.n$.

4) Each domain M_k, $k = 1, ..., n$, should be appended by the counterparts $\Upsilon'_r(g)$ and $\Upsilon'_r(g)$ of the border areas $\Upsilon_l(g)$ and $\Upsilon_r(g)$, respectively, at all its borders.

5) At each g-th stage, $g = 1, ..., q$, the next cell states of border areas $\Upsilon_l(g) \subseteq M_l$ are copied into its counterpart $\Upsilon_r(g)' \subseteq M_r$ in all domains $M_k \in M$.

Example 1. A bright example of a CA with multi-cell updating is a Margolus' diffusion model $\aleph_\beta = \langle A, M, \Theta \rangle$, proposed in [3], and proved to be equivalent to Laplace PDE in [10]. $A = \{0, 1\}$, $M = \{(i, j) : i, j = 0, ..., N\}$. In M two subsets are defined: $M^{even} = \{(i, j) : i(mod_2) = 0, j(mod_2) = 0\}$ and $M^{odd} = \{(i, j) : i(mod_2) = 1, j(mod_2) = 1\}$. They induce on M two partitions by 2×2 blocks given by a template $T(i, j) = \{(i, j), (i, j + 1), (i + 1, j + 1), (i + 1, j)\}$. If $(i, j) \in M^{even}$ the template represents the even partition, otherwise it represents the odd one. The local operator is as follows

$$\Theta(i, j): \begin{array}{l} \{(v_0, (i, j)), (v_1, (i, j + 1)), (v_2, (i + 1, j + 1)), (v_3, (i + 1, j))\} \\ \rightarrow \{(u_0, (i, j)), (u_1, (i, j + 1)), (u_2, (i + 1, j + 1)), (u_3, (i + 1, j))\}, \end{array} \quad (12)$$

$$\text{where } u_k = \begin{cases} v_{k-1}(mod_4), & \text{with probability} \quad \pi \\ v_{k+1}(mod_4), & \text{with probability} \quad 1 - \pi \end{cases}, \qquad k = 0, 1, 2, 3.$$

The mode of operation is two-stage synchronous, i.e. at even t $\Theta(i, j)$ is applied to M^{even}, at odd t – to M^{odd}. The model is used for simulating flow propagation of water through a porous substance under the influence of isotropic diffusion. (Fig. 1).

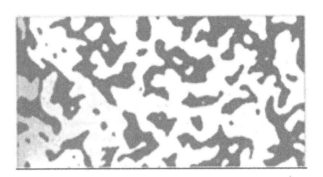

Fig. 1. A snapshot ($t = 4 \cdot 10^5$) of the simulation process or flow propagation in porous medium under isotropic diffusion. A fragment 300×600 cells is shown. Black cells correspond to solid walls, grey pixels - to fluid, white - to empty space.

Proceeding from the given physical parameters of the sample under simulation the cellular naming set is chosen as $M = \{(i, j : i = 0, ..., 8N, j = 0, ..., N\}$, with $N = 1000$. According to the above method the parallel algorithm is as follows.

1. The cellular array is decomposed into $n = 16$ domains with naming sets $M_k = \{(i, j) : i = 0, ..., 499, j = 0, ..., 999\}$, $k = 1, ..., n$, and $N(mod_2) = 0$.

2. On each domain M_k, $k = 1, ..., 16$, two subsets of names $M^{even} \subseteq M_k$ and $M^{odd} \subseteq M_k$ are defined.

3. Border areas and their counterparts are determined for the even and the odd stages as follows.

Even stage. Since the number of cells in any domain is even, then according to (11) for any pair of adjacent domains $M_l^{even} \subseteq M_l, M_r^{even} \subseteq M_r$ $T_S(i, j)_l^{even} \cap M_r^{even} = \emptyset$ for all $((i, j)_l(even)) \in M_l$, which yields in

$$\Upsilon_l = \Upsilon_r = \Upsilon_l' = \Upsilon_r' = \emptyset$$

Odd stage. The underlying template $T_S(N - 1, j) = \{(N - 1, j)(N - 1, j + 1)(N, j)(N + 1, j)\}$ of the border cells of M_l indicates that cells included in two last terms – (N, j) and $(N + 1, j)$ – are allocated in M_r, being named there as $\{0, j), (0, j + 1)\}$, j=0,...,N-1. Substituting it into (11) yields for j=0,...,N-1,

$$\Upsilon_r = \{(0, j)\}, \quad \Upsilon_l = \{(N - 1, j)\}, \quad \Upsilon_l' = \{(N, j)\}, \quad \Upsilon_l' = \{(-1, j)\},$$

and Υ_l' and Υ_r' are appended adjoining the borders of M_l and M_r, respectively. The similar is true for all adjacent borders.

4. After the even stage is completed no exchanges are done because the border areas for even stage are empty.

5. After the odd stage is completed data exchange is performed between all adjacent pairs of the domains: cell states of Υ_l are copied to the corresponding cells of Υ_r' and cell states of Υ_r are copied to the corresponding cells of Υ_l'.

The algorithm has been programmed and implemented in 16 processors of the cluster MVS-1000/128 in Siberian Supercomputer Center. Implementation of the algorithm in 16 processors showed the run time 1.012 times greater than that of a CA with the array size of one domain.

3.2 Asynchronous CA Parallelization

As distinct from the CA, whose parallel implementation is extremely efficient, the asynchronous case exhibits a problem for parallel simulation. The reason is in the impossibility of forming packages for data exchange. Each state $m_l \in \Upsilon_l$ is to be copied to Υ_r' of the adjacent domain just after the cell is updated. No delay for even a single time-step τ is allowed, because at the same time-step the cell (u, m_l) may be updated by the application of Θ to its neighbor, which violates the noncontradictoriness condition. It is evident that transferring data to adjacent processor after each updating of a border cell results in a very low efficiency of parallel implementation, because of transfer latency time, which is usually some orders larger than the transmission of a data bit. Moreover, in those random intercommunications one should avoid the deadlocks, which is an additional task. So, the above direct data exchange method should be rejected. The advantages of synchronous CA parallel implementation inspires the search of a transformation of the given asynchronous CA into a synchronous one having the same evolution. Unfortunately, there is no transformations which provide equality of evolutions in general case. Thus, the attempt is made to find a multi-stage synchronous CA, whose evolution approximates that of a given asynchronous $\aleph_\alpha$. It has been used for particular cases in [16,?], and considered in detail in [15]. The term "approximation" is used in the following sense. Some order is imposed to the random choice of cells to be updated, which brings no distortion in the evolution progress, but only restricts the ensemble of all possible transition sequences to the next global state. The algorithm for constructing $\aleph_\beta =$ which approximats the given $\aleph_\alpha = \langle A, M, \Theta \rangle$ is as follows.

1. Parameters A, M, and Θ are the same than those of $\aleph_\alpha$, where $\Theta : S(m) \to Q(m)$ with $|T_Q(m)| = q$.

2. A template T_B is defined, such that

$$T_B(m) \supseteq T_Q(m). \tag{13}$$

Naturally, $T_B(m)$ should be chosen of minimum cardinality, because it results in a less amount of stages.

3. On the main naming set $M' \in M$ the subsets $\{M_0', ..., M_b'\}$, $b = |T_B(m)|$ are defined satisfying the condition (8) for multi-stage CA. Moreover, for any M_g', $g = 1, ..., b$, the noncontradictoriness condition should be met, i.e.

$$T_B(m_k) \cap T_B(m_l) = \emptyset \quad \forall (m_g, m_h) \in M_g, \qquad \bigcup_{m_g \in M_g} T_B(m_g) = M. \quad (14)$$

4. Each iteration is divided into b stages. At each gth stage Θ is applied synchronously to all cells $m \in M'_g$, the subsets M'_g being chosen in any order.

In [15] it is proved that $\aleph_\beta$ obtained by the above algorithm is the restriction of $\aleph_\alpha$ in the sense that the set of its evolutions is included in the ensemble of all possible evolutions of $\aleph_\beta$, being far less in cardinality. By the above transformation he parallelization method of the $\aleph_\alpha$ is reduced to that of multi-stage CA parallelization.

Example 2. When anisotropy imposed by the pore walls properties and an additional pressure are to be taken into account, probabilistic asynchronous diffusion CA called a "naive diffusion" is used, $\aleph_\alpha = \langle A, M, \Theta \rangle$, $A = \{0, 1\}$, $M = \{(i, j)\}$, The application of Θ to a cell $(i, j) \in M$ makes the cell (i, j) to exchange states with one of its nearest neighbors $\phi_k(i, j)$ chosen with probability $p = p_k$, $k = 1, 2, 3, 4$.

$$\Theta(i, j) : \{(v_0, (i, j)), (v_1, (i - 1, j)), (v_2, (i, j + 1)), (v_3, (i + 1, j)), (v_4, (i, j_1))\}$$
$$\rightarrow \quad \{(u_0, (i, j)), (u_1, (i - 1, j)), (u_2, (i, j + 1)), (u_3, (i + 1, j)), (u_4, (i, j_1))\},$$

where

$$(u_0 = v_k) \& (v_k = u_0) \quad \text{if} \quad \begin{cases} (v_0 = 1 \& v_k = 0) & \text{with } p = p_k, \\ (v_0 = 0 \& v_k = 1) & \text{with } p = 1 - p_k. \end{cases}$$

The probabilities are determined by physical properties of the medium. Particularly, in case of hydrophobic pores and presence of a convective flow in the direction of the jth axis they are as follows.

$$p_1 = p_3 = 0.25 p_d, \quad p_2 = 0.3 p_d, \quad p_4 = 0.2 p_d \quad p_d = \sin \frac{\pi}{20} d,$$

where d is the distance between the cell (i, j) and the nearest wall. The local operator is applied to all cells of the array, i.e. $M' = M$. Parallel application of the model has been tested in simulation of flow propagation through the sample of porous substance having the same dimensions than those of Example 1. The parallel algorithm consists of two phases: 1)constructing the multistage approximation $\aleph_\beta$, and 2) determining the parameters of the data exchange procedure.

Phase 1
1. The template $T_B = \{(i + k, j + l) : k, l = -1, 0, 1\}$, satisfying (12) is defined with $s = |S(m)| = 9$.
2. Stage-subsets M_g, g=0,1,...,8, are formed according to (8) as follows:

$$(i, j) \in M_g \quad \text{if} \quad g = 3i(mod3) + j(mod3), \quad (15)$$

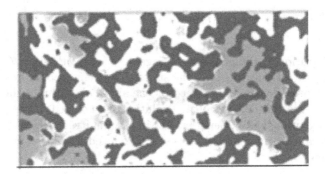

Fig. 2. A snapshot ($t = 70 \cdot 10^3$) of the simulation process or flow propagation in hydrophobic porous medium under anisotropic diffusion. A fragment 300×600 cells is shown. Black cells correspond to solid walls, grey pixels - to fluid, white pixels - to empty space.

Phase 2

1. The array is decomposed in 16 domains of 501×1002 cells, $N = 501$ is chosen being a multiple to $|S(m)| = 3 \times 3$, which allows to distribute the cells of M among the stage-subsets according to the rule (15).

2. Border areas and their counterparts are computed following (11) as follows.

$$
\begin{aligned}
&\text{if } g(mod_3) = 0: \quad \Upsilon_l = \Upsilon_r' = \emptyset, \quad \Upsilon_r = \{(i, N-2), (i, N-1),\\
&\hspace{4.2cm} \Upsilon_l' = \{(i, -1), (i, -2)\},\\
&\text{if } g(mod_3) = 1: \quad \Upsilon_l = \Upsilon_r' = \emptyset, \quad \Upsilon_r = \Upsilon_l' = \emptyset,\\
&\text{if } g(mod_3) = 2: \quad \Upsilon_r = \Upsilon_l' = \emptyset, \quad \Upsilon_l = \{(i, 0), (i, 1)\}, \quad \Upsilon_r' = \{(i, N), (i, N+1),\}\\
&\text{for } \quad i = 0, ..., N-1.
\end{aligned}
$$

$$(16)$$

The algorithm has been programmed and implemented in 16 processors of the cluster MVS-1000/128 in Siberian Supercomputer Center. The running time in 16 processors is 1.056 times greater than that for running the same amount of iterations in a single domain in a single processor.

3.3   Parallelization of Composed CA

Real life simulation tasks require several simple CA-models to operate in common for being adequate to a phenomenon under study. A number of methods are known [18] for composing some simple CA to obtain a CA-model of a complicated phenomenon. Two basic methods are the most used: a sequential composition called *superposition*, and a *parallel composition*, which are worth to be considered concerning coarse grained parallelization.

When *superposition* is used the process under simulation is composed of n component CA $\aleph_\rho^{(k)} = \langle A, M, \Theta^{(k)} \rangle$, $k = 1, ..., n$, which have identical alphabets and naming sets, but may differ in local operators and modes of operation. The composed CA $\aleph_\rho = \langle A, M, \Phi \rangle$, $\Phi = \{\Theta^{(1)}, ..., \Theta^k, ..., \Theta^n\}$, operates as follows.

Each iteration $\Omega(t) \xrightarrow{\Phi} \Omega(t+1)$ consists of n sequential transitions $\Omega^{(k)}(t) \xrightarrow{\Theta^{(k)}}$
$\Omega^{(k)}(t)$, $k = 1, ..., n$, each kth transition being an iteration of $\aleph_\rho^{(k)}$. It is worth
to notice, that any component CA performs its transition operating in its own
mode. Moreover, a component CA may be itself a composed CA, in what case the
composition exhibits an hierarchial construction. The method of parallelization
of a global superposition reduces to construction of the iteration of $\aleph_\rho$ as a
sequence of n iterations of the parallel algorithms of $\aleph_\rho^{(k)}$, developing the data
exchange procedures according to the rules, corresponding to their modes of
operation.

More complicated is coarse grained parallelization of CA which is a *parallel
composition*, when two[1] CA operate each on its own cellular array, using cell
states of the other as variables in its transition functions. Let two component
CA be $\aleph_\rho^{(1)} = \langle A^{(1)}, M^{(1)}, \Theta^{(1)} \rangle$, and $\aleph_\rho^{(2)} = \langle A^{(2)}, M^{(2)}, \Theta^{(2)} \rangle$. They should
have identical modes of operation, identical naming sets, but may have different
alphabet and different local operators.

$$\Theta^{(1)}((i,j)^{(1)}) : S^{(1)}((i,j)^{(1)}) \rightarrow Q^{(1)}((i,j)^{(1)}),$$

$$\Theta^{(2)}((i,j)^{(2)}) : S^{(2)}((i,j)^{(2)}) \rightarrow Q^{(2)}((i,j)^{(2)}).$$

The basic template

$$T_{S^{(1)}}(m) = \{\phi_0(m), ..., \phi_l(m), \phi_{(l+1)}(m), ..., \phi_s(m)\}, \quad m \in M^{(1)}$$

has the first l naming functions defined in $M^{(1)}$, and the last $s - l$ ones – defined
in $M^{(2)}$. Similarly,

$$T_{S^{(2)}}(m) = \{\phi_0(m), ..., \phi_h(m), \phi_{h+1}(m), ..., \phi_g(m)\}, \quad m \in M^{(2)}$$

has the first h naming functions defined in $M^{(2)}$, and the last $g - h$ ones – defined
in $M^{(1)}$. Each t-th iteration of a composed CA comprises next state computation
in all cells of both CA.

Parallelization method for a composed CA should follow all the rules given in
Subsection 2.3, being slightly modified as follows.

Step 1. Cellular arrays of both CA are cut into n compact equal parts $M_k = M_k^{(1)} \cup M_k^{(2)}$.

Step 2. Border areas are determined according to (11) for all pairs of adjacent
domains $M_l^{(1)}, M_r^{(1)}$ and $M_l^{(2)}, M_r^{(2)}$.

$$\Upsilon_r^{(11)} = \bigcup_{m_l \in M_l^{(1)}} \left(T_S^{(1)}(m_l) \cap M_r^{(1)} \right), \quad \Upsilon_r^{(12)} = \bigcup_{m_l \in M_l^{(1)}} \left(T_S^{(1)}(m_l) \cap M_r^{(2)} \right),$$
$$\Upsilon_r^{(22)} = \bigcup_{m_l \in M_l^{(2)}} \left(T_S^{(2)}(m_l) \cap M_r^{(2)} \right), \quad \Upsilon_r^{(21)} = \bigcup_{m_l \in M_l^{(2)}} \left(T_S^{(2)}(m_l) \cap M_r^{(1)} \right),$$

$$(17)$$

---

[1] The amount of component CA is confined to 2 because there is no experience of
testing parallel composition of more than 2 CA, though there is no principal objection
for the method to be extended to any numbers of component CA.

Their counterparts $\Upsilon_l'^{(11)} \cup \Upsilon_l'^{(12)}$ are to be appended to $M_l^{(1)}$, and $\Upsilon_l'^{(22)} \cup \Upsilon_l'^{(21)}$ - to $M^{(2)}$. The similar should be done to all other borders of both domains.

Step 3. Data exchange procedure consists of copying cell states from all border areas of each component array to their counterparts in the adjacent domains.

The above global parallel composition is used for simulation reaction-diffusion phenomena, where diffusion may be modeled by a Boolean CA $\aleph_\rho^{(1)}$), and reaction - by a CA with real alphabet [11] At each iteration transition functions (4) of $\aleph_\rho^{(1)}$ have to transform real variables from $\Omega^{(2)}$ into Boolean form in order to compute Boolean function. On its turn $\aleph_\sigma^{(2)}$ has to transform Boolean cell states of $\Omega^{(1)}$ into reals for computing its transition functions. The latter transformation includes averaging the Boolean states over the given *averaging area* which plays the role of basic local configuration $S^{(2)}(m)$, which is allocated in $\Omega^{(2)}$.

Example 3. Simulation of flow propagation through porous medium, where the fluid is exposed to a chemical reaction (oxidation), is modeled by a parallel composition of $\aleph_\beta^{(1)} = \langle A^{(1)}, M^{(1)}, \Theta^{(1)} \rangle$, simulating Boolean isotropic diffusion , and $\aleph_\sigma^{(2)} = \langle A^{(2)}, M^{(2)}, \Theta^{(2)} \rangle$ simulating reaction in reals. The diffusion CA $\aleph_\beta^{(1)} = $ in its turn is the superposition of $\aleph_{trans}^{(1)} = \langle \{0,1\}, M^{(1)}, \Theta_{trans} \rangle$, which performs transformation of real array $\Omega^{(2)}$ into a Boolean form, and $\aleph_{diff} \langle \{0,1 \, M^{(1)}, \Theta_{diff} \rangle$ simulating diffusion of Example 1, Θ_{diff} being equal to (12).

$$\Theta_{trans} : S_1^{(1)}(m^{(1)}) \to Q_1^{(1)}(m^{(1)}), \text{ where} S_1^{(1)}(m^{(1)}) = \{(v, m^{(1)}, (u, m^{(2)})\},$$
$$Q_1^{(1)}(m^{(1)}) = \{(f_1(u), m^{(2)})\}, \qquad f_1(u) = 1 \text{ with } \pi = u.$$

The local operator $\Theta^{(2)}$ is applied to the cells of $\Omega^{(2)}$ with states in $A^{(2)} = [0,1]$, where

$$S^{(2)}(m)^{(2)} = \{(u, m^{(2)}), (v_0, m^{(1)}), (v_1, \phi_1(m^{(1)})), ..., (v_s, \phi_s(mm^{(1)}))\},$$
$$Q^{(2)}(m) = \{(u\prime, m^{(2)}\},$$

where s is the averaging area size $5 \times 5 - 1$, $s = 24$ and

$$u\prime = 0.2w(1-w), \quad w = \frac{1}{s}\sum_l^s v_k.$$

Parallel application of the model has been tested on the flow propagation through the sample of porous medium having the same size than in Example 1. An iteration of the parallel algorithm is as follows.

Step 1. Both arrays are decomposed into 16 domains 500×1000 cells $\{M_k\}$, $k = 1, ..., 16$.

Step 2. Border areas and their counterparts are determined according to (11).

$$\Upsilon_l^{(1)}(\Theta_{trans}) = \Upsilon_r^{(1)}(\Theta_{diff}) = \emptyset,$$

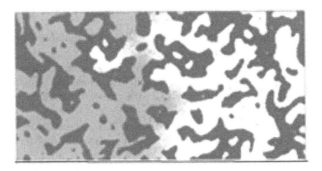

Fig. 3. A snapshot($t = 120 \cdot 10^3$) of the simulation process of flow propagation in porous medium under isotropic diffusion and oxidation. A fragment 300×600 cells is shown. Black cells correspond to solid walls, grey pixels - to fluid, white pixels - to empty space.

$\Upsilon_l^{(1)}(\Theta_{diff})$ and $\Upsilon_r^{(1)}(\Theta_{diff})$ are equal to those from Example 1 (step 3).

$$\Upsilon_r^{(1)}(\Theta^{(2)}) = \{(i,j) : i = 0, ...5\} \qquad \Upsilon_l^{(1)}(\Theta^{(2)}) = \{(i,j) : i = N-1, ..., N-6\},$$
$$\Upsilon_r^{(1)\prime}(\Theta^{(2)}) = \{(i,j) : i = -1, ... -5\}, \;\; \Upsilon_l^{(1)\prime}(\Theta^{(2)}) = \{(i,j) : i = N, ..., N+5\},$$
$$j = 0, .., N-1.$$

Step 3. In all domains M_k next states of $\Omega_k^{(1)}$ and $\Omega_k^{(2)}$ are computed and data exchange is performed between all pairs $(M_l^{(1)}, M_r^{(1)})$ of the adjacent domains.

Implementation of the algorithm in 16 processors showed the run time to be 1.021 times greater than that of the same simulation with the size 16 times less.

4   Conclusion

A general approach to domain decomposition methods for coarse-grained parallellization of CA algorithms is proposed. The approach is based on the fundamental principles of parallel processes correct behavior, which are formulated in the form of conditions to be met when organizing data exchange between domains. It is shown that the intrinsic cellular parallellism of CA-models does not garantee simple and correct coarse-grained parallelization methods, which differ esentially for different modes of CA operation. For asynchronous mode of operation high parallelization efficiency may be acheived by transformation CA in a multi-stage synchronous one. At any case parallelization efficiency is close to 0.9-1.

References

1. Toffolli, T.: Cellular Automata as an Alternative to (rather than Approximation of) Differential Equations in Modeling Physics. Physica D 10, 117–127 (1984)
2. Wolfram, S.: A new kind of science. Wolfram Media Inc., Champaign, Ill., USA (2002)

3. Toffolli, T., Margolus, N.: Cellular Automata Machines. MIT Press, Cambridge (1987)
4. Rothman, B.H., Zaleski, S.: Lattice-Gas Cellular Automata. Cambridge Univ. Press, Complex Hydrodynamics. London (1997)
5. Latkin, E.I., Elokhin, V.I., Gorodetskii, V.V.: Spiral concentration waves in the Monte-Carlo model of CO oxidation over Pd(110) caused by synchronization via CO_{ads} diffusion between separate parts of catalytic surface. Chemical Engineering Journal 91, 123–131 (2003)
6. Neizvestny, I.G., Shwartz, N.L., Yanovitskaya, Z.S., Zverev, A.V.: 3D-model of epitaxial growth on porous {111} and {100} Si surfaces. Computer Physics Communications 147, 272–275 (2002)
7. Sipper, M.: Evolution of Parallel Cellular Machines: The Cellular Programming Approach. Springer, Heidelberg (1997)
8. Bandini, S., Erbacci, G., Mauri, G.: Implementing Cellular Automata Based Models on Parallel Architectures: The CAPP Project. In: Malyshkin, V. (ed.) Parallel Computing Technologies. LNCS, vol. 1662, pp. 167–179. Springer, Heidelberg (1999)
9. Carotenuto, L., Mele, F., Furnari, M.M., Napolitano, R.: Pecans: A parallel environment for cellular automata modeling. Complex Systems 10, 23–41 (1996)
10. Malinetski, G.G., Stepantsov, M.E.: Modeling Diuffusive Processes by Cellular Automata with Margolus Neighborhood. Zhurnal Vychislitelnoy Matematiki i Matematicheskoy Phiziki (in Russian) 36(6), 1017–1021 (1998)
11. Bandman, O.: Simulation Spatial Dynamics by Probabilistic Cellular Automata. In: Bandini, S., Chopard, B., Tomassini, M. (eds.) ACRI 2002. LNCS, vol. 2493, pp. 10–19. Springer, Heidelberg (2002)
12. Achasova, S., Bandman, O., Markova, V., Piskunov, S.: Parallel Substitution Algorithm. In: Theory and Application, World Scientific, Singapore (1994)
13. Park, J.K., Steiglitz, K., Thurston, W.P.: Soliton-like behavior in automata. Physica D 19, 423–432 (1986)
14. Medvedev, Y.G.: Experimental study of Computational characteristic of parallel implementation of 3D cellular Automata model of viscous flow. In: Proceedings of Scientific Confernce Parallel Programming Technology, pp. 79–82. Moscow Univ. Press (2006)
15. Bandman, O.: Parallel Implementation of Asynchronous Cellular Automata Algorithm. In: El Yacoubi, S., Chopard, B., Bandini, S. (eds.) ACRI 2006. LNCS, vol. 4173, pp. 41–47. Springer, Heidelberg (2006)
16. Nedea, S.V., Lukkien, J.J., Jansen, A.P.J., Hilbers, P.A.J.: Methods for parallel simulation of surface reaction. In: Werner, B. (ed.) 4th Int. Workshop on Parallel and Distributrd Scientific and Engineering Computing with Applications, pp. 7–16. IEEE Comp. Society, Nice, France (2003)
17. Chen, N., Glazier, J.A., Alber, M.S.A: A Parallel Implementation of the Cellular Potts Model for Simulation of Cell-Based Morphogenesis. In: El Yacoubi, S., Chopard, B., Bandini, S. (eds.) ACRI 2006. LNCS, vol. 4173, pp. 58–67. Springer, Heidelberg (2006)
18. Bandman, O.: Composing Fine-graned Parallel Algorithms for Spatial Dynamics Simulation. In: Malyshkin, V. (ed.) PaCT 2005. LNCS, vol. 3606, pp. 99–113. Springer, Heidelberg (2005)

Cellular Automata Models for Complex Matter

Dominique Désérable, Pascal Dupont,
Mustapha Hellou, and Siham Kamali-Bernard

Laboratoire de Génie Civil & Génie Mécanique,
Institut National des Sciences Appliquées,
INSA, 20 Avenue des Buttes de Coësmes, 35043 Rennes, France
{Dominique.Deserable,
Pascal.Dupont,Mustapha.Hellou,Siham.Kamali-Bernard}@insa-rennes.fr
http://www.insa-rennes.fr

Abstract. Complex matter may lie in various forms from granular matter, soft matter, fluid-fluid or solid-fluid mixtures to compact heterogeneous material. Cellular automata models make a suitable and powerful tool to catch the influence of the microscopic scale onto the macroscopic behaviour of these complex systems. Rather than a survey, this paper will attempt to bring out the main concepts underlying these models and to give an insight for future work.

Keywords: cellular automata (CA) for complex matter (CACM), sandpile models, lattice-gas, lattice-grain, hybrid models.

1 Introduction

Complex matter may lie in various forms, from granular matter, soft matter, fluid-fluid or solid-fluid mixtures to compact heterogeneous material, and involves a diversity of dynamical processes including sandpile equilibrium or avalanches, mixing, stratification or segregation, emulsion or sedimentation in multiphase suspensions, miscible or immiscible flows in porous media and so forth. Long range propagative phenomena may include the void propagation in a porous medium, the force transmission in a granular packing, the progression of wavefronts in active media or the evolution of a fissuration at the onset of a defect in a compact material. Various aspects of critical phenomena are encountered in the behaviour of complex matter: liquid-solid transitions from free flows to arching effects in hoppers, mixed-unmixed transitions of bidisperse mixtures, laminar to turbulent evolution in fluid flows or instabilities near percolation thresholds are such transition examples. A thorough investigation of the behaviour of complex matter is therefore of major importance for industrial and scientific applications.

The theoretical methods currently used split up into continuum models, particle dynamics and cellular automata. Cellular automata make a suitable and powerful tool to catch the influence of the microscopic scale onto the macroscopic behaviour of complex systems. In short, a cellular automata network ("CA") is

V. Malyshkin (Ed.): PaCT 2007, LNCS 4671, pp. 385–400, 2007.

a space-time discretization of time into steps and space into interconnected cells taking on integer values and where the time evolution is governed by a transition function that updates the new state of the cells synchronously from the current state of their local neighbourhood. A CA can be one or multidimensional. In the simplest case, the $1d$ Wolfram's elementary cellular automata ("ECA") is constructed from the binary-valued ("$k = 2$") transition rule acting from nearest-neighbours ("$r = 1$") so that there exist 256 possible transitions denoted by their rule number [1]. Even with this minimal definition, a very complex dynamics may be revealed in the space-time diagram, depending on the random initial configuration. Starting now from the fact that complex matter may behave like a *particulate* system, a CA for complex matter ("CACM") can thereby be viewed as an extreme simplification of particle dynamics. Moreover, observing that such primitive CA rules are able to capture the essence of such complex behaviours readily leads to agree with the *"rather than"* Toffoli's paradigm that CA are the outstanding alternative to find the ordinary (ODE) or partial (PDE) differential equation of a phenomenon in complex matter [2].

Rather than a survey, this paper will attempt to bring out the main concepts underlying CACM models and to give an insight for future work. A taxonomy is presented as a proposal intended to tidy up the broad world of CACM. The CACM set is divided into the four following sections devoted to: the *sandpile* models underlying the universal concept of self-organized criticality; the *lattice-gas* models in which the reasons why they evolved from pure lattice-gas to lattice-Boltzmann until extended lattice-Boltzmann are highlighted; the *lattice-grain* models in their miscellaneous aspects including the related traffic-flow model lying far beyond our scope of complex matter; and a unified subset of *hybrid* models including a neural approach in reaction-diffusion, an environment dealing with the rheology of composite pastes, and movable cellular automata. A discussion is proposed afterwards about general questions related to CA, namely grain-size, synchronization, topology and scalability, consistency of the models. We focus on *models* and applications, not on CACM architectures. For this reason and except in specific cases, such names as von Neumann, Ulam, Burks, Margolus, Vichniac, Clouqueur, Adamatsky, Latkin, Yepez and other pioneers not forgotten will neither be referenced nor mentioned. For brevity's sake, the reader is also requested in data mining for a more detailed bibliography. This work is an extension of a previous study of CA for granular matter presented elsewhere [3].

2   Sandpile Models

This section may show how from a simple sandpile model, when poured at the top with a flow of grains, can rise a universal concept of self-organized criticality.

2.1   Self-organized Criticality in the Sandpile

The primary sandpile model is the "BTW" CA of Bak, Tang, Wiesenfeld [4] where a $1d$ CA simulates a $2d$ heap. At each timestep, a cell n contains an integer

z_n which denotes the height difference (or local slope) between two neighbouring sites. Adding a grain is yielded by an elementary operation. Whenever a critical state $z_n > z_c$ is reached, where z_c is a user-defined local critical slope, then grains fall. As a matter of fact, the transition which yields the new state of cell n follows a simple but nonlinear (because of the threshold condition) discretized diffusion equation. Although this rule is really plain, the model exhibits complex phenomena at macroscopic level, introducing the concept of self-organized criticality (SOC): the equilibrium of the heap is noised by multiscale fluctuations between an angle of stability and an angle of repose, with avalanches of all sizes. Rules of $2d$ CA for $3d$ heaps acting on square cells were also defined by the authors.

According to Kadanoff et al. [5], the process is shown to be self-similar with scale invariance. Since the sandpile algorithm acts on systems of finite size and in order to understand how this fact affects the behaviour of the system, the techniques of finite-size scaling (borrowed from the Wilson's renormalization procedure) and of multifractal analysis are used to extract the power-laws and critical exponents which govern the sizes and frequencies of avalanches.

2.2 Stratification and Segregation in a Binary Sandpile

The sandpile paradigm is applied by Makse et al. [6,7] to granular mixtures of two different species where four different generalized angles of repose can coexist. The angle of repose depends on the size of (small or large) rolling grains and on the aspect of their (rough or smooth) surface. At each timestep, a set of grains of two different species is poured at the top of the pile. Two macroscopic phenomena are observed: either a stratification of a mixture of large rough grains and small smooth grains or a complete segregation of a mixture of small rough grains and large smooth grains. Moreover, the stratification displays the formation of a two-layered kink moving uphill at constant velocity whereas the segregation shows a clear bipartition separated by a thin mixed barrier.

This twofold dynamics is confirmed experimentally, and theoretically, using a recent continuum formalism introduced first by Mehta, and by Bouchaud et coworkers ("BCRE") for a single species sandpile, then extended by Boutreux et de Gennes ("BdG") to bidisperse mixtures. The resulting set of "convective-diffusion" equations which governs the interface between the "fluid" surface and the underlying "solid" bulk is argued to include the essential features of the physics of granular flow (see [7] and references therein).

2.3 Self-organization and Stratigraphy in Aerolian Sand Ripples

A well-known self-organized process derived from the dynamics of the sandpile and commonly found in sand deserts, atop dunes, or sandy beaches is the metamorphosis of a flat sandy surface into a periodic rippled pattern due to the action of an external force, from wind or water. This process can be explained by the combination of two types of sand grain movement: saltation and reptation.

Similar artifacts are also observed during surface erosion via ion-sputtering in amorphous material.

A first self-organized CA approach for the analysis of sand ripple is the "worm" model of Haff *et* coworkers (see [8] and references therein): the time evolution is governed by the advancement of a worm's head incrementing its size and simultaneously decrementing the size of the worm in front; since short worms run faster than long ones, a merge between two successive worms should occur. Werner *et* Gillespie focus on average size and standard deviation resulting from random fluctuations of the worm's size: the evolution of the system is a Markov process whose analysis follows a mean-field approximation.

A different approach is the "NO" CA of Nishimori *et* Ouchi which maps a linear, continuous saltation-reptation process onto a $2d$ lattice wherein the saltation length depends on the local slope and the reptation follows a 2-dimensional diffusion equation. Whenever the wind force exceeds a critical value, ripple patterns spontaneously appear. Besides, Barchan dune-like patterns are yielded by a large-scale model which affects the saltation procedure. The drawback of the NO CA is that the growth of a ripple's height is unbounded. It was recently improved by the saltation-creep-avalanche model of Caps *et* Vandewalle by reintroducing the angle of repose into the system [9].

Anderson *et* Bunas focus on the stratigraphy carried out by a binary mixture but the relevant result of Makse [8], whose BCRE-BdG formalism takes again into account the interactions within the fluid-solid interface, leads to realistic morphologies of either inverse-graded or normal-graded lamination or cross-stratification depending on the size and shape of the grains.

2.4   Self-organized Criticality in Natural Hazards

The unified concept of SOC was applied to earthquakes by Bak *et* Tang [10] as a consequence of the earth crust being in a self-organized critical state. A simple CA "stick-slip" model yields $2d$ and $3d$ exponents as a prediction for the Gutenberg-Richter power-law distribution for energy released at earthquakes. Their pioneer-work gave rise to a broad research field in geophysics. A simplification of the stick-slip motion of the Burridge-Knopoff slider-block is the $1d$ CA of Nakanishi which shows a behaviour similar to the Carlson-Langer formalism describing the Newtonian equations of motion by coupled ODE. In the $2d$ "OFC" CA of Olami, Feder, Christensen a nonconservative, quasistatic rule yields a dynamical phase transition from localized to nonlocalized effects. By observing that a short-range interaction may lead to unphysical stress distributions, Weatherley *et* al. defined a new type of CA with long-range energy transfer. In the same way, the CA of Castellaro *et* Mulargia includes effects due to the transient loads of elastic waves, from the observation that a loading rate acts at a time-scale larger than the one of fracture propagation, which is assumed comparatively instantaneous [11].

Landslides are commonly caused by a trigger such as an earthquake, a downpour or a sudden snowmelt and their study gave also rise to various approaches of sandpile-type CA in order to extract the critical exponents of their power-law behaviour. Most of the authors have calibrated their theoretical results from thorough inventories of topographic databases to forecast the risk conditions of real events: debris-flows or snow avalanches [12,13]. More theoretically, the SOC of the landslide model of Hergarten *et* Neugebauer is implicitly based on a set of PDE that includes the aspects of slope stability and mass movement. Recently, the CA of Piegari *et al.* which is claimed to be at the edge of the SOC limit, is a dissipative, anisotropic version of the OFC CA including a space-time dependent factor of safety derived from the stability criterion of Terzaghi.

It should be notified that an earthquake has nothing to do with a pile of sand, except for its self-organized behaviour, which emphasizes the universal character of self-organized criticality. Turcotte *et* Malamud propose an inverse-cascade model of metastable clusters as a general explanation for the power-law frequency-size statistics produced by these self-organized CA and their associated natural hazards which may lie far beyond our scope of complex matter.

3   Lattice-Gas Models

Owing to the copious amount of literature about lattice-gas, lattice-Boltzmann and extended lattice-Boltzmann models and to the wide diversity of their application fields spreading from hydrodynamics of homogeneous or multicomponent fluid flows, thermohydrodynamics, magnetohydrodynamics to particle suspensions, soft matter, reaction-diffusion processes, crystallisation or growth process and even to other areas observed in some granular systems, we should refer the reader for more general questions to the monograph of Wolf-Gladrow [14] and to some recent reviews on the subject (Boghosian [15], Chopard *et al.* [16]).

3.1   Pure Lattice-Gas Models

Applied first to hydrodynamics, lattice-gas CA ("LGA") define a fluid "particle" as a large group of molecules. A first emergence of discrete velocity models comes from Broadwell near ten years before the "HPP" gas of Hardy, Pomeau *et* de Pazzis wherein a two-stage transition follows a collision-propagation scheme (the term "collision-advection" is now preferred because of the risk of confusion with a long-range propagative interaction). In the input step, two particles can collide on a site of a square lattice; the output step starts the advection, where density (namely the number of particles), momentum and energy are conserved at each site; upon completion of the advection stage, particles have moved to their nearest-neighbour site.

The "FHP" gas of Frisch, Hasslacher, Pomeau deals with a hexagonal lattice where up to three particles can collide. The reader is also referred to Wolfram who produced a similar LGA for fluids. It was shown by the authors that the HPP lattice-gas could not be consistent with the Navier-Stokes equation while the FHP symmetries ensure consistency: the evolution equation of the FHP can be averaged from Boltzmann's molecular chaos approximation and expanded in a Taylor series up to the second order; the equilibrium state follows a Fermi-Dirac distribution from which a Chapman-Enskog analysis yields the hydrodynamic equations of the FHP, but under condition of low Mach number.

An extended FHP model includes all possible conservative collisions, with up to a 7-velocity template (one particle may stay at rest). From this model, a $3d$ gas may handle $3d$ problems on a face-centered hypercubic lattice with up to a 27-velocity template [17].

An important feature of LGA is their capability of handling complicated geometries and boundary conditions: slip, no-slip or partial slip conditions are easily carried out by reflection, bounce-back or by a combination of both schemes for particle-wall as well as particle-particle interaction. Therefore, LGA have proved their efficiency in various applications in hydrodynamics: miscible or immiscible fluids or flow through porous media (as in Rothman *et* Keller [18], Stockman *et* al. [19]) are some relevant examples where classical computational methods may fail or involve extra difficulty to model.

3.2 Lattice-Boltzmann Models

Pure LGA have nevertheless some shortcomings which appear through the above mentioned analytical transformation of the evolution equation, that is: statistical noise, lack of Galilean invariance, spurious unphysical quantities resulting from the symmetries of the network and, at least in the $3d$ case, huge collision matrices or lookup tables. Indeed one can overcome some of them: for example the noisy effect may be shortened by averaging the results of simulation in space and time or by running a lot of samples with different seeds for their random sequence. But the best way seems to average the microdynamics *before* a simulation, whence the intrinsic specificity of lattice-Boltzmann models.

In lattice-Boltzmann "LB" models, the evolution equation no longer contains the Boolean motion of actual particles but a real-valued probability of presence, namely the single distribution function. McNamara *et* Zanetti [20] introduced the Bhatnagar-Gross-Krook "BGK" approximation, an ODE which equalizes the Lagrangian derivative of the distribution along the local velocities with the difference between Maxwell-Boltzmann equilibrium distribution and single distribution, normalized by a relaxation time due to collisions. The moments should ensure the conservation of density, momentum and energy. The BGK equation yields the evolution equation, again expanded in a Taylor series up to the second order, from which a Gaussian-type quadrature yields the hydrodynamic Navier-Stokes equation. It should be pointed out that the collision operator is now linearized [21].

To prevent inconsistency due to the insufficient symmetries in the HPP grid, the above development dealt with a 9-velocity template. Similar developments may be derived from $2d$ 7-velocity or $3d$ 15-velocity or 27-velocity templates depending on the symmetry required. More details about the theoretical aspects of LB models can be found in Lallemand *et* Luo [22].

Typical applications of LB models to hydrodynamics show relevant phenomena in fluid flow, complex fluids or multicomponent fluids in complicated geometries [23,24]. We should also mention the problem of particle suspensions, which is difficult to tackle by classical computational methods [25].

3.3 Extended Lattice-Boltzmann Models

The "pure" LB model may suffer itself from some limitations depending on particular situations. For instance, although LB simulations show a good behaviour for laminar flow or slightly turbulent flow, new extensions are needed for turbulent flow at high Reynolds number. However, knowing that momentum and configuration spaces are allowed to be freely discretized from BGK construction, this property was explored to redefine arbitrary mesh grids for a significant increase of the Reynolds number [26]. The lattice-Boltzmann equation turns into a discretized Boltzmann equation and the collision-advection into a three-stage collision-advection-interpolation process.

Another weakness of the LB model appears in situation of compressible flow. A quite different approach leading to a "gas kinetic scheme" is proposed to simulate shocks of interfaces and high Mach number flows [27]. Besides, a generalized LB model has been carried out to prevent a risk of numerical instability of the constrained BGK approximation and to release the Prandtl number, fixed to unity because of the uniform relaxation time [22].

New extensions of the LB model are likely to appear and continue to evolve from fine-grain to coarse-grain in the future, in order to tackle new open or still unsolved problems or problems which remain up to now the private area of classical computational fluid dynamics [28].

4   Lattice-Grain Models

The fact that granular media are neither a gas nor a liquid nor a solid or that they can encompass the three phases as a whole was likely to induce the concept of "lattice-grain" or "granular media lattice-gas" owing to the lack of terminology about this kind of complex matter.

4.1   Cellular Automata for Granular Flow

Historicity of discrete models of granular flow under gravity covers a period of forty years, from the pioneer-work of Litwiniszyn [29]. His model is a $2d$ random-walk within a brickwork pattern of "cages" with a stepwise grain-cavity exchange rule acting under gravity and wherein a trough pattern is induced by an output of dry sand through a bottom slot. In addition, a memory effect, that can be likened to an inertial effect, allows the cavity to "remember" its left-right direction at the previous step. Later on, Müllins [30] claims that these problems can be converted to boundary values problems in ordinary diffusion theory. Caram *et* Hong reintroduce a similar "diffusing void model" but dealing with free surfaces and obstacles.

From the above terminology, prototypes of CA applied to granular flow were brought out by Savage and Osinov. The underlying process is proved to follow a Fokker-Planck equation, reducible into a simple diffusion equation in the memoryless case. Although this model is able to display some patterns like funnel or Couette flows, insufficiencies are due to the physical limitations in the local interaction law. Some correlative attempts, sometimes with somewhat sophisticated transition rules, were applied again to hopper and Couette flows or to the free surface segregation of a binary mixture: Gutt *et* Haff mimic the Newton's law of particle dynamics where the gravitational acceleration is simulated by an integer "position offset"; Fitt *et* Wilmott adopt a mesoscopic approach where a cell stands for a box containing a volume of small and large particles.

A conclusive contribution to lattice-grain CA is the energetic model of Baxter *et* Behringer [31]. It deals with a hexagonal lattice where an anisotropy of (long) grains is considered. The two-stage transition follows an interaction-collision rule using a criterion of energy minimization. Applied to hoppers, the process displays realistic patterns of grain segregation as well as density waves in the flow. The main contribution of our model is the use of crystal-like exclusion rules in a multiphase context [32]. The time evolution follows a two-stage request-exchange transition using a criterion of kinematic exclusion. Realistic patterns may appear in various configurations: mass or funnel flow, density waves, arching effect in hoppers; mixing or segregation of a bidisperse medium in rotating drums are such examples.

4.2   Lattice-Gas Related Models

A modified version of lattice-gas CA is introduced by Peng *et* Herrmann [33] to reveal the phenomena of density waves formation in granular flow through a vertical pipe under gravity. A power-law distribution of the power spectrum of the density fluctuations shows that interparticle dissipation and roughness of the pipe's walls are responsible for the generation of waves, similar to the kinetic waves observed in traffic jams. The basic model is a FHP-gas but wherein the dissipation is simulated in a simple way by added collision rules: while the FHP-gas must satisfy the principle of single-occupancy, here an off-site collision mechanism is created, where colliding particles may be driven back to their source site during a transient state until equilibrium.

A similar approach is the granular media "GMLG" lattice-gas proposed by Károlyi, Kertész *et* al. [34], applied to the study of the friction-induced segregation. Extra rules are created in order to include energy dissipation through particle collisions and friction: a neat scheme defines one restitution coefficient as the probability of energy conservation and four friction coefficients (since we are in a binary mixture) for moving particles as probabilities of either to scatter or to stop upon advection. Although this model uses the same BdG formalism as in the Makse's sandpile [7], it should be emphasized that we deal here with a right FHP extended model.

4.3   Force Chains in Granular Packing

Another model deals with the process of formation of force chains in a granular packing. As notified by Liu et al. [35], no confusion should be made with the BTW sandpile, which is more a concept than a bead pack. In all cases, a $2d$ CA simulates a $2d$ heap. Liu et al. introduce a probabilistic "q" model and assume that the dominant physical mechanism leading to force chains is the inhomogeneity of the packing. It is a random walk process where each particle transmits its weight to exactly one neighbour in the layer below. The network of force distribution is carried out by a mean-field theory approach. The "HHR" sandpile of Hemmingsson, Herrmann, Roux [36] gives a description of static forces in a granular system. The relevant fact is the dip observed under the heap, where the force network displays a depression underneath the apex. The related model of Goles et al. is provided with an additional parameter of inertia. Finally, the introduction of force transmission into our kinetic version [32] by a top-down scheme allows the model to take into account the influence of the initial stress state and of the wall roughness in silo flow modelling [37].

This new field focusing on the formation of force networks in granular packing seems still to be somewhat immature and would likely open gates for further research. Moreover, as notified in the HHR CA, the downward sequential approach of these models suffers from a lack of Galilean invariance which should be somehow restored.

4.4   Traffic-Flow Related Models

A somewhat surprising observation is that granular flow may in some cases behave as road traffic flow. Therefore, traffic flow theory may help to clarify our understanding of the complex behaviour of granular matter. Whence this emergence of works with Leibig, Kurtze et Hong, Helbing, Nagatani... and from [38] to [39] to bridge the gap. The study of road traffic flow is not a recent deal: $1d$ models fit into one or multilane traffic whereas $2d$ models fit into urban traffic. The theory of traffic flow arose with the "car-following" model of Lighthill et Whitham who state some analogy with the pressure in compressible flow in fluid-dynamics. Although a first single-bit CA was due to Gerlough some decades ago, it is only recently that a lot of "particle hopping models" were carried out: see the theory now unified with the "ASEP" asymmetric stochastic exclusion process and "STCA" stochastic traffic cellular automata models, in Nagel [40] and references therein.

Let us now consider the Wolfram's "ECA-184" constructed from Rule 184 [1]. Its space-time diagram from single site seeds shows a car moving alone with constant velocity; but from an initial disordered state, it exhibits complex phenomena with critical points in phase transitions from jams to congestion depending on the density of the flow. It can be observed that the ECA-184 is the deterministic limit of the STCA. Related works focus on the formation of kink solitons which appears in the physics of traffic jams [41]. The particle hopping models are consistent with the nonlinear diffusion Burger's equation (ECA-184) or the noisy Burger's equation (STCA, ASEP) whereas the density waves are described by the associated Korteweg-de Vries KdV equation.

5 Hybrid Models

The three following CACM which are related to different species of matter and did not take place in any previous category are gathered here into a unified set of hybrid models.

5.1 Cellular-Neural Models of Reaction-Diffusion

Reaction-diffusion processes, often referred to "autowave" phenomena, arise in various types of active media in complex matter. First CA approaches displaying realistic patterns of crystal-growth forms, stripes and streaks, Belouzov-Zhabotinski rings, spirals, turbulence or Liesegang fronts highlight such physical, biological or chemical examples. More recently, lattice-gas and lattice-Boltzmann theories were successfully applied to those reactive systems in a more unified way: see Boon *et al.* and Weimar [42], and Chopard *et al.* [16].

The outcome of Bandman and Pudov's works is a hybrid, special-purpose "CA-CNN" system devoted to the study of reaction-diffusion phenomena [43]. It is a novel, fine-grain application of the "parallel substitution algorithm" which compounds the discrete character of the CA with the intelligency of neural networks [44], lying within a range between extended CA with real numbers and restricted NN with local connections. The time evolution follows a stepwise, two-stage transition until equilibrium: the cell performs the diffusion rules, a neural function performs the reaction *explicitly* from a given PDE. Note that this model departs distinctly from the Toffoli's paradigm [2] wherein the task of PDE solving is implicit. The system is intended to avoid the shortcoming of redundant discrete-continuous-discrete transformations that often cause problems of inaccuracy or instability in numerical computation. Simulations in the square lattice are carried out with promising issues [45].

5.2 Cellular Automata for Hydration of Cement-Based Materials

Cement paste is probably one of the most complex material, which can contain up to 15 different phases arranged into a complex microstructure. This complexity further increases in mortar where cement powder and medium grains coexist, even more in concrete as coarse aggregates are added in the mixture. A hybrid VCCTL (Virtual Cement and Concrete Testing Laboratory) environment is provided at NIST for simulation of hydration of cement-based materials and prediction of their physical properties by virtual testing [46].

The hydration code of VCCTL is a CA whose input is a $3d$ microstructure of a mixture of cement grains and water. This microstructure is obtained using a $2d$ digital image of the cement powder, its particle-size distribution and a given water-to-cement ratio. The output is the cement paste microstructure after hydration. The simulation runs during a user-defined number of hydration cycles. The hydration cycle splits into three steps: dissolution; random-walk diffusion of the mobile agents; reaction between colliding pixels. The result serves then as input of continuum methods to extract macroscopic properties, that is, elastic Young's modulus and Poisson ratio.

Besides its use for a normal hydration process, VCCTL can also simulate degradations like leaching, a dissolution of one or more phases that causes harmful effects to quality and durability of the material. The simulation consists in replacing the pixels representing the leached phases by water-pixels. The influence of dissolution on the porous network percolation [47] as well as on the global capillary porosity of the paste serves again, as in the unleached case, as input data to evaluate the effect on the degraded elastic moduli [48]. Multiscale simulations on mortar are also carried out [49] and where representative elementary volumes are defined for both micro and meso different scales by a homogenization procedure.

5.3   Movable Cellular Automata

The movable cellular automata "MCA" method of Psakhie, Horie and their coworkers [50] which may also be termed as "movable lattice particles" according to Popov's terminology [51] provides a novel, alternative approach to the conventional finite-element method applied to the elastoplastic behaviour of materials under the action of small or large deformations. This hybrid model combines the advantages of cellular automata and molecular dynamics within a mesoscopic representation of the material.

Like the fictitious "fluid" particles in the hexagonal symmetry of the FHP lattice-gas, "solid" particles are created, but the basic concept is a pairwise switching parameter that defines a linked state as a "chemical bond" whenever two neighbouring particles overlap. The distance between centers is considered and, during a local deformation, the time evolution of their linked or unlinked state acts as in a bistable medium. The particle's motion is governed by a set of translational and rotational equations following the Newton-Euler interaction law. In this sense, the method may be related to the Cundall-Strack granular dynamics except that particles are here fictitious and constrained by the lattice structure. Moreover, a (micropolar) Cosserat continuum is provided by additional degrees of freedom for each material point [52].

The effectiveness of MCA is revealed in various critical situations: behaviour of steel under load at the onset of fracture, response of heterogeneous structures like concrete under static or dynamic loads, strength properties of anisotropic material like lignite, roughness at surface interface, friction and melting in rail-wheel contact, wear phenomena in combustion engines, or crash tests [50,53].

6   Discussion

This attempt of taxonomy of CACM will call several relevant questions and problems. The following ones are pointed out. Where can be the border between fine-grain and coarse-grain CACM? Should the time evolution be synchronous? What about topology and scalability of the network? How to valid the consistency of a model? We focus on and limit ourselves to this non-exhaustive list of often unsolved questions, issued from our local experience and knowledge.

6.1   From Fine-Grain to Coarse-Grain CACM

From bitscale Wolfram's ECA to sophisticated models, the range of complexity in CACM may be extremely wide. The increasing complexity in lattice-gas models, from pure lattice-gas to lattice-Boltzmann until extended lattice-Boltzmann as described in the related section is a relevant example thereupon: while a monophase fluid particle is encoded with a 4-bit (resp. 6-bit) word in the HPP (resp. FHP) cell, a real-valued distribution function is encoded in the lattice-Boltzman cell, whereas arbitrary meshes are redefined to encode the discretized Boltzmann equation in the extended models. Some models are essentially coarse-grained: the movable cellular automata give a typical example in nature.

Let us consider as a coarse paradigm in parallel computing the subdivision of a spatial problem into cells according to a given tessellation and in the framework of a cell-processor allocation strategy, whatever the computational method of the solver might be. Each cell solves its own subproblem at mesoscale and should exchange data with its near-neighbours at each timestep according to a predefined neighbourhood template. Why this grid-based network would not be a CA? This odd question should raise a frequently claimed assertion that cellular automata would have lost their attractiveness over against the growing computational power of today computers. Observing that a simple HPP gas is able to reveal realistic phenomena, though possibly inconsistent, is sufficient to take this assertion as wrong. Cellular automata will remain a genuine approach *per se* and the finer the grain will be, the better the model. Anyhow, the model-to-architecture correspondence from fine-grain to special-purpose and from coarse-grain to general-purpose is straightforward.

6.2   Synchronous or Asynchronous Time Evolution

In several CACM, the time evolution is sometimes governed by asynchronous rules. The principle of simultaneity of a transition rule is not respected in the asynchronous case, when some models adopt a bottom-up or top-down scanning of the cells in the case of gravity flows or a partial scanning in order to avoid coupling between a moving particle and its vicinity. During the force network generation in granular systems, the time evolution is based on a downward row-by-row computation in the triangular lattice [35,36,37].

Our idea, which can be denied, is that "there is always something happening *at* a complex medium" and that top-down, bottom-up (gravity-based) or partial (implementation-based) asynchronous modes should be avoided. A sequential, non synchronous mode breaks the capability for an effective parallel implementation of the model. Moreover and more physically, it may break the Galilean invariance of the physical process [36,22]. So, the question is: how to yield a pure, synchronous transition rule?

Let us focus on a particular case, namely, our crystal-like granular CA [32]. The basic two-stage transition is unable to allow a void to propagate and solid grains to tumble down simultaneously. Other similar observations arise in situation of long-range interactions [11]. Including a synchronous propagative mode leads to consider the transition and the time evolution at two different scales and to consider the process as *instantaneous* within one timestep. This condition needs to set up a mechanism to stop this transitional sequence, namely, a criterion of *termination* for the current timestep. This criterion is carried out by a global all-to-all communication over the whole network.

In the general case, synchronizing a transition in CA is relevant to the Myhill's "firing squad" problem (see Mazoyer [54] and references therein).

6.3 Topology and Scalability of the Network

The *local* topology of a CA may have an important impact on the behaviour of the model. In general, nearest-neighbour interactions are considered. For the $1d$ case, that means that the individual computation works upon Wolfram's triplet ("$r = 1$") centered on the cell [1]. The $2d$ case allows several nearest-neighbour templates, the usual ones being either the (4-valent) von Neumann or the (8-valent) Moore neighbourhood in the square tiling and, on the other hand, either the (3-valent) star or the (6-valent) honeycomb neighbourhood in the hexagonal tiling. Note that the brickwork Litwiniszyn's template [29] is homeomorphic to the honeycomb. As in [45], the Margolus split-swap seesaw in the Moore template is sometimes encountered in CA rules.

The good properties of the hexavalent grid are important to notify: more symmetries, isotropy with maximal number of degrees of freedom, maximal coordinence. A relevant observation is the inconsistency of the (von Neumann) HPP gas and the consistency of the (honeycomb) FHP gas with the Navier-Stokes equation. In the $3d$ case, the face-centered hypercubic lattice is unfortunately the least frustrating solution, since there exists no isotropic tessellation of the $3d$ space.

At *global* level, the question of scalability should be pointed out: is a recursive network needed for scaling laws? Scaling laws are concerned by the choice of the size of the model, power-laws, renormalization or homogenization, critical phenomena and critical exponents. The property of scalability for the underlying CA network is able to facilitate this kind of procedure. For the $1d$ case, it is easy to choose a periodic ring of length 2^n in ergodic conditions. For the $2d$ chessboard, one can refer to the recursive framework of Kadanoff for the ferromagnetic Ising model when 4 spins in a cell are condensed into one single spin in the renormalization procedure [55]. What about the hexagonal case? We show that it is also the case, where the underlying graph is a hierarchical Cayley graph with periodic boundaries and maximal symmetries compared with the skewed framework of Niemeijer and van Leeuwen [56].

6.4 Consistency of the Models

Although difficult, the question of proving whether a CA model is consistent with mathematical equations involves the most challenging problems which depend upon a diversity of factors. Proofs of consistency are never easy even for simple cases and the deal may often be worse. Whence the renormalization-homogenization procedures and the need of comparative studies with other methods, at least when these methods are practicable. In several cases, the useful information of power-laws and critical exponents can yet be somehow extracted, the context of self-organized criticality being a quite meaningful example.

It is worth while keeping track of the diversity of PDE that occurred throughout our enumeration of simple CACM models: the simple diffusion equation, the Fokker-Planck equation, the Navier-Stokes equation, the Burger's one with its correlated Korteweg-de Vries equation and the recent outcome of, say, the Boutreux-de Gennes equation. Incidentally, the CA-neural hybrid environment [43] that might be extended beyond the area of active media jointly with the "programmable matter" methods [2,57] provide, by their respective explicit and implicit approach, an idealized laboratory of prospective studies and investigations upon the CA-PDE relationship.

References

1. Wolfram, S.: Statistical mechanics of cellular automata. Rev. Mod. Phys. 55, 601–644 (1983)
2. Toffoli, T.: Cellular automata as an alternative to (rather than an approximation of) differential equations in modeling physics. Physica 10 D, 117–127 (1984)
3. Désérable, D.: Cellular automata for granular matter: what trends? In: Bainov, D., Nenov, S. (eds.) Second Int. Conf. on Applied Math. SICAM'05, Plovdiv, p. 64 (2005)
4. Bak, P., Tang, C., Wiesenfeld, K.: Self-organized criticality. Phys. Rev. A 38, 364–374 (1988)
5. Kadanoff, L.P., Nagel, S.R., Wu, L., Zhou, S.M.: Scaling and universality in avalanches. Phys. Rev. A 39, 6524–6537 (1989)
6. Makse, H.A., Herrmann, H.J.: Microscopic model for granular stratification and segregation. Europhys. Lett. 43, 1–6 (1998)
7. Cizeau, P., Makse, H.A., Stanley, H.E.: Mechanisms of granular spontaneous stratification and segregation in two-dimensional silos. Phys. Rev. E 59, 4408–4421 (1999)
8. Makse, H.A.: Grain segregation mechanism in aeolian sand ripples. Eur. Phys. J. E 1, 127–135 (2000)
9. Caps, H., Vandewalle, N.: Ripple and kink dynamics. Phys. Rev. E 64(041302), 1–6 (2001)
10. Bak, P., Tang, C.: Earthquakes as a self-organized critical phenomena. J. Geophys. Res. 94(B11), 15635–15637 (1989)
11. Weatherley, D., Mora, P., Xia, M.: Long-range automaton models of earthquakes: power-law accelerations, correlation evolution, and mode-switching. Pure and Applied Geophys. 159(10), 2469–2490 (2002)
12. Iovine, G., Di Gregorio, S., Lupiano, V.: Debris-flow susceptibility assessment through cellular automata modelling: an example from 15–16 December 1999 disaster at Cervinara and San Martino Valle Caudina (Campania, southern Italy). Natural Hazards Earth Syst. Sc. 3, 457–468 (2003)

13. Kronholm, K., Birkeland, K.W.: Integrating spatial patterns into a snow avalanche cellular automata model. Geophys. Res. Lett. 32(19), L19504 (2005)
14. Wolf-Gladrow, D.A.: Lattice-gas cellular automata and lattice Boltzmann models. Springer, Heidelberg (2000)
15. Boghosian, B.M.: Lattice gases and cellular automata. Fut. Gen. Comp. Sys. 16, 171–185 (1999)
16. Chopard, B., Dupuis, A., Masselot, A., Luthi, P.: Cellular automata and lattice Boltzmann techniques: an approach to model and simulate complex systems. Advances in Complex Systems 5(2-3), 103–246 (2002)
17. Frisch, U., d'Humières, D., Hasslacher, B., Lallemand, P., Pomeau, Y., Rivet, J.P.: Lattice-gas hydrodynamics in two and three dimensions. Complex Systems 1, 649–707 (1987)
18. Rothman, D.H., Keller, J.M.: Immiscible cellular-automaton fluids. J. Stat. Phys. 52, 1119–1127 (1988)
19. Stockman, H.W, Li, Ch., Wilson, J.L.: A lattice-gas and lattice Boltzmann study of mixing at continuous fracture junctions: importance of boundary conditions. Geophys. Res. Lett. 24(12), 1515–1518 (1997)
20. McNamara, G.R., Zanetti, G.: Use of the Boltzmann equation to simulate lattice-gas automata. Phys. Rev. Lett. 61(20), 2332–2335 (1988)
21. Higuera, F.J., Succi, S., Benzi, R.: Lattice-gas dynamics with enhanced collisions. Europhys. Lett. 9, 345–349 (1989)
22. Lallemand, P., Luo, L.-S.: Theory of the lattice Boltzmann method: dispersion, dissipation, isotropy, Galilean invariance, and stability. Phys. Rev. E 61, 6546–6562 (2000)
23. Chen, S., Doolen, G.D.: Lattice-Boltzmann method for fluid flow. Ann. Rev. Fluid Mech. 30, 329–364 (1998)
24. Flekkøy, E.G., Herrmann, H.J.: Lattice Boltzmann models for complex fluids. Physica A 199, 1–11 (1993)
25. Ladd, A.J.C., Verberg, R.: Lattice Boltzmann simulations of particle-fluid suspensions. J. Stat. Phys. 104(5), 1191–1251 (2001)
26. Chen, H., Succi, S., Orszag, S.: Analysis of subgrid scale turbulence using the Boltzmann Bhatnagar-Gross-Krook kinetic equation. Phys. Rev. E 59, R2527–2530 (1999)
27. Xu, K., Prendergast, K.H.: Numerical Navier-Stokes solutions from gas kinetic theory. J. Comp. Phys. 114, 9–17 (1993)
28. Talia, D., Sloot, P. (eds.): Cellular automata: promise and prospects in computational science. Special issue of Fut. Gen. Comp. Sys. 16, 157–305 (1999)
29. Litwiniszyn, J.: Application of the equation of stochastic processes to mechanics of loose bodies. Archivuum Mechaniki Stosowanej 8(4), 393–411 (1956)
30. Müllins, W.W.: Stochastic theory of particle flow under gravity. J. Appl. Phys. 43, 665–678 (1972)
31. Baxter, G.W., Behringer, R.P.: Cellular automata models of granular flow. Phys. Rev. A 42, 1017–1020 (1990)
32. Désérable, D.: A versatile two-dimensional cellular automata network for granular flow. SIAM J. Applied Math. 62(4), 1414–1436 (2002)
33. Peng, G., Herrmann, H.J.: Density waves of granular flow in a pipe using lattice-gas automata. Phys. Rev. E 49, R1796–1799 (1994)
34. Károlyi, A., Kertész, J., Havlin, S., Makse, H.A., Stanley, H.E.: Filling a silo with a mixture of grains: friction-induced segregation. Europhys. Lett. 44(3), 386–392 (1998)
35. Coppersmith, S.N., Liu, C.H., Majumdar, S., Narayan, O., Witten, T.A.: Model for force fluctuations in bead packs. Phys. Rev. E 53, 4673–4685 (1996)

36. Hemmingsson, J., Herrmann, H.J., Roux, S.: Vectorial cellular automaton for the stress in granular media. J. Phys. I 45, 853–872 (1997)

37. Masson, S., Désérable, D., Martinez, J.: Modélisation de matériaux granulaires par automate cellulaire. Revue Française de Génie Civil 5(5), 629–650 (2001)

38. Wolf, D.E., Schreckenberg, M., Bachem, A. (eds.): Traffic and Granular Flow'95, Jülich. World Scientific Publishing, Singapore (1996)

39. Schadschneider, A., Pöschel, T., Kühne, R., Schreckenberg, M., Wolf, D.E. (eds.): Traffic and Granular Flow'05. Springer, Heidelberg (2007)

40. Nagel, K.: Particle hopping models and traffic flow theory. Phys. Rev. E 53, 4655–4672 (1996)

41. Nagatani, T.: The physics of traffic jams. Rep. Prog. Phys 65, 1331–1386 (2002)

42. Boon, J.-P., Dab, D., Kapral, R., Lawniczak, A.: Lattice gas automata for reactive systems. Phys. Rep. 273, 55–148 (1996)

43. Bandman, O.L.: Cellular-neural automaton: a hybrid model for reaction-diffusion simulation. Fut. Gen. Comp. Sys. 18(6), 737–745 (2002)

44. Pudov, S.: First order 2d cellular neural networks investigation and learning. In: Malyshkin, V. (ed.) PaCT 2001. LNCS, vol. 2127, pp. 94–97. Springer, Heidelberg (2001)

45. Malinetski, G.G., Stepantsov, M.E.: Modelling diffusive processes by cellular automata with Margolus neighborhood. Zh. Vych. Mat.Mat. Phys. 36(6), 1017–1021 (1998)

46. Haecker, C.J., Bentz, D.P., Feng, X.P., Stutzman, P.E.: Prediction of cement physical properties by virtual testing. Cement International 1(3), 86–92 (2003)

47. Bentz, D.P., Garboczi, E.J.: Modelling the leaching of calcium hydroxide from cement paste: effects on pore space percolation and diffusivity. J. Mat. Struct. 25(9), 523–533 (1992)

48. Kamali, S., Moranville, M., Garboczi, E., Prené, S., Gérard, B.: Hydrate dissolution influence on the Young's modulus of cement pastes. In: FraMCos'04, Vail, Colorado, pp. 631–638 (2004)

49. Bernard, F., Kamali-Bernard, S., Prince, W., Hjaj, M.: 3D multi-scale modeling of mortar mechanical behavior and effect of changes in the microstructure. In: FraMCos'07, Catania, Italy (in press)

50. Psakhie, S.G., Horie, Y., Ostermeyer, G.P., Korostelev, S.Y., Smolin, A.Y., Shilko, E.V., Dmitriev, A.I., Blatnik, S., Spegel, M., Zavsek, S.: Movable cellular automata method for simulating materials with mesostructure. Theor. Appl. Fract. Mech. 37, 311–334 (2001)

51. Popov, V.L., Filippov, A.E.: Method of movable lattice particles. Tribol. Int. 40(6), 930–936 (2007)

52. Popov, V.L., Psakhie, S.G.: Theoretical principles of modelling elastoplastic media by movable cellular automata method. I. Homogeneous media. Phys. Mesomech. 4(1), 15–25 (2001)

53. Dmitriev, A.I., Popov, V.L., Psakhie, S.G.: Simulation of surface topography with the method of movable cellular automata. Tribol. Int. 39(5), 444–449 (2006)

54. Mazoyer, J.: An overview of the firing squad synchronization problem. In: Choffrut, C. (ed.) Automata Networks. LNCS, vol. 316, pp. 82–94. Springer, Heidelberg (1988)

55. Kadanoff, L.P.: Scaling laws for Ising models near T_c. Physics 2(6), 263–272 (1966)

56. Désérable, D.: A framework for scaling and renormalization in the triangular lattice. In: Fourteenth Int. Symp. on Math. Theory of Networks & Systems MTNS' 2000, Perpignan, p. 109 (2000)

57. Toffoli, T.: Programmable matter methods. Fut. Gen. Comp. Sys. 16, 187–201 (1999)

Hysteresis in Oscillatory Behaviour in CO Oxidation Reaction over Pd(110) Revealed by Asynchronous Cellular Automata Simulation

Vladimir Elokhin, Andrey Matveev, Vladimir Gorodetskii, and Evgenii Latkin

Boreskov Institute of Catalysis SB RAS
Prosp. Akad. Lavrentieva, 5, 630090, Novosibirsk, Russian Federation
elokhin@catalysis.ru

Abstract. The dynamic behaviour of the CO oxidation reaction over Pd(110) has been studied by means of probabilistic asynchronous cellular automata (Dynamic Monte-Carlo). The influence of the internal parameters on the shapes of surface concentration waves obtained in simulations under the limited surface diffusion intensity conditions has been studied. The hysteresis in oscillatory behaviour has been found under step-by-step variation of oxygen partial pressure. Two different oscillatory regimes could exist at one and the same parameters of the reaction. The parameters of oscillations (amplitude, period and the shape of spatio-temporal patterns on the surface) depend on the kinetic prehistory of the system. The possibility for the appearance of the cellular and turbulent patterns, spiral, target and stripe oxygen waves on the surface in the cases under study has been shown.

Keywords: CO oxidation, palladium, oscillations, surface waves, asynchronous cellular automata, hysteresis in oscillatory regimes.

1 Introduction

The complex dynamic behaviour in oxidation reaction over platinum metals (bistability, oscillations, surface autowaves, etc.) can be directed by the structure of the reaction mechanism, specifically by the laws of physicochemical processes in the «reaction medium - catalyst» system. The most popular factors used to interpret the critical effects are the following [1]: i) phase transformations on the catalyst surface, including the formation and decomposition of subsurface oxygen during the reaction (e.g., Pd(110)), ii) structural phase transitions of the surface and its reconstruction due to the influence of the reaction media (e.g., Pt(100)).

In our opinion, the imitation (or stochastic) simulation is the most efficient tool for describing the spatio-temporal dynamics of the behaviour of adsorbates on the real catalytic surface, whose structure can change during the reaction. Recently the statistical lattice models for imitating the oscillatory and autowave dynamics in the adsorbed layer during CO oxidation over Pd(110) [2] and Pt(100) [3] single crystals, differing by the structural properties of catalytic surfaces, has been studied.

V. Malyshkin (Ed.): PaCT 2007, LNCS 4671, pp. 401–409, 2007.

2 Formulation of the Reaction Mechanism

The aim of this contribution is to study the influence of surface diffusion intensity on the shapes of surface concentration waves obtained in simulations. Let us restrict our consideration by CO oxidation reaction over Pd(110).

Based on our experimental FEM, TPR, XPS and MB data of CO oxidation oscillatory reaction on Pd tip surface [4, 5], some elementary steps have been added to L–H scheme, and a model (probabilistic asynchronous cellular automata) for the kinetic oscillations in CO + O_2 over Pd has been developed. The parameters of the elementary steps were partly taken from the literature [4]. The following detailed mechanism of the reaction was used for simulations:

1) $O_{2(gas)} + 2* \rightarrow 2O_{ads}$;
4) $O_{ads} + *_v \rightarrow [*O_{ss}]$;
2) $CO_{gas} + * \leftrightarrow CO_{ads}$;
5) $CO_{ads} + [*O_{ss}] \rightarrow CO_{2(gas)} + 2* + *_v$;
3) $CO_{ads} + O_{ads} \rightarrow CO_{2(gas)} + 2*$;
6) $CO_{gas} + [*O_{ss}] \leftrightarrow [CO_{ads}*O_{ss}]$;
7) $[CO_{ads}*O_{ss}] \rightarrow CO_{2(gas)} + * + *_v$ - «cork-screw» reaction

Here $*$ and $*_v$ are the active centres of the surface and subsurface Pd layer, respectively. Formation of the subsurface oxygen (modified surface) proceeds according to step 4, reduction of the initial surface – due to reactions 5 and 7 "cork-screw" reaction. The adsorbed CO_{ads} species can diffuse over the surface according to the following rules: (i) $CO_{ads} + * \leftrightarrow * + CO_{ads}$, (ii) $CO_{ads} + [*O_{ss}] \leftrightarrow * + [CO_{ads}*O_{ss}]$; (iii) $[CO_{ads}*O_{ss}] + [*O_{ss}] \leftrightarrow [*O_{ss}] + [CO_{ads}*O_{ss}]$. According to [6], we suppose that the heat of CO adsorption on the "oxidised" centres $[*O_{ss}]$ is less than that on the initial unoxidised $[*]$ one, i.e. the probability of $[CO_{ads}*O_{ss}]$ desorption (step 6) is greater than of CO_{ads} (step 2) one.

3 Algorithm of Simulation

The sequence of steps 1)-5) is often used for modelling of oscillations in catalytic oxidation reactions including the stochastic models, e.g. [7]. In our study, in addition to steps 1)-5), the possible process of $[CO_{ads}*O_{ss}]$ complex formation has been considered both because of CO adsorption (step 6) and the CO_{ads} diffusion over the surface. Besides, the possibility of the "cork-screw" reaction 7 is assumed. Step 4 is supposed to be irreversible. The model catalyst surface was represented by the square lattice N×N (N = 500 – 8000) with periodic boundary conditions (surface of torus). Each lattice cell can exist in one of five states: $*$, CO_{ads}, O_{ads}, $[*O_{ss}]$, $[CO_{ads}*O_{ss}]$. For steps (1), (2), (-2), (4), (5), (6), (-6), (7), the values of k_i were specified as a set of numbers, which can be considered as the rate constants of these elementary steps taking into account the partial pressures of O_2 (step 1) and CO (steps 2 and 6). The method for processing both step 3 and steps (i)-(iii) of CO_{ads} diffusion over the surface will be discussed below. The prescribed constants were recalculated as the probabilities of the realization of elementary processes w_i by the formula: $w_i = k_i / \Sigma k_i$.

Using a generator of random numbers uniformly distributed over the (0, 1) interval, we chose one of these processes according to the specified ratio of their occurrence. Then, also using pairs of random numbers, the coordinates of one cell or two adjacent cells, depending on the chosen process, were determined from N×N cells of lattice. This algorithm (first, choice of the process and, second, choice of the cell) makes it possible to take into account the dependence of the step rates on the adsorbate coverage.

The states of the cells are determined according to the rules prescribed by the detailed reaction mechanism. Let us show now the realisation of the chosen process, e.g., for the reaction 5: $CO_{ads} + [*O_{ss}] \rightarrow CO_{2(gas)} + 2* + *_v$ (the realization of the rest of reaction steps is similar). When two cells randomly chosen contain a $\{CO_{ads}, [*O_{ss}]\}$ pair, the states of both cells are changed to the state *, and one more molecule of carbon dioxide formed was put in the reaction rate counter. If the required pair is not found out, the attempt is rejected. After every choice of one of the above-named processes and an attempt to perform this process the inner cycle of CO_{ads} diffusion was processed, which included M attempts of random choice of a pair of adjacent cells of the lattice (M = 20-100). If the $\{CO_{ads}, *\}$, $\{CO_{ads}, [*O_{ss}]\}$, $\{*, [CO_{ads}*O_{ss}]\}$, $\{[*O_{ss}], [CO_{ads}*O_{ss}]\}$ pairs turned out to be these pairs, the states in these cells were interchanged according to the rules (i)-(iii), i.e. diffusion took place. Otherwise, the attempt of diffusion was rejected. The diffusion is necessary for the spatio-temporal processes synchronization occurring on the local regions of the model surface.

In our model we suppose that reaction 3) proceeds immediately as soon as adsorbed CO_{ads} and O_{ads} appear in the situation of nearest neighbourhood. After each successful attempt of CO or O_2 adsorption as well as of CO_{ads} diffusion, the neighbouring cells were checked to find the partners in reaction 3). If the partners were found, then the cells were given the state *, and one more CO_2 was added to the reaction rate counter. The so-called MC-step consisting of N×N attempts of choice and realization of "main" elementary processes 1)-2), 4)-7) is used as a time unit in the Monte Carlo models. During the MCS, each cell is tested on the average once. The reaction rate and surface coverages were calculated after each MCS as a number of CO_2 molecules formed or the number of cells in the corresponding state divided by the total value of the lattice cells N^2.

4 Results and Discussions

The synchronous oscillations of the reaction rate and surface coverages are exhibited within the range of the suggested model parameters under the conditions very close to the experimental observations – e.g., Fig 1. These oscillations are accompanied by the autowave behaviour of surface phases and adsorbate coverages, Fig. 2. One can see from the Figs. 1 and 2 that the oscillations are quite regular, and the shape of oxygen waves is of prominent cellular pattern of change: the initiation of oxygen fronts propagation proceeds simultaneously at different local regions of the model surface, and the O_{ads} and CO_{ads} coverages alternate during the period of oscillations. The

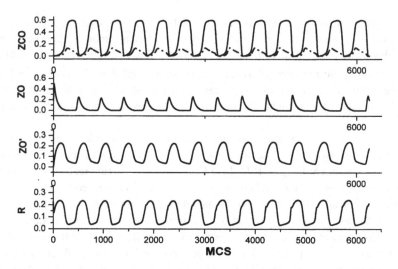

Fig. 1. Dynamics of changes in the surface coverages CO_{ads} (ZCO - solid line), $[CO_{ads}*O_{ss}]$ (ZCO - dash-dotted line), O_{ads} (ZO), $[*O_{ss}]$ (ZO'), reaction rate (R) - for CO oxidation over Pd(110). N = 1000, M = 100. The values of the rate constants of steps (s^{-1}) (see scheme): $k_1=1$, $k_2=1$, $k_{-2}=0.2$, $k_3=inf$, $k_4=0.03$, $k_5=0.01$, $k_6=1$, $k_{-6}=0.5$, $k_7=0.02$. The partial pressures of reagents (CO and O_2) are included in the rate constants of adsorption (k_1, k_2, k_6).

intensity of CO_2 formation in the CO_{ads} layer is low, inside oxygen island it is intermediate and the highest intensity of CO_2 formation is related to narrow zone between the moving O_{ads} island and surrounding CO_{ads} layer - «reaction zone», characterised by the elevated concentration of the free active centres [2]. The presence of the narrow reaction zone was found experimentally by means of the field ion probe-hole microscopy technique with 5 Å resolution [8]. The important role of the diffusion rate and of the lattice size on the synchronisation and stabilisation of surface oscillations has been demonstrated. Particularly, in the case of Pt(100), the decrease of the diffusion intensity (parameter M) from 100 to 30 leads to the irregular oscillations and to the turbulent patterns on the model surface – in this case the mobile islands of O_{ads} shaped as cellular waves, spiral fragments, etc., are formed [3]. Similar spatiotemporal behavior was experimentally observed in $CO+O_2/Pt(100)$ using the Ellipso-Microscopy for Surface Imaging (EMSI) technique [9].

Let us study the influence of diffusion intensity M on the shape of the surface waves in the case shown in the Fig. 2. Decrease of M up to value M = 50 doesn't change significantly the oscillatory and wave dynamics, but decreasing M to value M = 20 drastically change both the shape of oscillations and the spatiotemporal behaviour of simulated surface waves.

Period and amplitude of oscillations decrease considerably, the dynamic behaviour of reaction rate and surface coverages demonstrate the intermittence (oscillatory regime I). During these oscillations oxygen (O_{ads}) is always present on the surface (as

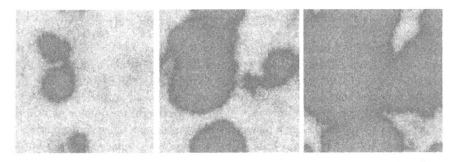

Fig. 2. The distribution of different adsorbates over the surface at the moment when the coverage change on the Pd(110) surface. Dark grey regions indicate the propagating oxygen islands, light grey regions – CO_{ads} layer. The lattice size N = 1000, diffusion intensity parameter M = 100.

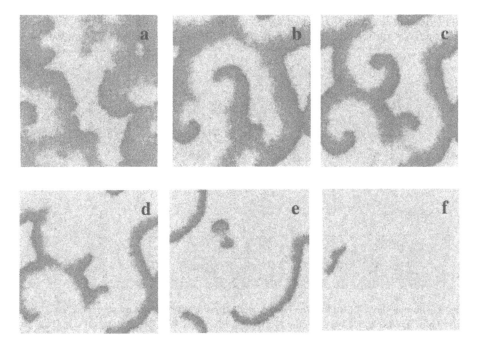

Fig. 3. Typical snapshots of the adsorbate distribution over the surface (N = 1000) at step-by step reducing of k_1 in the case of restricted diffusion intensity of CO_{ads} (M=20). The values of partial pressure of oxygen (i.e., k_1) are the following (from left to right): 1 (a), 0.9 (b), 0.85 (c), 0.8 (d), 0.73 (e), and 0.71 (f). The designations of adsorbate are the same as for Fig. 2.

opposed to the case of Figs. 1 and 2) in the form of turbulent spatiotemporal structures (Fig. 3a). It is seen from Fig. 3a that the whole surface is divided in several islands oscillating with the same period but with a phase shift relative to each other, therefore the reaction rate and coverage's time dependencies demonstrate the intermittence peculiarities. Here one can observe on the surface the spatio-temporal pattern of complicated turbulent shape. The colliding oxygen islands form the spiral-like patterns. Step-by step decrease of oxygen partial pressure (remember, that the values for O_2 and CO adsorption coefficients, k_1, k_2, and k_6 (s^{-1}), can be treated as the product of the impingement rate ($k_i \times P_i$) and of the sticking coefficient (S_i)) leads to the gradual thinning of oxygen travelling waves (Fig. 3b-e). At low values of k_1 (Fig. 3d-f) the long and thin oxygen stripe (or "worm"-like) patterns are formed on the simulated surface, and the clear tendency of turbulent patterns to combine into spirals disappeared at $k_1 < 0.8$. The amplitude of oscillations diminished with decreasing of k_1. At last, at $k_1 = 0.71$ (Fig. 3f), the oxygen stripe wave vanish slowly from the surface and the system transform to the low reactive state (the surface is predominantly covered by CO_{ads}).

The reverse increasing of k_1 leads to hysteresis in oscillatory behaviour. The oscillation appears only at $k_1 = 0.85$ via very fast "surface explosion" (Fig. 4a-h). It is surprising that the characteristics of oscillations differ drastically from those observed at gradual decreasing of k_1 at the same value of $k_1 = 0.85$. Now the amplitude of oscillations in the regime II (coverage's and reaction rate) is larger than in regime I, and instead of turbulent spiral-like pattern (Fig. 3c) we observe the alternately change

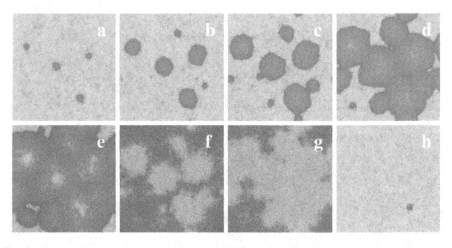

Fig. 4. The snapshots illustrating the rise of oscillations at inverse step-by-step increasing of k_1, $k_1 = 0.85$. The difference between the frames is 5 MC steps. The designations of adsorbate are the same as for Fig. 2.

of O_{ads} and CO_{ads} layers via growing cellular oxygen islands (Fig. 4) similar to the case with large diffusion intensity (Fig. 2). The interval of existence of these oscillations increased significantly. Noteworthily, that the simulations at higher lattice size N=8000 in regime II ($k_1 = 0.83$) gave us the "target"-like structures, which were observed experimentally [10], Fig 5.

Only at $k_1 = 1$ occurs the transformation from the regime II to the regime I – we observe again the turbulent patterns over the surface (Fig. 3a). In the cases discussed

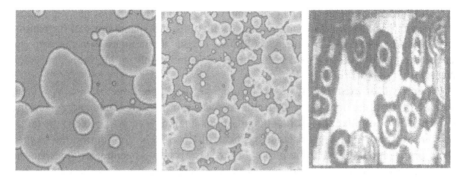

Fig. 5. Simulated "target" structures at N=8000 (a, b), and adsorbed oxygen and carbon monoxide structures on the Pt(110) experimentally observed by Photo Emission Electron Microscopy (PEEM) (c) [10]. The designations of adsorbate are the same as for Fig. 2.

above we perform the simulation experiments with constant P(CO), i.e., k_2 and k_6, changing over and back the O_2 partial pressure (k_1).

When we performed the simulations with constant $k_1 = 1$, M=20 and changing step-wise k_2 and k_6 (i.e., P(CO)) from 0.5 to 1.5 and back, we also obtained the hysteresis in oscillatory regime with similar spatiotemporal patterns on the surface.

It has been found in experiments, that the different oscillatory windows could exist in the parameter space of the particular system, e.g., CO oxidation over Pt(100) [9],

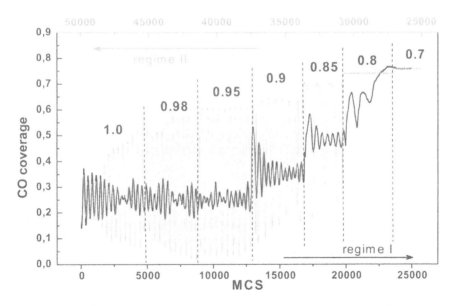

Fig. 6. The characteristics of two different oscillatory regimes at step-wise decreasing of P(O_2) from $k_1 = 1.0$ to $k_1 = 0.7$ (regime I) and at increasing from $k_1 = 0.8$ to $k_1 = 1.0$ (regime II): $k_1 = k_{ads}(O_2) \times S(O_2) \times P(O_2)$. Only oscillations of CO coverage have been shown.

i.e., at different parameters (temperature and CO/O$_2$ ratio) two regions has been found at a constant total pressure where the rate oscillations and spatiotemporal formations have been observed. In our case two different oscillatory regimes with discriminate spatiotemporal dynamics have been found in simulations *in the same* variation interval of P(O$_2$) (and P(CO)), Fig. 6.

The interval of existence of oscillatory regime II is quite large: $0.98 > k_1 > 0.82$. Increase of k_1 in this interval leads to the increasing of the amplitude and decreasing of the period of oscillations. At low bound of this interval (i.e., at $k_1 = 0.83$) the target structures of growing oxygen islands has been observed (Fig. 5) – during the oxygen island propagation CO have the possibility to adsorb into its centre. In this case the period of oscillations increased significantly ($\sim$ 2000 MCS). And only if we fall outside the upper limit of oscillatory regime II (at $k_1 = 1$) the transformation occurs from the regime II to the regime I – we observe again the turbulent patterns over the surface (Fig. 4a). When we switch over from $k_1 = 1$ to $k_1 = 0.85$, we observe again the oscillatory regime I. Fig. 6 illustrates the whole scenario of k_1 change during our simulation experiments, exemplified by CO$_{ads}$ dynamics. First we carried out the simulations at restricted CO$_{ads}$ diffusion intensity (M = 20) with P(O$_2$) (or k_1) equal to 1.0. Then we began to decrease the k_1 parameter (or, the same, P(O$_2$)) step-by-step manner down to the vanishing of the oscillatory regime I at P(O$_2$) = 0.71. The inverse step-by-step increase of P(O$_2$) leads to the rise of oscillatory regime II at P(O$_2$) = 0.85 (Fig. 6). The characteristics of oscillations (period and amplitude) differ drastically in these two oscillatory regimes, and what is more, the spatio-temporal patterns are distinctly different (Figs. 3 and 4). Whereas in oscillatory regime I oxygen is always present on the surface in the form of small islands, spirals and stripes, oscillatory regime II characterised by alternate high and low reactive states changing due to periodic oxygen cellular patterns propagation (cf. Figs. 3 and 4). The transition to the P(O$_2$) = 1 both from the value 0.98 and 0.85 (Fig. 6) leads to the oscillatory regime I. After the establishment of the regime I we can turn back to the P(O$_2$) = 0.85 and observe again the spiral-like spatio-temporal structures of oxygen on the surface (Fig. 3c). That means, that at the same value of the key parameter (e.g., $k_1 = 0.85$) two different «cycles» could exist. The shape of «integral» oscillations and spatio-temporal patterns depends on the dynamic prehistory (shape-memory effect).

5   Conclusion

Thus, the hysteresis in oscillatory behaviour has been found by kinetic asynchronous cellular automata modelling of CO oxidation reaction over Pd(110). Two different oscillatory regimes could exist at one and the same parameters of the reaction. The parameters of oscillations (amplitude, period and the shape of spatiotemporal patterns on the surface) depend on the dynamic prehistory of the system (shape-memory effect). The possibility for the appearance of the cellular, target and turbulent patterns, spiral, ring and "worm"-like waves on the surface in the cases under study has been shown. The results obtained make possible to interpret the surface processes on the atomic scale.

Acknowledgements. This work was supported by Russian Fund for Basic Research Grant # 05-03-32971, INTAS Grant # 05-109-5039 and Russian Science Support Foundation.

References

1. Imbihl, R., Ertl, G.: Oscillatory kinetics in heterogeneous catalysis. Chem. Rev. 95, 697–733 (1995)
2. Latkin, E.I., Elokhin, V.I., Matveev, A.V., Gorodetskii, V.V.: The role of subsurface oxygen in oscillatory behavior of CO + O_2 reaction over Pd metal catalysts: Monte Carlo model. J. Molec. Catal. A, Chem. 158, 161–166 (2000)
3. Latkin, E.I., Elokhin, V.I., Gorodetskii, V.V.: Monte-Carlo model of oscillatory CO oxidation having regard to the change of catalytic properties due to the adsorbate-induced Pt(100) structural transformation. J. Molec. Catal. A, Chem. 166, 23–30 (2001)
4. Gorodetskii, V.V., Matveev, A.V., Kalinkin, A.V., Niewenhuys, B.E.: Mechanism for CO oxidation and oscillatory reactions on Pd tip and Pd(110) surfaces: FEM, TPR, XPS studies. Chem. for Sustain. Dev. 11, 67–74 (2003)
5. Gorodetskii, V.V., Matveev, A.V., Podgornov, E.A., Zaera, F.: Study of the low-temperature reaction between CO and O_2 over Pd and Pt surfaces. Topics in Catalysis 32, 17–28 (2005)
6. Ertl, G.: Oscillatory catalytic reactions at single-crystal surfaces. Adv. Catal. 37, 213 (1990)
7. Vishnevskii, A.L., Latkin, E.I., Elokhin, V.I.: Autowaves on catalyst surface caused by carbon monoxide oxidation kinetics: Imitation model. Surf. Rev. Lett. 2, 459–469 (1995)
8. Gorodetskii, V.V., Drachsel, W.: Kinetic oscillations and surface waves in catalytic CO+O_2 reaction on Pt surface: Field electron microscope, field ion microscope and high resolution electron energy loss studies. Appl. Catal. A: General 188, 267–275 (1999)
9. Lauterbach, J., Bonilla, G., Fletcher, T.D.: Non-linear phenomena during CO oxidation in the mbar pressure range: a comparison between Pt/SiO_2 and Pt(100). Chem. Eng. Sci. 54, 4501–4512 (1999)
10. Jakubith, S., Rotermund, H.H., Engel, W., von Oertzen, A., Ertl, G.: Spatio-temporal concentration patterns in a surface reaction: Propagating and standing waves, rotating spirals, and turbulence. Phys. Rev. Lett. 65, 3013–3016 (1990)

CAOS: A Domain-Specific Language for the Parallel Simulation of Cellular Automata

Clemens Grelck[1,2], Frank Penczek[1,2], and Kai Trojahner[2]

[1] University of Hertfordshire
Department of Computer Science
c.grelck@herts.ac.uk, f.penczek@herts.ac.uk
[2] University of Lübeck
Institute of Software Technology and Programming Languages
trojahner@isp.uni-luebeck.de

Abstract. We present the design and implementation of CAOS, a domain-specific high-level programming language for the parallel simulation of extended cellular automata. CAOS allows scientists to specify complex simulations with limited programming skills and effort. Yet the CAOS compiler generates efficiently executable code that automatically harnesses the potential of contemporary multi-core processors, shared memory multiprocessors, workstation clusters and supercomputers.

1 Introduction

Cellular automata are a powerful concept for the simulation of complex systems; they have successfully been applied to a wide range of simulation problems [1,2,3,4,5,6,7,8]. This work is typically done by scientists who are experts in their field, but generally not experts in programming and computer architecture. Programming complex simulations correctly and efficiently quickly turns into a painful venture distracting from the interesting aspects of the simulation problem itself. Current advances in computer architecture make the situation considerably worse. Abundance of parallel processing power through multicore technology and the need to parallelise simulation software to effectively use standard computing machinery confronts us with the notorious hazards of parallel programming. The model of cellular automata naturally lends itself to parallel execution. However, the effective utilisation of parallel processing resources on whatever level requires very specific programming skills and is difficult, time-consuming and error-prone.

We propose a new domain-specific programming language named CAOS (Cells, Agents and Observers for Simulation) that is tailor-made for programming simulation software based on the model of cellular automata. Since it is restricted to this single purpose, it provides the scientist with little programming experience support for the rapid prototyping of complex simulations on a high level of abstraction. Nevertheless, the CAOS compiler fully automatically generates portable and efficiently executable code for a wide range of architectures. We support both shared memory systems through OPENMP and distributed

V. Malyshkin (Ed.): PaCT 2007, LNCS 4671, pp. 410–417, 2007.

memory systems through MPI. In fact, both approaches may be combined having the compiler generate multithreaded OPENMP code within MPI processes for hybrid architectures. Thus, CAOS not only supports today's multicore processors, but likewise clusters of workstations, traditional supercomputers and combinations thereof.

The remainder of the paper is organised as follows: In Sections 2, 3 and 4 we introduce cells, agents and observers, respectively. Section 5 outlines some implementation aspects and reports on performance measurements. We addresses related work in Section 6 and conclude in Section 7.

2 Cells

Fig. 1 shows the general layout of a CAOS program, which is organised into a sequence of sections. Following a set of declarations, which we will only sketch out briefly, we find the basic constituents of CAOS: cells, agents and observers. This section is concerned with cells; agents and observers are explained in the following sections. Cells consist of attribute declarations (the state space), an initialisation (the initial state) and a behaviour definition (the state transition function). This specification of a single cell is complemented by a grid definition that defines the assemblage of these uniform cells to a cellular automaton.

Program	$\Rightarrow$	*Declarations Cells Agents Observers*
Cells	$\Rightarrow$	*Grid Attributes Init Behaviour*
Grid	$\Rightarrow$	**grid** *Axis* $\lceil$, *Axis* $\rceil^*$;
Axis	$\Rightarrow$	*Index* .. *Index* : *Id* **<.>** *Id* : *Boundary*
Index	$\Rightarrow$	*IntConstant* | *Id*
Boundary	$\Rightarrow$	**static** | **cyclic**
Attributes	$\Rightarrow$	**cells** $\{$ $\lceil$ *Type Id* ; $\rceil+$ $\}$

Fig. 1. Grammar of CAOS programs

As mentioned earlier, the state space of CAOS cells can be quite complex: Following the key word `cells` we have a sequence of attribute declarations each associated with a type. This part very much resembles the definition of attributes in class definitions of an object-oriented languages. As types CAOS currently supports boolean values (`bool`), integer numbers (`int`), double precision floating point numbers (`double`) and user-defined enumeration types. The latter are very similar to those in C and can be defined in the declaration section of a CAOS program. Enumeration types are handy to use symbolic names whenever the state space is rather small. For example, in the Game of Life it may be more expressive to use an enumeration type

```
enum dead_or_alive {dead, alive};
```
than representing the state by boolean or integer values. The corresponding cell definition could look like

```
cells { dead_or_alive state; }
```

Cells are arranged to multi-dimensional grids using the grid declaration. Following the key word **grid** we have a sequence of axis specifications. Each axis specification itself consists of three parts separated by colons. First, we specify the extent of the grid along this axis. Grid sizes may be hard-coded using an integer constant. However, in most cases it is more convenient to use a symbolic constant defined in the declaration section or a symbolic parameter, which allows us to determine the grid size at runtime. A parameter declaration of the form

```
param int size = 100;
```

makes the CAOS compiler automatically generate a command line option `-size` *num* that can be used to overrule the default value specified (100 in this example). Of course, parameters can be used throughout the CAOS program at any appropriate expression position and not only in grid specifications.

The second part of an axis specification introduces two new identifiers as symbolic names for neighbouring cells along decreasing (left of <.> symbol) and increasing (right of <.> symbol) indices. These symbolic *directions* are the only means to access attributes of neighbouring cells; they avoid the error-prone use of explicit numerical indices and calculations on them.

Any grid has a finite size which raises the question of how to handle cells on the boundary. By putting one of the key words **static** and **cyclic** into the last part of the axis specification we offer the choice between an additional layer of constant cells and cyclic neighbourship relations. As an example, consider the following specification of a 2-dimensional grid using compass names for directions:

```
grid 1..100  : north <.> south : static,
      1..size : west <.> east   : cyclic;
```

Cells may be initialised by the available set of constants and parameters. Furthermore, entire start configuration can be read from files. We skip this part of the language and head straight on to the more interesting behaviour specification, i.e. the state transition function of our cells. Fig. 2 defines the syntax. Essentially, a CAOS behaviour specification is a C- or Java-like block of assignments. In addition to the state identifiers declared in the cells section of a CAOS program, we have local variables in the behaviour section. Such local variables are pure placeholders for intermediate values. Apart from them, the body of a behaviour specification is a sequence of assignments to either local variables or state variables.

Behaviour	$\Rightarrow$	**behaviour** { [*Type Id* [= *Expr*] ;]* [*Instruction*]* }
Instruction	$\Rightarrow$	*Assignment* | *Cond* | *ForEach* | *Switch*
Assignment	$\Rightarrow$	*Id* = *Expr* ;
Cond	$\Rightarrow$	**if** (*Expr*) *Block* **else** *Block*
ForEach	$\Rightarrow$	**foreach** (*Type Id* **in** *Set*) *Block*
Switch	$\Rightarrow$	**switch** (*Id*) { [*Case*]+ [*Default*] }
Case	$\Rightarrow$	**case** *CaseVal* [, *CaseVal*]* : *Block*
Block	$\Rightarrow$	*Instruction* | { [*Instruction*]* }

Fig. 2. Syntax of the behaviour section

Expressions are made up of local and state variables as well as the usual operators on the basic types supported by CAOS. The most noteworthy part here is the access to state variables of neighbouring cells. Whereas the existing values of a cell's own state variables are accessed simply by the variable's name, neighbouring cell's state variables are referred to using the *directions* introduced in the grid specification. Given the above cell and grid specifications, a cell may access the state of its left neighbour by state[west] or its upper neighbour by state[north]. CAOS also provides an associative and commutative operator on directions: With state[north^west] we can easily address the upper left neighbour without complicated and error-prone numerical index computations. Neighbourhoods are not limited to immediate neighbours: state[north^north] is perfectly fine. As the boundary condition on this axis was defined as static, the CAOS compiler will introduce a constant boundary layer of sufficient size.

CAOS provides a set of versatile control constructs. The C- or Java-like conditional, for example, allows us to implement the Game of Life:

```
behaviour { int cnt = 0;
            if (state[north]       == alive) cnt = cnt + 1;
            if (state[south]       == alive) cnt = cnt + 1;
            if (state[east]        == alive) cnt = cnt + 1;
            if (state[west]        == alive) cnt = cnt + 1;
            if (state[north^east]  == alive) cnt = cnt + 1;
            if (state[north^west]  == alive) cnt = cnt + 1;
            if (state[south^east]  == alive) cnt = cnt + 1;
            if (state[south^west]  == alive) cnt = cnt + 1;

            if (state == alive) {
              if (cnt == 2 || cnt == 3) state = alive;
              else state = dead;
            }
            else {
              if (cnt == 3) state = alive;
              else state = dead;
            } }
```

A more concise specification of the counting process can be achieved using the foreach construct:

```
foreach (dir d in [north, south, east, west,
                   north^east, north^west, south^east, south^west]) {
  if (state[d] == alive) cnt = cnt + 1;
}
```

The body code is executed for each element of the set of directions, represented by the local variable d of type dir. Likewise, the decision making code may be written more intuitively thanks to the switch-construct:

```
switch (state) { case alive: switch (cnt) { case 2,3: state = alive;
                                            default:  state = dead;
                                          }
                case dead:  switch (cnt) { case 3:   state = alive;
                                            default:  state = dead;
              }                                    }
```

CAOS provides further variations of the `foreach` and `switch` constructs using explicit guard expression. Moreover, there is a range of probabilistic constructs that allow programmers to introduce non-determinism. However, due to the limited space we cannot elaborate on them.

3   Agents

Agents are similar to cells in that they consist of a set of attributes. Agents move from cell to cell; at any step during the simulation an agent is associated with exactly one cell. A cell in turn may be associated with a conceptually unlimited number of agents. Like the cells, agents have a behaviour (or state transition function). The behaviour of an agent is based on its existing state and the state of the cell it resides at as well as all other agents and cells in the neighbourship as described above. In addition to updating its internal state, an agent (unlike a cell) may decide to move to a neighbouring cell. Conceptually, this is nothing but an update of the special attribute location. Agents also have a life time, i.e. rather than moving to another cell, agents may decide to die and agents may create new agents.

4   Observers

It is paramount for any simulation software to make the result of simulation, and in most cases intermediate states at regular intervals as well, visible for interpretation. Observers serve exactly this purpose. They allow us to observe the values of certain attributes of cells and agents or cumulative data about them (e.g. averages, minima or sums) at certain regular intervals of the simulation or just after completing the entire simulation.

Each observer is connected with a certain file name (not a certain file). The parallel runtime system takes full advantage of parallel I/O both when using MPI and OPENMP as backend. This file system handling is particularly tricky if it is to be hand-coded. An auxiliary tool suite provides a comfortable user-interface to observer data produced through parallel file I/O.

5   Implementation and Evaluation

We have implemented a fully fledged CAOS compiler[1] that generates sequential C code. On demand, the grid is automatically partitioned for multiple MPI processes. The process topology including the choice and number of partitioned grid axes are fully user-defined. A default process topology provided at compiler time may be overwritten at program startup. Additionally, each MPI process may be split either statically or dynamically into a user-defined number of OPENMP threads, provided that the available MPI implementation is thread-safe. Proper

---

[1] The current version does not yet support agents.

and efficient communication between MPI processes including the organisation of halo or ghost cells at partition boundaries is taken care of by the compiler without any user interaction. For implementation details see [16].

We use 2-dimensional Jacobi iteration as the basis for some performance evaluating experiments. Fig. 3 shows the complete CAOS code, which also serves as a reference example for CAOS programs. Note the observers that, at a certain time step (usually the last one) save the entire state as well as the average. Our experiments use two different machines: a 72-processor SUN SF15k with NUMA shared address space and an 8-node PC cluster with Intel Pentium IV processors and a gigabit ethernet connection.

```
param int atTstep = 1;
param int size = 100;

grid 0..size : left <.> right : static,
     0..size :   up <.> down  : static;

cells { double state; }

init { state = 0.0; }

init[down] { state = 500.0; }

behaviour { double a = 0.0;
            foreach (dir d in [up,down,left,right]) {
              a = a + state[d];
            }
            state = a / 4.0;
          }

observeall ("jacobi.outfile.all", timestep==atTstep) {
  double "state" = state;
}

observe ("jacobi.outfile.reduce", timestep==atTstep) {
  double "avgState" = avg(state);
}
```

Fig. 3. Jacobi iteration specified in CAOS

Fig. 4 shows the outcomes of our experiments on the shared address space (left) and on the distributed memory (right) architecture. While the latter figures show good speedups and scalability in the range of available nodes, the former provide some interesting insights into the suitability of MPI, OPENMP and a combination of the two as low-level execution models for CAOS (and similar numerical codes), at least on the given machinery. Using our purely MPI-based code generator achieves substantially better performance values than the purely OPENMP-based one. Likewise, using 2 or 4 OPENMP threads inside each MPI process does not pay off, although this organisation exactly matches the SF15k architecture. The SUN MPI implementation seems to be considerably more advanced than the OPENMP support in the C compiler. We also assume that the

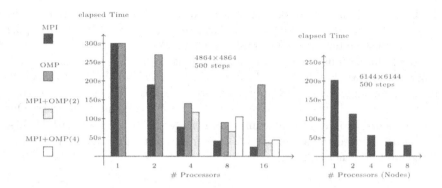

Fig. 4. Execution Times of CAOS Jacobi iteration on a shared address space system (left) using either MPI or OPENMP or a combination of both as execution platform and on a distributed memory workstation cluster (right) using only MPI

Solaris operating system may not schedule threads in a way that harnesses the hierarchical memory organisation.

6 Related Work

Mathematica and MatLab are well-known general-purpose systems that are also suitable for implementing cellular automata on a level of abstraction that exceeds that of standard programming languages. As examples for domain-specific languages and systems we mention CANL [9], CDL [10], TREND [11], CARPET/CAMEL [12,13], CELLANG [14] and JCASim [15]. Limited space does not allow us to discuss their relationship with CAOS in the desirable detail. A similar purpose inevitably results in certain similarities; differences lie in the number of axes supported, the concrete syntactical support for high-level programming, the way concurrency in the cellular automaton model is exploited (if at all) and the orientation towards runtime performance in general.

7 Conclusion

CAOS is a new domain-specific programming language that supports specification of multidimensional extended cellular automata at a high level of abstraction. Our automatically parallelising compiler exploits the restricted pattern of communication for generating efficiently executable code for both shared and distributed memory architectures. It provides access to the potential of modern computer architectures with modest programming skills. Space limitations prevent us from giving a complete introduction to the CAOS language. Further information on the project, including a technical report that covers compilation in-depth [16] and a source distribution with demos for download, is available at http://caos.isp.uni-luebeck.de/

References

1. Ermentrout, G.B., Edelstein-Keshet, L.: Cellular automata approaches to biological modeling. Journal of Theoretical Biology 160, 97–133 (1993)
2. Gutowitz, H.: Cryptography with Dynamical Systems, pp. 237–274. Kluwer Academic Publishers, Boston (1993)
3. Nagel, K., Schreckenberg, M.: A cellular automaton model for freeway traffic. J. Phys. I France 2 (1992)
4. Guisado, J., de Vega, F.F., Jiménez-Morales, F., Iskra, K.: Parallel implementation of a cellular automaton model for the simulation of laser dynamics. In: Alexandrov, V.N., van Albada, G.D., Sloot, P.M.A., Dongarra, J.J. (eds.) ICCS 2006. LNCS, vol. 3993, pp. 281–288. Springer, Heidelberg (2006)
5. Stevens, D., Dragicevic, S., Rothley, K.: iCity: A GIS-CA modelling tool for urban planning and decision making. Environmental Modelling & Software 22 (2007)
6. Georgoudas, I.G., Sirakoulis, G.C., Scordilis, E.M., Andreadis, I.: A cellular automaton simulation tool for modelling seismicity in the region of Xanthi. Environmental Modelling & Software 22 (2007)
7. D'Ambrosio, D., Iovine, G., Spataro, W., Miyamoto, H.: A macroscopic collisional model for debris-flows simulation. Environmental Modelling & Software 22 (2007)
8. Canyurt, O., Hajela, P.: A cellular framework for structural analysis and optimization. Computer Methods in Applied Mechanics and Engineering 194 (2005)
9. Calidonna, C., Furnari, M.: The cellular automata network compiler system: Modules and features. In: International Conference on Parallel Computing in Electrical Engineering, pp. 271–276 (2004)
10. Hochberger, C., Hoffmann, R., Waldschmidt, S.: Compilation of CDL for different target architectures. In: Malyshkin, V. (ed.) Parallel Computing Technologies. LNCS, vol. 964, pp. 169–179. Springer, Heidelberg (1995)
11. Chou, H., Huang, W., Reggia, J.A.: The Trend cellular automata programming environment. SIMULATION 78, 59–75 (2002)
12. Spezzano, G., Talia, D.: A high-level cellular programming model for massively parallel processing. In: Proc. 2nd Int. Workshop on High-Level Programming Models and Supportive Environments (HIPS'97), pp. 55–63. IEEE Press, New York (1997)
13. Spezzano, G., Talia, D.: Programming high performance models of soil contamination by a cellular automata language. In: Hertzberger, B., Sloot, P.M.A. (eds.) High-Performance Computing and Networking. LNCS, vol. 1225, pp. 531–540. Springer, Heidelberg (1997)
14. Eckart, D.: A cellular automata simulation system: Version 2.0. ACM SIGPLAN Notices 27 (1992)
15. Freiwald, U., Weimar, J.: The Java based cellular automata simulation system JCASim. Future Generation Computing Systems 18, 995–1004 (2002)
16. Grelck, C., Penczek, F.: CAOS: A Domain-Specific Language for the Parallel Simulation of Extended Cellular Automata and its Implementation. Technical report, University of Lübeck, Institute of Software Technology and Programming Languages (2007)

Parallel Hardware Architecture to Simulate Movable Creatures in the CA Model

Mathias Halbach and Rolf Hoffmann

TU Darmstadt, FB Informatik, FG Rechnerarchitektur
Hochschulstraße 10, D-64289 Darmstadt, Germany
Phone: +49 6151 16 {3713, 3606}; Fax: +49 6151 16 5410
{halbach, hoffmann}@ra.informatik.tu-darmstadt.de

Abstract. The general question of our investigation is: how can the simulation of moving objects (or agents) in a cellular automaton (CA) be accelerated by hardware architectures. We exemplify our approach using the creatures' exploration problem: n creatures are moving around in an unknown environment in order to visit all cells in shortest time. This problem is modeled as CA because this model is massively parallel and therefore it can be perfectly supported by hardware (FPGA technology). We need a very fast simulation because we want to observe and evaluate the collaborative performance for a different number of creatures, different behaviors of the creatures and for many different environments. As a main result from these simulations and evaluations we expect to find the best algorithms which can fulfill the task with the lowest work units (generations × creatures). In this contribution we have investigated the question how the creatures' exploration problem can be accelerated in hardware with a minimum of hardware resources. We have designed and evaluated five different architectures that vary in the combination or separation of the logic for the environment, for the creatures and for the collision detection. A speedup in the range of thousands compared to software can be reached using an architecture which separates the environment from the creatures and makes use of the memory banks embedded in the FPGA.

1 Introduction

The repeated simulation of complex Cellular Automata (CA) models under varying parameters is very time consuming on a single computer. As the CA model is inherently massively parallel, a hardware implementation is a promising alternative to multiprocessor simulation systems.

Previous investigations [1], [2], [3], [4] have shown that a speed up of hundreds to thousands is possible by the use of dedicated FPGA logic compared to software simulation on a personal computer. The resources needed to implement a Cellular Automaton in hardware depend on the number of cells in the field, the kind of neighborhood and the complexity of the rule.

In this contribution, we are solving a frequently encountered problem in which an automaton consists of two types of cells, many simple ones and few complex

V. Malyshkin (Ed.): PaCT 2007, LNCS 4671, pp. 418–431, 2007.

ones. The goal is to find efficient parallel hardware architectures which allow to simulate and evaluate such CA systems much faster than by software on a PC.

The problem used as an example is the so called "creature's exploration problem": A number of creatures with local intelligence are moving around autonomously in an environment in order to visit all empty cells in shortest time (with a minimum number of time steps, i. e. generations). The *environment* is given by a field of cells, called the *environment cells*. The environment cells are either of type *empty* or of type *obstacle*. A creature can move to an empty cell if no other creature tries to move to the same position (otherwise it is a conflict situation). The creatures behavior is given by a state machine, which reacts on an input signal m (move, creature can move). If the creature cannot move, it will turn to the right or to the left. The state machine is implemented by a state table.

The challenge is to find out the optimal behaviors for n collaborating creatures to perform the given task in shortest time. It is already very time consuming to find out the optimal behavior for a single creature if the number of states are larger than 5 or 6. The problem becomes much more difficult with multiple creatures and different behaviors.

We found an optimal behavior for one creature for a given set of initial configurations (environment plus the initial position and state of the creature) by the use of FPGA logic. Even with FPGA technology, it is not easy to find the optimum because the set of solutions is growing exponentially with the number of states. Like in software, the hardware implementation must try to simplify the complexity of the search procedure, e. g. by avoiding to test equivalent state machines and by not generating state machines with less states than required.

The problem of finding an optimal solution of moving agents using a state machine has also been addressed in [5], and the problem has practical applications like mowing a lawn [6] or exploring an unknown environment by robots.

In our preceding investigations optimal 6-state algorithms for a single creature were detected by the aid of FPGA acceleration [7]. These algorithms were used in further software evaluations for multiple creatures [8]. It turned out that the given task can be performed with a minimum number of work units using a certain number of creatures with an appropriate algorithm.

The goal of the presented work was to find an efficient parallel hardware architecture in order to simulate and test the performance of CA environments with complex creatures as fast as possible.

2   Formal Description of the Problem

The CA consists of two types of cells: (a) environment cells and (b) creatures. The environment cells are simple, static in their state and have four fixed links to their neighbors. The creatures are variable in their location and they have a variable state (direction, control state). Moreover, a creature has only one dynamic link to the neighbor in front of its moving direction. In the classical uniform CA model the union of these types forms a complex cell, which can be switched dynamically to the actual needed type. Environment cells carry either the value *free* or *obstacle*. Free cells can be visited whereas obstacles cannot. The border of an environment must be defined by cells of type obstacle. A rectangular environment can be described by

- the size n_x and n_y with $n_x, n_y \in \mathbb{N}$,
- the positions of the obstacles including the border positions $\mathbb{H} \subset \{c \mid c = (x, y) \in \mathbb{N}_0 \times \mathbb{N}_0 \wedge 0 \leq x < n_x \wedge 0 \leq y < n_y\} =: \mathbb{P}$,
- the border $\{c \mid c = (x, y) \in \mathbb{P} \wedge (x \in \{0, n_x - 1\} \vee y \in \{0, n_y - 1\})\} \subseteq \mathbb{H}$

where $\mathbb{P}$ is the set of all possible positions. The free cells are given by $\mathbb{F} := \mathbb{P} \backslash \mathbb{H}$.

Each creature (with index $i \in \mathbb{I}$, $|\mathbb{I}|$ = number of creatures) is defined by its actual position, direction and control state at the time step $t \in \mathbb{N}_0$:

- position: $p_{i,t} \in \mathbb{F}$,
- direction: $r_{i,t} \in \{0, 1, 2, 3\} =: \mathbb{D}$, where 0 represents north, 1 represents east etc.,
- control state: $s_{i,t} \in \mathbb{S} = \{v \mid v \in \mathbb{N}_0 \wedge 0 \leq v < S\}$ with $s_{i,0} := 0$

The number of possible control states is S which is a measure for the "brain power" of the creature. The creature looks one cell ahead in its actual moving direction $r_{i,t}$ and is able to read information from this position. We call the corresponding cell *front cell* and this position *front position*, which is defined as $\dot{p}_{i,t} \in \mathbb{F}$ by

$$\dot{p}_{i,t} := \begin{cases} (x_{i,t}, \, y_{i,t} + 1) & \text{if } r_{i,t} = 0 \text{ (north)} \\ (x_{i,t} + 1, \, y_{i,t}) & \text{if } r_{i,t} = 1 \text{ (east)} \\ (x_{i,t}, \, y_{i,t} - 1) & \text{if } r_{i,t} = 2 \text{ (south)} \\ (x_{i,t} - 1, \, y_{i,t}) & \text{if } r_{i,t} = 3 \text{ (west)} \end{cases} \quad \text{with } (x_{i,t}, y_{i,t}) = p_{i,t}.$$

Other front cell's features are tagged in the same way, e.g. $\dot{h}$ is the obstacle information of the front cell.

A creature must move to its front position if the front cell is reachable. The front cell is reachable (1) if the environment cell is free (not an obstacle) and (2) not occupied by another creature and (3) there is no conflict. If more than one creature wants to move to the same front cell, a conflict exists that must be resolved.

In general there are two solutions to resolve the conflicts: (1) either all creatures are stopped or (2) exactly one creature is selected to move on. The detection of the conflict requires a neighborhood distance of two, or a two phase algorithm [9]. In a fully parallel hardware implementation with uniform cells [4] we have placed a special collision detection logic in the front cell. This logic detects the conflicts and in such a case sends a stop signal to the creatures. Thereby in one phase only the creatures in conflict are prevented from moving.

The *moving condition* $m_{i,t}$ describes whether the creature i can move or not:

$$m_{i,t} := \begin{cases} \text{true when } \dot{p}_{i,t}' \in \mathbb{F} \wedge \forall_{j \in \mathbb{I}} \left((i = j) \vee (\dot{p}_{i,t}' \neq p_{j,t} \wedge \dot{p}_{i,t}' \neq \dot{p}_{j,t}') \right) \\ \text{false otherwise} \end{cases}$$

Depending on the moving condition the next position at time $t+1$ is

$$p_{i,t+1} := \begin{cases} \dot{p}_{i,t} \text{ if } m_{i,t} = \text{true} \\ p_{i,t} \text{ if } m_{i,t} = \text{false} \end{cases}.$$

Simultaneously with a possible move, the creature may change its state $s_{i,t}$ and its direction $r_{i,t}$ according to the next state function f and the output function g (turn right or left) which both are stored in the "brain" of the creature, i. e. in a memory table.

$$s_{i,t+1} \leftarrow f(s_{i,t}, m_{i,t})$$

$$r_{i,t+1} \leftarrow (r_{i,t} + g(s_{i,t}, m_{i,t})) \bmod 4$$

A state machine is formed by connecting the memory with a state register s and a direction register r as shown in figure 1a. The output actions of the creature are

moving condition = false:
R = turn right if the creature can't move, coded by "0"
L = turn left if the creature can't move, coded by "1"
moving condition = true:
Rm = move and turn right, if the creature can move, coded by "0"
Lm = move and turn right, if the creature can move, coded by "1"

Note that the state machine belongs to the creature and also has to move if the creature moves. A move of a creature in the CA model can be accomplished by copying the creature's state to the front cell and deleting the creature on its current position.

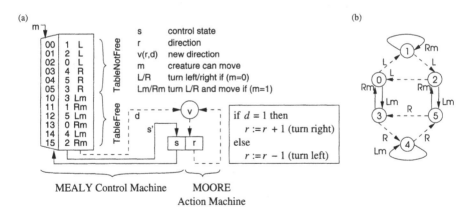

Fig. 1. (a) Table driven control machine and action machine; (b) corresponding 6-state algorithm G

A creature is implemented with a control machine (MEALY automaton) and an action machine (MOORE automaton) which is controlled by the control machine (fig. 1a). The behavior of the action machine is predefined and fixed. The state of the action machine is the direction r. The action machine reacts on the control signal d. If $d = 1$ the creature turns to the right $(r := r + 1)$, otherwise to the left $(r := r - 1)$.

The behavior of the control machine (also called algorithm for short in this context) is variable and can be configured by loading a state transition table. The control state is called s and the number of different states is n. Input to the state table is the control state s and the grant signal. Output of the state table is the control signal d and the next state s'. Note that the union of the control machine with the action machine results in a MOORE automaton. An algorithm is defined by the contents of the table. We are coding an algorithm by concatenating the contents to a string line by line, e. g.

1L2L0L4R5R3R-3Lm1Rm5Lm0Rm4Lm2Rm // string representation

= 1L2L0L4R5R3R-3L1R5L0R4L2R   // simplified string representation

The state table can be represented more clearly as a state graph (fig. 1b). If the state machine uses n states, we call such an algorithm n-state algorithm. The number of M of all algorithms which can be coded by a table oriented state machine is

$$M = (\#s \times \#y)^{(\#s \times \#x)}$$

where $n = \#s$ is the number of states, $\#x$ is the number of different input states and $\#y$ is the number of different output actions. Note that M increases dramatically, especially with $\#s$, which makes it very difficult or even impossible to check the quality of all algorithms in reasonable time for $\#s > 6$ with $\#x = \#y = 2$.

In preceding investigation [8], [10] we could discover the best 6-state algorithms for one creature. Using hardware support (FPGA technology) a large set of relevant algorithms was selected for five initial configurations by hardware enumeration, simulation and evaluation. From this set the best algorithms were selected during a software evaluation process applying 21 additional configurations.

The 10 best algorithms with respect to (1) success, (2) coverage and (3) speed are the following:

1. G: 1L2L0L4R5R3R-3L1R5L0R4L2R   6. E: 1R2L0R4L5L3L-3R4R5R0L1L2R
2. B: 1R2R0R4L5L3L-3R1L5R0L4R2L   7. F: 1R2L0L4R5R3R-3L4L5L0R1L2R
3. C: 1R2R0R4L5L3L-3R4R2L0L1L5R   8. H: 1L2L3R4L2R0L-2L4L0R3L5L4R
4. A: 0R2R3R4L5L1L-1R5R4R0L2L3L   9. I: 1L2L3L4L2R0L-2L4L0R3R5L4R
5. D: 1R2R3R1L5L1L-1R0L2L4R3L1L   10. J: 1R2R3R0R4L5L-4R5R3L2L0L1L

3 Alternative Architectures

The following variants have been considered

1. **Uniform:** classical uniform cellular automata,
2. **Augmented A:** The environment is augmented with parts of the creatures state and additional logic,
3. **Augmented B:** The environment is augmented with an index and additional logic,

4. **Separated 1:** separate creatures (complex rule) attached to the environment,
5. **Separated 2:** separate creatures with multiple memories as environment.

The variants 1 to 4 have already been discussed in [4] in more detail. In the uniform variant, the cell are the union of all types (creature, obstacle, empty). Therefore they are relatively complex. A type field is used to describe the actual usage of the cell. In the separated variant, the creatures are stored as individuals which can read the environment. In the augmented variants the environment is augmented with additional information such as creature's index (identification number), creature's direction or index (own position) of the environment cell, as can be seen in figure 2 for instance.

In the **Uniform Architecture** each cell has the same capabilities (attributes and rules). Only parts of all the capabilities are used in every generation depending on the actual type of the cells. It is possible to say that the cells are polymorphic.

The capabilities that must be combined in such an uniform cell are

- h: environment attribute – obstacle (true/false)
- c: type selection – creature is on the cell (true/false)
- s: control state of the creature
- r: direction of the creature
- ST: state table defining the creature's behavior
- CD: collision detection logic which generates a move signal m

The attributes c, s and r have to be variables. The environment attribute h shall be implemented as a variable (register or memory bit) in order to be able to change the environment during the simulation.

A state table ST or an equivalent logic defines the behavior of the creatures. It shall be variable, meaning that it should consist of registers which contents may be changed dynamically (e.g. in an optimization procedure). Optionally additional information for statistics (e.g. if the cell was already visited) may be stored in each cell. The next state (s') and next direction (r') of the uniform cell are given by the following formulas

$$\dot{m}^w := c^w \wedge (r^w \equiv w + 2 \bmod 4) \quad \text{for } w \in \mathbb{D}$$

$$\dot{m} := \exists_{w_1 \in \mathbb{D}} \dot{m}^{w_1} \wedge \neg\exists_{w_2 \in \mathbb{D}, w_2 \neq w_1} \dot{m}^{w_2}$$

$$\dot{s} := \begin{cases} s^{\text{north}} & \text{if } c^{\text{north}} \wedge r^{\text{north}} \equiv \text{south} \\ s^{\text{east}} & \text{if } c^{\text{east}} \wedge r^{\text{east}} \equiv \text{west} \\ s^{\text{south}} & \text{if } c^{\text{south}} \wedge r^{\text{south}} \equiv \text{north} \\ s^{\text{west}} & \text{if } c^{\text{west}} \wedge r^{\text{west}} \equiv \text{east} \end{cases}$$

$$s' = \begin{cases} f(s, \text{false}) & \text{if } c \wedge h \\ f(\dot{s}, \text{true}) & \text{if } \neg c \wedge \dot{m} \\ \text{any} & \text{otherwise} \end{cases}$$

$$r' = \begin{cases} r + g(s, \text{false}) \bmod 4 & \text{if } c \wedge \dot{h} \\ \dot{r} + g(\dot{s}, \text{true}) \bmod 4 & \text{if } \neg c \wedge \dot{m} \\ \text{any} & \text{otherwise} \end{cases}$$

with the same definition for $\dot{r}$ as for $\dot{s}$.

The CD logic for collision detection generates the signal m (move) which decides whether the creature can move or not. This signal move becomes false if (1) the front cell is an obstacle, (2) a creature is placed on the front cell, (3) two or more creatures want to move to the same front cell if the front cell is free.

Each creature can check the first and second condition by testing the front cell. The testing of the third condition is more complicated: First, the front cell checks if there are more than one creature in the neighborhood, which want to move to it (conflict). Second, the conflict situation is send back to all the creatures, which have caused the conflict.

In the implementation of **Augmented A Variant**, the cells of the field consist of so called *augmented cells* which are the union of the environment h, the direction r of a creature and the index c_i of the creature which is active on that cell. The state of the augmented cells is (h, c_i, r). The creature index c_i is stored decoded, which means that for each creature an active bit is reserved. If such an active bit is set, automatically a connection is routed to the appropriate creature via a bus system. Each creature drives an output bus d_i (one bit wide: turn left/right as output from the state machine) and listens to an input bus (one bit wide: move yes/no).

Each active augmented cell which is occupied by a creature i sends a request to its front cell defined by r_i. The front cell computes the move signal m_i by checking all the conditions that were mentioned above for the uniform variant. The move condition is then sent to the appropriate creature. After inspecting the state table, the creature returns d_i (turn left/right). If the creature cannot move, the augmented cell will change its direction accordingly. In the case, the creature can move to the front cell and copies the active bit from the augmented cell and the new direction from the bus.

In **Augmented B Variant**, the implementation of the environment cells are augmented only with an index (own position of the cell). The index is used to connect automatically the appropriate creature to the environment cell. A creature sends its current position p_i via a bus to all cells. If a dedicated cell detects its own position on that bus, it connects to it. In conjunction the direction r_i of that creature is also connected to that cell, and a backward connection m_i is established. This is illustrated in figure 2. The environment cell is augmented with special logic in order to compute the move signal, which is send back via a bus to the appropriate creature.

An interesting feature is the conflict detection. An active cell (environment cell connected to a creature) asks the front cell (the neighbor in the current direction r_i), if there might be a conflict. The front cell checks if its neighbors may cause conflicts and returns the required information. The active cell then sends the required move signal back to the creature. By this technique, the creatures can perceive indirectly that conflicting creatures are two cells ahead or right/left in

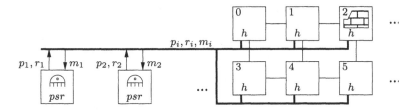

Fig. 2. Augmented, Variant B – mixture of Variant A and Multiplexer with enumerated area cells

front. Using the logic of a front cell during the computation of the next generation (asynchronously) the neighborhood of a creature can be indirectly increased. The hardware implementation causes no problem and asynchronous oscillation does not occur, because the logic of the front cell uses only local inputs.

Separated Architecture 1: Another way is to separate the environment and the creature, such that the changing state of the creatures is separated and therefore minimized, see figure 3. The advantage is that complex rules for the creatures need not to be replicated in the cells, which would result in a poor utilization of the hardware.

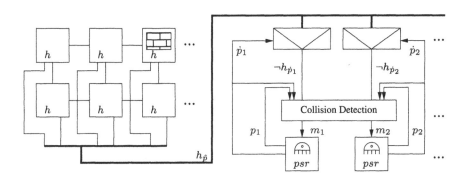

Fig. 3. Each creature is connected the environment, the collision detection logic is placed between the creatures (Separated Architecture 1)

Each creature has to be able to read the status of the environment cell (obstacle or not) from the current front position. This can be achieved in hardware by the use of a multiplexer. A technical problem arises when the number of cells exceeds a certain limit with our current FPGA technology. When exceeding the limit, the hardware needs too many resources (wires and cascaded multiplexers) or the time delay will be too large. Therefore, the multiplexer technique is limited to a small field.

Another problem arises with the detection of several creatures that are in conflict. There must be a central logic that detects and resolves the possible conflicts. This logic becomes very complex when the number of creatures is increasing. For a creature i this conflict exists if $p_i \equiv p_j \vee p_i \equiv \dot{p}_j$ gets true for any j with $i \neq j \in \mathbb{I}$. Unfortunately the complexity of the logic increases quadratically with the number of creatures. Therefore this architecture is limited to a certain number of creatures.

Comparison of the Architectures 1 to 4: The architectures were synthesized and configured for the Altera FPGA Cyclone EP1C20F324C7 using the Quartus II tools. The most relevant parameters are the size of the field, the number of control states of the state machine and the number of creatures. The resources are counted in the number of needed logic elements for that FPGA. The results of the syntheses are shown in figure 4. The maximum clock rate depends on the architecture, the field size and the number of creatures. The highest reached clock rate was 81 MHz, the lowest was 40 MHz.

The comparison of the architectures show that the architecture "Separated 1" needs the least resources. Therefore we concentrated in optimizing the architecture for bigger field sizes and more than 8 creatures. This architecture is called "Separated architecture 2" and is described in the following paragraph.

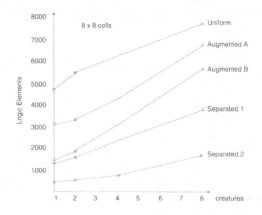

Fig. 4. Resources needed for a FPGA implementation

Separated Architecture 2: This architecture separates the simple environment cells from the complex creature cells like in the "Separated Architecture 1". In order to increase the field size and the number of creatures embedded memory banks of the FPGA are used instead of registers. In addition a signal is generated by the hardware which becomes true when all cells have been visited.

The hardware design (figure 5) consists of the following units

- n creatures
- collision detection logic
- obstacle detection unit
- success observer unit

Each creature consists of a control state machine and an action machine defining the individual behavior. Input to the control machine is the move signal m (creature can move) which becomes false if an obstacle (signal o) or a conflict (signal c) is detected: $m_i = \neg(o_i \vee c_i)$. The output signals of the creature are the current position p and the front position $\dot{p}$.

The central collision logic is connected to all creatures. It computes for each creature the collision signal c_i depending on all other positions and all front positions. This logic becomes quadratically more complex with the number of creatures. It could be synthesized for 16 creatures in our prototype FPGA implementation.

The obstacle detection unit indicates obstacles by the signal o_i for each creature. This signal becomes true if the front position of the creature is an obstacle. This information is hold in a look-up table. Dual port memories are used which are efficiently supported by the FPGA technology. Each pair of two creatures shares one dual port memory. Altogether $\frac{n}{2}$ dual port memories with the capacity of one bit per cell are needed.

The success observer unit implements a cyclic hardware process (watchdog process) which runs in parallel to the hardware simulation process. This unit generates a signal success, if all cells have been visited in a predefined time interval. In principle a register bit field can be used to store the information "cell visited". The problem is that each creature has to be connected to all the register bits through multiplexers. Such an implementation would require too many hardware resources. Therefore another approach was favored: The information "visited" is stored in memories. Each pair of two creatures shares one memory. First the creature with the odd index writes its position into the memory and afterwords the second creature with the even index. Thus two phases are needed to store the information.

Dual port memories are used in the implementation. The write port is configured for `datawidth` $= 1$ and `address` $= \dot{p}$. The read port is configured wider in order to parallelize the evaluation of the success signal (all cells visited). The read port is configured for the `datawidth` $= 16$ which implies that the read address can be shortened by 4 bits.

The observer process needs 256 clock cycles to check the whole field of 4 096 cells. In one clock cycle 16 cells are checked in parallel. For that purpose all outputs of the "visited" RAMs are OR-ed together. The result is AND-reduced and than AND-ed with the result from the previous clock cycle. A small logic with one flipflop is used for the AND-ing among the cycles.

There are two operational modes: *fuzzy mode* and *precise mode*. In the fuzzy mode the success signal is delayed with respect to the simulation because the checking process is slower than the simulation process. When the simulation is stopped by the success signal, the generation counter may be already higher $(g_{\max}+\delta,\ 0 \leq \delta \leq \frac{256}{3})$ than the exact number $g_{\max}$ of generations needed to visit all cells. For a general performance estimation the fuzziness is unimportant. If the

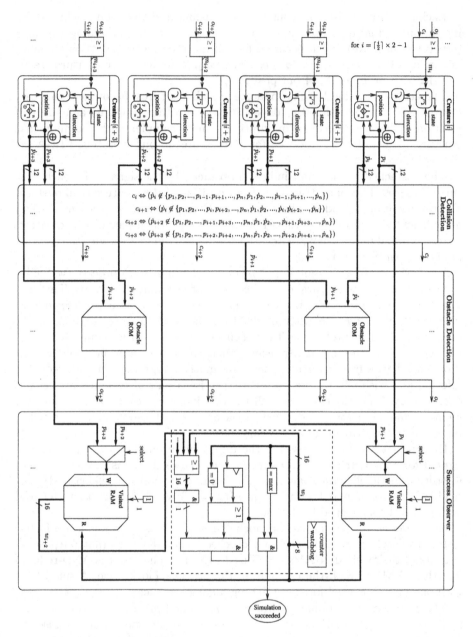

Fig. 5. Data Flow and Units of the Separated Architecture 2

exact generation g_{max} is needed for a precise performance evaluation, the precise mode can be chosen. In this mode the next simulation of the next generation is delayed until the success observer process has finished checking all cells.

The hardware simulation of one generation is performed in three phases.

1. phase A:
    - obstacle detection memory cycle 1,
    - collision detection logic cycle 1,
    - write position of odd creatures into Visited-RAMs cycle 1
2. phase B:
    - obstacle detection memory cycle 2,
    - collision detection logic cycle 2,
    - write position of even creatures into Visited-RAMs cycle 1
3. phase C:
    - updating the creatures' states (control, direction, position)

In the fuzzy mode each phase needs one clock cycle and the watchdog counter is incremented in each phase. In the precise mode phase B is delayed for 255 clock cycles in order to allow the watchdog counter to scan the whole information stored in the Visited-RAMs.

The Separated Architecture 2 was synthesized for the Altera Cyclone EP1C20-F324C7 FPGA using the Quartus II software. The needed resources and clock frequency are given in table 1.

Table 1. Synthesis results with time for one generation of 4 096 cells (used area size is 35 × 35), including time for software simulation

n creatures	clock rate	logic elements	memory bits	time	SW time
precise mode:					
1	167.00 MHz	301	8 192	1 539 ns	112 μs
4	180.73 MHz	692	16 384	1 422 ns	298 μs
8	160.10 MHz	1 622	32 768	1 605 ns	616 μs
16	144.32 MHz	4 691	65 536	1 781 ns	1 355 μs
32	71.34 MHz	16 849	131 072	3 603 ns	2 625 μs
fuzzy mode:					
1	181.79 MHz	303	8 192	16 ns	
4	174.61 MHz	744	16 384	17 ns	
8	162.65 MHz	1 630	32 768	18 ns	
16	145.62 MHz	4 730	65 536	21 ns	
32	75.68 MHz	17 046	131 072	40 ns	

In order to rate the FPGA implementation a functional equivalent software simulation was implemented optimally in C++. The platform is a PC with Pentium 4, 3.20 GHz, running with Microsoft Windows XP and Cygwin gcc version 3.4.4.

It is an impressive result of the comparison that the hardware simulation is many thousand times faster than the software simulation (see figure 6). Even if the hardware is in the precise mode, the speedup is in the range 21 to 1 081 (fuzzy mode: 1 870 to 55 369), depending on the number of creatures (1 to 64).

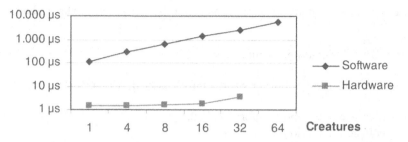

Fig. 6. Time for calculating one generation of 4 096 cells, separated architecture 2, precise mode

The hardware platform is used to test the performance for many different obstacle environments (robustness) and for different creature algorithms. From another investigation [8] and [10] we have already learned that a given task can be performed with minimal cost using the appropriate algorithm and a certain amount of collaborating creatures.

4   Conclusion

For the creatures exploration problem as an example for moving objects (hardware agents) in the CA we have designed and evaluated five different hardware architectures in order to speed up the simulation. The most promising architecture is "Separated Architecture 2". This architecture consists of creature modules, a central collision logic, an obstacle detection logic and a success observer. This architecture can compute a new generation of 4 096 cells with 32 creatures within 3 clock cycles in the fuzzy mode and in 257 clock cycles in the precise mode. The architecture was synthesized using Verilog for the ALTERA Cyclone Device. 84 % of the available logic cells and 44 % of the embedded memory bits were used for 4 096 cells and 32 creatures. The maximal reachable clock rate is 71.34 MHz. Compared to software simulation in C++ on a PC a speedup in the rage of many thousands was reached. The platform will be used for exhaustive simulations and evaluations in order to find out how a task for collaborating creatures can be accomplished with lowest cost.

References

1. Halbach, M., Heenes, W., Hoffmann, R., Tisje, J.: Optimizing the Behavior of a Moving Creature in Software and in Hardware. In: Sloot, P.M.A., Chopard, B., Hoekstra, A.G. (eds.) ACRI 2004. LNCS, vol. 3305, pp. 841–850. Springer, Heidelberg (2004)
2. Hoffmann, R., Heenes, W., Halbach, M.: Implementation of the Massively Parallel Model GCA. In: Parallel Computing in Electrical Engineering (PARELEC), Parallel System Architectures (September 2004)

3. Halbach, M., Hoffmann, R.: Implementing Cellular Automata in FPGA Logic. In: International Parallel & Distributed Processing Symposium (IPDPS), Workshop on Massively Parallel Processing (WMPP), IEEE Computer Society, Los Alamitos (2004)
4. Halbach, M., Hoffmann, R.: Minimising the Hardware Resources for a Cellular Automaton with Moving Creatures. In: Karl, W., Becker, J., Gropietsch, K.E., Hochberger, C., Maehle, E. (eds.) ARCS'06. 19th International Conference on Architecture of Computing Systems, Workshop Proceedings. Lecture Notes in Informatics (LNI). vol. P-81, pp. 323–332. Frankfurt, Germany (March 2006)
5. Mesot, B., Sanchez, E., Pena, C.A., Perez-Uribe, A.: SOS++: Finding Smart Behaviors Using Learning and Evolution. In: Standish, Abbass, Bedau. (eds.) Artificial Life VIII, p. 264. MIT Press, Cambridge (2002)
6. Koza, J.R.: Genetic Programming: On the Programming of Computers by Means of Natural Selection. MIT Pres, Cambridge (1992)
7. Halbach, M., Hoffmann, R.: Optimal Behavior of a Moving Creature in the Cellular Automata Model. In: Malyshkin, V. (ed.) PaCT 2005. LNCS, vol. 3606, pp. 129–140. Springer, Heidelberg (2005)
8. Halbach, M., Hoffmann, R., Both, L.: Optimal 6-State Algorithms for the Behavior of Several Moving Creatures. In: El Yacoubi, S., Chopard, B., Bandini, S. (eds.) ACRI 2006. LNCS, vol. 4173, pp. 571–581. Springer, Heidelberg (2006)
9. Hochberger, C.: CDL – Eine Sprache für die Zellularverarbeitung auf verschiedenen Zielplattformen. PhD thesis, TU Darmstadt, Darmstädter Dissertation D17 (1998)
10. Hoffmann, R., Halbach, M.: Are several creatures more efficient than a single one? In: El Yacoubi, S., Chopard, B., Bandini, S. (eds.) ACRI 2006. LNCS, vol. 4173, pp. 707–711. Workshop Crowds and Cellular Automata (C&CA) at ACRI 2006. Springer, Heidelberg (2006)

Comparison of Evolving Uniform, Non-uniform Cellular Automaton, and Genetic Programming for Centroid Detection with Hardware Agents

Marcus Komann, Andreas Mainka, and Dietmar Fey

Institute of Computer Science, University of Jena
Ernst-Abbe-Platz 2, 07743 Jena, Germany
marcus.komann@web.de, dietmar.fey@uni-jena.de

Abstract. Current industrial applications require fast and robust *image processing* in systems with low size and power dissipation. One of the main tasks in industrial vision is fast detection of centroids of objects. This paper compares three different approaches for finding *geometric algorithms* for centroid detection which are appropriate for a fine-grained parallel hardware architecture in an embedded vision chip. The algorithms shall comprise emergent capabilities and high problem-specific functionality without requiring large amounts of states or memory. For that problem, we consider *uniform* and *non-uniform cellular automata* (CA) as well as *Genetic Programming*. Due to the inherent complexity of the problem, an *evolution*ary approach is applied. The appropriateness of these approaches for centroid detection is discussed.

1 Introduction

Fast, robust, and reliable image processing with small embedded vision chips is a sophisticated task in industrial environments. Opposing requirements of high speed along with low size of the complete vision system, which has to integrate image capturing and processing in one intelligent CMOS camera chip, further complicate the design process. This makes the use of massively-parallel System-on-Chip architectures inevitable.

In order to simplify the design of future VLSI vision chips, we favor a fine-grained parallel architecture based on cellular automaton (CA) [10,11]. In this context, we already proposed the idea of so-called *Marching Pixels* in [4],[3]. Marching Pixels can be considered as a swarm of virtual hardware agents which are directly integrated in the hardware of vision chips. Inside these chips, they are crawling within a pixel field in order to fulfill tasks like the detection of centroid position, area, and the rotation of pre-known objects. The pixels of the input image are implemented in a large array of simple processor elements (PEs) which are working together synchronously. Each image pixel is attached to one PE in the ideal case. The so-called Marching Pixels start their march e.g. from the edges of an object, i.e. from a PE which hosts an edge pixel, towards the object's interior while collecting specific data. The behavior of Marching Pixels

V. Malyshkin (Ed.): PaCT 2007, LNCS 4671, pp. 432–441, 2007.

can be modeled as a CA which is specialised for vision chips. The advantage of using such virtual hardware agents is a gain of robustness due to their emergent capabilities and in particular the exploitable high degree of parallelism. For example, multiple objects are investigated by different swarms of hardware agents simultaneously.

We have already found several solutions for Marching Pixels' behavior in order to detect convex and concave formed objects in images using manually designed CAs [6],[5]. Depending on the complexity of the objects' shapes, the propagation of each Marching Pixel requires a state machine consisting of eight to twelve states. Usually, it holds that the higher the number of states is the higher is the chip area occupied by each PE and, thus, the larger is the whole chip die. Reducing the number of states makes it possible to install larger pixel resolutions on the same die or allows reducing the vision chip's size and power dissipation. In this paper, we therefore investigate if it is possible to decrease the number of required states we found with hand-made designs by means of evolving [2] corresponding CA rules. We apply that investigation to both *uniform* and *non-uniform CAs* as well as to an approach with *Genetic Programming*. All these approaches are compared and evaluated for our purpose of the design of a control algorithm for Marching Pixels hardware agents.

The remainder of the paper is structured as follows. In Sections 2 and 3, we describe the approaches of finding parallel image processing algorithms for centroid detection by evolving uniform and non-uniform cellular automata. We discuss their strengths and weaknesses and the general success of that approach. In Section 4, we present results achieved by considering Genetic Programming which is somehow similar to classic evolution of CAs but further allows modelling arithmetic operations and memory. Finally, we finish the paper with conclusions in Section 5.

2   Evolving Uniform Rules

We start with a binary image where the background is white and objects are black. Given this input image, the goal is to create an output image containing exactly one distinguished black pixel per object by modelling the image with a CA and executing specific CA rules on it. The distinguished pixel (resp. its CA cell, this is interchangeable from now on) shall correspond to the centroid pixel and shall contain a special state in the output image (resp. CA). All other pixels shall have the value of the background. Due to the discreteness of a pixel image, a deviation of up to one pixel is seen as a success.

2.1   Encoding the Rule Table

Expecting the reader to be familiar with basic concepts of CA and evolutionary algorithms, we only describe details of the implementation. State transition of the single cells is realised in form of direct encoding of the transition function (the "rules") in a look-up table. Because it is not known in advance how many and which rules are required, encoding of the complete rule table is necessary. The size of the rule table, measured by its number of entries s, depends on the state set Q and the applied neighborhood N. The size of the rule table grows exponentially in dependence of number of states and neighborhood, so minimising these values is worthwhile.

$$s = |Q|^{|N|}$$

2.2 Details of the Evolutionary Algorithm and the Applied Fitness Function

Creation of the rule tables of the cellular automaton can be done in two different ways. The first one is manual engineering using plausibility considerations. It is not dicussed here. The second one is exploiting the capabilities of evolutionary algorithms (EA). Looking at the size of the search space, which has z^{z^r} possible rule tables with $z = |Q|$ and $r = |N|$, the use of evolutionary algorithms seems feasible because this size is already large for small numbers of states and simple neighborhoods.

The evolutionary algorithm we use belongs to the class of elitarian genetic algorithms. The complete rule table is encoded as binary strings and starts with random initial values. The half of the population for the next generation is selected out of the 50% best evaluated individuals according to their fitness. The rest of the population is formed with the usual selection, crossover and mutation operations applied to these fittest individuals. Fitness calculation is obviously a neuralgic part of every evolutionary algorithm. It is the connection between the EA and the problem on one hand and the decider about the quality of found solutions on the other.

Our fitness function consists of two major parts. The first part is responsible for determination of the amount of wrong pixels, resp. states, in the output image after one of the CA algorithms belonging to the population was applied. They are determined by comparison with the ideal output image. For one pixel holds:

$$Q_{false}(o_{ij}, t_{ij}) = \begin{cases} 1 & (t_{ij} = 0 \wedge o_{ij} \neq 0) \vee (t_{ij} \neq 0 \wedge o_{ij} = 0) \\ 0 & otherwise \end{cases}$$

with o being the resulting image of the CA calculation (cells have state zero for background and state one for centroids), with t being the desired output image containing the centroid pixel, for $1 \leq i \leq n, 1 \leq j \leq m$. The pixels of the respective images are denoted by $o_{ij}, t_{ij}, 1 \leq i \leq n, 1 \leq j \leq m$. The dimension of the images is n, m. This leads to

$$f_{false} = \sum_{i=1}^{n} \sum_{j=1}^{m} Q_{false}(o_{ij}, t_{ij})$$

for the amount of detected wrong pixels in the complete output image after this specific CA computation.

A critical case arises when all pixels of the output image are white (all cells are in state zero) meaning they belong to the background. This leads to a very small failure in the above function although it is severely wrong semantically to have no meaningful pixels after the computation. Because of this, a control flag $bCenterFound$ and a penalty term nm are introduced in order to take care of that possibility. The control flag is set simply if the centroid pixel has the correct value and the penalty is used if all pixels have state zero. We then have

$$f_1 = \begin{cases} nm & , \neg bCenterFound \wedge f_{false} = 1 \\ f_{false} & , otherwise \end{cases}$$

for the first part of the fitness function.

The second part of the fitness function takes positions of wrongly calculated pixels into account. These are pixels of value other than zero. It is of advantage if these pixels settle around the real centroid pixel making it possible for them to be moved to the centroid pixel in later steps. We therefore need a distance measure for the second part of the fitness function, e.g Euclidean, Manhattan or Chequerboard. We favor Euclidean distance because diagonal distances are weighed a little worse than vertical and horizontal ones. This accommodates the von-Neumann neighborhood in the CA which we prefer in order to limit interconnects in the aspired real vision chip.

$$dist(o_{ij}, t_{gxgy}) = \begin{cases} \sqrt{(i - gx)^2 + (j - gy)^2} & o_{ij} \neq t_{ij} \\ 0 & otherwise \end{cases}$$

with $1 \leq i \leq n, 1 \leq j \leq m$. Values gx and gy refer to the coordinates of the centroid. Summing these distances up over all pixels results in the second part of the fitness function:

$$f_2 = \sum_{i=1}^{n} \sum_{j=1}^{m} dist(o_{ij}, t_{ij}) \ .$$

The final fitness function f, which is going to be minimised, is the sum of both parts f_1 and f_2:

$$f = f_1 + f_2 \ .$$

2.3   Results for the Uniform Case

We now show the evolution of a concrete rule table for a specific application. Given 10 example images of tools and their dedicated output images (see Figure 1), we use a discretised version of the tools images using a size of 16×16 in order to limit computing times, a population size of 300, and a maximal state number of 3. Thus, the size of the rule table equals 243. The applied CA has von-Neumann neighborhood and boundary values defined as zero (equals background). 6163 generations were needed to find the final rules which solve the

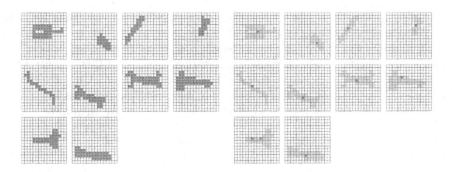

Fig. 1. Left: Simple input images of tools; Right: Calculated output images (Grey pixels represent the objects and are not present in the original output image. They can be seen here just for orientation).

problem. The resulting CA rules are able to detect the centroid of any tool in just 12 steps with the rule table seen in Table 1. This number would of course rise if larger object sizes were given.

A major drawback is the unrobustness of the resulting algorithm. Finding the centroids of other, unlearned objects is nearly not possible. This is no problem in industrial vision systems because, there, mostly pre-known objects have to be detected. However, also for learned objects, minor defects in the input image or at the edges of the objects cause severe detection failures. Apart from that, also rotation of the objects sometimes creates errors. The algorithm is indeed able to detect the centroids of objects as learned from the original input images but this weakness against smallest deviations makes it inapplicable to real environments where disturbances simply happen.

Table 1. Evolved rule table with 243 entries for centroid detection of tools. The number of the entry corresponds to the order (center north west south east); each component $\in \{0, 1, 2\}$.

```
0 1 1 0 0 0 0 1 1 0 0 0 0 0 1 1 1 0 0 0 0 1 1 0 1 0 1 0 0 1 2 1 0 1 1 1 0 2 0 1 2 0 0 1 0 0
0 1 2 0 0 0 1 2 0 0 0 1 1 0 1 0 1 1 0 2 1 2 2 2 2 0 1 0 0 0 2 0 0 2 1 0 0 0 0 0 1 2 2 2 1 1
2 0 0 0 2 2 0 1 1 0 1 1 1 0 0 1 0 1 0 1 0 1 2 0 0 1 2 1 0 2 1 1 0 2 0 0 0 1 0 2 2 1 2 0 0 0
2 1 1 1 0 0 0 0 0 2 0 1 2 1 1 1 1 1 1 2 2 1 0 1 0 2 0 0 0 0 2 0 1 0 1 0 2 1 0 0 0 0 2 0 1 0
2 0 0 1 0 0 2 0 2 1 0 1 2 1 0 0 1 1 1 2 0 1 0 2 2 1 2 1 1 0 1 1 2 1 0 0 0 0 1 0 0 0 0 2 0 0
                    2 1 0 0 0 0 1 0 1 2 1 2 1
```

3   Extension to Non-uniformity

3.1   Short Introduction of Non-uniformism and Related Work

Whereas all cells use the same rule table in a uniform CA, each cell or group of cells may have a different transition function in a non-uniform CA. Sipper introduced that kind of CAs [8] and their strengths if being evolved [9]. He showed that it is possible to realise universal computability with a non-uniform CA needing only two states whereas uniform CAs require at least three states to achieve the same. Furthermore, he proved that, for some global tasks, a non-uniform CA is more efficient than a uniform CA concerning the number of required states and the success rate of correct cell states in the CA after computation. These tasks were CA-global, e.g. the density problem in which all cells of a CA shall have the same state in the end as the majority of all cells had initially. Another example is the ordering problem in which all initial 1 and 0 states of a 1-dimensional toroidal two-state CA with neighborhood radius of one shall be shifted to opposite sides of the CA in the end. These tasks have a similar global character like our problem of reducing the number of states required for geometric algorithms, e.g. the centroid detection. In another work, non-uniform CAs and evolution have been successfully used for the deduction of a classifier system for car plate detection [1]. Therefore, we also try to evolve non-uniform CAs in addition to uniform CAs.

As for uniform CAs, each rule table is encoded as a binary string. Of course, the possibility of cells having an own table increases the size of the search space dramatically. With M being the amount of cells, z the number of states, and r the number of neighbor cells we now have to search in $\left(z^{z^r}\right)^M$ possible automata. The fitness function has also to be adapted and is now calculated separately for every single cell only in its local neighborhood. This makes it easier or maybe even possible at all to solve problems with local characteristics.

In detail, fitness is calculated as the ratio of correctly recognised cells to all cells for all applied input images after an iteration. Then, the fitness of each cell is compared to its neighbored cells. If no neighbor is better, nothing is done. If one neighbor is fitter, the current cell's rule table is substituted by that cell's table and mutated with a certain possibility. If more neighbors have a higher fitness, their tables are crossed and used for the current cell. Before we applied this so-called coevolution scheme to our problem of centroid detection, we carried out some pre-investigations in order to find out if non-uniform CAs are appropriate for our problem. For the mentioned density problem, it showed [8] that a co-evolved non-uniform CA has an image success rate of at least 93% whereas the absolute peak performance of a uniform CA is 83% for the same dimension (1D CA with 149 cells, $|Q|=2$, $|N|=1$).

3.2   Investigating Non-uniform CAs in Detail

Starting with the above mentioned ordering problem, we used an automaton with 32 states and 33 steps resulting in a search space of size $\left(2^{2^3}\right)^{32} = 256^{32}$ whereas the corresponding uniform CA has 256 possible tables.

The best possible fitness for the uniform case lies approx. at just 0.71. Compared to the optimal fitness of 1, this means that the problem can not be solved that way. The non-uniform CA with the same attributes has a medium fitness value of 0.9377. But this value has to be handled with care concerning our task of centroid detection because it just signalises the amount of correct pixels. If the location of single pixels is more important than others, like in the case of centroid detection, this might be misleading. Testing the procedure with the ordering problem, we only got 7 correctly detected objects out of a set of 50 although the fitness function showed a value of 0.93% correct pixels per image. The ordering was executed correctly in every case but the exact number of zeros and ones was wrong in most cases.

Furthermore, we investigated the possibility of finding boundary boxes. A boundary box is simply the smallest possible axis-parallel rectangle which completely encloses an object. We tried to find a non-uniform CA with two states by teaching 16 patterns, allowing maximal 35 steps. Table 2 shows the result. It can be seen that only 8 different rule tables were used in cells of the CA which differ only in one to three bits hinting that they semantically do not differ at all. To prove this deduction, we executed the same experiment with 100 example patterns. The result of that experiment was that all cells use the same rule 0, now changing the non-uniform CA to a uniform one.

Table 2. Rule table of a non-uniform CA with 16 example patterns

Rule table number	Rule table as binary string
0	010101110111111110110111111011111
1	010101110111111110111111111011111
2	010101110111110001111111111011111
3	011101110111111110111111111011111
4	010101110111111110111111111111111
5	010101110111111110111011111111111
6	010101100111111110111011111111111
7	010101100111111110111011111011111

Observations made in this section hint that using non-uniform CAs might help for some kind of problems. Another observation we made is that it is difficult to solve translation-invariant problems with this approach. The automata always developed towards a uniform CA in that case. We assume that, for completely translation-invariant problems, non-uniform CAs will outperform uniform CAs only if markers mounted on the objects are used to center the object pixels before a non-uniform CA is applied. E.g., the detection of car plates as shown in [1] falls in that class because the signs and the single letters can be centred in advance to CA computation.

4 A Third Approach: Genetic Programming

Since the results based on evolving CA rules were not completely satisfying we moved to a different approach allowing a higher degree of abstraction. This approach uses *Genetic Programming* (GP) and was intoduced in [7]. In GP, solutions are represented in form of trees containing computer programs. These small programs replace the rules of the cells of a CA and expand the possibilities by also modelling memory and arithmetic operations. Of course, the genetic operators like mutation and crossing have to be adjusted to this new representation. The crossing operator gets two trees as parents where one node respectively is randomly chosen. The subtrees under these nodes are then exchanged creating two new individuals. This approach reveals high dynamics since it can make the new trees simpler or more complex. Mutation is done very similar. One node is randomly chosen and substituted by a completely new one.

The applied evolutionary algorithm differs only slightly from a genetic algorithm [7]. After filling the initial population with random programs, the fitness of each program is determined by applying it to the problem. Then again, selection, replication, mutation, and crossing are exhibited creating a new set of individuals which are again evaluated. This is done until any exit criterion is reached.

In order to find centroids in images, an approach is used where virtual agents or ants which are able to carry out simple operations move along a pixel field. The goal is now to use several of these agents collectively in order to reach the goal in an emergent way. The most simple form of solution for the centroid problem is the collecting of all object pixels while the coordinates of the visited pixels are accumulated. After all pixels have been visited, the accumulated values are divided by the number of accumulated pixels and the centroid of arbitrary objects is found. We first started with a program for one agent. The best programs, measured in shortness of program length, let the hardware agents move along a spiral starting from the outer edge pixels towards the interior of the object. These programs determine the centroid exactly.

In order to further speed up the detection process, we evolved programs with two hardware agents which are a priori forced by their instruction set to move around the edge pixels. We also let two agents start from random positions looking into opposite directions. The price for that speed-up is that the object must not contain large holes in order to be detected correctly. The functionality of the evolved agent consists of elementary actions like e.g. *turn left, turn right, step forward*, and *noop*, contained in the set T, and simple functions, contained in the set F. The function prog2 gets two arguments as input which are applied one after another. The conditional function if_pixel_ahead executes the first argument in case a pixel is ahead and argument two otherwise while function if_agent_ahead does the same if an agent is ahead.

$$F = \{\text{prog2, if\_pixel\_ahead, if\_agent\_ahead}\}$$
$$T = \{\text{turn\_left, turn\_right, step\_forward, noop}\}$$

We operate on an image where an edge detection has been applied before in a pre-processing step. Figure 2 left shows the best evolved program for the fitness function displayed in the equation below, in which w_0, w_1 refer to adjustable weights that represent the priorities. Our empiric studies showed that $w_0 = 150, w_1 = 15$ are appropriate values. *Agents* refers to the number of used agents, *pixel − found* to unvisited pixels, and *program_size* to the size of the evolved program. Aim of the evolution is to minimise f. The evolved program steers two agents to traverse the edges and to unify into one agent in the end. There, only one agent survives. The dying agent must of course first transmit its information of counted pixels to the surviving one. The agents again have to accumulate the pixel positions they visit during their march. These pixels are then marked to prevent them from being counted twice. The surviving agent divides the accumulated value by the number of visited pixels in the end. Figure 2 right shows the propagation of two agents which started their march in the upper left corner.

$$f = w_0 \cdot (w_1 \cdot agents + (pixel - found)) + program\_size \qquad (1)$$

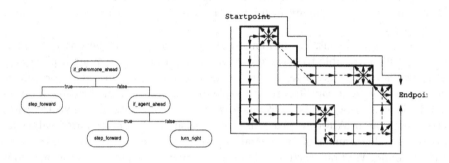

Fig. 2. Left, Evolved program; right, example propagation of two hardware agents

5   Conclusions

In this paper, we compared three different opportunities for the evolution of data-parallel geometric algorithms capable of detecting centroids of objects in images. The work is motivated by an existing hardware architecture designed by hand and the desire for algorithms which require smaller amounts of states in order to reduce chip area. For that goal, we evolved uniform as well as non-uniform CAs and used Genetic Programming.

By applying different example patterns, we found out that both CA types can be used to develop algorithms for object detection but not without problems. Both CA approaches had difficulties of delivering robust algorithms which are capable of finding the centroids also in slightly noisy images and none of them was able to detect unlearned objects.

Comparing uniformity and non-uniformity, the strength of the non-uniform approach lies in problems where local information in the images can be fixed, e.g. detection of letters on a centred car plate. If locality is not given, i.e. if the objects' positions in the image are not known in advance, the non-uniform CA converges towards uniformity. Then, both approaches lead to the same algorithmic rules for specific problems and non-uniform CAs lose their advantage.

The main problem of evolving CAs is the forced limitation to a small number of states because otherwise a dramatic increase in search space and thus in time to find an optimal rule set is caused. E.g., evolving CAs with five states was not possible for us in reasonable time. Future work should comprise using more states and evolving more sophisticated CAs with several objects on large clusters or computing grids easing this drawback.

The third presented approach Genetic Programming exploits the useage of memory and simple arithmetic operations. At the moment, it seems to be the best choice to evolve the functionality for hardware agents implemented in arrays of processor elements. With GP, we were able to evolve simple programs which found the centroids with high robustness. The evolved agents always found the centroid correctly and fast. The prize to pay for this higher effectivity of course is a different requirement for the functional cells in the array which must have the capabilites to execute these evolved little programs.

References

1. Adorni, G., Bergenti, F., Cagnoni, S.: A cellular-programming approach to pattern classification. In: Banzhaf, W., Poli, R., Schoenauer, M., Fogarty, T.C. (eds.) EuroGP 1998. LNCS, vol. 1391, pp. 142–150. Springer, Heidelberg (1998)
2. Baeck, T.: Evolutionary algorithms in theory and practice: evolution strategies, evolutionary programming, genetic algorithms. Oxford Univ. Press, New York (1996)
3. Fey, D., Schmidt, D.: Marching-pixels: a new organic computing paradigm for smart sensor processor arrays. In: Proceedings of the 2nd conference on Computing Frontiers CF'05, pp. 1–9. ACM Press, New York (2005)
4. Fey, D., Schmidt, D.: Marching pixels: A new organic computing principle for smart cmos camera chips. In: Proc. Workshop on Self-Organization and Emergence – Organic Computing and its Neighboring Disciplines, LNI, pp. 123–130 (2005)
5. Komann, M., Fey, D.: Marching pixels - using organic computing principles in embedded parallel hardware. In: International Conference on Parallel Computing in Electrical Engineering (PARELEC06), pp. 369–373 (2006)
6. Komann, M., Fey, D.: Realising emergent image pre-processing tasks in cellular-automaton-alike massively parallel hardware. Int. Journ. of Parallel, Emergent and Distributed Systems 22, 79–89 (2007)
7. Koza, J.R.: Genetic Programming: On the Programming of Computers by Means of Natural Selection (Complex Adaptive Systems). MIT Press, Cambridge (1992)
8. Sipper, M.: Evolution of parallel cellular machines: the cellular programming approach. Springer, Heidelberg (1997)
9. Sipper, M., Tomassini, M.: Computation in artificially evolved, non-uniform cellular automata. Theor. Comput. Sci. 217(1), 81–98 (1999)
10. Neumann, J.v.: Theory of Self-Reproducing Automata. University of Illinois Press, Urbana (1966)
11. Wolfram, S.: A new kind of science. Wolfram Media, Champaign, IL, USA (2002)

Associative Version of Italiano's Decremental Algorithm for the Transitive Closure Problem

Anna Nepomniaschaya

Institute of Computational Mathematics and Mathematical Geophysics,
Siberian Division of the Russian Academy of Sciences,
pr. Lavrentieva, 6, Novosibirsk, 630090, Russia
anep@ssd.sscc.ru

Abstract. We propose a natural implementation of Italiano's algorithm for updating the transitive closure of directed graphs after deletion of an edge on a model of associative (content addressable) parallel systems with vertical processing (the STAR–machine). The associative version of Italiano's decremental algorithm is given as procedure **DeleteArc**, whose correctness is proved and time complexity is evaluated. We compare implementations of Italiano's decremental algorithm and its associative version and enumerate the main advantages of the associative version.

1 Introduction

The dynamic graph algorithms maintain some property of a changing graph more efficiently than recomputation of the entire graph with a static algorithm after every change. Typical changes include insertions or deletions of vertices or edges. An algorithm is called *fully dynamic* if the update operations include both insertions and deletions of edges or vertices, and it is called *partially dynamic* if only one type of an update, either insertions or deletions, is allowed. A partially dynamic algorithm is called *incremental* if it supports only insertions, while it is called *decremental* if it supports only deletions.

The transitive closure (or reachability) problem in a directed graph G with n vertices and m edges consists in finding whether there is a directed path between any two vertices in G. In the fully dynamic transitive closure problem, a directed graph is updated under an intermixed sequence of edge insertions, edge deletions, and the following two types of queries: a *Boolean* query for vertices i and j that returns *yes* if there is a path from i to j and *no* otherwise, and a *path* query that returns an actual path from i to j if it exists.

We focus on decremental algorithms for the transitive closure problem. The first decremental algorithm for the transitive closure was given by Ibaraki and Katoh [4]. Their algorithm takes $O(n^2)$ time for a deletion. Italiano [6] and La Poutré and Leeuwen [9] improved this estimation to $O(m)$ worst-case time per a deletion on a directed acyclic graph (DAG). In [10], Yellin proposed a decremental algorithm which requires $O(dm^*)$ time for m deletions on a DAG, where d is the maximum outdegree of the initial graph G and m^* is the number

V. Malyshkin (Ed.): PaCT 2007, LNCS 4671, pp. 442–452, 2007.

of edges in the initial transitive closure of G. In [2], Frigioni et al. proposed a variant of Italiano's algorithms [5, 6], called *Ital-Gen*, whose decremental part applies to a general graph and any sequence of edge deletions takes $O(m^2)$ worst-case time. All of these algorithms perform a Boolean query in $O(1)$ time. The decremental algorithm by La Poutré and Leeuwen [9] does not support a path query but the other above–mentioned algorithms perform a path query in time proportional to the length of a path. In [3], Henzinger and King presented a randomized decremental transitive closure algorithm for general directed graphs, which takes $O(nlog^2n)$ amortized time per update and $O(n/\log n)$ time per a Boolean query.

In this paper we propose the new data structure that allows us to implement in a natural way Italiano's decremental algorithm on the associative (content addressable) parallel processors, which are mainly oriented to solving non–numerical problems. To this end, we employ the STAR–machine [7] that simulates the run of associative parallel systems of the SIMD type with bit–serial (vertical) processing. Following Foster [1], *time complexity* of an algorithm is measured by counting all elementary operations of the STAR–machine (its *microsteps*) performed in the worst case. It is assumed that each elementary operation takes one unit of time. The associative version of Italiano's decremental algorithm is given as procedure DeleteArc whose correctness is proved. We show that on the STAR–machine this procedure takes $O(n \log n)$ time per a deletion. We also obtain that the associative algorithm performs a Boolean and a path queries in the same time as Italiano's decremental algorithm. Finally, we compare implementations of Italiano's decremental algorithm and its associative version and enumerate the main advantages of the associative version.

2   A Model of Associative Parallel Machine

Here, we propose a brief description of our model. It is defined as an abstract STAR–machine of the SIMD type with the vertical data processing [7]. It consists of the following components:

– a sequential control unit (CU), where programs and scalar constants are stored;
– an associative processing unit consisting of p single–bit processing elements (PEs);
– a matrix memory for the associative processing unit.

The CU passes an instruction to all PEs in one unit of time. All active PEs execute it in parallel, while inactive PEs do not perform it. Activation of a PE depends on data.

The input binary data are loaded in the memory in the form of two–dimensional tables, in which each data item occupies an individual row, and it is updated by a dedicated processing element. The rows are numbered from top to bottom and the columns – from left to right. Both a row and a column can easily be accessed. Some tables may be loaded in the memory.

An associative processing unit is represented as h vertical registers, each consisting of p bits. Vertical registers can be regarded as a one-column array. The bit columns of the tabular data are stored in the registers that perform the necessary Boolean operations.

Its run is described by means of the language STAR being an extension of Pascal. Let us briefly consider the STAR constructions needed for the paper. To simulate the data processing in the matrix memory, we use data types word, slice, and table. Constants for the types slice and word are represented as a sequence of symbols of a set $\{0, 1\}$ enclosed within single quotation marks. The types slice and word are used for the bit column access and the bit row access, respectively, and the type table is used for defining the tabular data. Assume that any variable of the type slice consists of p components which belong to $\{0, 1\}$. For simplicity, let us call *slice* any variable of the type slice.

Now we present some elementary operations and a predicate for slices.

Let X, Y be variables of the type slice and i be a variable of the type integer. We use the following operations:

SET(Y) sets all components of Y to $'1'$;

CLR(Y) sets all components of Y to $'0'$;

$Y(i)$ selects the i-th component of Y;

FND(Y) returns the number i of the first (the uppermost) $'1'$ of Y, $i \geq 0$;

STEP(Y) returns the same result as FND(Y) and then resets the first $'1'$ found to $'0'$.

In the usual way, we introduce the bitwise Boolean operations: $X\,and\,Y$, $X\,or\,Y$, $not\,Y$, $X\,xor\,Y$.

The predicate SOME(Y) results in true if and only if there is at least a single component $'1'$ in the slice Y.[1]

Note that the predicate and all operations for the type slice are also performed for the type word. We will also employ the bitwise Boolean operations between a variable w of the type word and a variable Y of the type slice, where the number of bits in w coincides with the number of bits in Y.

Let T be a variable of the type table. We employ the following elementary operations:

ROW(i, T) returns the i-th row of the matrix T;

COL(i, T) returns its i-th column.

Note that the STAR statements are defined in the same manner as for Pascal. We will use them later for presenting our procedures.

We will employ the basic procedure MATCH(T, X, v, Z) [8] that uses the given global slice X to select by $'1'$ positions of rows which will be processed. It defines in parallel the positions of those rows of a given matrix T which coincide with a given pattern v. It returns a slice Z, where $Z(i) =' 1'$ if and only if ROW(i, T) $= v$ and $X(i) =' 1'$. In [8], we show that this procedure takes $O(k)$ time, where k is the number of bit columns in the matrix T.

---

[1] For simplicity, the notation $Y \neq \Theta$ denotes that the predicate SOME(Y) results in true.

3   Preliminaries

Let $G = (V, E)$ be a *directed graph (digraph)* with a set of vertices V and a set of directed edges (arcs) E. We assume that $V = \{1, 2, \ldots, n\}$, $|V| = n$, and $|E| = m$.

An arc e from i to j is denoted by $e = (i, j)$, where the vertex i is *head* of e (or *father*) and the vertex j is its *tail* (or *son*). Also, if $(i, j) \in E$, then j is called to be *adjacent* to i.

A sequence of arcs $e_1, e_2, \ldots, e_k$ is a *path* from the head of e_1 to the tail of e_k if the tail of e_i is the head of e_{i+1} for $1 \leq i \leq k - 1$.

A vertex v is *reachable* from u if there is a path from u to v ($u - v$ path). In such a case, u is called *ancestor* of v, and v is called *descendant* of u.

The *transitive closure* of a digraph $G = (V, E)$ is a digraph $G^* = (V, E^*)$ such that an arc $(u, v) \in E^*$ if and only if v is reachable from u in G.

A *spanning tree* T_u is a connected acyclic subgraph of G with the root vertex u that cointains all the descendants of u.

An *adjacency matrix* $Adj = [a_{ij}]$ of a digraph G is an $n \times n$ Boolean matrix, where $a_{ij} = 1$ if and only if there is an arc (i, j) in the set E.

4   Italiano's Decremental Algorithm for the Transitive Closure

We first recall the data structure proposed by Italiano to support the efficient deletion of arcs in a digraph and the *Boolean* and *path* queries.

The transitive closure of a graph G is represented by associating to each vertex $u \in V$ a set $Desc[u]$ of all descendants of u in G. Any $Desc[u]$ is organized as a spanning tree rooted at the vertex u. In addition, an $n \times n$ matrix of pointers *Index* is used for fast access to vertices in the trees. It is defined as follows. $Index[i, j]$ points to the vertex j in the tree $Desc[i]$ if $j \in Desc[i]$ and it is *Null* otherwise.

Let an arc (i, j) be deleted from G. If (i, j) does not belong to any spanning tree, then the data structure does not change. Otherwise, this arc is deleted from all spanning trees in which it appears. Let (i, j) belong to $Desc[u]$. Then $Desc[u]$ is updated as follows. After deleting the arc (i, j) from $Desc[u]$ it splits into two subtrees. To obtain a new tree, it is necessary to check whether there is such a vertex z in $Desc[u]$ that $(z, j) \in E$ and the corresponding $u - j$ path avoids the vertex i. If such a vertex z exists, then it is called a *hook* for j. In this case, the arc (i, j) is replaced by the arc (z, j), which joins two subtrees and $Desc[u]$ does not change. Otherwise, the vertex j along with all its outgoing edges are deleted from $Desc[u]$, and the seach for a hook for each son of j is recursively performed.

A Boolean query for vertices i and j is performed in $O(1)$ time by checking $Index[i, j]$. If every vertex in each spanning tree is provided with an additional pointer to the parent, then a path query is carried out by means of a bottom-up traversal in $Desc[i]$ from j to the root i and it takes $O(l)$ time, where l is the length of $i - j$ path.

5   An Associative Version of Italiano's Decremental Algorithm

In the STAR–machine memory, a graph is represented as association of matrices *Left* and *Right*, where every arc (u, v) occupies an individual row, and $u \in Left$ and $v \in Right$.

To design the associative version of Italiano's algorithm, we will use the following data structure:

– an association of matrices *Left* and *Right* and a global slice X, where positions of arcs belonging to G are marked with $'1'$;

– an $n \times \log n$ matrix *Code*, whose every i-th row saves the binary representation of the vertex i;

– an $m \times n$ Boolean matrix *Trans*, whose every i-th column saves by $'1'$ the positions of arcs belonging to the spanning tree T_i;

– an $n \times n$ Boolean matrix *Nodes*, whose every i-th column saves by $'1'$ all vertices that belong to the spanning tree T_i;

– an $n \times n$ Boolean matrix *Adj*, whose every i-th column saves by $'1'$ all the sons of the vertex i.

Let us enumerate the following two properties of the matrices *Trans* and *Adj*.

Property 1. Every i-th row of the matrix *Trans* saves by $'1'$ the roots of trees that include the arc written in the i-th row of the graph representation.

Property 2. Every i-th row of the matrix *Adj* saves by $'1'$ the heads of arcs entering the vertex i.

We first propose the associative parallel algorithm for updating a spanning tree after deleting an arc.

Let an arc (i, j) be deleted from the spanning tree T_p, the graph representation and the matrix *Adj*. The associative parallel algorithm uses a slice $A1$ to save the sons of a deleted arc tail and a slice A to save all descendants of j that have not been updated yet. Initially, the slice A consists of zeros.

The algorithm carries out the following steps.

Step 1. Save the j-th row of the matrix *Adj* by means of a variable, say $u1$.

Step 2. Save the p-th column of the matrix *Nodes* using a slice, say $A2$.

Step 3. Perform the statement $u := u1 \, and \, A2$. Note that positions of vertices that can be used as a hook for j are marked with $'1'$ in the variable u.

The following two cases are possible.

Case 1. $u \neq \Theta$. Then determine the position r of the leftmost bit $'1'$ in the row u. Further determine the position of the arc (r, j) in the graph representation and include it in the p-th column of the matrix *Trans*. Check whether there is a descendant of j that has not been updated yet in the slice A. If $A = \Theta$, go to the exit. Otherwise, go to Step 4.

Case 2. $u = \Theta$. Then determine the positions of arcs outgoing from j in the tree T_p and delete them from the p-th column of the matrix *Trans*. After that, delete the vertex j from the p-th column of the matrix $Nodes$. Further, by means of a slice, say $A1$, save the sons of the deleted arc tail in the tree T_p. Finally, include these vertices into the slice A.

Step 4. While $\text{SOME}(A)$ results true, determine the current descendant t of j that corresponds to the uppermost bit $'1'$ in the slice A and replace this bit by $'0'$. Then go to Step 1 to determine a hook for t in the tree T_p.

On the STAR–machine, this algorithm is implemented as procedure Hook.

The associative parallel algorithm for the dynamic updating of the transitive closure of a directed acyclic graph after deleting an arc (i, j) performs the following steps.

Step 1. Determine the position k of the arc (i, j) in the association of matrices $Left$ and $Right$.

Step 2. Save the k-th row of the matrix $Trans$ by means of a variable, say v.

Step 3. Delete the arc (i, j) from the matrices Adj, $Trans$, and the graph representation.

Step 4. While $\text{SOME}(v)$ results true, determine the position p of the leftmost bit $'1'$ in v and replace this bit by $'0'$. Then maintain the spanning tree T_p using the associative parallel algorithm for finding a hook.

On the STAR–machine, this algorithm is realized as procedure DeleteArc.

6   Implementation of the Associative Version of Italiano's Decremental Algorithm on the STAR-Machine

In this Section, we present the procedures Hook and DeleteArc and prove their correctness. We first consider the procedure Hook that maintains a spanning tree T_p after deleting an arc (i, j). It returns a slice A for the matrix $Nodes$ and the updated p-th column in matrices $Trans$ and $Nodes$. Initially $A = \Theta$.

```
procedure Hook(Left,Right: table; Code: table; Adj: table;
   C: slice(Code); X: slice(Left); j,p: integer;
   var A: slice(Nodes); var Trans: table; var Nodes: table);
/* The arc (i,j) has been deleted from the given graph. */
var Z,Z1,Z2: slice(Left);
   A1,A2: slice(Nodes);
   C1: slice(Code);
   w1,w2: word(Code);
   u,u1: word(Adj);
   i1,r,t: integer;
   label 1,2;
1. Begin Z:=COL(p,Trans);
2.    w2:=ROW(j,Code);
3.    u1:=ROW(j,Adj);
/* The word u1 saves by '1' the heads of arcs entering j. */
4.    A2:=COL(p,Nodes);
```

```
/* All vertices from T_p are marked with '1' in the slice A2. */
5.   u:=u1 and A2;
/* The word u saves by '1' the vertices that may be used
   as a hook for j. */
6.   if SOME(u) then
/* There is a hook for the vertex j. */
7.     begin r:=FND(u); w1:=ROW(r,Code);
8.       MATCH(Left,X,w1,Z1); MATCH(Right,Z1,w2,Z2);
9.       i1:=FND(Z2); Z(i1):='1';
10.      COL(p,Trans):=Z;
/* We include the arc (r,j) into the tree T_p. */
11.        if SOME(A) then goto 1 else goto 2;
12.    end else
/* There is no a hook for the vertex j. */
13.    begin MATCH(Left,Z,w2,Z1);
/* In the slice Z1, we save positions of arcs outgoing
   from the vertex j in the tree T_p. */
14.      Z:=Z and (not Z1); COL(p,Trans):=Z;
/* We delete positions of arcs outgoing from j in T_p. */
15.      A2(j):='0'; COL(p,Nodes):=A2; CLR(A1);
/* We delete j from the p-th column of the matrix Nodes. */
16.      while SOME(Z1) do
17.        begin i1:=STEP(Z1); w1:=ROW(i1,Right);
18.          MATCH(Code,C,w1,C1);
19.          t:=FND(C1); A1(t):='1';
/* In the slice A1, we save a son of the deleted arc tail. */
20.        end;
21.      A:=A or A1;
/* In the slice A, we save vertices that will be updated. */
22.    1: while SOME(A) do
23.        begin t:=STEP(A);
/* Here, t is the descendant of the vertex j. */
24.          Hook(Left,Right,Code,Adj,C,X,t,p,A,Trans,Nodes);
25.        end;
26.    end;
27. 2: End;
```

Theorem 1. *Let a directed acyclic graph G be given as association of matrices Left and Right and its transitive closure be given as matrix Trans. Let matrices Code, Adj, and Nodes be also given. Let an arc (i,j) be deleted from the graph representation, the matrix Adj, and the p-th column of the matrix Trans. Then after performing the procedure Hook, the updated spanning tree T_p is written into the p-th column of the matrix Trans and the updated set of its vertices is written into the p-th column of the matrix Nodes.*

Proof (Sketch). We will prove this by induction on the number of vertices l which are deleted from T_p during its maintenance.

Basis is checked for $l \leq 1$, that is, no more than one vertex is deleted from T_p during its maintenance. After performing lines 1–4, the slice Z saves the p-th column of the matrix $Trans$, where the position of the arc (i, j) is marked with $'0'$, the variable $w2$ saves the binary code of the deleted arc tail, the variable $u1$ saves the heads arcs entering j, and the slice $A2$ saves the vertices of the spanning tree T_p. After performing line 5, the variable u saves the vertices of T_p that can be used as a hook for j.

The following two cases are possible.

Case 1. $u \neq \Theta$. Then after performing line 7 we determine the binary code of the leftmost hook r for j in the row u. After performing lines 8–10, we determine the position of the arc (r, j) in the graph representation and include it into the spanning tree T_p. Since initially $A = \Theta$, we run to the procedure end after performing line 11. In addition, the p-th column of the matrix $Nodes$ does not change.

Case 2. $u = \Theta$. Then after performing lines 13–14, we determine positions of arcs outgoing from j in T_p and delete them from the p-th column of the matrix $Trans$. Further we delete the vertex j from the p-th column of the matrix $Nodes$ and set zeros in the slice $A1$ (line 15). After performing the cycle wlile SOME(Z1) do (lines 16–20), we determine all sons of j in T_p and accumulate them in the slice $A1$. After performing line 21, we include these vertices into the slice A. While $A \neq \Theta$, we select the current son t of j and perform the procedure Hook (lines 22–25). Since a single arc is deleted from T_p, there is a hook for every son of the vertex j in T_p. We determine such a hook as described in Case 1. As soon as $A = \Theta$, we go to the procedure end.

Step of induction. Let the assertion be true when no more than l vertices are deleted from T_p during its maintenance. We will prove this for $l + 1$ vertices.

By the inductive assumption, after deleting l vertices from T_p the updated spanning tree is written into the p-th column of the matrix $Trans$ and the updated set of vertices is written into the p-th column of the matrix $Nodes$. Let q be the $(l+1)$-th vertex being deleted from T_p. Then we reason by analogy with Case 2 of the basis but with the difference that after performing lines 13–21, the slice A saves the sons of q along with other descendants of j that have not been updated yet in T_p. Since q is the last deleted vertex, we determine a hook for every descendant of j as described in Case 1. $\square$

Let us consider the procedure DeleteArc that maintains the transitive closure after deleting the arc (i, j) from the graph G. It returns the global slice X for the graph representation and the updated matrices Adj, $Trans$, and $Nodes$.

```
procedure DeleteArc(Left,Right: table; Code: table; i,j: integer;
    var X: slice(Left); var Adj,Nodes: table; var Trans: table);
var Y,Z: slice(Left);
  A,A1: slice(Nodes);
  C: slice(Code);
  w1,w2: word(Code);
  v,v1: word(Trans);
```

```
   k,p: integer;
1. Begin CLR(v1); CLR(A); SET(C);
2.   w1:=ROW(i,Code); w2:=ROW(j,Code);
3.   MATCH(Left,X,w1,Y); MATCH(Right,Y,w2,Z);
4.   k:=FND(Z);
/* The arc (i,j) is written in the k-th row of the graph
   representation. */
5.   v:=ROW(k,Trans);
/* The word v saves the k-th row of the matrix Trans. */
6.   A1:=COL(i,Adj); A1(j):='0'; COL(i,Adj):=A1;
7.   X(k):='0';
8.   ROW(k,Trans):=v1;
/* We delete the arc (i,j) from the matrices Adj and Trans
   and from the graph representation. */
9.   while SOME(v) do
10.     begin p:=STEP(v);
11.       Hook(Left,Right,Code,Adj,C,X,j,p,A,Trans,Nodes);
12.     end;
13. End;
```

Theorem 2. *Let a directed acyclic graph G be given as association of matrices Left and Right and its transitive closure be given as matrix Trans. Let the matrices Code, Adj, and Nodes be also given. Let the arc (i,j) be deleted from G. Then after performing the procedure DeleteArc, this arc is deleted from the matrix Adj and all spanning trees in which it appears. Moreover, the updated spanning trees are written in the corresponding columns of matrices Trans and Nodes.*

Proof (Sketch). We prove this by induction on the number of spanning trees l in the matrix $Trans$, where the arc (i,j) appears.

Basis is checked for $l = 1$. After performing lines 1–4, we first initialize the slice A for the procedure Hook and the variable $v1$ for the matrix $Trans$. Then we determine the k-th row of the graph representation, where the arc (i,j) is stored. After performing lines 5–8, we first save the k-th row of the matrix $Trans$ by means of the variable v. Then we delete the arc (i,j) from matrices $Trans$, Adj, and the graph representation. After performing lines 9–12, we determine the single spanning tree T_p that includes the arc (i,j) and update it by means of the procedure Hook.

Step of induction. Let the assertion be true when no more than l spanning trees include the arc (i,j). We prove this for the case when $l+1$ spanning trees include this arc. By the inductive assumption after selecting the first l spanning trees, whose roots are marked with '1' in v, we write the updated trees into the corresponding columns of matrices $Trans$ and $Nodes$. We can apply the procedure Hook to the spanning tree whose root corresponds to the leftmost bit '1' in v in view of initializing the slice A in the procedure DeleteArc. Since $A = \Theta$ after updating any spanning tree by means of the procedure Hook, we can apply it to other $l - 1$ spanning trees whose roots are marked with '1' in v. After updating the l-th spanning tree, we select the root of the $(l + 1)$-th spanning tree in which the arc (i, j) appears and update it by means of the procedure Hook.   □

Now we evaluate time complexity of the procedure DeleteArc. To this end, we have to determine the total number of vertices being updated after deleting an arc from the transitive closure. In view of performing the procedure Hook, at most all vertices of a subtree rooted at the tail of the deleted arc are updated. Therefore the procedure DeleteArc takes $O(n \log n)$ time per a deletion, where the factor $\log n$ appears due to the use of the basic procedure MATCH.

One can check that space complexity of the procedure DeleteArc is $O(mn)$.

On the STAR–machine, a *Boolean* query for the vertices i and j is carried out in $O(1)$ time by checking the j-th bit of the i-th column in the matrix *Nodes*. A *path* query is performed by means of a bottom-up traversal from j to i in the i-th spanning tree, located in the i-th column of the matrix *Trans*, using the procedure MATCH. It takes $O(l \log n)$ time, where l is the length of the path.

Let us compare implementations of Italiano's decremental algorithm and its associative version:

– for every vertex i, Italiano's algorithm maintains a set $Desc[i]$ which cointains all descendants of i. The associative version maintains the arcs from T_i whose positions are selected by $'1'$ in the i-th column of the matrix *Trans*;

– Italiano's algorithm maintains a matrix *Index*, where $Index[i, j]$ points to the vertex j in the tree $Desc[i]$. The associative version maintains the Boolean matrix *Nodes*, where every i-th column saves the positions of vertices from T_i;

– for every vertex j, Italiano's algorithm maintains a list of vertices $ln(j) = \{i \in V \mid (i, j) \in E\}$. The associative version maintains the j-th row of the matrix *Adj*, where heads of arcs entering j are marked with $'1'$;

– for every vertex j, Italiano's algorithm uses an additional pointer to its parent. The associative version determines the parent of any vertex by means of the basic procedure MATCH;

– to improve the efficiency of finding a hook, Italiano's algorithm associates to each vertex j in each $Desc[u]$ a bookeeping pointer that points to the first vertex in $ln(j)$, which has not been scanned yet. The associative version immediately determines a hook for j in a given tree T_p.

7   Conclusions

We have proposed the new data structure used for a natural and efficient implementation of Italiano's decremental algorithm on the STAR–machine having no less than m PEs. Note that this data structure can be also used for designing an associative version of Italiano's incremental algorithm for the transitive closure [5]. The associative version of Italiano's decremental algorithm is represented as procedure DeleteArc whose correctness is proved. We have obtained that this procedure takes $O(n \log n)$ time per a deletion assuming that each microstep of the STAR–machine takes one unit of time and its space complexity is $O(mn)$ bits. We have also compared the implementations of Italiano's decremental algorithm and its associative version and enumerate the main advantages of the associative version.

We are planning to design an associative version of the Ital–Gen algorithm proposed by Frigioni et al. [2] that generalizes Italiano's algorithms [5, 6].

References

1. Foster, C.C.: Content Addressable Parallel Processors. Van Nostrand Reinhold Company, New York (1976)
2. Frigioni, D., Miller, T., Nanni, U., Pasqualone, G., Schaefer, G., Zaroliagis, C.: An Experimental Study of Dynamic Algorithms for Directed Graphs. In: Bilardi, G., Pietracaprina, A., Italiano, G.F., Pucci, G. (eds.) ESA 1998. LNCS, vol. 1461, pp. 368–380. Springer, Heidelberg (1998)
3. Henzinger, M.R., King, V.: Fully Dynamic Biconnectivity and Transitive Closure. In: Proc. 36th IEEE Symposium on Foundations of Computer Science (FOCS'95), pp. 664–672 (1995)
4. Ibaraki, T., Katoh, N.: On-Line Computation of Transitive Closure for Graphs. Information Processing Letters 16, 95–97 (1983)
5. Italiano, G.F.: Amortized Efficiency of a Path Retrieval Data Structure. Theoretical Computer Science 48(2-3), 273–281 (1986)
6. Italiano, G.F.: Finding Paths and Deleting Edges in Directed Acyclic Graphs. Information Processing Letters 28, 5–11 (1988)
7. Nepomniaschaya, A.S.: Language STAR for Associative and Parallel Computation with Vertical Data Processing. In: Mirenkov, N. (ed.) Proc. of the Intern. Conf. Parallel Computing Technologies, pp. 258–265. World Scientific, Singapore (1991)
8. Nepomniaschaya, A.S., Dvoskina, M.A.: A Simple Implementation of Dijkstra's Shortest Path Algorithm on Associative Parallel Processors. In: Fundamenta Informaticae, 43th edn., pp. 227–243. IOS Press, Amsterdam (2000)
9. La Poutré, J.A., van Leeuwen, J.: Maintenance of Transitive Closure and Transitive Reduction of Graphs. In: Göttler, H., Schneider, H.-J. (eds.) WG 1987. LNCS, vol. 314, pp. 106–120. Springer, Heidelberg (1988)
10. Yellin, D.M.: Speeding up Dynamic Transitive Closure for Bounded Degree Graphs. Acta Informatica 30(4), 369–384 (1993)

Support for Fine-Grained Synchronization
in Shared-Memory Multiprocessors

Vladimir Vlassov[1], Oscar Sierra Merino[1],
Csaba Andras Moritz[2], and Konstantin Popov[3]

[1] Royal Institute of Technology (KTH), Stockholm, Sweden
[2] University of Massachusetts (UMASS), Amherst, MA, U.S.A.
[3] Swedish Institute of Computer Science (SICS), Stockholm, Sweden

Abstract. It has been already verified that hardware-supported fine-grain synchronization provides a significant performance improvement over coarse-grained synchronization mechanisms, such as barriers. Support for fine-grain synchronization on individual data items becomes notably important in order to efficiently exploit thread-level parallelism available on multi-threading and multi-core processors. Fine-grained synchronization can be achieved using the full/empty tagged shared memory. We define the complete set of synchronizing memory instructions as well as the architecture of the full/empty tagged shared memory that provides support for these operations. We develop a snoopy cache coherency protocol for an SMP with the centralized full/empty tagged memory.

1 Introduction

There are two general types of synchronization that guarantee correctness of execution in shared-memory programming model: mutual exclusion and condition synchronization. With mutual exclusion, only one process (thread) may execute its critical session at a time, whereas with condition synchronization a process may be suspended until some certain condition is met. There exist several synchronization mechanisms that allow to achieve mutual exclusion or condition synchronization, such as locks and barriers.

Barriers are an example of synchronization that ensure the correctness of a producer-consumer behavior. They are coarse-grain in the sense that all processes participating in a barrier have to wait at a common point, even though the data a waiting process truly depends on can be already available.

The main advantage of fine-grain synchronization arises from the fact that synchronization is provided at data-level [6]. As a consequence, false data dependencies and unnecessary delays caused by the coarse-grained synchronization can be avoided. Communication overhead due to global barriers is also avoided, because each process communicates only with the processes it depends on. Thus, the serialization of program execution is notably reduced and more parallelism can be exploited, in particular for large number of processors. While the overhead of fine-grain synchronization remains constant, that of a coarse-grain operation typically increases with the number of processors.

V. Malyshkin (Ed.): PaCT 2007, LNCS 4671, pp. 453–467, 2007.
© Springer-Verlag Berlin Heidelberg 2007

Fine-grain synchronization is most commonly provided by three different mechanisms [28]: *(a)* language-level support for expressing data-level synchronization operations, *(b)* full/empty bits storing the synchronization state of each memory word, and *(c)* processor operations on full/empty bits. Write-once I-structures [4] and M-structures [5] support fine-grain synchronization in data arrays. As another example, J-structures provide consumer-producer style of synchronization, while L-structures guarantee mutual exclusion access to a data element [1]. Both data types associate a state bit with each element of an array.

Synchronization failures can be handled by polling the memory location until the synchronization condition is met, or by blocking the thread and returning the control at a later stage. The latter scheme requires more support as it is necessary to save and restore context information. A combination of both is another option, polling first for a given period and then blocking the thread. The waiting algorithm may depend on the type of synchronization being executed [16].

Most research regarding multiprocessors show that fine-grain synchronization is a valuable alternative for improving the performance of many applications. Hardware support can be worthwhile for fine-grain synchronization [14].

The challenge of programming multiprocessors turned to mainstream [22] with the proliferation of multi-threaded [23] and multi-core [20] processors caused, in turn, by difficulties with increasing processor frequencies [13] and diminishing returns from ever more complex processor architectures [21]. The study [25] reveals that existing applications possess inherent parallelism that cannot be fully exploited on practical superscalar architectures but on multi-core processors with 8-16 cores. The amount of available parallelism is measured by analysing data dependencies between program statements. Fine-grained synchronization mechanisms can allow to fully exploit the available data-flow parallelism. At the same time, the main memory becomes relatively less expensive reducing the cost of overhead of storing full/empty bits.

Multi-core chips possess high-bandwidth, low-latency interconnects which can be exploited also for efficient implementation of full/empty bit-based fine-grained synchronization. A cache design that implements synchronization primitives would relieve the processor from the need to access the main memory, which we believe would substantially improve the efficiency of synchronization.

In this paper we present a snoopy cache coherency protocol that supports full/empty bit-based fine-grained synchronization. We took the MESI protocol and extended it with additional states and state transitions that allow the cache to differentiate between "full" and "empty" states of synchronization bits. We also show how threads blocked due to wrong state of synchronization bits can be handled similarly to threads waiting for cache miss processing.

In [18] we presented a directory-based cache coherency protocol supporting full/empty bit-based fine-grained synchronization, and its simulation-based evaluation. The evaluation demonstrated significant performance and scalability benefits of the fine-grained synchronization over the coarse-grained one. Evaluation of our bus-based cache coherency protocol is still a pending work.

2   Related Work

The MIT Alewife machine is a cache-coherent **shared memory** multiprocessor [1] with non-uniform memory access (NUMA). Although it is implemented with an efficient message-passing mechanism, it provides an abstraction of a global shared memory to programmers. Each node contain a communication and memory management unit (CMMU) which deals with cache coherency and synchronization protocols. Cache coherency is achieved through LimitLESS, a software extended directory-based protocol. The home node of a memory line is responsible for the coordination of all coherence operations for that line.

Support for fine-grain synchronization in Alewife includes full/empty bits for each 32-bit data word and fast userlevel messages. Colored load and store instructions are used to access synchronization bits. The alternate space indicator (ASI) distinguishes each of these instructions. Full/empty bits are stored in the bottom four bits of the coherency directory entry (at the memory) and as an extra field in the cache tags (at the cache), so they do not affect DRAM architecture nor network data widths. The Alewife architecture also defines language extensions to support both J- and L-structures.

The aim is that a successful synchronization operation does not incur much overhead with respect to a normal load or store. In the ideal case, the cost of both types of operations is expected to be the same. This is possible because full/empty bits can be accessed simultaneously with the data they refer to. The cost of a failed synchronization operation depends much on the specific hardware support for synchronization. The overhead of software-supported synchronization operations is expected to be much higher than their hardware counterparts. However, Alewife minimizes this by rapidly switching between threads on a failed synchronization attempt or a cache miss, requiring the use of lockup-free caches.

Handling failed synchronization operations in software has the advantage of being less complex in terms of hardware and more flexible. The basis of Alewife support for fine-grain synchronization is that, as synchronization operations are most probably successful, overhead due to such failures is not expected to notably reduce overall system performance.

Support for fine-grained synchronization in cache coherency protocols has also been suggested for **message-passing architectures**, such as Tera [2], StarT-NG [3], and Eldorado [8]. For instance, StarT-NG is a high-performance message passing architecture in which each node consists of a commercial symmetric multiprocessor (SMP) that can be configured with up to 3 processors, which are connected to the main memory by a data crossbar. A low-latency high-bandwidth network interconnects every node in the system.

Handling of Coherence in StarT-NG are fully implemented in software and is therefore very flexible. In [27] a cache coherency protocol with support for fine-grained synchronization using I-structures is introduced. According to the results of that study, performance improvements in an integrated coherence protocol are two-fold. First, the write-once behavior of I-structures allows writes to be performed without the exclusive ownership of the respective cache line. Once a write has been carried out, stale data in other caches is identified because its full/empty bit is unset. In a directory-based protocol, a synchronized load in a remote location will find the full/empty bit unset and forward the request to the proper node. Another advantage of a coherence protocol integrated with fine-grain synchronization is the efficiency in the management of pending requests by reducing the number of transactions needed to perform some particular operations. As an example, a synchronized load in traditional coherence protocols usually requires the requesting node to obtain the exclusive ownership of the affected block in order to set the full/empty bit to the empty state.

Several authors proposed mechanisms for **hardware support of coarse-grained synchronization**, such as QOLB(QOSB) ("queue on lock(sync) bit") [9,12] and lock box [24].

The hardware **transactional memory** is a non-blocking synchronization mechanism [11,10,17,19] that aims to replace the lock-based synchronization. A transaction is a sequence of memory operations executed by a single thread, which is guaranteed to be atomic and serializable. Transactional memory systems provide a simple programming model, but require also extensive hardware support. LogTM [19] detects also transaction execution conflicts at the cache level, yielding better performance.

3   Synchronizing Memory Operations

Synchronization operations require tagged memory, in which each location is associated to a state bit in addition to a value stored in the location. The state bit is known as full/empty (FE) bit, and it controls the behavior of synchronized loads and stores. For example, a set FE-bit indicates that the corresponding memory reference has been written by a successful synchronized store. On the contrary, an unset FE-bit means either that the memory location has never been written since it was initialized or that a synchronized load has read it.

The full/empty-tagged memory, shortly FE-memory, is the memory in which each word has a FE-bit associated with it. In general, the FE-memory can be composed of two parts: (1) the data memory which holds data, and (2) the state memory which holds FE-bits. A memory operation on the FE-memory can access either of these parts or both. The joint diagram depicted in Figure 1 shows possible combinations of read (Rd) or write (Wr) operations that access the data memory with operations set-to-Empty (E) and set-to-Full (F) that access the state part of the memory. Combined operations such as Rd&E (read and set to Empty) and Wr&F (write and set to Full) are atomic.

A categorization of the different synchronizing memory operations as proposed earlier [26] is depicted in Figure 2. The simplest type of operations includes unconditional (ordinary) load and store, setting and resetting the full/ empty bit or a combination of these. As they do not depend on the previous value of the full/empty bit, unconditional operations always succeed. Conditional operations depend on the value of the full/empty state bit to successfully complete. A conditional read, for instance, is only performed if the state bit of the location being accessed it set. The complimentary applies for a conditional write. Conditional

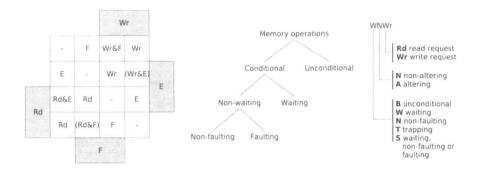

Fig. 1. Memory Operations **Fig. 2.** Categories of the FE- **Fig. 3.**   Opcode
                               Memory Operations   Notation

memory operations can be either waiting or non-waiting. In the former case, the
operation remains pending in the memory until the state miss is resolved. This
introduces non-deterministic latencies in the execution of synchronizing memory
operations. Lastly, conditional non-waiting operations can be either faulting or
non-faulting. While the latter do not treat the miss as an error, faulting operations fire a trap on a state miss and either retry the operation immediately or
switch to another context.

All memory operations, regardless of the classification made in Figure 2, can
be further catalogued into altering and non-altering operations. While the former
modify the full/empty bit after a successful synchronizing event, the latter do
not touch this bit in any case. According to this distinction, ordinary memory
operations fall into the unconditional non-altering category. Figure 3 explains
our memory opcode notation.

4   Memory Architecture

In a multiprocessor system providing fine-grain synchronization, each shared
memory word is tagged with a full/empty bit that indicates the synchronization
state of the referred memory location. Assuming that a memory word is 32-bit
long, this implies an overhead of just 3%. Although many variations exist when
implementing this in hardware, the structure of shared memory is conceptually
as shown in Figure 4.

Each shared memory location (a word) has three logical parts, namely:

- The shared data itself.
- State bits associated with the location. The full/empty bit is placed within
  the state bits. This bit is set to 1 if the corresponding memory location
  has already been written by a processor and thus contains valid data. If
  the architecture has cache support other state bits such as the dirty bit may
  exist. The dirty bit is set if the memory location is not up-to-date, indicating
  that it has been modified in a remote node.

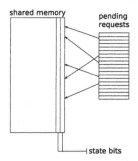
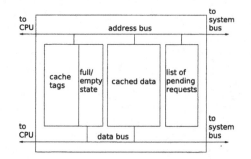

Fig. 4. Memory Operations   **Fig. 5.** Categories of the FE-Memory Operations

- The list of pending memory requests. Synchronization misses fired by conditional waiting memory operations are placed in this list. When an appropriate synchronizing operation is performed, the relevant pending requests stored in this list are resumed. If the architecture has cache support, the list of pending memory requests also stores ordinary cache misses. The difference between both types of misses is that synchronization misses store additional information, such as the accessed slot index in the corresponding cache block.

When a memory word is cached, its full/empty bit must also be stored at the cache side as an extra field in the cache tag, allowing checking the synchronization state in the same step as the cache lookup. A structure for a cache supporting fine-grain synchronization proposed in this report is depicted in Figure 5. The coherence protocol has two logical parts, one for the data and another for the synchronization bit.

Our design assumes that the smallest synchronizing element is a word. As a cache line is usually longer, it may contain multiple elements, including both synchronized and ordinary words. A tag for a cache line includes the full/empty bits for all the words that are stored in that line even though some of the FE-bits can be not in use. Note that while a dirty bit refers to a complete cache line, a full/empty bit refers to a single word in a cache line.

In the proposed architecture, lists of pending requests (unresolved synchronization misses) are maintained in hardware at the cache level, more concretely in the miss status holding registers (MSHR) [15]. In order to store synchronization misses in these registers, two more fields have to be added containing the slot's index accessed by the operation and the specific variant of synchronized operation that will be performed.

5   Cache Coherence with Support for Fine-Grain Synchronization

Caches in multiprocessors must ensure that modifications to data that is resident in a cache are seen in the rest of the nodes that share a copy of the data. This can be achieved in several ways, which may depend on the particular system architecture. In bus-based system cache coherence can be implemented by a snooping mechanism, where each cache is continuously monitoring the system bus and updating its state according to the relevant transactions seen on the bus. On the contrary, mesh network-based multiprocessors use a directory structure to ensure cache coherence. In these systems, each location in the shared memory is associated with a directory entry that keeps track of the caches that have a copy of the referred location. Both, snoopy and directory-based mechanisms can be further classified into write-invalidate and write-update protocols. In the former case, when a processors writes shared data in its cache, all other copies, if any, are set as invalid. Update protocols change copies in all caches to the new value instead of marking them as invalid.

The performance of multiprocessor systems is partially limited by cache misses and node interconnection traffic. Consequently, cache coherence mechanisms play an important role in solving the problems associated with shared data. Another performance issue is the overhead imposed by synchronizing data operations. In the case of systems that provide fine-grain synchronization, this overhead is due to the fact that synchronization is implemented as a separate layer over the cache coherence protocol. Indeed, bandwidth demand can be reduced if no data is sent in a synchronization miss. This behavior requires the integration of cache coherence and fine-grain synchronization mechanisms. However, both mechanisms are conceptually independent.

In the proposed architecture, failing synchronizing events are resolved in hardware. The cache controller deals not only with coherency misses, but also with full/empty state misses. Synchronization is thus integrated with cache coherency operations, as opposed to e.g. Alewife where which the synchronization protocol is implemented separately from the cache coherency system.

This approach can be extended to the processor registers by adding a full/ empty tag to them. This would allow an efficient execution of synchronization operations from simultaneous threads on the registers. However, additional modifications are needed in the processor architecture to implement this feature.

6 Fine-Grain Synchronization with a Snoopy Cache Coherency Protocol

Our cache coherency protocol is based on the MESI – four-state write-invalidate protocol for a write-back cache with the following state semantics [7]:

- *Modified* (M) – this cache has the only valid copy of the block; the location in main memory is invalid.
- *Exclusive clean* (E) – this is the only cache with a copy of the block; the main memory is up-to-date. A signal S is available to the controller in order to determine on a BusRd if any other cache currently holds the data.

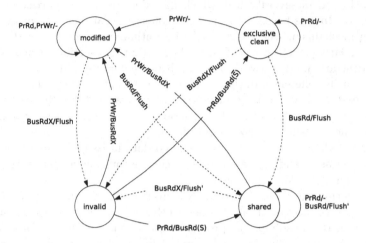

Fig. 6. State Diagram for the MESI Protocol

– *Shared* (S) – the block is present in an unmodified state in this cache, main memory is up-to-date and zero or more caches may also have a shared copy.
– *Invalid* (I) – the block does not have valid data.

The state diagram corresponding to the MESI protocol without fine-grain synchronization support is shown in Figure 6. In the figure, we use the notation A/B, where A indicates an observed event and B is an event generated as a consequence of A [7]. Dashed lines show state transitions due to observed bus transactions, while continuous lines indicate state transitions due to local processor actions. Finally, the notation Flush' means that data is supplied only by the corresponding cache. Note that this diagram does not consider transient states used for bus acquisition.

We extended the MESI protocol such that the full/empty state of the accessed word is explicitly indicated by splitting each state of the original MESI protocol into two states: one where FE-bit is Full and another where FE-bit is Empty. The modified protocol is called FE-MESI protocol; it is sketched in Figure 9. The transactions not shown in this figure are not relevant for the corresponding state and do not cause any transition in the receiving node. See [18] for the detailed description of state transition rules and some examples.

For simplicity yet without loosing generality, the description here considers only two types of FE-memory operations issued by the processor: waiting non-altering read (PrWNRd) and waiting altering write (PrWAWr). As an implementation option, the altering read operation can be achieved by issuing non-altering read in combination with an operation that clears the full/empty bit without retrieving data, i.e. sets FE-bit to Empty. This operation can be named unconditional altering clear, or PrUACl according to the nomenclature previously described. PrUACl operates on a full/empty bit without accessing or altering the associated data.

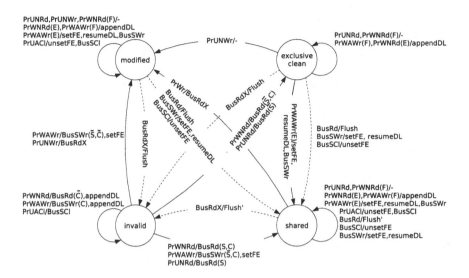

Fig. 7. Simplified State Diagram for the FE-MESI Protocol

Clearing of full/empty bits is necessary in order to reuse synchronized memory locations (see [14] for the detailed description). While a PrUARd could be used for this end, the PrUACl instruction completes faster, as it alters the full/empty bit without actually reading data from the corresponding location.

Using the operations PrWNRd (waiting non-altering reads), PrWAWr (waiting altering write) and PrUACl (unconditional altering clear), one can implement I-structures (write-once variables) and M-structures (reusable I-structures).

Waiting operations constitute the most complex sort of synchronizing operations, as they require additional hardware in order to manage deferred lists and resume pending synchronization requests. The behaviour of other types of memory operations is a simplified version of waiting operations. Most of the transitions depicted in Figure 9 are identical in the rest of the cases, with exception of the behaviour when a synchronization miss is detected. Instead of being added to the list of pending requests, other variants of missing operations either fire an exception or are silently discarded. Two additional bus transactions are needed in order to integrate fine-grain synchronization into the MESI protocol:

BusSWr. A node has performed an altering waiting write. The effect of this operation in observing nodes is to set the full/empty bit of the referring memory location and resume the relevant pending requests.

BusSCl. A node has performed an altering read or an unconditional clear operation. The effect of this operation in observing nodes is to clear the full/empty bit of the referring memory location, thus making it reusable.

We introduce a new signal C in order to determine whether a synchronized operation misses. This bus signal will be called shared-word signal, as it indicates whether any other node is sharing the referring word. The shared-word signal can be implemented as a wired-OR controller line, which is asserted by each cache that holds a copy of the relevant word with the full/empty bit set. According to this notation, a waiting read request written in the form $\mathrm{PrWNRd}(C)$ successfully performs, while an event of the form $\mathrm{PrWNRd}(\overline{C})$ causes a synchronization miss. Note also that, as each cache line may contain several synchronized data words, it is necessary to specify the specific word to which the synchronized operation is to be performed. Consequently, a negated synchronization signal $(\overline{C})$ causes a requesting read to be appended to the list of pending operations whereas a requesting write to be performed successfully. If the synchronization signal is otherwise asserted (C), then a synchronized read is completed successfully whereas a requesting write is suspended.

In addition to the shared-word signal already introduced, three more wired-OR signals are required for the protocol to operate correctly, as described in [7]. The first signal (named S) is asserted if any processor different than the requesting processor has a copy of the cache line. The second signal is asserted if any cache has the block in a dirty state. This signal modifies the meaning of the former in the sense that an existing copy of a cache line has been modified and then all the copies in other nodes are invalid. A third signal is necessary in order to indicate whether all the caches have completed their snoop, that means, if it is reliable to read the value of the first two signals.

Figure 7 shows a more compact state transition specification in which information about the full/empty state of the accessed word is implicit. Instead, the value of the C line or the full/empty bit is specified as a required condition between parentheses. Figure 9 and Figure 7 do not consider neither transient states needed for bus acquisition nor the effects due to real signal delays.

Correspondence between processor instructions and bus transactions.
When a processing node issues a memory operation, the cache of the node interprets the request and, in case of a miss, it later translates the operation into one or more bus transactions. The correspondence between the different processor instructions and the memory requests seen on the bus is shown in Figure 8. Unconditional non-altering read and write requests generate ordinary read and write transactions on the bus. On the contrary, an unconditional altering read requires a BusRd transaction followed by a BusSCl transaction. Effectively, apart from retrieving the data from the corresponding memory location, a PrUARd request also clears the full/empty state bit of the referring location. This is performed by BusSCl, which does not access nor modifies the data but only the full/empty bit. It is important to observe that an unconditional altering read cannot be performed by just a BusSCl transaction, as it just alters the full/empty bit without retrieving any data. The last unconditional operation, PrUAWr, generates a specific bus transaction, namely BusAWr, which unconditionally sets the full/empty bit after writing the corresponding data to the accessed memory location.

The behavior of all conditional memory operations depends on the value of the shared-word bus signal. A conditional non-altering read generates an ordinary read bus transaction after checking whether the shared-bus signal is asserted.

Request from processor	Bus transaction issued on a miss
PrUNRd	BusRd (ordinary read)
PrUNWr	BusWr (ordinary write)
PrUARd	BusRd & BusSCl
PrUAWr	BusAWr
PrSNRd	BusRd(C)
PrSNWr	BusWr(C)
PrSARd	BusRd(C) & BusSCl
PrSAWr	BusSWr(C)

Fig. 8. Correspondence Between Processor Instructions and Memory Requests

A conditional altering read generates a BusSCl transaction in addition to the ordinary read transaction. Finally, a conditional altering write causes a BusSWr transaction to be initiated on the bus. This transaction sets the full/empty bit after writing the data to the referred memory location.

Note that all synchronized operations generate the same bus transactions regardless of their particular type (waiting, non-faulting or faulting). The difference resides in the behavior when a synchronization miss is detected and not in the bus transactions issued as a consequence of the request.

Management of pending requests
Each processing node keeps a local deferred list. This list holds both ordinary presence misses and synchronization misses. It is possible also for both types of misses to happen for a single access. In this case, not only the accessed line is not present in the cache, but also the synchronization state is not met at the remote location where the copy of the word is held. After a relevant full/empty bit change is detected, any operation that matches a required synchronization state is resumed at the appropriate processing node.

Certain requests can be merged together, in particular – non-altering pending read requests with incoming read requests (see [18] for the detailed rules).

Apart from coalescing of requests, it is also crucial to specify how resuming of pending requests is done. As explained at the beginning of this section, coherence of full/empty state bits is ensured by proper bus transactions, to be precise, BusSWr and BusSCl. This means that all caches that have pending requests for a given memory location will know when the synchronization condition is met by snooping into the bus and waiting for a BusSWr or a BusSCl transaction. When such transaction is noticed, a comparator checks if there is an entry in any MSHR matching the received bus transaction. In this case, action is taken so as to resume the pending request.

Due to this feature, it is possible for a cache to have pending requests for a memory location that is not cached or is cached in an invalid state. The location will be brought again into the cache when the synchronization miss is resolved. The ability of replacing cache lines that have pending requests allows efficient management and resuming of pending requests with minimum risk of saturating the cache hierarchy.

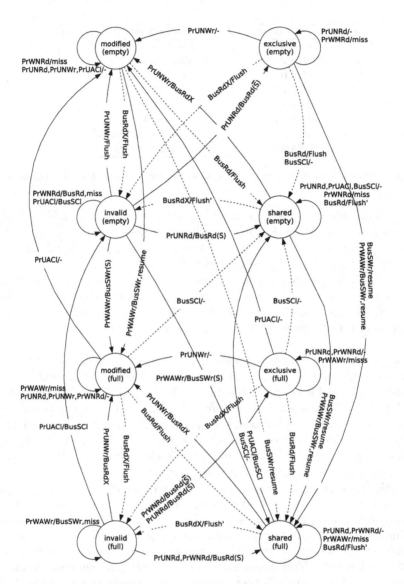

Fig. 9. State Diagram for the FE-MESI Protocol

Imagine a scenario when nodes A, B and C have pending requests to a location (X) in their MSHR. While nodes A and B have invalid copies in their caches, node C has the exclusive ownership of the referred location, whose full/empty state bit is unset. After node C successfully performs a conditional altering write to location X, this event is notified on the bus by a BusSWr transaction. This transaction informs nodes A and B that they can resume the pending request to location X, which happens to be a conditional altering read. As a consequence, only one of these nodes will be able to successfully issue the operation at this point. This is imposed by bus order. For instance, if node B gets the bus ownership before node A, the pending request from the former will be resumed and the operation at node A will stay pending in the MSHR.

7   Conclusions

Fine-grain synchronization is a valuable mechanism for speeding up the execution of parallel algorithms by avoiding false data dependencies and unnecessary process waiting. However, the implementation of fine-grain synchronization introduces additional complexity in both hardware and software.

A novel architecture with support for fine-grain synchronization at the cache coherence level is introduced. We propose a model that can be efficiently implemented in modern multiprocessors. The hardware overhead required by this architecture is not expected to be excessive.

We propose a cache coherence protocol with support for fine-grain synchronization for bus-based multiprocessors. Our proposal includes the rules for management and resuming pending requests, which is a key issue for the correct operation of the presented architecture. We believe our protocol can be used in multi-core multiprocessors.

Acknowledgments

This work was supported in part by a research grant from the Swedish Foundation for International Cooperation in Research and Higher Education (STINT), Sweden, and in part by by a research grant from the National Science Foundation (NSF), USA. We would like to thank Diganta Roychowdhury and Raksit Ashok, former students at the Electrical and Computer Engineering Department at the University of Massachusetts Amherst (UMASS); and the former members of the MIT Alewife Project Donald Yeung and Matthew Frank for providing excellent advises and comments.

References

1. Agarwal, et al.: The MIT Alewife machine: architecture and performance. In: ISCA '95: Proceedings of the 22nd Annual International Symposium on Computer Architecture, Margherita Ligure, Italy, pp. 2–13. ACM Press, New York (1995)
2. Alverson, et al.: The Tera computer system. In: ICS '90: Proceedings of the 4th International Conference on Supercomputing, Amsterdam, The Netherlands, pp. 1–6. ACM Press, New York (1990)
3. Ang, B., Arvind, Chiou, D.: StarT the Next Generation: Integrating global caches and dataflow architecture. In: Advanced Topics in Dataflow Computing and Multithreading, IEEE Press, New York (1995)
4. Arvind, R.N., Pingali, K.: I-structures: data structures for parallel computing. ACM Transactions on Programming Languages and Systems (TOPLAS) 11(4), 598–632 (1989)

5. Barth, P., Nikhil, R., Arvind.: M-structures: extending a parallel, non-strict, functional language with state. In: Proceedings of the 5th ACM Conference on Functional Programming Languages and Computer Architecture, Cambridge, MA, U.S, pp. 538–568. Springer, Heidelberg (1991)
6. Chen, D.-K., Su, H.-M., Yew, P.-C.: The impact of synchronization and granularity on parallel systems. In: ISCA '90: Proceedings of the 17th Annual International Symposium on Computer Architecture, Seattle, Washington, pp. 239–248. ACM Press, New York (1990)
7. Culler, D.E., Singh, J.P., Gupta, A.: Parallel Computer Architecture. Morgan Kaufmann, Seattle (1997)
8. Feo, J., Harper, D., Kahan, S., Konecny, P.: ELDORADO. In: CF '05: Proceedings of the 2nd Conference on Computing Frontiers, Ischia, Italy, pp. 28–34. ACM Press, New York (2005)
9. Goodman, J., Vernon, M., Woest, P.: Efficient synchronization primitives for large-scale cache-coherent multiprocessors. In: ASPLOS-III: Proceedings of the 3rd International Conference on Architectural Support for Programming Languages and Operating Systems, Boston, Massachusetts, pp. 64–75. ACM Press, New York (1989)
10. Hammond, et al.: Transactional memory coherence and consistency. In: Proceedings of the 31st Annual International Symposium on Computer Architecture, p. 102. IEEE Computer Society, Los Alamitos (2004)
11. Herlihy, M., Moss, J.: Transactional memory: architectural support for lock-free data structures. In: Proceedings of the 20th Annual International Symposium on Computer Architecture, San Diego, California, pp. 289–300. ACM Press, New York (1993)
12. Kägi, A., Burger, D., Goodman, J.: Efficient synchronization: Let them eat QOLB. In: Proceedings of the 24th Annual International Symposium on Computer Architecture, Denver, Colorado, pp. 170–180. ACM Press, New York (1997)
13. Kim, N., Austin, T., Blaauw, D., Mudge, T., Flautner, K., Hu, J., Irwin, M., Kandemir, M., Narayanan, V.: Leakage current: Moore's Law meets static power. IEEE Computer 36(12), 68–75 (2003)
14. Kranz, D., Lim, B.H., Agarwal, A., Yeung, D.: Low-cost support for fine-grain synchronization in multiprocessors. In: Multithreaded Computer Architecture: A Summary of the State of the Art, pp. 139–166. Kluwer Academic Publishers, Boston (1994)
15. Kroft, D.: Lockup-free instruction fetch/prefetch cache organization. In: ISCA '98: 25 years of the International Symposia on Computer Architecture (selected papers), Barcelona, Spain, pp. 195–201. ACM Press, New York (1998)
16. Lim, B.-H., Agarwal, A.: Reactive synchronization algorithms for multiprocessors. In: ASPLOS-VI: Proceedings of the 6th International Conference on Architectural Support for Programming Languages and Operating Systems, San Jose, CA, U.S, pp. 25–35. ACM Press, New York (1994)
17. McDonald, A., Chung, J., Carlstrom, B., Minh, C., Chafi, H., Kozyrakis, C., Olukotun, K.: Architectural semantics for practical transactional memory. ACM SIGARCH Computer Architecture News 34(2), 53–65 (2006)
18. Merino, O.S., Vlassov, V., Moritz, C.A.: Performance implication of fine-grained synchronization in multiprocessors. Technical Report TRITAIMITLECS R 02:02, Department of Microelectronics and Information Technology (IMIT) Royal Institute of Technology (KTH), Stockholm, Sweden (2002)
19. Moore, K., Bobba, J., Moravan, M., Hill, M., Wood, D.: LogTM: Log-based transactional memory. In: Proceedings of the 12th International Symposium on High-Performance Computer Architecture, pp. 254–265 (February 2006)

20. Olukotun, K., Nayfeh, B., Hammond, L., Wilson, K., Chang, K.: The case for a single-chip multiprocessor. In: ASPLOS-VII: Proceedings of the 7th International Conference on Architectural Support for Programming Languages and Operating Systems, Cambridge, Massachusetts, pp. 2–11. ACM Press, New York (1996)
21. Ronen, R., Mendelson, A., Lai, K., Lu, S.-L., Pollack, F., Shen, J.P.: Coming challenges in microarchitecture and architecture. Proceedings of the IEEE 89(3), 325–340 (2001)
22. Sutter, H.: The free lunch is over: A fundamental turn toward concurrency in software. Dr. Dobb's Journal 30(3) (March 2005)
23. Tullsen, D., Eggers, S., Levy, H.: Simultaneous multithreading: Maximizing on-chip parallelism. In: The 22th Annual International Symposium on Computer Architecture, Santa Margherita Ligure, Italy, pp. 392–403. ACM Press, New York (1995)
24. Tullsen, D., Lo, J., Eggers, S., Levy, H.: Supporting fine-grained synchronization on a simultaneous multithreading processor. In: HPCA '99: Proceedings of the 5th International Symposium on High Performance Computer Architecture, pp. 54–58. IEEE Computer Society, Los Alamitos (1999)
25. Vachharajani, N., Iyer, M., Ashok, C., Vachharajani, M., August, D., Connors, D.: Chip multi-processor scalability for single-threaded applications. SIGARCH Computer Architecture News 33(4), 44–53 (2005)
26. Vlassov, V., Moritz, C.A.: Efficient fine grained synchronization support using full/empty tagged shared memory and cache coherency. Technical Report TRITA-IT-R 00:04, Deptartment of Teleinformatics, Royal Institute of Technology (KTH) (December 2000)
27. Xiaowei, S.: Implementing global cache coherence in *T-NG. Master's thesis, Department of Electrical Engineering and Computer Science, MIT (May 1995)
28. Yeung, D., Agarwal, A.: Experience with fine-grain synchronization in MIMD machines for preconditioned conjugate gradient. In: PPOPP '93: Proceedings of the 4th ACM SIGPLAN Symposium on Principles and Practice of Parallel Programming, San Diego, CA, U.S, pp. 187–192. ACM Press, New York (1993)

Self-organised Criticality in a Model of the Rat Somatosensory Cortex

Grzegorz M. Wojcik[1], Wieslaw A. Kaminski[1], and Piotr Matejanka[2]

[1] Institute of Computer Science
Maria Curie-Sklodowska University
pl. Marii Curie-Sklodowskiej 5, 20-031-Lublin, Poland
gmwojcik@gmail.com
[2] Motorola Polska Electronics
ul. Wadowicka 6, 30-415 Krakow, Poland

Abstract. Large Hodgkin-Huxley (HH) neural networks were examined and the structures discussed in this article simulated a part of the rat somatosensory cortex. We used a modular architecture of the network divided into layers and sub-regions. Because of a high degree of complexity effective parallelisation of algorithms was required. The results of parallel simulations were presented. An occurrence of the self-organised criticality (SOC) was demonstrated. Most notably, in large biological neural networks consisting of artificial HH neurons, the SOC was shown to manifest itself in the frequency of its appearance as a function of the size of spike potential avalanches generated within such nets. These two parameters followed the power law characteristic of other systems exhibiting the SOC behaviour.

1 Introduction

In physics, a critical point is a point at which a system changes radically its behaviour or structure. Self-organised critical phenomena is exhibited by driven systems which reach a critical state by their intrinsic dynamics, independently of a value of any control parameter. An archetype of a self-organised critical system is a sand pile. The sand is slowly dropped onto a surface, forming a pile. As the pile grows, avalanches occur which carry the sand from the top to the bottom of the pile. At least in model systems, the slope of the pile becomes independent of the rate at which the system is driven by dropping sand. This exemplifies (self-organised) critical slope [16].

One of the oldest numerical models describing the sand-pile problem is presented i.e., in [1],[3],[6]. In this model, a one-dimensional pile of sand comprising a system of columns is considered. Grains of sand are contained in the aforementioned columns. The dynamics of the system is defined by a collection of equations describing the effect of a one-grain addition. After a proper number of grains have been added to the appropriate columns, a critical inclination of the sand pile occurs that causes disorder and relaxation of the whole system. This disorder is referred to as an avalanche.

V. Malyshkin (Ed.): PaCT 2007, LNCS 4671, pp. 468–476, 2007.

Critical states of a system are signalled by a power-law distribution in some observable. In the case of sand-piles, one can measure the size distribution of the avalanches. A frequency of an avalanche appearing in the system is a function of its size and can be expressed by the power law [1]:

$$D(S) \sim S^{-k}, \tag{1}$$

where k stands for a characteristic number for a given system.

In particular, systems exhibiting behaviour predicted by the SOC model have attracted widespread attention [4],[5],[8],[10],[11],[12]. Earthquakes, forest fires, biological evolution, to name just a few, have all been successfully modelled this way [1]. The aim of the research discussed in this contribution was to investigate if the SOC occurs in large and biologically realistic neural networks modelling the mammalian somatosensory cortex. There are experiments confirming the existence of frequency tuning and adaptation to stimulus statistics in neurons of the rat somatosensory cortex [7]. Finding the SOC in the model will allow us to design a new series of experiments with a large number of neurons leading to a discovery of a new class of neurodynamic phenomena are taking place in real brains.

Computer-based models and simulations of microcircuits consisting of numerically complicated HH neurons [9] are power consuming. However, the simulation time can be shortened by using cluster-based parallelised computing. All the simulations discussed in this paper were conducted in a parallel version of GENESIS compiled for the MPI environment [14]. The choice of the GENESIS simulator allowed us to use many processors (for parallelisation effectiveness, the time of a typical run and other details see Appendix A). Remarkably, in this article we demonstrate that in large HH neural networks, critical relaxation phenomena also occur and we show that the size and frequency of the spike potentials appearing in such networks follow the power law. Consequently, the system can be represented by the SOC model and the occurrence of the SOC depends on the number of synaptic connections present in the simulated part of the discussed brain.

2   Model and Method of Parallelisation

The somatosensory pathways bring sensory information from the periphery into the brain, e.g., from a rat's whisker to the somatosensory cortex. Information from the snout passes along the trigeminal nerve, projecting to the trigeminal complex in the brainstem, which sends projections to the medial ventral posterior nucleus of the thalamus (VPm). Each whisker has a representative physical structure in the brain, forming 2-D maps of the whisker pad throughout the pathway. In the cortex, these structures are known as barrels. They are formed from clusters of stellate cortical neurons, with the cell bodies arranged in a ring and dendrites filling the middle "hole". The dendrites form synapses with multiple axons rising from the VPm [15].

The neurons used in the simulations were built according to a slightly modified version of the HH model [9] and are relatively simple (for detail, see Appendix B). The modification was arranged in the model of the neuron in order to avoid a rapid synchronisation of the whole simulated system. An additional parameter responsible for the probability of exocitosis was added for each synaptic connection in post-synaptic neuron. The change required a simple modification of original GENESIS code. Changed version of GENESIS, compiled for Linux and MPI, can be downloaded from [14].

The subsequently constructed net consisted of 2025 of the above-mentioned neurons that were placed on a square-shaped 2-D grid with 45 rows and 45 columns. A pair of numbers ranging from 0 to 44 identified each neuron. All the cells were divided into 22 groups, called layers, numbered from 1 to 22. Communication between neurons was established based on the following principles - the input signal from each neuron from the m-th layer was transported to all the cells from layers: $m + 1, m + 2, m + 3, ..., m + N_s$, where N_s was the integer number, not greater than the number of layers (see Fig. 1). Note that such a structure (2-D with dense "neural rings") imitates the structure of rat cortical barrels. Such a structure can be easily parallelised, so we decided to simulate the

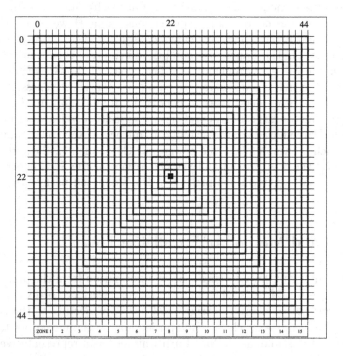

Fig. 1. The scheme of the simulated network. Layers are highlighted by the thick lines. Stimulating neuron is marked with the black square. The coordinates of the neurons are marked on the top and the left side of the scheme. In each zone there are 3 columns of neurons as marked at the bottom. The choice of columns belonging to particular zones is arbitrary.

problem on 15 processors. We divided the network into 15 zones. In each zone the same number of neurons were simulated. The zones were named from 1 to 15 and the way in which they were arranged is presented in Fig.1. Such a choice allowed us to run simulations in optimal way, without the barriers being timed out. The complexity of the system increases rapidly with N_s, so does the time of simulation. A good parallelisation of the model not only shortens its simulation time, but most often makes it executable at all. That is why parallelisation techniques are in such demand for HH systems with large number of synapses.

Synaptic connections are characterised by three parameters: weight w, time delay τ, and the probability p of transporting the signal, which corresponded to the mentioned probability for the occurrence of exocitosis. The probability p is set to a constant and was the same for all the synapses ($p = 0.5$). Values of two other parameters depend on the position of both the pre-synaptic and post-synaptic neuron. For each pair of neurons, one of which is in the m-th layer and the other belongs to the n-th layer, the parameters w and τ are chosen according to following rules:

$$w = \frac{w_0}{|m - n|}, \tag{2}$$

$$\tau = 10^{-4}|m - n| \; [s], \tag{3}$$

where w_0 is a positive constant (in our simulations $w_0 = 2$). The system was stimulated by the neuron $N[23, 23]$ that is the main receptor of activities from the outside of the net (i.e., a glass capillary stimulating the whisker [7] or an electrode transmitting some random stimulus directly into the cortex). As a result, the receptor was producing a periodic spike potential with a frequency of about 80 Hz. In addition, the net is characterised by the parameter T that corresponds to the system's working time (usually, in our simulations usually $T = 15$ s).

3   Simulations and Results

During the simulation, all the data necessary to calculate the time of spike potential occurrence for each neuron were collected. The stimulus was transported to all the cells through the connections in agreement with their architecture. The activity of the whole neural network was examined. In this case by avalanche we understand the group of neurons that are active in the same and small interval of time (i.e., $t_i = 1$ ms). The algorithm used to compute the number of avalanches was implemented in C++ and its main idea was to analyse typical text files containing the time and value of membrane potential in search for the spiking neurons in the same time.

For a system with a small number of connections ($N_s < 6$), the power law cannot precisely describe the number of spike-potential avalanche appearances as a function of its size (Fig. 2). In the case of a net with a small number of connections, a different behaviour in the range of small size avalanches was observed and a clear deviation from the power law for small size avalanches could

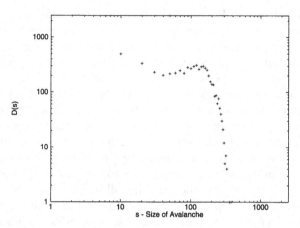

Fig. 2. Frequency $D(s)$ as a function the size of avalanche for $N_s = 1$ and $T = 15$ s

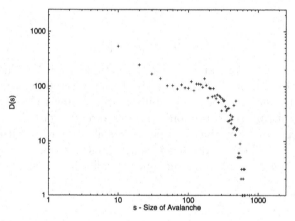

Fig. 3. Frequency $D(s)$ as a function of the size of avalanche for $N_s = 3$ and $T = 15$ s

be noted (Fig. 3). Presumably, it is the result of the correlation of spike potentials occurring on neurons that are situated near the centre of the net. Their work is both highly regular and synchronised with the central neuron receiving impulses from the outside. Despite this, a quite good agreement with the above-mentioned law could be observed that improves as the number of connections in the system increases ($N_s = 6$). A very clear transitional area could be distinguished that disappears as the net becomes more complex (Fig. 4).

Supposedly, the avalanches of a very large size do not obey the power law, either (Figs. 5,6). In this case, however, it can be easily rationalised as the avalanches appear very rarely (no more than several times during the entire simulation). Consequently, an agreement with the law of the SOC should not be expected there. We also suggest that with an increased degree of complexity and longer working time of the system, the law Eq. (1) would be obeyed more closely.

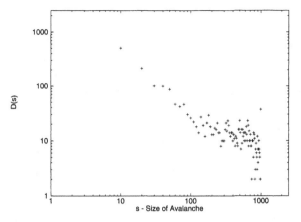

Fig. 4. Frequency $D(s)$ as a function of the size of avalanche for $N_s = 6$ and $T = 15$ s

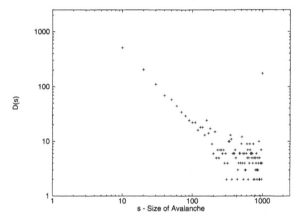

Fig. 5. Frequency $D(s)$ as a function of the size of avalanche for $N_s = 9$ and $T = 15$ s

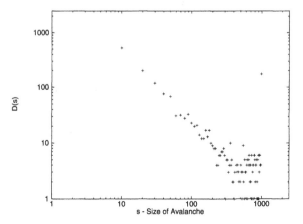

Fig. 6. Frequency $D(s)$ as a function of the size of avalanche for $N_s = 12$ and $T = 15$ s

4   Conclusions

In this paper we report results of rat somatosensory cortex simulations. The modular structure of the cortex makes possible the application of good parallelisation as the particular zones can be simulated on separate nodes. Our model is scalable and we can easily increase the number of neurons in each zone which lets us run simulations consisting of even more than 256 thousand HH neurons on the local cluster. This helps us build more realistic models of a mammalian cortex. Most of the discussed simulations were conducted on the local cluster. The cluster is part of the CLUSTERIX grid project [13]. With access to 800 processors and by increasing the number of simulated zones and neurons, a structure consisting of several millions of neural cells simulated in a similar way can be imagined.

Initially we simulated about 2000 of the HH neurons. Some biologically-inspired topology was arranged and results proved that processes pertinent to complex systems characterised by a critical state take place. In particular, such systems follow a simple, empirical power principle that is known from other phenomena in Nature. Nevertheless, in the planned experiments we are going to investigate theoretically the biological reasons for such a behaviour. A good theoretical and experimental understanding of self-organisation of brain micro-circuits may result in new field of computational neuroscience research.

Acknowledgements

This work has been supported by the Polish State Committee for Scientific Research under the grant number N519 017 32/2120. The initial stage of parallelisation has been performed within the HPC-EUROPA Project (RII3-CT-2003-506079), with the support of the European Community - Research Infrastructure Action within the FP6 Structuring the European Research Area Programme. The author (GMW) would like to thank the EPCC and HPC-Europa organisation, especially his hosts: Prof. L. Smith, Dr. B. P. Graham and Dr. M. Hennig of Stirling University, Scotland.

References

1. Bak, P.: How nature works: The Science of Self-Organised Criticality. Copernicus Press, New York (1996)
2. Bower, J.M., Beeman, D.: The Book of GENESIS - Exploring Realistic Neural Models with the GEneral NEural SImulation System. Telos, New York (1995)
3. Jensen, H.J.: Self Organizing Criticality. Cambridge University Press, Cambridge (1998)
4. Aegerter, C.M., Gnther, R., Wijngaarden, R.J.: Avalanche dynamics, surface roughening, and self-organized criticality: Experiments on a three-dimensional pile of rice Phys. Rev. E 67 (2003) 051306
5. Bak, P., Christensen, K., Danon, L., Scanlon, T.: Unified Scaling Law for Earthquakes Phys. Rev. Lett. 88 (2002) 178501

6. Bak, P., Tang, C., Wisenfeld, K.: Self-organized criticality: An explanation of the 1/f noise Phys. Rev. Lett. 59, 381–384 (1987)
7. Garcia-Lazaro, J.A., Ho, S.S.M., Nair, A., Schnupp, J.W.H: Adaptation to Stimulus in Rat Somatosensory Cortex. FENS Abstr. 3, A109.4 (2006)
8. Lubeck, S.: Crossover phenomenon in self-organized critical sandpile models Phys. Rev. E 62, 6149–6154 (2000)
9. Hodgkin, A.L., Huxley, A.F.: A Quantitative Description of Membrane Current and its Application to Conduction and Excitation in nerve. J. Physiol. 117, 500–544 (1952)
10. Paczuski, M., Bassler, K.E.: Theoretical results for sandpile models of self-organized criticality with multiple topplings Phys. Rev. E. E 62, 5347–5352 (2000)
11. Pastor-Satorras, R., Vespignani, A.: Corrections to scaling in the forest-fire model Phys. Rev. E 61, 4854–4859 (2000)
12. Yang, X., Du, S., Ma, J.: Do Earthquakes Exhibit Self-Organized Criticality? Phys. Rev. Lett. 92 (2004) 228501
13. CLUSTERIX - The National Cluster of Linux Systems: http://www.clusterix.pcz.pl
14. The GENESIS compiled for Linux MPI: http://complex.umcs.lublin.pl/gmwojcik/modgenesis4mpi.tgz
15. The Rat Somatosensory Pathway: http://www.bris.ac.uk/Depts/Synaptic/info/pathway/somatosensory.htm
16. A definition of an SOC: http://www.wikipedia.org

Appendix A: Details of the Hardware and Software Environment of the Simulations

The local cluster used for all the simulations was built of 13 machines including one special machine - the so-called "access node". Each SMP machine had two 64-bit 1.4 GHz Itanium2 IA64 processors with 4 GB of RAM memory. The cluster works under control of Debian Linux Sarge (v. 3.1) and 2.6.8-1 kernel version. The model is simulated in GEneral NEural SImulation System GENESIS v.2.2.1 with its MPI extension. A gcc compiler was used for the general system configuration. The compilation of GENESIS for Linux MPI required some tuning of its code and can be found in [14].

The length of a typical run for $N_s = 1$ and $T = 15$ s was about 12000 s. (3.3 hours) when the problem was parallelised for 15 nodes. Some benchmarking was done for the parallelisation. For the discussed simulations the speedup of 2.8 if compared to 3-processor run was obtained. At the first sight it is not very optimistic, however, for networks with $N_s > 6$ simulation on one SPARC 400 MHz node takes longer than three weeks.

Appendix B: Properties of HH Neurons

Our model consisted of multicompartmental neurons with two dendrite compartments, a soma and an axon. The dendrites contained a synaptically activated channel and the soma had voltage activated HH sodium and potassium channels.

The behaviour of each compartment was equivalent to the behaviour of some electrical circuit [2]. Thus, each circuit was characterised by a typical for GENESIS group of parameters set as follows: resistances $R_a = 0.3\ \Omega$, $R_m = 0.33\ \Omega$, capacity $C_m = 0.01$ F, and potential $E_m = 0.07$ V. For the soma compartment $E_k = 0.0594$ V and for the dendrite $E_k = 0.07$ V. Conductance for each type of ionic channels was chosen to be: $G_K = 360\ \Omega^{-1}$ and $G_{Na} = 1200\ \Omega^{-1}$. These parameters originated from neurophysiological experiments [2] and were chosen to make the model biologically more realistic. The soma had a circular shape with the diameter of 30 μm, dendrites and axon were cable-like with the length of 100 μm. All the other parameters were chosen as suggested by GENESIS authors to simulate the behaviour of the biological-like neurons [2]. More details concerning the HH model can be found elsewhere [2], [9].

Control of Fuzzy Cellular Automata: The Case of Rule 90

Samira El Yacoubi[1] and Angelo B. Mingarelli[2]

[1] MEPS/ASD - University of Perpignan
52, Paul Alduy Avenue, 66860 Perpignan, Cedex, France
yacoubi@univ-perp.fr
http://www.univ-perp.fr/see/rch/cef/index.html
[2] School of Mathematics and Statistics, Carleton University,
Ottawa, Canada, K1S 5B6
amingare@math.carleton.ca
http://www.math.carleton.ca/~amingare/

Abstract. This paper is dedicated to the study of fuzzy rule 90 in relation with control theory. The dynamics and global evolution of fuzzy rules have been recently investigated and some interesting results have been obtained in [10,15,16]. The long term evolution of all 256 one-dimensional fuzzy cellular automata (FCA) has been determined using an analytical approach. We are interested in this paper in the FCA state at a given time and ask whether it can coincide with a desired state by controlling only the initial condition. We investigate two initial states consisting of a single control value u on a background of zeros and one seed adjacent to the controlled site in a background of zeros.

Keywords and Phrases: control, fuzzy, cellular automata, Rule 90.

1 Introduction

Control theory is the area of application-oriented mathematics that deals with the basic principles underlying the analysis and design of control systems. It states that systems behavior is caused by a response to an outside stimulus and may be influenced so as to achieve a desired goal.

A wide literature has been devoted to the control of dynamical continuous (discrete) time systems in both finite and infinite dimensional cases, [2,5,13,14]. These systems have been studied in terms of inputs and outputs using classical approaches based on ordinary/partial differential equations or integral equations. However, the complexity of real world systems leads to serious difficulties both in control theory and in the model implementation.

New approaches based on cellular automata (CA) and their variants are presented as a good alternative. They constitute very promising tools for describing complex natural systems in terms of local interactions between a large number of identical components.

CA in their classical form are autonomous systems. An appropriate way to introduce control in these models to make them more useful in systems theory

V. Malyshkin (Ed.): PaCT 2007, LNCS 4671, pp. 477–486, 2007.

has been given in [6]. Some concepts related to the control theory (regional controllability, identification, spreadability) has been studied mainly in the case of additive CA [7,8,9]. However, the problem of obtaining analytical results is still posed.

We investigate in this paper the case of fuzzy CA as a real-valued version of CA which seems to provide best results regarding the control problems. *Fuzzy CAs* are an attempt to perform the reverse process; i.e., to start from a CA and "fuzzify" the disjunctive normal form which describes its rule [3]. Introduced to study the impact that state-discretization has on the behavior of these systems, they have been used to investigate the result of perturbations (e.g. noisy sources, computation errors, mutations, etc.) on the evolution of Boolean CA [11]. In this sense, this continuous-state CA model is a particular case of coupled map lattices (CML) [1].

For the control issue, one consider a system on a time interval $[0, T]$ and ask whether some particular target state is reachable starting from a specific initial condition. Its defined on a background of zeros and consisting first, of an unknown single value (the control value) and then on a single seed adjacent to a controlled site.

We specifically study rule 90 because of its symmetry, additivity and some intricate features.

2 Basic Definitions

2.1 Cellular Automata Approach

A cellular automaton is a collection of cells arranged on a graph. All cells share the same local space (i.e., the set of values cells range in), the same neighborhood structure (i.e., the cells to which a cell is connected), and the same local function (i.e., the function defining the effect of neighbors on each cell, also called transition function or rule). The global evolution is defined by the synchronous update of all values according to the local function applied to the neighborhood of each cell. A configuration of the automaton is a state of all lattice cells [19].

Furthermore, CA were one of the first parallel computing abstract models. Conceived by John von Neumann [17] in the 1950's to investigate self-reproduction, CA have been mainly used for studying parallel computing methods and the formal properties to model systems.

Given a linear bi-infinite lattice of cells, the local Boolean space $\{0, 1\}$, the neighborhood structure $\langle$ left neighbor, itself, right neighbor $\rangle$, and a local rule $g : \{0, 1\}^3 \longrightarrow \{0, 1\}$, the global dynamics of an *elementary CA* is defined by:

$$f : \{0, 1\}^{\mathbb{Z}} \longrightarrow \{0, 1\}^{\mathbb{Z}}$$

$$\forall i \in \mathbb{Z}, f(x)_i = g(x_{i-1}, x_i, x_{i+1}).$$

The *local rule* is defined by the 8 possible local configurations a cell can detect in its direct neighborhood:

$$(000, 001, 010, 011, 100, 101, 110, 111) \to (r_0, \cdots, r_7),$$

where each triplet represents a local configuration of the left neighbor, the cell itself, and the right neighbor. In general, the value $\sum_{i=0:7} 2^i r_i$ is used as the name of the rule. The local rule of any Boolean CA is canonically expressed as a *disjunctive normal form*:

$$g(x_1, x_2, x_3) = \vee_{i|r_i=1} \wedge_{j=1:3} x_j^{d_{ij}}$$

where d_{ij} is the j-th digit, from left to right, of the binary expression of i, and x^0 (resp. x^1) stands for $\neg x$ (resp. x).

2.2 Fuzzy Cellular Automata

The initial string now consists of a set of fuzzy states, that is a collection of arbitrary but fixed real numbers in the closed interval $[0,1]$. Inherent in this procedure is the fact that fuzzification allows one to move from the discrete (boolean) to the continuous (fuzzy) by extending the domain of definition of the rule. We describe such a method of fuzzifying a rule herewith, the source of which is in [3]. Our fuzzification is somewhat *natural* as we will see next. Throughout, we adopt the terminology from Flocchini *et al*, [10].

Definition 1. *In this paper a CFMS CA, or "fuzzy" CA for brevity, is obtained by fuzzification of the local function of a given boolean CA as follows: In the DNF we redefine for real numbers $a, b \in [0,1]$, the quantities $(a \vee b)$ to be $(a+b)$, $(a \wedge b)$ to be (ab), and $(\neg a)$ to be $(1-a)$. In other words, $a \vee b = a+b$, $a \wedge b = a \cdot b$, and $\neg a = 1 - a$, where $+$ and "." are ordinary addition and multiplication of real numbers.*

Example 1. Since $90 = 2^1 + 2^3 + 2^4 + 2^6$ we see that the rule number, $90 = \sum_{i=0}^7 r_i 2^i$, forces $r_i = 1$ only for $i = 1, 3, 4, 6$. Use of the disjunctive normal form expression above gives us

$$
\begin{aligned}
g_{90}(x_1, x_2, x_3) &= \vee_{i|r_i=1} \wedge_{j=1}^3 x_j^{d_{ij}}, \\
&= (x_1^{d_{11}} \wedge x_2^{d_{12}} \wedge x_3^{d_{13}}) \vee (x_1^{d_{31}} \wedge x_2^{d_{32}} \wedge x_3^{d_{33}}) \vee (x_1^{d_{41}} \wedge x_2^{d_{42}} \wedge x_3^{d_{43}}) \\
&\quad \vee (x_1^{d_{61}} \wedge x_2^{d_{62}} \wedge x_j^{d_{63}}), \\
&= (x_1^0 \wedge x_2^0 \wedge x_3^1) \vee (x_1^0 \wedge x_2^1 \wedge x_3^1) \vee (x_1^1 \wedge x_2^0 \wedge x_3^0) \vee (x_1^1 \wedge x_2^1 \wedge x_3^0), \\
&= (\neg x_1 \wedge \neg x_2 \wedge x_3) \vee (\neg x_1 \wedge x_2 \wedge x_3) \vee (x_1 \wedge \neg x_2 \wedge \neg x_3) \vee \\
&\quad \vee (x_1 \wedge x_2 \wedge \neg x_3) \\
&= (1 - x_1)(1 - x_2)x_3 + (1 - x_1)x_2 x_3 + x_1(1 - x_2)(1 - x_3) + \\
&\quad x_1 x_2 (1 - x_3), \\
&= x_1 + x_3 - 2 x_1 x_3.
\end{aligned}
$$

$$(1)$$

$$(2)$$

Note that in "fuzzifying" the DNF (1), we replaced $\neg x$ by $1 - x$, $x \vee y$ by $x + y$, and $x \wedge y$ in (1) by their product, xy, so as to find the fuzzy form (or rule) given by (1) or equivalently (2), in accordance with the fuzzification process defined above. In this case, the local rule maps the triples of zeros and ones as follows:

$$000, 001, 010, 011, 100, 101, 110, 111 \rightarrow 0, 0, 1, 1, 1, 0, 1, 0.$$

Thus, (boolean) rule 90 is given by (1) above while fuzzy rule 90, given by (2), may be written as

$$g_{90}(x, y, z) = x + z - 2xz,$$

for any value of $(x, y, z) \in [0, 1]^3$.

3   Control of Fuzzy Rule 90

3.1   The Case of a Single Controlled Cell in Zero Backgrounds

CA have been extensively used as a modelling tool to approximate nonlinear discrete and continuous dynamical systems in a wide range of applications.

However the inverse problem of determining the CA that satisfies some specified constraints has received little attention. An interesting inverse problem is to find an appropriate CA rule capable of steering a given system from an initial state to a desired configuration during a time horizon T. If the rule has the form : $s_{t+1} = F_u(s_t, u_t)$, the problem is usually referred to as the controllability problem, consists in finding a control $u = (u_0, u_1, \cdots, u_{T-1})$ in an appropriate control space such that, for some $T \geq 0$,

$$s(T) = S_d$$

where S_d is a desired state, given in a suitable space of reachable states.

An example of a controllability problem with CA models has been considered in a previous work [7], but only from a numerical point of view. The approach used is based on genetic programming techniques in the case of additive CA. The results obtained are quite promising and stimulate further research in this direction.

Controllability is related to the possibility of forcing the system into a particular state by using an appropriate control signal. In this work we consider the case where the signal is applied only at $t = 0$ so as to influence only the initial state in order to achieve a desired state at time T.

In this analysis all cells but one are initially set to 0. For example, starting from a single value $a = \frac{1}{8}$ in a zero background, the space-time diagram is represented in Table 1. Generally speaking we note that, for any $a \in [0, 1]$, we have $g(x, \bullet, a) = g(a, \bullet, x) = a + x(1 - 2a)$. We give the following definitions :

Definition 2. *The spatio-temporal diagram (or space-time diagram) from an initial configuration x^0 is the double sequence (x_i^t) where $i, t \in \mathbb{N}$, t denotes time steps, and i denotes cell indices.*

Definition 3. *The light cone from a cell x_i^t is the set $\{x_j^{t+p} \mid p \geq 0 \text{ and } j \in \{i - p, \cdots, i + p\}\}$.*

In [10] the authors proved the following interesting result (Proposition 1 below) which we will make use of in various parts in the sequel. Let

$$f(t, i) = \binom{t}{\frac{t+i}{2}}, \text{ where } \binom{a}{b} = \frac{a!}{b!(a-b)!}.$$

Table 1. Evolution from $\frac{1}{8}$ in a zero background

Time		Local states						
	$\cdots$	-3	-2	-1	0	1	2	$3 \cdots$
0	$\cdots$	0	0	0	$\frac{1}{8}$	0	0	$0 \cdots$
1	$\cdots$	0	0	$\frac{1}{8}$	0	$\frac{1}{8}$	0	$0 \cdots$
2	$\cdots$	0	$\frac{1}{8}$	0	$\frac{7}{32}$	0	$\frac{1}{8}$	$0 \cdots$
3	$\cdots$	$\frac{1}{8}$	0	$\frac{37}{128}$	0	$\frac{7}{32}$	0	$\frac{1}{8} \cdots$
4	$\cdots$	0	$\frac{175}{512}$	0	$\cdots$	0	$\frac{175}{512}$	$0 \cdots$

Proposition 1. *The spatio-temporal diagram from a single value $a \in [0,1]$ in a zero background is given explicitly by: $\forall t \in \mathbb{N}$,*

$$x_i^t = \begin{cases} \frac{1}{2}(1 - (1 - 2a)^{f(t,i)}) & \text{if } t + i \text{ is even and } i \in \{-t, \cdots, t\} \\ 0 & \text{otherwise} \end{cases}$$

We motivate our result with the following question: **Given a cell i, t and a desired value $A \in (0,1]$, can one find a real control u which acts at $t = 0$ such that the light-cone from u has the property that $x_i^t = A$?**

Theorem 1. *Given a cell i, t, with $i \in \{-t, \cdots, t\}$, and cell value A, there exists a control $u \in [0,1]$ such that, in a homogeneous background of zeros, we have that $x_i^t = A$. Such a control is given explicitly as follows:*

- *If $0 \leq A \leq 1/2$, and $t + i$ is even, we choose $u = (1 - (1 - 2A)^{1/f(t,i)})/2$,*
- *If $1/2 \leq A \leq 1$, $t + i$ is even and $f(t, i)$ is odd, we can choose $u = (1 + (2A - 1)^{1/f(t,i)})/2$,*
- *If either $f(t, i)$ is even or $t + i$ is odd then no such control exists.*

Proof: For $0 \leq A \leq 1/2$ and $t + i$ an even number, $x_i^t = (1 - (1 - 2u)^{f(t,i)})/2$ by Proposition 1. By assumption, $1 - 2A \geq 0$ and $x_i^t = A$, thus $1 - 2u = (1 - 2A)^{1/f(t,i)}$ and the first claim follows. For $1/2 \leq A \leq 1$ and $t + i$ even, we note that $(2A - 1)^{f(t,i)} = -(1 - 2A)^{f(t,i)}$ since f is odd. Thus, as before, we can choose u as $u = (1 + (2A - 1)^{1/f(t,i)})/2$. The last claim follows since u cannot be real if $f(t, i)$ is even and $A = 0$ if $t + i$ is odd, each of which is excluded from the discussion.

3.2 Case of a Controlled Cell with a Single Seed in a Zero Background

We consider the case where the initial string consists of two cells, one of which is the control, in a background of zeros. The discussion is now complicated by the fact that at each cell value x_i^t the value A is generally a polynomial of high degree in u. Thus, the finding of a control requires showing that the polynomial equation $x_i^t = A$ has a real root $u \in (0,1)$.

The procedure involves as a basis the technique described in detail in [15]. In this case we define the initial point $x_0^0 = u$ as the unknown control variable, and $x_1^0 = a$ where $a \in (0,1)$ is fixed but otherwise arbitrary. All other entries in the initial string are set initially to zero. Now consider the *left diagonals* $\mathcal{L}_k^-$: these are the sequences defined by $\{x_{-j}^{j+k}\}_{j=0}^{\infty}$. Thus, in Table 1 the main left diagonal $\mathcal{L}_0^-$ consists of the sequence $\{1/8, 1/8, \ldots\}$, the diagonal $\mathcal{L}_2^-$ forms the sequence $\{7/32, 37/128, 175/512, \ldots\}$ and so on. As is shown in [10] and more generally in [15] in the two-seed case we are considering here, these left-diagonal sequences all converge to $1/2$, that is, for each $k \geq 0$, the sequence $x_{-j}^{j+k} \to 1/2$ as $j \to \infty$.

We consider the earlier problem of determining given a cell i, t and a desired value $A \in (0,1]$, whether one can find a real control u such that the light-cone from u has the property that $x_i^t = A$? To set the framework for the discussion that follows we consider the Table below, Table 2, where only the evolution to the left of the initial cell is displayed.

Table 2. Evolution from a controlled cell and one seed in a zero background

	$\cdots$ -3	-2	-1	0	1
0	$\cdots$ 0	0	0	u	a
1	$\cdots$ 0	0	u	a	0
2	$\cdots$ 0	u	a	$2u - 2u^2$	$\cdots$
3	$\cdots$ u	a	$4u^3 - 6u^2 + 3u$	$4a^3 - 6a^2 + 3a$	$\cdots$
4	$\cdots$ a	$4u - 12u^2 + 16u^3 - 8u^4$	$\cdots$	$\cdots$	$\cdots$

To begin with we determine whether elements A in the second left diagonal (the one beginning with $2u - 2u^2$) can be reached by means of a real control $u \in (0,1)$. The first such result follows:

Lemma 1. *Consider the cell value x_{-j}^{j+2} where $j \geq 0$ is arbitrary but fixed. Then there is a control u such that the light cone from u contains the cell value $x_{-j}^{j+2} = A$ if either $j + 2$ is even and $A \in [0, 1/2]$ or $j + 2$ is odd and $A \in [0, 1]$. In fact, the controls can be chosen as follows:*

$$u = \begin{cases} \frac{1}{2}(1 \pm (1 - 2A)^{1/(j+2)})/2 & \text{if } j + 2 \text{ is even and } A \in [0, 1/2] \\ \frac{1}{2}(1 - (1 - 2A)^{1/(j+2)})/2 & \text{if } j + 2 \text{ is odd and } A \in [0, 1] \end{cases}$$

Finally, $x_{-j}^{j+2} = A$ is not reachable by a real control if $j + 2$ is even and $A > 1/2$.

Proof: Let $j = 0$. Now, $x_0^2 = A = 2u - 2u^2$ has the roots $u = (1 + (1 - 2A)^{(1/2)})/2$ and $u = (1 - (1 - 2A)^{(1/2)})/2$, both real and less than 1 (u is real only if $A \leq 1/2$). Thus, if $A \in [0, 1/2]$, either root is a possible control and no real control exists if $A > 1/2$.

The case $j = 1$: In this case, $x^3_{-1} = 3u - 6u^2 + 4u^3$ and we note that, for any $A \in [0, 1/2]$, a direct calculation shows that $3u - 6u^2 + 4u^3 = A$ admits the root $u = (1 - (1 - 2A)^{1/3})/2$, with $u \in [0, 1/2]$. For $A \in [1/2, 1]$ the root is given by the same value, since we take into account the relation that $(1 - (1 - 2A)^{1/3})/2 = (1 + (2A - 1)^{1/3})/2$. In either case, our $u \in [0, 1]$.

The case $j \geq 2$: We observe that, by definition, $x^4_{-2}(u) = u + (1 - 2u)x^3_{-1}(u)$, where the explicit dependence of x^3_{-1} and the left side on u is noted. Since $x^3_{-1}((1 - (1 - 2A)^{1/3})/2) = A$ holds for every appropriate value of A, it follows that $x^3_{-1}(u) = ((2u - 1)^3 + 1)/2$. It follows that

$$x^4_{-2}(u) = u + (1 - 2u)x^3_{-1}(u)$$
$$= u + (1 - 2u)((2u - 1)^3 + 1)/2$$
$$= 1/2 - (2u - 1)^4/2,$$

and so $x^4_{-2}(u) = A$ as well for $u = (1 - (1 - 2A)^{1/4})/2$ and $A \leq 1/2$. Note that the rest of the argument can now proceed by induction on the (left) column number j.

This said, let $x^{j+2}_{-j}(u) = u + (1 - 2u)x^{j+1}_{-j+1}(u)$, where $x^{j+1}_{-j+1}(u) = A$ for $u = (1 - (1 - 2A)^{1/(j+1)})/2$ for $j = 0, 1, 2, \ldots, k - 1$. Then, as before, $x^{j+1}_{-j+1}(u) = (1 - (1 - 2u)^{j+1})/2$ for $j = 0, 1, 2, \ldots, k - 1$. As before, we now see that for $j = k - 1$,

$$x^{k+1}_{-k+1}(u) = u + (1 - 2u)x^k_{-k+2}(u)$$
$$= u + (1 - 2u)(1 - (1 - 2u)^k)/2$$
$$= (1 - (1 - 2u)^{k+1})/2,$$

which is our statement for $j = k$. Therefore, for any j (even or odd)

$$x^{j+2}_{-j}(u) = (1 - (1 - 2u)^{j+2})/2$$

From this we see that $x^{j+2}_{-j} = A$ for $u = (1 - (1 - 2A)^{1/(j+2)})/2$. The remaining case where $j + 2$ is even and there is the additional control $u = (1 + (1 - 2A)^{1/(j+2)})/2$ is similar and so is omitted. This concludes the proof of the lemma.

Lemma 2. *Consider the fourth diagonal, $\mathcal{L}_4$, consisting of cells of the form x^{j+3}_{-j} where $j \geq 0$ is arbitrary but fixed. Then there is NO real control u such that $x^{j+3}_{-j} = A$ unless $A = (1 - (1 - 2a)^{j+3})/2$.*

Proof: An easy induction argument shows that, for any initial seeds u, a, $x^{j+3}_{-j} = (1 - (1 - 2a)^{j+3})/2$. The result follows.

In order to handle the general case we need to relate the degree of the general polynomial in u in the i, j-cell to the cell itself and its value. We observe that whenever k is odd, then x^{j+k}_{-j} consists of powers of a only, that is, the polynomial is independent of u, in which case a result similar to the one in Lemma 2 above holds.

Theorem 2. *Cells of the form x_{-j}^{j+k}, where $k > 0$ is odd and $j \geq 0$ is arbitrary but fixed, are independent of u. So, generally, there is no real control u such that $x_{-j}^{j+k} = A$ unless A takes on a specific a-value also dependent upon k.*

Proof: Consider for example, the case $k = 3$, that is, x_{-j}^{j+3} with $j = 0$. Since $x_0^3 = a + x_1^2 - 2ax_1^2$ and $x_1^2 = 2a - 2a^2$, it follows that x_0^3 is a function of a alone. Next, by definition, for $j = 1$, $x_{-1}^4 = a + x_1^3 - 2ax_1^3$ and since x_1^3 is a function of a alone as we have shown then so is x_{-1}^4. The general result, that x_{-j}^{j+3} is independent of a, now follows by a straightforward induction argument on the column number. Next, a moment's notice shows us that a similar induction argument also gives us that for k odd, x_0^k is independent of u (since the cell values x_{-1}^{k-1}, x_1^{k-1} are independent of u). Once it is known that x_0^k is independent of u it follows using an argument similar to the case where $k = 3$ that x_{-j}^{j+k} is independent of u.

To determine some of these exceptional A-values we note that by the proof of Lemma 2, $x_{-j}^{j+3} = (1 - (1 - 2a)^{\delta(j,3)})/2$, for every $j \geq 0$ where

$$\delta(j,3) = j + 3.$$

In addition, $x_0^5 = (1 - (1 - 2a)^9)/2$, $x_{-1}^6 = (1 - (1 - 2a)^{14})/2$, etc. Generally, one can show by induction that $x_{-j}^{j+5} = (1 - (1 - 2a)^{\delta(j,5)})/2$, where

$$\delta(j,5) = 8 + 3j + (j+1)(j+2)/2,$$

for every $j \geq 0$. Expressions are more complicated for x_{-j}^{j+k} with $k \geq 7$, but they are of the form $x_{-j}^{j+k} = (1 - (1 - 2a)^{\delta(j,k)})/2$, where δ is given by solving the recurrence relation $\delta(j,7) - \delta(j-1,7) = \delta(j+1,5)$. Solving this gives

$$\delta(j,7) = 9\,j + 25 + (j+1)\,(j+2)\,(j+3)\,/6 + 2\,(j+1)\,(j+2)$$

for every $j \geq 0$. Generally, $\delta(j,k)$ for odd $k \geq 9$, $k = 2m+1$, involves a polynomial of degree m arising from linear combinations of various binomial coefficients. It can be found recursively using the methods adopted above.

Remark 1. Insight into the method for obtaining the degree of x_{-j}^{j+k} where $k \geq 0$ is even can be extracted from the case where $k = 2$ above; for simplicity we write down the result for $k = 4$ below. Once again, the number of controls depends on various parity considerations, but whenever k is even there is always at least one control for any cell value $A \in [0, 1/2]$.

Lemma 3. *For the left diagonal x_{-j}^{j+4} where $j \geq 0$ is arbitrary but fixed, there is at least one control u such that the light cone from u contains the cell value $x_{-j}^{j+4} = A$. The control can be chosen as*

$$u = 1/2 - (1 - 2A)^{1/\delta(j,4)}/2$$

when $A \in [0, 1/2]$ and

$$\delta(j, 4) = 4 + 2j + (j + 1)(j + 2)/2 = \binom{k + 4}{\frac{4}{2}} - 1,$$

so that δ and d agree for even k.

Thus, the only cases where some form of controllability may arise are those in which $k > 0$ is even. In these cases where k is even, we have that for any $j \geq 0$,

$$\deg x_{-j}^{j+k} = \binom{j + k}{\frac{k}{2}} - 1 = \delta(j, k).$$

4 Concluding Remarks

The work presented in this paper is related to the most general problem of control theory using Cellular Automata models. We attempted to solve it in a special yet more complicated case where the control acts only at the initial state.

A current study considers the case of finding a control vector $u = (u_0, u_1, \cdots, u_{T-1})$ which forces the system during the discrete time interval $\{0, 1, T-1\}$ at a localized cell in both zero background and a single seed on a zero background cases. The space-time diagram is then of the form:

		-3	-2	-1	0	1
0	$\cdots$	0	0		a	u_0
1	$\cdots$	0	0	a	u_0	u_1
2	$\cdots$	0	a	u_0	$.$	u_2
$\cdots$						
$\vdots$					$\vdots$	
$T-1$	$\cdots$	$.$	$.$	$.$	$.$	u_{T-1}
T	$\cdots$	A_{-3}	A_{-2}	A_{-1}	A_0	$.$

and the problem is to reach a state $(\cdots, 0, 0, x_{-T}^T, \cdots, x_{-1}^T, x_0^T)$ which coincides with a desired one A at time T.

Finally, regarding the results obtained in this paper, some transformations and operations on the rules (which preserve qualitative and/or quantitative dynamic properties) could be used to extend the class of rules to which our method applies. In fact, building homomorphisms between known and new systems, composing known rules to obtain new ones, and combining individual properties to get homomorphically global ones, the methods described in this paper can be applied, with minor modifications, to the Fuzzy Rules 60, 102, 153, 165, and 195 where we find similar convergence and control properties.

References

1. Bunimovich, L.A.: Coupled Map Lattices: one Step Forward and two Steps Back. Physica D 86, 248–255 (1995)
2. Callier, F.M., Desoer, C.A.: Linear System Theory. Springer, Heidelberg (1991)
3. Cattaneo, G., Flocchini, P., Mauri, G., Santoro, N.: Cellular automata in fuzzy backgrounds. Physica D 105, 105–120 (1997)
4. Culik II, K., Yu, S.: Undecidability of CA classification schemes. Complex Systems 2, 177–190 (1988)
5. Curtain, R.F., Zwart, H.: An introduction to Infinite-dimensional linear systems theory. Springer, Heidelberg (1995)
6. El Yacoubi, S., El Jai, A.: Notes on control and observation in Cellular automata models. WSEAS Transaction on Computers 2(4), 1086–1092 (2003)
7. El Yacoubi, S., El Ja, A., Ammor, N.: Regional controllability with cellular automata models. In: Bandini, S., Chopard, B., Tomassini, M. (eds.) ACRI 2002. LNCS, vol. 2493, pp. 357–367. Springer, Heidelberg (2002)
8. El Yacoubi, S., El Jai, A.: Cellular Automata and Spreadability. Journal of Mathematical and Computer Modelling 36, 1059–1074 (2002)
9. El Yacoubi, S., Jacewicz, P.: A genetic programming approach to structural identification of cellular automata models. Journal Of Cellular Automata (to appear)
10. Flocchini, P., Geurts, F., Mingarelli, A., Santoro, N.: Convergence and aperiodicity in fuzzy cellular automata: revisiting rule 90. Physica D 42, 20–28 (2000)
11. Flocchini, P., Santoro, N.: The chaotic evolution of information in the interaction between knowledge and uncertainty. In: Stonier, R.J., Yu, X.H. (eds.) Complex Systems: Mechanism of Adaptation, pp. 337–343. IOS Press, Amsterdam (1994)
12. Lasiecka, I., Triggiani, R.: Control Theory for Partial Differential Equations- Continuous and Approximation Theories. Cambridge University Press, Cambridge (2000)
13. Lee, K.Y., Chow, S., Barr, R.O.: On the control of discrete-time distributed parameter systems. Siam J. Control 10(2) (1972)
14. Lions, J.L.: Contrôle optimal de systèmes gouvernés par des équations aux dérivées partielles, Dunod et Gauthier- Villars, Paris (1968)
15. Mingarelli, A.B.: The global evolution of general fuzzy cellular automata. J. Cellular Automata 1(2), 141–164 (2006)
16. Mingarelli, A.B., El Yacoubi, S.: On the decidability of the evolution of the fuzzy cellular automata, FCA 184. In: Alexandrov, V.N., van Albada, G.D., Sloot, P.M.A., Dongarra, J.J. (eds.) ICCS 2006. LNCS, vol. 3993, pp. 360–366. Springer, Heidelberg (2006)
17. Von Neumann, J.: Theory of Self-Reproducing Automata. University of Illinois Press, Urbana (1966)
18. Sontag, E.D.: Mathematical Control Theory: Deterministic Finite Dimensional Systems, 2nd edn. Springer, New York (1998)
19. Wolfram, S.: Cellular Automata and Complexity. Collected Papers. World Scientific, Singapore (1994)

Intensive Atmospheric Vortices Modeling Using High Performance Cluster Systems

A.I. Avetisyan, V.V. Babkova, S.S. Gaissaryan, and A.Yu. Gubar

Institute for System Programming RAS
109004, Russia, Moscow, B. Kommunisticheskaya, 25
{arut,barbara,ssg}@ispras.ru, parkAG@yandex.ru
http://www.ispras.ru/groups/ctt/parjava.html

Abstract. The goal of the paper is development of a scalable parallel program calculating the numerical solution of the system of equations modeling the processes and origin conditions of intensive atmospheric vortices (IAV) in 3D compressible atmosphere according to the theory of mesovortice turbulence by Nikolaevskiy. Original system of non-linear equations, and its initial and boundary conditions are discussed. The structure of a parallel program for high performance cluster is developed. The problems concerning to optimization of the program in order to increase its scalability are studied. In summary the results of numerical computations are discussed.

1 Inroduction

Presently the parallel programming became conventional, and scientists have an opportunity to verify their ideas and models concerned with large computational expenses. In this paper we discuss a scalable parallel program calculating numerical solution of non-linear system of equations, modeling the processes and origin conditions of intensive atmospheric vortices (IAV) in 3D compressible atmosphere according to the theory of mesovortice turbulence by Nikolaevskiy. The system of equations was obtained in [1,2] and is a strongly non-linear system of the mixed type. The program was developed in the Institute for System Programming RAS in collaboration with the Institute of Physics of Earth RAS using ParJava environment and is intended to be executed using high-performance clusters.

2 ParJava

Integrated ParJava Environment [3] was designed and implemented in ISP RAS and is intended to support development and maintenance of data-parallel programs. Assurance of program's efficiency and scalability needs additional tuning of a program to detect and remove possible bottlenecks preventing to achieve needed level of its scalability. It is very useful to know program's dynamic properties (profiles, traces, slices, etc.) when it is tuned. However the analysis of the program's dynamic properties usually is coupled with necessity of numerous executions of a parallel program on the target computing system (high-performance cluster).

V. Malyshkin (Ed.): PaCT 2007, LNCS 4671, pp. 487–495, 2007.

The ParJava Environment provides an original mechanism of interpretation of a parallel program allowing to obtain precise estimates of the parallel program's dynamic properties. The advantage of the interpretation vs. execution of a program is that the former is made using instrumental computer (PC or Workstation) instead of the target computing system (high-performance cluster). It essentially reduce the price and precipitates the development and modifying of parallel applications. +

ParJava Integrated Environment is installed on ISP RAS cluster, as well as on high-performance clusters in JSCC RAS and RCC MSU. ParJava Environment is used in education process on system programming departments in MSU and MIPT.

One of advantages of ParJava Environment is that a parallel program developed using this environment can be executed using an arbitrary scalable computing system without any modifications or transformations preserving its scalability. It removes many problems concerning the distribution of parallel programs.

3 Mathematical Model and Computational Implementation

With dry-adiabatic atmosphere hypothesis accepted [5], from the basic theory of mesoscale turbulence [6], one can derive the following set of equations of motions of the air, which are conservation laws for mass, impulse, moment of inertia and angular momentum:

$$\frac{da'}{dt} = -(U_3 a_{0z} + Div) \tag{1}$$

$$\frac{dU_i}{dt} = A_1(f(\Delta U_i + \frac{\partial Div}{\partial X_i}) + U_{ij}\varphi_j) + $$
$$A_2 \varepsilon_{ijk} \hat{A}_j [f\omega_k] + \delta_{i3}g \cdot 0.4a'(1 + 0.2a') - c^2 \frac{\partial a'}{\partial X_i} \tag{2}$$

$$\frac{dJ}{dt} = A_4(f\Delta J + \varphi_j \frac{\partial J}{\partial X_j}), \tag{3}$$

$$\frac{dF_i}{dt} = A_3(f\Delta F_i + \varphi_j \frac{\partial F_i}{\partial X_j}) + \frac{f}{J}\left((A_3 + A_4)\frac{\partial F_i}{\partial X_j}\frac{\partial J}{\partial X_j} - 2A_2\omega_i\right) - \frac{g}{J}\varepsilon_{ij3}\hat{A}_j[J], \tag{4}$$

where $i, j = 1, 2, 3$, the axis $z = X_3$ is directed upwards; U_i is the wind velocity, $Div = \frac{\partial U_i}{\partial X_i}$, $\Delta = \frac{\partial^2}{\partial X_i^2}$; $\frac{d}{dt} = \frac{\partial}{\partial t} + U_i \frac{\partial}{\partial X_i}$, $a = \ln(\rho/\rho_0) - a_0(z)$ is the perturbation of the air density logarithm, $a_0(z) = \frac{5}{2}\ln(1 - \gamma_a z)$, $\gamma_a = \frac{g}{C_p T_0}$,

$C_p = \frac{7}{2}R_a \approx 1005$ J/(kg K) is the specific heat capacity [5], T_0 and ρ_0 are the temperature and the density at $t = 0$, $z = 0$, g is the gravity acceleration,

$f = f(\omega) = \dfrac{\omega_{bk} + \omega}{\omega_0}$, ω_0 and ω_{bk} are initial and background mesovorticities, A_j are

initial values of coefficients of turbulent viscosity [1]; $F_k = \Omega_k + \omega_k$ is the total

vorticity, $\Omega_k = \dfrac{1}{2}\varepsilon_{kij}\dfrac{\partial U_j}{\partial X_i}$ is the macrovorticity, ω_k is the mesovorticity,

$c^2 = \dfrac{7}{5}R_aT_0 \cdot (1 - \gamma_a z) \cdot (1 + 0.4a)$ is the square of the speed of the sound,

$U_{ij} = 2e_{ij} = \dfrac{\partial U_i}{\partial X_j} + \dfrac{\partial U_j}{\partial X_i}$, $\hat{A}_j[B] \equiv \dfrac{\partial B}{\partial X_j} + B\left(\dfrac{\partial a}{\partial X_j} + \delta_{j3}a_{0z}\right)$, $\varphi_j = \hat{A}_j[f]$. The

members $o(a^2)$ are neglected in (1)-(4).

In the co-ordinates (r, z, φ) with center at $r = 0$ $(x, y = L/2)$, the initial conditions
are   as   follows:

$U_\varphi = U_0 f_{ur}(r, R_0) f_{uz}(z)\sigma(R_0 - r)$, $\omega_z = \omega_0 f_{ur}(r, R_1(z)) f_{uz}(z)\sigma(R_1(z) - r)$,

$J = (J_0 - J_{bk})\left[1 - \left(\dfrac{r}{R_1(z)}\right)^2\right]f_{uz}(z)\sigma(R_1(z) - r) + J_{bk}\sigma(r - R_1(z))$, where $R_0 < L/2$ is

the radius of a "cloud" of mesovortices, U_0, ω_0, J_0 are the initial amplitudes, $\sigma(r)$ is

the   Heaviside   function, $R_1(z) = \sqrt{J_{bk}} + (0.5R_0 - \sqrt{J_{bk}}) \cdot \dfrac{2z}{H} \cdot \exp(1 - \dfrac{2z}{H})$,

$f_{ur}(r, R_0) = 4\dfrac{r(R_0 - r)}{R_0^2}$, $f_{uz}(z) = \dfrac{\ln(1 + z/z_{rgh})}{\ln(1 + H/z_{rgh})}$, H is the area height. The other

components equal to zero.

The task (1)-(4) is set in the rectangular area $D = \{|x|, |y| < L; 0 < z < H\}$. The
boundary conditions for the wind and pressure correspond to a common model [7].
The MTN approach allows setting the turbulent stresses which all equal to zero with
the exception for the tangential stresses near the Earth calculated by the Shiffrinson
formulae [8].

The task (1)-(4) has been numerically solved by using a modified Runge-Kutta-
Adams scheme where the finite difference method for Eq. (1) is based on the leapfog
scheme with averaging over three half-levels in time [4]. The whole scheme is
hereafter referred to as the MRKAL scheme. This is a conditionally stable scheme of
the second order of accuracy both in space and time, with the criteria of stability
found to be close to those of explicit MacCormack schemes [4].

4 Parallel Algorithm

The program may be divided in two parts: loading and initialization of data and the
main cycle. Resulting data retention is made during the execution of the main cycle.
The program's input information is kept in a text file and includes physical
parameters of the model and auxiliary data needed for the program, e.g., number of
outputs of significant results along a trace. Then the arrays are filled by initial data.

After the initialization the program keeps the zero level of the data and begins the execution of its main loop. The function "Layer" is called four times during each iteration, calculating the values of the main arrays in the loops with regard to X, Y, and Z. If the current iteration needs data retention, the function "Eplus" is called three times.

The loops were examined for admissibility of parallelization using distance test, which showed the absence of dependencies between the array elements, being processed in loops. This fact allowed to divide the arrays into blocks and distribute the blocks obtained among the cluster's processors. Since the chosen difference scheme was "three-point" it is necessary for blocks to collide. The collision areas are called shade sides, during calculation being necessary to pass the values of the shade sides from the processors their values were calculated to the processors they are used. For the three-point difference scheme each shade side has a width in one space layer. During the current iteration only data obtained during previous iterations are used. It allows updating shade sides only once for each layer, reducing overheads for data transfer. It was stated that two-dimension partition is more effective than one-dimension partition, so the two-dimension partition was used.

Significant results are preserved by each processor on its local hard disc as binary arrays. After the termination of the computation the combination of all these results is performed. Transfer of such amounts of data during the program execution would cause strong mistiming on each step and would essentially increase the total time of the program execution.

Besides, a breakpoint mechanism was implemented to support long-time calculations. Only a few arrays and several parameters are preserved to provide the opportunity of breaking calculation in order to continue it afterwards. At the next startover these arrays and parameters are loaded and provide the restoring of the whole context of the abortive task. Thus, in contrast to the standard breakpoint mechanism, when the whole context of a task is preserved, we preserve only about 25% of the whole task's memory, providing the essential economy of the disc space. From the same reasons the arrays for visualization were thinned out, i.e. only each second point was preserved. It had no influence on the quality of visualization, however decreased the length of visualized data in eight times.

Calculations were performed on MVS1000M Cluster (Power 2,2 GHz processors, Myrinet (2 Gbit/s)), in JSCC RAS. Each launching of a program needs to spend the time needed not only to perform calculation, but also to wait the cluster become free in a queue.

Since physicists needed many launchings of the program using various initial values, the problem of determining of optimal number of processors for the program using given size of the matrix was critical. Besides, the process of the tornado modeling is iterative in nature, that means that the parallel version of the program is constantly being modified, and the tornado modeling algorithm is often modified as well. These changes cause the consequent changes in the parallel program, which may cause the changes in its scalability properties and may change the optimal number of processor nodes. Thus, regular determination of the scalability interval is needed. Performing metering using the target computing system, being shared, would essentially slow down our work. The task was solved using interpreter from ParJava Environment [3].

The interpreter allows predicting execution time of a parallel program using instrumental computer. The interpreter uses the following initial data: (1) the model of the parallel program, (2) byte-code of the program's basic blocks, and (3) the estimate of the execution time of each of the program's basic blocks on the target computing system. The estimate of the execution time of basic blocks is obtained by measuring the duration of their execution on the target computing system. Since at that each basic block is executed independently, the user must assign initial data providing their correct execution. User puts the set of initial data in configuration file. in the case in question was needed to set about 270 values of local variables and members of the classes, to measure the execution time of all (more, than 1200) basic blocks.

It took just 1 hour of running on a single processor node to obtain the estimates for all basic blocks. Note, that techniques used allows to take account the effects of cache, and jit-compiler.

Since the interpreter uses hybrid techniques including elements of direct execution the problem of lack of storage on instrumental computer was critical. Tornado modeling requires several large arrays of data, that is impossible to place in the instrumental computer's storage. To gain the solution of the problem a transformation of the model was performed. The transformation consisted in removing from the basic blocks all the expressions values of which had no effect on control flow. First of all the arrays holding velocity fields, values of turbulence, mesovortices, etc. were removed.

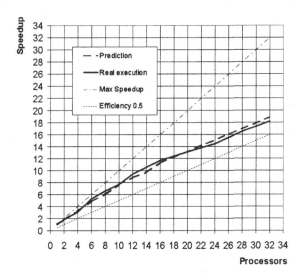

Fig. 1. Comparison of predicted and actual speed-up of program. In case of processor number more than 24 degradation of efficiency can be seen.

This allowed to change appreciably storage requirements reducing them to 2MB per logical process, out of dependency on the size of the difference equation.

The interpreter allowed to obtain the estimates of program's speed-up (Fig. 1) which were precise enough: the error did not exceed 10%, and was 5% in average.

For parallel program execution huge computational capability are used (hundreds of Gflps or more). Duration of program execution may achieve several days. Interpretation of a model, representing entire program, on a PC, which capacity comparable to just one node of a cluster, may take unacceptable amount of time. Two kinds of program model transformations are the solution of this problem. The meaning of the first one is that a resultant model contains control flow affected calculations only. As far as basic block work time defined a priori, such a separation of computations doesn't affect on program work time estimation.

The second transformation, so called reduction, intends changing the interpreted fragment of a program model on just one node, which uses already obtained program work time estimation. The reduction allows avoiding alternating interpretation of all the loops, essentially reducing interpreter overhead charges. In the limit these charges shouldn't depend on program input data.

The computation separation during our program interpretation allowed cutting speed vectors array, density array and so on from the model. This led to 2 MB memory requirements of every logical processor and made it possible to reduce most of the cycle iterations.

The degradation of efficiency may be explained by several reasons. First of all, the parallelization of the program hasn't done the most effective way. The version presented is just a pilot version, where two-dimension partition were used. The second, while number of processors is growing up and amount of calculation on one processor is falling down, we still waste a time on message passing. So for any matrix there will be some optimal number of processors, exceeding which degradation will take place.

5   Results of Numerical Modeling of 3D Tornado

The task (1)-(4) is solved in cube with $L = H = 1500$ m, N varying from 70 to 200, $U_0 = 1.5$ m/s, $R_0 = 300$ m, $z_{rgh} = 0.1$ m, $A_1 = 1000$ m^2/s; the dimensionless parameters of mesoscale interaction close to those used in [1]: $S_v = 0.5A_2/A_1 = 0.01$, $M_v = A_3/A_1 = 1$, $I_v = A_4/A_1 = 1$, $\Pi_m = 0.25(I_v+M_v)(1+\omega_{rel})J_{rel} = 750 \div 3000$, $\Pi_v = S_v(1+\omega_{rel}) = 100 \div 300$ ($\omega_{rel} = \omega_0 R_0/U_0$; $J_{rel} = J_{rel}/R_0^2$), $J_{bk}/J_0 = 0.05$, $\omega_{bk}/\omega_0 = 0.01$, and with the "standard atmosphere" thermodynamics used at the Earth surface [5]. Like in [1], under these conditions, the meso-to-macro energy ratio $(E_{mes}/E_{mac})_0 \sim \Pi_m\Pi_v$ is greater than the critical one, so a tornado arises: the wind energy E_{mac} increases abruptly (at the expense of the mesoenergy E_{mes}) to reach some peak value proportional to $\Pi_m\Pi_v$, and then slowly fades out. Total energy $E = E_{mac} + E_{mes} + E_{in}$ (E_{in} is the internal one) always decreases because the whole system is closed while the subsystem of macromotions of the wind is open since it interacts with the subsystem of mesoscale motions. This is the reason of IAV arising in the MTN as a self-organization phenomenon in open dissipative systems.

The particular features of tornado arising in 3D compressible dry-adiabatic atmosphere are considered for a concrete computation with $\Pi_m = 750$, $\Pi_v = 120$.

Initially (at $t_0 = 0$ s), zero vertical and radial wind velocities has been set, with only a calm local cyclonic wind with the maximum speed of 1.5 m/s. Typical for tornado vertical-radial circulation is formed in about a minute. At $t_5 = 51.7$ s, the uprising speed reaches 31 m/s at 600 m height, the maximum radial inflow ($--U_r$) is about 7 m/s at 500 m height and 230 m distance from center (with those for outflow, $+U_r$, respectively, 5 m/s at 1200 m height and 330 m radius). On the whole, a typical mushroom-like structure of tornado is formed in about a minute.

The 3D wind speed visualization (in VisAD library) at t_{16}=165.4 s is shown in Fig.2. The structure shown is permanent for few minutes, with the wind speed maximum varying, for the time of modeling, within 43 ÷ 35 m/s, then, it slowly decreases to 12 m/s in half an hour.

Fig. 2. 3D visualization of tornado at $t_{16} = 165.4$ s

Fig. 3. Hurricane in Montana, USA, 94- highway, Yellowstone River Valley. (Photo by A.V. Panshin © 2005).

Such a behavior is common for small and medium tornados (with measured intensiveness varying from T2 to T4): a rapid, within a minute, rose of the wind energy up to 0.8 of its maximum value, with slowly fading afterwards.

A local hurricane (or a tornado of T3 intensity) is shown in Fig. 3. The photo has been made in Montana, USA, in August of 2005. The phenomenon has been being observed for some minutes.

Both in temporal and scaled parameters, the near resemblance to the parallel computational results got with using the MTN task (1)-(4) is practically certain.

Note that such a phenomena can be rarely observed. A local hurricane (splashed down waterspout) with similar parameters has been observed near Gosport, Hampshire, England, 5.11.1999 [9]. When reaching the land, it quickly moves 750 m inside the Hill Head village, near Gosport, then, "after lifting up to the air a dozen of pigs", it died out in an hour.

On the whole, the numerical results on 3D tornado modeling in the Mesovortice Turbulence theory by Nikolaevsky (MTN) [6] describe the phenomena of tornado or local hurricane origination due to accumulated energy of mesovortices, even under the dry-adiabatic atmosphere hypothesis used in (1)-(4). As well as in a simplified model studied in [1], the excess energy of mesovortices $(E_{mes}/E_{mac})_0 \sim \Pi_m \Pi_v > (E_{mes}/E_{mac})_{cr} \sim 10000$ leads to IAV origination. When using a sufficient number of spatially distributed air velocity sensors and appropriate processing of the measurements, the excess energy of mesovortices can be measured at weather stations, giving a possibility for tornado and other local IAV forecast in a given region.

It is clear that once the dry-adiabatic atmosphere hypothesis accepted, it is impossible to model the slow processes of mesovortice activity accumulation leading to IAV arising. To make it possible, one should take into account the following factors: the solar radiation (i.e. heating of the underlying surface), the air moisture and pollution, sludging, the Earth's rotation, the mass and energy exchange with global vortices (i.e. hurricanes and tropycal cyclones), changes in climate, geo-electromagnetic effects, and so on [5]-[9].

6 Conclusion

The results were presented by the Institute of Physics of the Earth to Hydrometeorological Center of Russia/ as well as on Methods of Aerophysical Research 13th International Conference (ICMAR 2007).

Naturally, with all these factors get into consideration, the computational model comes to be more complicated. However, these factors seem to have a small affect upon the rapid process of tornado arising.

The main computational problems remain as follows: searching for the optimal partition of parallel data processing through the nodes, intermediate data traffics, and final processing for 1D ÷ 3D visualization.

The work has been supported by the RFBR, Project NN 05-01-00995 and 05-07-90308, and by the Pr. RAS, Project N 13-6-1/06.

Acknowledgments. The authors are grateful to M.D. Kalugin for developing 3D visualization and GUI, and to V.N. Nikolaevsky, V.A.Padaryan and S.A. Arsenyev for useful critics, discussions and support.

References

1. Arsenyev, S.A., Yu, G.A., Nikolaevskiy, V.N.: Self-Organization of Tornado and Hurricanes in Atmospheric Currents with Meso-Scale Eddies. Doclady Earth Science 396(4), 588–593 (2004)
2. Nikolaevskiy, V.N.: Vortexes and waves. M: Mir, pp. 266–335 (1984)
3. Ivannikov, V., Gaissaryan, S., Avetisyan, A., Padaryan, V.: Improving properties of a parallel program in ParJava Environment. In: Dongarra, J.J., Laforenza, D., Orlando, S. (eds.) Recent Advances in Parallel Virtual Machine and Message Passing Interface. LNCS, vol. 2840, pp. 491–494. Springer, Heidelberg (2003)
4. Fletcher, C.A.J.: Computational Techniques for Fluid Dynamics. Springer, Heidelberg (1991)
5. Hrgian, A.H.: Fizika Atmosfery (in Russian). M. Izd-vo MSU, 240 (1986)
6. Nikolaevskiy, V.N.: Angular Momentum in Geophysical Turbulence: Continuum. Spatial Averaging Method. Kluwer (Springer), Dordrecht 245 (2003)
7. Khain, A.P., Sutyrin, G.G.: Tropical Cyclones and its Interaction with the Ocean (in Russian). L. Gidrometeizdat, 272 (1983)
8. Emtsev, B.T.: Tekhnicheskaya Gidromekhanika (in Russian). M. Mashinostroeniye, 463 (1978)
9. Anthony, G.: Tornado With a Measured Intensity of T3 at Hill Head, Hampshire, 5. J.Meteorol. 25(254), 361–367 (2000)

Dynamic Strategy of Placement of the Replicas in Data Grid

Ghalem Belalem[1] and Farouk Bouhraoua[2]

[1] Dept. of Computer Science, Faculty of Sciences,
University of Oran - Es Senia, Oran, Algeria
Ghalem1dz@Yahoo.fr
[2] Institute of Computer Science, Faculty of Science and Engineering,
University of Mostaganem, Algeria
farouk622000@yahoo.fr

Abstract. Grid computing is a type of parallel and distributed systems, that is designed to provide pervasive and reliable access to data and computational resources over wide are network. Data Grids connect a collect of geographically distributed computers and storage resources located in different parts of the world to facilitate sharing of data and resources. These grids are concentrated on the reduction of the execution time of the applications that require a great number of processing cycles by the computer. In such environment, these advantages are not possible unless by the use of the replication. This later is considered as an important technique to reduce the cost of access to the data in grid. In this present paper, we present our contribution to a cost model whose objective is to reduce the cost of access to replicated data. These costs depend on many factors like the bandwidth, data size, network latency and the number of the read/ write operations.

Keywords: Data Grid, Replication, Data placement, Cost model, CERN.

1 Introduction

Today, the utility of many internet services is limited by the availability rather than the execution. The replication is the most used approach to offer the highest availability of data. The experiment on the distributed systems show that the reproduction promotes high data availability, low bandwidth consumption, increased fault tolerance and improved scalability [1]. The replication is the process of creation and placement of the copies of entities software. The phase of creation consists in reproducing the structure and the state of the replicated entities, whereas the phase of placement consists in choosing the suitable slot of this new duplication, according to the objectives of the replication. The replication cost is often linked to the deployment cost of the reproduction to the dynamic creation cost of the reproduction and to the emplacement replication costs towards the client. In our approach, the placement algorithm of the replicas was designed by the cost model, formulated as an optimization problem that

V. Malyshkin (Ed.): PaCT 2007, LNCS 4671, pp. 496–506, 2007.

reduces at least the global cost of access to data, further to a focusing on the influence of the read/ write operations on the replication cost (report: number of readings, number of writings) in grids at a given moment. What will facilitate us to take a decision for the creation or the moving of replicas to adequate sites as well as their deleting. In order to evaluate this cost model, a simulator called *"GREP-SIM"* was developed and implemented under a tree hierarchical topology inspired from *CERN* data grid architecture (the European Organization for Nuclear Research) [3]. The results show that the performances of the replications depend strongly on the replicas emplacement, and the number of the read/write operations effected on these replicas.

The remainder of the paper is organized as follows. In the second section we presents an overview of some costs models for the data replications. The third section will be reserved for our contribution in a cost model for replication in data grids. Experimentation results of our model on tree topology are the object of the fourth section. Finally, section five will be reserved for the conclusion and some future works.

2   Related Works

The primary reason to use a cost model is the ability to take optimal decisions for accessing to data replicas in the future use. The execution of such multidimensional and complex optimizations in a centralized way is very difficult, since the planning domain (attributes of resources) is very huge. The optimisation service of grid must be scalable in items of the number of network nodes (tens, hundreds, or even thousands) [4]. The grid is a dynamic environment where the resources status can change without any warning. By employing a model, we can exploit this dynamism to take decisions during the execution time of the work. Recently, there has been a noteworthy interest for the proposition of cost models in the grids environment.

The presented works in [5], in order to insure the efficient and rapid access to enormous and largely distributed data, the authors suggest a set of services and protocols of replication management, which offer higher data availability, a low bandwidth consumption and a great faults tolerance. Replication decisions have been taken according to cost model, which evaluate the data access cost and execution gain. This model is function of many parameters just like the response time, the bandwidth, and the reproduction costs accumulated by execution time. To guarantee the scalability, the duplications are organized combining of hierarchical and flat topologies. This suggested model based on Fat-Tree topology [6], where the bandwidth increase leaves towards the root. Very interesting results were produced by the simulator *NS* [7]. The cost model proposed in[8] is well adapted to machines *MIMD*. However, it can't be applied to machines of *SIMD* type where the performances analysis in communication is more complex, because of the difficulty of separating the calculus. This model is according to routing time of a message between processors, initiation time (start up) and bandwidth. This work has shown that routing time of a message and the initiation time have an important influence on the choice of processors interconnection topology, data organisation, load balancing, the number of acceptable synchronization and the messages size. For the suggested model $CASEY$ in [9] which concentrate on data placement problem. It depends on the sites number, the read number effected by a site by a time unity called: read volume by site, the cost of a read by a given site on the copy placed in another site, the write number effected by a given site by a time unity, write cost realized by a given site of the copy placed on another site. Finally, the storage cost, by time unity, of a copy placed on a given site. The optimal placement returns back to minimize a global objective function made up of parameters group described in above passage. This model is not well adapted on a large-scale environment, because it belongs to the NP-complete problems class. Extra hypothesis can simplify it neglecting storage and write costs.

3   Cost Model and Replicas Placement

A possible data distribution of important sizes consists in replicating them so as to place them on a set of servers. The interest of this fragmentation and this distribution is to dispatch up the load on different servers, and to avoid the bottlenecks appearance. Many placement strategies can be used in these types of systems [12,11,10]. In this paper, we have used a distribution on a tree network topology.

3.1   Grid Topology

The data grid topology used as a support for the proposed model is described below in figure 1, and inspired of the architecture $CERN$. It is made up of 5 levels: the root (level 0), three sublevels that contain nodes (level 1 till 3), and the last level is for leaves (level 4). All the nodes including the root, representing the servers, can have data replicas, except the last level of the leaves, which represents the clients from where the requests come.

In this topology, every node admits one child or many except the leaves, and every node has only one immediate father except the root.

3.2   A Cost Model

The replication cost model suggested in our approach is designed as an optimization problem of replicas placement, which reduces at least the sum of the access cost in a grid, basing on the described parameters in *(Table. 1)*.

Let $n \in R_d$, the nearest node serving a set of clients that query (read and write) data d. We are going to calculate the global access cost of data d situated in the node n, which is the sum of: transfer cost of data d, processing calculus cost of operation (write or read) by the node n, and the propagation cost of data d updating towards the other nodes belonging to R_d.

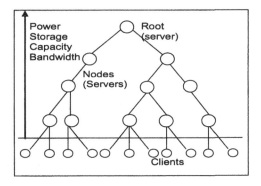

Fig. 1. Logical topology of the grid $CERN$

Table 1. Parameters used in the model

Parameter	Description
pn	The immediate father of a node n
R_d	The group of nodes containing a replica of data d
$BW(n)$	Bandwidth between the nodes n and pn; ($BW(n)$ =1/ bandwidth(n, pn))
$Size(d)$	Size of data d
$Way_d(n_1, n_2)$	A set of nodes met along the way of node n_1 till node n_2, except node n_2
TE_{dn}	Processing cost of write operation on data d situated at the node n
TL_{dn}	Processing cost of read operation on data d situated at the node n
NE_{dn}	Write number affected on the data d passed through the node n
NL_{dn}	Read number affected on the data d passed through by the node n

Let be $CT_d(n_1, n_2)$ transfer cost of data d from node n_1 to node n_2, defined by

$$CT_d(n_1, n_2) = Size(d) \sum_i BW(i); \qquad i \in Way_d(n_1, n_2) \qquad (1)$$

To maintain the replicated data coherence, we use strict protocol ROWA [2], from where CU_{dn} : propagation cost of updating data d situated at node n.

$$CU_{dn} = \sum_k CT_d(n, k); \qquad k \in R_d - \{n\} \qquad (2)$$

When a client c interrogates data d located in the closest node n, the costs are evaluated to:
CE_{dn} : write cost on data d situated at node n.

$$CE_{dn} = CT_d(c, n) + TE_{dn} + CU_{dn} \qquad (3)$$

CL_{dn}: read cost on data d situated at node n,

$$CL_{dn} = CT_d(c, n) + TL_{dn} \qquad (4)$$

Let's admit, in what follows, that all the nodes of the same level have the same characteristics (power and high storage capacity), and the same bandwidth between a node and its sons. Therefore, we can deduce that the write cost of the node $n(CE_{dn})$ is fixed for the interrogations of descending clients (leaves) of this node n. The same for the read cost (CL_{dn}). Consequently, we can evaluate the global access cost:

$CostG_{dn}$: global access cost to data d situated at node n,

$$CostG_{dn} = NL_{dn} * CL_{dn} + NE_{dn} * CE_{dn} \tag{5}$$

The optimization problem of the global cost function will be to find the minimum cost of N servers containing asked data d, we will have:

$$Cost\_Min = \underbrace{Min}_{i \in N} \quad \{NL_{di} * CL_{di} + NE_{di} * CE_{di}\} \tag{6}$$

3.3   Placement Algorithm

A node can serve several clients that formulate requests on data, when this last is the nearest node to them containing a reply of this data. Going by the described cost model above, placement algorithm takes the decision of moving, creating or even deleting the replicas. This decision is taken according to the number of writings and readings effected on the data replica d situated in node n by the clients in a given time. It has to be noticed that in case of only reads are occurred by clients ($NE_{di} = 0 \forall i \in R_d$), it is evident that The best solution is the one where all the replicas will be placed on all the nodes of the before last level (level 3). Yet, for the case where exist writes only ($NL_{di} = 0 \forall i \in R_d$), the best solution is to have no replica. This is because of updating propagations.

Let $Asc(n)$ a set of ascendants (ancestors) of node n and $Des(n)$ a set of descendants of node n. Let's suppose at the given moment, that the global cost $CostG_{dn}$ is the smallest cost among the ones of $Asc(n) + Des(n)$. The increase of the number of writings NE_{dn} by a certain value (to be identified) modifies the least cost which will be equal to another cost of node an $Asc(n)$ ($Cost\_Min = CostG_{dan}$), while the increase of the number of reading by a certain value (to be identified) modifies the least cost value which will be equal to another cost of node $d_n \in Des(n)$ ($Cost\_Min = CostG_{ddn}$). Therefore, the aim is to find the interval of NE_{dn} values and the interval of the NL_{dn} values so that the cost $CostG_{dn}$ stays always the lowest ($Cost\_Min = CostG_{dn}$), in other words, the replica of data d will always be situated at the node n. This leads us to find a trade-off between the number of writings NE_{dn} and the number of readings NL_{dn}.

Let T_{dn} the ratio of the read number on the write number occurred on data d situated in node n.

$T_{dn} = NL_{dn}/NE_{dn}$

So that the replica of the data d stays in the node n and doesn't migrate in the node pn father of the node n, it's necessary that $CostG_{dn} < CostG_{dpn}$

i.e.: $NL_{dn} * CL_{dn} + NE_{dn} * CE_{dn} < NL_{dpn} * CL_{dpn} + NE_{dpn} * CE_{dpn}$

With: $NL_{dn} = NL_{dpn}$, $NE_{dn} = NE_{dpn}$ and $T_{dn} = NL_{dn}/NE_{dn}$

After the resolution of this equation with NL_{dn} and NE_{dn} as unknowns, we obtain:

$$T_{dn} > \frac{CE_{dn} - CE_{dpn}}{CL_{dpn} - CL_{dn}}$$

Let $Son(n)$ a set of nodes, which are at the same moment the immediate sons of node n , the ancestors of clients that interrogates data d, and which don't contain replica of the data d.

However, so that the replica of the data d stays in the node n and doesn't migrate in the nodes sn immediate sons of node n ($\forall sn \in Son(n)$), it's necessary that $CostG_{dn} < CostG_{dsn}$ i.e.:

$$NL_{dn} * CL_{dn} + NE_{dn} * CE_{dn} < \sum_{sn \in Son(n)} NL_{dsp} * CL_{dsn} + \sum_{sn \in Son(n)} NE_{dsn} * CE_{dsn}$$

With : $T_{dn} = NL_{dn}/NE_{dn}$,

$$NL_{dn} = \sum_{sn \in Son(n)} NL_{dsn}$$

and

$$NE_{dn} = \sum_{sn \in Son(n)} NE_{dsn}$$

After the resolution of this equation with NL_{dn} and NE_{dn} as unknowns, we obtain: $T_{dn} < \frac{CE_{dsn} - CE_{dn}}{CL_{dn} - CL_{dsn}}$

So that $CostG_{dn}$ the cost of node n be the smallest cost of all nodes belonging to $Asc(n) + Des(n) + n$

$$CostG_{dn} = min\{NL_{di} * CL_{di} + NE_{di} * CE_{di}\}; \qquad \forall i \in Asc(n) + Des(n) + n$$

T_{dn} must check the following equations:

$$\left\{ \begin{array}{lll} \forall s_n \in Son(n) & & \\ \text{If} \quad n = root & \text{Then} & T_{dn} < \frac{CE_{dsn} - CE_{dn}}{CL_{dn} - CL_{dsn}} \\ \text{If} \quad n \in before-last-Level & \text{Then} & T_{dn} \geq \frac{CE_{dn} - CE_{dpn}}{CL_{dpn} - CL_{dn}} \\ \text{Else} \quad \frac{CE_{dn} - CE_{dpn}}{CL_{dpn} - CL_{dn}} \leq T_{dn} < \frac{CE_{dsn} - CE_{dn}}{CL_{dn} - CL_{dsn}} & & \end{array} \right\} \quad (7)$$

Let a replicas distribution on the grid in a given moment, and let the cost of the node n the smallest cost of all nodes belonging to $Asc(n) + Des(n) + n(Cost_{M}in = CostG_{dn})$. Placement algorithm applied on the node n whose its T_{dn} value has changed will be as follows:

Algorithm 1. PLACEMENT

1: x,z : node
2: $x \leftarrow n$
3: **if** T_{dx} value do not check equation 7 **then**
4:
5:     **if** $T_{dx} < (CE_{dx} - CE_{dpx})/(CL_{dpx} - CL_{dx})$ **then**
6:
7:         **while** $T_{dx} < (CE_{dx} - CE_{dpx})/(CL_{dpx} - CL_{dx})$ **do**
8:             $NE_{dx} \leftarrow NE_{dx} + NE_{dpx}$
9:             $NL_{dx} \leftarrow NL_{dx} + NL_{dpx}$
10:        **end while**
11:        Move the replica of node n towards the node x
12:        **for all** $((z \in Des(x))$ **and** $(z$ is server of $d))$ **do**
13:            $OldCostG_{dx} \leftarrow CalculateCostG_{dx}$
14:            $NE_{dx} \leftarrow NE_{dx} + NE_{dz}$
15:            $NL_{dx} \leftarrow NL_{dx} + NL_{dz}$
16:            $NewCostG_{dx} \leftarrow CalculateCostG_{dx}$
17:            **if** $NewCostG_{dx} \leq OldCostG_{dx}$ **then**
18:                Delete the replica of data d from node z
19:            **end if**
20:        **end for**
21:    **else**
22:        **for all** $z \in Son(x)$ **do**
23:            Create a replica of data d on node z
24:        **end for**
25:        Delete the replica of data d from node x
26:    **end if**
27: **end if**

After the arrival of the requests, we check the T_{di} values $\forall d$ and $\forall i \in R_d$. Thus, according to T_{di}'s values, we take decisions of the emplacement of concerned replicas. We notice that the suppression of replicas, which the requests number produced by the clients for these replicas is inferior at a given threshold, gives rise to a clear and remarkable amelioration in the global access cost to the grid data.

4   Simulation

The presented cost model seems to be very well adapted to hierarchical architectures. A simulator called "*GREP-SIM*" was developed in order to evaluate this model. This simulator allows us to generate a hierarchical topology of a tree inspired of data grid architecture *CERN*. In this simulator, every node in the network is able to specify its storage capacity, its processor performance, the local replicas, and a detailed history of the requests passing through this node (the passage of a request by this node at the time of its routing from a client toward its server node), where we can associate two variables for every data in the grid specifying respectively the read and write number occurred on this data and that are passed through this node. This detailed history of nodes will indicate us the number of the produced requests by every client on every data. If the number of produced requests on data exceeds a certain threshold, the concerned client will be considered as the best client for this data. Many algorithms were proposed for the emplacement of replicas in the closest server to the best client, by using several solutions to select the most appropriate server to contain its replicas [13]. In order to compare our model, we shall use two other placement models. The first one is based on the best client algorithm where the replica will be placed on the closest node of this client [14]. The second one is based on the common father algorithm. Contrary to the first model, which favours the best client and penalizes another client, which have produced a number of requests exceeding the threshold, the common father place the replica on the closest common node of the two clients.

4.1   Simulated Grid Model

The topology of simulated grid, described in the following schema in *figure. 2*, is compound of 15 nodes. A root, 14 intermediary nodes and 16 leaves representing the clients. The bandwidth improves from inferior level to the superior one.

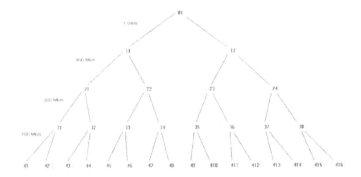

Fig. 2. Simulated model of the Grid topology

4.2   Experimentations and Results

The experimentations were held on definite simulation parameters in *table. 2*.

In the beginning, a random distribution of replicas has been done and saved along the simulation. The simulator calculates the response times of every request for this distribution. Then, it recalculates the responses time for the same requests but by applying models of the best client, common father and finally our model, which we have named it, the best ancestor. For the same distribution, we execute five different experimentations (scenarios), where the read and write numbers produced by the clients are modified, as it is mentioned in the following *table. 3*.

Table 2. Simulation parameters

Data number	4
Data size	From 1 Gb to 4 GB
Replicas number	From 1to 8 per data
Requests number	800
Threshold	50

Table 3. Read/Write per scenario

Scenario	Read number	Write number
1	800	0
2	770	30
3	740	60
4	600	200
5	450	350

The obtained results are illustrated by two graphs. The *figure. 3* represents the average time response per scenario and the *figure. 5* represents the average time response per clients of the third scenario.

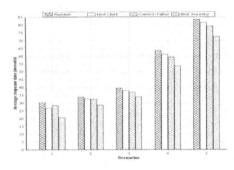

Fig. 3. Average time response per scenario

Fig. 4. Average time response per scenario after suppression

The results show that the global access cost in the grid is clearly improved when using our model. Indeed, we notice in the first graph a decrease of 11,41% of the average time response of this model compared to the common father model, of 12,72% compared to the model of the best client and of 16,51% compared with the random distribution.

We were anxious to present the second graph *(figure. 5)* to show some exceptional cases that can appear. For instance, the averages time response for the clients 413 and 416 that are favoured by the model of the best client are the best times, versus the clients 414 and 415 that are penalized.

During the simulation study, we have noticed that if we make dynamic suppression of replicas weakly requested (the requests number produced on these replicas doesn't exceed a certain threshold), the performances will improve even more. After the suppression of the replicas that the request number produced on them doesn't exceed a threshold equal 10, the results presented in *figure. 4* show a decrease of 13,39% of the average time response of this model compared to the common father model, of 14,78% compared to the model of the best client and de 18,37% compared with the random distribution.

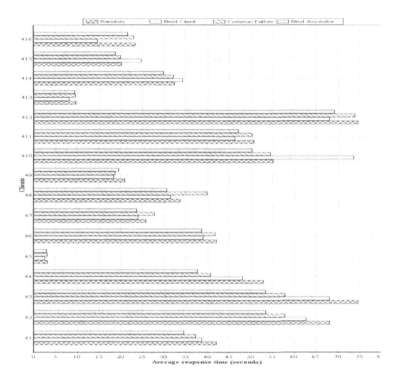

Fig. 5. Average time response per clients

5   Conclusion and Future Works

In this work, we have studied the problem of the global access cost in a grid system for the replicated data. The problem was formulated such as an optimization subject of a cost model linked mainly to two cost functions: read cost and write cost by node, and linked to two essential parameters: reads number and writes number by node. So, this model allowed us to conceive an efficient algorithm of dynamic placement of replicas. The logical data grid model is based on a tree architecture where the bandwidth is variable according the tree levels and the nodes of the same level have the same characteristics. The results show that the use of the dynamic replication algorithm based on our model improves the access performances to data in the grid. These results are promising. Nevertheless, they are based on specific work environments. In the future work we project to validate our model on real data grids by implementing the proposed approach in a more realistic environment such as Globus. Furthermore, this approach studies will be focused on the contribution of the prediction of the requests types'arrival by using the statistic laws (normal distribution, Poisson distribution,...).

References

1. Deris, M.M., Abawajy, J.H., Suzuri, H.M.: An Efficient Replicated Data Access Approach for Large-Scale Distributed Systems, IEEE International Symposium CCGrid 2004, Chicago, Illinois, USA (April 19-22, 2004)
2. Goel, S., Sharda, H., Taniar, D.: Replica Synchronization in Grid Databases. Int. Journal Web and Grid Services 1(1), 87–112 (2005)
3. The European Organization for Nuclear Physics CERN DataGrid Project, http://grid.web.cern.ch/grid/
4. Foster, I., Kesselman, C., Tuecke, S.: The Anatomy of the Grid: Enabling Scalable Virtual Organizations. Int. Journal Supercomputer Applications 15(3) (2003)
5. Lamehamedi, H., Szymanski, B., Deelman, E.: Data Replication Strategies in Grid Environments. In: Proc. 5th International Conference on Algorithms and Architecture for Parallel Processing, ICA3PP'2002, Bejing, China, pp. 378–383 (2002)
6. Leiserson, C.H.: Fat-Trees: Universal Networks for Hardware-Efficient Supercomputing. IEEE Trans. on Comp. C-34(10), 892–901 (1985)
7. NS Network Simulator, http://www.mash.cs.berkeley.edu/ns
8. Parhamu, B.: Introduction to Parallel Processing: Algorithms and Architectures, Plenum (1999)
9. Raynal, M.: Gestion des Donnees Reparties: Problemes et Protocoles. Tome3: Introduction aux principes des systemes repartis, Eyrolles, France (1992)
10. Michalewicz, Z.: Genetic Algorithms + Data Structures = Evolution Programs, 3rd edn. Springer, Heidelberg (1996)
11. Xu, J., Li, B., Lun Lee, D.: Placement Problems for Transparent Data Replication Proxy Services. IEEE Journal on Selected Areas in Communications 20(7) (September 2002)
12. Milojicic, D.: Peer to Peer Techbology, HP Labs Technical Report, HPL-2002-57, http://www.hpl.hp.com/techreports/2002/HPL-2002-57.html
13. Guyton, J.D., Michael, F.S.: Locating Nearby Copies of Replicated Internet Servers, University of Colorado, TR CU-CS-762-95
14. Ranganathan, K., Foster, I.: Identifying Dynamic Replication Strategies for a High Performance Data Grid. In: Proc. of the International Grid Computing Workshop, Denver, CO (November 2001)

ISO: Comprehensive Techniques Toward Efficient GEN_BLOCK Redistribution with Multidimensional Arrays

Shih-Chang Chen and Ching-Hsien Hsu[*]

Department of Computer Science and Information Engineering
Chung Hua University, Hsinchu 300 Taiwan
scc@sclab.csie.chu.edu.tw, chh@chu.edu.tw

Abstract. Runtime data redistribution is usually required in parallel algorithms to enhance data locality, achieve dynamic load balancing and reduce remote data access on distributed memory multicomputers. In this paper, we present comprehensive techniques to implement GEN_BLOCK redistribution in parallelizing compilers, including *Indexing* schemes for communication sets generation, a contention-free communication *Scheduling* algorithm and an *Optimization* technique for improving communication efficiency. Both theoretical analysis and experimental results show that the proposed techniques can efficiently perform GEN_BLOCK data redistribution during runtime.

1 Introduction

The data-parallel programming model extends sequential programming language with parallel constructs for handling large aggregates of data such as arrays. To efficiently execute a program written with this paradigm, appropriate data distribution is critical to the performance. Appropriate distribution of data can balance the computational load, improve data locality, and reduce inter-processor communication. However, in many data parallel algorithms, an optimal distribution of data depends on the characteristics of an algorithm, as well as on the attributes of the target architecture. Because the optimal distribution changes from one phase to another, data redistribution turns out to be a critical operation during runtime.

In general, data redistribution can be classified into two categories, regular and irregular. Regular redistribution employs BLOCK, CYCLIC, or BLOCK-CYCLIC(c) to specify array decomposition while irregular data redistribution employs user-defined function to specify size of data segments.

To map unequal sized segments of arrays onto processors, High Performance Fortran version 2 (HPF2) provides GEN_BLOCK directive to facilitate generalized block distributions. The following code segment demonstrates an example of High Performance Fortran version 2 (HPF2) irregular data redistribution with GEN_BLOCK format. The source and destination distributions are defined by *old* = /22, 23, 46, 9/ and *new* = /8, 47, 21, 24/, respectively, where *old* and *new* are declared as templates for

---

[*] Corresponding author.

V. Malyshkin (Ed.): PaCT 2007, LNCS 4671, pp. 507–515, 2007.

mapping data segments onto processors. Consequently, the DISTRIBUTE directive decomposes array A onto 4 processors according to the *old* parameters in the source distribution phase. The REDISTRIBUTE directive realigns data elements in array A with processors according to *new* parameters in the destination distribution phase.

> PARAMETER (*old* = /22, 23, 46, 9/)
> !HPF$ PROCESSORS P(4)
>   REAL A(100), *new* (4)
> !HPF$ DISTRIBUTE A (GEN_BLOCK(*old*)) onto **P**
> !HPF$ DYNAMIC
>   *new* = /8, 47, 21, 24/
> !HPF$ REDISTRIBUTE A (GEN_BLOCK(*new*))

In general, data redistribution has two important issues to be handled in order to achieve good algorithm performance during runtime, the indexing scheme and communication scheduling approach. In recent years, most researches focused on proposing different communication scheduling heuristics to minimize communication costs of irregular data redistribution during runtime. Without precedent, this study integrates comprehensive techniques to implement GEN_BLOCK (irregular) redistribution, including an *Indexing* scheme for generating communication sets with multi-dimensional arrays, a communication *Scheduling* method, termed as Two-Phase Degree Reduction (*TPDR*) algorithm, for GEN_BLOCK redistribution, and an *Optimization* technique, named Local Message Reduction (*LMR*), for enhancing efficiency of the algorithm.

2   Related Work

Techniques for dynamic data redistribution are usually classified into regular and irregular instances. There are many researches have been done with regular block-cyclic data distribution format. Due to the different definition of GEN_BLOCK, methods on irregular problems can be varied from regular ones.

For regular instances, the *PITFALLS* algorithm [10] is a representative research for communication sets identification. Similar researches include algorithms for BLOCK-CYCLIC data redistribution between processor sets proposed by Park *et al.* [8], the algorithmic redistribution methods for BLOCK-CYCLIC decompositions proposed by Dongarra *et al.* [9], the *Generalized Basic-Cycle Calculation* method [3] and redistribution algorithms using MPI User-Defined Datatypes proposed by Bai *et al.* [1].

For communication efficiency, the communication scheduling technique proposed by Dongarra *et al.* [2] is a representative research. Other techniques include the multiphase redistribution strategy proposed by Kaushik *et al.* [6] to minimize message startup cost and the processor mapping techniques for minimizing data transmission overheads presented in [4] and [7].

Researches on irregular array redistribution include data indexing and communication optimization. For data indexing category, a symbolic analysis method was proposed by Guo *et al.* [5] to generate messages and reduce communication cost. For communication efficiency, Lee *et al.* [7] presented a logical processor reordering algorithm on irregular array redistribution. This algorithm reordered processor id to reduce communication overheads. Guo *et al.* [11] proposed a divide-and-conquer scheduling algorithm for performing irregular array redistribution. Yook and Park proposed a relocation scheduling algorithm [13]. It was a two-phase scheduling algorithm which consisted of a list scheduling phase and a reallocation phase. Hui *et al.* [12] proposed an improved algorithm based on relocation algorithm. However, it reports very high algorithm complexity due to the constitution of divide-and-conquer algorithm and the relocation process.

3 Communication Sets Identification

3.1 Single Dimensional Array

Definition 1: Given a $S = (s_1, s_2, ..., s_m)$ to $D = (d_1, d_2, ..., d_m)$ GEN_BLOCK redistribution over m processors, the parameters $s_1, s_2, ..., s_m$ and $d_1, d_2, ..., d_m$ are quantities of source data and destination data for processors $P_1, P_2, ..., P_m$, respectively. For source processor SP_i, the lower bound and upper bound of source data denoted by SD^l_i and SD^u_i, are defined as $SD^l_i = 1 + \sum_{k=0}^{i-1} s_k$ and $SD^u_i = \sum_{k=0}^{i} s_k$. For destination processor DP_j, the lower bound and upper bound of destination data denoted by DD^l_j and DD^u_j, are defined as $DD^l_j = 1 + \sum_{k=0}^{i-1} d_k$ and $DD^u_j = \sum_{k=0}^{i} d_k$.

Definition 2: Given a $S = (s_1, s_2, ..., s_m)$ to $D = (d_1, d_2, ..., d_m)$ GEN_BLOCK redistribution over m processors, for source processor SP_i, its destination processor set denoted by DPS_i, is the set of destination processors with consecutive ids start from DPS_i^l and end at processor DPS_i^u; for destination processor DP_j, its source processor set denoted by SPS_j, is the set of source processors with consecutive ids start from SPS_j^l and end at processor SPS_j^u;

According to the this definition, DPS_i and SPS_j can be formulated as follows,

$$DPS_i^l = \{ j \mid DD^l_j \leq SD^l_i \leq DD^u_j \}, \quad DPS_i^u = \{ j \mid DD^l_j \leq SD^u_i \leq DD^u_j \},$$
$$SPS_j^l = \{ i \mid SD^l_i \leq DD^l_j \leq SD^u_i \}, \quad SPS_j^u = \{ i \mid SD^l_i \leq DD^u_j \leq SD^u_i \}$$

To simplify the presentation, table 1 summarizes notations used in this paper and its corresponding terminology.

Table 1. Mapping table of notations used in this paper

Abbreviation	Full Name
SD	Source Data
DD	Destination Data
DPS	Destination Processor Set
SPS	Source Processor Set

Fig. 1 shows two distribution schemes on array A[1:100] over 4 processors. Scheme I represents array decomposition for SP_i and scheme II represents array decomposition for DP_i. Parameters in Fig. 1 are the quantity of data segment that will be distributed to corresponding processors.

Distribution Scheme I (for Source Processor)					Distribution Scheme II (for Destination Processor)			
Processor ID	SP_0	SP_1	SP_2	SP_3	Processor ID	DP_0	DP_1	DP_2	DP_3
Data size	22	23	46	9	Data size	8	47	21	24

(a)   (b)

Fig. 1. Irregular array distribution schemes. (a) Distribution scheme for source processors. (b) Distribution scheme for destination processor.

To facilitate identification of communication sets, array S and array D are associated with a dummy head entry, storing parameters in scheme I and scheme II, respectively. Accordingly, for example, $S = \{0, 22, 23, 46, 9\}$ and $D = \{0, 8, 47, 21, 24\}$.

Applying the above definitions, equations (1) and (2) can be used to generate communication messages between source and destination processors. Given a $S = (s_1, s_2, ..., s_m)$ to $D = (d_1, d_2, ..., d_m)$ GEN_BLOCK redistribution on a one-dimensional array A, for source processor SP_i, the message to be sent to destination processor DP_j is a consecutive data segment, can be formulated as

$$msg_{i \to j}^{send} = (x, y) \tag{1}$$

where $x < y$.[1]

$x = \max(1 + \sum_{a=0}^{i} S[a], 1 + \sum_{b=0}^{j} D[b])$, is the left index of the message in local array of SP_i.

$y = \min(\sum_{a=0}^{i+1} S[a], \sum_{b=0}^{j+1} D[b])$, is the right index of the message in local array of SP_i.

For destination processor DP_j, the message to be received from source processor SP_i can be formulated as follows,

$$msg_{j \leftarrow i}^{receive} = (p, q) \tag{2}$$

where $p < q$.[2]

$p = \max(1 + \sum_{a=0}^{j} S[a], 1 + \sum_{b=0}^{i} D[b])$, is the left index of the message in local array of DP_j.

---

[1] if $x>=y$, means SP_i does not need to send message to DP_j.
[2] if $p>=q$, means DP_j does not need to receive message from SP_i.

$q = \min(\sum_{a=0}^{j+1} S[a], \sum_{b=0}^{i+1} D[b])$, is the right index of the message in local array of DP_j.

Because of no repetition communication pattern in irregular GEN_BLOCK array redistribution, according to definition 2, Equations (3) and (4) can be used to calculate the total number of messages for SP_i to send and for DP_j to receive.

$$|DPS_i| = DPS_i^u - DPS_i^l + 1 \tag{3}$$

$$|SPS_j| = SPS_j^u - SPS_j^l + 1 \tag{4}$$

3.2 Multi-dimensional Array

For the reason of simplicity, we use 2-D equation model to explain the multi-dimensional indexing method. Following is an example, given a 2*2 processor grid and distribution schemes (6, 4) in the first dimension and (2, 3) in the second dimension, representing the source distribution scheme. Fig. 2 shows that data block $(1, 6)*(1, 2)$ is allocated to P_{00}, the data block $(7, 10)*(1, 2)$ is allocated to P_{10} and so on.

Fig. 3 shows another example of GEN_BLOCK distribution, representing destination distribution with distribution scheme (8, 2) in the first dimension and (4, 1) in the second dimension, denoted by dotted lines. By overlapping the two distribution layouts in Fig. 2 and Fig. 3, it results nine separated data blocks, $m_{00}, m_{01}, .., m_{22}$. The data block m_{00} is allocated to P_{00} in both source and destination distributions. Similarly, m_{22} belongs to P_{11} in both source and destination distributions. Unlike m_{00}, data blocks m_{01}, m_{10} and m_{11} are allocated to P_{01}, P_{10} and P_{11}, respectively, in the source distribution and will all be allocated to P_{00} in the destination phase. Similar situation on m_{12} and m_{21}, the two blocks are both allocated to P_{11} in source phase and will be redistributed to P_{01} and P_{10} in the destination phase.

Similar to 1-D scheme, the $Sx = \{0, 6, 4\}$ and $Dx = \{0, 8, 2\}$ are arrays for representing source and destination distribution parameters in the first dimension; $Sy = \{0, 2, 3\}$ and $Dy = \{0, 4, 1\}$ are arrays for representing distribution parameters in the second dimension. Therefore, given a $S = (Sx\{\}, Sy\{\})$ to $D = (Dx\{\}, Dy\{\})$ GEN_BLOCK redistribution on a two-dimensional array A, for source processor SP_{xy}, the message to be sent to destination processor DP_{xy} can be formulated as

$$msg_{xy \rightarrow x'y'}^{send} = ((r, s), (t, u)), \text{ where } r \leq s \text{ and } t \leq u \tag{5}$$

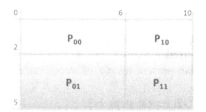 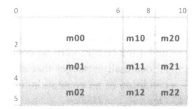

Fig. 2. 2-D array decomposition with GEN_BLOCK distribution

Fig. 3. The generated messages for 2-D GEN_BLOCK redistribution

$$r = \max(1+\sum_{a=0}^{x} Sx[a], 1+\sum_{b=0}^{x'} Dx[b]), \quad s = \min(\sum_{a=0}^{x+1} Sx[a], \sum_{b=0}^{x'+1} Dx[b]),$$

$$t = \max(1+\sum_{a=0}^{y} Sy[a], 1+\sum_{b=0}^{y'} Dy[b]), \quad u = \min(\sum_{a=0}^{y+1} Sy[a], \sum_{b=0}^{y'+1} Dy[b]).$$

For example, data blocks that SP_{10} sends to DP_{00}, DP_{01}, DP_{10} and DP_{11} are ((7, 8), (1, 2)), ((9, 10), (1, 2)), ((7, 8), (5, 2)) and ((9, 10), (5, 2)), respectively. Because of the validation conditions are $r \le s$ and $t \le u$, only $m_{01} = ((7, 8), (1, 2))$ and $m_{02} = ((9, 10), (1, 2))$ are valid. Thus SP_{10} sends m_{01} and m_{02} to DP_{00} and DP_{01}, respectively. Note that although Equation (5) is a 2-D indexing scheme, it can be extended and applied to multi-dimensional instances.

4 Communication Scheduling

Prior to demonstrate the proposed scheduling algorithm, we first clarify common restrictions in this problem. In general, to avoid communication conflicts, no two or more messages sent/received by the same processor can be scheduled in the same communication step.

Definition 3: Given a directed bipartite graph $G = (V, E)$ and vertex $v_i \in V$, the degree of vertex v_i denoted by *degree*(v_i), is the sum of in-degree or out-degree of v_i. *Degree*$_{max}$ denotes the maximum degree(v_i).

The *TPDR* scheduling algorithm is consisted of two parts. The first part is a degree reduction iteration phase which can be applied when *Degree*$_{max} > 2$. The second part is an adjustable coloring mechanism, which employs a coloring method and an adjustable mechanism to arrange communications remained in G, used when *Degree*$_{max} \le 2$. Since the optimality of graph theory, this phase is guaranteed to be optimal in terms of minimum number of communication steps and total costs.

The degree reduction iteration phase operates as following steps:

1. If *Degree*$_{max} = d > 2$, let $V_{max} = \{v_1, v_2, ..., v_k\}$ be the set of vertices with degree equal to d. Sort vertices $v_1, v_2, ..., v_k$ in an non-increasng according to accumulated costs of communication messages that adjacent to the vertex.
2. Schedule the minimum message from each of vertices $\{v_1, v_2, ..., v_k\}$ into step d under the condition of no contention incurred.
3. Allocate all messages that are smaller than present length[3] of step d under the condition of no contention incurred.
4. *Degree*$_{max} = $ *Degree*$_{max} - 1$. If *Degree*$_{max} > 2$, repeat steps 1-3.

---

[3] Length of a step is equal to the maximum message size in that scheduling step.

5   Local Message Reduction Optimization

As discussed in section 4, a good scheduling algorithm could arrange messages to be sent / received in proper communication steps. In order to minimize synchronization delay among different communication steps, messages with close size will be scheduled into the same step. However, this adoption is inadequate to derive a good schedule in practice due to the different access time of local and remote data. In other words, a good schedule of communications can be desired if the scheduling algorithm is performed upon actual communication costs instead of theoretical message sizes. Namely, the local communication should be distinguished from remote ones.

The *Local Message Reduction* (*LMR*) optimization scheme first defines ratio of remote access time to local access time as follows,

$$RLR = \frac{RAT}{LAT} \,{}_4 \tag{6}$$

In *LMR* implementation, the *RLR* is then used to regulate costs of local messages in order to reflect the actual communication costs. Upon the reduced message sizes, *TPDR* can be employed to give a more precise scheduling result.

A minor issue worthy to mention, although it is not reasonable to say that the scheduling result obtained by *LMR* outperforms the ordinary schedule by only comparing the theoretical-reduced costs, the improvement of *LMR* scheme can still be observed in further experiments which will be addressed in next section.

6   Performance Evaluation

To evaluate the performance of proposed *techniques*, we have implemented these algorithms along with two other methods, the *Coloring* and *List-Coloring* scheduling algorithms, with C+MPI codes. The former employs a pure coloring mechanism and the later is combination of *Coloring* method and list scheduling method. The experimental results are based on an array A[1:1000] over 4, 8, 12 and 16 processors. The size of array A is 1 GB. Each executing time in the following Figures is the average time of 10 randomly generated GEN_BLCOK redistribution cases.

Fig. 4 shows the performance results of *TPDR*, *Coloring* and *List-Coloring* scheduling algorithms. The *Coloring* method paid all attention on optimizing communication steps without considering the overall schedule length. On the other hand, the *List-Coloring* algorithm adopted a size-oriented list scheduling approach to minimize overall communication costs and a coloring mechanism to ensure minimum number of communication steps during the redistribution operation. We observe that both *TPDR* and *List-Coloring* outperforms the pure coloring mechanism in terms of total execution time. Moreover, because both of the two algorithms aim at improving scheduling length and guarantee the minimum number of communication step, they do not have significant difference from performance results.

---

[4] *RLR* is short for Remote to Local Ratio; *RAT* is short for Remote Access Time; *LAT* is short for Local Access Time.

Fig. 5 gives comparisons of three algorithms implemented with *LMR* scheme. We have similar observations that both *TPDR* and *List-Coloring* outperforms the pure coloring mechanism in terms of total execution time. There is one thing worthy to mention is that the *LMR* technique improves all scheduling algorithms as compare to Fig. 4 and resulting *TPDR* and *List-Coloring* have almost the same performance when number of processors increased.

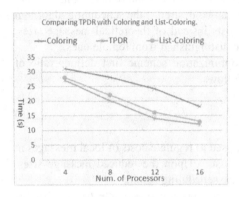

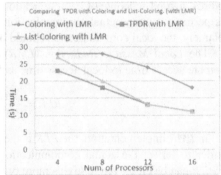

Fig. 4. Performance results of three scheduling algorithms

Fig. 5. Performance results of the three scheduling algorithms when LMR is applied (RLR=8)

7 Conclusions

Without precedent, this paper presented comprehensive techniques to implement GEN_BLOCK redistribution, which includes an *Indexing* scheme for communication sets generation, a contention-free communication *Scheduling* algorithm and an *Optimization* technique for improving communication efficiency. Both theoretical analysis and experimental results show that the proposed techniques can efficiently perform GEN_BLOCK data redistribution during runtime.

Acknowledgements

This paper is based upon work supported by National Science Council (NSC), Taiwan, under grants no. NSC95-2213-E-216-006. Any opinions, findings, and conclusions or recommendations expressed in this material are those of the authors and do not necessarily reflect the views of the NSC.

References

[1] Bai, S.-W., Yang, C.-S., Huang, T.-C.: Packing/Unpacking using MPI User-Defined Datatypes for Efficient Data Redistribution. IEICE Transaction on Information and Systems E87-D, 1721–1728 (2004)

[2]   Desprez, F., Dongarra, J., Petitet, A.: Scheduling Block-Cyclic Data redistribution. IEEE Transactions on Parallel and Distributed Systems 9, 192–205 (1998)

[3]   Hsu, C.-H, Bai, S.-W, Chung, Y.-C, Yang, C.-S: A Generalized Basic-Cycle Calculation Method for Efficient Array Redistribution. IEEE Transactions on Parallel and Distributed Systems 11, 1201–1216 (2000)

[4]   Hsu, C.-H, Yang, D.-L., Chung, Y.-C., Dow, C.-R.: A Generalized Processor Mapping Technique for Array Redistribution. IEEE Transactions on Parallel and Distributed Systems 12, 743–757 (2001)

[5]   Guo, M., Pan, Y., Liu, Z.: Symbolic Communication Set Generation for Irregular Parallel Applications. The Journal of Supercomputing 25, 199–214 (2003)

[6]   Kaushik, S.D., Huang, C.H., Ramanujam, J., Sadayappan, P.: Multi-phase data redistribution: Modeling and evaluation. In: Proceeding of IPPS'95, pp. 441–445 (1995)

[7]   Lee, S., Yook, H., Koo, M., Park, M.: Processor reordering algorithms toward efficient GEN_BLOCK redistribution. In: Proceedings of the ACM symposium on Applied computing, pp. 539–543 (2001)

[8]   Park, N., Prasanna, V.K., Raghavendra, C.S.: Efficient Algorithms for Block-Cyclic Data redistribution Between Processor Sets. IEEE Transactions on Parallel and Distributed Systems 10, 1217–1240 (1999)

[9]   Petitet, A.P., Dongarra, J.J.: Algorithmic Redistribution Methods for Block-Cyclic Decompositions. IEEE Transactions on Parallel and Distributed Systems 10, 1201–1216 (1999)

[10] Ramaswamy, S., Simons, B., Banerjee, P.: Optimization for Efficient Data redistribution on Distributed Memory Multicomputers. Journal of Parallel and Distributed Computing 38, 217–228 (1996)

[11] Wang, H., Guo, M., Wei, D.: Divide-and-conquer Algorithm for Irregular Redistributions in Parallelizing Compilers. The Journal of Supercomputing 29, 157–170 (2004)

[12] Wang, H., Guo, M., Wei, D.: Message Scheduling for Irregular Data Redistribution in Parallelizing Compilers. IEICE Transactions on Information and Systems E89-D, 418–424 (2006)

[13] Yook, H.-G., Park, M.-S.: Scheduling GEN_BLOCK Array Redistribution. The Journal of Supercomputing 22, 251–267 (2002)

A New Memory Slowdown Model for the Characterization of Computing Systems

Rodrigo Fernandes de Mello[1], Luciano José Senger[2], Kuan-Ching Li[3], and Laurence Tianruo Yang[4]

[1] Dept. of Computer Science - ICMC, University of São Paulo, São Carlos, SP Brazil
mello@icmc.usp.br
[2] Dept. of Information Technology, University of Ponta Grossa, PR Brazil
ljsenger@uepg.br
[3] Dept. of Computer Science (CSIE), Providence University, Shalu, Taichung Taiwan
kuancli@pu.edu.tw
[4] Dept. of Computer Science, St. Francis Xavier University, Antigonish, NS Canada
lyang@stfx.ca

Abstract. Performance measurements were extensively conducted to characterize parallel computer systems by using modelling and experiments. By analyzing them, we corroborate current models did not provide precise memory characterization. After detailed result observation, we conclude that the performance slowdown is linear when using the main memory, and exponential when using the virtual memory.

In this paper, we propose a characterization model composed of two regressions which represent the slowdown caused by memory usage. Experimental results confirm the memory slowdown model improves the quality of computing system characterization, allowing to carry out simulations and the use of such results as a way to design real systems, minimizing project design costs.

1 Introduction

The computer system evaluation allows the analysis of technical and economic feasibility, safety, performance and correct execution of processes. The evaluation comprises the application of techniques to estimate the behavior on different situations. Such techniques provide numerical results which allow the comparison among different solutions for the same problem [7]. The computer system evaluation may use elementary or indirect techniques. The elementary ones are directly employed on the system, consequently the system has to be previously implemented. Indirect techniques allow the system evaluation before implementing, what is relevant at the project design phase [8,9,14,15,12].

Indirect techniques employ mathematical models to represent the main system component behavior. Such models should be as similar as possible to the real computing system, allowing to obtain the nearest real results without being necessary to implement the system [12]. The main advantage of this approach is that the system can be evaluated and investigated before its implementation stage, reducing the total amount of investment. A number of models have been proposed for the evaluation of execution time and process delay. They consider CPU usage, the performance slowdown due to the use of the virtual memory [1] and the time spent in message transmissions [6].

V. Malyshkin (Ed.): PaCT 2007, LNCS 4671, pp. 516–524, 2007.

Amir *et al.* [1] have proposed a method for job assignment and reassignment on cluster computing. This method utilizes a queuing network model to represent the slowdown caused by virtual memory usage. In such model, the static memory $m(j)$ used by the process is known and load to each computer is defined according to equation 1, where: $L(t, i)$ is the load of computer i at the instant t; $l_c(t, i)$ is the CPU occupation; $l_w(t, i)$ is the amount of main memory used; $r_w(i)$ is maximum capacity of the main memory; and β the slowdown factor due to the use of virtual memory. Such factors increase the process response time, what consequently reflects in a lower final performance. This work attempts to minimize the slowdown by means of scheduling operations.

$$L(t, i) = \begin{cases} l_c(t, i) & \text{if } l_w(t, i) \leq r_w(i) \\ l_c(t, i) * \beta & \text{otherwise} \end{cases} \tag{1}$$

Mello *et al.* [10] have proposed improvements to the slowdown model by Amir *et al.* [1], investigating in parallel modelling of message transmission delays [6, 18]. That work includes new parameters which allow better modelling of process slowdown. However, such model presents similar limitations to the work previously presented by Amir *et al.* [1], since it neither model the delay caused by the virtual memory usage (represented in equation 1 by the parameter β), nor consider other execution delays generated by message transmissions, hard disk accesses and other input/output operations.

Culler *et al.* [6] have proposed the LogP model to quantify the overhead and network communication latency among processes. The overhead and latency cause delays among communicating processes. This model is composed of the following parameters: L which represents the high latency limit or delay incurred in transmitting a message containing a word (or a small number of words) from the source computer to a target; o represents the overhead which is the time spent to prepare a message for sending or receiving; g is the minimum time interval between consecutive message transmissions (sending or receiving); P is the number of processors. The LogP model assumes a finite capacity network with the maximum transmission defined by L/g messages.

Sivasubramaniam [18] used the LogP model to propose a framework to quantify the overhead of parallel applications. In such framework, aspects such as the processing capacity and the communication system usage are considered. This framework joins efforts of actual experiments and simulations to refine and define analytic models. Though, this approach still presents limitations, due to its incompleteness.

The LogP model can be aggregated to the model by Amir *et al.* [1] and Mello *et al.* [10], permitting to evaluate the process execution time and slowdowns considering CPU, memory and network messages. Unfortunately, the composition of these three models is still incomplete, since the spatial and message generation probability distributions are not considered. Motivated by such limitations, some studies have been proposed [11, 20].

Chodnekar *et al.* [11] have presented a study to characterize the probability distribution of messages on communication systems. In such work, the 1D-FFT and IS [19], Cholesky and Nbody [17], Maxflow [2], 3D-FFT and MG [3] parallel applications are evaluated and executed on real computing systems. In the experiments, some information has been captured such as the message sending and receiving moments, message size and destination. Such information were analyzed by using statistic tools, and the spatial and message generation probability distributions were obtained. The spatial distribution defines the frequency that each process communicates to others, while the message generation distribution defines the probability that each process sends messages to others.

They have concluded that the most usual message generation probability distribution for parallel applications is the exponential, hyperexponential and Weibull. It has also been concluded that the spatial distribution is non-uniform and there are different traffic patterns during the application execution. In most of the applications, there is a process which receives and sends large number of messages to others (like a master node in PVM and MPI applications). The work also presents some features on message volume distribution, though precise analysis about the message size, overhead and latency can not be provided.

Vetter and Mueller [20] have studied the communication behavior of scientific applications using MPI. This study quantifies the average volume of transmitted messages and their size, and the result is that in peer-to-peer systems, 99% of the transmitted messages vary from 4 to 16384 bytes, while in collective calls, this number varies from 2 to 256 bytes. This was combined to the studies on spatial and message generation distributions by Chodnekar *et al.* in [11] and to the LogP model [6] which allow the identification of overhead and communication latency in computing systems.

All models previously presented try to represent and characterize a real computing system. Each model focus on a specific subject such as processing, memory and network. Experiments conducted using such models and comparing to results obtained from real environments. The results proved that models are not able to completely represent real environments. We expect that, when joining all the characteristics of such models, it is possible to characterize and replicate the behavior to be observed in computer systems. By replicating, we can simulate such systems and better understand before implementing the production version. This may reduce costs related to the design, on-the-fly modifications, and also allows the simulation of environments not easily available to common users (such as Grids). Unfortunately, even in such way we cannot understand the actual system behavior, because some parameters are not well defined and studied. Such problem has motivated this work which proposes a new memory model to characterize the delays caused by the main and virtual memory on process executions. By modelling such delays or slowdowns caused to the process execution, we can better represent a real environment.

To study such memory delay, we have developed a suite of benchmark tools called BenchSim. In this suite, there are applications to measure the CPU, hard disk and network performances.

This paper is organized as following. In section 2, we present the proposed memory model, while validation results are presented in section 3, and finally, some concluding remarks are presented in section 4.

2   The Model

By joining all previously presented models, researchers may study and evaluate different system techniques without the need to run applications on real computing systems.

This reduces the time to evaluate such techniques, allowing to consider more time in the design than implementation phase. This is also very important because some environments are easily available (such as clusters and grids). Our motivation in this paper is to improve the system characterization by better represent the slowdowns caused by memory.

The work by Amir *et al.* [1] presents adequate equation in which there is a delay in the process execution from the moment the virtual memory starts to be used. Though, we have to improve such characterization to better represent real systems. Based on this research, we decided to propose a suite of benchmark tools to evaluate system capacity, including memory. From experiments, we noticed the memory was not well characterized by previous models and we decided to propose a static and virtual memory parameter to improve related work.

From experimental results, we corroborate the other models did not provide the precise memory characterization. We observed the performance slowdown is linear during the main memory usage and exponential from the moment the virtual memory starts to be used. So, we should model the memory usage with different parameters.

The proposed memory benchmark creates child processes until the main and virtual memories are filled up, measuring the delays of the context switches among processes. Child processes only allocate memory and then sleep for some seconds, and thus, it does not consider the processor usage. We assume this context switch time as the slowdown time to resume a process execution, and this is considered as the memory delay parameter to complement other models.

We have conducted experiments on a personal computer consisting of one Intel Pentium 4 2.4 GHz CPU, 512 MB RAM, 512 MB virtual memory, 7200 rpm hard disk and one 100 Mb Fast Ethernet network card. The results are very interesting, and they are shown in figure 1.

We confirmed the main memory slowdown has a linear behavior. Though, from the moment the virtual memory starts to be used, the slowdown becomes exponential and tends to be infinite after occupying both memories. Such results invalidate the multiplicative constant delay proposed by Amir *et al.* [1]. For generating memory delay parameters, data regressions is proposed in table 1, which are based on the figure 1. Such equations are used as memory slowdown parameter, instead of β in the equation 1, in the Amir's model. The memory occupation is applied in the regressions of table 1 and the resultant y is used as β. If only the main memory is used, we adopt the linear regression, otherwise, the exponential.

Besides measuring the memory slowdown, the suite of benchmark tools, named BenchSim[1], contains applications to measure objectively the CPU capacity, hard disk read and write throughput and the message transmission delays. Such tools evaluate these characteristics until they reach a minimum sample size based on the central limit theorem, allowing to apply statistical summary measures such as confidence interval, standard deviation and mean [21]. This suite is composed of the following tools:

1. `mips` – it measures the processor capacity, in millions of instructions per second. This tool uses a `bench()` function implemented by Kerrigan [13];

---

[1] Source code available at http://www.icmc.usp.br/~mello

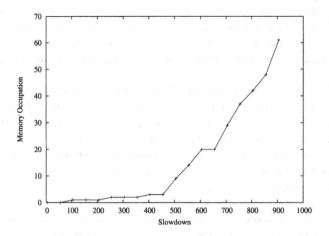

Fig. 1. Main and Virtual Memory Slowdown

Table 1. Regressions of the Main and Virtual Memory Slowdown

Used Memory	Regression	Equation	R^2
Main memory	Linear	$y = 0.0069x - 0.089$	0.9377
Main and virtual Memory	Exponential	$y = 1.1273 * e^{0.0045x}$	0.9691

2. memo – it creates child processes until the main and virtual memories are filled up, measuring the delays of the context switches among processes. Child processes only allocate memory and then sleep for some seconds, thus it does not consider the processor usage;
3. discio – it measures the write mean throughput (buffered and unbuffered) and the read mean throughput in local storage devices (hard disks) or remote storage devices (via network file systems);
4. net – it is composed of two applications, a client and a server, which allow the evaluation of the time spent to send and receive messages on communication networks.

Afterwards, a real environment was parameterized to validate the memory slowdown model adaptation and also the way resource capacities are obtained by the BenchSim. Results are presented in the next section.

3   Validation

In order to validate the proposed memory model characterization, all the previously presented models were joint and real and simulation experiments conducted. The real experiments considered executions of a parallel application developed in PVM [4] in a scenario composed of two homogeneous computers. This application is composed of a master and worker processes. The master process launches one worker on each computer and defines three parameters: the problem size, that is, the number of mathematic operations executed to solve an integral (eq. 2) defined between two points a and b by using the trapezium rule [16, 5], while the workers present four stages: message receiving, processing and message sending. The message exchange happens between master and worker at the beginning and at the end of the worker execution. The workers are instrumented to count the time consumed in operations.

$$\int_a^b 2 * \sin x + e^x \tag{2}$$

Scenario details are presented in the table 2 and they have been obtained by the benchmark suite. A message size of 32 bytes has been considered for the benchmark *net*. The table 3 presents the slowdown equations generated by using main and virtual memories, respectively, on the computers c_1 and c_2. Such equations have were obtained by the experiments with the benchmark *memo*. The linear format of the equations is used when the main memory is not completely filled up, for instance, in the case of computers c_1 and c_2 not exceed 1 GB of the memory capacity. After exceeding such limit, the virtual memory is used and the delay is represented by the exponential function.

Table 2. System details

Resource	c_1	c_2
CPU (Mips)	1145.86	1148.65
Main memory (Mbytes)	$1Gbyte$	$1Gbyte$
Virtual memory (Mbytes)	$1Gbyte$	$1Gbyte$
Disk writing throughput (MBytes/seg)	65.55	66.56
Disk reading throughput (MBytes/seg)	76.28	75.21
Network overhead and latency (seconds)	0.000040	

Table 3. Memory slowdown functions for computers c_1 and c_2

Memory	Regression	Equation	R^2
Main memory	Linear	$y = 0.0012x - 0.0065$	0.991
Main and Virtual memory	Exponential	$y = 0.0938 * e^{0.0039x}$	0.8898

Experimental results are presented in the table 4. We may observe that the error among the curves is low, close to zero. Ten experiments have been conducted for a different number of applications, each one composed of two workers executing on two computers. Such experiment was applied to saturate the capacity of environment resources. The figure 2 shows the experiment and simulation results.

Table 4. Simulation results for computers c_1 and c_2

Processes	Actual	Simulation	Error (%)
10	151.40	149.51	0.012
20	301.05	293.47	0.025
30	447.70	437.46	0.022
40	578.29	573.58	0.008
50	730.84	714.92	0.021
60	856.76	862.52	0.006
70	1002.10	1012.17	0.009
80	1147.44	1165.24	0.015
90	1245.40	1318.37	0.055
100	1396.80	1471.88	0.051

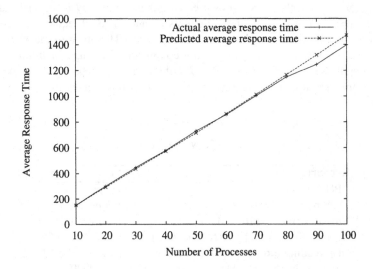

Fig. 2. Actual and simulated mean response times for computers c_1 and c_2

Simulation results confirm the ability to reproduce the real system behavior. Errors start to increase when the system executes large number of processes (ranging from 90 to 100).

Real executions, using 90 and 100 processes, overload the computers and some processes were killed by PVM. The premature stopping of processes (about 5 processes where killed) decreases the computer loads, justifying the model error. The simulator was used aiming to predict the system behavior.

4   Conclusions and Future Work

After studied extensively performance models introduced by Amir *et al.* [1], Mello *et al.* [10], Culler *et al.* [6], Sivasubramaniam [18], Chodnekar *et al.* [11], Vetter and

Mueller [20], we have noticed such models are not capable to completely represent a computing environment. Such drawbacks have motivated this work which proposes a new memory model to characterize the delays caused by the main and virtual memory on process executions and the development of a suite of benchmarks, named BenchSim.

As observed by experimental results obtained from real and simulated environments, the proposed memory model can better represent a real computing system under investigation.

Acknowledgments

This paper is based upon work supported by CAPES, Brazil under grant no. 032506-6 and NSC, Taiwan under grants no. NSC95-2911-I-216-001 and NSC95-2221-E-126-006-MY3. Any opinions, findings, and conclusions or recommendations expressed in this material are those of the authors and do not necessarily reflect the views of the CAPES or NSC.

References

1. Amir, Y.: An opportunity cost approach for job assignment in a scalable computing cluster. IEEE Transactions on Parallel and Distributed Systems 11(7), 760–768 (2000)
2. Anderson, R.J., Setubal, J.C.: On the parallel implementation of goldberg's maximum flow algorithm. In: Proceedings of the fourth annual ACM symposium on Parallel algorithms and architectures, San Diego, California, United States, pp. 168–177. ACM Press, New York (1992)
3. Bailey, D.H., Barszcz, E., Barton, J.T., Browning, D.S., Carter, R.L., Dagum, D., Fatoohi, R.A., Frederickson, P.O., Lasinski, T.A., Schreiber, R.S., Simon, H.D., Venkatakrishnan, V., Weeratunga, S.K.: NAS Parallel Benchmarks. The International Journal of Supercomputer Applications 5(3), 63–73 (1991)
4. Beguelin, A., Gueist, A., Dongarra, J., Jiang, W., Manchek, R., Sunderam, V.: PVM: Parallel Virtual Machine: User's Guide and tutorial for Networked Parallel Computing. MIT Press, Cambridge (1994)
5. Burden, R.L., Faires, J.D.: Análise Numérica. Thomson (2001)
6. Culler, D.E., Karp, R.M., Patterson, D.A., Sahay, A., Schauser, K.E., Santos, E., Subramonian, R., von Eicken, T.: LogP: Towards a realistic model of parallel computation. In: Principles Practice of Parallel Programming, pp. 1–12 (1993)
7. de Mello, R.F.: Proposta e Avaliacão de Desempenho de um Algoritmo de Balanceamento de Carga para Ambientes Distribuídos Heterogêneos Escaláveis. PhD thesis, SEL-EESC-USP (November 2003)
8. Lazowska, E., et al.: Quantitative System Performance: Computer System Analysis Using Queueing Networks Models. Prentice-Hall, Englewood Cliffs (1984)
9. Bratley, P., et al.: A Guide to Simulation. Springer, Heidelberg (1987)
10. Mello, R.F., et al.: Analysis on the significant information to update the tables on occupation of resources by using a peer-to-peer protocol. In: 16th Annual International Symposium on High Performance Computing Systems and Applications, Moncton, New-Brunswick, Canada (June 2002)
11. Chodnekar, S., et al.: Towards a communication characterization methodology for parallel applications. In: Proceedings of the 3rd IEEE Symposium on High-Performance Computer Architecture (HPCA '97), p. 310. IEEE Computer Society Press, Los Alamitos (1997)

12. Jain, R.: The Art of Computer Systems Performance Analysis: Techniques for Experimental Design, Measurements, Simulation and Modeling. John Wiley & Sons, England (1991)
13. Kerrigan, T.: Tscp benchmark (2004)
14. Kleinrock, L.: Queueing Systems - Volume II: Computer Applications. Wiley, England (1976)
15. Lavenberg, S.S.: Computer Performance Modeling Handbook. Academic Press, San Diego (1983)
16. Pacheco, P.S.: Parallel Programming with MPI. Morgan Kaufmann, Seattle (1997)
17. Singh, J.P, Weber, W., Gupta, A.: Splash: Stanford parallel applications for shared-memory. Technical report (1991)
18. Sivasubramaniam, A.: Execution-driven simulators for parallel systems design. In: Winter Simulation Conference, pp. 1021–1028 (1997)
19. Sivasubramaniam, A., Singla, A., Ramachandran, U., Venkateswaran, H.: An approach to scalability study of shared memory parallel systems. In: Measurement and Modeling of Computer Systems, pp. 171–180 (1994)
20. Vetter, J.S., Mueller, F.: Communication characteristics of large-scale scientific applications for contemporary cluster architectures. J. Parallel Distrib. Comput. 63(9), 853–865 (2003)
21. Shefler, W.C.: Statistics: Concepts and Applications. The Benjamin/Cummings (1988)

SCRF – A Hybrid Register File Architecture

Jer-Yu Hsu, Yan-Zu Wu, Xuan-Yi Lin, and Yeh-Ching Chung

Department of Computer Science, National Tsing Hua University,
Hsinchu, 30013, Taiwan, R.O.C.
{zysheu, ocean}@sslab.cs.nthu.edu.tw,
{xylin, ychung}@cs.nthu.edu.tw

Abstract. In VLIW processor design, clustered architecture becomes a popular
solution for better hardware efficiency. But the inter-cluster communication
(ICC) will cause the execution cycles overhead. In this paper, we propose a
shared cluster register file (SCRF) architecture and a SCRF register allocation
algorithm to reduce the ICC overhead. The SCRF architecture is a hybrid register file (RF) organization composed of shared RF (SRF) and clustered RFs
(CRFs). By putting the frequently used variables that need ICCs on SRF, we
can reduce the number of data communication of clusters and thus reduce the
ICC overhead. The SCRF register allocation algorithm exploits this architecture
feature to perform optimization on ICC reduction and spill codes balancing.
The SCRF register allocation algorithm is a heuristic based on graph coloring.
To evaluate the performance of the proposed architecture and the SCRF register
allocation algorithm, the frequently used two-cluster architecture with and
without the SRF scheme are simulated on Trimaran. The simulation results
show that the performance of the SCRF architecture is better than that of the
clustered RF architecture for all test programs in all measured metrics.

Keywords: VLIW processor, cluster processor architecture, register architecture, register allocation algorithm.

1 Introduction

The clustered RF architecture is one of the solutions for this scalability problem of the
wide-issue architecture [1,2,3]. In the clustered RF architecture, the functional units
and the RF are partitioned into clusters and functional units can only have intra-
cluster accessibility to their local RFs. Therefore, the complexity of RFs and bypass
network can be reduced significantly.

In this paper, we propose a shared clustered RF architecture, *SCRF*, to reduce the
ICC overhead. The *SCRF* is a hybrid architecture by combining the clustered RF
architecture and the RF replication scheme. In the *SCRF* architecture, the RF and
functional units are divided into clusters. The RF in each cluster contains one shared
RF and one local RF. The shared RFs (*SRFs*) act as the replicated RFs in the RF
replication scheme and the local RFs (*CRFs*) act as the RFs in the clustered RF
architecture. Any one of the ICC models mentioned above can be used as the ICC
model of the *SCRF* architecture. When a functional unit in a cluster wants to access
data in another cluster, it can access the data through either the ICC or the *SRF* in its

V. Malyshkin (Ed.): PaCT 2007, LNCS 4671, pp. 525–536, 2007.

cluster. By putting the frequently used variables that need ICCs on the *SRF*, we can reduce the number of data communication of clusters and thus reduce the ICC overhead. In the clustered RF architecture, some registers will be used for calling convention. These registers are called macro registers [4]. The ICCs generated to access these macro registers cannot be optimized by the clustering algorithm. In the *SCRF* architecture, we can define these macro registers in the *SRF* and the ICC overhead can be reduced a lot.

In the *SCRF* architecture with macro registers in the *SRF*, the execution cycles, the ICC overhead, the spill codes overhead, and the code density can get 11.6%, 55.6%, 52.7%, and 18.2% reduction in average, respectively.

The rest of the paper is organized as follow. In Section 2, we will give brief descriptions for some related research work. Section 3 will describe the *SCRF* architecture and discuss some hardware design issues. In Section 4, we will give the details of the *SCRF* register allocation algorithm. Section 5 will give the experiment evaluation and analysis.

2 Related Work

The clustered RF architecture has advantage in hardware efficiency, but the drawback is the extra ICC overhead [5]. Many new RF organizations have been proposed in the literature to eliminate ICC overhead and remain hardware efficient [1,6,7,8].

Narayanasamy *et al.* propose a clustered superscalar architecture. The RF organization is similar as that of the *SCRF*. But their ICC is decided by hardware, and shared RF is only used for ICC. Zhang *et al.* [9] also proposed a similar *SCRF* architecture. They design a two destination write operation to write registers in shared RF and clustered RF simultaneously. This way can remove the anti-dependency to speed up the software pipelining. But they did not propose any compiler algorithms for this architecture.

Some researchers try to solve the problem of binding variables to clustered *RF*s. In our work, we want to bind variables to *SRF* and *CRF*s. Hiser *et al.* do variables binding before the instruction clustering. The authors proposed a heuristic to do the variables binding for ICC reduction. Terechko *et al.* [10] proposed several global values binding algorithms for the clustered *RF*s architecture. Since the global values are long live range variables, the binding of global values is more important. The authors proposed a feedback-directed two-pass assignment. The assignment does variable binding after initial assignment, clustering and scheduling for accurate ICC estimation. But it dose not take spill pressure into consideration.

3 The Architecture Models

3.1 The Clustered RF Architecture

The clustered RF architecture and its instruction set used in this paper are based on the EPIC processor architecture [4] (see Fig. 1).

In the EPIC processor architecture, each cluster contains an integer unit, a floating unit, a branch unit, a general purpose RF (GPR), a floating point RF (FPR), a branch target RF (BTR), and a memory unit. In this clustered RF architecture, it has the following disadvantages:

- Since the ICC uses communication units to move date between RFs in different clusters, it will lead to several performance overheads such as extra issue slots occupation, the schedule length increasing, and the code size increasing.
- Since the spill codes pressure will aggregate to one cluster under certain situations in the register allocation phase, this imbalance of the spill code pressure will cause more spill codes overhead.

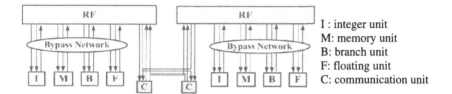

Fig. 1. The clustered RF architecture

3.2 The *SCRF* Architecture

In the *SCRF* architecture, each cluster contains two types of RF, *SRF* and *CRF* (see Fig. 2). The *SRF* can be accessed by all functional units and the *CRF* can be accessed only by functional units in its local cluster.

The ICC is solved by using communication units to move date between *CRF*s in different clusters. The *SCRF* architecture has the following advantages:

- The *SRF* provides a shared storage to allocate variables. Functional units can access these variables on *SRF* without the ICC. An efficient *SRF* register allocation scheme is needed for variables binding in order to optimize the ICC reduction.
- In addition to the ICC reduction, the balanced spill codes pressure is another advantage of the *SCRF* architecture. In the *SCRF* architecture, we can allocate some variables from high spill codes pressure cluster to the *SRF*. Therefore the unbalanced situation of spill codes pressure can be eliminated.

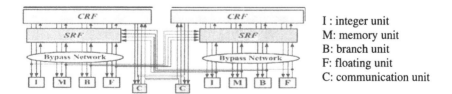

Fig. 2. The *SCRF* architecture

4 The *SCRF* Register Allocation Algorithm

The notations used in the following sections are listed below:

- *CLR*: the set of all variables.
- *SLR*: the set of meta-variables.
- C_i: the ith cluster of the *SCRF* architecture.
- v_i: a variable in *CLR*.
- S_i: a variable in *SLR*.
- cr_{ij}: the ith register of the *CRF* in the jth cluster.
- sr_i: the ith register of the *SRF*.
- $C\_LR(v_i)$: the live range of variable v_i.
- $S\_LR(S_i)$: the live range of variable S_i.
- $icc\_cost(v_i)$: the ICC overhead of variable v_i.
- $icc\_cost(S_i)$: the ICC overhead of variable S_i.
- $sp\_code(v_i)$: the spill code overhead of variable v_i.
- $sp\_code(S_i)$: the spill code overhead of variable S_i.
- $icc\_relation(v_i)$: the set of variables that have an *ICC relation* with v_i.
- $in\_relation(v_i)$: the set of variables that have an *interference relation* with v_i.
- $node(v_i)$: the corresponding vertex of variable v_i in a variable graph.
- $(node(v_i), node(v_j))$: an edge of a variable graph.
- $W(node(v_i))$: the weight associated to vertex $node(v_i)$ in a variable graph.
- $W((node(v_i), node(v_j)))$: the weight associated to edge $(node(v_i), node(v_j))$ in a variable graph.
- $color(cr_{ij})$: the color of register cr_{ij}.
- $color(sr_i)$: the color of register sr_i.
- $color(v_i)$: the color of variable v_i.
- $color(S_i)$: the color of variable S_i.

Fig. 3 shows the compilation flow used in the *SCRF* architecture. In Fig. 3, the clustering phase performs clustering for instructions and variables. In this phase, each variable is assigned to one cluster. If ICC is needed, the clustering algorithm will generate new variables and insert communication instructions for data transfer. The new generated variables are assigned to the demand cluster.

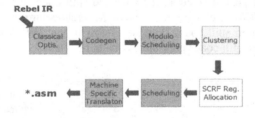

Fig. 3. The compilation flow of the *SCRF* architecture

Before modeling the variable binding problem, we need the following definitions:

Definition 1: If two variables v_i and v_j in *CLR* are on different clusters and they are used in an ICC code, then $C\_LR(v_i)$ and $C\_LR(v_j)$ have an *ICC relation*.

Definition 2: If $C\_LR(v_i)$ and $C\_LR(j_i)$ have intersections, then $C\_LR(v_i)$ and $C\_LR(j_i)$ have an *interference relation*.

If $C\_LR(v_i)$ and $C\_LR(v_j)$ have an *ICC relation*, the ICC overhead occurred between variables v_i and v_j. If $C\_LR(v_i)$ and $C\_LR(v_j)$ have an *interference relation*, variables v_i and v_j cannot be allocated to the same register.

Definition 3: A variable graph $VG = (V, E)$ is defined as a weighted graph, where $V = \{node(v_i) \mid \forall\ v_i \in CLR\}$, $E = E_{icc} \cup E_{in} = \{(node(v_i), node(v_j)) \mid \forall\ v_i, v_j \in CLR,\ v_j \in icc\_relation(v_i)\} \cup \{(node(v_x), node(v_y)) \mid \forall\ v_x, v_y \in CLR,\ v_y \in in\_relation(v_x)\}$, $W(node(v_i)) = sp\_code(v_i)$ for all $v_i \in CLR$, $W((node(v_i), node(v_j))) = icc\_cost(v_i)$ for all $(node(v_i), node(v_j)) \in E_{icc}$, and $W((node(v_x), node(v_y))) = 0$ for all $(node(v_x), node(v_y)) \in E_{in}$.

Given a variable graph VG and the colors of $CRFs$ and SRF, the variable binding problem can be modeled as a graph coloring problem as follows:

Input:

A variable graph $VG = (V, E)$ and the colors of $CRFs$ and SRF

Constrains:

1. For all $(node(v_x), node(v_y)) \in E_{in}$, $color(v_x) \neq color(v_y)$.
2. If v_i is assigned to cluster C_j, v_i can only be colored by the colors of registers in C_j or the colors of registers in SRF

Goal:

Based on the constraints, do a graph coloring on VG using the colors of registers in CRFs and SRF such that the following cost function is minimized:

$$Cost(VG) = Cost(V) + Cost(E_{icc}) \qquad (1)$$

where $Cost(V) = \displaystyle\sum_{v_i \in CLR} W(node(v_i))$ if v_i is not colored,

and $Cost(E_{icc}) = \displaystyle\sum_{(node(v_i), node(v_j)) \in E_{icc}} W((node(v_i), node(v_j)))$ if

$color(v_i) \neq color(v_j)$.

Since the graph coloring problem above is *NP*-complete, we propose a greedy algorithm, the *SRF* register allocation algorithm, to find a suboptimal solution. Given *CLR* and the variable graph *VG* of *CLR*, the proposed algorithm consists of the following phases:

4.1 Phase 1

Since our goals are to reduce the ICC and the spill code overheads, if variables used in ICCs can be binding to *SFR*, the ICCs and the spill code overheads of variables can be eliminated. Therefore, in this phase, we want to construct the set *SLF* from *CLF* by merging variables in *CLF* that have the same ICC relation as a variable in *SLF*. We called the variables in *SLF* as meta-variables. Note that a meta-variable in *SLF* contains at least one variable in *CLF*. The meta-variables are candidates for *SRF* binding. The construct of *SLF* from *CLF* is given as follows:

Algorithm SLR_gen(CLR)
1. Let $SLR = \varnothing$; **for** $(i=1; i< |CLR|; i++)$ mark$[i] = 0$;
2. **for** $(i=1; i< |CLR|; i++)$ {
3.   **if** (mark$[i] == 0$) **then** {
4. $S_i = \{v_i\}$; $S\_LR(S) = C\_LR(v_i)$;
5.   **for** $(j=i+1; j<= |CLR|; j++)$
6.   **if** (mark$[j] == 0$ && $(v_j \in icc\_relation(v_i))$ **then**
7.   { $S_i = S_i \cup \{v_j\}$; $S\_LR(S) = S\_LR(S) \cup C\_LR(v_j)$; mark$[j] = 1$;}
8. $SLR = SLR \cup S_i$;
9.   }
10. }
End_of_SLR_gen

4.2 Phase 2

Given a colored or uncolored *VG*, in this phase, the *CRF-coloring* algorithm will color those uncolored vertices in *VG* such that *Cost(VG)* in Equation (1) is minimized. This problem is similar to the traditional Chaitin's style graph coloring register allocation problem [11]. In the *CRF-coloring* algorithm, the weights of vertices are used to decide the coloring order of vertices. Initially, all uncolored vertices are sorted as a list, *CAN*, according to their weights in descending order. Then, vertex *node*(v_i) in *CAN* is colored one by one according to the colors of neighbors of *node*(v_i). During the coloring process, a vertex may be colored or uncolored. However, the number of colors used should be the minimum. The *CRF-coloring* algorithm is given as follows:

Algorithm CRF_coloring(VG)
1. Let *CAN* be a sorted uncolored vertices of *VG* according to the weights of vertices in descending order; /* *CAN(k)* denotes the *k*th element in *CAN* */
2. **for** $(k=1; k<= |CAN|; k++)$ {
3.   Let *CAN(k)* be the corresponding vertex v_i of variable in *VG* and v_i is a variable assign to cluster C_j;
4.   Let *neighbor_color*(v_i) = {*color*(v_i)| $v_l \in in\_relation(v_i)$};
5. $m = 1$; **while** (*color*(cr_{mj}) $\in$ *neighbor_color*(v_i)) $m++$;
6.   **if** ($m <=$ the number of register of *CRF* in C_j)
7.   **then** *color*(*node*(v_i)) = *color*(cr_{mj})
8. }
End_of_CRF_coloring

4.3 Phase 3

Given the colored *VG* obtained in the Phase 2, in this phase, we want to find the variable S_i in *SLF* such that the binding of S_i to *SRF* can lead to a maximum gain of the ICC and the spill code overheads reduction. After binding S_i to *SRF*, we change the colors of vertices in *VG* that corresponding to variables in S_i to the color of S_i, that is, for each variable v_i in S_i, set *color*(v_i) = *color*(S_i). Since the change of variable colors will release some colors for other uncolored variables, we call algorithm

CRF_coloring to color those uncolored variables. Then, we continue the binding of variables in *SLF* to *SRF* process until all variables in *SLR* are binding to *SRF* or no variable in *SLR* can be binding to *SRF*. The following algorithm performs the tasks mentioned above.

Algorithm SRF_coloring(VG, SLF)
1. $n = 1$; **for** $(k=1; k <= |SLF|; k++)$ mark$[k] = 0$; $VG_2 = VG$;
2.   **do** {
3. $gain = 0$; $i = 0$; $VG_1 = VG$;
4.   **for** $(k=1; k <= |SLF|; k++)$
5.   **if** (mark$[k] == 0$) **then** {
6.   **call** *color_S$_k$(VG, S$_k$)*;
7. $temp = Cost(VG_1) - Cost(VG)$;
8.   **if** ($temp > gain$) **then** { $gain = temp$; $VG_2 = VG$; $i = k$;}
9. $VG = VG_1$;
10.   }
11. $VG = VG_2$; $n++$; mark$[i] = 1$;
12. } **until** ($n > |SLF|$)
End_of_SRF_coloring

Algorithm color_S$_k$(VG, S$_i$)
1. $neighbor\_color(S_i) = \underset{v_j \in S_i}{\cup} \{color(v_l)| v_l \in in\_relation(v_j)\}$;
2. $m=1$;**while**($color(sr_m) \in neighbor\_color(S_i)$) $m++$;
3.   **if** ($m <=$ the number of register of *SRF*) **then** {
4. $color(S_i) = color(sr_m)$;
5. $\forall v_j \in S_i, color(v_j) = color(S_i)$;
6.   **call** *CRF_coloring(VG)*;
7.   }
End_of_color_S$_k$

4.4 Phase 4

The coloring process will be terminated as one of the following conditions is satisfied;

- All variables in *SLR* are binding to *SRF*.
- No variable in *SLR* can be binding to *SRF*.

If the first case is satisfied, all variables can be binding to *SRF*, the ICC and the spill codes overheads of variables can be eliminated. For the second case, if all variables are colored, the spill code overheads of variables can be eliminated. Otherwise, some variables will be spilled to memory. The corresponding spill codes, callee-saved codes, and caller-saved codes will be generated.

4.5 An Example to Illustrate the SCRF Register Allocation

In the *SCRF* register allocation, we calculate the *CLR*, interference relations and ICC relations as the input data. In this example, these input data is listed as follow.

- $CLR = \{ v_0, v_1, v_2, v_3, v_4, v_5, v_6, v_7, v_8, v_9, v_{10}, v_{11} \}$
- Interference relations $= \{(v_0, v_1), (v_0, v_2), (v_0, v_5), (v_1, v_2), (v_1, v_3), (v_1, v_4),$
$(v_1, v_6), (v_2, v_4), (v_3, v_4), (v_4, v_5), (v_5, v_7), (v_6, v_7),$
$(v_8, v_9), (v_8, v_{10}), (v_8, v_{11}), (v_{10}, v_{11})\}$
- ICC relations $= \{(v_0, v_8), (v_3, v_9), (v_5, v_8), (v_7, v_{10})\}$

According to **Definition 3,** *VG* can be build as the Fig. 4. In Fig. 4, Fig. 5 and Fig. 6, the interference relations are show as the solid lines and the ICC relations are show as dash lines.

The goal of the *SCRF* register allocation is to minimize Equation (1). The following will show the state transition of this example in these four phases of the *SCRF* register allocation.

In phase 1, *SLR* is computed from *CLR* by merging variables in *CLR* based on the *ICC* relations of variables in *CLR*. Variables in *SLR* are candidates that can be binding to *SRF*. The following is the computed result by *SLR_gen* algorithm.

$SLR =\{ S_0, S_1, S_2, S_3, S_4, S_5, S_6, S_7\},$
$S_0 = \{ v_0, v_5, v_8\}, S_1 = \{ v_1\}, S_2 = \{ v_2\}, S_3 = \{ v_3, v_9\},$
$S_4 = \{ v_4\}, S_5 = \{ v_6\}, S_6 = \{ v_7, v_{10}\}, S_7 = \{ v_{11}\}$

In phase 2, the *CRF-coloring* algorithm is performed to color *VG* such that the $Cost(VG)$ in Equation (1) is minimized. In this example, CRF_i denotes the *CRF* in cluster i and cr_i denotes the register i in *CRF*. In *SRF*, sr_i denotes the register i in *SRF*. In Fig. 5 and Fig. 6, if one node is colored by cr_i or sr_i, we color the node as green or blue respectively and mark the number i inside this node. In this example, there are two registers in each CRF_i and one register in *SRF*.

$CRF_0 = \{ cr_0, cr_1 \}, CRF_1 = \{ cr_2, cr_3 \}, SRF = \{ sr_0 \}$

After the *CRF-coloring* algorithm, the state of *VG* is show as Fig. 5.

In phase 3, the *SRF-coloring* algorithm is performed to bind variables in *SLF* to *SRF* such that the $Cost(VG)$ is minimized. The *SRF-coloring* algorithm will terminate when all variables in *SLR* are binding to *SRF* or no variable in *SLR* can be binding to *SRF*.

In *SRF-coloring* algorithm, the variable S_{max} in *SLR* is found such that the binding of S_{max} to *SRF* can lead to a maximum gain based on the current colored *VG*. Each gain of S_i in *SLR* is calculated as follow and S_0 is found as S_{max}.

$gain(S_0) = 155, gain(S_1) = 22, gain(S_2) = 34, gain(S_3) = 101,$
$gain(S_4) = 78, gain(S_5) = 0, gain(S_6) = 89, gain(S_7) = 25.$
$=> S_{max} = S_0$

After the *SRF-coloring* algorithm, the state of *VG* is show as Fig. 6.

In phase 4, the termination condition of *SRF-coloring* is checked. If one of the termination conditions is occurred, the *SRF-coloring* is finished. Otherwise, *SRF-coloring* is repeated until one of the termination conditions is occurred. In Fig. 6, the termination condition is occurred in no variable in *SLR* can be binding to *SRF*. The following lists each S_i state in Fig. 6.

S_0:colored, S_1:un-colorable, S_2: un-colorable, S_3: un-colorable, S_4: un-colorable, S_5:gain<0, S_6: un-colorable, S_7: un-colorable.
=> No more variable in *SLR* binding to *SRF* is possible

After *SRF-coloring*, the un-colored node variables are spilled to memory. In this example, v_4 is spilled to memory and the corresponding spill codes are generated.

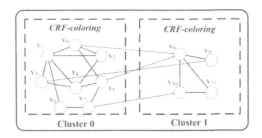

Fig. 4. The initial graph for *SCRF* register allocation

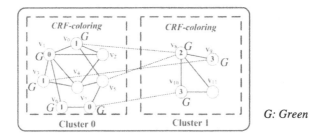

Fig. 5. The state of *VG* after *CRF-coloring*

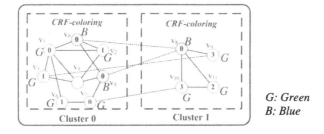

Fig. 6. The state of *VG* after *SRF-coloring*

4.6 Macro Register Allocation

In the *SCRF* architecture, if the macro registers are defined in *CRFs*, variable v_i used for the dedicated functionalities cannot be merged with variables in *icc_relation*(v_i) and the improvement of the ICC overhead reduction and the spill code balance is constrained. If we define some frequent used macro registers in *SRF*, the ICC and the spill code overheads of variables binding to these macro registers are eliminated. In the *SCRF* register allocation phase, we can define some frequent used macro registers in *SRF* and bind variables used for the dedicated functionalities to their macro registers before performing algorithm *SLR_gen*. From the simulation results, we can see that the proposed register allocation algorithm with macro register defined in *SRF* has better performance than that with macro register defined in *CRFs*.

5 Performance Comparisons

To evaluate the proposed the *SCRF* register allocation algorithm, we have implemented the *SCRF* architecture shown in Fig. 3 and the *SCRF* register allocation algorithm on a compiler framework, Trimaran [12], from CCCP project [13] along with the clustered RF architecture shown in Fig. 2. We use a set of multimedia research benchmarks, MediaBench [14], as test programs. The BUG [15] is used as the clustering algorithm for instructions and variables. We compare the performance of the benchmarks in terms of the execution cycles, the ICC overhead, the spill codes overhead, and the code density for the clustered RF architecture and the *SCRF* architecture under different architecture parameters. Table 1 shows the settings of these architecture parameters used in the performance evaluation. In Table 1, the *CRF* size field indicates the number of registers in a *CRF* (GPR, FPR, BTR). The *SRF* size field indicates the number of registers in the *SRF*. The Macro Reg. field dedicates what RF is the frequent used macro registers.

Fig. 7 to Fig. 10 shows the simulation results of execution cycles, ICC overhead, spill code overhead and code size, respectively.

Table 1. The architecture parameter settings

Architecture	*CRF* size	*SRF* size	Macro Reg.
CRF{16, 16}	16	0	*CRF*
CRF{20, 20}	20	0	*CRF*
SCRF{16, 16, 8}	16	8	*CRF*
SCRF_m{16, 16, 8}	16	8	*SRF*

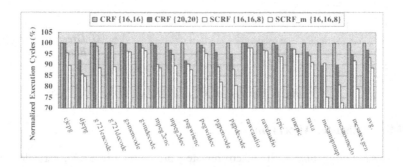

Fig. 7. The execution cycles benchmark result

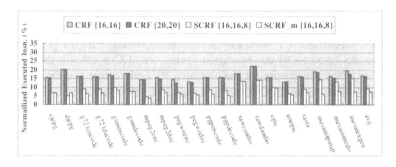

Fig. 8. The ICC overhead benchmark result

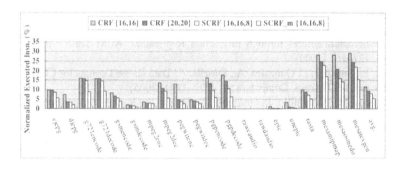

Fig. 9. The spill code overhead benchmark result

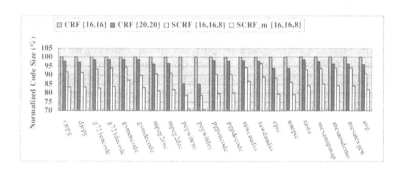

Fig. 10. The code size benchmark result

6 Conclusions

In this paper, we propose the *SCRF* architecture and the *SCRF* register allocation algorithm. We use replication techniques in *SRF* for hardware efficiency. The *SCRF* register allocation algorithm is a heuristic and priority based algorithm. It not only considers the ICC reduction but also the spill code pressure balance. To evaluate the proposed the *SCRF* register allocation algorithm, we have implemented the *SCRF* architecture and the *SCRF* register allocation algorithm on a compiler framework, Trimaran, along with the clustered RF architecture. A set of multimedia research benchmarks, MediaBench, is used as test programs. We compare the performance of the benchmarks in terms of the execution cycles, the ICC overhead, the spill codes overhead, and the code density for the clustered RF architecture and the *SCRF* architecture under different architecture parameters. The simulation results show that the performance of the *SCRF* architecture is better than that of the clustered RF architecture for all test programs. In the *SCRF* architecture with specific registers in the *SRF*, the execution cycles, the ICC overhead, the spill codes overhead, and the code density can get 11.6%, 55.6%, 52.7%, and 18.2% reduction in average, respectively.

References

1. Aleta, A., Condina, J.M., Gonzalez, A., Kaeli, D.: Removing Communications in Clustered Microarchitectures through Instruction Replication. ACM Trans. Arch. and Code Opt. 1, 127–151 (2004)
2. Gibert, E., Sanchez, J., Gonzalez, A.: Distributed Data Cache Designs for Clustered VLIW Processors. IEEE Trans. Computers 54, 1227–1241 (2005)
3. Parcerisa, J.M., Sahuquillo, J., Gonzalez, A., Duato, J.: On-chip Interconnects and Instruction Steering Schemes for Clustered Microarchitectures. IEEE Trans. Parallel and Distributed Systems 16, 130–144 (2005)
4. Terechko, A., Garg, M., Corporaal, H.: Evaluation of Speed and Area of Clustered VLIW Processors. In: Proc. 18th Int. Conf. VLSI Design, pp. 557–563 (2005)
5. Gangwar, A., Balakrishnan, M., Kumar, A.: Impact of Inter-cluster Communication Mechanisms on ILP in Clustered VLIW Architectures. In: 2nd Workshop on Application Specific Processors, in conj. 36th IEEE/ACM Annual Int. Symp. Microarchitecture (2003)
6. Lin, Y.-C., You, Y.-P., Lee, J.-K.: Register Allocation for VLIW DSP Processors with Irregular Register Files. In: Proc. Compilers for Parallel Computers, pp. 45–59 (2006)
7. Nagpal, R., Srikant, Y.N.: Integrated Temporal and Spatial Scheduling for Extended Operand Clustered VLIW Processors. In: Proc. 1st Conf. Computing Frontiers, pp. 457–470 (2004)
8. Zalamea, J., Llosa, J., Ayguade, E., Valero, M.: Hierarchical Clustered Register File Organization for VLIW Processors. In: Proc. 17th Int. Symp. Parallel and Distributed Processing, p. 77.1 (2003)
9. Zhang, Y., He, H., Sun, Y.: A New Register File Access Architecture for Software Pipelining in VLIW Processors. In: Proc. Conf. Asia and South Pacific Design Automation, vol. 1, pp. 627–630 (2005)
10. Terechko, A., Le Thenaff, E., Corporaal, H.: Cluster Assignment of Global Values for Clustered VLIW Processors. In: Proc. Int. Conf. Compilers, Architecture and Synthesis for Embedded Systems, pp. 32–40 (2003)
11. Chaitin, G.J.: Register allocation and spilling via graph coloring. In: Proc. ACM SIGPLAN Symp. Compiler Construction, pp. 98–105 (1982)
12. Trimaran Consortium: The Trimaran Compiler Infrastructure (1998) http://www.trimaran.org
13. CCCP research group: Compilers Creating Custom Processors. http://cccp.eecs.umich.edu
14. Lee, C., Potkonjak, M., Mangione-Smith, W.H.: MediaBench: A Tool for Evaluating and Synthesizing Multimedia and Communications Systems. In: Proc. 30th ACM/IEEE Int. Symp. Microarchitecture, pp. 330–350 (1997)
15. Ellis, J.: Bulldog: A Compiler for VLIW Architectures. MIT Press, Cambridge (1985)

Model Based Performance Evaluation for MPI Programs*

Victor Ivannikov, Serguei Gaissaryan, Arutyun Avetisyan, and Vartan Padaryan

Institute for System Programming Russian Academy of Sciences,
25 B. Kommunisticheskaya st., Moscow, 109004, Russia
Phone (+7-495) 912-46-14; Fax (+7-495) 912-15-24
{ivan, ssg, arut, vartan}@ispras.ru
http://www.ispras.ru/groups/ctt/parjava.html

Abstract. The paper considers the model of a parallel program, which can be effectively interpreted using an instrumental computer, allowing for fairly exact prediction of the actual runtime of a parallel program on a specific parallel computing system. The model has been developed for parallel Java-programs with explicit exchange of messages by means of the MPI library. The model is part of the ParJava environment. The model is derived by converting the program control tree, which, for the Java-program, can be built by modifying the abstract syntax tree. Communication functions are modeled by using the LogGP model, allowing to account for the specific features of a distributed computational system.

1 Introduction

At present, parallel computations are widely used to solve engineering and scientific problems. Efficient parallel computations require knowledge of dynamical characteristics of a parallel program, used not only for its debugging but also for tuning. The existing technologies can yield such characteristics only through the use of a target computational system, which, due to specific features of access, increases the time and, consequently, the cost of the design.

Many scientific centers study the possibility of performing this stage of parallel program development to an instrumental computer. These studies are based on the modeling of parallel programs, when an adequate model of the parallel program is studied and interpreted on an instrumental computer. We believe that novel model-based technologies of parallel programming not only will make it possible to transfer most of the design to the instrumental computer but also will extend the capabilities of an application programmer in investigating and modifying the program to be designed.

In this paper, we consider a model of a parallel program that can efficiently be interpreted on an instrumental computer, making it possible to accurately predict the time of its actual execution on a given parallel computational system. The model is

---

* This work is supported by RFBR, grants 05-01-00995, 05-07-90308, 06-07-89119.

V. Malyshkin (Ed.): PaCT 2007, LNCS 4671, pp. 537–543, 2007.

designed for parallel programs with explicit message passing written in Java with calls to the MPI library and is a part of the ParJava environment [1].

2 Model of a Parallel Java Program

Let us consider the structure of a Java program. According to Java Language Specification, a Java program is a set of classes that can be regarded as types of the corresponding objects. Each class contains methods, static blocks, and variables. The methods and variables can be either static (related to all objects of a given class) or object (related to each individual object of a given class). The values of static and object variables govern the state of the object, and the methods make it possible to change this state. The static blocks are executed when a corresponding class is loaded into the JVM and compute the initial values of static variables.

A *model of a parallel Java program* is defined as the set of models of all classes of the program. A *model of a class* c of a parallel Java program is the list of models of all methods of the class. The first element of the list is named c._ and models the set of static and object variables of the class c, as well as the static blocks defined in class c. The class constructor is modeled as the method named c.<init>. If overloaded methods (or constructors) are defined in the class, the method name is appended with a suffix constructed by the method signature.

The model of the method body is obtained from the abstract syntax tree (AST) of the method by replacing the AST subtrees corresponding to the expressions and calls of other methods and functions by basic blocks. The computations performed in each basic block are represented in the Java byte-code. The tree resulting from these transformations contains internal nodes corresponding to the following statements of the source program: {}, if, if-else, do, for, while, switch, try, break, continue, return, throw, sync and the leaves of the model are the basic blocks.

To describe the semantics of communication functions, the following ten *basic exchange operations* are introduced: Init, Free, Pack, Unpack, Post, Get, Process, Copy, MakeThread, and Idle. The operations Init and Free describe the selection and initialization (the release, respectively) of service data structures used in the communication. Pack(buf, n, type) and Unpack(buf, n, type) are transformations performed by the MPI over the data arrays buf of type type and size n bytes. Here, we mean the conversion of float and double data into a machine-independent form, shift of bytes in data of integer types, conversion of data of type MPI_CHAR (*representation conversion*). The operations Post(buf, n, dest) and Get(buf, n, source) describe sending of the buffer buf of length n bytes to the processor with number dest (receiving the buffer buf of length n bytes from a processor with number source). Together with the buffer, a fixed-length service message is always sent. If only a service message is to be sent, neither the buffer name nor its length is specified; therefore, in these cases, the operations Post(nul, 0, dest) and Get(nul, 0, source) are used. Process(serv_msg) handles the service message. Copy(buf, n) copies the buffer buf of size n bytes into the memory of a computational node.*MakeThread* creates a job stream in the program based on tools provided by the user or operating system.

Consider a blocking receive operation (MPI_RECV). The operation scenario of this function depends on the operational mode of the corresponding message sending. If the message has already been buffered in the memory of the process-receiver, the function MPI_RECV duplicates data from the system (or intermediate, in the case of the buffered sending) buffer to the user buffer. Besides, it is necessary to take into account the operation of the runtime support system aimed at keeping data in the intermediate memory.

```
MPI_RECV(buf, count, datatype, suorce, tag, comm, status)
::=
{Get(buf, count, source);}RTS ||
{Init;
 Copy(buf, count);
 Unpack(buf, count, datatype);
 Free;}Program
```

If the message has not yet arrived to the buffer, the function MPI_RECV stops the operation of the computational node until an appropriate message arrives. It is possible that the function will have to respond to the request of the authorization of data sending in the case where the sending process sends a message in the synchronous mode or in the buffered mode based on the "lazy" algorithm. Thus, in the case when the sending starts after the start of the receiving, the operation of the function is described as follows:

```
MPI_RECV(buf, count, datatype, suorce, tag, comm, status)
::=
{Init;
 Wait(request, source)
 Post(nul, 0, source);
 Wait(buf, source);
 Get(buf, count, source);
 Unpack(buf, count, datatype);
 Free;}Program
```

If the sending begins before starting MPI_RECV, the request will be processed in the runtime support system:

```
{Get(nul, 0, source);
 Process(request)}RTS ||
{Init;
 Post(nul, 0, source);
 Wait(buf, source);
 Get(buf, count, source);
 Unpack(buf, count, datatype);
 Free;}Program
```

In the remaining cases, when the authorization is not requested (sending in the readiness mode or by the "greedy" algorithm), the function MPI_RECV operates as follows:

```
{Init;
 Wait(buf, source);
 Get(buf, count, source);
 Unpack(buf, count, datatype);
 Free;}Program
```

3 Interpretation of the Model

The aim of the interpretation is to calculate the attribute *Time* for each *interpreted node*, which can be a basic block, an internal node, or a method (function). When the time of execution has been computed, the corresponding node of the model can be *reduced*; i.e., it can be replaced by a node of the type reduced basic block by means of the reduction operation.

The *interpretation of the model of a parallel Java-program* consists in the interpretation of the model of method main from one of the classes of the program. The name of this class is specified by the user. The user can also specify values of the parameters of method main.

The *interpretation of the model of a function (method)* represents an interpretation of its root. The *interpretation of an internal node* v is the recursive computation of the attribute *Time* by the values $Time(r_1)$, $Time(r_2)$, ..., where r_1, r_2, ... being direct descendants of the node v. The choice of the descendent is determined by the value of the selector.

For example, the interpretation of the node $v = <id$, if-else, I, O, C, (r_1, r_2), $id(S)$, *Time*> representing the if statement consists in computing values of the selector $s = val(S)$ resulting from the interpretation of the expression S and in the subsequent interpretation of a node r_1 (if $s = true$) or r_2 (when $s = false$). Note that $Time(v) = Time(S) + Time(r_i)$, where $i = 1$ if $s = true$ and $i = 2$ if $s = false$.

The preliminary estimation of the time of execution of computational basic blocks makes it possible to reduce the overheads of the subsequent interpretation, since this approach estimates the time of execution of each basic block only once. Comparative analysis of different methods for estimating the time of execution of computational basic blocks is conducted in [2]. It is noted that the methods based on measurement of the time of execution of computational basic blocks on an instrumental computer and subsequent scaling of the measured time by multiplying it by some coefficient do not provide the required accuracy because of the complexity of deriving the scaling coefficient. Other methods considered in that paper assume the specification of the time of execution by the user or the use of a hardware emulator of a node of the target computational system.

Since the duration of execution of a communication function may depend on the moment of its call, as well as on the moment when the response communication function is called, it is necessary to introduce the notion of model time. Following [3], we assume that a parallel program is interpreted in n independent logical processes. Each logical process has its own model clock, mapping $T^i(v)$ of nodes v of the model interpreted in the logical process i (where i is the number of the process within the communicator MPI_COMM_WORLD) into the time instants (readings of model timer).

The initial readings of model timers of all logical processes are equal to zero. The readings of the model timer of a logical process are updated after the interpretation in this process of each basic block by adding the value of the attribute *Time* of the basic block to the current value of the model time. The interpretation of the communication functions uses the readings of model timers of different processes in order to choose a scenario for the communication and estimate its duration. During the interpretation of a communication function, we assume that the interpreter of the parallel program has determined the logical processes involved in the communication and that the readings of model timer of each process are available.

The MPI functions were modeled by means of ten basic operations. Let us divide these operations into three groups: (1) operations the execution time of which depends only on the features of the computational node, (2) operations the execution time of which depends only on the features of the network, and (3) operation Wait, the execution time of which depends on the readings of the model timer of another logical process.

The first group includes also basic operations whose features are determined for each realization of the MPI: *Init*, *Free*, *Pack*, *Unpack*, *Copy*, *MakeThread*, and *Process*. The time of execution of these operations is predefined and kept in a service table. The time of execution of the operations *Pack* and *Unpack* are not equal to zero only if the elements of the array to be sent are objects (and, consequently, the array needs to be serialized/deserialized). If the array elements are of a basic type, the tools of the package java.nio make it possible to obtain data at the C-code level without overheads. The operation *MakeThread* allows the basic communication operations in a logical thread to be executed independently and can be represented in the MPI realization in different ways (for example, by callbacks). The duration of these basic communication operations is determined with the help of benchmarks.

The second group consists of operations *Post* and *Get*. In work [4], it was shown that LogGP model of a network adequately describes real scalable networks (for example, Quadrics, Myrinet, SCI, etc.). Thus, the durations of operations *Post* and *Get* are given by the formulas

$$Time(Post\,(data)) = b*(n+k) + d_P(n+k),\ d_P\,(0) = l$$
$$Time(Get\,(data)) = b*n + d_G(n),\ d_G\,(0) = l$$

The parameters b (bandwidth) and l (latency) are taken from the characteristics of the communication hardware. The parameter k is the size of the service data that are always sent together with the message. The values of the overhead functions $d_P(n)$ and $d_G(n)$ are determined from a table, which, for each computational system, can be obtained by means of benchmarks using the technique proposed in [5].

To compute the waiting time, one needs only readings of the model timer at the beginning and end of operation Wait(event). To determine the beginning of the waiting, it is sufficient to compute the time when the previous operation terminated. The CPU idling ends when the message arrives at the receiving node. This moment is called the time mark of the message and denoted as *TM(message)*. The time mark of the message is determined by the process-sender of this message on the basis of readings of the model timer at the moment when the sending starts and the estimate of the time needed for the message to arrive at the receiving computational node. Thus, the value of $TM(message)$ is determined by the formula

$$TM(message) = T_b(Post(message)) + d_P(n + k),$$

where n is the message size, k is the size of service data, $T_b()$ are readings of the model timer at the message start time, $d_P()$ is the function of message sending overheads.

4 Conclusions

The proposed model has been implemented and included into the instrumental environment for development of parallel programs ParJava.

In order to validate our modeling method, we have compared the actual running time of the several programs (as synthetic benchmarks, as real application programs) with our interpretation of it. The application of the model to the prediction of the time of execution of model programs for clusters of different architectures has shown quite acceptable results: the prediction error is less than 10%. We used SCI-cluster at RCC MSU, Myrinet-cluster at ISP RAS, and the fragment of the Myrinet-cluster at Joint SuperComputer Center (JSCC) Russian Academy of Sciences.

The ParJava environment was used for the development of several application programs and packages: the package of alphanumeric solving linear algebra problems (Tambov State University), programs for modeling the origination of intense atmospheric eddies (Institute of Physics of the Earth, Russian Academy of Sciences), parallel implementation of genetic algorithms for local adaptive control systems (Division of Modeling Systems, Institute of System Programming, Russian Academy of Sciences), and the like. The application of the model to the development of these programs will assist in revealing their bottlenecks and, at the same time, will make it possible to detect drawbacks of the model and its interpreter. In addition, it will be clarified what instrumental programs should be implemented for successful exploitation of the model.

At present, on the basis of the model described in this paper, analyzers of parallel traces aimed at revealing bottlenecks, cross-blockings, etc. are being developed. These tools will allow us to investigate a parallel program under development on an instrumental computer, thus essentially reducing the development time and cost.

References

1. Ivannikov, V., Gaissaryan, S., Avetisyan, A., Padaryan, V.: Improving Properties of a Parallel Program in ParJava Environment. In: Dongarra, J.J., Laforenza, D., Orlando, S. (eds.) Recent Advances in Parallel Virtual Machine and Message Passing Interface. LNCS, vol. 2840, pp. 491–494. Springer, Heidelberg (2003)
2. Zheng, G., Wilmarth, T., Jagadishprasad, P., Kale, L.V.: Simulation-Based Performance Prediction for Large Parallel Machines. Int. J. Parallel Programming 33(2-3), 183–207 (2005)

3. Prakash, S., Bagrodia, R.: MPI-SIM: Using Parallel Simulation to Evaluate MPI Programs. In: Proc. of the Winter Simulation Conf., USA, IEEE, pp. 467–474 (1998)
4. Alexandrov, A., Ionescu, M.F., Schauser, K.E., Scheiman, C.: LogGP: Incorporating Long Messages into the LogP Model — One Step Closer Towards a Realistic Model for Parallel Computation, Technical Report TRCS95-09, Univ. of California at Santa Barbara (1995)
5. Martin, R.P., Vahdat, A.M., Culler, D.E., Anderson, T.E.: Effects of Communication Latency, Overhead, and Bandwidth in a Cluster Architecture. In: Proc. 24th Annual Int. Symposium on Comp. Architecture, USA, pp. 85–97 (1997)

Runtime System for Parallel Execution of Fragmented Subroutines[*]

K.V. Kalgin[1,2], V.E. Malyshkin[1,2,3], S.P. Nechaev[1,2], and G.A. Tschukin[1,3]

[1] Supercomputer Software Department
Institute of Computational Mathematics and Mathematical Geophysics,
Russian Academy of Sciences
{kalgin,malysh, nechaev}@ssd.sscc.ru
[2] Novosibirsk State University
[3] Novosibirsk State Technical University
gera_lord@mail.ru

Abstract. The architecture of a runtime system supporting parallel execution of fragmented library subroutines on multicomputers is proposed. The approach makes possible to develop the library of parallel subroutines and to provide automatically their dynamic properties such as dynamic load balancing. Usage of the MPI for communications programming provides good portability of an application.

1 Introduction

This paper presents a runtime system supporting execution of the fragmented parallel subroutines. The project deals with to the development of the library of standard parallel subroutines (LPS) for numerical modeling. This is the part of a wider Assembly Technology project [1,2]. The LPS is developed on the basis of some libraries of sequential subroutines like Intel MKL [3], or any other library. Every subroutine of MKL is used for construction of its LPS version. Instead of parallelization of the code of a certain subroutine from MKL, this subroutine is applied not to its whole input data but to the data parts. The subroutine applications to the data parts are permitted to be executed in parallel. For example, a matrices multiplication subroutine sgemm is used for construction of fragmented parallel matrices multiplication subroutine lps_sgemm in the following way. The matrices A, B and C are represented as sets of minors, (see fig. 1) The algorithm of lps_sgemm consists of the applications of the sgemm to every pair of minors A_{ik} and B_{kj} for calculation of the partial results C_{ij}^k and then calculation of the resulting sum $C_{ij} = \sum_k C_{ij}^k$. A fragment F_{ij}^k consists of sgemm code, input matrices A_{ik} , B_{kj} and output matrix C_{ij}^k. Therefore, the lps_sgemm consists of the set of fragments F_{ij}^k and fragments for C_{ij}^k summing, that may (but do

---

[*] This work is partially supported by the grants of NWO-RFBS contracts NWO-RFBS 047.016.007 and NWO-RFBS 047.016.018, Russian Ministry of Education, contract PHII.2.2.1.1.3653 and PhD grant from the French Ministere Education Nationale (MEN-DRIC).

V. Malyshkin (Ed.): PaCT 2007, LNCS 4671, pp. 544–552, 2007.
© Springer-Verlag Berlin Heidelberg 2007

Fig. 1. Matrix multiplication fragmentation

not have to) be executed in parallel. The subroutine `lps_sgemm` is included into the LPS. Every LPS subroutine is described as an asynchronous program, the fragments of which can be executed in parallel, if the data dependencies between fragments are not violated. Setting apart the details of the fragmented module representation we consider the architecture of the runtime system and the results of its testing.

2   Related Work

MapReduce [4] is a programming model and an associated implementation used at Google for processing and generating large data sets. Users specify a map function that processes a key/value pair to generate a set of intermediate key/value pairs, and a reduced function that merges all intermediate values associated with the same intermediate key. This idea is based on a similar operator in the functional language Lisp. The map function computation is split into several amounts of *splits*, which have the same functionality as fragments in the architecture proposed. Dynamic load balancing is attained by having much more splits, than the processors available and re-distributing splits during runtime. The MapReduce runtime system uses a centralized dispatching mechanism. There is one dedicated process – master, which takes care of splits distribution during runtime.

2.1   Parallel Libraries

IBM PESSL [5] is a scalable mathematical subroutine library that supports parallel processing applications on clusters of processor nodes optionally connected by a high-performance switch. The parallel ESSL supports the Single Program Multiple Data (SPMD) programming model using the Message Passing Interface (MPI) library. For communications programming, the Parallel ESSL contains Basic Linear Algebra Communications Subroutines (BLACS), which use MPI. For programming of the computations Parallel ESSL uses the ESSL subroutines. Global data structures (vectors, matrices, or sequences) must be distributed by the user in a special way across the processes prior to calling the Parallel ESSL subroutines.

Intel Cluster MKL is a superset of Intel MKL and includes also ScaLAPACK software and Cluster DFT software for solving computational problems on distributed-memory parallel computers. In order to use ScaLAPACK routines, it is necessary to do the following:

1. Initialize the processes grid;
2. Distribute data onto the processes grid;
3. Call the computation routine;
4. Free the processes grid

MPI or BLACS communication routines are used for programming of communications. The main problem with the use of these libraries is the necessity to distribute data and to program communications properly. Library routines encapsulate only high-performance sequential implementations of computations and communications inside a certain subroutine. All the necessary dynamic properties of a program should be implemented by the user.

The key feature of the proposed runtime system is to put together data and code, whereas the mentioned above libraries keep them separate, and to implement fragments migration. This provides universal mechanism for implementation of dynamic properties of a subroutine execution.

2.2 Complex Projects

The program fragmentation and the architecture of a supporting computer system were proposed in [6] as comprehensive project. On the basis of this suggestion, in the middle 80s, the 24 nodes multicomputer ES-2704 was developed, oriented to support execution of the fragmented programs [7]. Each node of ES-2704 was in its turn the multiprocessor with three specialized processors with common memory. These processors were functionally specialized for computation, scheduling of computation and communications correspondingly. The main objective of this work was providing a high reliability of computations.

The above mentioned Assembly Technology [1,2] is based on two principal ideas. First, the program, as a whole is assembled out of ready made fragments. Second, the fragmented structure of the assembled program is kept during runtime in order to automatically provide the dynamic properties of the program. The technology was used for parallel implementation of the large scale numerical models of natural phenomena.

The main difference between the runtime system proposed and the above systems are the following:

- Fragmented parallel subroutines can be called even from sequential programs for parallel execution.
- Dynamic properties of an application are provided automatically.

In the above mentioned projects, runtime systems were used because the high quality solutions of program construction cannot sometimes be statically found before computation, in particular, in the course of compilation. In construction of a parallel program, many good solutions, for example proper resources allocation, can also be found only during runtime. In such a way, a high quality execution of fragmented programs should be supported by a runtime system in order to provide the implementation ofdynamic properties of fragmented subroutines.

3   Fragments Creation and Execution

3.1   Implementation of a Fragment

The runtime system considers a fragment as a data structure, which encapsulates both data and methods (class). This class inherits interface doWork() from the base class. A data to be processed is the class member. So, if two data elements are processed by the same code, then two fragments should be created.

The runtime system only has to call doWork() method in order to obtain the result. This method has void return type, so it has to manage what to do with intermediate results: send them to another fragment, write them to file, etc.

3.2   Creation of Fragments

All the fragments must be created before the runtime system starts their execution. When calling a LPS routine from a serial code, the following auxillary functions are required:

- lps_*routine_name*_create_fragments() – creation and initial distribution of appropriate fragments out of lps_*routine_name*() parameters During construction each fragment obtains a unique identifier – fragment rank, which does not depend on fragment's current location and does not change during execution.
- lps_init() – Initialization of LPS runtime system
- lps_finalize() – Finalization of LPS runtime system and return to serial control flow

If two or more LPS subroutines are called one after another, some interpocedural optimizations should be performed to avoid redundant inter-fragment communications. The interprocedural optimizer is one of purposes of future work.

Only existing LPS subroutines can be called out of serial code. In order to create new subroutines a special high-level programming language for fragmented program description is under development. Fragments are created during translation of program, written in this language, into C++ + MPI.

4   The Outline of the Runtime System Architecture

4.1   The Runtime System Functions

A parallel subroutine is considered as a set of fragments, which communicate with each other by message passing. So, runtime system should provide the following functions:

- Execution of ready fragments
- Passing messages between fragments
- Fragment lookup service
- Fragment migration support

4.2   Execution of Ready Fragments

A fragment is considered to be ready, when the runtime system process running in corresponding node has received all the messages for this fragment. This condition is sufficient to avoid deadlocks, because sends are non-blocking, and recvs will not block execution of fragment, cause all the messages for it are already received by the runtime system process. Situation, when several fragments have been left unprocessed and none of them can start, is easy to detect. In that case, runtime system finishes its work and produces an error message.

Inter-fragment communications are time-consuming operations, when fragments are processed by different processes. In this case it is suitable to have several worker threads in SMP node instead of several processes.

In such a way, fragments in a certain node are being processed by a pool of workers, containing as many threads, as amount of CPUs/CPU cores are present in the node.

4.3   Data Exchanges and Implementation of Information Dependencies

Due to MPI implementations limitations, MPI functions cannot be called from fragments directly. In order to overcome this, the base class Job has methods send and recv to communicate with other fragments. Both methods work with structures, encapsulating MPI_Send family functions parameters. send method places an outgoing message in a special queue, and recv method asks for data, already received by the system.

Information dependencies between fragments are defined in a subroutine by developers of the library subroutine. The dependence should be specified explicitly in the code of a fragments. This is done in the following way. A fragment receives a value of every input variable with recv() method. A fragment outputs a value of an output variable with send() method. Therefore, adding message from fragment A to fragment B makes fragment A to be run before fragment B. The runtime system starts a certain fragment only if it has received all its input messages.

4.4   Fragment Lookup Service

During runtime, fragments can communicate with each other. In outgoing messages, the recipient is identified by a fragment rank. In the MPI_Send family of functions the recipient is identified by the process rank in MPI communicator. Because fragments can migrate between processors, it is necessary to detect current location of a certain fragment during runtime. Each process should track the locations of fragments initially included into its work queue. So, only one extra message is required to detect the location of a necessary fragment. The components work in asynchronous manner, temporary inconsistency between FLS entry and a real location of a fragment may occur. If a message arrives for a fragment, which has already left its location, the message will be redirected to the fragment current location.

4.5   Fragment Migration Support

The dynamic load balancing is implemented by providing the fragments migration support. The decentralized heuristic load balancing algorithm "receiver initiates" [8] is used. If some node has no fragments for processing, then the runtime system asks its neighbors for extra fragments. In order to identify the neighbors of each node, the MPI communicator with different virtual topologies associated with it is used. It provides good tunability of a subroutine execution to the network interconnections topology. Fragments migrate with all the incoming messages runtime system has already received for it. The outline of this architecture is shown on the fig. 2 (Only one worker of thread pool is shown;)

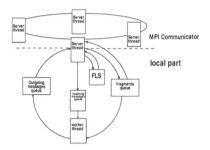

Fig. 2. Outline of runtime support system

5   Experiments

5.1   Hardware

The tests were accomplished on the following hardware:

- NKS-160: 45 x dual Itanium2 processors, 3GB RAM each, interconnected with InfiniBand
- MVS-1000: 64 x dual Alpha 21264 processors, 2GB RAM each, interconnected with Myrinet
- smp4x64: 2 x dual core Itanium2 processor with 64 GB RAM
- woodcrest: 2 x dual core Xeon processor with 8GB RAM

5.2   Measurement Program

The matrix-by-matrix multiplication was selected for performance measurements. There are two kinds of fragments here: "Scatter", which generates source matrices and scatters it between "Worker" fragments, and "Worker", which multiplies submatrices (see fig. 3).

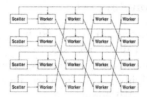

Fig. 3. Scheme of fragmented matrix multiplication

5.3 Overhead Costs

In this series of tests fragmentation maintenance cost is measured. The runtime system is started at a single processor using a single worker thread and changing the amount of fragments. The total amount of computations remains constant because each fragment becomes smaller. The multiplication of matrices 1024 x 1024 of floats was tested. The figure 4 shows that the fragmentation overhead in this particular case is smaller than $\ln(n+1)$, where n stands for the amount of fragments, while n does not exceed some certain value. This means, that fragments must not be too small in order to keep low overheads. Finally, this series of test shows that fragmentation offers dynamic properties of a program for a reasonable price

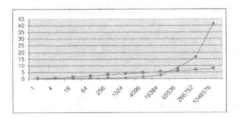

Fig. 4. Fragmentation Overheads

5.4 Speedup and Efficiency

In this series of tests speedup of a fragmented program is measured. Changing the amount of cluster nodes is used. The amount of fragments remains constant and, so, the total amount of computations remains constant, too. Program consists of 16 fragments, load disbalance is missing;

5.5 Load Balancing Possibility Tests

In this series of tests the cost of the dynamic load balancing of a fragmented program is measured. Changing the amount of cluster nodes is used. The amount of fragments remains constant and, so, the total amount of computations remains constant, too. The following criteria are used: the total execution time and a

Table 1. Speedup and efficiency. Execution time in seconds.

	NKS-160	MVS-1000	smp4x64	woodcrest
1 processor	24.35394	126.3	25.9	13.22319
2 processors	12.91473	65.2	13.4	7.05442
4 processors	7.04837	34.6	7.2	4.45204
8 processors	4.96530	18.4	—	—
16 processors	2.68926	10.6	—	—

Table 2. Dynamic load balancing. Time in seconds.

	NKS-160	smp4x64	woodcrest
1 processor	24.615423	25.97979	13.21207
2 processors	15.76361	16.20747	9.96568
4 processors	10.15956	11.61100	6.72279
8 processors	6.21874	—	—
16 processors	3.53200	—	—

maximum difference between the nodes execution times. As result of the implementation peculiarities, messages between fragments located at the same nodes are delivered much faster, than those between fragments located at different nodes of a cluster. In the previous test, communicating "Scatter" and "Worker" fragments were initially distributed on the same node, and in this test they were distributed randomly.

6   Conclusions and Future Work

On the basis of LPS, where many necessary subroutines are accumulated, even execution of a sequential program with many calls to the LPS subroutines might be done in parallel very well. Certainly, usage of fragmented programming demands to reconstruct the numerical algorithms into fragmented form. It is clear, that not any numerical algorithm can be reconstructed into fragmented form. Such algorithms cannot be used for development of parallel applications and selection of the suitable algorithms should be done. Therefore, one of the first needs is reconstruction of the most widely used numerical algorithms into fragmented form. in order to simplify work of an application programmer and to provide better performance of an application program the implementation of the runtime system also should be improved. First, the optimization of subroutines execution should be done. For this the manager of dynamic memory should be developed in order to simplify the implementation of the memory allocation and re-allocation, dynamic load balancing, etc. Secondly, the global optimization of the data allocation should be done. Future work includes also improvement of the load balancing and message dispatching algorithms. Implementation of runtime system for GRID is planned, too.

References

1. Valkovskii, V.A., Malyshkin, V.E.: Synthesis of Parallel Programs and Systems on the Basis of Computational Models. Nauka, Novosibirsk (in Russian) (1988)
2. Kraeva, M.A., Malyshkin, V.E.: Assembly Technology for Parallel Realization of Numerical Models on MIMD-Multicomputers. The International Journal on Future Generation Computer Systems 17(6), 755–765 (2001)
3. Intel MKL reference. http://www.intel.com/cd/software/products/asmo-na/eng/341976.htm
4. Dean, J., Ghemawat, S.: MapReduce: Simplified Data Processing on Large Clusters http://216.239.37.132/papers/mapreduce-osdi04.pdf
5. IBM PESSL reference. http://www.pdc.kth.se/doc/SP/manuals/pessl/pessl.pdf
6. Glushkov, V.M., Ignatyev, M.V., Myasnikov, V.A., Torgashev, V.A.: Recursive machines and computing technologies. In: Proceedings of IFIP Congress, vol. 1, pp. 65–70, North-Holland Publish. Co (1974)
7. Torgashev, V.A., Tsarev, I.V.: Sredstva organizatsii parallelnykh vychislenii i programmirovaniya v multiprocessorakh s dynamicheskoi architechturoi. Programmirovanie (in Russian) 4, 53–67 (2001)
8. Tanenbaum, A.S.: Modern Operating Systems, 2nd edn.

Application of Simulation Approaches to Creation of Decision Support System for IT Service Management

Yuri G. Karpov, Rostislav I. Ivanovsky, and Kirill A. Sotnikov

St.Petersburg State Polytechnical University,
Distributed Computing and Networking Department,
21, Politekhnicheskaya ul., St. Petersburg, Russia, 194021
tel./fax: +7 812 297 1639
{karpov, iri, sotnikov}@dcn.infos.ru
http://dcn.infos.ru

Abstract. The paper presents a simulation-based approach to creation of decision support system for IT Service Management. The presented approach includes monitoring of stochastic data IT Services and calculation of measure of alignment to business goals with its characteristic basing on SLA/SLO. The approach combines the benefits of two kinds of models: analytical and simulation ones. The key idea of the paper is to demonstrate how modern methods of stochastic process analysis may enhance trustworthiness and quality of decision making along business goals within IT Services.

Keywords: Simulation, Stochastic analysis, SLA, SLO, IT Service Management, Decision support.

1 Problem Statement

Managing IT systems and services (ITS) is the main challenge enterprise IT organisations are facing today. There is a number of Enterprise Resource Planning (ERP) systems presented on the market now, which include considerably powerful tools covering gathering and analysing statistical data, planning and scheduling of miscellaneous tasks, fixing and ordering of data, automation of flows of various natures, etc. But the fact is that most of these ERP systems lack in means of ITS optimisation and decision support.

We present a simulation-based approach to decision support system which uses monitored stochastic data and calculates the measure of alignment to business goals with its characteristic basing on SLA/SLO. The approach combines the benefits of two kinds of models: analytical and simulation ones. The parameters of analytical model are defined by monitoring the real-life system and then simulation model parameters are adjusted basing on analytical one together with data obtained from real system. The presentation demonstrates how modern methods of stochastic process analysis (like sensitivity analysis, regression analysis, risk analysis, factor analysis

V. Malyshkin (Ed.): PaCT 2007, LNCS 4671, pp. 553–558, 2007.

with finding most leverage factors influencing results, etc.) may enhance trustworthiness and quality of decision making along business goals by the example of managing IT infrastructure.

The goal of this paper is to suggest an approach to IT service management (ITSM) according the business goals of the enterprise with measure of trustworthiness and risk analysis.

2 Proposed Approach

Processes in the ITS possess a stochastic character, so all the predictions about system's future behaviour basing on the analysis of these processes are stochastic as well. We propose to calculate such characteristics as reliability and confidence interval for every parameter obtained from the analysis of ITS processes. As in general such estimates cannot be obtained analytically we use in our work the simulation model [1] which is described in more detail in section 3.

Before running the simulation model we select a criteria J (in general a combination of weighted *key goal indicators* (*KGI*) [4]) and preliminarily select and analyze:

- set of influencing factors x_i, ($i = 1,.., n$);
- set of controls u_k, ($k = 1,.., m$);
- set of disturbing influences q_r, ($r = 1,.., l$).

Simulation model of a complex system has numerous parameters and selection of *KGIs* among them is a non-trivial task, but there's a number of methods to solve it. We use sensitivity analysis and regression analysis to specify valuable *KGIs* before using model for decision making.

Using simulation model as a basis for decision support is possible only when its reliability is proved (guaranteed). For this purpose we consequently analyse different approximations inside simulation model (SM_j), starting from the very first ($j = 1$, initial estimation), with the subsequent periodic calibration of our model to the real life data [2]. The data about the real processes in IT system may be obtained from the repository. Every following variant of model is characterized by a higher degree of reliability and confidence. In general the sequence of SM_j possesses the convergence by probability:

$$\lim_{j \to \infty} P\{| SM_j - ITS | < \varepsilon\} = 1; \ \varepsilon > 0 \tag{1}$$

where P is probability, ITS – genuine IT system.

While running the simulation model between the calibration moments the following range of tasks is solved:

- by analyzing the sensitivity of $J(x_i, u_k, q_r)$ to variations of factors x_i, controls u_k and disturbances q_r ranking by the degree of impact to J is done.
- disturbances q_r are simulated, class of every disturbance is determines (random variable, random process) and parameters of their distributions are defined;

- by multiple runs of the model (considering significant x_i, q_r) in the defined time interval $[t_0, t_f]$ the set of possible meanings random variable $J_f(u_k) = \sup J(t_f)$ is obtained and sum polygon of this random variable is defined. Here $J_f(u_k)$ is the upper bound of criteria value achievable in the current conditions;
- by obtaining the sum polygon we estimate the possibility of random variable $J_f(u_k)$ to hit in areas (fair Q_F, tolerant Q_T and critical Q_C) and determine thus the possibility of risk of hitting Q_C area. The area (Q_F, Q_T, Q_C) borders are defined by business goals.

As during the simulation criteria values may be obtained on every step within the interval $[t_0, t_f]$ the regression analysis method may be applied to calculate the mathematical dependence to describe the behaviour of $\sup J(t)$ at the average. Additionally, not only point estimates of regression correlations, but also dispersions of these parameters may be received. This in turn allows to fulfil the prediction of $\sup J(t^*)$ value, where $t^* > t_f$ is a fixed time, with the estimate in increasing error while increasing $\tau = t^* - t_f$.

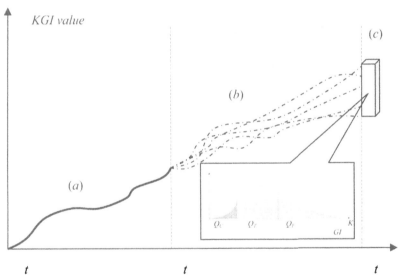

(a) modeled observation interval, periodically calibrated

(b) prediction modeling

(c) KGI values estimation obtained from multiple runs of prediction modeling

Fig. 1. Prediction process diagram

The reliability of prediction grows as well while calibrating the simulation model. In mathematical terms every next calibration may be considered as a shift of observation's left bound to the right and decrease prediction interval. On every step we gain the best knowledge about the current situation. Using the calibrated prehistory we make a forecast with such characteristics as reliability and risk analysis of hitting the critical area. The simulation modeling allows us to get the numeric estimates of prediction's reliability increase. Graphical representation of our approach is presented on Figure 1.

3 Application Example

The structure of example solution is presented on figure 2. The upper level of our system, repository, may be in particular considered as any ERP solution which provides the detailed and comprehensive information about system processes. Data from the repository is used for periodical calibration of the model to achieve higher reliability of prediction results.

The simulation model simulates the real structure behaviour including customers, IT infrastructure and financial flow modelling. One of the main advantages of simulation modelling is the fact that one can build a model of sufficiently complex system just having in mind understanding of only behaviour of each element of the system and interconnection rules. For example a model of IT infrastructure (ITI) may be specified as an interconnection of a number of servers, switches, communication channels, etc. The model of server may be expressed as a random delay depending on number of concurrently processed transactions; the switching rules may be specified using policies. While running simulation model the processing time of each transaction may be obtained and possible SLA violations, penalties, etc. may be calculated using SLA expressions and rules.

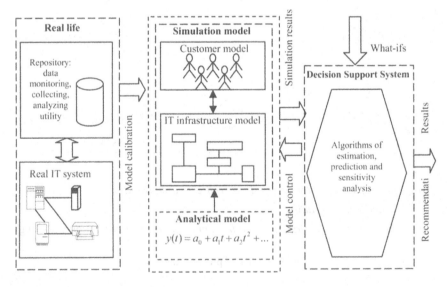

Fig. 2. Example solution structure

The customer uses the resources the provider company (IT infrastructure in our case) by generating various types of transactions according to SLA, pays for this usage and receives penalty payments if SLA is violated. The customer may experience technical problems as well which are to be resolved by IT system services.

ITI model includes models of its elements with proper behavior characteristics, breakdowns (incidents and problems in ITS), recovery times and downtimes with the corresponding stochastic specifications. In addition, techniques for modeling financial flows for IT services leading to compliance models for SLAs/SLOs. We stress that incidents are one of the key points of our simulation model as they are a starting point for possible loses in system. Incidents as well as customers' technical problems are resolved by technical department which is also included in our structure. Incidents resolution time depends on IT Management strategy. The other task of technical department is to trace the operations fulfilment and disclose SLA violations. The infrastructure model also includes a financial department which calculates appropriate invoices for customers and calculates penalties if SLA is violated. Financial department may be used as output showing the current situation in terms of business goals or *KGIs*.

Decision Support System realises algorithms of prediction, estimation and analysis described in section 2. In addition to calculations it may provide answers to what-if questions and be a foundation for decision making.

When using simulation models one of the key problems is proof of model validity. In addition to traditional approach of model calibration basing on scenarios of real system functioning we use adjustment of model parameters at every time step using analytical model based on parameters monitoring which represents integral system characteristic. The calibration affects the stochastic description of the process flow in the ITS and allows to achieve higher reliability simulation results.

4   Further Development and Application Area

The range of tasks which may be solved using the presented approach is rather wide and is not certainly restricted by just ITI management. It may also be used for business management, application management, etc.

Considering ITSM we may excrete the following range of tasks which may be solved using and within the frames of our approach.

In application to analytical methods of prediction and forecasting:

- Sensitivity analysis and regression analysis. One may extract a variety of indicators, characterizing the ITS functioning. Sensitivity and regression analysis allows specifying the most valuable indicators, key performance indicators (KPIs) which may be used for future decision making.
- Selection and analysis of influencing factors, controls and disturbing influence factors in ITS. Ranking of factors, controls and disturbances by the degree of impact to KPIs using the sensitivity analysis. This type of analysis may be also applied to the criteria selected in accordance with business goals.
- Application of analytical models for prediction and forecasting. As usage of the simulation model gives a possibility to obtain every value at every time step, the regression analysis method may be applied to calculate the mathematical dependence to describe the behavior of selected criteria at the average. Additionally, not only point estimates of regression correlations, but also dispersions of these parameters may be received. This in turn allows fulfilling the

prediction of criteria value with such characteristics as reliability and risk analysis of hitting the critical area (for the criteria).

In application to decision support for ITSM:

- Selection and ranking of key performance indicators that measure the performance of IT service delivery and operations with respect to the value they contribute to the business supported by the IT.
- Investigation of dependencies between IT metrics and business objectives, business rules and policies.
- Investigation of optimization techniques for decision support within IT service management processes.

Our approach may also cover ITI processes like change management, incident management, service level management, etc. thus giving the new possibilities for these spheres.

5   Conclusion

The paper presents the simulation-based approach to IT service management. The main benefits of this approach lie in combination to two kinds of models, analytical and simulation ones, and in constant calibration to the real system's behavior. The example provided covers the IT infrastructure management, but the general approach is not restricted by this area and may also be used for business management, application management as well as covering of specific ITS processes.

We do not consider our approach as a separate tool or system; we expect it to be a supplemental tool to huge enterprise systems providing powerful means of gathering and structuring the information but lacking in decision support capabilities.

References

1. Popkov, T., Karpov, Yu., Garifullin, M.: Using Simulation Modelling for IT Cost Analysis. In: 10th HP OpenView University Association Workshop (July 2003) http://www.hpovua.org
2. Schmid, M., Schaefer, J., Kroeger, R., Sotnikov, K., Karpov, Yu.: Combining Application Instrumentation and Simulation to Forecast Costs and Revenue in Application Service Provisioning Scenarios Using Simulation Modelling for IT Cost Analysis. In: 13th HP OVUA Workshop (June 2006)
3. Aib, I., Sallé, M., Bartolini, C., Boulmakoul, A.: A Business Driven Management Framework for IT Systems Management. In: IFIP/IEEE International Symposium on Integrated Management, poster session, Nice, France (September 2005)
4. Control Objectives for Business Information-related Technology COBIT. http://www.isaca.org/cobit.htm

Using Analytical Models to Load Balancing in a Heterogeneous Network of Computers

Jean M. Laine and Edson T. Midorikawa

Department of Computer Engineering and
Digital Systems - Polytechnic School
University of São Paulo
Av. Prof. Luciano Gualberto, trav. 3, 158
São Paulo – SP – 05508-900, Brazil
{jean.laine, edson.midorikawa}@poli.usp.br

Abstract. An effective workload distribution has a prime rule on reducing the total execution time of a parallel application on heterogeneous environments, such as computational grids and heterogeneous clusters. Several methods have been proposed in the literature by many researchers in the last decade. This paper presents two approaches to workload distribution based on analytical models developed to performance prediction of parallel applications, named PEMPIs VRP (*Vector of Relative Performances*). The workload is distributed based on relative performance ratios, obtained by these models. In this work, we present two schemes, static and dynamic, in a research middleware for a heterogeneous network of computers. In the experimental tests we evaluated and compared them using two MPI applications. The results show that, using the VRP's dynamic strategy, we can reduce the imbalance, among the execution time of the processes, in relation to average time from 25% to near of 5%.

1 Introduction

Load balancing strategies can improve the performance of parallel and distributed applications, dividing the workload among the machines, in order to exploit each of them properly. Different approaches can be applied for that objective, both for homogeneous and heterogeneous environments of distributed computing. In high-performance homogeneous environments, such as homogeneous clusters, generally, a static strategy is used to divide the work into a number of pieces equal to the number of nodes or processors in the environment, in order to distribute equally the computation among the machines. On the other hand, in heterogeneous systems, such as heterogeneous network of computers, heterogeneous clusters or computational grids [1, 2], the workload is divided according to the computational power of each host, and then, all machines will receive a workload proportional to its processing capacity and load situation. A static workload partition and distribution generates a low overheads compared to dynamic strategies. Generally, these strategies are based on the divide-and-conquer techniques, where the problem is divided into a number of sub-problems that can be solved separately.

V. Malyshkin (Ed.): PaCT 2007, LNCS 4671, pp. 559–568, 2007.

A strategy that can be used is, partitioning the workload equally and distributing the parts to the nodes; each node should receive more or less slices according to own capacity. Another approach is, dividing the workload not equally, then each node would receive slices suitable to own computational power. An advantage of the last one is the reduction of the total message exchange on the network and consequently lower overhead to communication.

This paper presents two approach to PEMPIs VRP: static and dynamic. It's a set of techniques of workload distribution in heterogeneous environments. We intend to verify how analytical performance prediction models can aid load balancing, considering the individual capacity of the machines. We use two MPI (Message Passing Interface) [3,4] parallel programs as case studies: matrix multiplication and a simulator for the interaction of particles under gravitational forces.

The remainder of this paper is organized as follows. Section 2 presents some considerations about workload distribution in homogeneous and heterogeneous systems. Section 3 describes our methodology for workload distribution for heterogeneous environments. In section 4 we introduce the applications used in our experimental tests, present some characteristics of our experimental environment and we detail how our experiments were conducted. The experimental results are showed in section 4.2. Some related works are presented in section 5. The conclusions of our paper and some future work are discussed in section 6.

2   Workload Distribution

In distributed and heterogeneous systems there are many factors able to influence the application performance and affect the total execution time of programs. For instance, we can quote the CPU processing power, CPU load, operating system overhead, network bandwidth and amount of memory. The individual processing power is not related only with CPU processing power but also with available amount of memory, memory latency, cache size, interconnection structures and I/O bandwidth. However, other factors can influence the performance of distributed applications, such as, bad load balance and huge message exchange. To efficiently utilize computing resources, provided by the environment, and to increase the global system performance, we have to adopt an efficient mechanism of load balancing.

In heterogeneous environment, a load balancing strategy should consider the computational power of each machine and the communication cost for exchanging data on the network before partitioning and distributing the tasks to hosts. In the literature is possible to find some strategies, such as, Self-Scheduling (SS), Chunk Self-Scheduling (CSS), Guided Self-Scheduling (GSS) and Trapezoidal Self-Scheduling (TSS) [5, 6, 7, 8, 9] that were developed to this kind of environment.

In homogeneous systems, the simplest load balancing strategy only divide the problem size (n) by the number of processes (p) and distributes the tasks among the machines. Then, each process will receive the same amount of work $\left(\frac{n}{p}\right)$.

There are some strategies developed to this purpose, such as, Block Scheduling, Cyclic Scheduling and Block-D Scheduling [10].

The main objective of load balancing is, to distribute workload uniformly to all nodes, in order to prevent some machines with idle or under-utilized resources and also overloaded. Otherwise, the load concentration or imbalance can affect not only the global system performance, but also, a particular distributed application running in the environment.

In this context, we present and discuss in this paper two strategies, static and dynamic, applicable to heterogeneous network of computers, such as, clusters [11] or computational grids [12,1]. Both strategies uses performance prediction models, elaborated by a methodology named PEMPIs to load balance. The master divides the workload according to relative performance ratios defined by VRP (*Vector of Relative Performances*).

3   Developed Strategy

This section describes a strategy developed for workload balance, based on analytical performance prediction models generated by PEMPIs, a methodology to performance analysis and prediction of MPI programs [13]. The strategy, named VRP, has two possible approachs: static and dynamic. The static scheme can be used in homogeneous environment, while the second approach is more suitable to heterogeneous and dynamic environment.

The analytical models developed by PEMPIs to represent the application's behavior can be applied to performance prediction and workload balance, as will be explained later in this paper. To elaborate these analytical models, is necessary to analyze, before, the complexity of the applications algorithm. For instance, the model used to represent particles under gravitational forces application, that is $(O(\frac{n^2}{p}))$, can be written as following:

$$t(n,p) = \frac{a}{p}n^2 + \frac{b}{p}n + \frac{c}{p} \qquad (1)$$

So, PEMPIs VRP is a strategy developed to provide workload balance in distributed systems by assigning an adequate workload for each node. The workload distribution algorithm is based on a set of values, related to the performance of each node. These values consider many factors, such as processing, memory resources and communication capabilities.

Basically VRP is a vector of m positions, where each value is associated with a machine and characterizes its relative performance in the environment. The values of VRP are ordered by processing power, where $VRP[1]$ represent the slowest machine of the system and $VRP[m]$ stores the relative performance ratio of the fastest machine, as following:

$$VRP = \{\varphi_1, \varphi_2, \varphi_3, ..., \varphi_{m-1}, \varphi_m\} \qquad (2)$$

where:

$$\varphi_m = \frac{\delta_1(n,p)}{\delta_m(n,p)} \qquad (3)$$

φ_m: represents the relative performance value of the mth machine and the parameters $\delta_m(n, p)$ and $\delta_1(n, p)$ represent the analytical models developed by PEMPIs to machine 1 and m, respectively;

φ_1: represents the relative performance value of the slowest machine of the system and the value of φ_1 is 1.

So, the relative performance value calculated to each machine indicates the amount of load that will be processed by this machine. The parameters of this unitary load and partition is computed by the following formulas:

$$ul = \frac{\tau}{\displaystyle\sum_{i=1}^{m} VRP[i]} \qquad (4)$$

$$\Delta_m = \lceil ul \times VRP[m] \rceil \qquad (5)$$

where ul is the unitary load, τ is the total workload and Δ_m is the assigned workload to mth machine.

So, we apply these formulas to each test configuration in the environment in order to generate the most adequate VRP to our load balancing strategy. We can use two different approachs to obtain the VRP. The first method to load balancing is static, and the values used to VRP are the same to all configurations of the environment and the problem. The second strategy is dynamic, and we define the values of VRP in function of the number of processes (p) and size of the problem (m). The tasks will be distributed based on VRP values. We can observe during the tests that, the dynamic approach is more suitable and reach better results than the static strategy.

4   Case Studies

In order to test and evaluate the PEMPIs VRP strategy we have applied it to some parallel applications. Firstly, we modeled two MPI programs (the traditional matrix multiplication and a simulator of particles interaction under gravitational forces) with PEMPIs. These applications were executed on the environment showed in the figure 1.

4.1   Computational Environment

The experimental tests were executed on a heterogeneous network of computers composed by different processing nodes. There are three types of machines, named intel, bio and taurus. The intel machines have an Intel Pentium D 950 processor, 2GB of DDR2 SDRAM, dual gigabit Ethernet interfaces and run Fedora Core 5. The bio machines are composed by dual AMD Athlon MP 2400+ nodes, with 1GB DDR SDRAM, dual Intel Ether-Express Pro Fast Ethernet boards and run RedHat Linux. The taurus machines have an Intel Celeron 433MHz, 256 MB SDRAM, Fast Ethernet interfaces and run RedHat Linux. The parallel applications use the LAM-MPI implementation. The figure 1 shows our testbed environment.

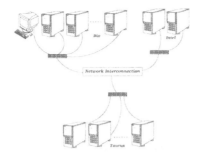

Fig. 1. Network testbed (logical diagram)

4.2 Workload Balancing

In this section we describe the application programs used in our experimental tests, presenting some information about their respective algorithms and parallelization techniques, and then, we discuss the evaluation results of our load balancing strategy.

Matrix Multiplication - MM. Matrix multiplication is present in the majority of scientific computing and computer graphics applications. So, it is an important efficient implementation of this application on parallel and distributed systems. Several works have been developed considering new parallel algorithms for matrix multiplication on different environment, distributed or not, showing its importance.

In our tests we used the conventional $O(n^3)$ algorithm. The program was, initially, executed in each node type, in order to obtain the PEMPIs analytical models. To evaluate our proposed strategy, we analyzed the execution time of each parallel task. The Figure 2 shows the load balancing using a static strategy to VRP. Some processes have presented an unbalancing up to 25% in relation to average time $(DFAT)$ for some problem sizes.

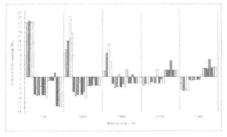

Fig. 2. MM with static VRP

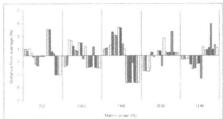

Fig. 3. MM with dynamic VRP

The $DFAT_p$ (*Distance From Average Time*) represents how much time the execution of slave p (x_p) is distant from average time of all slaves ($\overline{x}$), as following:

$$DFAT_p = \frac{x_p - \overline{x}}{\overline{x}} \qquad (6)$$

Depending on the configuration of the problem size (n) and the number of processes (p), the static VRP cant be efficient and the imbalance can be high. Based on these results and observations, we decide to improve our technique and modified the form used to obtain the values of VRP. In the second approach, the VRP is determined dynamically and adjusted to each problems configuration (p,n). Figure 3 shows the new results after these modifications to the same problems configuration. As can be seen, all tasks presented a maximum distance close to 5%, showing that the dynamic strategy was successful in adequately distribute the workload among the heterogeneous nodes, generating a more homogeneous distribution.

Particles under Gravitational Forces - PGF. The program *gravity* implements an application similar to the well known *n-body problem* [14], with the simulation of the interaction of a number of particles under gravitational forces. A total of N particles composes the system to be simulated, each of them are characterized by its mass, position and momentum. The used algorithm adopts the particle-particle (PP) method to compute the interaction forces among the particles.

The application parallelization is based on partitioning the computation task among the processing nodes through the data distribution: each node gets a set of particles to the process. The data structure, describing the current state of all particles, is maintained by the master and is broadcasted in the beginning of a time step computation.

Before starting the computation of each step, each node must communicate with the master in order to send the current state of its particles. After the master have collected all the information, it broadcasts the data structure to all tasks. Each parallel task is mapped in only one node. The memory used to store all data structures is dynamically allocated, minimizing the total memory requirements for each task.

The Figure 4 presents the DFAT for all slaves, using the static VRP approach. As we can observe, the maximum distance from average time was about 5.5%

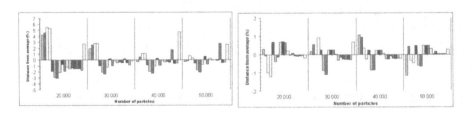

Fig. 4. PFG with static VRP   **Fig. 5.** PFG with dynamic VRP

in some problems configuration. To solve this imbalance we used analytical performance models for different workload ranges, in order to get a more accurate prediction and then a more balanced execution across a dynamic VRP strategy, as done and presented to matrix multiplication. After these modifications the balancing was improved and the new results are showed in the figure 5. After adjusting the models and the VRP, we reduced the maximum distance to near 1% of the worse situation of unbalancing. This represent an improvement of 80% in the workload distribution (load balancing) if compared with static approach.

4.3   Comparing the PEMPIs VRP with SS Strategy

After these promising results, we have executed another evaluation using our strategy and comparing it with the self-scheduling (SS) method. The reason for the choice of self-scheduling method is the following: a natural way to dynamically adjust the workload in an heterogeneous environment is to assign the computational task at run-time, depending on the availability of the nodes. This approach is widely used for many heterogeneous systems, such as task-of-bags grid applications.

Figure 6 presents the experimental tests to MM using 18 processors (4 intel, 7 bio and 7 taurus) and the speed-up curve comparing the VRP and SS strategy. A simple inspection in the figure is possible to verify that our strategy outperforms the self-scheduling method and the speedup increases in function of n. For example, to $n = 1440$ the speedup is approximately 1.5 and to $n = 2880$ this value is near to 3.

We can note that for matrices with order 720 and 1080, PEMPIs VRP presented a performance a little lower than SS, with speed-up factors of 0.92 and 0.97, respectively. We consider the following reasons for this result: the overhead of our strategy compared to the simplicity of SS and the lack of a more optimized implementation. But the main reason is, due to the fact that PEMPIs VRP makes use of an analytical performance model for the workload distribution. After adjusting the analytical models we improved the speed-up, in relation to previous results, as far as 5% to $n = 720$ and $n = 1080$. The accuracy of this performance model is very important in our strategy.

The figure 7 compared our strategy with Self-scheduling method to PGF using 18 processors (4 intel, 6 bio and 8 taurus). The experimental tests show that PEMPIs VRP outperforms SS by around 10%, allowing us to conclude the usability of our proposal.

5   Some Related Works

With the growing adoption of heterogeneous distributed environments, mainly clusters and computational grids, many researches have dedicated to research many subjects relative to these platforms. Among these subjects we can quote the performance analysis and prediction of parallel and distributed applications. The execution time is much important for applications designed to solve complex

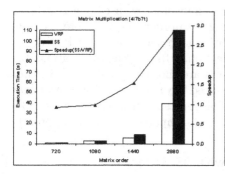

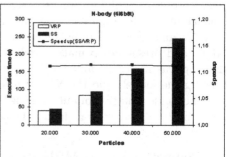

Fig. 6. PEMPIs VRP x SS - MM   **Fig. 7.** PEMPIs VRP x SS - PGF

problems using such platforms. So it is always meaningful to create mechanisms to improve the applications response time.

Vraalsen [15] presents a strategy for performance prediction of applications designed to grid environments. Also, the strategy intends to detect unexpected behavior caused by systems dynamic. Among the causes for this behavior are the resource sharing and the load balance.

For the real time monitoring of the application it is used a tool named Autopilot [16]. The tool was developed to dynamic environments and can execute real time measurement of the application in heterogeneous computational grids. For that, Autopilot uses sensors and actuators spread across the environment.

In the Self-Scheduling strategy (SS) each process requests a piece of work when it is idle. This piece of work is the smaller possible. In the literature we can find others strategies, as Chunk Self-Scheduling (CSS), Guided Self-Scheduling (GSS) and Trapezoidal Self-Scheduling (TSS) [5, 6, 7, 8, 9].

In the [17] a study of dynamic schemes for loops with step dependencies for heterogeneous clusters has been reported. The work extends three dynamic schemes (CSS, TSS and DTSS) by introducing synchronization points at certain intervals so that processors compute in pipelined fashion.

A study about the overhead of a dynamic load balancing library (DLBL) for large irregular data-parallel scientific applications on general-purpose cluster is described in [18]. The DLBL is based on dynamic loop scheduling techniques.

In the paper [19] is presented a game theoretic approach to solve the static load balancing problem in a distributed system. The solution adopted is based on the Nash Bargaining Solution (NBS) and, different of our work, they use simulation to test the proposed scheme.

6   Conclusions

In this paper we have discussed an alternative approach to workload distribution in heterogeneous environments using performance prediction analytical models, named PEMPIs VRP. The main contribution of our strategy is the adoption of these analytical performance prediction models to load balancing.

The analysis of the execution times distribution of the parallel tasks in the application programs, showed that the computational workload for each processing node in the heterogeneous cluster was adequate, presenting a more uniform execution times distribution after the application of our strategy. For most cases, the execution time of parallel tasks was under 5% (MM) and 2% (PGF) off the average. The imbalance presented by the VRP's static strategy was minimized when the values of VRP were determined dynamically. To some configurations, the imbalance was reduced from 25% to 5%. The new approach uses different analytical models to determine the VRP values and produces a more homogeneous workload distribution than the static approach.

For future works, we intend to extend our strategy to consider multiple processors or cores in SMP nodes to compute the workload for each task. Preliminary studies show that dual-processor nodes has better performance than dual-core processors. One possible explanation for this consideration is, the memory bus that is shared by both cores to the main memory. A more detailed investigation is being conducted.

The application of our strategy in a computational grid requires take into consideration many other subjects, such as, the ratio of workload and communication times and network latency. These aspects are being studied and developed in a research middleware project.

References

1. Németh, Z., Sunderam, V.: Characterizing grids: Attributes, definitions, and formalisms. Journal of Grid Computing 1(1), 9–23 (2003)
2. Foster, I., Kesselman, C., Nick, J.M., Tuecke, S.: The physiology of the grid: An open grid services architecture for distributed systems integration. Technical Report OGSI WG, Global Grid Forum (June 2002)
3. Snir, M., Otto, S.: MPI — The Complete Reference: The MPI Core. MIT Press, Cambridge (1998)
4. Gropp, W., Huss-Lederman, S., Lumsdaine, A., Lusk, E., Nitzberg, B., Saphir, W., Snir, M.: MPI — The Complete Reference: the MPI-2 Extensions, vol. 2. MIT Press, Cambridge (1998)
5. Polychronopoulos, C.D., Kuck, D.J.: Guided self-scheduling: a practical scheduling scheme for parallel supercomputers. IEEE Transactions on Computers C-36(12), 1425–1439 (1987)
6. Tzen, T.T., Ni, L.M.: Trapezoidal self-scheduling: A practical scheduling scheme for parallel compilers. IEEE Transactions on Parallel and Distributed Systems 4(1), 87–98 (1993)
7. Shih, W.C., Yang, C.T., Tseng, S.S.: A performance-based approach to dynamic workload distribution for master-slave applications on grid environments. In: GPC 73–82 (2006)
8. Yang, C.T., Shih, W.C., Tseng, S.S.: A dynamic partitioning self-scheduling scheme for parallel loops on heterogeneous clusters. In: International Conference on Computational Science, vol. (1), pp. 810–813 (2006)

9. Yang, C.T., Chang, S.C.: A parallel loop self-scheduling on extremely heterogeneous pc clusters. In: International Conference on Computational Science, pp. 1079–1088 (2003)
10. Li, H., Tandri, S., Stumm, M., Sevcik, K.C.: Locality and loop scheduling on NUMA multiprocessors. In: Proceedings of the 1993 International Conference on Parallel Processing. Volume II - Software, pp. II-140–II-147. CRC Press, Boca Raton (1993)
11. Buyya, R.: High Performance Cluster Computing: Architectures and Systems. Prentice Hall PTR, Upper Saddle River (1999)
12. Foster, I., Kesselman, C.: The Grid 2: Blueprint for a New Computing Infrastructure. Morgan Kaufmann Publishers Inc., San Francisco (2003)
13. Midorikawa, E.T., Oliveira, H., Laine, J.M.: Pempis: A new methodology for modeling and prediction of mpi programs performance. International Journal of Parallel Programming 33(5), 499–527 (2005)
14. Franklin, M., Govindan, V.: The n-body problem: Distributed system load balancing and performance evaluation. Technical Report 93-16, Department of Computer Science and Engineering, Washington University, St. Louis (2003)
15. Vraalse, F., Aydt, R.A., Mendes, C.L., Reed, D.A.: Performance contracts: Predicting and monitoring grid application behavior. In: Lee, C.A. (ed.) GRID 2001. LNCS, vol. 2242, pp. 154–165. Springer, Heidelberg (2001)
16. Ribler, R.L., Vetter, J.S., Simitci, H., Reed, D.A.: Autopilot: Adaptive control of distributed applications. In: 7th IEEE Symposium on High-Performance Distributed Computing (HPDC), pp. 172–179 (1998)
17. Ciorba, F.M., Andronikos, T., Riakiotakis, I., Chronopoulos, A.T., Papakonstantinou, G.: Dynamic multi phase scheduling for heterogeneous clusters. In: 20th International Parallel and Distributed Processing Symposium (IPDPS' 06), Rhodes Island, Greece, p. 10. IEEE Computer Society Press, Los Alamitos (2006)
18. Banicescu, I., Carino, R.L., Pabico, J.P., Balasubramaniam, M.: Overhead analysis of a dynamic load balancing library for cluster computing. In: 19th IEEE International Parallel and Distributed Processing Symposium (IPDPS'05) - Workshop 1, Washington, DC, USA, IEEE Computer Society Press, Los Alamitos (2005)
19. Penmatsa, S., Chronopoulos, A.T.: Cooperative load balancing for a network of heterogeneous computers. In: 20th IEEE International Parallel and Distributed Processing Symposium (IPDPS 2006), 15th Heterogeneous Computing Workshop, p. 10. IEEE Computer Society Press, Los Alamitos (2006)

Block-Based Allocation Algorithms for FLASH Memory in Embedded Systems

Pangfeng Liu[1], Chung-Hao Chuang[1], and Jan-Jan Wu[2]

[1] Department of Computer Science and Information Engineering
National Taiwan University, Taipei, Taiwan
pangfeng@csie.ntu.edu.tw
[2] Institute of Information Science, Academia Sinica, Taipei, Taiwan

Abstract. A flash memory has write-once and bulk-erase properties so that an intelligent allocation algorithm is essential to providing applications efficient storage service. This paper first demonstrates that the online version of FLASH allocation problem is difficult, since we can find an adversary that makes every online algorithm to use as many number of blocks as a naive and inefficient algorithm. As a result we propose an offline allocation algorithm called *Best Match* (BestM) for allocating blocks in FLASH file systems. The experimental results indicate that BestM delivers better performance than a previously proposed First Re-arrival First Serve (FRFS) method.

1 Introduction

The recent rapid developments of embedded systems have changed many aspects of our daily life. More and more embedded systems are deployed in household appliances, office machinery, transportation vehicles, and industrial controllers. These tiny devices, with the help from increasing computing power of modern microprocessors, are able to perform and control complex operations. With this advancing embedded system technology more and more "smart" devices are able to provide inexpensive and reliable controlling capability.

There are two special properties in the flash file system management – *write-once* and *bulk-erasing*. The term write-once means that if there is a data in a storage space, it cannot be overwritten in place. The new data must be placed into another available place and the original data is declared out-of-date. If a data is updated multiple number of times the correct location of the data will change with time. This characteristic makes the management of flash file system very different from disk file systems.

A *bulk-erasing* operation is performed when there are a large number of un-marked and marked storage spaces mixed together in the flash file system. Before a "erase" operation the latest data within the regions that will be erased needs to be copied to other space with no data. These copy operations and reusing the space occupied by the old version of data are managed by the *garbage collection*.

There have been various techniques proposed to improve the performance of garbage collection for flash memory [6,7,4]. Kawaguchi, et al. proposed a

V. Malyshkin (Ed.): PaCT 2007, LNCS 4671, pp. 569–578, 2007.
© Springer-Verlag Berlin Heidelberg 2007

cost-benefit policy [6], which uses a value-driven heuristic function as a block-recycling policy. Chiang, et al. [4] refined the work by considering the locality in the run-time access patterns. Kim, et al. [7] proposed to periodically move live data among blocks so that blocks have more even life-cycles.

Although researchers have proposed excellent garbage-collection policies, there is little work done in providing a deterministic performance guarantee for flash-memory storage systems. It has been shown that garbage collection could impose almost 40 seconds of blocking time on time-critical tasks without proper management [8]. As a result, Chang, et al. [3] proposed a deterministic garbage collection mechanism to provide a predictable garbage collection mechanism. If the allocation method uses less blocks, the number of flash memory blocks requested to update reduces when the system executes garbage collection. Therefore, a good allocation algorithm improves garbage collection time. This motivates us to develop great allocation algorithms to reduce the resource consumption for flash memory systems.

Chou, et al. [5] proposed several allocation algorithms, including a First Re-arrival First Serve (FRFS) method that provides excellence performance. FRFS sorts the page access sequence by their re-arrival time and assigns each of them an ordinal order accordingly. The algorithm then allocates blocks for page access request according to this ordinal number. In this paper we compare our algorithm with FRFS by examining their performance.

2   Flash Memory Allocation Model

A flash memory system consists of some blocks and each block has a fixed number of cells. We assume that the number of cells in each block is denoted by B. Every cell has the same amount of capacity for data, and every block has the same number of cells. We denote the cells in every block by $C[0]$, $C[1]$, $C[2]$, ..., $C[B-1]$.

Every flash memory cell is in one of the three states – *free*, *valid* and *invalid*. A cell is free means that there is no data in it. A cell is valid means that there is data valid stored in it. A cell is invalid indicates that the data in it is no longer valid while the valid data is actually stored elsewhere. From the status of its cells we define that a block is either *active* or *inactive*. A block is active means that there is at least one valid cell in it, otherwise it is inactive. In other words an inactive block has only free or invalid cells. Note that only inactive blocks can be erased and reused.

Initially all cells are free and all blocks are inactive. When a data is placed into a free cell, the cell becomes valid and the block which contains the cell becomes active. If an inactive block becomes active, we assign an index to the block. Unlike a disk file system, a valid cell cannot be written in place. If we want to relocate a valid cell, we need to put the data into another free cell so that the original cell becomes invalid. Then the invalid cells can be transformed into free cells by an *erase* operation, which erases all cells in a block simultaneously. After the erase operation all cells of an inactive blocks return to the free state and can be reused. On the other hand, an active block, which has at least a valid cell in it, cannot be erased.

2.1 Page Access Sequence

We assume that a file is partitioned into pages of the same size, and every page is denote by a letter (e.g., a, b, c). Each page has the same amount of data as a cell in the flash memory system, so that any page can fit into any cell. We access a file by pages, therefore file access can be modeled as a sequence of page access. This sequence is defined as *page access sequence*.

A page can appear multiple times in a page access sequence, and we need to make a distinction among these appearances. For the purpose of assigning pages to cells, we actually mean assigning a particular appearance of a page to a cell. To avoid further confusion in notation, we will use the notation p_i to denote a i-th appearance of a page p.

2.2 Flash Memory Allocation

For a page access sequence, we only need to allocate free cells for page write operation, since reading operations do not change the status of any cell. We need to allocate free cells for page writes and set the status of those cells they previously resided to invalid. Consequently, given a page access sequence, we can focus on page writes and neglect pages reads.

After we retain only the writing operations in a page access sequence, we must assign a free cell for each page write. We use a *page allocation function* for this purpose, that is, an allocation function F maps a page appearance p_i to a block $F(p_i)$ and puts page appearance p_i into the first free cell C in block $F(p_i)$, then changes the state of C from free to valid. If the block $F(p_i)$ is inactive, we set it to "active". In addition, if p_i is not the first appearance of page p in this sequence, we set the status of the cell it previously resided, which is in block $F(p_{i-1})$, to be invalid. If all cells of the block become invalid or free, we can reuse the block and set it to be "inactive".

3 Algorithms

3.1 The Online Problem

We first consider a naive algorithm for the online page allocation problem. Let us assume that there are N different pages in the input sequence. The algorithm simply place all the requests for the same pages into the same block. As a result each block contains only a single most up-to-date content of a page, plus all the previous contents that all have been marked invalid. This simple minded algorithm uses N blocks, which is much more than the obvious lower bound $\frac{N}{B}$, where B is the number of cells in a block.

We design an online adversary that makes every online algorithm to use N blocks, where N is the number of different pages in the input sequence. The adversary first asks the algorithm to allocate a cell for the first page appearance a_0. Then the adversary asks the algorithm to allocate a cell for the second page appearance b_0. If the algorithm puts b_0 into the same block as a_0 is in, the adversary asks the algorithm to allocate a cell for the same page again – the page appearance will be b_1. That is, the adversary keeps asking the algorithm to allocate a cell for the same page b until the algorithm allocates a block *different* from the block page appearance a_0 is in. The adversary keeps doing this for page c, d and so on. Eventually every page has to be in its "own" block, therefore, every online algorithm needs to use up to N blocks in the worst case.

Theorem 1. *There exists an adversary that will find an input consisting of N different pages, for any algorithm so that the algorithm must use N blocks.*

First-Come-First-Serve Algorithm. For the online problem Chou and Liu proposed a simple First Come First Serve (FCFS) algorithm [5]. The idea of FCFS is to assign blocks to page appearances according to their arrival time, so that we can use new blocks as late as possible. FCFS is simple enough to be used in the online model. However, the experimental results from [5] indicate that it does not provide superior performance.

3.2   The Offline Problem

We first review a previously proposed First-Re-arrival-First-Served (FRFS) algorithm [5]. Chou and Liu showed that FRFS produces good schedules for inputs taken from the actual disk tracing [5].

First-Rearrival-First-Serve. The idea of FRFS is to assign blocks to page appearance according to when the page will *re-arrive*, so that those page appearances that will re-arrive earlier will be placed together, and the block they reside can be reused as early as possible.

Although FRFS reuses blocks as soon as possible, it may use many new blocks before reusing a block. For example, let the page access sequence be 1, 2, $\ldots$, N, 1, 2, 1, 3, $\ldots$, 1, N, and each block has two cells. FRFS allocates the first N page appearances to N different blocks according to their re-arrival time. As a result FRFS uses N different blocks before reusing the first block. Given any page access sequence of N different pages, the worst possible case is to use N blocks. For the given sequence above, FRFS actually produces the *worst* possible schedule, thus we propose a new method called *Best Match* (BestM) so that this worst case behavior is avoided.

Best Match. The idea of the Best Match algorithm is to assign page appearances to cells according to their *difference*. A difference between two page appearances is defined as the sum of the difference of their arrival time and the difference of their re-arrival time. The reason that we use difference to allocate cells is that it is likely that all cells in the same block will be set to valid (and invalid) at about at the same time, so the flash memory allocation could use the minimal number of blocks.

Best match allocation algorithm uses a data structure called *block list* to store the flash memory blocks. Every block contains B cells and a block index. Initially the block list does not contain any block. When a page appearance arrives, the BestM algorithm computes a block index i for it. We then search the block list for block i. If block i is not in the block list yet, we insert a new block into the block list and set its index to i. After BestM decides the block index for an incoming page appearance, BestM places this page appearance into the first free cell of the assigned block. If a block becomes inactive and we want to recycle it, we just delete it from the block list.

BestM algorithm has two stages. In the first stage, BestM computes the re-arrival time for every page appearance. After knowing the re-arrival time of every page appearance, we decide the block indices for those page appearances that will *not* appear again. Since these pages will not be relocated, we reserve the first $\lceil N/B \rceil$ blocks for them. Specifically, we sort these "never-again" page appearances by their arriving time, and those B page appearances having the earliest arrival time are assigned to block index 0, and those next earliest B page appearances are assigned to block index 1, and so on. The total number of blocks used in this stage is $\lceil N/B \rceil$, so the first block indices that be be assigned in the second stages is $\lceil N/B \rceil$.

In the second stage, we compute the *length* for those page appearances that the corresponding pages *will* appear again. The length of p_i is defined as $A(p_{i+1}) - A(p_i)$, where $A(p_i)$ is the arrival time of page appearance p_i. Then we sort the page access sequence according to their lengths. We first select the page appearance that has the longest length, which is denoted by p_j. When there are multiple page appearances that have the same longest length, we randomly pick one. We then select $B - 1$ page appearances that have the minimum sum of the difference from page appearance p_j. That is, we selected $B - 1$ page appearances that have the smallest sum of differences from p_j among all other page appearances, and place them into the same block as p_j. We repeat this process until all page appearances are assigned to blocks.

After each page appearance is assigned to a block, we know when every block is used and when it can be recycled. thus we can compute the necessary number of blocks for the sequence. BestM places the page appearances into the block according to the block indices. When a page appearance arrives, we put it into the first free cell of the assigned block. We insert a new block into the block list and increase the number of active blocks by one, if it is the first page appearance that is put into this block. When a page re-arrives, we also need to set the status of the cell it previously resided to be invalid. If all cells of a block are invalid or free, the block is inactive and can be reused, therefore we can delete the block in the block list and decrease the number of active blocks by one. We maintain the number of active blocks and at the end we know the maximum number of blocks required by the algorithm BestM.

4   Experimental Results

4.1   Implementation Issues

For the longest page appearance p_j that has not yet been selected, we select other $B - 1$ page appearances that have the minimum difference from p_j and assign them to the same block. Obviously, BestM can be implemented in $O(M^2)$ time, where M is the number of page appearances. When the length of page access sequence is very longer, we will spend a great amount of time to pack page appearances together. Consequently the time complexity of BestM will be much higher than FRFS, which runs in $O(M log M)$ time. Fortunately, we use an *interval tree* data structure plus a *bounded search* technique to reduce the time complexity of matching page appearances.

We consider a page appearances as a "time windows". The time window of page appearance p_i is from $A(p_i)$ to $A(p_{i+1})$, where $A(p_i)$ is the time when the page appearance p_i arrives. For the longest page appearance p_j, other page appearances may intersect with it, be contained in it, or be disjoint from it. BestM will find the most suitable page appearances from these three categories.

Intersected Intervals. We use an interval tree to find the most suitable page appearances from the first category, that is, those that intersect with p_j. First, we build the interval tree using a standard technique [9]. Since there are at most N distinct pages, and the page appearances from the same page do not intersect, the time to query the interval tree in order to find all intervals that intersect with p_j is bounded to $O(N + log M)$ [9]. The number of page appearances we will find is at most $2N$, since each endpoint of p_j intersects with at most N page appearances, and p_j is the longest interval. From these $2N$ intervals, we select the $B-1$ appearances that have the smallest difference from p_j. Let S_0 denote the set of these intervals. The set S_0 can be computed in time $O(N \log B)$ – we simply maintain a heap of the $B - 1$ elements, and the number of insertion/deletion is bounded by $O(N)$. The total number of selections is $O(\frac{M}{B})$ so the total time is $O(\frac{M}{B}(N + \log M + N \log B))$.

Contained Intervals. We now consider the intervals that are *contained* in p_j. An interval q_k is contained in another interval p_j if and only if the arrival time of q_k is no earlier than the arrival time of p_j, and the re-arrival time of q_k is no later than the re-arrival time of p_j.

The length of the longest interval p_j can be up to M time steps in the extreme case. If we examine each individual page appearance to determine those that are contained in p_j, the time complexity is $\Omega(M)$, which is unacceptable. However, for a page appearance that is contained in p_j, the longer its length, the smaller its difference from p_j, so if we examine these page appearances according to their lengths, we can reduce the time to find the most suitable appearances that should be put together with p_j.

By using the same interval tree described earlier, we can find all page appearances that are contained in every page appearance efficiently. First we sort the page appearances according to their lengths, then the appearances query the interval tree in non-decreasing length order. For every page appearance q_k, we find the intervals that intersect it by querying the interval tree. If both end points of q_k intersect with the same page appearance p_i, then q_k is contained in p_i. In addition, since a long page appearance queries the interval tree before a short appearance, each appearance will have a list of appearances that it contains in non-decreasing length order. The time complexity for this preprocessing is bounded by $O(N + \log M)$ per page appearance, and is $O(M(N + log M))$ for all appearances.

We now need to find the $B - 1$ longest intervals that are contained in p_j. For each page appearance, it can be contained by at most N intervals, so the total number of entries in the "contained list" for all appearances is bounded by $O(MN)$. A page appearance can easily determine the longest remaining $B - 1$ appearances by scanning through its list. Hence, the total time to find best $B - 1$ intervals that every page appearance contains is $O(MN)$. The total time including the preprocessing is therefore $O(M(N + log M))$. We use S_1 to denote the set of the best $B - 1$ intervals that are contained in p_j.

Disjoint Intervals. Now we describe the selection process of finding the best $B-1$ page appearances that do not intersect with, or are not included by p_j. For each page q, we consider the last appearance q_b that appears before p_j but do not have intersection with p_j. It is obvious that any page appearance $q_c, c < b$ has a larger difference than q_b has. Similarly, let the first appearance q_a that appears after p_j but does not have intersection with p_j. Any page appearance $q_c, c > a$ will have a larger difference than q_a has.

We can think of these appearances as $2N$ queues, where each page has two queues of appearances that are before or after the intervals of p_j. The elements in these $2N$ queues are sorted in increasing "difference" order so that the first element has the minimum difference in the queue.

Now we need to find the $B - 1$ appearances the have the minimum difference from these $2N$ queues. We can accomplish this in two steps. First we construct a heap of size $B - 1$ with the first element from these $2N$ queues. This heap is constructed by repeated inserting the first element of each queue, and those that are not among the $B - 1$ smallest elements are discarded. Second we start removing elements from the heap. Once we remove the minimum element from the heap, we insert the next element from the same queue into the heap. We repeatedly remove $B-1$ elements from this heap, and the these elements are the $B - 1$ appearances that has the minimum difference from p_j. Let S_2 denote the set of these intervals found. The total time complexity is bounded by $O((N + B) \log B)$ per p_j, and $O(\frac{M}{B}(N + B) \log B)$ overall.

Time Complexity. We now calculate the time complexity. The time to find $B-1$ intersected page appearances with minimum difference is $O(\frac{M}{B}(N+\log M + N \log B))$. The time to find best $B - 1$ contained intervals is $O(MN)$. The time to find the best $B - 1$ disjoint page appearances is $O(\frac{M}{B}(N + B) \log B)$. The time to choose the best $B - 1$ intervals from S_0, S_1, and S_2 is $O(B)$ per p_j, and

$O(M)$ overall. The total time combined is therefore $O(MN + \frac{M}{B} \log M)$ When B is a constant the overall time complexity is $O(M(N + logM))$.

4.2 Experimental Settings

We have three different trace files collected from three computer systems. The first file is collected from a NTFS file system. The applications that access this file system include text editor, web browser and P2P software. It is collected with Microsoft trace-log and analyzed by Microsoft tracedmp. The second trace file is downloaded from BYU Trace Distribution Center [1]. It is from a database system Postgres 7.1.2, Redhat Linux with one client running 20 iterations. The third file is downloaded from flash-memory research group in CSIE, NTU. [2]. It is a FAT32 file system over a portable device. The applications have emails sending/receiving, movie playing and downloading, web surfing and so on.

4.3 Effect of the Length of Page Access Sequence

Figure 1 shows the relation between the length of page access sequence and the average number of used blocks for the first, second and third trace files respectively. FCFS performs worst because when there are a large number of pages that will not re-appear, FRFS and BestM allocate them in the same block area, but FCFS may put them into different blocks so that FCFS cannot reuse those blocks.

In Figure 1 although FRFS reuses block faster than BestM does, it may assign those page appearances that arrive at very different time to the same blocks. Consequently, FRFS may allocate a lot of blocks before it can reuse any. On the other hand, BestM places page appearances whose arrival and re-arrival time are close to each other into the same blocks, BestM combines the advantage of reusing blocks as early as possible and using new blocks as late as possible. Consequently BestM performs much better than FRFS, except for this kind of trace file that there are very few pages that usually re-arrive and so many pages that will not re-appear. FCFS performs badly for any kind of trace file.

4.4 The Effects of Cell Number

Figure 2 shows the ratio of the average numbers of blocks used by FCFS and BestM using three different file system traces under different B values. The ratio between the number of blocks used by FCFS and BestM rapidly increases because FCFS may not be able to decrease the number of used blocks but BestM is. However, when B reaches 256 for the first trace file this ratio actually drops because FCFS luckily puts some page appearances that do not re-arrive into the same block.

Figure 2 also shows the ratio of the average numbers of blocks used by FRFS and BestM using three file traces. When the number of cells in a block (B) increases the ratio increases for all three trace files. When B increases, FRFS is more likely and mistakenly to put page appearances with very different arrival time into the same blocks, and consequently use more blocks.

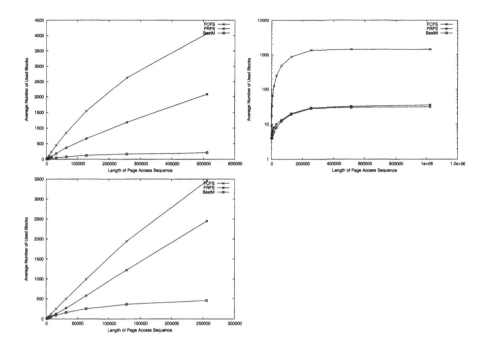

Fig. 1. The number of blocks used by FCFS, FRFS and BestM when given different sized prefix of the NTFS file system trace, BYU Trace Distribution Center trace log, and FAT32 portable device trace

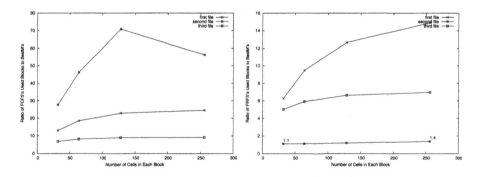

Fig. 2. Effects of the number of cells in each block on the ratio of the number of used blocks used by FCFS and BestM, and used by FRFS to BestM

5   Conclusion

This paper proposes an allocation problem in the context of flash memory systems. We use an online adversary argument to show that when the page access sequence is given one page appearance at a time, for every algorithm we can always find a bad input so that the performance is as bad as a simple naive algorithm.

We propose a BestM allocation algorithm that puts those page appearances whose arrival time and re-arrival time are close to each other into the same block. To overcome the aggressive behavior of a previously proposed FRFS, BestM matches together those page appearances whose arrival time and re-arrival time are close to each other. The idea is that by doing so we may obtain a balance between having to use new blocks and being able to reuse blocks.

We evaluate the performance BestM by experiments. We compare the allocation results with a previous First Re-arrival First Serve algorithm (FRFS), and show that BestM outperforms FRFS when given real trace data. When the length of page access sequence or the number of cells in every block grows, this advantage becomes more obvious. Although the $O(M(N + logM))$ time complexity of BestM is slightly higher than FRFS, the number of required blocks is reduced by a factor of 5 from FRFS to BestM.

References

1. Byu trace distribution center. `http://tds.cs.byu.edu/tds/index.jsp`
2. Chang, L.-P., Kuo, T.-W.: An adaptive stripping architecture for flash memory storage systems of embedded systems. In: IEEE Eighth Real-Time and Embedded Technology and Applications Symposium, pp. 601–606 (2002)
3. Chang, L.-P., Kuo, T.-W., Lo, S.-W.: Real-time garbage collection for flash-memory storage systems of real-time embedded systems. ACM Transaction on Embedded Computing Systems 3(4), 837–863 (2004)
4. Chiang, M.-L., Lee, C.-H., Chang, R.-C.: Manage flash memory in personal communicate devices. In: Proceedings of IEEE International Symposium on Consumer Electronics, pp. 177–182 (1997)
5. Chou, L.-F., Liu, P.: Efficient allocation algorithms for flash file systems. In: 11th International Conference on Parallel and Distributed Systems, pp. 634–641 (2005)
6. Kawaguchi, A., Nishioka, S., Motoda, H.: A flash memory based file system. In: Proceedings of the USENIX Technical Conference, pp. 155–164 (1995)
7. Kim, H.-J., Lee, S.-G.: Memory management for flash storage system. In: Proceedings of the Computer Software and Applications Conference, pp. 284–293 (1999)
8. Malik, V.: Jffs2 is broken. In: Mailing List of Memory Technology Device (MTD) Subsystem for Linux (June 28, 2001)
9. Rivest, R.L., Cormen, T.H., Leiserson, C.E., Stein, C.: Introduction to Algorithms. MIT Press, Cambridge (2001)

Variable Reassignment in the T++ Parallel Programming Language

Alexander Moskovsky, Vladimir Roganov, Sergei Abramov,
and Anton Kuznetsov

Program Systems Institute of the Russian Academy of Sciences,
Pereslavl-Zalessky, 152020, Yaroslavl region, Russia
moskov@lcc.chem.msu.ru, var@pereslavl.ru,
abram@botik.ru, tonic@pereslavl.ru
http://www.botik.ru/PSI

Abstract. The paper describes the OpenTS parallel programming system that provides the runtime environment for T++ language. T++ is an extension for C++ that adds a set of keywords to C++, allowing smooth transition from sequential to parallel applications. In this context the support of repeated assignments to a variable is an important feature. The paper focused on semantics and implementation of such variables in T++. Applications written in T++ can be run on computational clusters, SMPs and GRIDs, either in Linux or Windows OS.

Keywords: OpenTS, T++, parallel computing, variable reassignment.

1 Introduction

There are a lot of academic and industry projects exist in the field of high-level parallel programming, many of which are successful and well-known [1, 4, 2, 5, 3, 6, 7, 8, 9, 10, 11, 12, 13, 14, 17, 18]. However, none of them has widespread adoption outside high-performance computing community. Today, when parallel processors are more accessible to mass market than ever before (multi-core CPUs, small clusters), parallel programming tools has to be simple enough for mainstream use. That makes further research in the parallel programming field more necessary than ever before.

Our new and original OpenTS (Open T-system) approach has many advantages due to combination of simplicity and high performance. The main project goal is to ease the process of writing parallel programs for moderately experienced programmers. Therefore OpenTS users don't have to be able to write very efficient code, but nevertheless they can make quick though efficient parallel applications.

Three ideas are basic for the OpenTS:

- Parallel graph reduction is used as a programming model [11](coarse grain dataflow).
- Extending a sequential programming language (C,C++) with additional keywords to express parallelism.

V. Malyshkin (Ed.): PaCT 2007, LNCS 4671, pp. 579–588, 2007.

– Dynamic parallelization at runtime on basis of directives (T++ attributes) specified by a programmer.

T++ is a native input language for OpenTS and is a transparent attribute-based extension of C++ [16] that supports parallelism. It is simple, intuitively obvious and easy to learn.

In this paper we focus on T++ language distinctive feature: ability to reassign variables. This feature differentiates our project from the other parallel programming systems based on functional programming (e.g. SISAL [14]).

The paper is organized as following. First, OpenTS programming model and language are described. Then, underlying shared memory mechanism is outlined. Finally, there are performance measurements and comparison of OpenTS application with an analogue.

2   OpenTS Programming Model

The OpenTS programming model is very similar to a coarse-grain dataflow model [10, 3]. In OpenTS in order to write a parallel program, a programmer must designate the following:

– Independent parts (pure functions) of the program (parallelism granules or T-functions), that can be moved over the network and computed remotely.
– Variables that are used to exchange data between parallelism grains (T-variables).

The rest of work is performed by the OpenTS components: T++ compiler and runtime support library.

It should be kept in mind that granules of parallelism must be large enough (coarse grains) to avoid overhead inflicted by the runtime system operating with relatively small grains. So, a grain with, say, a single floating-point multiplication would not be efficient, because time needed to transfer such grain to a computing node can be much greater than grain computing time. On the other hand, large grain size is often the cause of a small number of grains and unbalanced computational load in multiprocessor.

Granule aggregation technique is available in OpenTS for recursive programs, similar to "task inlining" technique of Multilisp [6]. In order to create an input programming language for OpenTS, existing programming language should be extended with extra keywords or pseudo-comments. Currently, only C++ extension "T++" is implemented, Refal [15] version is underway.

3   T++ Language

The T++ language adds the following keywords (attributes) to C++:

– **tfun** — a function attribute which designates a T-function that may return a non-ready value. T-function represents a granule of parallelism. As for now, a T-function cannot be a class method but must be an ordinary C function.

- **tval** — a variable attribute which enables variables to contain a non-ready value (T-value). Such values are produced by T-functions. At any moment of time T-values can be in one of two possible states: non-ready, when producer T-function is still working, or ready, when producer finished and returned a result. The T-variable can be cast to the original C++ type variable, what makes producer T-functions running and the thread of execution suspend until T-value becomes ready. That it very similar to "dataflow variable" [10] or "mentat variable" [3] or "futures" [6]. That also differs T++ from standard data-flow models, where task is ready for execution only after all incoming data is ready — in opposite, threads in OpenTS can be launched before any incoming data for a granule is ready.
- **tptr** — T-pointer, a T++ analogue of C++ pointer that can hold reference to a non-ready value (T-value).
- **tout** — a function parameter attribute used to specify parameters whose values are produced by the function. This is a T++ analog of the "by-reference" parameter passing in C++.
- **tct** — an explicit T-context specification. This keyword is used for specification of additional attributes of T-entities.
- **tdrop** — a T++-specific function that makes a variable value ready. It may be very helpful in optimization when it's necessary to make non-ready values ready before the producer function finishes.
- **twait** — a T++-specific function that causes waiting for an argument expression to be ready.

Open C++ [21] is used for conversion of T++ programs into C++. It translates all T++ attributes into the pure C++ code.

The recursive calculation of the given Fibonacci number is the simplest parallel program:

```
#include <stdio.h>
tfun int fib(int n) {
    return (n < 2) ? n : fib(n-1) + fib(n-2);
}
tfun int main (int argc, char *argv[]) {
    if (argc != 2) {return 1;}
    int n = atoi(argv[1]);
    printf("Fibonacci %d is %d\n",n,(int)fib(n));
    return 0;
}
```

In this case, invocations of **fib** functions are treated as independent tasks that can be computed in parallel in independent threads, or on the remote computational nodes. You can see that minimal modifications differ the T++ from the C++ code: attributes of T-functions and explicit cast of **fib** function result to **int**. That casting not only extracts value from T-value, which is returned by **fib**, but also makes **main** function to wait for the **fib** result. However, runtime support library may implement a C-call for **fib**. In that case, overhead of calling T-function drops dramatically, and parallelism granules (T-function calls) "aggregated" in a single granule, technique, similar of "task inlining" for MultiLisp [6].

Some specific of the T++ language should be underlined:

- It is a "seamless" C++ extension, which means that evident C++ macrodefinitions of T++ keywords can enable T++ program compilation by a C++ compiler. If some good coding style in T++ is adhered to, such compilation (which is done via "-not" command line option) will result in correct sequential program.
- Garbage collection is supported. Non-ready values that are no longer necessary are detected and destroyed by the runtime system.
- Function execution can be postponed, not necessarily generating any computation after invocation, depending on execution strategy. By default, if no thread is waiting for function result, function execution will be omitted.
- T-variables support repeated assignments. This is done by the tricky protocol of assignment and readiness of the variable values, related to the thread lifecycle.

4   Implementation of Variable Reassignment

The latter T++ feature deserves a more detailed description. Each T-variable is linked with its T-value. T-variables are type-safe: it is possible to assign values of the same type only. A T-variable can have multiple values during its lifetime. T-variables may share the same T-value. In other words, T-variables are wrappers for their values, however, variables may change their values in a way that C++ smart pointers [19] do. T-value can be either non-ready or an ordinary C-value. An assignment of a T-variable to a C-variable makes execution thread to wait until T-value is ready — a usual approach for "futures-based" [6] systems like OpenTS.

```
tval int x;
int y;
x = some_tfun();
y = x;  // will wait until x has a ready value
```

Contrary, assignment of a C-value to a T-variable immediately causes T-value of that variable to be ready.

```
tval int x;
x = some_tfun(); // assigns a non-ready value to x
x = 1; // assigns a ready value to x
x = 2; // unlinks the old value, creates a new one
```

The capability to assign multiple values for a single T-variable required us to introduce "producer" thread concept. For the sake of simplicity, let us consider each T-function call to be executed in a separate thread of execution (a "lightweight thread"). Then, we consider thread as a producer for all values that are allocated in its context. When producer thread is destroyed, all T-values produced by this thread are no longer changed (frozen). Consumer threads don't have any access to T-values, unless values are frozen. Frozen values are also produced when a T-function is called with T-variable as a parameter — snapshot copy of current value is produced. Such frozen values then can be easily shared among concurrent threads or across multiple cluster nodes. Consider the following example of T-variable reassignments:

```
#include <stdio.h>
#define N 10
tfun int tproducer(int i) {
    tval int x;
    x = 2*i;
    return x;
}
tfun int tconsumer(tval int t, int i) {
    return t+i;
}
tfun int main(int argc, char *argv[]) {
    tval int tmp;
    tval int res[N];
    for (int i = 0; i < N; ++i) {
        tmp = tproducer(i);
        res[i] = tconsumer(tmp,i);
    }
    for (int i = 0; i < N; ++i)
        printf("%d\n",(int)res[i]);
    return 0;
}
```

First, take a look at first loop inside main function. On each iteration, the tmp T-variable is assigned a new value — an output of tproducer for i-th iteration. On the next line, tmp is a parameter for tconsumer invocation: tmp value is passed as input to tconsumer. If tmp value was "hot" (like after tmp=i instead of tmp=tproducer(i) assignment), the value would be copied and the copy would be frozen. Inside the tproducer, the x value was initially allocated as "hot" and the tproducer is the value producer. Then the x variable is assigned with 2*i value of type int. On the next line, the value of x variable is assigned to the return value of tproducer call. When the tproducer thread stops, the return value is "frozen" and delivered to consumers (to tmp and t variables). The tconsumer job is trivial — it awaits of its input value (produced by tproducer) and conducts a summation of two integers. On the next interation of the loop, reassignment to tmp will unlink tmp's value of last iteration and the process will continue.

5   Distributed Shared Memory in OpenTS

The OpenTS implementation relies on object-oriented distributed shared memory (OODSM) [20] for storing T-values. The garbage collection is supported for T-values. When OpenTS runtime detects that there is no more links to a given T-value, the value is scrapped and memory address is reused. Each cell has "seqNo" attribute in order to distinguish between various "generations" of objects sharing the same cell.

OpenTS employs MPI [4] as a low-level transport layer. In this case, a "naive" reference count implementation of garbage collection is inapplicable. For instance, MPI library [4] can deliver a bunch of "decrement" messages ahead of corresponding "increments", which could result in premature value destruction. OpenTS utilizes a more sophisticated technique — weighted reference counting. In this approach, each reference has an integer "weight" depending on "weight" of value. A T-value is considered no longer necessary when its weight equals to the original weight assigned at value creation.

6   POV Ray Parallelization with OpenTS

There are a lot of applications that utilize OpenTS as a parallel programming platform. Most of them are simulation tools. Some are developed by groups outside of our institution, like [24, 25]. Here we present our case-study example: implementation of patch for POV Ray (Persistence Of Vision) ray-tracer. In order to evaluate the programming technique as a whole, not only the runtime support library effectiveness and scalability is an issue, but programming language qualities as well. Despite programming language beauty is a subjective matter, we believe that some sharp differences in code statistics, such as the number of lines of code, can be rather convincing.

The well-known POV Ray application is widely used to obtain realistic images using ray-tracing rendering technology. POV Ray is freely distributed with source code evolved from C to C++ during last years. Since ray-tracing consumes a lot of computation resources even for simple scenes, a few parallel versions of POV Ray have been developed and contributed by different authors. There are several approaches to parallelize POV Ray to make it work on multicomputers: from trivial rsh-based scripts, invoking POV Ray executable for parts of target scene on different UNIX hosts, to the most effective PVM and MPI-based implementations, supporting dynamic load balancing and features like animation and interactive display functions.

There are two well-known MPI-based POV Ray ports:

- MPI POVRay, based on POV Ray 3.1g., written in C with MPI patch applied.
- ParaPov, based on POV Ray 3.50c., written in C++ with MPI patch applied.

Total size of POV Ray 3.1g MPI-related source files (mpipov.c and mpipov.h) is more than 1500 lines of code, with multiple changes scattered over many files.

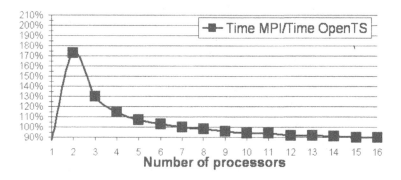

Fig. 1. Performance comparison of T++ and MPI versions of POV Ray

However, an intention to minimize changes in POV Ray code resulted in coding style that sometimes can be challenging to the reviewer. POV Ray 3.50c MPI patch is written in more straightforward C++, about 3000 lines total.

To make comparison more correct, we made our patch applicable to both original POV Ray versions (3.1g and 3.50c). OpenTS port is straightforward: most of porting work consisted in removing unnecessary task management MPI code, replacing it by only two T-functions. Result code is written in C/C++ with T++ patch applied, and no MPI code. T++ source file tpovray.tcc is shorter than 200 lines. Also a few minor changes were made in file povray.c.

Table 1. Benchmark results (in seconds) for scalar, MPI and T++ versions of POV Ray

N procs	C-POVRay	MPI-POVRay	T-POVRay
1	1 364.40	1 368.16	1 578.34
2		1 361.05	787.00
3		682.97	526.33
4		455.81	395.96
5		342.22	318.64
6		273.56	265.79
7		228.26	228.74
8		197.56	200.63
9		171.29	179.21
10		152.27	161.38
11		137.30	146.65
12		125.00	136.00
13		114.95	125.00
14		105.89	116.96
15		98.82	109.59
16		91.97	102.42

Performance comparison has been done with the "chess board scene" taken from the original POV Ray distribution with the scene width and height set to 1500 pixels. The chess board scene has 430 primitives in objects and 41 in bounding shapes. The graph, displaying the ratio between execution times of MPI POV Ray 3.50c and OpenTS is shown on Fig. 1. In table 1 there are execution times for scalar, MPI and T++ versions of POV Ray.

The computational cluster used had the following configuration:

- operating system: Red Hat Linux, kernel 2.4.27.
- 16 cluster nodes; each node: 2CPUs AMD Athlon MP 1800+ RAM 1GB, HDD 40GB.

The performance advantage of T++ version is due to suboptimal load balancing of MPI version. The latter reserves one CPU for management work, and advantage gradually degrades when number of CPUs increases.

7   Related Work

The comprehensive review of all research, conducted in the field of high-level parallel programming tools, extends far beyond limits of this paper. The review by D. Talia [17] which was written in 2000 has 62 citations in bibliography. Since then, interest to parallel programming tools only grew, since multi-core microprocessors appeared on commodity market and cluster computing became very popular.

We would like to stress distinctive features of OpenTS approach:

- OpenTS borrows many ideas from the world of parallel functional programming [8], that differentiates OpenTS from many parallel C++ extensions [18]. At the same time, OpenTS relies on C++ runtime, that overcomes performance limitations of functional programming languages.
- OpenTS has features like reassignment of variables and distributed garbage collector implemented. That differentiates OpenTS approach from the dataflow and future-based approaches like Mentat [3] or Oz [10].
- OpenTS adopts more higher-level implicit approach to parallelism than MPI [4].
- OpenTS has no means to parallelize computations in loops, like OpenMP [1], however, it is oriented primarily on computational clusters.

The way how values of variables in T++ become ready is similar to transaction concept of modern relational databases, however, OpenTS does not follow "transactional memory" approach to parallel programming [22, 23].

8   Conclusion

OpenTS is a tool for high-level parallel programming, providing a runtime for T++ language. It supports variable reassignment that helps in development of complex though efficient parallel applications. T-variable can be assigned a value multiple times, that conforms to a usual imperative style of programming. This feature considerably distinguishes OpenTS from many analogue parallel programming systems. As POV Ray case-study shows, only 200 lines of T++ code is required to parallelize it, while independently developed MPI version is more than 1500 lines long. At the same time, application performance is affected in a very little extent. Many aspects of the system are not covered in this paper, load balancing is the most important. We refer to our previous publication here [16]. The OpenTS approach to parallelism is implicit, since runtime library and compiler together should be able to adapt programs to a wide variety of parallel computers that exist today: multi-cores, SMPs, computational clusters with different kind of interconnects, and GRIDs. At the same time, computational source code of OpenTS is separated from management code (scheduling, task aggregation and so on). We hope that these features together will make OpenTS a useful tool for parallel computing. The OpenTS is available for download at `www.opents.net`.

Acknowledgments. This work is supported by Russian Foundation of Basic Research grant N 050708005ofi_a and basic research program of Presidium of the Russian Academy of Sciences "Development of basics for implementation of distributed scientific informational-computational environment on GRID technologies".

As well, we thank Igor Zagorovsky, German Matveev, Alexandr Inyukhin, Alexandr Vodomerov, Eugene Stepanov, Ilya Konev, Elena Shevchuk, Yuri Shevchuk, Alexei Adamovich, Philip Koryaka, Maxim Kovalenko and others who contributed to the design and implementation of OpenTS and T++.

References

1. Chandra, R., Menon, R., Dagum, L., Kohr, D., Maydan, D., Mcdonald, J.: Parallel Programming in OpenMP. Morgan Kaufmann, Seattle (2000)
2. Kaleev L. V. ,Krishnan S. Charm++: Parallel Programming with Message-Driven Objects in [18], pp. 175–213
3. Grimshaw, A.S.: Easy to Use Object-Oriented Parallel Programming with Mentat IEEE Computer, pp. 39–51 (May 1993)
4. Lusk, E., et al.: MPI-2: Extensions to the Message-Passing Interface MPI Forum (2001)
5. Cilk, R.K.H.: Efficient Multithreaded Computing, Ph. D. Thesis. MIT Department of Electrical Engineering and Computer Science (June 1998) `http://supertech.lcs.mit.edu/cilk/`
6. Halstead, R.: MULTILISP: a language for concurrent symbolic computation ACM Transactions on Programming Languages and Systems (TOPLAS) 7(4), 501–538 (1985)
7. Zhang, L., Krintz, C., Soman, S.: Efficient Support of Fine-grained Futures in Java International Conference on Parallel and Distributed Computing Systems (PDCS), Dallas, TX (November 2006)

8. Pointon, R.F., Trinder, P.W., Loidl, H-W.: The Design and Implementation of Glasgow distributed Haskell. In: Mohnen, M., Koopman, P. (eds.) IFL 2000. LNCS, vol. 2011, pp. 53–70. Springer, Heidelberg (2001)

9. Lastovetsky, A.: mpC — a Multi-Paradigm Programming Language for Massively Parallel Computers ACM SIGPLAN Notices 31(2), 13–20 (February 1996)

10. Smolka, G.: The Development of Oz and Mozart. In: Van Roy, P. (ed.) MOZ 2004. LNCS, vol. 3389, p. 1. Springer, Heidelberg (2005)

11. Loidl, H-W.: Granularity in Large-Scale Parallel Functional Programming PhD. Thesis. University of Glasgow (March 1998) Available online http://www.dcs.gla.ac.uk/~hwloidl/publications/PhD.ps.gz

12. Goodale, T., et al.: The Cactus Framework and Toolkit: Design and Applications. In: Palma, J.M.L.M., Sousa, A.A., Dongarra, J.J., Hernández, V. (eds.) VECPAR 2002. LNCS, vol. 2565, pp. 197–227. Springer, Heidelberg (2003)

13. Cantonnet, F., El-Ghazawi, T.: Performance and Potential: A NPB Experimental Study Supercomputing Conference (2002) http://sc-2002.org/paperpdfs/pap.pap316.pdf

14. Cann, D.: Retire Fortran? Debate Rekindled. Supercomputing Conference, New-Mexico, USA (November 1991)

15. Turchin, V.F.: REFAL-5 programming guide and reference manual New England Publishig Co., Holyoke (1989)

16. Abramov, S., Adamovich, A.I., Inyukhin, A., Moskovsky, A., Roganov, V., Shevchuk, E., Yu, S., Vodomerov, A.: OpenTS: An Outline of Dynamic Parallelization Approach. In: Malyshkin, V. (ed.) PaCT 2005. LNCS, vol. 3606, pp. 303–312. Springer, Heidelberg (2005)

17. Talia, D.: Advances in Programming Languages for Parallel Computing in Annual Review of Scalable Computing, Yuen C. K., pp. 28–58 (2000)

18. Wilson, G.V., Lu, P. (eds.): Parallel Programming Using C++. MIT Press, Cambridge (1996)

19. Stroustrup, B.: The Design and Evolution of C++. Addison-Wesley, London (2004) (in Russian translation: Piter, St.Petersburg, 2007)

20. Carter, J.B., Khandekar, D., Kamb, L.: Distributed shared memory: where we are and where we should be headed Fifth Workshop on Hot Topics in Operating Systems (HotOS-V), Orcas Island, Washington (May 04-05, 1995)

21. Chiba, S.: A Metaobject Protocol for C++ Proceedings of the ACM Conference on Object-Oriented Programming Systems, Languages, and Applications (OOPSLA), pp. 285–299 (October 1995)

22. Harris, T., Fraser, K.: Language Support for Lightweight Transactions Object-Oriented Programming, Systems, Languages, and Applications. pp. 388–402 (October 2003)

23. Herlihy, M., Moss, J.E.B.: Transactional Memory: Architectural Support for Lock-Free Data Structures Proceedings of the 20th Annual International Symposium on Computer Architecture, pp. 289–300 (1992)

24. Arslambekov, R.M., Potemkin, V.A., Guccione, S.: Parallel version of MultiGen for multi-conformational analysis of biological activity of compounds XII International Conference CMMASS' 2003, Book of abstracts (2003)

25. Kornev, A.: On globally stable dynamic processes Russian Journal of Numerical Analysis and Mathematical Modelling 17(5), 472

Parallel Construction of Moving Adaptive Meshes Based on Self-organization*

Olga Nechaeva[1] and Mikhail Bessmeltsev[2]

[1] Supercomputer Software Department
ICMMG, Siberian Branch
Russian Academy of Science
Pr. Lavrentieva, 6, Novosibirsk, 630090, Russia
nechaeva@ssd.sscc.ru
[2] Department of Mechanics and Mathematics
Novosibirsk State University
Pirogova, 2, Novosibirsk, 630090, Russia
bmpix@mail.ru

Abstract. A new highly parallelizable method of moving mesh construction based on the Kohonen's Self-Organizing Maps (SOM) is proposed. This method belongs to a class of methods in which the mesh is an image under an appropriate mapping of a fixed mesh over a computational domain. Unlike the conventional methods of this class, the proposed method doesn't require solving complicated systems of nonlinear partial differential equations and is able to work with arbitrary time-dependent mesh density function. High efficiency of parallelization is conditioned by the inherent parallelism of the underlying stochastic SOM algorithm. Sequential as well as detailed parallel algorithms for moving mesh construction are proposed.

1 Introduction

Adaptive mesh methods are commonly used for solving partial differential equations with large solution variations, and play an important role in a variety of areas such as solid and fluid dynamics, material science, heat transfer simulation, etc [1]. It has been shown that improvements in accuracy and efficiency can be gained by concentrating mesh nodes around areas of large solution variation [2]. For the numerical solution of time-dependent differential equations, moving adaptive mesh methods are used in which a mesh density adapts to the solution behavior. Moving meshes are efficient especially if the solution singularities are concentrated in a small region and change rapidly [3].

Within the scope of all moving mesh methods, there is a class of methods in which at each time step the mesh is an image under an appropriate mapping of a fixed mesh

---

* This work was supported in part by the Grant of Rosobrazovanie, contract РНП.2.2.1.1.3653 and Program for Basic Research of RAS Presidium No. 14.15-2006.

V. Malyshkin (Ed.): PaCT 2007, LNCS 4671, pp. 589–598, 2007.
© Springer-Verlag Berlin Heidelberg 2007

over a computational domain. It is important that there is no need to insert and delete mesh nodes while adaptation. This class of methods is attractive for parallel computations because of the following properties. First, all methods of this class use simple data structures and do not require, e.g., to store mesh nodes and connections between them in a tree- or list-structure. Second, the moving mesh always has a fixed number of nodes even though the nodes remain concentrated in moving regions of rapid variation of the solution, and there is no need to employ expensive load balancing techniques after adaptive refinement at each time step [4].

However, all methods of this class, e.g. those proposed in [5-9], are very complicated since they require solving systems of nonlinear partial differential equations (PDEs) just to obtain an appropriate mapping that defines a mesh and controls mesh nodes movements. That is why this class of moving mesh methods has been relatively less developed. Deriving a reliable equation for the mapping is a difficult task even in 1D space. But real-world problems usually need complex 3D simulations. Additionally, the necessity of solving the nonlinear PDEs leads to overwhelming difficulties in parallelization for both static and moving mesh construction. Therefore, the task is to develop a method of moving mesh construction that is applicable to any dimensionality and simple to parallelize efficiently.

In our previous research, an alternative neural network approach to adaptive mesh construction based on self-organization has been proposed [10]. The core of this approach is the Kohonen's Self-Organizing Maps (SOM) [11]. In the case of static adaptive meshes, the approach have been shown to provide highly parallelizable neural network methods for construction of qualitative adaptive meshes in a sense of generally accepted quality criteria [12].

In this paper, the approach is extended to the moving mesh construction. Due to the self-organizing principles and stochastic nature of the underlying SOM algorithm, the new method (1) allows us to obtain a good mesh with arbitrary mesh density function that can be even unsmooth or vanishing; (2) is able to work with large solution deformations while the PDE-based methods can produce qualitative meshes only for relatively small deformations and, thus, require decreasing the time step; (3) is expected to be applicable to any dimensionality without essential modifications and, thus, provides us the opportunity to solve 3D large-scale simulation problems. Finally, the most important property is that the proposed method for moving mesh construction is fine-grained, has an inherent parallelism and can be parallelized with high efficiency.

When solving a problem by the moving mesh methods, each time step of the numerical algorithm usually contains two independent parts: a solution algorithm substep and a mesh-deformation algorithm substep [3]. If each of the parts has different requirements on data decomposition for an efficient parallelization, then it can lead to an inefficient general parallel algorithm. Therefore, it is important to provide the consistency between parallel implementation of these two parts.

In the proposed neural network method, all mesh nodes are processed according to the same rule independently of each other. This property guarantees high efficiency of parallel implementation of the mesh deformation algorithm for any uniform mesh nodes distribution over the processors regardless of their locations in the physical and computational domain. Consequently, the data decomposition can be done in accordance with the requirements only on the parallel implementation of the solution algorithm, and there is no need, e.g. to assemble all of the nodes on one processor or to perform a large amount of communication between processors.

The paper is organized as follows. In Section 2, sequential algorithm of moving mesh construction is proposed. Section 3 contains the detailed parallel version of the algorithm of mesh construction and experimental results. Section 4 concludes the paper.

2 Moving Mesh Construction Based on Self-organization

For static adaptive meshes, the process of mesh construction using Kohonen's Self Organizing Maps (SOM) is as follows [13]. Starting with an arbitrary initial mesh, the SOM algorithm transforms it iteratively into a desired adaptive one, preserving the structure of a fixed mesh. At each iteration of the SOM algorithm, mesh nodes get displacements towards a random point generated from the physical domain. The displacements decrease gradually because they are multiplied by the time dependant decreasing learning rate. Density distribution of the obtained mesh approximates the probability distribution used for the random point generation. The number of iterations for the mesh construction process is fixed beforehand depending on the number of mesh nodes.

In the case of moving meshes, the similar iterative process is performed at each time step but with the less number of iteration and special learning rate, since the mesh is to be adapted only around changing areas of solution variations and doesn't need to fit the whole physical domain.

In this paper, the neural network approach for moving mesh construction is illustrated in the 2D case. At each time step, the physical domain is assigned by a bit-mapped image where grayscale pixels reflect the desired mesh density function in such a way that dark areas correspond to the higher mesh density.

Let G be a physical simply-connected domain in a 2D Euclidean space with spatial coordinates $x = (x^1, x^2)$. Since the physical domain is assigned by a bitmapped image, G consists only of a finite number of pixels, i.e. $|G| < \infty$. A moving adaptive mesh $G_N(t) = \{x_1(t), ..., x_N(t)\}$ is to be constructed on G, where $x_i(t) \in G$, $i = 1, ..., N$ are moving mesh nodes, t is a discrete time step. Let Q be a computational domain in a 2D Euclidean space with coordinates $q = (q^1, q^2)$ with a fixed mesh $Q_N = \{q_1, ..., q_N\}$, where $q_i \in Q$, $i = 1, ..., N$ are independent of time. For simplicity, let us consider the case when Q_N is a rectangular uniform mesh (a widely used type of a fixed mesh). Also, let $w(t, x)$ be a mesh density function. In our experiments, at each time step, the function $w(t, x)$ is defined by the intensity of grey on the bitmapped image G. Density of the adaptive mesh is to be proportional to the values of w. To use $w(t, x)$ in the SOM algorithm, this function should be normalized to obtain the probability distribution $p(t, x)$ for random point generation.

$$p(t,x) = \frac{w(t,x)}{\sum_{z \in G} w(t,z)} \cdot \qquad (1)$$

If large solution variations occur only within small regions, there is no need to move the nodes which are far from these regions. It also improves accuracy of the solution. Therefore, let us denote by $\Delta w(t,x) = |w(t,x) - w(t-1,x)|$, $t > 0$, the difference between values of mesh density function at two adjacent time steps. Mesh deformation is to be carried out around non zero values of Δw. To control the deformation within the physical domain, the function $v(t,x)$ is defined depending on Δw, where $0 \le v(t,x) \le 1$.

At each time step, the proposed mesh deformation algorithm is performed by the procedure *Deform* which is based on the modified learning algorithm for SOM. The input parameters for the procedure are the following: t is a time step, *StartIter* is the iteration number from which the procedure starts, M is the maximum number of iterations ($1 \le StartIter \le M$). The maximum number of iterations is fixed beforehand depending on N.

Algorithm 1. The procedure *Deform(t, StartIter, M)*.
Perform the following operations at each iteration $s = StartIter$,..., M.

a) *Point generation.* Generate a random point $y \in G$ according to the probability distribution $p(t,x)$ given in (1).

b) *Winner determination.* Calculate the Euclidean distances between y and all the nodes $x_i^s(t)$ and choose the node $x_m^s(t)$ which is the closest to y, i.e.

$$\left\| y - x_m^s(t) \right\| \le \left\| y - x_i^s(t) \right\| \qquad (2)$$

for all $i = 1, ..., N$. The node $x_m^s(t)$ is called a *winner*.

c) *Node coordinates correction.* Adjust locations of the mesh nodes using the following rule:

$$x_i^{s+1}(t) = x_i^s(t) + v(t, x_i^s(t)) \theta_{q_m}^M (s, q_i)(y - x_i^s(t)) \qquad (3)$$

for all $i = 1, ..., N$, where $\theta_{q_m}^M(t, q_i) \in [0,1]$ is a *learning rate*.

The rule (3) defines the displacement of each mesh node $x_i^s(t)$ towards the random point y. The displacement magnitude is controlled by the learning rate $\theta_{q_m}(t, q_i)$ (depending on the locations of the node q_i and the winner q_m in the computational domain) and by the value of $v(t,x)$ at the old node position $x_i^s(t)$.

To evaluate the function $v(t,x)$, a neighborhood of the point x is denoted by $B_\gamma(x)$, where an integer γ is the radius of the neighborhood. Then, the function $v(t,x)$ is as follows.

$$v(t,x) = \begin{cases} 0, & if \ B_\gamma(x) \cap \{z : \Delta w(t,z) > 0\} = \varnothing \\ e^{-\dfrac{\rho(x)^2}{2(\gamma/2)^2}}, & otherwise \end{cases} \qquad (4)$$

where $\rho(x) = \min\limits_{z \in B_\gamma(x) \cap \{z:\Delta w(t,z)>0\}} \| x - z \|$. This function is equal to 1 at all points x for

which $\Delta w(t,x) > 0$, takes values from (0,1) in the neighborhood around the areas

with $\Delta w(t,x) > 0$ and is equal to 0 over the rest of the physical domain.

In our previous investigations, the learning rate has been thoroughly selected to
provide the good mesh quality with reasonable computational speed [13], and looks

like $\theta_{q_m}^M(s,q_j) = \delta(s)\,\eta_{q_m}(s,q_j)$, where $\delta(s) = s^{-0.2}\chi(s)$ is a learning step,

$\eta_{q_m}(s,q_i) = 0.05^{\left(\dfrac{d(q_m,q_i)}{r(s)}\right)^2}$ is a learning radius, $\chi(s) = 1 - e^{5(s-M)/M}$,

$r(s) = r(M) + \chi(s)\big(r(1)0.05^{s/M} - r(M)\big) s^{-0.25}$. The maximum number of iterations M

is fixed beforehand depending on N; $r(1)$ and $r(M)$ are values of a learning radius
that are selected depending on distances between nodes in the computational domain Q, $r(1) > r(M)$. The functions $\chi(s)$, $\delta(s)$ and $r(s)$ are shown in Fig. 1.

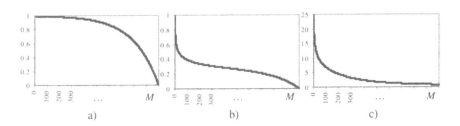

Fig. 1. Diagrams of functions taking part in the learning rate: a) function $\chi(s)$, b) function $\delta(s)$,
c) function $\rho(s)$

The iterative process in the procedure *Deform* can be conventionally divided into
two stages: ordering stage ($s = 1,...,M/2$) and refining stage ($s = M/2,...,M$) [11].
During the ordering stage, the learning step is sufficiently large and it makes the mesh
roughly take the form of the physical domain. The refining stage allows the mesh to
fit the domain and the probability distribution more accurately. For mesh deformation
at each time step, only the refining stage is needed and, then, the parameter *StartIter*
is equal to $M/2$. As it tuned out from our experiments, mesh deformation for $t > 0$
requires a smaller value of M than the first mesh construction (at $t = 0$) which has to
obtain the mesh from arbitrary nodes positions. Therefore, at zero time step, the mesh
is constructed using the procedure *Deform* with maximum number of iterations equal
to $2M$.

Algorithm 2. Moving mesh algorithm.

0. Set up arbitrary initial locations of the mesh nodes $x_i^0(0)$, $i = 1, ..., N$.

1. Perform the procedure $Deform(0, 1, 2M)$ using the function $v(0, x) = 1$, $\forall x \in G$.

2. For each time step $t > 0$ repeat the following operations:

　a) *Density function modification*. Obtain a new mesh density function $w(t, x)$. Calculate the functions $p(t, x)$ and $\Delta w(t, x) = |\, w(t, x) - w(t - 1, x)\,|$ for all $x \in G$.

　b) *Calculation of $v(t, x)$*. For each $x \in G$ search for the point $z \in B_\gamma(x)$ at which $\Delta w(t, z) > 0$ and the distance $\|\, x - z\,\|$ reaches a minimum value. If there is no such a point z, then $v(t, x) = 0$. Otherwise, calculate

$$\rho(x) = \min_{z \in B_\gamma(x) \cap \{z : \Delta w(t, z) > 0\}} \|\, x - z\,\| \text{ and } v(t, x) = e^{-\frac{\rho(x)^2}{2(\gamma/2)^2}}.$$

　c) *Mesh deformation*. Perform the procedure $Deform(t, M/2, M)$ using $v(t, x)$ obtained at 2.b).

3 Parallel Adaptive Mesh Construction

Both the Algorithm 1 and 2 in the previous Section have an inherent parallelism which makes it possible to parallelize them efficiently. In this section, parallel algorithms for distributed memory systems are proposed. Let a multicomputer consist of k processors $P_0, ..., P_{k-1}$.

The most time consuming operations in the algorithm 1 are the calculation of distances $\|y - x_i^s(t)\|$ in (2) and the correction of node locations $x_i^{s+1}(t)$ in (3), since they require processing of all mesh nodes. Fortunately, all mesh nodes are processed in the same way independently of each other. So, these steps can be parallelized by distributing the set of mesh nodes G_N over the processors. It has to be noted that mesh nodes distribution can be done in accordance with the requirements on parallel implementation of the PDE solution algorithm (the first substep of a time step). Let $G_N^{(j)}$ be a subset of the mesh nodes stored in the processor P_j, $j = 0, ..., k-1$, where

$$G_N(t) = \bigcup_{j=0}^{k-1} G_N^{(j)}, \ G_N^{(p)} \cap G_N^{(q)} = \varnothing, \ p \neq q.$$ Let also a fixed mesh Q_N be distributed

over the processors in such a way that the processor P_j contains a subset of the fixed mesh nodes $Q_N^{(j)}$ and if $x_i(t) \in G_N^{(j)}$, then $q_i \in Q_N^{(j)}$. To perform the random points generation, the whole image G is to be stored in all the processors. It is important to ensure that the same sequence of random points is generated at each processor. Also the correction of mesh nodes requires to store the function $v(t, x)$, $\forall x \in G$, in all the processors. Parallel version of the mesh deformation algorithm (Algorithm 1) suitable for the implementation on MPI is as follows.

Parallel Algorithm 1. The procedure $ParDeform(t, StartIter, M)$.

All processors perform the following operations at each iteration $s = StartIter, ..., M$.

a) *Point generation.* In each processor, the same random point $y \in G$ is generated according to the probability distribution $p(t, x)$ given in (1).

b) *Winner determination.* According to (2), each processor P_j searches for the node $x_{m(j)}^s(t) \in G_N^{(j)}(t)$ that is the closest to y ($x_{m(j)}^s(t)$ is a local winner) and performs MPI_Allreduce with the operation MPI_MINLOC to distribute $\| y - x_{m(j)}^s(t) \|$ and determine the global winner $x_m^s(t)$. Then, if the local winner computed by the processor P_j is the global winner, then this processor broadcasts the node q_m to all other processors.

c) *Node coordinate correction.* Each processor P_j adjusts locations of the mesh nodes by applying the rule (3) to all $x_i^s(t) \in G_N^{(j)}$.

It has to be point out that interprocessor communications occur only for winner selection. Due to the low amount of communications, this parallel algorithm of mesh deformation is highly efficient.

Parallelization of the Algorithm 2 is reduced to parallel calculation of the function $v(t, x)$. Even though the whole image is stored in all processors, each of the processors processes its own part of the image while calculation of $v(t, x)$ and then broadcasts it to all other processors.

Let $G^{(j)}(t)$ be a part of the bitmapped image which is to be processed by the processor P_j. Let us denote by $\bar{G}_\gamma^{(j)}(t) = G^{(j)}(t) \cup \{B_\gamma(x) : x \in G^{(j)}(t)\}$ the extension of the part $G^{(j)}(t)$ which is surrounded by the neighborhood of radius γ. The extension $\bar{G}_\gamma^{(j)}(t)$ is quite easy to calculate. For example, if $G^{(j)}(t)$ is a horizontal stripe region of the image and $B_\gamma(x)$ is square-shaped, then $\bar{G}_\gamma^{(j)}(t)$ is a stripe with the height that is greater by 2γ than those of $G^{(j)}(t)$.

Parallel Algorithm 2. Parallel moving mesh algorithm.

0. Each processor P_j, $j = 0, ..., k-1$, sets up arbitrary initial locations of mesh nodes $x_i^0(0) \in G_N^{(j)}$

1. Each processor P_j performs the procedure $ParDeform(0, 1, 2M)$ using the function $v(0, x) = 1$, $\forall x \in G$ with the set of nodes $G_N^{(j)}$.

2. For each time step $t > 0$ repeat following operations:

a) *Density function modification.* The processor P_j calculates the functions $p(t, x)$ for all $x \in G$ using the mesh density function $w(t, x)$. Calculate $\Delta w(t, x) = | w(t, x) - w(t-1, x) |$ for all $x \in \bar{G}_\gamma^{(j)}(t)$.

b) *Calculation of* $v(t, x)$. The processor P_j calculates the function $v(t, x)$ for all $x \in G^{(j)}(t)$ in the same way as it is done at the step 2.b) of Algorithm 2, and then performs the procedure MPI_Allgather to distribute the obtained part of $v(t, x)$ over all other processors.

c) *Mesh deformation.* Each processor P_j performs the procedure *ParDeform*$(t, M/2, M)$ using $v(t, x)$ obtained at 2.b).

The proposed parallel algorithms have been implemented using MPI library. Fig.2 shows computation time and efficiency dependence on the number of processors. Time has been measured for 1 time step of the parallel algorithm 2 in which the procedure *ParDeform* has been performed with $M = 80000$, i.e. during 40000 iterations. The mesh G_N size has been 300 by 600 of nodes. All measurements have been made in Siberian Supercomputer Center using MVS-1000/128 system that consists of 128 processors Alpha, 667MHz, connected to each other by Myrinet. The efficiency of parallelization obtained is greater then 90%.

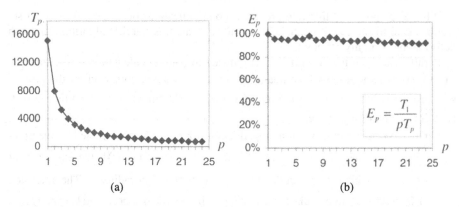

(a)   (b)

Fig. 2. Computation time (a) and efficiency (b) measured for 1 time step with $M = 80000$ and mesh size 300×600 nodes

In Fig. 3, an example of the moving mesh obtained by the proposed method is shown. In this example, an area with high mesh density given by the black color moves within the physical domain. Let us notice that the mesh density function is not smooth, and the mesh adapts to it successfully as shown in Fig. 3(d). Since the mesh density function changes in a local area, the mesh nodes also move only around this area as we can see it in Fig. 3(b) and Fig. 3(c) where the mesh nodes trajectories are shown. In the top of Fig. 3(c), the nodes tend to form high mesh density as their trajectories are directed towards the black area at the second time step. On the contrary, the bottom part of Fig. 3(c) shows the nodes moving out of previous location of this black area. Locations of nodes lying far from the black area don't change at all, and trajectories are points.

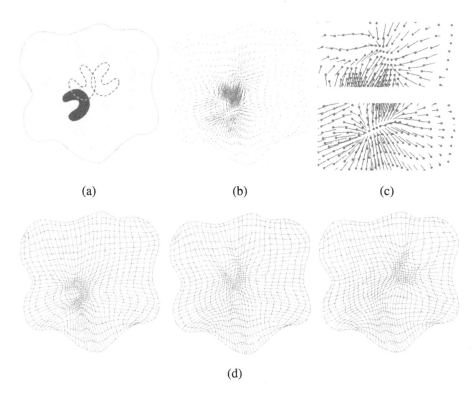

(a)   (b)   (c)

(d)

Fig. 3. The moving mesh obtained by the proposed neural network method; (a) physical domain with varying density function at three different time steps; (b) trajectories of mesh nodes moved from their locations at the first time step to those at the second time step; (c) detailed view of the trajectories in top and bottom parts of (b); (d) the resulting moving mesh at three time steps

4   Conclusion

In this paper, the new moving mesh method based on self organization is proposed. Due to the inherent parallelism of the algorithms, the method is simple to parallelize efficiently in accordance with the requirements only on the parallel implementation of the solution algorithm. Also, the method doesn't require solving complicated systems of nonlinear PDEs and is able to work with arbitrary mesh density function even with large deformations in time. It is expected that in the 3D case the algorithm of moving mesh construction will remain the same as in the 2D cases.

In the future, the proposed moving mesh method will be extended for 3D moving surface and volume meshes with preservation of all the above properties.

References

1. Lebedev, A.S., Liseikin, V.D., Khakimzyanov, G.S.: Development of methods for generating adaptive grids. Vychislitelnye tehnologii 7(3), 29 (2002)
2. Khakimzyanov, G.S., Shokin, Y.I., Barakhnin, V.B., Shokina, N.Y.: Numerical Modelling of Fluid Flows with Surface Waves. SB RAS, Novosibirsk (2001)

3. Cao, W., Huang, W., Russell, R.D: Approaches for generating moving adaptive meshes: location versus velocity. Applied Numerical Mathematics 47, 121–138 (2003)

4. Tsai, H.M., Wong, A.S.F., Cal, J., Zhu, Y., Liu, F.: Unsteady flow calculations with a parallel multiblock moving mesh algorithm. AIAA J. 39, 1021–1029 (2001)

5. Bochev, P., Liao, G., Pena, G.: Analysis and computation of adaptive moving grids by deformation, Numer. Meth. PDEs qw, pp. 489–506 (1996)

6. Liao, G.J., Anderson, D.: A new approach to grid generation. Appl. Anal. 44, 285–298 (1992)

7. Thompson, J.F., Warsi, Z.U.A., Mastin, C.W.: Numerical grid generation, foundations and applications. North-Holland, Amsterdam (1985)

8. Knupp, P.M., Robidoux, N.: A framework for variational grid generation: conditioning the Jacobian matrix with matrix norms. SIAM J. Sci. Comput. 21, 2029–2047 (2000)

9. Cao, W., Huang, W., Russell, R.D.: A moving mesh method based on the geometric conservation law. SIAM J. Sci. Comput. 24, 118–142 (2002)

10. Nechaeva, O.I.: Neural network approach for adaptive mesh construction. In: Proc. of VIII National scientific conference "NeuroInformatics-2006," Part 2. MEPhI, Moscow, pp. 172–179 (2006)

11. Kohonen, T.: Self-organizing Maps. Springer Series in Information Sciences, vol. 30, p. 501. Springer, Heidelberg (2001)

12. Nechaeva, O.: Neural Network Approach for Parallel Construction of Adaptive Meshes. In: Malyshkin, V. (ed.) PaCT 2005. LNCS, vol. 3606, pp. 446–4513. Springer, Heidelberg (2005)

13. Nechaeva, O.: Composite Algorithm for Adaptive Mesh Construction Based on Self-Organizing Maps. In: Kollias, S., Stafylopatis, A., Duch, W., Oja, E. (eds.) ICANN 2006. LNCS, vol. 4131, pp. 445–454. Springer, Heidelberg (2006)

Data Transfer in Advance on Cluster

Nilton Cézar de Paula[1], Gisele da Silva Craveiro[2], and Liria Matsumoto Sato[1]

[1] Polytechnic School
[2] School of Arts, Science and Humanities,
University of São Paulo, Brazil
nilton.paula@poli.usp.br, giselesc@usp.br,
liria.sato@poli.usp.br

Abstract. Scientific applications are increasingly challenging computational platforms and software tools. In this scenario of improving performance demand, computer cluster users require for mechanisms that could reduce data transfer delay. To contribute to this question, we proposed a data transfer in advance mechanism that improved overall system performance by diminishing data-intensive job wait. We also designed and implemented the Integrated Scheduling System (ISS) to analyze and evaluate our proposal. This system automates the preparation, submission and tracking of job executions in a cluster. The mechanism is also combined with an I/O file operation and computation overlapping idea that results in significant improvement of performance rates, confirmed by some experiments.

Keywords: data staging, job scheduling, data scheduling.

1 Introduction

Current scientific applications have been handling a huge volume of data and this tends to increase year by year. An efficient execution of this kind of application also requires great computational power to accomplish complex task processing. With this goal, scientists all over the world have been using clusters so as to ensure processing power and storage capacity. In order to perform the processing of those applications, data and execution must be divided through cluster nodes, which can be done manually or automatically [1].

In case of manual distribution, the user should choose the execution node, make available all data required, start application execution and finally collect the results when it is completed.

The manual distribution becomes undesirable when the number of applications or machine pool size increases. In this sense, automatic distribution through a scheduler can free users from the difficult decision imposed by manual distribution. The scheduler will handle information about resource status in order to ideally allocate the most compatible ones to the application execution. There is a number of schedulers for clusters and the most well known ones among cluster computing users are: PBS/OpenPBS [2], LSF [3], LoadLeveler [4] and Condor [5]. For readers interested in this subject, we suggest [6].

V. Malyshkin (Ed.): PaCT 2007, LNCS 4671, pp. 599–607, 2007.

Many applications that access data via some shared file system can suffer from significant overhead caused by inefficient utilization of the computing resources [7]. This is due to the concurrent access bottleneck to the I/O node. One alternative to this situation is the data set transference to and from local disks. However, the transfer operation of large files takes a significant amount of time and consequently this cause CPUs idleness, as shown in [8].

Another transfer mechanisms limitation is that a transfer cannot be started before node allocation. During the time elapsed from node allocation until all file(s) transfer completion, there is no job execution in that node and consequently a low CPU use. This idle time could be minimized by some coordination between the data transference scheduler and the job scheduler in order to stage data as soon as the job scheduler chooses a specific cluster node to run a data-intensive job.

An overlapping strategy between file operations and computation [9, 10] could achieve resource usage optimization resulting in an increasing CPU utilization while a transfer operation occurs.

This work presents a mechanism called data transfer in advance where the coordination between job scheduler and data scheduler is achieved transparently. We also designed and implemented a system to analyze and evaluate our proposal. It automates the preparation, submission and the execution tracking of independent jobs. Two tools were used in our system: Condor [11, 12] that manages the scheduling and execution of distributed computation and Stork [13] that manages the data placement in heterogeneous environments.

The rest of this paper is organized as follows. Section 2 discusses some related work. In Section 3 we describe the data transfer in advance mechanism and some detail our system are presented in Section 4. Tests have their results presented and analyzed in Section 5. Finally, we conclude our work and indicate further questions in Section 6.

2 Related Work

This work is indebted to a large body of research on file system from principles of overlapping I/O and computing instructions [9], going through a variety of data-movement systems embedded in job schedulers for computer clusters (PBS/OpenPBS [2], LSF [3], LoadLeveler [4], Condor [5] to cite some). In these systems, the data transfer occurs after node allocation, causing resource idleness until all input files are moved to the execution node.

Some alternatives to overcome the problem of low resource utilization have been proposed. In [14] a system called Kangaroo is presented and their approach is based in some overlapping of I/O and CPU instructions, hiding network storage devices behind memory and disk buffers. However, in this work, there is an option to start managing outputs instead of inputs. It is stated that input anticipation is harder, as it claims explicit information or accurate speculation.

Machida et al. propose in [8] strategies to solve the low utilization of resources in data grid through tightly coupling of replica staging and computation scheduling and that computation and communication overlapping. A compute bound job may start or resume its execution while there is a data movement to that node. If the transfer finishes earlier than the computation, then the compute bound job is suspended or migrated.

We understand that update replica cost in a cluster can make unfeasible efficient resource utilization for some applications that access large amount of data spread in many copies in the platform. It is also worth to mention that reasonable complex mechanism of replica consistency is needed.

One important difference is that the concept of overlapping communication and computation in their approach is mainly applied to minimize CPU idleness, while in our proposal it is adopted aiming to reduce data-intensive job execution time in a cluster. In our system, job execution order is preserved according to its arrival time.

3   Mechanism of Data Transfer in Advance

The main goal of the data transfer in advance mechanism is to minimize the data staging phase and, as a consequence, the job execution could be stated as sooner as than possible because all necessary input files would be already transferred to the execution node. In the next subsections we detail the data transfer in advance mechanism regarding node selection decision and the job execution order assurance.

3.1   Selecting the Destination Node to the Data Transfer

At the moment that the user submits a job, he must classify it as data-intensive or compute-intensive. Based on this classification, our system will be able to detect the transfer demand of input data and can divide the cluster in three pools: idle machines, machines that are running compute-intensive jobs and those that are executing data-intensive jobs. This mapping will be used in the process of node selection division in order to achieve a favorable overlapping between file operation and computation.

The node that will receive the data is selected according to some job requirements such as memory size, disk space, processors amount, operating system, and other criteria. An idle node that provides all job requirements will be the preferred choice. If there are some suitable nodes but they are all busy, it will be selected the one that is executing a compute-intensive job. It is important to mention that the selected node that will receive all data via data transfer in advance mechanism will be also the execution node.

3.2   Ensuring the Data-Intensive Job Execution

The job execution must be started after the input data transfer is finished. In the best case, the input data transfer finishes before a node to job execution is located by the job scheduler. However, if the transfer is not complete, strategies must be applied to guarantee the job execution only after the transfer.

We present a strategy to solve this problem so that the job scheduler activities are not modified. This strategy consists in representing the data-intensive job (J) through a special job (J´). When the user submits a job, it sends a job specification file to the submission node. This file contains information about the job requirements, input data and executable files. The job specification file of J´ is generated including all information about J and it is submitted to the job scheduler. J´ executes the following actions which must guarantee the J execution: (i) if data transfer is complete then execute J; (ii) otherwise, waits it to be finished and execute J. Overlapping between data transfer and computation as suggested in [8, 9] could be applied aiming to improve the use of the execution node.

4   Integrated Scheduling System - "ISS"

Our system, called Integrated Scheduling System (ISS), provides functionalities that allow main activities of job execution on cluster to be automated through of an adequate coordination between a job scheduler and a data scheduler to provide better resource utilization. Other benefits that may be mentioned: more users will be able to use a job scheduler, environment learning time is reduced, fewer errors in simple activities, better potential extraction from job scheduler services.

In addition to the advantages presented, our system also provides simultaneous use of idle resource and output data transfer, because a transfer can be perfectly accomplished while another job is in execution.

4.1   Architecture of ISS

ISS architecture as presented in Figure 1 is composed of two parts: **Management Node** and **Execution Node**. **Management Node** is responsible for job execution request reception and preparation to its later execution by **Execution Node**. In the **Management Node** we identify two modules of system that are needed to prepare the job for execution: the Job Management Integrator (JMI) and the Data Management Integrator (DMI). In the following we present its components in detail.

The *Job Receiver* component accepts jobs submitted from the user. Each job consists in an executable file, an input files set and, optionally, an output file set and some job execution restrictions. *Job Receiver* prepares a disk area to receive the job in data structure. This data structure behaves as an index and will ensure requests processing order, from its arrival to submission to job scheduler (JS). It is also a communication interface among different system components and this indirect interaction was designed to best provide fault recovery mechanisms according to safety levels desired to each component.

The *Job Specification Maker* component builds a job specification file for JS from an execution request. In such request the user must inform: input/output files, executable and its arguments, execution requirements, job classification and other information.

The *Resource Discover* is responsible to find an appropriate resource to a data-intensive job (J) and to build its correspondent special job (J´). Information collected by JS will be used in this matching process. As soon as the resource is chosen, additional information are written in the job specification file of J´ in order to guide *Job Submitter* in its submission process and *Data Movement Manager* in its data transfer in advance process. For J, there will be no alteration in the specification file.

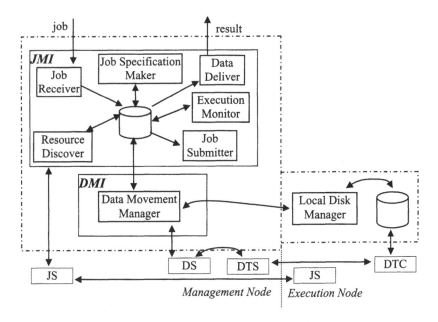

Fig. 1. ISS architecture. Components of the proposed system are in the dotted line area.

The job submission to JS is performed by *Job Submitter*. This component analyzes all job specification files information, submits the job and keeps track in a log file.

Another module identified in the proposed system is the Data Management Integrator (DMI), which has only one component: the *Data Movement Manager*. It is responsible for executable transfer and anticipated data movement. To accomplish this, a data movement specification file is created, then it is delivered to Data Scheduler (DS) and finally all data transfer tracking is done.

Data are placed in a previously prepared area in the execution node and the component responsible for such task is the *Local Disk Manager*, which resides in the **Execution Node**. LDM´s activities comprise: to allocate/free disk space and to create/remove a temporary area. The part of the system that runs the transfers is represented in our architecture by the DTS (Data Transfer Server) and DTC (Data Transfer Client) modules.

The *Execution Monitor* will collect and analyze information about jobs submitted to JS. As soon as it detects that a job execution is finished, it will make results accessible to the user. The results are sent to users through the *Data Deliver*.

In our system implementation Condor represents JS and Stork was chosen for DS. Condor provides resource monitoring capacity and jobs queueing mechanism. In order to make scheduling decisions, Condor works on some specifications written in resource description language [15]. The specifications describe nodes characteristics and jobs restrictions that Condor will consider during resource selection phase, when the matchmaking technique [16] is applied to find the resource. Stork [13] is specialized in data storage on heterogeneous environments and to transfer data performs the following activities: data preparation, control access verification and data transmission. Stork can queue, schedule, monitor, manage data transfers and ensure that they will be completed.

5 Evaluation

Experiment results were obtained executing some jobs on the system in a cluster running GNU/Linux 2.4. Each cluster node is an AMD Athlon 1.5 GHz, with 256Mb RAM interconnected via a *Fast Ethernet* network. Condor package used was 6.8.2 version that also brings Stork package. The cluster was used in the following scheme. One node runs the JMI and DMI modules, Central Manager, Condor's job submission functionality and Stork data transfer server. All jobs are submitted from this machine. In remaining nodes were installed the *Local Disk Manager* component, Condor job execution functionalities. In addition, safety module and GridFTP data transfer protocol [17] were configured in all cluster nodes. It is important to mention that this protocol was used by Stork.

First of all, two jobs were implemented in C programming language. In order to make a clear characterization, one is computing intensive and the other mainly executes file operations. The computing intensive one, briefly named here A, multiplies two 2000x2000 matrices. The data-intensive job, called B, handles a data file with size varying from 32Mb to 2048Mb. After some calculation on each input file entry, a resulting output file is produced with the same size. Job execution time was calculated since job waits in execution queue with "*running*" state. In this situation, no job is scheduled before that state changes from "*running*" to "*completed*".

Figure 2(a) presents Job B execution times, obtained from only one execution node in the cluster. We have also considered the inexistence of job in execution queue in two modalities: with (*with DTA*) and without data transfer in advance mechanism (*without DTA*). When *with DTA* execution modality is applied, execution performance improves to files with size over 128Mb in contrast to *without DTA*. Thus, the time spent waiting for scheduling will be used to partial data transfer in advance. In addition to this, the time for output file transfer does not increment job execution time, as it only passes to "*completed*" state before data transfer starts.

As file size increases, the execution performance becomes better, because GridFTP protocol is designed to transfer bigger data blocks [17]. Therefore, special job (J') execution time can be decreased, as it waits for input data transfer to execution node. The same does not occur in transfers of files inferior to 128Mb, when the performance gets worse to jobs *with DTA*, because input data transfer time is almost the same in both the execution modalities.

Data transfer in advance mechanism gains are much more interesting when input data are ready at the time the scheduler attends the job. An improvement can be exhibited in the line graph of Figure 2(b), which shows execution times of Job A and B, combined with execution modalities *without DTA* and *with DTA*.

Jobs were executed similarly to the previous test, running in only one cluster node, so showing the same execution behavior pattern. In this test, input data transfer occurs during Job A processing. Results showed that there is significant performance improvement with increasing file size because there is no wait for input data transfers. On the other hand, we have no improvement with files smaller than 128Mb, explained by the same reasons previously discussed.

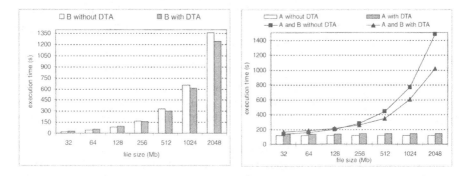

Fig. 2. (a) Execution times of Job B.   (b) Execution times of Job A and B.

An interesting fact should be observed in the bar graph of Figure 2(b) is that input data transfers have slightly affected Job A execution time. This happens due to an I/O operations overlapping with computation associated to GridFTP protocol that consumed few resources during data transfer. We used *top* Linux command in order to keep track of resources usage during job execution.

Figure 3 presents next test results, with the execution of ten Jobs B that have run in four cluster nodes, in execution modalities *with DTA* and *without DTA*.

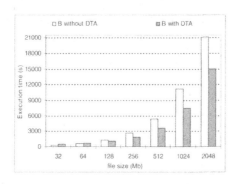

Fig. 3. Execution times of ten Jobs B

As observed, *with DTA* modality demonstrates a very interesting contribution to job execution time reduction again. The difference becomes more expressive as file size increases because, on average, 7 jobs have started their execution with all necessary data already downloaded in execution node. Besides, the bigger the output files to be transferred, the longer is the time available for the scheduler to make decisions about another jobs. This way, our mechanism contributes to an increase in jobs execution throughput.

6 Conclusions and Future Works

We have presented in this work a mechanism that improves data-intensive job execution time through data staging of all input files to an execution node. In addition to this, an I/O operations and CPU bound jobs overlapping is applied. ISS (Integrated Scheduling System) was designed and implemented to verify the concepts application. The job preparation, submission and execution tracking in a cluster were supported by the system.

Experimental results obtained from two job types (namely A and B) have revealed that the proposed mechanism influenced in the increased performance of jobs that access data files greater than 128Mb. Gains are much more remarkable when all necessary data have been already received by the execution workstation before job is sent to it.

It is also very important to point out that the system architecture contributed to an increased execution throughput as the execution node becomes available before output data transfer to submission node. As results proved, additional cost imposed by shared resource used was considered acceptable.

In extension to this work, we intend to implement more sophisticated scheduling policies in order to better determine the node that will receive data transfer in advance. We are also motivated to propose further extensions that would comprise the case of dependent and parallel jobs.

Finally, new scalability tests with more simultaneous jobs running in a greater number of nodes will bring additional information which may lead us to identify new behavior patterns.

Acknowledgments. We would like to thank Pró-reitoria de Pesquisa e Pós-graduação (PROPP) from Universidade Estadual de Mato Grosso do Sul (UEMS) and also to Fundação de Apoio ao Desenvolvimento do Ensino, Ciência e Tecnologia do Estado de Mato Grosso do Sul (FUNDECT) for allowing advanced studies.

References

1. Basney, J.: Network and CPU Co-Allocation in High Throughput Computing Environments. Ph.D. dissertation, University of Wisconsin-Madison (2001)
2. Henderson, R.L., Tweten, D.: Portable Batch System-PBS: Requirements Specification. NASA Ames Research Center (1998)
3. Zhou, S.: LSF: Load Sharing in Large-Scale Heterogeneous Distributed Systems. In: Proceedings of the Workshop on Cluster Computing, Florida (1992)
4. IBM.: Using and Administering LoadLeveler: Release 3.0, 4th edn. IBM Corporation (1996)
5. Litzkow, M.J., Livny, M., Mutka, M.W.: Condor: A Hunter of Idle Workstations. In: 8th International Conference on Distributed Computing Systems, Washington (1988)
6. Baker, M., Fox, G., Yau, H.: Cluster Computing Review. Northeast Parallel Architectures Center, Syracuse University, Technical Report SCCS-748 (1995)
7. Livny, M., Basney, J., Raman, R., Tannenbaum, T.: Mechanisms for High Throughput Computing. SPEEDUP Journal 11. 1 (1997)

8. Machida, Y., Takizawa, S., Nakada, H., Matsuoka, S.: Multi-Replication with Intelligent Staging in Data-Intensive Grid Application. In: The 7th IEEE/ACM International Conference on Grid Computing (2006)
9. Hellerman, H., Smith, H.J.: Throughput Analysis of Some Idealized Input, Output, and Compute Overlap Configurations. ACM Computing Surveys (1970)
10. Reid, K.L., Stumm, M.: Overlapping Data Transfer with Application Execution on Clusters. In: Proceedings of the Second Workshop on Cluster-Based Computing, New Mexico (2000)
11. Basney, J., Livny, M., Tannenbaum, T.: High Throughput Computing with Condor, HPCU news 1(2) (1997)
12. Thain, D., Tannenbaum, T., Livny, M.: Distributed Computing in Practice: The Condor Experience. Concurrency and Computation: Practice and Experience 17 (2004)
13. Kosar, T., Livny, M.: Stork: Making Data Placement a First Class Citizen in the Grid. In: Proceedings of 24th IEEE Int. Conference on Distributed Computing Systems (ICDCS), Tokyo (2004)
14. Thain, D., Basney, J., Son, S., Livny, M.: The Kangaroo Approach to Data Movement on the Grid. In: Proceedings of the 10th IEEE Symposium on High Performance Distributed Computing (HPDC10), San Francisco (2001)
15. Raman, R., Livny, M., Solomon, M.: Matchmaking: Distributed Resource Management for High Throughput Computing. In: Proceedings of the 7th IEEE Int. Symposium on High Performance Distributed Computing, Chicago (1998)
16. Raman, R., Livny, M., Solomon, M.: Resource Management through Multilateral Matchmaking. In: Proceedings of the 9th IEEE Symposium on High Performance Distributed Computing, Pittsburgh (2000)
17. Allcock, B., Bester, J., Bresnahan, J., Chervenak, A.L., Foster, I., Kesselman, C., Meder, S., Nefedova, V., Quesnal, D., Tuecke, S.: Data Management and Transfer in High Performance Computational Grid Environments. Parallel Computing Journal 28(5) (2002)

A Trust-Oriented Heuristic Scheduling Algorithm for Grid Computing

Mingjun Sun, Guosun Zeng, Lulai Yuan, and Wei Wang

Department of Computer Science and Technology, Tongji University,
Shanghai 201804, China
Tongji Branch, National Engineering & Technology Center of
High Performance Computer, Shanghai 201804, China
Jacob.m.sun@gmail.com

Abstract. Security and reliability are major concerns in Grid computing systems. Trust mechanism has been focus of much research in recent years providing a safety and reliable Grid computing environment. Based on EigenTrust model, in this paper, we extend the traditional job scheduling strategies and present a new algorithm named Trust-Oriented Sufferage algorithm. Simulations are performed to evaluate the performance of the new algorithm.

Keywords: Grid computing; trust model; job scheduling; Sufferage algorithm.

1 Introduction

Grid is a unified computing platform which tries to connect and share all resources in the Internet, including computation resource, storage resource, information resource, knowledge resource and equipments for scientific research, and then solves the problems of large-scale scientific engineering computing [1]. And how to obtain trustworthy resource is an important issue. As resource in Grid environment is inevitably unreliable and unsafe, a kind of algorithm is needed to schedule the jobs over the trusty nodes to execute, reduce the jobs execution time, lower the ratio of failure execution, and improve the security of execution environment of important data [2].

Large-scale controlled sharing and interoperation among distributive resources are enabled in Grid computing system [3]. Trust is a major concern of the resource consumers and providers on a Grid. Resource providers may not want their resources used by consumers they do not trust, and similar concerns apply from the consumer side as well. Based on this scenario, we can see that if the resource management systems are aware of the security requirement of both resource providers and consumers it could minimize the cost of job scheduling. The aim of our study is to incorporate a certain trust mechanism in scheduling algorithm and provide Grid resource consumers and providers a more secure environment. Based on EigenTrust [9] model, we present a new algorithm named Trust-Oriented Sufferage algorithm. Simulations are performed to evaluate the performance of the new algorithm.

V. Malyshkin (Ed.): PaCT 2007, LNCS 4671, pp. 608–614, 2007.

There has been several research efforts related to our work. Azzedin and Maheswaran [3] presented a trust-aware model between the resource producers and consumers. Abdul-Rahman and Hailes [4] developed a model for supporting trust based on experience and reputation; this model allows entities to decide which other entities are trustworthy. S.Song and K.Hwang [5] enhanced the Min-min and Sufferage heuristics and proposed a novel Space-Time Genetic Algorithm for trusted job scheduling. Abawajy [6] presented Distributed Fault-Tolerant Scheduling (DFTS) to provide fault-tolerance to task execution in Grid systems.

This paper is organized as follows. Section 2, defines the concept of trust. Section 3, introduces EigenTrust algorithm. Trust-Oriented Sufferage algorithm is presented in Section 4. The simulation and its analysis are showed in Section 5. Conclusions is discussed in Section 6.

2 Definition of Trust

Trust is a complex notion so that its study is often limited. Until now, a consensus of the trust's definition could not be found in the literatures [7], [8]. We found the definition in [4] is instructive as follows:

Trust is the firm belief in the competence of an entity to act as expected such that this firm belief is not a fixed value associated with the entity but rather it is subject to the entity's behavior and applies only within specific context at a given time.

Ranging from very trustworthy to very untrustworthy, the trust level is built on the past experiences of Grid nodes in a specified context. Since one could beyond each individual's resources to evaluate all aspects of a given situation when making a trust decision, Grid nodes could rely on information from others. The definition of reputation [4] we use in this paper is as follows:

A reputation is an expectation about an agent's behaviors based on information or about observations of its past behavior.

3 EigenTrust Algorithm

EigenTrust Algorithm provides eigenvector computation for the trust mechanism in P2P networks, enabling peers could distinguish trustable peers from malicious peers. Here we introduce it to job scheduling in Grid.

In the Grid environment, nodes often rate each other after transactions. For instance, every time when node i executes a task from node j, it may rate the transaction as successful ($tr(i,j) = 1$) or unsuccessful ($tr(i,j) = -1$). So the local trust value of node i to j could be defined as:

$$ltr_{ij} = \sum tr_{ij} \tag{1}$$

In order to aggregate local trust value, it is necessary to normalize them. In this way, malicious nodes could not get high local trust value from one another by frequent transactions. A *normalized local trust value*, C_{ij}, is defined as follows:

$$c_{ij} = \begin{cases} \dfrac{\max(ltr_{ij},0)}{\sum_j \max(ltr_{ij},0)}, if \sum_j \max(ltr_{ij},0) \neq 0 \\ p_j, otherwise \end{cases} \tag{2}$$

p_i is defined as

$$p_i = \begin{cases} \dfrac{1}{|P|}, i \in P \\ 0, i \notin P \end{cases} \tag{3}$$

In formula (3), the P is defined as a set containing the pre-trusted nodes. The system should choose a very few number of pre-trusted nodes, such as the designers of the network or the first few nodes to join the network.

Then, we could aggregate the normalized local trust values. In the Grid environment, node i could get recommendations from its acquaintances about other nodes:

$$t_{ij} = \sum_k c_{ik} c_{kj} \tag{4}$$

If we write formula (4) in matrix notation, then we could get the trust vector $\vec{t_i} = C^T \vec{c_i}$, where C is defined to denote the matrix $[c_{ij}]$, $c_i = [c_{i1}, c_{i2}, \ldots c_{in}]^T$ contains c_{ij}, and $t_i = [t_{i1}, t_{i2}, \ldots t_{in}]^T$ contains t_{ij}.

Each node could gain a wider view by asking his friends' friends, then $\vec{t_i} = (C^T)^2 \vec{c_i}$. If he continues in this manner ($\vec{t_i} = (C^T)^n \vec{c_i}$), he could get a complete view of the global Grid environment.

In the Grid system, there is potential for malicious collectives to form. A malicious collective is a group of malicious nodes who know each other, who give each other high local trust values and give all other nodes low local trust values in an attempt to subvert the system order. This issue could be solved by taking:

$$\vec{t}^{(k+1)} = (1-\alpha)C^T \vec{t}^{(k)} + \alpha \vec{p} \tag{5}$$

where α is a constant between 0 and 1. In this way, we could break collective by having each node place at least some trust in the accessible nodes in Grid that are not parts of a collective.

Each node in Grid system is supposed to compute and store its own global trust value t_i:

$$t_i^{(k+1)} = (1-\alpha)(c_{1i}t_1^{(k)} + \ldots + c_{ni}t_n^{(k)}) + \alpha p_i \tag{6}$$

The detail algorithm is shown as Figure 1:

EigenTrust(){

Each Node i do{

    Query all nodes $j \neq i, t_i^{(0)} = p_i$

    repeat

        compute $t_i^{(k+1)} = (1-\alpha)(c_{1i} t_1^{(k)} + ... + c_{ni} t_n^{(k)}) + \alpha p_i$;

        send $c_{ij} t_i^{(k+1)}$ to all nodes;

        compute $\delta = |t_i^{(k+1)} - t_i^{(k)}|$;

        wait for all nodes return $c_{ji} t_i^{(k+1)}$;

    until $\delta < \varepsilon$

    }

}

Fig. 1. EigenTrust Algorithm

4 Trust-Oriented Scheduling Algorithm

Trust-oriented job scheduling is NP-harder, so the heuristics are needed. Traditional scheduling algorithms, which aim at finishing tasks in the minimum complete time, includes OLB, Greedy, Fast Greedy, Min-min, Max-min, Sufferage[12], A*, simulated Annealing, Tabu Search, Genetic algorithms, etc. Experiments show that Min-min, Genetic algorithm, A* and Sufferage have better performance. However, Genetic algorithm and A* run slowly, and could not adapt to the large-scale Grid computing. Min-min algorithm has some problems in balancing the load, while Sufferage has a best comprehensive performance in Grid environment.

The basic idea of Trust-Oriented Sufferage is as follows: Every node should be assigned one task which will suffer the most lost of trust value if the task is not assigned to this node.

Trust scope is introduced to Trust-Oriented Sufferage here. The scope of 0 to 1 is equally divided into n (n is a positive integer) parts, which named trust scope. n is an important factor to the performance of the algorithm. Experiments show that algorithm performance will be reduced by either too high value or too low value of n. So we choose $n = 6$ for our algorithm simulation. Trust value of all nodes could be mapped to trust scope, which denotes as TSN. Similarly, task trust requirement denotes as TTR.

As a batch mode scheduling algorithm, Trust-Oriented Sufferage will not map tasks onto nodes as they arrive. Tasks are collected in set which is examined for mapping at prescheduled times. In algorithm, Task T is the current task set, while Task T' is the next one.

Algorithm 1. Trust-Oriented Sufferage Algorithm

Input: Task trust requirement TTR and initial trust values of nodes
Output: Task-node map scheme

```
Trust-Oriented Sufferage (Task T, Task T') {
1.   EigenTrust ();
2.   Map trust value of all nodes to trust scope TSN.

3.   for all tasks t_i in T
4.       for all nodes n_j
5.           c_ij = e_ij + r_j
6.       endfor
7.   endfor
8.   do until( all tasks in T are scheduled )
9.       for each task t_i in T
10.          calculate minimum complete time
11.          if the minimum complete time of ti larger
             than D_i
             //D_i is user-defined deadline of task
             completion
12.          delete t_i from T, and insert it into T'
             //in this case, t_i could not be scheduled
             in this execution T.
13.      endfor
14.      sort tasks in T in ascending order by their
         minimum complete time
15.      mark all nodes available
16.      for each task t_i in T
17.             find node n_j that gives the minimum
                complete time as well as TSN_j > TTR_i
18.          sufferage value = (TSN_j - TTR_i)*(SCT - MCT)
                //SCT - second minimum complete time
19.          if n_j is unassigned
20.              assign t_i to node n_j , delete t_i in T
21.              mark n_j assigned
22.          else if sufferage value of task t_n already
                assigned to n_j is less than the sufferage
                value of task t_i
23.              unassign task t_n , add it back to T
24.              assign task t_i to node n_j , delete t_i in T
25.          endfor
26.      update vector r which contains tasks assigned
         to nodes
27.      update matrix C, the expected completion time
         matrix
28. enddo
}
```

In the above algorithm, e_{in} is the expected executing time for task t_i on node n_j when n_j has no other loads; r_j is the complete time of current tasks on node n_j; C_{ij} is the expected complete time for task t_i on node n_j.

Trust-Oriented Sufferage sorts the tasks in Task T in ascending order by their minimum complete time. It is similar with Min-min by some way. And sufferage value is determined by both TSN and TTR. Thus, Trust-Oriented Sufferage could integrate trust into traditional job scheduling, and get better performance.

5 Experiments and Results Analysis

Simulations were performed to evaluate the performance of our algorithm. The GridSim[10] toolkit provides a general infrastructure for simulation of different classes of Grid resources, Grid nodes, and job schedulers. 8 Grid nodes and 200 tasks were simulated in the experiments. And we found [11] instructive for our experiments.

In GridSim environment, the initial trust degrees of the nodes are generated randomly. Several nodes with the highest trust values were chosen as the pre-trusted nodes. In formula (5), we can see α is an important factor to solve malicious collectives. Our Experiments show that the algorithm performance will be reduced by either too high or too low value of α. So we set 0.2 as its value in the following experiments.

Figue 2 shows the makespan of the algorithms. Min-min and Sufferage algorithms without trust mechanism will be more probable to reschedule the tasks than the Trust-Oriented Sufferage (TOS), for the unsuccessfully executed tasks will not assigned until the next schedule event.

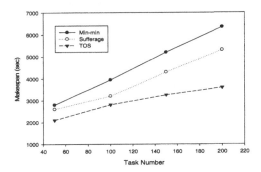

Fig. 2. Makespan of Algorithms

Site utilization rate is the percentage of calculating power allocated to tasks on a Grid node. Table 1 shows the site utilization rate of 8 nodes. Site 2 and site 5 were pre-trusted, so they take more tasks than average.

Table 1. Site Utilization

	0	1	2	3	4	5	6	7
Min-min	90	17	70	44	96	22	97	34
Sufferage	79	30	50	57	88	46	37	90
TOS	50	20	90	54	95	96	32	18

6 Conclusions

It's a crucial issue to integrate the trust mechanism into job scheduling in Grid computing. Based on EigenTrust, the famous Sufferage algorithm was modified to Trust-Oriented Sufferage. And simulation shows that our algorithm does perform well to match the risky and unstable Grid computing environment. Further enhancement of the trust-oriented job scheduling algorithms will be studied in our future work.

Acknowledgements

This research was partially supported by the National Natural Science Foundation of China under grant of 60673157, the Ministry of Education key project under grant of 105071 and SEC E-Institute: Shanghai High Institutions Grid under grant of 200301.

The first author would like to thank Wenyu Hu for the frequent discussions, her advice and insights that shaped this paper.

References

1. Foster, I., Kesselman, C., Tuecke, S.: The Anatomy of the Grid: Enabling Scalable Virtual Organizations. International Journal of Supercomputer Application (2001)
2. Wang, W., Zeng, G.S.: Trusted Dynamic Level Scheduling Based on Bayes Trust Model. Science in China: Series F Information Sciences 37(2), 285–296 (2007)
3. Azzedin, F., Matheswaran, M.: Integrating trust into grid resource management systems. In: 2002 International Conference on Parallel Processing (ICPP 2002), pp. 47–54. IEEE Press, Canada (2002)
4. Abdul-Rahman, A., Hailes, S.: Supporting trust in virtual communities. In: Hawaii Int'l Conference on System Sciences (January 2000)
5. Song, S., Kwok, Y.-K., Hwang, K.: Security-Driven Heuristics and A Fast Genetic Algorithm for Trusted Grid Job Scheduling. In: Proceedings of the 19th IEEE International Parallel and Distributed Processing Symposium (IPDPS'05) (2005)
6. Abawajy, J.H.: Fault-Tolerant Scheduling Policy for Grid Computing Systems. In: Proc. IPDPS (2004)
7. Misztal, B.: Trust in Modern Societies [M]. Polity Press, Cambridge (1996)
8. Grandison, T., Sloman, M.: A survey of trust in Internet applications. IEEE Communications Surveys & Tutorials 4(4), 2–16 (2000)
9. Kamvar, S.D., Schlosser, M.T., Garcia-Molna, H.: The eigentrust algorithm for reputation management in p2p networks. In: Proceedings of the 12th International World Wide Web Conference (WWW '03), Budapest, Hungary (2003)
10. Buyya, R., Murshed, M.: A Deadline Budget Constrained Cost-Time Optimisation Algorithm for Scheduling Task Farming Applications on Global Grids, CoRR cs.DC/0203020 (2002)
11. Li, K., He, Y., Liu, X., Wang, Y.: Security-Driven Scheduling Algorithms Based on EigenTrust in Grid. In: pdcat, Sixth International Conference on Parallel and Distributed Computing Applications and Technologies (PDCAT'05), pp. 1068–1072 (2005)
12. Maheswaran, M., Ali, S., Siegel, H.J., Hensgen, D., Freund, R.F.: Dynamic Matching and Scheduling of a Class of Independent Tasks onto Heterogeneous Computing Systems. In: Proceedings of the Eighth Heterogeneous Computing Workshop (HCW '99), San Juan, Puerto Rico, pp. 30–44 (April 1999)

3-Points Relationship Based Parallel Algorithm for Minimum Ultrametric Tree Construction

Kun-Ming Yu[1], Jiayi Zhou[2,*], Chun-Yuan Lin[3], and Chuan Yi Tang[4]

[1] Department of Computer Science and Information Engineering, Chung Hua University
[2] Institute of Engineering Science, Chung Hua University
[3] Institute of Molecular and Cellular Biology, National Tsing Hua University
[4] Department of Computer Science, National Tsing Hua University
yu@chu.edu.tw, jyzhou@pdlab.csie.chu.edu.tw,
cyulin@mx.nthu.edu.tw, cytang@cs.nthu.edu.tw

Abstract. To construct an evolutionary tree is an important topic in computational biology. An evolutionary tree can symbolize the relationship and histories for a set of species. There are many models had been proposed to resolve these problems. However, most of them are NP-hard problem. Ultrametric tree is one of the most popular models, it is used by a well-accepted tree construction method--Unweighted Pair Group Method with Arithmetic Mean, which is widely used by biologists to observe the relationship among species. However, it is a heuristic algorithm. In this paper, we proposed a 3-Points relationship (3PR) based parallel algorithm to solve this problem. 3PR is a relationship between distance matrix and constructed evolutionary trees. The main concept is for any triplet species, two species closer to each other in distance matrix should be closer to each other in evolutionary tree. Then we combined this property and branch-and-bound strategy to reduce the computation time to obtain the optimal solution. Moreover, we put the lower ranked path which is determined by 3PR to delay bound pool (DBP) to accelerate the algorithm execution. DBP is a mechanism which can store the lower ranked path and can be helping algorithm to find a better bounding values speedily. The experimental results show that our proposed algorithm can reduce the computation time compared with algorithm without 3PR. Moreover, it also shows 3PR can reduce the computation time when number of computing nodes increasing.

1 Introduction

An evolutionary tree can represent the histories for a set of species, it is a useful tool for biologist to observe existent species or evaluate the relationship of them. However, the real evolutionary histories are unknown in practice. Therefore, there are many methods had been proposed to construct a meaningful evolutionary tree, which is closing to the real one. The majority of these methods are all based on two inputs: the sequences and the distance matrix [9]. In the input of sequences, an evolutionary

---

[*] The corresponding author.

V. Malyshkin (Ed.): PaCT 2007, LNCS 4671, pp. 615–622, 2007.

tree is usually constructed according to the multiple sequence alignment (*MSA*). However, it has been shown to be nondeterministic polynomial (NP)-hard to obtain an optimal result for *MSA* problem [10].

In the input of distance matrix, the distance matrix is composed of a set of user-defined values for any two species (e.g., edit distance). Many models [10,10] and methods had been proposed to represent the evolutionary tree. However, to construct an optimal evolutionary tree had been shown to be NP-hard [3,7] for many proposed methods. One of the most commonly used models is ultrametric tree (UT), it is a rooted and leaf label and edge weighted binary tree. The internal node represents the hypothesis ancestors which evolved from one common ancestor, and the leaf stand for present-day species. Moreover, it assumes the rate of evolution is constant. Due to it is a NP-hard problem, biologists usually use heuristic algorithm to find an *UTs*. The Unweighted Pair Group Method with Arithmetic mean (*UPGMA*, [10,11]) is one of the popular heuristic algorithms to construct *UTs*.

In this paper, we would like to find an ultrametric tree which the sum of edge weight is minimal, we call it as minimum ultrametric tree (*MUT*) problem. Although it had been show to be a NP-hard problem [3,12], to construct middle size of tree is useful for biologists to observe the evolutionary relationship. Therefore, it seems possible to find *MUT* by exhaustive search, however, the trees grown very rapidly. For example, $A(10) > 10^7$, $A(20) > 10^{21}$, $A(30) > 10^{37}$. Thus it can be seen when the number of species grown, it seems impossible to exhaustively search.

Wu [12] proposed a branch-and-bound algorithm for construct *MUT* to avoid exhaustive search, and it is useful to solve NP-hard problem. The experimental result shows that [12] can find a *MUT* for 25 species in reasonable time. However, the computation time grows rapidly when the number of species increasing. Therefore, in previous work, we proposed an efficient parallel branch-and-bound algorithm for this problem [12]. The experimental result shows that the proposed parallel algorithm can solve 35 species in reasonable time with 16 computing nodes PC cluster. The number of candidate *UTs* for 35 species is $9*10^8$ times than the number of candidate *UTs* for 25 species. The results show that the proposed parallel branch-and-bound algorithms can efficient bounding *UTs* and reducing the computation time.

Moreover, we observe the relationship between distance matrix and evolutionary tree. We assume for any three species, two species closer to each other in distance matrix should be closer to each other in evolutionary tree, then we named this relationship as 3-Points Relationship (*3PR*). In [14], we apply this property when branching third species. The experimental results show that it can reduce at most 25% of computation time when we apply this property. However, we do not use this property thoroughly when we select branching path in the proposed algorithm, we only apply in branching third species (depth 0). Since [1] shows there may have the contradictory relationship among them for any four species.

In this paper, we proposed a *3PR* based parallel algorithm for *MUT* problem. In order to prevent the four points contradiction situation, we use sliding window strategy when applying *3PR* to select branching path. Moreover, we proposed a delay bound pool (DBP) mechanism to guarantee the optimal solution can be found. In the branch-and-bound strategy, how to find a better bounding value as soon as possible is an important issue. Therefore, the *DBP* mechanism can store the lower ranked path and help the algorithm to find a better bounding value quickly. The experimental results show that our parallel algorithm with *3PR* can reduce the computation time for Human Mitochondrial DNAs data set and random generated data set.

This paper is organized as follows. In section 2, some preliminaries for sequential branch-and-bound algorithm and *3PR* are given. *3PR* based parallel algorithm is described in section 3 and section 4 shows our experimental results. Finally, conclusions and future work are given in section 5.

2 Preliminaries

An ultrametric tree is a rooted, leaf labeled binary tree, and each edge associates with a weight, the length from root to any leaf is equal. To simplify the presentation, notations and terminologies used in this paper are prior defined as follows. We denote a weighted graph as $G=(V, E, w)$ with vertex set V and edge set E with an edge weighted function w.

Definition 1: A distance matrix of n species is a symmetric $n \times n$ matrix M such that $M[i,j] \geq 0$ for all $M[i,i]=0$, and for all $0 \leq i, j \leq n$.

Definition 2: Let $T = (V, E, w)$ be an edge weighted tree and $u, v \in V$. The path length from u to v is denoted by $d_T(u,v)$. The weight of T is defined by

$$w(T) = \sum_{e \in E} w(e).$$

Definition 3: For any M, MUT for M is T with minimum $w(T)$ such that $L(T) = \{1,...,n\}$ and $d_T(i,j) \geq M[i,j]$ for all $1 \leq i, j \leq n$. The problem of finding MUT for M is called MUT problem.

Definition 4: Let P be a topology, and $a, b \in L(P)$. $LCA(a,b)$ denotes the lowest common ancestor of a and b. If x and y are two nodes of P, we write $x \rightarrow y$ if and only if x is an ancestor of y.

Definition 5: The distance between distance matrix and rooted topology of evolutionary trees is consistent if $M[i,j] < \min(M[i,k], M[j,k])$ if and only if $LCA(i,j) < LCA(i,k) = LCA(j,k)$ for any $1 \leq i, j, k \leq n$. Otherwise is contradictory.

2.1 Sequential Branch-and-Bound Algorithm for MUT

In [3], a sequential branch-and-bound algorithm was presented by Hendy and Penny to construct a minimum evolutionary tree of 11 species. Wu [12] proposed an efficient sequential branch-and-bound algorithm which was presented to construct *MUT*s from a metric distance matrix. An optimal solution of 25 species can be found in a reasonable time (in 24 hours). The results showed that the branch-and-bound algorithm is useful for *MUT* problem. In the proposed branch-and-bound algorithm, it repeatedly searches the branch-and-bound tree (*BBT*) to find a better solution until optimal one is found. The *BBT* can represent the *UT*. Assume the root of *BBT* is depth 0, therefore each node with depth I in *BBT* represent a topology with a leaf set $\{1,...,i+2\}$. The algorithm of [12] is shown in following.

Sequential Branch-and-Bound Algorithm

Input: A $n*n$ distance matrix M
Output: The minimum ultrametric trees

1: Load distance matrix and re-labels the species by maxmin permutation as leaf set
    $\{1,2,...n\}$.
2: Creates the root v of the *BBT* which v represent the topology with leaves 1 and 2.
3: Run UPGMA and use the result as the initial upper bound (UB).
4: **while** Count(BBTs) !=0
        if LB(v) >= UB
                Delete v and all its children.
        Select a node s in *BBTs* according to selection rule, whose children of s has not been
generated.
        Generate the children of s by using branching rule.
        If a better solution is found, then update *UB* as a new upper bound.
5: Report the minimum ultrametric trees for M.

2.2 3-Point Relationship (*3PR*)

Fan [1] proposed *3PR* for evaluate the quality of the evolutionary tree. 3PR is a
logical method to check the *LCA* relation for any triplet of species (a, b, c) in distance
matrix and constructed evolutionary tree. The definition is shown in *Definition 5*. For
example, Table 1 is the distance matrix and Figure 1 show two candidate of *BBT*. We
can observe that M[a,c] =20 > M[b,c]=15, therefore b, c should be closer to each
other in the evolutionary tree. Thus, we denote the Figure 1 (a) is a cntradictory tree.
Moreover, there are many methods had been proposed to construct evolutionary tree,
we can evaluate each constructed tree with *3PR* and count number of contradictory
set. Less contradiction set means the tree construction method is more ble for given
data.

Table 1. Distance matrix

	a	b	c
a	0	25	20
b	25	0	15
c	20	15	0

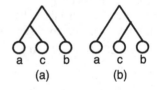

Fig. 1. Candidate BBTs

3 The Proposed Parallel Branch-and-Bound Algorithm

The branch-and-bound algorithm is a general technique to solve combinatorial search
problems. Many theoretical properties for sequential and parallel branch-and-bound
algorithm had been discussed. For a branch-and-bound algorithm, it consists of four
parts: branching rule, selection rule, bounding rule, and termination rules. The
branching, bounding, and termination rules are problem dependent, and the selection
rule is algorithm dependent. The selection rule will be an important factor for the

performance of a designed algorithm. Four well-know search methods, breadth-first [3], depth-first, best-first, and random [9], have been presented for the selection rule.

There are many aspects to choose the selection rules. In our algorithm, breadth-first search will use up the memory, and random search strategy may be useful for our application to find a better bounding value in global view. Moreover, best-first search should have a mechanism to balance the memory usage, when memory will be using up, it should use depth-first search instead of best-first search to reduce the memory usage. Among them, the depth-first search and the best-first search are two efficient and commonly used methods.

In this paper, we proposed a branch-and-bound algorithm with a *3PR* selection strategy in parallel computing environment. Moreover, we proposed a delay bound pool (*DBP*) mechanism to speed-up the better bounding value finding process and guarantee the optimal solution can be found. Since for any four species, there may be existence a contradictory relationship. [1] illustrates for any four species *a*, *b*, *c*, *d*, if there exist a relationship sets ((*a*,*b*),*c*), ((*a*,*b*),*d*), ((*a*,*c*),*d*), ((*b*,*d*),*c*) or ((*a*,*b*),*c*), ((*a*,*b*),*d*), ((*a*,*c*),*d*), ((*c*,*d*),*b*) then there existed a contradictory relationship. Therefore, we only use *3PR* when we insert third species instead of using it in all branching steps in previous work. In this paper, we use sliding window technique to apply *3PR* in our proposed parallel algorithm. First, we re-label the species by maxmin permutation and get the species array. Second, set the sliding window size to three, each time we compare three species and choose the suitable *BBT* then we put other candidate *BBTs* to *DBP*.

For example, Figure 2 is the species after maxmin permutation and we want to insert fourth species (species 4) into BBT. Figure 3 represents two candidate *BBTs*, then we compare $M[3,4]$ and $M[2,4]$. Assumed $M[3,4]$ is less then $M[2,4]$ then we select Figure 3 (b) and put the Figure 3 (a) to the *DBP*.

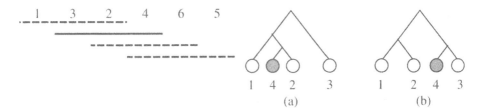

Fig. 2. Sliding Window   **Fig. 3.** Candidate BBTs

Since we should guarantee the optimal solution can be found, therefore we can't drop the lower ranked candidate *BBTs*. Moreover, according to *3PR*, we know the better bounding value can be found in the tree which conformed to a least count of contradictory sets. The candidate *BBTs* puts to *DBP* can help the running queue shorter and find the better bounding value quickly. After a new bounding value to be found, it can bound the *BBT* in Global Pool, Local Pool, and *DBP*. The detail of *3PR* based parallel algorithm is shown in following.

3PR based Parallel Algorithm for MUT Problem

Input: A $n*n$ distance matrix M, Level of 3PR, Time constraint.
Output: The ultrametric trees with minimum cost.

Master Processor (MP):

1: Load distance matrix and re-labels the species by maxmin permutation.
2: Creates the root of the BBT.
3: Run UPGMA and use the result as the initial upper bound (UB).
4: Branches the BBT according to 3PR with limit of level of 3PR, and move the contradictory BBTs to delay bound pool (DBP).
5: Until BBTs reaches 3 times of total number of computing nodes, it broadcasts the global UB and sends the BBT to computing nodes cyclically.
6: **while** Count(BBTs in LP) > 0 **or** Count(BBTs in GP) > 0 **or** Count(BBTs in DBP) >0
  if Count(BBT in LP) ==0 **and** Count(BBT in GP) !=0
    receive BBTs from GP
  v = get the *BBT* for branch according to *3PR*
  Put others *BBTs* to *DBP*
  if LowerBound(v) > *UB*
    continue
  Generate the children of v according to *3PR*
  if v branched completed
    if Cost(v) < *UB*
      Update the Global Upper Bound (*GUB*) to every computing nodes
      Add the v to the results set
  if Count(*BBTs* in *GP*) == 0
    Send last two *UT* in sorted *LP* to *GP*
  if Count(*BBTs* in *LP*) == 0 **and** Count(*BBTs* in *GP*)
    LP = DBP
7: Gather all solutions from each computing node and then output it.

Each of Slave Processors (SP):

1: **while** Count(*BBT* in *LP*) > 0 **and** execution time < T_C
  if LowerBound(v) > *UB*
    continue
  v = get the *BBT* for branch according to *3PR*
  Put others *BBTs* to *DBP*
  Generate the children of v according to *3PR*
  if v branched completed
    if Cost(v) < *UB*
      Update the Global Upper Bound (*GUB*) to every computing nodes
      Add the v to the results set
  If there is a request from *MP* and the number of computing nodes in *LP* >2, then send 2 nodes to *MP*.
2: **if** Count(*BBTs* in *LP*) == 0
  Send a request to *MP*
  If receive 2 nodes from *GP* in *MP*, then go to *step 1*.
3: Send all nodes in *LP* to *MP*.

4 Experimental Results

To evaluate the performance of the proposed algorithm, we have implemented our algorithm in C++ and Message Passing Library 2. The program executes in a PC cluster with 16 computing nodes, the hardware specification is an AMD Athlon PC with a clock rate 2.0 GHz and 1 GB memory. The PCs are interconnected by 100 Mb fast ehternet switch. The system architecture is master/slave architecture, we choose one PC as master and the master will dispatch jobs, handle global pool and collect results from slave PCs. Two data sets are used to verify the performance of our proposed algorithm. One is randomly generated data set, which the range of distance between 1 and 100. Another is a practical data set of 136 Human Mitochondrial DNAs (*HMDNA*), which is obtained from [11]. We run five different instances of each number of species to eliminate the data dependence situation.

Figure 4 is the computation time of *HMDNA* data set with 16 computing nodes, we can observe that *3PR* could reduce the execution time when the number of species grows. Figure 5 is the computation time of Random data set with 16 computing nodes, the experimental results show that our algorithm also perform well on the random generated data set. According to our observation, it can reduce about 20% and 10% of computation time for *HMDNA* data set and random data set, respectively.

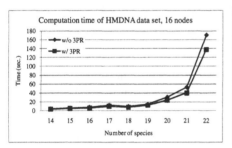

Fig. 4. Computation time of HMDNA

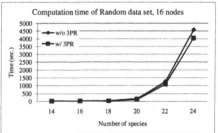

Fig. 5. Computation time of Random Data

5 Conclusions

In this paper, we proposed a *3PR* based branch-and-bound parallel algorithm for *MUT* problem. *3PR* is a property between distance matrix and evolutionary tree. We apply this property with sliding window technique to accelerate the process of selecting branching path in the parallel branch-and-bound algorithm. Moreover, we propose a delay bound pool (*DBP*) mechanism to store the lower ranked path to reduce the influence of selecting new path in branch-and-bound strategy; it can help the branch-and-bound algorithm to find a better bounding value quickly. The experimental results show that our algorithm can reduce the computation time compared with the algorithm without applying *3PR*. In the future, we would like to observe how the sliding windows size affects the computation time.

References

1. David, M.H., James, J.B., Mary, E.W., Marty, R.B., Ian, J.M.: Experimental Phylogenetics: Generation of a Known Phlogeny. Science 255(5044), 589–592 (1992)
2. Fan, C.T.: The evaluation of evolutionary tree. Master Thesis, National Tsing Hua University (2000)
3. Farach, M., Kannan, S., Warnow, T.: A robust model for finding optimal evolutionary trees. Algorithmica 13, 155–179 (1995)
4. Gusfield, D.: Algorithms on Strings, Trees, and Sequences, computer science and computational biology. Cambridge University Press, Cambridge (1997)
5. Hendy, M.D., Penny, D.: Branch and bound algorithm to determine minimal evolutionary trees. Mathematical Biosciences 59, 277–290 (1982)
6. Janakiram, V.K., Agrawal, D.P., Mehrotra, R.: A randomized parallel branch-and-bound algorithm. In: Proc. Int. Conf. Prallel Process, pp. 69–75 (1988)
7. Krivanek, M.: The complexity of ultrametric partitions on graphs. Information Processing Letter 27(5), 265–270 (1988)
8. Lawler, E.L., Wood, D.W.: Branch-and-bound methods: A survey. Oper. Res. 14, 699–719 (1966)
9. Li, W.H.: Molecular Evolution. Sinauer Associates, Inc (1997)
10. Li, W.H., Graur, D.: Fundamentals of Molecular Evolution. Sinauer Associates (1991)
11. Linda, V., Mark, S., Henry, H., Kristen, H., Allan, C.W.: African Populations and the Evolution of Human Mitochondrial DNA. Science 253(5027), 1503–1507 (1991)
12. Wu, B.Y., Chao, K.M., Tang, C.Y.: Approximation and Exact Algorithm for Constructing Minimum Ultrametric Trees from Distance Matrices. J. of Combinatorial Optimization 3, 199–211 (1999)
13. Yu, K.-M., Zhou, J.-Y., Lin, C.-Y., Tang, C.Y.: Parallel Branch-and-Bound Algorithm for Constructing Evolutionary Trees from Distance Matrices. In: IEEE Proceedings of the 8th International Conference on High Performance Computing in Asia Pacific Region, pp. 66–72 (2005)
14. Yu, K.-M., Zhou, J., Lin, C.-Y., Tang, C.Y.: An Efficient Parallel Algorithm for Ultrametric Tree Construction Based on 3PR. In: Min, G., Di Martino, B., Yang, L.T., Guo, M., Ruenger, G. (eds.) Frontiers of High Performance Computing and Networking – ISPA 2006 Workshops. LNCS, vol. 4331, pp. 215–220. Springer, Heidelberg (2006)

Load Balancing Approach Parallel Algorithm for Frequent Pattern Mining

Kun-Ming Yu[1], Jiayi Zhou[2,*], and Wei Chen Hsiao[3]

[1] Department of Computer Science and Information Engineering, Chung Hua University
[2] Institute of Engineering Science, Chung Hua University
[3] Department of Information Management, Chung Hua University
[1]yu@chu.edu.tw, [2,3]{jyzhou, swch}@pdlab.csie.chu.edu.tw

Abstract. Association rules mining from transaction-oriented databases is an important issue in data mining. Frequent pattern is crucial for association rules generation, time series analysis, classification, etc. There are two categories of algorithms that had been proposed, candidate set generate-and-test approach (Apriori-like) and Pattern growth approach. Many methods had been proposed to solve the association rules mining problem based on FP-tree instead of Apriori-like, since apriori-like algorithm scans the database many times. However, the computation time is costly when the database size is large with FP-tree data structure. Parallel and distributed computing is a good strategy to solve this circumstance. Some parallel algorithms had been proposed, however, most of them did not consider the load balancing issue. In this paper, we proposed a parallel and distributed mining algorithm based on FP-tree structure, Load Balancing FP-Tree (LFP-tree). The algorithm divides the item set for mining by evaluating the tree's width and depth. Moreover, a simple and trusty calculate formulation for loading degree is proposed. The experimental results show that LFP-tree can reduce the computation time and has less idle time compared with Parallel FP-Tree (PFP-tree). In addition, it has better speed-up ratio than PFP-tree when number of processors grow. The communication time can be reduced by preserving the heavy loading items in their local computing node.

Keywords: FP-tree, data mining, association rules, parallel and distributed computing, load-balancing.

1 Introduction

The basic concept of frequent pattern is given a database which consists of many transactions, and each transaction is a list of items. After that, to find a pattern that occurs frequently in a data set named frequent pattern. It is useful in basket data analysis, sale campaign analysis, and DNA sequent analysis. To extract the frequent pattern from transaction databases is also an important problem in data mining research for mining association rules [1,11], time series analysis, classification [2], etc. Most of

---

* The corresponding author.

V. Malyshkin (Ed.): PaCT 2007, LNCS 4671, pp. 623–631, 2007.
© Springer-Verlag Berlin Heidelberg 2007

previous researches can be classified to candidate set generate-and-test approach (Apriori-like) and Pattern growth approach (FP-growth) [5,2].

For Apriori-like approach, many methods [1] had been proposed, which are based on Apiori algorithm [1,11]: if any length k pattern is not frequent in database, then the length (k+1) super-pattern never can be frequent. However, Apriori will generate huge number of candidate datasets and tests whether is frequent or not by repetitively scanning the database. For example, to mine the frequent pattern with size 50 items should generate more than 2^{50} (about 10^{15}) candidate sets and verify whether it is frequent or not by pattern matching from database.

Han et al. [5] had proposed a new approach for mining frequent pattern and introduced a data structure, Frequent Pattern (FP) Tree, which only store compressed, essential information about frequent patterns. Moreover, a mining algorithm for FP-tree was also developed, FP-growth. Opposite to Apriori-like algorithm, FP-growth only scan database twice and mining information can be obtained from FP-tree.

However, to discover frequent pattern will increase the computation time significantly when the database size is large. Javed et al. [8] had proposed a parallel frequent pattern tree mining algorithm (PFP-tree) to solve this problem, and parallel and distributed computing is a good strategy to solve this problem. There are many parallel and distributed methods had been proposed [6,8,9,10,12,6]. However, it does not consider the load balancing issue, some computing nodes will have heavy loading and some do not.

In this paper, we proposed a load balancing approach parallel algorithm for the frequent pattern mining problem, Load balancing FP-tree (LFP-tree). Moreover, a loading degree function is also developed. The goal of LFP-tree is to calculate each item's loading degree by calculating the weight and the depth of the FP-tree then dispatch different number of items to computing nodes to achieve the load balancing.

The experiment results show that LFP-tree has better balancing than PFP-tree. It can reduce the idle time and has the better speed-up ratio then PFP-tree. Moreover, the data exchanging time needed in LFT-tree is also less than in PFP-tree.

This paper is organized as follows. In section 2, FP-tree, FP-growth, and PFP-tree will be described. LFP-tree algorithm will be introduced in section 3 and section 4 shows our experimental results. Finally, conclusions and future work are given in section 5.

2 Related Work

First, we will define the frequent pattern mining problem. Let $I=\{a_1, a_2, ..., a_n\}$ be a set of items, and a transaction database $DB=<T_1, T_2, ..., T_n>$ be a set of transaction T_i ($i \in [1..n]$). The number of transaction in DB contains pattern A named support. A is frequent pattern if A's support is no less than a predefined *minimum support threshold* ξ. Give a transaction database DB and a minimum support threshold ξ, the problem of finding the complete set of frequent patterns is called the frequent pattern mining problem.

2.1 Frequent Pattern Growth (FP-Growth)

FP (Frequent Pattern)-growth [5] algorithm was proposed by Han et al. in 2000 A.D., FP-growth algorithm only scan the database twice. Firstly, it scans database to create header table, the frequent 1-item descend sorting in header table. Secondly, it scans database again to create FP-tree. Afterward, the algorithm uses FP-growth to get all frequent patterns via scanning FP-tree. FP-tree only stores frequent 1-itemset, it compresses the space requirement with huge database, and thus it can use the space more efficiently. FP-tree includes the node-link that node-link links the item which has the same name. Moreover, each link started from header table, thus for any item a_i can be efficiently obtained from the FP-tree's header table by following a_i's node-links.

FP-growth is a mining algorithm based on FP-tree. It begins by building header table, after selecting an item as mining target, it finds out all relative routes of this item data by node-link. Then it constructs the subtree item by the same concept of FP-tree construction, named conditional frequent tree. Afterward, the algorithm will select an item from subtree as a mining goal and construct a new subtree. To traverse the FP-tree recursively, finding all frequent item set.

2.2 Parallel FP-Tree Algorithm (PFP-Tree)

In order to shorten the mining time, Javed et al. proposed PFP-tree algorithm [8], which is developed for SIMD computing environment. PFP-tree is based on FP-tree data structure and divided into different partitions that equal the number of computing nodes. After that, each processor constructs local header table (*LHT*) with their own database. Then creates the global header table (*GHT*) by sending data from each slave computing node (*SN*) to master computing node (*MN*). Afterward, each *SN* has the *GHT* information and using the FP-tree construction algorithm to create local FP-tree. *MN* assigns each *SN* to mine the same number of items by block distribution. Then each *SN* should exchange portion of FP-tree and using FP-growth mining algorithm to find all frequent patterns.

The main characteristic of PFP-tree algorithm is to use special data exchanging method. The method groups the *SN* to reduce the repetition data exchange. Every *SN* needs to communicate to each other at most $\log p$ rounds. (*p* is the number of *SN*s) In order to exchange data for FP-growth, *SN*s will be divided into two groups, then exchange necessary information, and divide each group into two sub groups, and repeatedly until all *SN*s have been exchanged. After receiving necessary information from other *SN*s, each *SN* begins to mine frequent pattern by applying FP-growth method.

3 Load Balancing Frequent Pattern Tree (LFP-Tree)

After studying the previous FP-tree related algorithms. We find that the depth and width of the tree will influence the computation time tremendously in recursively mining process. Moreover, in parallel and distributed computing environment, unsuitable data distributions will increase the makespan and the idle time of each participate computing node.

Therefore, to evaluate load degree of processors and evaluate how much time will be used when mining each item is a crucial issue. A suitable evaluating function can evaluate the computation time accurately and balanced the load of each computing node. The procedure of the proposed LFP-tree will be described in detail as follows:

3.1 Global Header Table Construction Step

The Global Header Table construction step is based on FP-tree. The data will be distributed equally to each slave computing node (*SN*) from Master computing node (*MN*). After that, *SN*s receives the data (as local database, *LDB*) and scans the *LDB* for the first time. Then we will get all items and its support and create the local header table. Afterward, each *SN* transfers local header table to *MN* and then receives a combined global header table (*GHT*). (Fig. 1)

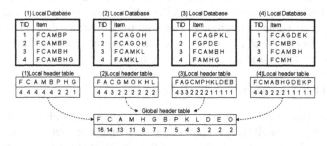

Fig. 1. An example of Global Header Table

3.2 FP-Tree Construction Step

According to tree construction rule in FP-tree, each *SN* constructs the local FP-tree by scanning the *LDB*. First of all, each *SN* creates a FP-tree that contains only a root node named *null*. Secondly, it selects and sorts the frequent item in transaction according to the order of *GHT* for each transaction in *LDB*. Then inserts the transaction into FP-tree. Each node of FP-tree stores *item-name*, *count*, and *node-link*, where *item-name* is the item of the node represents, *count* represent the number of transactions occurred by the portion of path, and *node-link* links to the next node which has the same *item-name* in FP-tree. For example, in fig. 2 each *SN* constructs their local FP-tree according to the order of *GHT*, then link each item from *GHT* by *node-link*.

3.3 The Load Degree Evaluation and Item Distribution Step

Since the computation time of mining process in each *SN* depends on how many items needed to mine. However, each item in FP-tree has different width and depth; the mining time also varies. Therefore, it is important to assign the mining items to *SN*. A suitable distribution of mining items can reduce the makespan and tge idle time. To evaluate each item processed on each *SN*, and then *MN* collects the results from *SN*s and assigns items to *SN* to mine the frequent patterns. Fig. 3 is an example of load degree evaluation procedure. For example, item A appears twice in FP-tree on

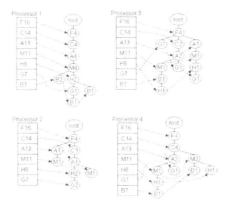

Fig. 2. An example of FP-tree

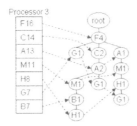

Item	Number Depth	No. 2	No.3	Average of depth	Total Number
F	1			1	1
C	2			2	1
A	3	2		2.5	2
M	4	3		3.5	2
H	6	4		5	2
G	2	4	5	3.6	3
B	5			5	1

Fig. 3. The depth and width of FP-tree

Processor 3. The first one of item A has depth equal to 3, and second one has depth 2. So the average of depth of item A is 2.5 ((2+3)/2).

The proposed loading evaluation formula is presented in equation (1), where P is the number of processors, S is all item set, C_t is the number of leaf nodes, and Dp_i is the depth of pattern in processor i. Each SN uses this loading evaluation function to determine the load degree of each item. Afterward send the evaluated value to MN, and then the MN assign items to mine to SN according to this value. In order to avoid exchange in large data between computing nodes, LFP-tree preserves the item which the loading is large in the local computing node. Then dispatch items according to the loading of each item.

Loading Evaluation of Item

$$L_j = \frac{\sum_{i=1}^{P} Dp_i}{P} \times \frac{Max\ (Ct_j) + Min\ (Ct_j)}{2}\ ,\ \ (1<i<P,\ 1<j<S) \tag{1}$$

3.4 Data Exchanging and Result Collection Step

After decided the load degree, the algorithm assigns mining items to each *SN*. *SN* should exchange FP-tree with other *SN*s to receive the required data for mining. In this step, we will apply group exchanging method in PFP-tree algorithm. The method could refer to 2.2, and Fig. 4 shows the exchanged and integrated FP-tree.

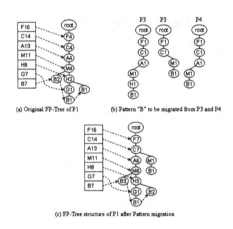

(a) Original FP-Tree of P1   (b) Pattern "B" to be migrated from P3 and P4

(c) FP-Tree structure of P1 after Pattern migration

Fig. 4. An example of exchange and integrate FP-tree

After that, each *SN* execute FP-growth algorithm to mining all frequent item set from local FP-tree, and the *MN* collects all mined data and store it back to database. Afterward, *MN* reports the mined results to user.

4 Experimental Results

In order to evaluate the performance of our proposed algorithm, we implement LPF-tree along with PFP-tree algorithms and executed in a 16-node Linux based PC-cluster. These two algorithms are implemented by message passing interface 2 (MPI-2) and C programming language. We use a practical blood biochemical testing data which contains 157,222 transactions and there are at most seven items of each transaction. Moreover, we also compare the degree of load balancing of PFP-tree and LFP-tree algorithms. Table 1 is the hardware and software specification.

Fig. 5 and Fig. 6 are the computation time with different number of processors of PFP-tree and LFP-tree respectively. The results show when the number of processors increased, the variation of computation time of each processor in PFP-tree is

Table 1. Hardware and Software Specification

Hardware Environment	
CPU	AMD Athlon Processor 2200+
Memory	1GB DDR Ram
Network	100 Mbps interconnection network
Disk	80GB IDE H.D.
Software Environment	
O.S.	ReadHat Linux 7.3
Library	MPICH2 1.0.3

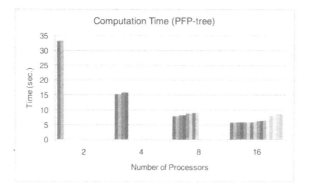

Fig. 5. Computation time of PFP-tree

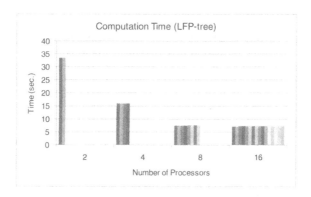

Fig. 6. Computation time of LFP-tree

increased. On the contrary, our proposed LFP-tree can balance the workload of each participated processor and reduce their idle time. In Fig 7, LFP-tree algorithm can save about 16% of computation time when the number of processors great than eight compared with PFP-tree. Fig. 8 shows the speed-up ratio of PFP-tree and LFP-tree, we can observe that LFP-tree algorithm has better ratio when the number of processors increases. We also observed that the data exchanging time rises when the number of processors grows. Moreover, Fig. 9 shows LFP-tree could preserve items

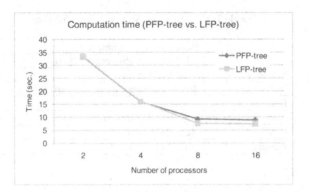

Fig. 7. Speed-up ratio of PFP-tree and LFP-tree

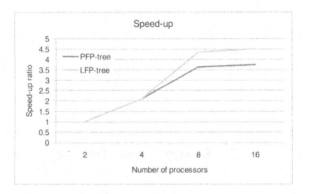

Fig. 8. Speed-up ratio of PFP-tree and LFP-tree

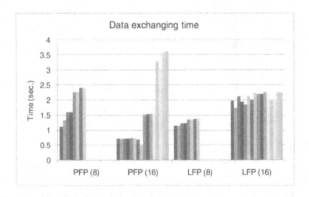

Fig. 9. Data exchange time

which loading is large in the local computing to save communication time. The experimental results shows FP-tree has better balancing capability and it can save about 16% of computation time. Moreover, the speed-up ratio is better than PFP-tree when the processors augmented.

5 Conclusions

To mine the frequent pattern from transaction-oriented database is an important issue in data mining research. There are lots of methods that had been proposed to solve this problem, and some of them are developed for parallel and distributed computingsystem. However, distributed mining item without considering the size of FP-tree will cause some computing node to idle and increasing the makespan. In this paper, we proposed an efficient parallel algorithm for frequent pattern mining problem and proposed an evaluation function to estimate the loading of each item. The experimental results show that our algorithm has better load balancing capability and can reduce the computation time. Moreover, the proposed algorithm can save the communication time by preserving the heavy loading items in their local computing node. In the future, we can extend this concept to grid computing system. In grid computing, the computing abilities are heterogeneous, we can dispatch mining item to computing node according to the computation power of nodes and reduce the overall computation time.

References

1. Agrawal, R., Srikant, R.: Fast algorithms for Mining Association Rules in Large Database. In: Proceedings of the 20th International conference on Very Large Data Base, pp. 487–499 (1994)
2. Almaden, I.: Quest synthetic data generation code. http://www.almaden.ibm.com/cs/quest/syndata.html
3. Coenen, F., Leng, P., Ahmed, S.: Data structure for association rule mining: T-trees and P-trees. IEEE Transactions on Knowledge and Data Engineering 16(6), 774–778 (2004)
4. Gorodetsky, V., Karasaeyv, O., Samoilov, V.: Multi-agent Technology for Distributed Data Mining and Classification. In: Proceedings of the IEEE/WIC International Conference on Intelligent Agent Technology, pp. 438–441 (2003)
5. Han, J., Pei, J., Yin, Y., Mao, R.: Mining Frequent Patterns without Candidate Generation: A Frequent-Pattern Tree Approach. J. of Data Mining and Knowledge Discovery 8(1), 53–87 (2004)
6. Holt, J.D., Chung, S.M.: Parallel mining of association rules from text databases on a cluster of workstations. In: Proceedings of 18th International Symposium on Parallel and Distributed Processing, p. 86 (2004)
7. Iko, P., Kitsuregawa, M.: Shared Nothing Parallel Execution of FP-growth. DBSJ Letters 2(1), 43–46 (2003)
8. Javed, A., Khokhar, A.: Frequent Pattern Mining on Message Passing Multiprocessor Systems. Distributed and Parallel database 16(3), 321–334 (2004)
9. Li, T., Zhu, S., Ogihara, M.: A New Distributed Data Mining Model Based on Similarity. Symposium on Applied Computing, pp. 432–436 (2003)
10. Lin, C.-R., Lee, C.-H., Chen, M.-S., Yu, P.S.: Distributed Data Mining in a Chain Store Database of Short Transactions. In: Conference on Knowledge Discovery in Data, pp. 576–581 (2002)
11. Park, J.S., Chen, M.-S., Yu, P.S.: An Effective Hash-Based Algorithm for Mining Association Rules. ACM SIGMOD Record 24(2), 175–186 (1995)
12. Tang, P., Turkia, M.P.: Parallelizing Frequent Itemset Mining with FP-Trees. Computers and Their Applications, pp. 30–35 (2006)

Author Index

Lecture Notes in Computer Science

For information about Vols. 1–4536

please contact your bookseller or Springer